T0211027

Lecture Notes in Computer Science   13874

Founding Editors

Gerhard Goos
Juris Hartmanis

Editorial Board Members

The series Lecture Notes in Computer Science (LNCS), including its subseries Lecture Notes in Artificial Intelligence (LNAI) and Lecture Notes in Bioinformatics (LNBI), has established itself as a medium for the publication of new developments in computer science and information technology research, teaching, and education.

LNCS enjoys close cooperation with the computer science R & D community, the series counts many renowned academics among its volume editors and paper authors, and collaborates with prestigious societies. Its mission is to serve this international community by providing an invaluable service, mainly focused on the publication of conference and workshop proceedings and postproceedings. LNCS commenced publication in 1973.

Said El Hajji · Sihem Mesnager ·
El Mamoun Souidi
Editors

Codes, Cryptology and Information Security

4th International Conference, C2SI 2023
Rabat, Morocco, May 29–31, 2023
Proceedings

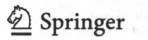

Editors
Said El Hajji [iD]
Mathematics Department, Faculty of Sciences
Mohammed V University
Rabat, Morocco

Sihem Mesnager [iD]
University of Paris VIII
Paris, France

El Mamoun Souidi [iD]
Computer Science Department, Faculty
of Sciences
Mohammed V University
Rabat, Morocco

ISSN 0302-9743   ISSN 1611-3349 (electronic)
Lecture Notes in Computer Science
ISBN 978-3-031-33016-2   ISBN 978-3-031-33017-9 (eBook)
https://doi.org/10.1007/978-3-031-33017-9

This Springer imprint is published by the registered company Springer Nature Switzerland AG
The registered company address is: Gewerbestrasse 11, 6330 Cham, Switzerland

Preface

These are the proceedings of the 4th edition of the International Conference on Codes, Cryptology and Information Security (C2SI 2023), organized in cooperation with the International Association for Cryptologic Research – IACR. The conference should have taken place in the beautiful city of Rabat (Morocco) from May 29 to May 31, 2023. This edition of the C2SI conference took place in 2021 but was postponed to 2023 due to the pandemic.

We are very grateful to the Program Committee members and the external reviewers for their professionalism and excellent hard work! The conference received 62 submissions, of which 21 contributed papers were finally selected for presentation after a single-blind peer review. At least two reviewers reviewed each paper.

All final decisions were taken only after a clear position could be clarified through additional reviews and comments. The submission and selection of papers were made using the Easychair software.

The Committee also invited Yvo G. Desmedt (University of Texas at Dallas, USA and University College London, UK), Philippe Gaborit (University of Limoges, France), David Naccache (ENS Paris and PSL University, Paris, France) and Pierangela Samarati (Università degli Studi di Milano, Italy) to present a talk on topics of their choice, and we thank them for having accepted! The first three invited speakers mentioned above have submitted an invited paper to be presented during the conference.

Special compliments go out to the Moroccan team and the local organizer of C2SI 2023, who brought the workshop much success. We also would like to thank all who provided us with excellent help with publicity and guidance regarding the website. We warmly thank several high institutes and organizations for their financial support, notably the Hassan II Academy of Sciences and Technology, CNRST (National Center for Scientific and Technical Research in Morocco) and ICESCO (Islamic World Educational, Scientific and Cultural Organization). Last but not least, we deeply thank Mohammed Regragui, Dean of the Faculty of Sciences of Rabat, for his financial support, encouragement, and continued unfailing support.

March 2023

Said El Hajji
Sihem Mesnager
El Mamoun Souidi

Organization

Co-chairs

Sihem Mesnager	University of Paris VIII, France
Said El Hajji	Mohammed V University in Rabat, Morocco
El Mamoun Souidi	Mohammed V University in Rabat, Morocco

Steering Committee

Abderrahim Ait Wakrime	Mohammed V University in Rabat, Morocco
Karima Alaoui Ismaili	Mohammed V University in Rabat, Morocco
Sophia Alami Kamouri	Mohammed V University in Rabat, Morocco
Mohammed Ammari	Mohammed V University in Rabat, Morocco
Mohamed A. Belhamra	Mohammed V University in Rabat, Morocco
Hafida Benazza	Mohammed V University in Rabat, Morocco
Youssef Bentaleb	ENSA, Kenitra, Morocco
Abdelkader Betari	Mohammed V University in Rabat, Morocco
Azzouz Cherrabi	Mohammed V University in Rabat, Morocco
Sidi Mohamed Douiri	Mohammed V University in Rabat, Morocco
Hassan Echoukairi	Mohammed V University in Rabat, Morocco
Abderrahim EL Abdllaoui	Mohammed V University in Rabat, Morocco
M. El Ghomari	Mohammed V University in Rabat, Morocco
Said El Hajji (Co-chair)	Mohammed V University in Rabat, Morocco
Ahmed El Yahyaoui	Mohammed V University in Rabat, Morocco
Mustapha Esghir	Mohammed V University in Rabat, Morocco
Mohamed Fihri	Mohammed V University in Rabat, Morocco
Allal Ghanmi	Mohammed V University in Rabat, Morocco
Ahmed Hajji	Mohammed V University in Rabat, Morocco
Ouafaa Ibrihich	Mohammed V University in Rabat, Morocco
Sihem Mesnager	Université Paris 8, France
Mounia Mikram	ESI, Rabat, Morocco
Ghizlane Orhanou	Mohammed V University in Rabat, Morocco
Ali Ouacha	Mohammed V University in Rabat, Morocco
Ali Ouadfel	Mohammed V University in Rabat, Morocco
El Mamoun Souidi	Mohammed V University in Rabat, Morocco
Youssef Zahir	Mohammed V University in Rabat, Morocco
Youssef Zaitar	Mohammed V University in Rabat, Morocco

Khalid Zine-Dine   Mohammed V University in Rabat, Morocco
Fouad Zinoun   Mohammed V University in Rabat, Morocco

Program Committee

Abderrahim Ait Wakrime   Mohammed V University in Rabat, Morocco
Elena Andreeva   TU Wien, Austria
Muhammad Rezal K. Ariffin   Universiti Putra Malaysia, Malaysia
François Arnault   Limoges University, France
Emanuele Bellini   Technology Innovation Institute, Abu Dhabi, UAE
Alexis Bonnecaze   Aix-Marseille University, France
Martino Borello   University of Paris 8, France
Ridha Bouallegue   Ecole Nationale d'Ingénieurs de Tunis, Tunisia
Lilya Budaghyan   University of Bergen, Norway
Claude Carlet   Univ. of Paris 8, France & Univ. of Bergen,
                                    Norway
Sumit Debnath   National Institute of Technology, Jamshedpur,
                                    India
Yvo Desmedt   University College London, UK
Said El Hajji   Mohammed V University in Rabat, Morocco
Philippe Gaborit   Université de Limoges, France
Cuiling Fan   Southwest Jiaotong University, China
Sylvain Guilley   Telecom-ParisTech and Secure-IC, France
Qian Guo   Lund University, Sweden
Abdelkrim Haqiq   Hassan 1st University, Morocco
Shoichi Hirose   University of Fukui, Japan
Vincenzo Iovino   University of Salerno, Italy
Michael-John Jacobson   University of Calgary, Canada
Juliane Krämer   University of Regensburg, Germany
Nian Li   Hubei University, China
Juan Antonio Lopez Ramos   Universidad de Almería, Spain
Subhamoy Maitra   Indian Statistical Institute, India
Edgar Martinez-Moro   University of Valladolid Castilla, Spain
Sihem Mesnager   University of Paris VIII, France
Marine Minier   Université de Lorraine, France
Abderrahmane Nitaj   CNRS - Université de Caen, France
Ferruh Ozbudak   Middle East Technical University, Turkey
Aris T. Pagourtzis   National Technical University of Athens, Greece
Raquel Pinto   University of Aveiro, Portugal
Elizabeth A. Quaglia   Royal Holloway, University of London, UK
Santanu Sarkar   Indian Institute of Technology Madras, India

Palash Sarkar   Indian Statistical Institute, India
El Mamoun Souidi   Mohammed V University in Rabat, Morocco
Pantelimon Stanica   Naval Postgraduate School, USA
Damien Stehlé   ENS Lyon, France
Leo Storme   Ghent University, Belgium
Deng Tang   Shanghai Jiao Tong University, China
Miguel Carriegos Vieira   Universidad de León, Spain
Zhengchun Zhou   Southwest Jiaotong University, China

Additional Reviewers

Paulo Almeida
Kévin Atighehchi
Gennaro Avitabile
Daniele Bartoli
Vincenzo Botta
Marco Calderini
Zhixiong Chen
Debendranath Das
Siemen Dhooghe
Samed Düzlü
Said El Kafhali
Mohammed Ennahbaoui
Luca De Feo
Loïc Ferreira
Tako Boris Fouotsa
Artem Grigor
Mohamed Hanini
Idrissi Hind
Zhao Hu
Nikolay Kaleyski

Michael Kiermaier
Lukas Kölsch
Julia Lieb
David Marquis
Michael Meyer
Tapaswini Mohanty
Miguel Ángel Navarro-Pérez
Abdellah Ouammou
Tapas Pandit
Leo Robert
Sushmita Sarkar
Vikas Srivastava
Sihong Su
Violetta Weger
Yanan Wu
Xi Xie
Haode Yan
Qin Yue
Lijing Zheng

C2SI Conference in Honor of Jean-Louis Lanet

J.-L. Lanet started his career as a technician researcher at Snecma, now part of the Safran group. He worked on hard real-time techniques for jet engine control (1984–1995). He designed a distributed architecture able to tolerate several failures while keeping its real-time capabilities. During that period, he got an engineering degree in computer science, and his PhD degree.

Next, he was a senior researcher at Gemplus Research Labs (1996–2007) the smart card manufacturer. During this period, he spent two years at Inria (2003–2004) as a senior research associate in the Everest team. At that time, he got his French Habilitation (Computer Science) from the University of Marseille, France.

He was a professor at the University of Limoges (2007–2014) at the Computer Science department, where he was the head of the Smart Secure Device group. He was also an associate professor at the University of Sherbrook and was in charge of the Security and Cryptology course of the USTH Master's (Hanoi). His research interests include the security of small systems like smart cards and software engineering, malware analysis and hardware security. Finally, he joined Inria-Rennes Bretagne Atlantique in September 2014 as director of the High-Security Labs (LHS) until 2020. He has more than 200 papers in the fields of security and software engineering in scientific journals and proceedings.

Contents

Information Security

Discrete Mathematics

Coding Theory

Invited Papers

Cryptologists Should Not Ignore the History of Al-Andalusia

Yvo Desmedt[✉]

Department of Computer Science, University of Texas at Dallas, Richardson, USA
`y.desmedt@cs.ucl.ac.uk`

Abstract. Most cryptographers believe our modern systems and proven secure protocols cannot be broken. Some are now convincing Treasure Departments to make their own versions of Bitcoin. Today cryptosystems are considered secure as long as academics have not broken them. Earlier we argued that this approach might be badly flawed, by presenting a minority viewpoint.

In this paper, we look at what the history of Al-Andalusia might teach us in regard to our research community. We also wonder how "open" our so called "open" research is.

Keywords: cryptography · cryptanalysis · the new dark ages

1 Introduction

The use of computational complexity allowed the introduction of public key cryptography [4,8]. It opened the door to a lot of research in academia, which was followed by having several conferences and journals on the topic. At Catacrypt 2014 (see [3] for the full paper), the author argued that this description is too optimistic. In Sect. 2 we briefly survey these viewpoints.

Besides using history as a way to motivate our minority viewpoint, we use two other approaches. First of all we look at the lack of major progress on cryptanalysis and analyze why this might be the case. For this we first look in Sect. 3 at closed research. In this context we will use history to motivate our viewpoints. We then consider the "open" research on the topic in Sect. 5. The last part is partially based on research on anthropology.

2 Earlier Viewpoints

We summarize the main viewpoints expressed by the author at Catacrypt 2014 (see [3]) about modern cryptologic research. These were:

A part of this work was presented at the Rump Session of Crypto 2020, August 18, 2020, with title: "40 years Advances in Cryptology: How Will History Judge Us?" Yvo Desmedt thanks the organizers for the invited paper and the Jonsson Endowment for, e.g., the airfare.

- **lack of cryptanalytic efforts:** "at the first Crypto conferences we had 33–48% of the papers on cryptanalysis. At Crypto 2012 it was only 6%".
- **related to RSA:** "no new algorithms—at least ignoring quantum computers—have been developed since 1990 on factoring (see [7])".
- **related to AES:** the attitude it was very carefully designed can not be justified when studying the history of cryptanalysis. From Kahn [6] we learn that the longest a cryptosystem withstood cryptanalysis was for roughly 300 years.
- **security of conventional cryptography:** "standards have primarily been developed based on work only presented at workshops, such as FSE, instead of at the flagship conferences such as Asiacrypt, Crypto and Eurocrypt."
- **academia:** "who in academia will "waste" years trying to break some cryptosystem"?

The talk (see [3]) also stated that:

> Modern cryptographers believe that the gap between encryption (signing, etc.) and cryptanalysis is superpolynomial (in the security parameter), but we have no proof!

and that we were not the first "scientific" discipline that was "believed" based. Indeed:

- "alchemists believed they would succeed in transforming lead into gold. Newton's work involved a lot of research on alchemy. It took until Mendeleev before we had chemistry.
- astrologists believed they could predict the future by looking at the movement of the stars." "Today astrology has fallen into disbelief (at least for scientists) and has been replaced by astronomy."

3   Closed Research

Huge closed research laboratories have been set up during (and after) WWII, which is more than 80 years ago. We try to estimate how much academia might have fallen behind in these 80 years.

With the development of the atomic bomb huge closed research laboratories have been set up. However, these are only the top of a huge iceberg. Indeed, besides govermental laboratories, several universities have closed research labs, such as the Institute for Advanced Study at Princeton.

One might easily speculate that most of the research done in that community remains classified. Seeing that these labs have existed for more than 80 years, one should wonder how much science and technology might have been created. To better understand this, consider the time period 1860–1940. One then finds that a whole range of technologies were developed, such as the Edison Lamb, Bell's telephone, the car, the airplane, electric trains, the cruise missile (V1) and the first ballistic missile (V2), which was the basis for the Saturn rocket. From a physics viewpoint, one sees the development of both Quantum Mechanics, and Relativity Theory.

One should also not forget that most of researchers in these labs have no teaching duties. This allows them to produce results much faster than these working in academia. Moreover, these labs/institutes were able to attract top researchers. Indeed the Princeton Institute was able to attract researchers such as Einstein and Weyl[1].

A question in this regard is whether there is a historic precedent that might help better speculate about the scale of science and technology that might have been created in secrecy.

3.1 Some Al-Andalusian History

It is well known that while Europe had its "Dark Ages," the Muslim Empire was flourishing. Less known is that Cordoba (Al-Andalusia) had the largest library[2] at that time. The (West) European Crusaders when conquering some land from the Muslims, quickly realized they were living in the Dark Ages. The existence of the Library of Cordoba did not remain secret. Gerard of Cremona translated more than 87 books of this library from Arabic science[3]. The rest of the history is well known and not relevant to our argument.

3.2 Comparing the Two Worlds

If we compare what is going on today with what happened during the Dark Ages, then until now, secrecy has been maintained much better. We can only speculate secret books exist which might be in secret libraries, of which the existence can not be verified.

4 Using Information Flow to Analyze "Leaks"

Seeing that the secrecy is maintained well, estimating how many decades the closed community is ahead on the academic one is very difficult.

An approach we suggest to use is the technique of Information Flow, see e.g. [2]. Anything which is declassified about x might leak something about y if there is a correlation. An interesting question is how to do this in a systematic way. This approach properly will require quite an extensive research before it can be used. Instead we only look at a few things that have been declassified and wonder whether that data might be useful.

---

[1] https://www.ias.edu/about/mission-history.
[2] https://islamicbridge.com/2021/10/the-lost-library-of-cordoba/.
[3] https://en.wikipedia.org/wiki/Toledo_School_of_Translators.

4.1   Some Heuristic Arguments

We now give a first example of something that was declassified.

It is now known that US President Carter did not have access to the US UFO files, despite having requested these while he was president. From this, one could conclude that data is only provided on a need to know basis. If that conclusion is true, the progress that the closed community might have made, could be very limited. Indeed, some research results have interdisciplinary impact. As an example, imagine a person who wants to do physics, but is not giving access to books on calculus.

So, if access to books in the secret library is controlled too strictly, then the use within the closed research community might not have lead to the explosion of science and technology we saw between 1860 and 1940 in the open community.

Using the last argument to claim that the closed community has made little progress is obviously wrong. The dropping of two atomic bombs on Japan leaked to the world the progress Los Alamos made.

4.2   Information Flow in Crypto Context

Churchill (or one of his advisors) realized quickly that each time the breaking of the Enigma or Lorenz cipher would be used by the military it might[4] leak to the Germans the breaking.

Misinformation is also used in our crypto context. As an example, consider what was known about the Colossus, i.e., the first computer. The author visited UK's "National Museum of Computing" twice. During his 1996 visit he was told that despite the order from Churchill to destroy all machines, "some were kept for practicing with similar machines." During his 2014 visit he was told that "some were kept to continue breaking Lorenz ciphers". The author told the guide of the previous visit. The guide then stated that "the Soviet Union knew the UK had broken Enigma, but did not know that they also broke the Lorenz cipher. Since they assumed the UK could not break it, they used the Lorenz cipher for a while. That information was still classified in 1996."

5   "Open" Research

We critically look at the research in the so called "open" community. We wonder:

– whether academia is the right environment for research?
– whether the research in academia is truly open?

---

[4] Rommel sent a message to Hitler in which he wondered Enigma had been broken, to which Hitler replied "impossible" [6].

5.1   How Anthropology Can Help

Anthropologist observed that in the last 40,000 years our brain has decreased by 10% in size [5]. Human biologists have wondered why we are "evolving" in such a way. One theory that has been put forward is that since we live in a society we no longer need individual intelligence, but instead need *collective intelligence* [10].

The argument that Stonier [10] used for collective intelligence is that the 1980's research on the W-boson involved 135 authors at CERN, while the work on X-rays was done by an individual, being Roentgen.

When comparing the closed laboratories with the current academic environment, in particular in the context of the research on cryptology, we see that academia is still relying heavily on the researcher as an individual. Indeed, for example, the tenure process in the US typically requires that the person has shown independence from the prior advisor. In computer science, having systematically 10 co-authors on a paper is not something that is encouraged. So, one can wonder whether academia is still the right environment for research.

Note that in cryptology some faculty members have been succesful in attracting a lot of funding and be able to build a research group with several PhD students. However, since there is typically a *single* advisor, such a group usually follows the advisor blindly. For example, we see such groups working on linear and differential cryptanalysis, without trying to come up with new cryptanalytic approaches.

5.2   Condoned Research

We now wonder whether modern research is truly open. The silencing during COVID of dissenting medical experts has now finally received some attention. Daley [1] for example wrote:

> We have returned to the world of Galileo vs the Vatican. Scientific dissidents are again silenced and ostracised for their opinions
> ... the comprehensive suppression of dissent even when it came from expert sources - and the prohibition on argument even when it was accompanied by counter-evidence ...

We now wonder whether

1. the approach of having govermental agencies be the main source for research, in particular on cryptologic research, and
2. the use of peer reviewers

might lead to suppression of dissent. First, at Catacrypt 2014 (see [3]) the author already pointed out that at Crypto 2012 only 6% of the papers were on cryptanalysis. Shamir [9] stated in a personal communication that:

> There were not so many papers on cryptanalysis at the Crypto conference because in the past, the US National Science Foundation did not tend to fund cryptanalysis.

Since the US attracts the top PhD students and has most of the top universities in the world, this NSF policy might have a dramatic negative impact on our understanding of the (in)security of our cryptosystems. So, this argues our first point we wanted to make.

Let us now consider the impact of peer review on the suppression of dissent. Kahneman (Nobel Prize winner) pointed out, in the context of economics, that humans are not rational. The same can be stated for peer reviewers. Moreover, peer reviewers tend to support the majority viewpoint, which unfortunately in science is sometimes the wrong one (see Sect. 2).

5.3 The Crypto Context

At Catacrypt 2014 (see [3]), related to block ciphers, the author stated:

> the emphasis is on developing systems that can only withstand some specific attacks, such as "linear" and "differential cryptanalysis."

At Catacrypt 2017, Courtois revealed that EPSRC has rejected all his proposals to fund research on Algebraic Cryptanalysis, which uses multivariate polynomials. By not having this funding, we currently do not know whether an alternative technology to Algebraic Cryptanalysis might be succesful in breaking block ciphers. Note that sometimes the first versions of an invention have limited use. Bell Labs invention of the transistor is such an example that needed extra technology to become useful[5].

6   Conclusions

With 80 years closed research, we suggested that we are living in the new dark ages. We briefly compared the current one with the one of the Middle Ages. We saw that the progress the Muslim World had made did not remain secret, while today most people are not aware they are living in the new dark ages. Many books of the library of Cordoba got translated. Today we can only guess a secret library with secret books exist.

To make matters worse, open research on the topic of cryptanalysis is quite limited, in particular in the USA. The implications of all that for cryptology are far going. Since our academic knowledge might be quite restricted, we should promote the use of unconditionally secure cryptosystems, a recommendation the author already made at Catacrypt 2014 (see [3]).

Acknowledgment. The author thanks Karel Desmedt, for having observed decades ago, the significant reduction in new life changing inventions between the 1940–1980 area compared to the 1900–1940 area.

---

[5] https://www.sony.com/en/SonyInfo/CorporateInfo/History/capsule/12/.

References

1. Daley, J.: Governments have learnt that fear works - and that is truly terrifying. The Telegraph (2022)
2. Denning, D.E.R.: Cryptography and Data Security. Addison-Wesley, Reading (1982)
3. Desmedt, Y.: What is the future of cryptography? In: Ryan, P.Y.A., Naccache, D., Quisquater, J.-J. (eds.) The New Codebreakers. LNCS, vol. 9100, pp. 109–122. Springer, Heidelberg (2016). https://doi.org/10.1007/978-3-662-49301-4_7
4. Diffie, W., Hellman, M.E.: Privacy and authentication: an introduction to cryptography. Proc. IEEE **67**, 397–427 (1979)
5. Henneberg, M.: Decrease of human skull size in the Holocene. Hum. Biol. **60**, 395–405 (1988)
6. Kahn, D.: The Codebreakers. MacMillan Publishing Co., New York (1967)
7. Lenstra, A.K., Lenstra, H.W., Jr., Manasse, M.S., Pollard, J.M.: The number field sieve. In: Proceedings of the Twenty Second Annual ACM Symposium Theory of Computing, STOC, 14–16 May 1990, pp. 564–572 (1990)
8. Merkle, R.C.: Secure communications over insecure channels. Comm. ACM **21**, 294–299 (1978)
9. Shamir, A.: Personal communication during CANS 2022 (2022)
10. Stonier, T.: Information technology, collective intelligence and the evolution of human societies. In: Stonier, T. (ed.) Beyond Information, pp. 85–106. Springer, London (1992). https://doi.org/10.1007/978-1-4471-1835-0_5

Compact Post-quantum Signatures from Proofs of Knowledge Leveraging Structure for the **PKP**, **SD** and **RSD** Problems

Loïc Bidoux[1] and Philippe Gaborit[2(✉)]

[1] Technology Innovation Institute, Abu Dhabi, UAE
[2] University of Limoges, Limoges, France
gaborit@unilim.fr

Abstract. The MPC-in-the-head introduced in [IKOS07] has established itself as an important paradigm to design efficient digital signatures. For instance, it has been leveraged in the Picnic scheme [CDG+20] that reached the third round of the NIST Post-Quantum Cryptography Standardization process. In addition, it has been used in [Beu20] to introduce the Proof of Knowledge (PoK) with Helper paradigm. This construction permits to design shorter signatures but induces a non negligible performance overhead as it uses cut-and-choose. In this paper, we introduce the *PoK leveraging structure* paradigm along with its associated *challenge space amplification* technique. Our new approach to design PoK brings some improvements over the PoK with Helper one. Indeed, we show how one can substitute the Helper in these constructions by leveraging the underlying structure of the considered problem. This new approach does not suffer from the performance overhead inherent to the PoK with Helper paradigm hence offers different trade-offs between security, signature sizes and performances. In addition, we also present four new post-quantum signature schemes. The first one is based on a new PoK with Helper for the Syndrome Decoding problem. It relies on ideas from [BGKM22] and [FJR21] and improve the latter using a new technique that can be seen as performing some cut-and-choose with a meet in the middle approach. The three other signatures are based on our new PoK leveraging structure approach and as such illustrate its versatility. Indeed, we provide new PoK related to the Permuted Kernel Problem (PKP), Syndrome Decoding (SD) problem and Rank Syndrome Decoding (RSD) problem. Considering (public key + signature), we get sizes below 9 kB for our signature related to the PKP problem, below 15 kB for our signature related to the SD problem and below 7 kB for our signature related to the RSD problem. These new constructions are particularly interesting presently as the NIST has recently announced its plan to reopen the signature track of its Post-Quantum Cryptography Standardization process.

S. El Hajji et al. (Eds.): C2SI 2023, LNCS 13874, pp. 10–42, 2023.
https://doi.org/10.1007/978-3-031-33017-9_2

1   Introduction

Zero-Knowledge Proofs of Knowledge (PoK) are significant cryptographic primitives thanks to their various applications. They allow a prover to convince a verifier that he knows some secret without revealing anything about it. Designing compact PoK is an important problem as one can convert such proofs into signature schemes using the Fiat-Shamir transform [FS86, PS96] or the Unruh [Unr15] transform. Over the years, many post-quantum signatures have been constructed following this approach using for instance the Syndrome Decoding problem [Ste93], the Multivariate Quadratic problem [SSH11] or the Permuted Kernel Problem [Sha89]. The Picnic [CDG+20] and MQDSS [CHR+20] signature schemes that have been submitted to the NIST Post-Quantum Cryptography Standardization process also follow this approach. More recently, Katz, Kolesnikov and Wang [KKW18] proposed a protocol based on the MPC-in-the-head paradigm [IKOS07] in the preprocessing model. Two years later, Beullens generalized their work by introducing the concept of PoK with Helper [Beu20]. The Helper is a trusted third party that can ease the design of PoK and later be removed using cut-and-choose. Since then, the PoK with Helper paradigm have been extensively used to design post-quantum signature schemes; see for instance [GPS21, FJR21, BGKM22, Wan22]. This approach is quite interesting as it produces shorter signatures than existing ones however using a Helper along with cut-and-choose also induces a non negligible performance overhead.

In this paper, we introduce the notion of PoK leveraging structure as a new paradigm to design PoK. Formally, our approach consists in using standard (to be read as without Helper) PoK however we believe that it is more easily understood when described by analogy to the PoK with Helper paradigm. Indeed, our new approach can be seen as a way to remove the trusted Helper without using cut-and-choose. In order to do so, we leverage some structure within the hard problem used to design the PoK. Interestingly, the required additional structure has generally either been already well studied in the literature or is closely related to the considered problem. PoK following our new framework differs from PoK with Helper ones in several ways. These differences motivate the introduction of a new technique called challenge space amplification that is particularly well suited for our new way to design PoK. In practice, PoK leveraging structure can lead to smaller signature schemes than PoK with Helper ones but rely on the use of some structure within the considered hard problem.

Contributions. We propose a new approach to design PoK as well as four new post-quantum signature schemes. Our main contribution is the introduction of the *Proof of Knowledge leveraging structure* paradigm along with its associated *challenge space amplification* technique. In addition, we present a new PoK with Helper for the SD problem that outperforms all existing constructions with the notable exception of the [FJR22] one. This new PoK is particularly interesting when combined with our PoK leveraging structure framework. Moreover, we demonstrate the versatility of our new approach by designing three post-quantum signature schemes respectively related to the Permuted Kernel Problem (PKP), Syndrome Decoding (SD) problem and Rank Syndrome Decoding (RSD) problem. Considering (public key + signature), we get sizes below 9 kB for our signature related to the PKP problem, below 15 kB for our signature related to the SD problem and below 7 kB for our signature related to the RSD problem.

Paper Organization. We provide definitions related to PoK, coding theory and hard problems in Sect. 2. Our PoK leveraging structure paradigm and our amplification technique are respectively described in Sects. 3 and 4. Our PoK with Helper for the SD problem is depicted in Sect. 5 while our PoK leveraging structure for the PKP, SD and RSD problems are presented in Sect. 6. To finish, we provide a comparison of resulting signature schemes with respect to existing ones in Sect. 7.

2 Preliminaries

Notations. Vectors (respectively matrices) are represented using bold lowercase (respectively upper-case) letters. For an integer $n > 0$, we use $\mathcal{S}_n$ to denote the symmetric group of all permutations of n elements. In addition, we use $\mathsf{GL}_n(\mathbb{F}_q)$ to denote the linear group of invertible $n \times n$ matrices in $\mathbb{F}_q$. For a finite set S, $x \xleftarrow{\$} S$ denotes that x is sampled uniformly at random from S while $x \xleftarrow{\$,\theta}$ denotes that x is sampled uniformly at random from S using the seed θ. Moreover, the acronym PPT is used as an abbreviation for the term "probabilistic polynomial time". A function is called negligible if for all sufficiently large $\lambda \in \mathbb{N}$, $\mathsf{negl}(\lambda) < \lambda^{-c}$, for all constants $c > 0$.

2.1 Proof of Knowledge and Commitment Schemes

We start by defining Proof of Knowledge (PoK) following [AFK21] notations. Let $R \subseteq \{0,1\}^* \times \{0,1\}^*$ be an NP relation, we call $(x, w) \in R$ a statement-witness pair where x is the statement and w is the witness. The set of valid witnesses for x is $R(x) = \{w \mid (x, w) \in R\}$. In a PoK, given a statement x, a prover P aims to convince a verifier V that he knows a witness $w \in R(x)$.

Definition 1 (Proof of Knowledge). *A $(2n + 1)$-round PoK for relation R with soundness error ϵ is a two-party protocol between a prover $\mathsf{P}(x, w)$ with input a statement x and witness w and a verifier $\mathsf{V}(x)$ with input x. We denote by $\langle \mathsf{P}(x, w), \mathsf{V}(x) \rangle$ the transcript between P and V. A PoK is correct if*

$$\Pr\left[\,\mathit{accept} \leftarrow \langle \mathsf{P}(x, w), \mathsf{V}(x) \rangle\,\right] = 1.$$

Definition 2 (Tree of Transcripts). *Let $k_1, \dots, k_n \in \mathbb{N}$, a $(k_1, \dots, k_n)$-tree of transcripts for a $(2n + 1)$-round public coin protocol PoK is a set of $K = \prod_{i=1}^{n} k_i$ transcripts arranged in a tree structure. The nodes in the tree represent the prover's messages and the edges between the nodes correspond to the* *challenges sent by the verifier. Each node at depth i has exactly k_i children corresponding to the k_i pairwise distinct challenges. Every transcript is represented by exactly one path from the root of the tree to a leaf node.*

Definition 3 $((k_1, \ldots, k_n)$**-out-of-**$(N_1, \ldots, N_n)$ **Special-Soundness).** *Let $k_1, \ldots, k_n, N_1, \ldots, N_n \in \mathbb{N}$. A $(2n+1)$-round public-coin PoK, where V samples the i-th challenge from a set of cardinality $N_i \geq k_i$ for $i \in [n]$, is $(k_1, \ldots, k_n)$-out-of-$(N_1, \ldots, N_n)$ special-sound if there exists a PPT algorithm that on an input statement x and a $(k_1, \ldots, k_n)$-tree of accepting transcripts outputs a witness w. We also say PoK is $(k_1, \ldots, k_n)$-special-sound.*

Definition 4 (Special Honest-Verifier Zero-Knowledge). *A PoK satisfies the Honest-Verifier Zero-Knowledge (HZVK) property if there exists a PPT simulator Sim that given as input a statement x and random challenges $(\kappa_1, \ldots, \kappa_n)$, outputs a transcript $\langle \mathsf{Sim}(x, \kappa_1, \cdots, \kappa_n), \mathsf{V}(x) \rangle$ that is computationally indistinguishable from the probability distribution of transcripts of honest executions between a prover $\mathsf{P}(x, w)$ and a verifier $\mathsf{V}(x)$.*

PoK with Helper introduced in [Beu20] are protocols that leverage a trusted third party (the so-called Helper) within their design. They can be seen as 3-round PoK following an initial step performed by the Helper. We defer the reader to [Beu20] for their formal definition. PoK are significant cryptographic primitives as they can be turned into digital signatures using the Fiat-Shamir transform [FS86, PS96, AFK21]. Hereafter, we define commitment schemes which are an important building block used to construct PoK.

Definition 5 (Commitment Scheme). *A commitment scheme is a tuple of algorithms $(\mathsf{Com}, \mathsf{Open})$ such that $\mathsf{Com}(r, m)$ returns a commitment c for the message m and randomness r while $\mathsf{Open}(c, r, m)$ returns either 1 (accept) or 0 (reject). A commitment scheme is said to be correct if:*

$$\Pr\left[b = 1 \mid c \leftarrow \mathsf{Com}(r, m), \ b \leftarrow \mathsf{Open}(c, r, m) \right] = 1.$$

Definition 6 (Computationally Hiding). *Let (m_0, m_1) be a pair of messages, the advantage of $\mathcal{A}$ against the hiding experiment is defined as:*

$$\mathsf{Adv}_{\mathcal{A}}^{\mathsf{hiding}}(1^\lambda) = \left| \Pr\left[b = b' \mid \begin{matrix} b \xleftarrow{\$} \{0,1\}, \ r \xleftarrow{\$} \{0,1\}^\lambda \\ c \longleftarrow \mathsf{Com}(r, m_b), \ b' \longleftarrow \mathcal{A}.\mathsf{guess}(c) \end{matrix} \right] - \frac{1}{2} \right|.$$

A commitment scheme is computationally hiding if for all PPT adversaries $\mathcal{A}$ and every pair of messages (m_0, m_1), $\mathsf{Adv}_{\mathcal{A}}^{\mathsf{hiding}}(1^\lambda)$ is negligible in λ.

Definition 7 (Computationally Binding). *The advantage of an adversary $\mathcal{A}$ against the commitment binding experiment is defined as:*

$$\mathsf{Adv}_{\mathcal{A}}^{\mathsf{binding}}(1^\lambda) = \Pr\left[\begin{matrix} m_0 \neq m_1 \\ 1 \longleftarrow \mathsf{Open}(c, r, m_0) \\ 1 \longleftarrow \mathsf{Open}(c, r, m_1) \end{matrix} \ \middle| \ (c, r, m_0, m_1) \longleftarrow \mathcal{A}.\mathsf{choose}(1^\lambda) \right].$$

A commitment scheme is computationally binding if for all PPT adversaries $\mathcal{A}$, $\mathsf{Adv}_{\mathcal{A}}^{\mathsf{binding}}(1^\lambda)$ is negligible in λ.

2.2 Coding Theory

We recall some definitions for both Hamming and rank metrics. Let n be a positive integer, q a prime power, m a positive integer, $\mathbb{F}_{q^m}$ an extension of degree m of $\mathbb{F}_q$ and $\beta := (\beta_1, \ldots, \beta_m)$ a basis of $\mathbb{F}_{q^m}$ over $\mathbb{F}_q$. Any vector $\mathbf{x} \in \mathbb{F}_{q^m}^n$ can be associated to the matrix $\mathbf{M_x} \in \mathbb{F}_q^{m \times n}$ by expressing its coordinates in β.

Definition 8 (Hamming weight). *Let* $\mathbf{x} \in \mathbb{F}_2^n$, *the Hamming weight of* $\mathbf{x}$, *denoted* $w_H(\mathbf{x})$, *is the number of non-zero coordinates of* $\mathbf{x}$.

Definition 9 (Rank weight). *Let* $\mathbf{x} \in \mathbb{F}_{q^m}^n$, *the rank weight of* $\mathbf{x}$, *denoted* $w_R(\mathbf{x})$, *is defined as the rank of the matrix* $\mathbf{M_x} = (x_{ij}) \in \mathbb{F}_q^{m \times n}$ *where* $x_j = \sum_{i=1}^m x_{i,j} \beta_i$.

Definition 10 (Support). *Let* $\mathbf{x} \in \mathbb{F}_{q^m}^n$, *the support of* $\mathbf{x}$ *denoted* $\mathrm{Supp}(\mathbf{x})$, *is the* $\mathbb{F}_q$-*linear space generated by the coordinates of* $\mathbf{x}$ *namely* $\mathrm{Supp}(\mathbf{x}) = \langle x_1, \ldots, x_n \rangle_{\mathbb{F}_q}$. *It follows from the definition that* $w_R(\mathbf{x}) = |\mathrm{Supp}(\mathbf{x})|$.

We define linear codes over a finite field $\mathbb{F}$ where $\mathbb{F} = \mathbb{F}_2$ in Hamming metric and $\mathbb{F} = \mathbb{F}_{q^m}$ in rank metric as well as quasi-cyclic codes and ideal codes. We restrict our definitions to codes of index 2 as they are the ones used hereafter.

Definition 11 ($\mathbb{F}$-linear code). *An* $\mathbb{F}$-*linear code* $\mathcal{C}$ *of length* n *and dimension* k *denoted* $[n, k]$ *is an* $\mathbb{F}$-*linear subspace of* $\mathbb{F}^n$ *of dimension* k. *A generator matrix for* $\mathcal{C}$ *is a matrix* $\mathbf{G} \in \mathbb{F}^{k \times n}$ *such that* $\mathcal{C} = \{\mathbf{xG}, \ \mathbf{m} \in \mathbb{F}^k\}$. *A parity-check matrix for* $\mathcal{C}$ *is a matrix* $\mathbf{H} \in \mathbb{F}^{(n-k) \times n}$ *such that* $\mathcal{C} = \{\mathbf{x} \in \mathbb{F}^n, \ \mathbf{Hx}^\top = 0\}$.

Definition 12 (Quasi-cyclic code). *A systematic binary quasi-cyclic code of index 2 is a* $[n = 2k, k]$ *code that can be represented by a generator matrix* $\mathbf{G} \in \mathbb{F}_2^{k \times n}$ *of the form* $\mathbf{G} = [\mathbf{I}_k \ \mathbf{A}]$ *where* $\mathbf{A}$ *is a circulant* $k \times k$ *matrix. Alternatively, it can be represented by a parity-check matrix* $\mathbf{H} \in \mathbb{F}_2^{(n-k) \times k}$ *of the form* $\mathbf{H} = [\mathbf{I}_k \ \mathbf{B}]$ *where* $\mathbf{B}$ *is a circulant* $k \times k$ *matrix.*

Definition 13 (Ideal matrix). *Let* $P \in \mathbb{F}_q[X]$ *a polynomial of degree* k *and let* $\mathbf{v} \in \mathbb{F}_{q^m}^k$. *The ideal matrix* $\mathcal{IM}_P(\mathbf{v}) \in \mathbb{F}_{q^m}^{k \times k}$ *is of the form*

$$
\mathcal{IM}_P(\mathbf{v}) = \begin{pmatrix} \mathbf{v} & \mod P \\ X \cdot \mathbf{v} & \mod P \\ \vdots & \\ X^{k-1} \cdot \mathbf{v} & \mod P \end{pmatrix}.
$$

Definition 14 (Ideal code). *Let* $P \in \mathbb{F}_q[X]$ *a polynomial of degree* k, $\mathbf{g} \in \mathbb{F}_{q^m}^k$ *and* $\mathbf{h} \in \mathbb{F}_{q^m}^k$. *An ideal code of index 2 is a* $[n = 2k, k]$ *code* $\mathcal{C}$ *that can be represented by a generator matrix* $\mathbf{G} \in \mathbb{F}_{q^m}^{k \times n}$ *of the form* $\mathbf{G} = [\mathbf{I}_k \ \mathcal{IM}_P(\mathbf{g})]$. *Alternatively, it can be represented by a parity-check matrix* $\mathbf{H} \in \mathbb{F}_{q^m}^{(n-k) \times k}$ *of the form* $\mathbf{H} = [\mathbf{I}_k \ \mathcal{IM}_P(\mathbf{h})]$.

Let $\mathbf{a} = (a_1, \ldots, a_k) \in \mathbb{F}_2^k$, for $r \in [1, k-1]$, we define the $\mathbf{rot}()$ operator as $\mathbf{rot}_r(\mathbf{a}) = (a_{k-r+1}, \ldots, a_{k-r})$. For $\mathbf{b} = (\mathbf{b}_1, \mathbf{b}_2) \in \mathbb{F}_2^{2k}$, we slightly abuse notations and define $\mathbf{rot}_r(\mathbf{b}) = (\mathbf{rot}_r(\mathbf{b}_1), \mathbf{rot}_r(\mathbf{b}_2))$. Whenever $\mathbf{H}$ is the parity-check matrix of a quasi-cyclic code or an ideal code, if one has $\mathbf{H}\mathbf{x}^\top = \mathbf{y}^\top$, then it holds that $\mathbf{H} \cdot \mathbf{rot}_r(\mathbf{x})^\top = \mathbf{rot}_r(\mathbf{y})^\top$.

2.3   Hard Problems

We introduce several hard problems along with some of their variants. They are used to design signature schemes in the remaining of this paper.

Definition 15 (PKP problem). *Let (q, m, n) be positive integers, $\mathbf{H} \in \mathbb{F}_q^{m \times n}$ be a random matrix, $\pi \in \mathcal{S}_n$ be a random permutation and $\mathbf{x} \in \mathbb{F}_q^n$ be a vector such that $\mathbf{H}(\pi[\mathbf{x}]) = 0$. Given $(\mathbf{H}, \mathbf{x})$, the Permuted Kernel Problem $\mathsf{PKP}(q, m, n)$ asks to find a permutation π.*

Definition 16 (IPKP problem). *Let (q, m, n) be positive integers, $\mathbf{H} \xleftarrow{\$} \mathbb{F}_q^{m \times n}$ be a random matrix, $\pi \in \mathcal{S}_n$ be a random permutation, $\mathbf{x} \in \mathbb{F}_q^n$ be a random vector and $\mathbf{y} \in \mathbb{F}_q^m$ be a vector such that $\mathbf{H}(\pi[\mathbf{x}]) = \mathbf{y}$. Given $(\mathbf{H}, \mathbf{x}, \mathbf{y})$, the Inhomogeneous Permuted Kernel Problem $\mathsf{IPKP}(q, m, n)$ asks to find π.*

Definition 17 (SD problem). *Let (n, k, w) be positive integers, $\mathbf{H} \in \mathbb{F}_2^{(n-k) \times n}$ be a random parity-check matrix, $\mathbf{x} \in \mathbb{F}_2^n$ be a random vector such that $w_H(\mathbf{x}) = w$ and $\mathbf{y} \in \mathbb{F}_2^{(n-k)}$ be a vector such that $\mathbf{H}\mathbf{x}^\top = \mathbf{y}^\top$. Given $(\mathbf{H}, \mathbf{y})$, the binary Syndrome Decoding problem $\mathsf{SD}(n, k, w)$ asks to find $\mathbf{x}$.*

Definition 18 (QCSD problem). *Let $(n = 2k, k, w)$ be positive integers, $\mathbf{H} \in \mathcal{QC}(\mathbb{F}_2^{(n-k) \times n})$ be a random parity-check matrix of a quasi-cyclic code of index 2, $\mathbf{x} \in \mathbb{F}_2^n$ be a random vector such that $w_H(\mathbf{x}) = w$ and $\mathbf{y} \in \mathbb{F}_2^{(n-k)}$ be a vector such that $\mathbf{H}\mathbf{x}^\top = \mathbf{y}^\top$. Given $(\mathbf{H}, \mathbf{y})$, the binary Quasi-Cyclic Syndrome Decoding problem $\mathsf{QCSD}(n, k, w)$ asks to find $\mathbf{x}$.*

Decoding One Out of Many Setting. We denote by $\mathsf{QCSD}(n, k, w, M)$ the QCSD problem in the decoding one out of many setting [Sen11]. In this setting, several small weight vectors $(\mathbf{x}_i)_{i \in [1, M]}$ are used along with several syndromes $(\mathbf{y}_i)_{i \in [1, M]}$ and one is asked to find any $\mathbf{x}_i$. This setting is natural for the QCSD problem as one can get additional syndromes using rotations.

Definition 19 (RSD problem). *Let (q, m, n, k, w) be positive integers, $\mathbf{H} \in \mathbb{F}_{q^m}^{(n-k) \times n}$ be a random parity-check matrix, $\mathbf{x} \in \mathbb{F}_{q^m}^n$ be a random vector such that $w_R(\mathbf{x}) = w$ and $\mathbf{y} \in \mathbb{F}_{q^m}^{(n-k)}$ be a vector such that $\mathbf{H}\mathbf{x}^\top = \mathbf{y}^\top$. Given $(\mathbf{H}, \mathbf{y})$, the Rank Syndrome Decoding problem $\mathsf{RSD}(q, m, n, k, w)$ asks to find $\mathbf{x}$.*

Definition 20 (IRSD problem). *Let $(q, m, n = 2k, k, w)$ be positive integers, $P \in \mathbb{F}_q[X]$ be an irreducible polynomial of degree k, $\mathbf{H} \in \mathcal{ID}(\mathbb{F}_{q^m}^{(n-k) \times n})$ be a* *random parity-check matrix of an ideal code of index 2, $\mathbf{x} \in \mathbb{F}_{q^m}^n$ be a random vector such that $w_R(\mathbf{x}) = w$ and $\mathbf{y} \in \mathbb{F}_{q^m}^{(n-k)}$ be a vector such that $\mathbf{Hx}^\top = \mathbf{y}^\top$. Given $(\mathbf{H}, \mathbf{y})$, the Ideal Rank Syndrome Decoding problem $\mathsf{IRSD}(q, m, n, k, w)$ asks to find $\mathbf{x}$.*

Definition 21 (RSL problem). *Let (q, m, n, k, w, M) be positive integers, $\mathbf{H} \in \mathbb{F}_{q^m}^{(n-k) \times n}$ be a random parity-check matrix, E be a random subspace of $\mathbb{F}_{q^m}$ of dimension ω, $(\mathbf{x}_i)_{i \in [1,M]} \in (\mathbb{F}_{q^m}^n)^M$ be random vectors such that $\mathrm{Supp}(\mathbf{x}_i) = E$ and $(\mathbf{y}_i) \in (\mathbb{F}_{q^m}^{(n-k)})^M$ be vectors such that $\mathbf{Hx}_i^\top = \mathbf{y}_i^\top$. Given $(\mathbf{H}, (\mathbf{y}_i)_{i \in [1,M]})$, the Rank Support Learning problem $\mathsf{RSL}(q, m, n, k, w, M)$ asks to find E.*

Definition 22 (IRSL problem). *Let $(q, m, n = 2k, k, w, M)$ be positive integers, $P \in \mathbb{F}_q[X]$ be an irreducible polynomial of degree k, $\mathbf{H} \in \mathcal{ID}(\mathbb{F}_{q^m}^{(n-k) \times n})$ be a random parity-check matrix of an ideal code of index 2, E be a random subspace of $\mathbb{F}_{q^m}$ of dimension ω, $(\mathbf{x}_i)_{i \in [1,M]} \in (\mathbb{F}_{q^m}^n)^M$ be random vectors such that $\mathrm{Supp}(\mathbf{x}_i) = E$ and $(\mathbf{y}_i)_{i \in [1,M]} \in (\mathbb{F}_{q^m}^{(n-k)})^M$ be vectors such that $\mathbf{Hx}_i^\top = \mathbf{y}_i^\top$. Given $(\mathbf{H}, (\mathbf{y}_i)_{i \in [1,M]})$, the Ideal Rank Support Learning problem $\mathsf{IRSL}(q, m, n, k, w, M)$ asks to find E.*

3   New Paradigm to Design PoK Leveraging Structure

3.1   Overview of Our PoK Leveraging Structure Approach

The PoK with Helper paradigm introduced in [Beu20] eases the design of PoK and has historically led to shorter signatures. It relies on introducing a trusted third party (the so called Helper) that is later removed using cut-and-choose. In this section, we introduce a new paradigm that can be seen as an alternate way to remove the Helper in such PoK. Formally, our approach consists in using standard (to be read as without Helper) PoK however we believe that it is more easily understood when described by analogy to the PoK with Helper paradigm.

PoK Leveraging Structure. Our main idea can be seen as using the underlying structure of the considered problem in order to substitute the Helper in the PoK with Helper approach. As a consequence, all the PoK designed following our paradigm share the framework described in Fig. 1. Indeed, all our PoK leveraging structure are 5-round PoK whose first challenge space $\mathcal{C}_{\mathsf{struct}}$ is related to some structure and whose second challenge space can be made arbitrarily large. This specific framework impacts the properties of the considered protocols which can be leveraged to bring an improvement over existing constructions. Indeed, removing the Helper provides an improvement on performances that can lead to smaller signature sizes when some additional conditions are verified. We describe in Table 1 how our new paradigm can be applied to the PoK with Helper from [Beu20] and Sect. 5 in order to design new PoK leveraging structure related to the PKP, SD and RSD problems. For instance, starting from the SD problem over $\mathbb{F}_2$, one may introduce the required extra structure by considering the QCSD problem over $\mathbb{F}_2$ or the SD problem over $\mathbb{F}_q$.

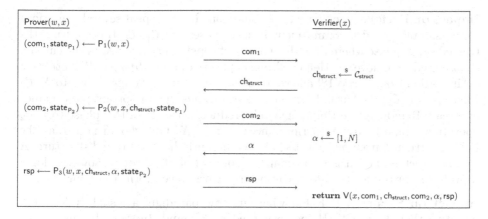

Fig. 1. Overview of PoK leveraging structure

Table 1. Substitution of the Helper using PoK leveraging structure

Scheme	First Challenge	Second Challenge	Problem
SUSHYFISH [Beu20]	Helper	Linearity over $\mathbb{F}_q$	IPKP
Section 6.1	Linearity over $\mathbb{F}_q$	Shared Permutation	IPKP
[FJR21,BGKM22]	Helper	(Shared Permutation)	SD over $\mathbb{F}_2$
Section 5	Helper	Shared Permutation	SD over $\mathbb{F}_2$
Section 6.2	Cyclicity	Shared Permutation	QCSD over $\mathbb{F}_2$
Section 5	Helper	Shared Permutation	RSD
Section 6.3	Cyclicity	Shared Permutation	IRSD
	Cyclicity, Linearity, Same Support	Shared Permutation	IRSL

3.2   Properties of PoK Leveraging Structure

Hereafter, we discuss the advantages and limits of our new approach by describing its impact on soundness, performance, security and size of the resulting signature scheme. We denote by $\mathcal{C}_1$ and $\mathcal{C}_2$ the sizes of the two considered challenge spaces and by τ the number of iterations that one need to execute to achieve a negligible soundness error for some security parameter λ.

Impact on Soundness Error. Removing the trusted setup induced by the Helper allows new cheating strategies for malicious provers. In most cases, this means that the soundness error is increased from $\max(\frac{1}{\mathcal{C}_1}, \frac{1}{\mathcal{C}_2})$ for protocols using a Helper to $\frac{1}{\mathcal{C}_1} + (1 - \frac{1}{\mathcal{C}_1}) \cdot \frac{1}{\mathcal{C}_2}$ for protocols without Helper. A malicious prover has generally a cheating strategy related to the first challenge that is successful with probability $\frac{1}{\mathcal{C}_1}$ as well as a cheating strategy related to the second challenge for the remaining cases that is sucessful with probability $(1 - \frac{1}{\mathcal{C}_1}) \cdot \frac{1}{\mathcal{C}_2}$. The aforementioned expression is equal to $\frac{1}{\mathcal{C}_2} + \frac{\mathcal{C}_2 - 1}{\mathcal{C}_1 \cdot \mathcal{C}_2}$ hence one can see that for challenge spaces such that $\mathcal{C}_2 \gg 1$, the resulting soundness error is close to $\frac{1}{\mathcal{C}_2} + \frac{1}{\mathcal{C}_1}$. In addition, if one has also $\mathcal{C}_1 \gg \mathcal{C}_2$, the soundness error is close to $\frac{1}{\mathcal{C}_2}$.

Impact on Performances. Using a Helper, one has to repeat several operations (some sampling and a commitment in most cases) $\tau \cdot C_1 \cdot C_2$ times during the trusted setup phase where C_1 is the number of repetitions involved in the cut and choose used to remove the Helper. While in practice the *beating parallel repetition* optimization from [KKW18] allows to reduce the number of operations to $X \cdot C_2$ where $X \leq \tau \cdot C_1$, the trusted setup phase still induces an important performance overhead. Removing the Helper generally reduces the cost of this phase to $\tau \cdot C_2$ operations thus improving performances as $\tau \leq X$. One should note that the PoK constructed from our new technique inherently have a 5-round structure. A common technique consists to collapse 5-round PoK to 3-round however doing so would re-introduce the aforementioned performance overhead in our case.

Impact on Security. PoK following our new paradigm are slightly less conservative than PoK with Helper collapsed to 3-round. Indeed, the underlying 5-round structure can be exploited as demonstrated by the attack from [KZ20]. In practice, one can increase the number of iterations τ to take into account this attack. One can also amplify the challenge spaces sizes in order to reduce the effectiveness of this attack as explained in Sect. 4. In addition, the security proofs of the PoK following our new paradigm might be a bit more involved. Indeed, one might need to introduce an intermediary problem and rely on a reduction from the targeted problem to this intermediary problem. This strategy was used in [AGS11] with the introduction of the DiffSD problem and its reduction to the QCSD problem. More recently, such a strategy has also been used in [FJR22] where the d-split SD problem is used as an intermediary problem along with a reduction to the SD problem. In practice, one generally need to increase the considered parameters for these reductions to hold securely.

Impact on Resulting Signature Size. Several of the aforementioned elements impact the signature size in conflicting ways. For instance, removing the Helper increases the soundness which impacts the signature size negatively however it also reduces the number of seeds to be sent which impacts the signature size positively. In addition, many PoK with Helper feature a trade-off between performances and signature sizes hence our performance improvement related to the Helper's removal directly translate into a reduction of the signature size in these cases. Moreover, using a 5-round structure reduces the number of commitments to be sent but requires to take into account the attack from [KZ20]. In practice, our new paradigm lead to smaller signature sizes over comparable PoK with Helper when the parameters are chosen carefuly. This is mainly due to the performance improvement related to the Helper's removal while the work from [KZ20] constitutes a limiting factor thus motivating the new technique introduced in Sect. 4.

Our new paradigm exploits the structure of the considered problems in order to build more compact PoK. As a result, our protocols differs from existing ones in several ways thus leading to different features when it comes to soundness, performances, security and resulting signature sizes. Interestingly, the required additional structure has been either already well studied (such as cyclicity for the QCSD and IRSD problems) or is closely related to the considered problem (such as linearity over $\mathbb{F}_q$ for the inhomegeneous IPKP problem).

4   Amplifying Challenge Space to Mitigate [KZ20] Attack

4.1   Overview of Our Challenge Space Amplification Technique

It was shown in [KZ20] that 5-round PoK that use parallel repetition to achieve a negligible soundness error are vulnerable to an attack when they are made non-interactive with the Fiat-Shamir transform. One can easily mitigate this attack by increasing the number of considered repetitions τ. This countermeasure increases the resulting signature size hence most designers choose to collapse 5-round schemes into 3-round ones instead. In the case of our new paradigm, such a strategy is not desirable as explained in Sect. 3. These considerations motivate the research for an alternate way to mitigate the [KZ20] attack.

Challenge Space Amplification. Our new mitigation strategy consists in amplifying the challenge space sizes rather than increasing the number of repetitions. In particular, we are interested in amplifying the first challenge space of our PoK leveraging structure. Hereafter, we show how such an amplification can be performed by increasing the size of the public key. Interestingly, in some cases, one may increase the size of the challenge space exponentially while increasing the size of the public key only linearly. In such cases, our new mitigation strategy is more efficient than increasing the number of repetitions τ.

4.2   The [KZ20] Attack Against 5-Round PoK

We start by recalling that most PoK from the litterature feature a soundness error ranging from $2/3$ to $1/N$ for N up to 1024. In order to achieve a negligible soundness error, one has to execute τ repetitions of the underlying protocol. The main idea of the [KZ20] result is to separate the attacker work in two steps respectively related to the first and second challenges. A malicious prover tries to correctly guess the first challenges for $\tau^* \leq \tau$ repetitions as well as the second challenges for the remaining $\tau - \tau^*$ repetitions leveraging the fact that a correct guess for any challenge allows to cheat in most protocols. The efficiency of the attack depends on the number of repetitions τ, the sizes of the challenge spaces $\mathcal{C}_1$ and $\mathcal{C}_2$ as well as a property of the PoK called the capability for early abort. PoK with Helper have the capability for early abort however schemes constructed following our new paradigm don't. As a consequence, finding a way to mitigate the [KZ20] attack is of great importance in our context. Our mitigation strategy relies on the fact that the attack complexity increases if the two challenges spaces $\mathcal{C}_1$ and $\mathcal{C}_2$ are not of equal size. Indeed, in our context (no capability for early abort), the attack complexity is equal to $\mathsf{Cost}(\tau) = \frac{1}{P_1(\tau^*,\tau,\mathcal{C}_1)} + (\mathcal{C}_2)^{\tau-\tau^*}$ where $P_1(r,\tau,\mathcal{C}_1)$ is the probability to correctly guess at least r amongst τ challenges in a challenge space of size $\mathcal{C}_1$ namely $P_1(r,\tau,\mathcal{C}_1) = \sum_{i=r}^{\tau} \left(\frac{1}{\mathcal{C}_1}\right)^i \cdot \left(\frac{\mathcal{C}_1-1}{\mathcal{C}_1}\right)^{\tau-i} \cdot \binom{\tau}{i}$ with τ^* being the number of repetitions in the first step of the attack that minimizes the attack cost namely $\tau^* = \underset{0 \leq r \leq \tau}{\arg\min} \frac{1}{P_1(r,\tau,\mathcal{C}_1)} + (\mathcal{C}_2)^{\tau-r}$.

4.3   Trade-Off Between Public Key Size and Challenge Space Size

In order to mitigate the attack from [KZ20], we propose to increase the size of the first challenge space. This decreases the probability that a malicious prover is able to correctly guess τ^* random challenges in the first step of the attack hence reduces its efficiency. In order to do so, one can introduce several instances of the considered hard problem in a given public key as suggested in [BBBG21]. Using the SD problem for illustrative purposes, one replaces the secret key $\mathsf{sk} = (\mathbf{x})$ where $w_H(\mathbf{x}) = \omega$ and public key $\mathsf{pk} = (\mathbf{H}, \mathbf{y}^\top = \mathbf{H}\mathbf{x}^\top)$ by M instances such that $\mathsf{sk} = (\mathbf{x}_i)_{i\in[1,M]}$ and $\mathsf{pk} = (\mathbf{H}, (\mathbf{y}_i^\top = \mathbf{H}\mathbf{x}_i^\top)_{i\in[1,M]})$ where $w_H(\mathbf{x}_i) = \omega$. In practice, this implies that the parameters of the schemes have to be chosen taking into account that the attacker has now access to M instances $(\mathbf{H}, (\mathbf{y}_i)_{i\in[1,M]})$. This setting has been studied within the code-based cryptography community and is commonly referred as decoding one out of many in the literature [Sen11]. Using this technique, the first challenge space size is increased by a factor M however the size of the public key is also increased by a factor M. Overall, the challenge space amplification approach reduces the (public key + signature) size as suggested by numbers in Sect. 7.

We now present a new idea that greatly improves the efficiency of the aforementioned amplification technique. Interestingly, in some cases, it is possible to increase the challenge space size *exponentially* while only increasing the public key size *linearly*. We illustrate such cases using the RSD problem namely the syndrome decoding problem in the rank metric setting. As previously, let us consider M instances such that $\mathsf{sk} = (\mathbf{x}_i)_{i\in[1,M]}$ and $\mathsf{pk} = (\mathbf{H}, (\mathbf{y}_i^\top = \mathbf{H}\mathbf{x}_i^\top)_{i\in[1,M]})$ where $w_R(\mathbf{x}_i) = \omega$. Moreover, if we choose the $\mathbf{x}_i$ such that they all share the same support E, then we end up working with the RSL problem. The RSL problem can be seen as a generalization of the RSD problem whose security has been studied in [GHPT17, DAT18, BB21]. Due to the properties of the rank metric, any linear combination of $\mathbf{x}_i$ has a support $E' \subseteq E$ (with $E' = E$ with good probability) and a rank weight equal to $\omega' \leq \omega$ (with $\omega' = \omega$ with good probability). One can leverage this property to design more efficient protocols by substituting a random choice of a $\mathbf{x}_i$ value by a random choice of a linear combination of the $\mathbf{x}_i$ values. Doing so, a random choice amongst M values is substituted by a random choice amongst q^M values thus amplifying the considered challenge space size exponentially rather than linearly while still requiring the public key size to be increased only linearly by the factor M. This makes our amplification technique quite efficient as a mitigation strategy against the [KZ20] attack as suggested by the numbers presented in Sect. 7.3. Indeed, one can see that amplifying the first challenge space size exponentially reduces the number of repetitions τ from 37 to 23 namely an improvement approximately greater than 35%.

5   New PoK with Helper for the SD Problem

The first efficient PoK for the SD problem was introduced by Stern in [Ste93]. Over the years, many variants and improvements have been proposed in [Vér97, AGS11, CVE11] for instance. Several PoK achieving an arbitrarily small soundness error have been proposed recently in [GPS21, FJR21, BGKM22, FJR22]. Most of these schemes (with the notable exception of [FJR22]) relies on permutations to mask the secret value $\mathbf{x}$ associated to the considered SD problem. Hereafter, we present a new PoK with Helper that outperforms previous permutation-based schemes. It is described in Fig. 2 and encompasses several ideas from [BGKM22], [FJR21] and [BGKS21]. Indeed, our protocol follows the same paradigm as PoK 2 from [BGKM22] as it introduces several permutations $(\pi_i)_{i \in [1,N]}$ and masks the secret $\mathbf{x}$ using the permutation π_α for $\alpha \in [1, N]$ while revealing the other permutations $(\pi_i)_{i \in [1,N] \setminus \alpha}$. A notable difference comes from the fact that it also leverages the shared permutations paradigm from [FJR21] where the permutations $(\pi_i)_{i \in [1,N]}$ are nested around a global permutation π such that $\pi = \pi_N \circ \cdots \circ \pi_1$. As a consequence, our protocol masks the secret $\mathbf{x}$ using $\pi_\alpha \circ \cdots \circ \pi_1[\mathbf{x}]$ for $\alpha \in [1, N]$. This differs from [FJR21] where the secret is masked by $\pi[\mathbf{x}]$ and where $\pi[\mathbf{u} + \mathbf{x}] + \mathbf{v}$ is computed without revealing π. This difference allows us to perform a *cut-and-choose with a meet in the middle approach* where the recurrence relation related to π is used in both directions rather than just one. Thanks to this new property, our protocol can benefit from an optimization introduced in [BGKS21] that allows to substitute a vector by a random seed. This improvement is of great importance as it implies that our PoK size scales with $1.5\,\tau\,n$ (where τ is the number of repetitions required to achieve a negligible soundness error and n is the vector length considered within the SD instance) while all previous protocols feature sizes scaling with a factor $2\,\tau\,n$ instead. As a consequence, our protocol outperforms the protocols from [BGKM22] and [FJR21]. We defer the reader to Tables 4 and 5 for a comparison with existing protocols including the recent [FJR22] proposal.

Inputs & Public Data

$w = \mathbf{x}$, $x = (\mathbf{H}, \mathbf{y})$

Helper(x)

$\theta \xleftarrow{\$} \{0,1\}^\lambda$, $\xi \xleftarrow{\$} \{0,1\}^\lambda$

for $i \in [1,N]$ **do**

   $\theta_i \xleftarrow{\$,\theta} \{0,1\}^\lambda$, $\phi_i \xleftarrow{\$,\theta_i} \{0,1\}^\lambda$, $\pi_i \xleftarrow{\$,\phi_i} S_n$, $\mathbf{v}_i \xleftarrow{\$,\phi_i} \mathbb{F}_2^n$, $r_{1,i} \xleftarrow{\$,\theta_i} \{0,1\}^\lambda$, $\mathsf{com}_{1,i} = \mathsf{Com}(r_{1,i}, \phi_i)$

end

$\pi = \pi_N \circ \cdots \circ \pi_1$, $\mathbf{v} = \mathbf{v}_N + \sum_{i \in [1,N-1]} \pi_N \circ \cdots \circ \pi_{i+1}[\mathbf{v}_i]$, $\mathbf{r} \xleftarrow{\$,\xi} \mathbb{F}_2^n$, $\mathbf{u} = \pi^{-1}[\mathbf{r} - \mathbf{v}]$

$\mathsf{com}_1 = \mathsf{Hash}(\mathbf{H}\mathbf{u} \,\|\, \pi[\mathbf{u}] + \mathbf{v} \,\|\, (\mathsf{com}_{1,i})_{i \in [1,N]})$

Send (θ, ξ) to the **Prover** and com_1 to the **Verifier**

$\mathsf{P}_1(w, x, \theta, \xi)$

Compute $(\theta_i, \pi_i, \mathbf{v}_i)_{i \in [1,N]}$ and $\mathbf{u}$ from (θ, ξ)

$\mathbf{s}_0 = \mathbf{u} + \mathbf{x}$

for $i \in [1,N]$ **do**

   $\mathbf{s}_i = \pi_i[\mathbf{s}_{i-1}] + \mathbf{v}_i$

end

$\mathsf{com}_2 = \mathsf{Hash}(\mathbf{u} + \mathbf{x} \,\|\, (\mathbf{s}_i)_{i \in [1,N]})$

$\mathsf{V}_1(x, \mathsf{com}_1)$

$\alpha \xleftarrow{\$} [1,N]$

$\mathsf{P}_2(w, x, \theta, \xi, \alpha)$

$\mathbf{z}_1 = \mathbf{u} + \mathbf{x}$, $z_2 = (\theta_i)_{i \in [1,N] \setminus \alpha}$, $z_3 = \xi$, $\mathbf{z}_4 = \pi_\alpha \circ \cdots \circ \pi_1[\mathbf{x}]$

$\mathsf{rsp} = (\mathbf{z}_1, z_2, z_3, \mathbf{z}_4, \mathsf{com}_{1,\alpha})$

$\mathsf{V}_2(x, \mathsf{com}_1, \mathsf{com}_2, \alpha, \mathsf{rsp})$

Compute $(\bar{\phi}_i, \bar{r}_{1,i}, \bar{\pi}_i, \bar{\mathbf{v}}_i)_{i \in [1,N] \setminus \alpha}$ from z_2 and $\bar{\mathbf{t}}_N = \bar{\mathbf{r}}$ from z_3

for $i \in \{N, \ldots, \alpha + 1\}$ **do**

   $\bar{\mathbf{t}}_{i-1} = \bar{\pi}_i^{-1}[\bar{\mathbf{t}}_i - \bar{\mathbf{v}}_i]$

end

$\bar{\mathbf{s}}_0 = \mathbf{z}_1$, $\bar{\mathbf{s}}_\alpha = \bar{\mathbf{t}}_\alpha + \mathbf{z}_4$, $\bar{\mathsf{com}}_{1,\alpha} = \mathsf{com}_{1,\alpha}$

for $i \in [1,N] \setminus \alpha$ **do**

   $\bar{\mathbf{s}}_i = \bar{\pi}_i[\bar{\mathbf{s}}_{i-1}] + \bar{\mathbf{v}}_i$

   $\bar{\mathsf{com}}_{1,i} = \mathsf{Com}(\bar{r}_{1,i}, \bar{\phi}_i)$

end

$b_1 \longleftarrow (\mathsf{com}_1 = \mathsf{Hash}(\mathbf{H}\mathbf{z}_1 - \mathbf{y} \,\|\, \bar{\mathbf{r}} \,\|\, (\bar{\mathsf{com}}_{1,i})_{i \in [1,N]}))$

$b_2 \longleftarrow (\mathsf{com}_2 = \mathsf{Hash}(\mathbf{z}_1 \,\|\, (\bar{\mathbf{s}}_i)_{i \in [1,N]}))$

$b_3 \longleftarrow (w_H(\mathbf{z}_4) = \omega)$

return $b_1 \wedge b_2 \wedge b_3$

Fig. 2. PoK with Helper for the SD problem over $\mathbb{F}_2$

Theorem 1. *If the hash function used is collision-resistant and if the commitment scheme used is binding and hiding, then the protocol depicted in Fig. 2 is an honest-verifier zero-knowledge PoK with Helper for the SD problem over $\mathbb{F}_2$ with soundness error $1/N$.*

Proof. Proof of Theorem 1 can be found in Appendix A.

6   New PoK Related to the PKP, SD and RSD Problems

6.1   PoK Leveraging Structure for the IPKP Problem

We present in Fig. 3 a PoK leveraging structure for the IPKP problem using linearity over $\mathbb{F}_q$ along with the shared permutation from [FJR21].

Theorem 2. *If the hash function used is collision-resistant and if the commitment scheme used is binding and hiding, then the protocol depicted in Fig. 3 is an honest-verifier zero-knowledge PoK for the IPKP problem with soundness error equal to $\frac{1}{N} + \frac{N-1}{N \cdot (q-1)}$.*

Proof. Proof of Theorem 2 can be found in Appendix B.

6.2   PoK Leveraging Structure for the QCSD Problem over $\mathbb{F}_2$

We apply results from Sects. 3 and 4 on top of the PoK with Helper from Sect. 5. This PoK leverages quasi-cyclicity over $\mathbb{F}_2$ and is depicted in Fig. 4.

Theorem 3. *If the hash function used is collision-resistant and if the commitment scheme used is binding and hiding, then the protocol depicted in Fig. 4 is an honest-verifier zero-knowledge PoK for the QCSD(n, k, w, M) problem with soundness error equal to $\frac{1}{N} + \frac{(N-1)(\Delta-1)}{N \cdot M \cdot k}$ for some parameter Δ.*

Proof. Proof of Theorem 3 can be found in Appendix C.

Remark. The parameter Δ is related to the security of the DiffSD problem. The QCSD problem reduces to the intermediary DiffSD problem for sufficient large values of Δ as showed in Appendix C. When Δ is not large enough, the security reduction does not hold which enable additional cheating strategies for the adversary hence impact the soundness of the protocol.

6.3   PoK Leveraging Structure for the IRSL Problem

One can adapt the protocols described in Sects. 5 and 6.2 to the rank metric setting by replacing permutations by isometries for the rank metric. Doing so, one get a PoK with Helper for the RSD problem as well as a PoK leveraging structure for the IRSD problem. In addition, one can apply the challenge space amplification technique presented in Sect. 4 in order to get a PoK leveraging structure for IRSL problem as depicted in Fig. 5. In practice, one has to take into account the cases where $\omega' < \omega$ mentioned in Sect. 4 however we omit such cases in Fig. 5 for conciseness.

Inputs & Public Data

$w = \pi$, $x = (\mathbf{H}, \mathbf{x}, \mathbf{y})$

$\mathcal{C}_{\text{struct}} = \mathbb{F}_q^*$, $\text{ch}_{\text{struct}} = \kappa$

$\underline{P_1(w, x)}$

$\theta \xleftarrow{\$} \{0,1\}^\lambda$

for $i \in \{N, \ldots, 1\}$ **do**

$\quad \theta_i \xleftarrow{\$, \theta} \{0,1\}^\lambda$, $\phi_i \xleftarrow{\$, \theta_i} \{0,1\}^\lambda$

$\quad$ **if** $i \neq 1$ **do**

$\qquad \pi_i \xleftarrow{\$, \phi_i} \mathcal{S}_n$, $\mathbf{v}_i \xleftarrow{\$, \phi_i} \mathbb{F}_q^n$, $r_{1,i} \xleftarrow{\$, \theta_i} \{0,1\}^\lambda$, $\text{com}_{1,i} = \text{Com}(r_{1,i}, \phi_i)$

$\quad$ **else**

$\qquad \pi_1 = \pi_2^{-1} \circ \cdots \circ \pi_N^{-1} \circ \pi$, $\mathbf{v}_1 \xleftarrow{\$, \phi_1} \mathbb{F}_q^n$, $r_{1,1} \xleftarrow{\$, \theta_1} \{0,1\}^\lambda$, $\text{com}_{1,1} = \text{Com}(r_{1,1}, \pi_1 \| \phi_1)$

$\quad$ **end**

end

$\mathbf{v} = \mathbf{v}_N + \sum_{i \in [1, N-1]} \pi_N \circ \cdots \circ \pi_{i+1}[\mathbf{v}_i]$

$\text{com}_1 = \text{Hash}(\mathbf{Hv} \| (\text{com}_{1,i})_{i \in [1,N]})$

$\underline{P_2(w, x, \kappa)}$

$\mathbf{s}_0 = \kappa \cdot \mathbf{x}$

for $i \in [1, N]$ **do**

$\quad \mathbf{s}_i = \pi_i[\mathbf{s}_{i-1}] + \mathbf{v}_i$

end

$\text{com}_2 = \text{Hash}((\mathbf{s}_i)_{i \in [1,N]})$

$\underline{P_2(w, x, \kappa, \alpha)}$

$\mathbf{z}_1 = \mathbf{s}_\alpha$

if $\alpha \neq 1$ **do**

$\quad z_2 = \pi_1 \| (\theta_i)_{i \in [1,N] \setminus \alpha}$

else

$\quad z_2 = (\theta_i)_{i \in [1,N] \setminus \alpha}$

end

$\text{rsp} = (\mathbf{z}_1, z_2, \text{com}_{1,\alpha})$

$\underline{V(x, \text{com}_1, \kappa, \text{com}_2, \alpha, \text{rsp})}$

Compute $(\bar{\phi}_i, \bar{r}_{1,i}, \bar{\pi}_i, \bar{\mathbf{v}}_i)_{i \in [1,N] \setminus \alpha}$ from z_2

$\bar{\mathbf{s}}_0 = \kappa \cdot \mathbf{x}$, $\bar{\mathbf{s}}_\alpha = \mathbf{z}_1$, $\bar{\text{com}}_{1,\alpha} = \text{com}_{1,\alpha}$

for $i \in [1, N] \setminus \alpha$ **do**

$\quad \bar{\mathbf{s}}_i = \bar{\pi}_i[\bar{\mathbf{s}}_{i-1}] + \bar{\mathbf{v}}_i$

$\quad$ **if** $i \neq 1$ **do**

$\qquad \bar{\text{com}}_{1,i} = \text{Com}(\bar{r}_{1,i}, \bar{\phi}_i)$

$\quad$ **else**

$\qquad \bar{\text{com}}_{1,1} = \text{Com}(\bar{r}_{1,1}, \bar{\pi}_1 \| \bar{\phi}_1)$

$\quad$ **end**

end

$b_1 \longleftarrow (\text{com}_1 = \text{Hash}(\mathbf{H}\bar{\mathbf{s}}_N - \kappa \cdot \mathbf{y} \| (\text{com}_{1,i})_{i \in [1,N]}))$

$b_2 \longleftarrow (\text{com}_2 = \text{Hash}((\bar{\mathbf{s}}_i)_{i \in [1,N]}))$

return $b_1 \wedge b_2$

Fig. 3. PoK leveraging structure for the IPKP problem

Inputs & Public Data

$w = (\mathbf{x}_i)_{i\in[1,M]}, \ x = (\mathbf{H}, (\mathbf{y}_i)_{i\in[1,M]}),$

$\mathcal{C}_{\text{struct}} = [1,M] \times [1,k], \ \mathsf{ch}_{\text{struct}} = (\mu, \kappa)$

$\underline{\mathsf{P}_1(w,x)}$

$\theta \xleftarrow{\$} \{0,1\}^\lambda, \ \xi \xleftarrow{\$} \{0,1\}^\lambda$

for $i \in [1, N]$ do

$\quad \theta_i \xleftarrow{\$,\theta} \{0,1\}^\lambda, \ \phi_i \xleftarrow{\$,\theta_i} \{0,1\}^\lambda, \ \pi_i \xleftarrow{\$,\phi_i} S_n, \ \mathbf{v}_i \xleftarrow{\$,\phi_i} \mathbb{F}_2^n, \ r_{1,i} \xleftarrow{\$,\theta_i} \{0,1\}^\lambda, \ \mathsf{com}_{1,i} = \mathsf{Com}(r_{1,i}, \phi_i)$

end

$\pi = \pi_N \circ \cdots \circ \pi_1, \ \mathbf{v} = \mathbf{v}_N + \sum_{i\in[1,N-1]} \pi_N \circ \cdots \circ \pi_{i+1}[\mathbf{v}_i], \ \mathbf{r} \xleftarrow{\$,\xi} \mathbb{F}_2^n, \ \mathbf{u} = \pi^{-1}[\mathbf{r} - \mathbf{v}]$

$\mathsf{com}_1 = \mathsf{Hash}(\mathbf{H}\mathbf{u} \,\|\, \pi[\mathbf{u}] + \mathbf{v} \,\|\, (\mathsf{com}_{1,i})_{i\in[1,N]})$

$\underline{\mathsf{P}_2(w,x,\mu,\kappa)}$

$\mathbf{x}_{\mu,\kappa} = \mathsf{rot}_\kappa(\mathbf{x}_\mu), \ \mathbf{s}_0 = \mathbf{u} + \mathbf{x}_{\mu,\kappa}$

for $i \in [1, N]$ do

$\quad \mathbf{s}_i = \pi_i[\mathbf{s}_{i-1}] + \mathbf{v}_i$

end

$\mathsf{com}_2 = \mathsf{Hash}(\mathbf{u} + \mathbf{x}_{\mu,\kappa} \,\|\, (\mathbf{s}_i)_{i\in[1,N]})$

$\underline{\mathsf{P}_3(w,x,\mu,\kappa,\alpha)}$

$\mathbf{z}_1 = \mathbf{u} + \mathbf{x}_{\mu,\kappa}, \ z_2 = (\theta_i)_{i\in[1,N]\setminus\alpha}, \ z_3 = \xi, \ \mathbf{z}_4 = \pi_\alpha \circ \cdots \circ \pi_1[\mathbf{x}_{\mu,\kappa}]$

$\mathsf{rsp} = (\mathbf{z}_1, z_2, z_3, \mathbf{z}_4, \mathsf{com}_{1,\alpha})$

$\underline{\mathsf{V}(x, \mathsf{com}_1, (\mu,\kappa), \mathsf{com}_2, \alpha, \mathsf{rsp})}$

Compute $(\bar{\phi}_i, \bar{r}_{1,i}, \bar{\pi}_i, \bar{\mathbf{v}}_i)_{i\in[1,N]\setminus\alpha}$ from z_2 and $\bar{\mathbf{t}}_N = \bar{\mathbf{r}}$ from z_3

for $i \in \{N, \ldots, \alpha+1\}$ do

$\quad \bar{\mathbf{t}}_{i-1} = \bar{\pi}_i^{-1}[\bar{\mathbf{t}}_i - \bar{\mathbf{v}}_i]$

end

$\bar{\mathbf{s}}_0 = \mathbf{z}_1, \ \bar{\mathbf{s}}_\alpha = \bar{\mathbf{t}}_\alpha + \mathbf{z}_4, \ \mathsf{c\bar{o}m}_{1,\alpha} = \mathsf{com}_{1,\alpha}$

for $i \in [1,N] \setminus \alpha$ do

$\quad \bar{\mathbf{s}}_i = \bar{\pi}_i[\bar{\mathbf{s}}_{i-1}] + \bar{\mathbf{v}}_i, \ \mathsf{c\bar{o}m}_{1,i} = \mathsf{Com}(\bar{r}_{1,i}, \bar{\phi}_i)$

end

$b_1 \longleftarrow (\mathsf{com}_1 = \mathsf{Hash}(\mathbf{H}\mathbf{z}_1 - \mathsf{rot}_\kappa(\mathbf{y}_\mu) \,\|\, \bar{\mathbf{r}} \,\|\, (\mathsf{c\bar{o}m}_{1,i})_{i\in[1,N]}))$

$b_2 \longleftarrow (\mathsf{com}_2 = \mathsf{Hash}(\mathbf{z}_1 \,\|\, (\bar{\mathbf{s}}_i)_{i\in[1,N]}))$

$b_3 \longleftarrow (w_H(\mathbf{z}_4) = \omega)$

return $b_1 \wedge b_2 \wedge b_3$

Fig. 4. PoK leveraging structure for the $\mathsf{QCSD}(n,k,w,M)$ problem over $\mathbb{F}_2$

Theorem 4. *If the hash function used is collision-resistant and if the commitment scheme used is binding and hiding, then the protocol depicted in Fig. 5 is an honest-verifier zero-knowledge PoK for the* IRSL *problem with soundness error equal to* $\frac{1}{N} + \frac{(N-1)(\Delta-1)}{N(q^{Mk}-1)}$ *for some parameter* Δ.

Proof. Proof of Theorem 4 can be found in Appendix D.

Inputs & Public Data

$w = (\mathbf{x}_i)_{i \in [1,M]}, \quad x = (\mathbf{H}, (\mathbf{y}_i)_{i \in [1,M]}),$

$\mathcal{C}_{\text{struct}} = (\mathbb{F}_q)^{Mk} \setminus (0, \cdots, 0), \quad \text{ch}_{\text{struct}} = \gamma = (\gamma_{i,j})_{i \in [1,M], j \in [1,k]}$

$\mathsf{P}_1(w, x)$

$\theta \xleftarrow{\$} \{0,1\}^\lambda, \; \xi \xleftarrow{\$} \{0,1\}^\lambda$

for $i \in [1, N]$ do

$\quad \theta_i \xleftarrow{\$,\theta} \{0,1\}^\lambda, \; \phi_i \xleftarrow{\$,\theta_i} \{0,1\}^\lambda, \; \mathbf{P}_i \xleftarrow{\$,\phi_i} \mathrm{GL}_m(\mathbb{F}_q), \; \mathbf{Q}_i \xleftarrow{\$,\phi_i} \mathrm{GL}_n(\mathbb{F}_q), \; \mathbf{v}_i \xleftarrow{\$,\phi_i} \mathbb{F}_{q^m}^n, \; r_{1,i} \xleftarrow{\$,\theta_i} \{0,1\}^\lambda, \; \text{com}_{1,i} = \text{Com}(r_{1,i}, \phi_i)$

end

$\mathbf{P} = \mathbf{P}_N \times \cdots \times \mathbf{P}_1, \; \mathbf{Q} = \mathbf{Q}_N \times \cdots \times \mathbf{Q}_1, \; \mathbf{v} = \mathbf{v}_N + \sum_{i \in [1,N-1]} \mathbf{P}_N \times \cdots \times \mathbf{P}_{i+1} \cdot \mathbf{v}_i \cdot \mathbf{Q}_{i+1} \times \cdots \times \mathbf{Q}_N$

$\mathbf{r} \xleftarrow{\$,\xi} \mathbb{F}_2^n, \; \mathbf{u} = \mathbf{P}^{-1} \cdot (\mathbf{r} - \mathbf{v}) \cdot \mathbf{Q}^{-1}$

$\text{com}_1 = \text{Hash}\big(\mathbf{Hu} \,\|\, \mathbf{P} \cdot \mathbf{u} \cdot \mathbf{Q} + \mathbf{v} \,\|\, (\text{com}_{1,i})_{i \in [1,N]}\big)$

$\mathsf{P}_2(w, x, \gamma)$

$\mathbf{x}_\gamma = \sum_{(i,j) \in [1,M] \times [1,k]} \gamma_{i,j} \cdot \mathbf{rot}_j(\mathbf{x}_i), \; \mathbf{s}_0 = \mathbf{u} + \mathbf{x}_\gamma$

for $i \in [1, N]$ do

$\quad \mathbf{s}_i = \mathbf{P}_i \cdot \mathbf{s}_{i-1} \cdot \mathbf{Q}_i + \mathbf{v}_i$

end

$\text{com}_2 = \text{Hash}\big(\mathbf{u} + \mathbf{x}_\gamma \,\|\, (\mathbf{s}_i)_{i \in [1,N]}\big)$

$\mathsf{P}_3(w, x, \gamma, \alpha)$

$\mathbf{z}_1 = \mathbf{u} + \mathbf{x}_\gamma, \; z_2 = (\theta_i)_{i \in [1,N] \setminus \alpha}, \; z_3 = \xi, \; \mathbf{z}_4 = \mathbf{P}_\alpha \times \cdots \times \mathbf{P}_1 \cdot \mathbf{x}_\gamma \cdot \mathbf{Q}_1 \times \cdots \times \mathbf{Q}_\alpha$

$\text{rsp} = (\mathbf{z}_1, z_2, z_3, \mathbf{z}_4, \text{com}_{1,\alpha})$

$\mathsf{V}(x, \text{com}_1, \gamma, \text{com}_2, \alpha, \text{rsp})$

Compute $(\bar{\phi}_i, \bar{r}_{1,i}, \bar{\mathbf{P}}_i, \bar{\mathbf{Q}}_i, \bar{\mathbf{v}}_i)_{i \in [1,N] \setminus \alpha}$ from z_2 and $\bar{\mathbf{t}}_N = \bar{\mathbf{r}}$ from z_3

for $i \in \{N, \ldots, \alpha + 1\}$ do

$\quad \bar{\mathbf{t}}_{i-1} = \bar{\mathbf{P}}_i^{-1} \cdot (\bar{\mathbf{t}}_i - \bar{\mathbf{v}}_i) \cdot \bar{\mathbf{Q}}_i^{-1}$

end

$\bar{\mathbf{s}}_0 = \mathbf{z}_1, \; \bar{\mathbf{s}}_\alpha = \bar{\mathbf{t}}_\alpha + \mathbf{z}_4, \; \tilde{\text{com}}_{1,\alpha} = \text{com}_{1,\alpha}$

for $i \in [1, N] \setminus \alpha$ do

$\quad \bar{\mathbf{s}}_i = \bar{\mathbf{P}}_i \cdot \bar{\mathbf{s}}_{i-1} \cdot \bar{\mathbf{Q}}_i + \bar{\mathbf{v}}_i$

$\quad \tilde{\text{com}}_{1,i} = \text{Com}(\bar{r}_{1,i}, \bar{\phi}_i)$

end

$b_1 \longleftarrow \big(\text{com}_1 = \text{Hash}\big(\mathbf{Hz}_1 - \sum_{(i,j) \in [1,M] \times [1,k]} \gamma_{i,j} \cdot \mathbf{rot}_j(\mathbf{y}_i) \,\|\, \bar{\mathbf{r}} \,\|\, (\tilde{\text{com}}_{1,i})_{i \in [1,N]}\big)\big)$

$b_2 \longleftarrow \big(\text{com}_2 = \text{Hash}\big(\mathbf{z}_1 \,\|\, (\bar{\mathbf{s}}_i)_{i \in [1,N]}\big)\big)$

$b_3 \longleftarrow \big(w_H(\mathbf{z}_4) = \omega\big)$

return $b_1 \wedge b_2 \wedge b_3$

Fig. 5. PoK leveraging structure for the IRSL problem

7   Resulting Signatures and Comparison

PoK can be transformed into signature schemes using the Fiat-Shamir transform [FS86]. Several optimizations can be employed in the process, we defer the interested reader to previous work such as [KKW18, Beu20, GPS21, BGKM22] for additional details. Hereafter, we keep the inherent 5-round structure of our PoK (except for the one from Sect. 5 that is collapsed to 3-round) hence parameters are chosen taking into account the attack from [KZ20]. Moreover, we only consider parameters for $\lambda = 128$ bits of security. The commitments are instantiated using hash functions along with some randomness. For the signatures, random salts are added to the hash functions.

7.1   Signatures Based on PoK Related to the **PKP** Problem

The signature size of our protocol from Sect. 6.1 is detailed in Table 2. Table 3 provides a comparison with respect to other PoK for the PKP problem. The complexity of the PKP problem has been studied in [KMRP19]. We consider parameters from [Beu20] for our comparison namely ($q = 997, n = 61, m = 28$). In addition, we use both ($N = 32, \tau = 42$) and ($N = 256, \tau = 31$).

Table 2. Signature sizes for our PKP based construction

	Signature size
Our Work (Sect. 6.1)	$5\lambda + \tau \cdot (n \cdot \log_2(q) + n \cdot \log_2(n) + \lambda \cdot \log_2(N) + 2\lambda)$

Table 3. Signatures based on PKP for $\lambda = 128$ (sorted by decreasing size)

	Type	pk	σ	Structure	Security Assumption
SUSHYFISH [Beu20]	Fast	0.1 kB	18.1 kB	3-round	IPKP
	Short	0.1 kB	12.1 kB		
[Fen22]	Fast	0.1 kB	16.4 kB	5-round	IPKP
	Short	0.1 kB	12.9 kB		
Our Work (Sect. 6.1)	Fast	0.1 kB	10.0 kB	5-round	IPKP
	Short	0.1 kB	8.9 kB		

7.2   Signatures Based on PoK Related to the **SD** Problem

Table 4 compares signature sizes of our new protocol with respect to existing ones. One can see that our signatures scale with a factor $1.5n \cdot \tau$ which bring an improvement with respect to previous (comparable) schemes that scale with a factor $2n \cdot \tau$. Table 5 provides a comparison to other code-based signatures constructed from PoK for the SD problem. Parameters are chosen taking into account attacks from [BJMM12] and [Sen11]. For our protocol from Sect. 5, we have used ($n = 1190, k = 595, \omega = 132$) as well as ($N = 8, \tau = 49, M' = 187$) and ($N = 32, \tau = 28, M' = 389$). In these cases, M' is the parameter related to the beating parallel repetition from [KKW18] namely M' instances are prepared during the preprocessing step amongst which τ are actually executed. For our protocol from Sect. 6.2, we have used ($n = 1306, k = 653, \omega = 132, \Delta = $

17) as well as $(N = 32, \tau = 42, M = 22)$ and $(N = 256, \tau = 33, M = 12)$. Numbers for [FJR22] are from the original paper while numbers for [FJR21] have been recomputed using the aforementioned parameters in order to provide a fair comparison.

Table 4. Signature sizes (sorted by decreasing size)

	Signature size
[BGKM22]	$2\lambda + \tau \cdot (2n + 3\lambda \cdot \log_2(N) + 3\lambda \cdot \log_2(M/\tau))$
[FJR21]	$2\lambda + \tau \cdot (2n + \lambda \cdot \log_2(N) + 2\lambda + 3\lambda \cdot \log_2(M/\tau))$
Our Work (Sect. 5)	$3\lambda + \tau \cdot (1.5n + \lambda \cdot \log_2(N) + 2\lambda + 3\lambda \cdot \log_2(M/\tau))$
Our Work (Sect. 6.2)	$5\lambda + \tau \cdot (1.5n + \lambda \cdot \log_2(N) + 2\lambda)$

Table 5. Signatures based on SD for $\lambda = 128$ (sorted by decreasing size)

	Type	pk	σ	Structure	Security Assumption
[BGKM22]	Fast	0.1 kB	26.4 kB	3-round	SD over $\mathbb{F}_2$
	Short	0.1 kB	20.5 kB		
[FJR21]	Fast	0.1 kB	23.3 kB	3-round	SD over $\mathbb{F}_2$
	Short	0.1 kB	16.9 kB		
Our Work (Sect. 5)	Fast	0.1 kB	19.6 kB	3-round	SD over $\mathbb{F}_2$
	Short	0.1 kB	14.8 kB		
Our Work (Sect. 6.2)	Fast	1.8 kB	15.1 kB	5-round	QCSD over $\mathbb{F}_2$
	Short	1.0 kB	13.5 kB		
[FJR22]	Fast	0.1 kB	17.0 kB	5-round	SD over $\mathbb{F}_2$
	Short	0.1 kB	11.8 kB		
	Fast	0.2 kB	11.5 kB	5-round	SD over $\mathbb{F}_q$
	Short	0.2 kB	8.3 kB		

7.3   Signatures Based on PoK Related to the RSD/RSL Problem

Parameters for our PoK based on the rank metric are chosen to resist best known attacks against RSD [GRS15, BBC+20] and RSL [BB21, GHPT17, DAT18]. For our protocol from Sect. 5, we have used $(q = 2, m = 31, n = 30, k = 15, \omega = 9)$ as well as $(N = 8, \tau = 49, M' = 187)$ and $(N = 32, \tau = 28, M' = 389)$. For our protocol from Sect. 6.3, we have used $(q = 2, m = 37, n = 34, k = 17, \omega = 9, \Delta = 10)$ as well as $(N = 32, \tau = 37)$ and $(N = 512, \tau = 25)$ for the variant relying on the IRSD problem. In addition, we have used $(q = 2, m = 37, n = 34, k = 17, \omega = 10, \Delta = 40, M = 5)$ as well as $(N = 64, \tau = 23)$ and $(N = 1024, \tau = 14)$ for the variant relying on the IRSL problem (Tables 6 and 7).

Table 6. Signature sizes for our RSD based constructions

	Signature size
Our Work (Sect. 5)	$3\lambda + \tau \cdot (mn + \omega(m + n - \omega) + \lambda \cdot \log_2(N) + 2\lambda + 3\lambda \cdot \log_2(M/\tau))$
Our Work (Sect. 6.3)	$5\lambda + \tau \cdot (mn + \omega(m + n - \omega) + \lambda \cdot \log_2(N) + 2\lambda)$

Table 7. Signatures based on RSD for $\lambda = 128$ (sorted by decreasing size)

	Type	pk	σ	Structure	Security Assumption
[BCG+19]	–	0.2 kB	22.5 kB	5-round	IRSD
Our Work (Sect. 5)	Fast	0.1 kB	17.2 kB	3-round	RSD
	Short	0.1 kB	13.5 kB		
Our Work (Sect. 6.3)	Fast	0.1 kB	12.6 kB	5-round	IRSD
	Short	0.1 kB	10.2 kB		
	Fast	0.5 kB	8.4 kB	5-round	IRSL
	Short	0.5 kB	6.1 kB		
[Fen22]	Fast	0.1 kB	7.4 kB	5-round	RSD
	Short	0.1 kB	5.9 kB		

8   Conclusion

In this paper, we have introduced a new approach to design PoK along with its associated amplification technique. Using this new paradigm, we have provided new post-quantum signatures related to the PKP, SD and RSD problems. Our signature related to the PKP problem features a (public key + signature) size ranging from 9 kB to 10 kB which is up to 45% shorter than existing ones. Our signature related to the SD problem features a (public key + signature) size ranging from 15 kB to 17 kB which outperforms existing constructions such as Wave [DAST19] and LESS [BBPS21] but is outperformed by [FJR22]. Our signature related to the RSL problem has a (public key + signature) size ranging from 7kB to 9kB which outperforms Durandal [ABG+19] but is outperformed by [Fen22]. One should nonetheless note that Wave and Durandal have smaller signature sizes (but bigger public key sizes) than our schemes. These constructions are interesting as they are also competitive with SPHINCS+ [BHK+19] that have been recently selected during the NIST Standardization Process. While the MPC-in-the-head approach have opened the way to several trade-offs between signature size and performances, our work extend these possibilities even more by leveraging structured versions of the considered hard problems. These new trade-offs are significant as they can lead to shorter signatures as demonstrated in this work. Future work will include applying our new approach to other hard problems such as the $\mathcal{MQ}$ problem and SD over $\mathbb{F}_q$ one (see Appendices E and F).

A   Proof of Theorem 1

Theorem 1. *If the hash function used is collision-resistant and if the commitment scheme used is binding and hiding, then the protocol depicted in Fig. 2 is an honest-verifier zero-knowledge PoK with Helper for the* SD *problem over* $\mathbb{F}_2$ *with soundness error* $1/N$.

Proof. We prove the correctness, special soundness and special honest-verifier zero-knowledge properties below.

Correctness. The correctness follows from the protocol description once the cut-and-choose with meet in the middle property $\bar{\mathbf{s}}_\alpha = \bar{\mathbf{t}}_\alpha + \mathbf{z}_4$ has been verified. From $\mathbf{s}_0 = \mathbf{u} + \mathbf{x}$ and $\mathbf{s}_i = \pi_i[\mathbf{s}_{i-1}] + \mathbf{v}_i$ for all $i \in [1, \alpha]$, one can see that $\bar{\mathbf{s}}_\alpha = \pi_\alpha \circ \cdots \circ \pi_1[\mathbf{u} + \mathbf{x}] + \mathbf{v}_\alpha + \sum_{i \in [1, \alpha-1]} \pi_\alpha \circ \cdots \circ \pi_{i+1}[\mathbf{v}_i]$. In addition, from $\bar{\mathbf{t}}_N = \pi[\mathbf{u}] + \mathbf{v}$, and $\bar{\mathbf{t}}_{i-1} = \pi_i^{-1}[\bar{\mathbf{t}}_i - \mathbf{v}_i]$ for all $i \in \{N, \ldots, \alpha+1\}$, one can see that $\bar{\mathbf{t}}_\alpha = \pi_\alpha \circ \cdots \circ \pi_1[\mathbf{u}] + \mathbf{v}_\alpha + \sum_{i \in [1, \alpha-1]} \pi_\alpha \circ \cdots \circ \pi_{i+1}[\mathbf{v}_i]$. As $\mathbf{z}_4 = \pi_\alpha \circ \cdots \circ \pi_1[\mathbf{x}]$, one can conclude that $\bar{\mathbf{s}}_\alpha = \bar{\mathbf{t}}_\alpha + \mathbf{z}_4$.

Special Soundness. To prove the special soundness, one need to build an efficient knowledge extractor Ext which returns a solution of the SD instance defined by $(\mathbf{H}, \mathbf{y})$ given two valid transcripts $(\mathbf{H}, \mathbf{y}, \mathsf{com}_1, \mathsf{com}_2, \alpha, \mathsf{rsp})$ and $(\mathbf{H}, \mathbf{y}, \mathsf{com}_1, \mathsf{com}_2, \alpha', \mathsf{rsp}')$ with $\alpha \neq \alpha'$ where $\mathsf{com}_1 = \mathsf{Setup}(\theta, \xi)$ for some random seeds (θ, ξ). The knowledge extractor Ext computes the solution as:

1. Compute $(\pi_i)_{i \in [1,n]}$ from z_2 and z_2'
2. Output $(\pi_1^{-1} \circ \cdots \circ \pi_\alpha^{-1}[\mathbf{z}_4])$

We now show that the output is a solution to the given SD problem. One can compute $(\bar{\pi}_i, \bar{\mathbf{v}}_i)_{i \in [1,N]}$ from z_2 and z_2'. From the binding property of the commitments $(\mathsf{com}_{1,i})_{i \in [1,N]}$, one has $(\pi_i, \mathbf{v}_i)_{i \in [1,N]} = (\bar{\pi}_i, \bar{\mathbf{v}}_i)_{i \in [1,N]}$. From the binding property of commitment com_1, one has $\mathbf{H}(\mathbf{z}_1 - \mathbf{u}) = \mathbf{y}$ and $\bar{\mathbf{t}}_N = \pi[\mathbf{u}] + \mathbf{v}$. Using $\bar{\mathbf{t}}_N$ and $(\pi_i, \mathbf{v}_i)_{i \in [1,N]}$, one has $\bar{\mathbf{t}}_\alpha = \pi_\alpha \circ \cdots \circ \pi_1[\mathbf{u}] + \mathbf{v}_\alpha + \sum_{i \in [1,\alpha-1]} \pi_\alpha \circ \cdots \circ \pi_{i+1}[\mathbf{v}_i]$. From the binding property of commitment com_2, one has $\bar{\mathbf{s}}_0 = \bar{\mathbf{s}}_0' = \mathbf{z}_1$. In addition, one has $\bar{\mathbf{s}}_i = \bar{\pi}_i[\bar{\mathbf{s}}_{i-1}] + \bar{\mathbf{v}}_i$ for all $i \in [1, N] \setminus \alpha$ as well as $\bar{\mathbf{s}}_i' = \bar{\pi}_i[\bar{\mathbf{s}}_{i-1}'] + \bar{\mathbf{v}}_i$ for all $i \in [1, N] \setminus \alpha'$. Using the binding property of commitment com_2 once again, one can deduce that $\bar{\mathbf{s}}_i = \bar{\pi}_i[\bar{\mathbf{s}}_{i-1}] + \bar{\mathbf{v}}_i$ for all $i \in [1, N]$ hence $\bar{\mathbf{s}}_\alpha = \pi_\alpha \circ \cdots \circ \pi_1[\mathbf{z}_1] + \mathbf{v}_\alpha + \sum_{i \in [1, \alpha-1]} \pi_\alpha \circ \cdots \circ \pi_{i+1}[\mathbf{v}_i]$. From the binding property of commitment com_2, one has $\bar{\mathbf{s}}_\alpha = \bar{\mathbf{t}}_\alpha + \mathbf{z}_4$ hence $\mathbf{z}_1 - \mathbf{u} = \pi_1^{-1} \circ \cdots \circ \pi_\alpha^{-1}[\mathbf{z}_4]$. As a consequence, one has $\mathbf{H}(\pi_1^{-1} \circ \cdots \circ \pi_\alpha^{-1}[\mathbf{z}_4]) = \mathbf{y}$ along with $w_H(\mathbf{z}_4) = \omega$ thus $\pi_1^{-1} \circ \cdots \circ \pi_\alpha^{-1}[\mathbf{z}_4]$ is a solution of the considered SD problem instance.

Special Honest-Verifier Zero-Knowledge. We start by explaining why valid transcripts do not leak anything on the secret $\mathbf{x}$. A valid transcript contains $(\mathbf{u} + \mathbf{x}, (\pi_i, \mathbf{v}_i)_{i \in [1,N] \setminus \alpha}, \pi[\mathbf{u}] + \mathbf{v}, \pi_\alpha \circ \cdots \circ \pi_1[\mathbf{x}], \mathsf{com}_{1,\alpha})$ namely the secret $\mathbf{x}$ is masked either by a random value $\mathbf{u}$ or by a random permutation π_α. The main difficulty concerns the permutation π_α as the protocol requires $\pi_\alpha \circ \cdots \circ \pi_1[\mathbf{u} + \mathbf{x}]$ to be computed while both $(\mathbf{u} + \mathbf{x})$ and $(\pi_i)_{i \in [1, \alpha-1]}$ are known. To overcome this issue, the protocol actually computes $\pi_\alpha \circ \cdots \circ \pi_1[\mathbf{u} + \mathbf{x}] + \mathbf{v}_\alpha + \sum_{i \in [1, \alpha - 1]} \pi_\alpha \circ \cdots \circ \pi_{i+1}[\mathbf{v}_i]$ for some random value $\mathbf{v}_\alpha$ hence does not leak anything on π_α. In addition, if the commitment used is hiding, $\mathrm{com}_{1,\alpha}$ does not leak anything on π_α nor $\mathbf{v}_\alpha$. Formally, one can build a PPT simulator Sim that given the public values $(\mathbf{H}, \mathbf{y})$, random seeds (θ, ξ) and a random challenge α outputs a transcript $(\mathbf{H}, \mathbf{y}, \mathrm{com}_1, \mathrm{com}_2, \alpha, \mathrm{rsp})$ such that $\mathrm{com}_1 = \mathsf{Setup}(\theta, \xi)$ that is indistinguishable from the transcript of honest executions of the protocol:

1. Compute $(\pi_i, \mathbf{v}_i)_{i \in [1, N]}$ and $\mathbf{u}$ from (θ, ξ)
2. Compute $\tilde{\mathbf{x}}_1$ such that $\mathbf{H}\tilde{\mathbf{x}}_1 = \mathbf{y}$ and $\tilde{\mathbf{x}}_2 \xleftarrow{\$} \mathcal{S}_\omega(\mathbb{F}_2^n)$
3. Compute $\tilde{\mathbf{s}}_0 = \mathbf{u} + \tilde{\mathbf{x}}_1$ and $\tilde{\mathbf{s}}_i = \pi_i[\tilde{\mathbf{s}}_{i-1}] + \mathbf{v}_i$ for all $i \in [1, \alpha - 1]$
4. Compute $\tilde{\mathbf{s}}_\alpha = \pi_\alpha \circ \cdots \circ \pi_1[\mathbf{u} + \tilde{\mathbf{x}}_2] + \mathbf{v}_\alpha + \sum_{i \in [1, \alpha - 1]} \pi_\alpha \circ \cdots \circ \pi_{i+1}[\mathbf{v}_i]$
5. Compute $\tilde{\mathbf{s}}_i = \pi_i[\tilde{\mathbf{s}}_{i-1}] + \mathbf{v}_i$ for all $i \in [\alpha + 1, N]$
6. Compute $\tilde{\mathrm{com}}_2 = \mathsf{Hash}\big(\mathbf{u} + \tilde{\mathbf{x}}_1 \,\|\, (\tilde{\mathbf{s}}_i)_{i \in [1, N]}\big)$
7. Compute $\tilde{\mathbf{z}}_1 = \mathbf{u} + \tilde{\mathbf{x}}_1$, $z_2 = (\theta_i)_{i \in [1, N] \backslash \alpha}$, $z_3 = \xi$, $\tilde{\mathbf{z}}_4 = \pi_\alpha \circ \cdots \circ \pi_1[\tilde{\mathbf{x}}_2]$
8. Compute $\tilde{\mathrm{rsp}} = (\tilde{\mathbf{z}}_1, z_2, z_3, \tilde{\mathbf{z}}_4, \mathrm{com}_{1,\alpha})$ and output $(\mathbf{H}, \mathbf{y}, \mathrm{com}_1, \tilde{\mathrm{com}}_2, \alpha, \tilde{\mathrm{rsp}})$

The transcript generated by the simulator Sim is $(\mathbf{H}, \mathbf{y}, \mathrm{com}_1, \tilde{\mathrm{com}}_2, \alpha, \tilde{\mathrm{rsp}})$ where $\mathrm{com}_1 \longleftarrow \mathsf{Setup}(\theta, \xi)$. Since $\tilde{\mathbf{x}}_1$ and $\mathbf{x}$ are masked by a random mask $\mathbf{u}$ unknown to the verifier, $\tilde{\mathbf{z}}_1$ and $\mathbf{z}_1$ are indistinguishable. Similarly, since $\tilde{\mathbf{x}}_2$ and $\mathbf{x}$ have the same Hamming weight and are masked by a random permutation π_α unknown to the verifier, $\tilde{\mathbf{z}}_4$ and $\mathbf{z}_4$ are indistinguishable. As $\tilde{\mathbf{z}}_1$ and $\mathbf{z}_1$ are indistinguishable, $\tilde{\mathbf{s}}_i$ and $\mathbf{s}_i$ are also indistinguishable for all $i \in [1, \alpha - 1]$. Since $\tilde{\mathbf{s}}_\alpha$ and $\mathbf{s}_\alpha$ both contains a random mask $\mathbf{v}_\alpha$ unknown to the verifier, they are indistinguishable. As $\tilde{\mathbf{s}}_\alpha$ and $\mathbf{s}_\alpha$ are indistinguishable, so do $\tilde{\mathbf{s}}_i$ and $\mathbf{s}_i$ for all $i \in [\alpha + 1, N]$. Finally, z_2 and z_3 are identical in both cases and $\mathrm{com}_{1,\alpha}$ does not leak anything if the commitment is hiding. As a consequence, $(\tilde{\mathrm{rsp}}, \tilde{\mathrm{com}}_2)$ in the simulation and $(\mathrm{rsp}, \mathrm{com}_2)$ in the real execution are indistinguishable. Finally, Sim runs in polynomial time which completes the proof.

B   Proof of Theorem 2

Theorem 2. *If the hash function used is collision-resistant and if the commitment scheme used is binding and hiding, then the protocol depicted in Fig. 3 is an honest-verifier zero-knowledge PoK for the* IPKP *problem with soundness error equal to* $\frac{1}{N} + \frac{N-1}{N \cdot (q-1)}$.

Proof. We prove the correctness, special soundness and special honest-verifier zero-knowledge properties below.

Correctness. The correctness follows from the protocol description once it is observed that $\mathbf{s}_N = \pi[\kappa \cdot \mathbf{x}] + \mathbf{v}$ which implies that $\mathbf{H}\mathbf{s}_N - \kappa \cdot \mathbf{y} = \mathbf{H}\pi[\kappa \cdot \mathbf{x}] + \mathbf{H}\mathbf{v} - \kappa \cdot \mathbf{y} = \mathbf{H}\mathbf{v}$.

$(q - 1, N)$**-Special Soundness.** To prove the $(q - 1, N)$-special soundness, one need to build an efficient knowledge extractor Ext which returns a solution of the IPKP instance defined by $(\mathbf{H}, \mathbf{x}, \mathbf{y})$ with high probability given a $(q-1, N)$-tree of accepting transcripts. One only need a subset of the tree to complete the proof namely the four leafs corresponding to challenges $(\kappa, \alpha_1), (\kappa, \alpha_2), (\kappa', \alpha_1)$ and (κ', α_2) where $\kappa \neq \kappa'$ and $\alpha_1 \neq \alpha_2$. The knowledge extractor Ext computes the solution as:

1. Compute $(\bar{\pi}_i)_{i \in [1,n]}$ from $z_2^{(\kappa, \alpha_1)}$ and $z_2^{(\kappa, \alpha_2)}$
2. Compute $\bar{\pi} = \bar{\pi}_N \circ \cdots \circ \bar{\pi}_1$
3. Output $\bar{\pi}$

One can compute $(\bar{\pi}_i^{(\kappa)}, \bar{\mathbf{v}}_i^{(\kappa)})_{i \in [1,N]}$ and $(\bar{\pi}_i^{(\kappa')}, \bar{\mathbf{v}}_i^{(\kappa')})_{i \in [1,N]}$ from $\left(z_2^{(\kappa, \alpha_i)}\right)_{i \in [1,2]}$ and $\left(z_2^{(\kappa', \alpha_i)}\right)_{i \in [1,2]}$ respectively. From the binding property of the commitments $(\mathsf{com}_{1,i})_{i \in [1,N]}$, one has $(\bar{\pi}_i, \bar{\mathbf{v}}_i)_{i \in [1,N]} = (\bar{\pi}_i^{(\kappa)}, \bar{\mathbf{v}}_i^{(\kappa)})_{i \in [1,N]} = (\bar{\pi}_i^{(\kappa')}, \bar{\mathbf{v}}_i^{(\kappa')})_{i \in [1,N]}$. By construction, one has $\bar{\mathbf{s}}_0^{(\kappa, \alpha_1)} = \bar{\mathbf{s}}_0^{(\kappa, \alpha_2)} = \kappa \cdot \mathbf{x}$. In addition, one has $\bar{\mathbf{s}}_i^{(\kappa, \alpha_1)} = \bar{\pi}_i[\bar{\mathbf{s}}_{i-1}^{(\kappa, \alpha_1)}] + \bar{\mathbf{v}}_i$ for all $i \in [1, N] \setminus \alpha_1$ as well as $\bar{\mathbf{s}}_i^{(\kappa, \alpha_2)} = \bar{\pi}_i[\bar{\mathbf{s}}_{i-1}^{(\kappa, \alpha_2)}] + \bar{\mathbf{v}}_i$ for all $i \in [1, N] \setminus \alpha_2$. From the binding property of commitment com_2, one can deduce that $\bar{\mathbf{s}}_i^{(\kappa)} = \bar{\pi}_i[\bar{\mathbf{s}}_{i-1}^{(\kappa)}] + \bar{\mathbf{v}}_i$ for all $i \in [1, N]$ hence $\bar{\mathbf{s}}_N^{(\kappa)} = \bar{\pi}[\kappa \cdot \mathbf{x}] + \bar{\mathbf{v}}$. Following a similar argument, one also has $\bar{\mathbf{s}}_N^{(\kappa')} = \bar{\pi}[\kappa' \cdot \mathbf{x}] + \bar{\mathbf{v}}$. From the binding property of commitment com_1, one has $\mathbf{H}\bar{\mathbf{s}}_N^{(\kappa)} - \kappa \cdot \mathbf{y} = \mathbf{H}\bar{\mathbf{s}}_N^{(\kappa')} - \kappa' \cdot \mathbf{y}$. It follows that $\mathbf{H}(\bar{\pi}[\kappa \cdot \mathbf{x}] + \bar{\mathbf{v}}) - \kappa \cdot \mathbf{y} = \mathbf{H}(\bar{\pi}[\kappa' \cdot \mathbf{x}] + \bar{\mathbf{v}}) - \kappa' \cdot \mathbf{y}$ hence $(\kappa - \kappa') \cdot \mathbf{H}\bar{\pi}[\mathbf{x}] = (\kappa - \kappa') \cdot \mathbf{y}$. This implies that $\mathbf{H}\bar{\pi}[\mathbf{x}] = \mathbf{y}$ thus $\bar{\pi}$ is a solution of the considered IPKP problem.

Special Honest-Verifier Zero-Knowledge. We start by explaining why valid transcripts do not leak anything on the secret π. A valid transcript contains $(\mathbf{s}_\alpha, (\pi_i, \mathbf{v}_i)_{i \in [1,N] \setminus \alpha}, \mathsf{com}_{1,\alpha})$ where the secret π is hiden by the unknown permutation π_α. In our protocol, one need to compute $\pi[\mathbf{x}]$ without leaking anything on the secret π. To overcome this issue, the protocol actually computes $\pi[\mathbf{x}] + \mathbf{v}$ for some value $\mathbf{v}$ that is masked by the unknown random value $\mathbf{v}_\alpha$. In addition, if the commitment used is hiding, $\mathsf{com}_{1,\alpha}$ does not leak anything on π_α nor $\mathbf{v}_\alpha$. Formally, one can build a PPT simulator Sim that given the public values $(\mathbf{H}, \mathbf{x}, \mathbf{y})$, random challenges (κ, α) outputs a transcript $(\mathbf{H}, \mathbf{x}, \mathbf{y}, \mathsf{com}_1, \kappa, \mathsf{com}_2, \alpha, \mathsf{rsp})$ that is indistinguishable from the transcript of honest executions of the protocol:

1. Compute $(\pi_i, \mathbf{v}_i, \tilde{\mathsf{com}}_{1,i})$ as in the real protocol except for $\tilde{\pi}_1 \xleftarrow{\$} S_n$
2. Compute $\tilde{\pi} = \pi_N \circ \cdots \tilde{\pi}_1$
3. Compute $\mathbf{v}$ and $\tilde{\mathsf{com}}_1$ as in the real protocol
4. Compute $\tilde{\mathbf{x}}$ such that $\mathbf{H}\tilde{\mathbf{x}} = \kappa \cdot \mathbf{y}$
5. Compute $\mathbf{s}_0 = \kappa \cdot \mathbf{x}$ and $\tilde{\mathbf{s}}_i = \pi_i[\tilde{\mathbf{s}}_{i-1}] + \mathbf{v}_i$ for all $i \in [1, \alpha - 1]$
6. Compute $\tilde{\mathbf{s}}_\alpha = \pi_\alpha[\tilde{\mathbf{s}}_{\alpha-1}] + \mathbf{v}_\alpha + \pi_{\alpha+1}^{-1} \circ \cdots \circ \pi_N^{-1}[\tilde{\mathbf{x}} - \pi[\kappa \cdot \mathbf{x}]]$
7. Compute $\tilde{\mathbf{s}}_i = \pi_i[\tilde{\mathbf{s}}_{i-1}] + \mathbf{v}_i$ for all $i \in [\alpha + 1, N]$
8. Compute $\tilde{\mathsf{com}}_2 = \mathsf{Hash}((\tilde{\mathbf{s}}_i)_{i \in [1,N]})$ and $\tilde{\mathbf{z}}_1 = \tilde{\mathbf{s}}_\alpha$
9. Compute $\tilde{z}_2 = \tilde{\pi}_1 \,||\, (\theta_i)_{i \in [1,N] \setminus \alpha}$ if $\alpha \neq 1$ or $\bar{z}_2 = (\theta_i)_{i \in [1,N] \setminus \alpha}$ otherwise
10. Compute $\tilde{\mathsf{rsp}} = (\tilde{\mathbf{z}}_1, \tilde{z}_2, \tilde{\mathsf{com}}_{1,\alpha})$ and output $(\mathbf{H}, \mathbf{x}, \mathbf{y}, \tilde{\mathsf{com}}_1, \kappa, \tilde{\mathsf{com}}_2, \alpha, \tilde{\mathsf{rsp}})$

The transcript generated by the simulator Sim is $(\mathbf{H}, \mathbf{x}, \mathbf{y}, \tilde{\text{com}}_1, \kappa, \tilde{\text{com}}_2, \alpha, \tilde{\text{rsp}})$. Since $\tilde{\mathbf{s}}_\alpha$ (in the simulation) and $\mathbf{s}_\alpha$ (in the real world) are masked by a random mask $\mathbf{v}_\alpha$ unknown to the verifier, $\tilde{\mathbf{z}}_1$ and $\mathbf{z}_1$ are indistinguishable. In addition, since $\tilde{\pi}_1$ is sampled uniformly at random in $\mathcal{S}_n$, $\tilde{z}_2$ and z_2 are indistinguishable. Finally, $\tilde{\text{com}}_{1,\alpha}$ does not leak anything on π_α nor $\mathbf{v}_\alpha$ if the commitment is hiding. As a consequence, $(\tilde{\text{com}}_1, \tilde{\text{com}}_2, \tilde{\text{rsp}})$ (in the simulation) and $(\text{com}_1, \text{com}_2, \text{rsp})$ (in the real execution) are indistinguishable. Finally, Sim runs in polynomial time which completes the proof.

C Proof of Theorem 3

Similarly to what was done in [AGS11], we introduce the intermediary DiffSD problem (Definition 23) in order to prove the security of the protocol depicted in Fig. 4. Its security (Theorem 3) relies of the DiffSD problem and is completed by a reduction from the QCSD problem to the DiffSD problem (Theorem 5). In our context, we consider QCSD instances with up to M vectors (decoding one out of many setting) which means that the adversary has access to Mk syndromes (M given syndromes combined with k possible shifts). In practice, one has to choose the QCSD parameters so that the PoK remains secure even taking into account both the number of given syndromes as well as the (small) security loss induced by the use of the DiffSD problem.

Definition 23 (DiffSD problem). *Let $(n = 2k, k, w, M, \Delta)$ be positive integers, $\mathbf{H} \in \mathcal{QC}(\mathbb{F}_2^{(n-k)\times n})$ be a random parity-check matrix of a quasi-cyclic code of index 2, $(\mathbf{x}_i)_{i\in[1,M]} \in (\mathbb{F}_2^n)^M$ be vectors such that $w_H(\mathbf{x}_i) = w$ and $(\mathbf{y}_i)_{i\in[1,M]} \in (\mathbb{F}_2^{(n-k)})^M$ be vectors such that $\mathbf{H}\mathbf{x}_i^\top = \mathbf{y}_i^\top$. Given $(\mathbf{H}, (\mathbf{y}_i)_{i\in[1,M]})$, the Differential Syndrome Decoding problem $\mathsf{DiffSD}(n, k, w, M, \Delta)$ asks to find $(\mathbf{c}, (\mathbf{d}_j, \kappa_j, \mu_j)_{j\in[1,\Delta]}) \in \mathbb{F}_2^{(n-k)} \times (\mathbb{F}_2^n \times [1,k] \times [1,M])^\Delta$ such that $\mathbf{H}\mathbf{d}_j^\top + \mathbf{c} = \mathrm{rot}_{\kappa_j}(\mathbf{y}_{\mu_j}^\top)$ and $w_H(\mathbf{d}_j) = w$ for each $j \in [1, \Delta]$.*

Theorem 5. *If there exists a PPT algorithm solving the $\mathsf{DiffSD}(n, k, w, M, \Delta)$ problem with probability $\epsilon_{\mathsf{DiffSD}}$, then there exists a PPT algorithm solving the $\mathsf{QCSD}(n, k, w, M)$ with probability $\epsilon_{\mathsf{QCSD}} \geq (1 - M \times p - (2^{(n-k)} - 2) \times p^\Delta) \cdot \epsilon_{\mathsf{DiffSD}}$ where $p = \frac{\binom{n}{w}}{2^{(n-k)}}$.*

Sketch of Proof. We start by highlighting the main steps of the proof. One should note that the DiffSD problem is constructed from a QCSD instance and as such always admit at least a solution namely the solution of the underlying QCSD instance. Indeed, any solution to the DiffSD problem satisfying $\mathbf{c} = (0, \cdots, 0)$ can be transformed into a solution to the QCSD problem with similar inputs. Hereafter, we study the probability that there exists solutions to the DiffSD problem for any possible value of $\mathbf{c}$. To do so, we consider two cases depending on weather $\mathbf{c}$ is stable by rotation or not. The first case implies that either $\mathbf{c} = (0, \cdots, 0)$ or $\mathbf{c} = (1, \cdots, 1)$ while the second case encompasses every other possible value for $\mathbf{c}$. We show that for correctly chosen values n, k, w and Δ, the probability that there exists solutions to the DiffSD problem satisfying $\mathbf{c} \neq (0, \cdots, 0)$ is small. Such solutions can't be transformed into solutions to the QCSD problem hence induce a security loss in our reduction.

Given a $[n, k]$ quasi-cyclic code $\mathcal{C}$, we restrict our analysis (and our parameters choice) to the case where (i) n is a primitive prime and (ii) the weight ω is lower than the Gilbert-Varshamov bound associated to $\mathcal{C}$ *i.e.* the value for which the number of words of weight less or equal to w corresponds to the number of syndromes. Thus, given a syndrome $\mathbf{y}$, the probability p that there exists a pre-image $\mathbf{x}$ of $\mathbf{y}$ such that $\mathbf{H}\mathbf{x}^\top = \mathbf{y}^\top$ and $w_H(\mathbf{x}) = \omega$ is $p = \binom{n}{w}/2^{(n-k)}$ namely the number of possible words of weight ω divided by the number of syndromes.

Let $\mathcal{A}_{\mathsf{DiffSD}}$ be an algorithm that given inputs $(\mathbf{H}, (\mathbf{y}_i)_{i \in [1,M]})$ generated following Definition 23 outputs a solution $(\mathbf{c}, (\mathbf{d}_j, \kappa_j, \mu_j)_{j \in [1,\Delta]})$ to the considered DiffSD instance. Let $\mathcal{A}_{\mathsf{QCSD}}$ be an algorithm that given access to $\mathcal{A}_{\mathsf{DiffSD}}$ and inputs $(\mathbf{H}, (\mathbf{y}_i)_{i \in [1,M]})$ corresponding to an instance of the QCSD problem in the decoding one out of many setting outputs a solution to this instance. We denote by $\mathcal{A}_{\mathsf{QCSD}}(\mathbf{H}, (\mathbf{y}_i)_{i \in [1,M]}) \neq \perp$ (respectively $\mathcal{A}_{\mathsf{DiffSD}}(\mathbf{H}, (\mathbf{y}_i)_{i \in [1,M]}) \neq \perp$) the fact that $\mathcal{A}_{\mathsf{QCSD}}$ (respectively $\mathcal{A}_{\mathsf{DiffSD}}$) outputs a *valid* solution to the QCSD (respectively DiffSD) problem.

$\underline{\mathcal{A}_{\mathsf{QCSD}}(\mathbf{H}, (\mathbf{y}_i)_{i \in [1,M]})}$:

1. Compute $(\mathbf{c}, (\mathbf{d}_j, \kappa_j, \mu_j)_{j \in [1,\Delta]}) \leftarrow \mathcal{A}_{\mathsf{DiffSD}}(\mathbf{H}, (\mathbf{y}_i)_{i \in [1,M]})$
2. If $\mathbf{c} = (0, \cdots, 0)$, output $\mathbf{x} = \mathbf{rot}_{k-\kappa_1}(\mathbf{d}_1)$
3. If $\mathbf{c} \neq (0, \cdots, 0)$, output $\perp$

Let $\mathbf{c}_0$ denote the event that the solution to the DiffSD problem is also the solution of the underlying QCSD instance. One has $\epsilon_{\mathsf{QCSD}} = P[\mathcal{A}_{\mathsf{QCSD}}(\mathbf{H}, (\mathbf{y}_i)_{i \in [1,M]}) \neq \perp] \geq P[\mathcal{A}_{\mathsf{QCSD}}(\mathbf{H}, (\mathbf{y}_i)_{i \in [1,M]}) \neq \perp \cap \mathbf{c}_0] = P[\mathcal{A}_{\mathsf{DiffSD}}(\mathbf{H}, (\mathbf{y}_i)_{i \in [1,M]}) \neq \perp \cap \mathbf{c}_0]$. Let $\mathbf{c}_{\mathsf{stable}}$ and $\mathbf{c}_{\mathsf{unstable}}$ denote the events that the DiffSD problem admits another solution than the one of its underlying QCSD instance where $\mathbf{c}$ is stable (respectively unstable) by rotation. One has $P[\mathcal{A}_{\mathsf{DiffSD}}(\mathbf{H}, (\mathbf{y}_i)_{i \in [1,M]}) \neq \perp] = P[\mathcal{A}_{\mathsf{DiffSD}}(\mathbf{H}, (\mathbf{y}_i)_{i \in [1,M]}) \neq \perp \cap \mathbf{c}_{\mathsf{stable}}] + P[\mathcal{A}_{\mathsf{DiffSD}}(\mathbf{H}, (\mathbf{y}_i)_{i \in [1,M]}) \neq \perp \cap \mathbf{c}_{\mathsf{unstable}}]$. We show bellow that if $\mathbf{c}$ is stable by rotation then $\mathbf{c} = (0, \cdots, 0)$ or $\mathbf{c} = (1, \cdots, 1)$. Let $\mathbf{c}_1$ denote the event that the DiffSD problem admits another solution than the one of its underlying QCSD instance where $\mathbf{c} = (1, \cdots, 1)$. It follows that $P[\mathcal{A}_{\mathsf{DiffSD}}(\mathbf{H}, (\mathbf{y}_i)_{i \in [1,M]}) \neq \perp \cap \mathbf{c}_0] = P[\mathcal{A}_{\mathsf{DiffSD}}(\mathbf{H}, (\mathbf{y}_i)_{i \in [1,M]}) \neq \perp] - P[\mathcal{A}_{\mathsf{DiffSD}}(\mathbf{H}, (\mathbf{y}_i)_{i \in [1,M]}) \neq \perp \cap \mathbf{c}_1] - P[\mathcal{A}_{\mathsf{DiffSD}}(\mathbf{H}, (\mathbf{y}_i)_{i \in [1,M]}) \neq \perp \cap \mathbf{c}_{\mathsf{unstable}}]$ hence $P[\mathcal{A}_{\mathsf{DiffSD}}(\mathbf{H}, (\mathbf{y}_i)_{i \in [1,M]}) \neq \perp \cap \mathbf{c}_0] = \epsilon_{\mathsf{DiffSD}} - P[\mathcal{A}_{\mathsf{DiffSD}}(\mathbf{H}, (\mathbf{y}_i)_{i \in [1,M]}) \neq \perp \cap \mathbf{c}_1] - P[\mathcal{A}_{\mathsf{DiffSD}}(\mathbf{H}, (\mathbf{y}_i)_{i \in [1,M]}) \neq \perp \cap \mathbf{c}_{\mathsf{unstable}}] = (1 - P[\mathbf{c}_1] - P[\mathbf{c}_{\mathsf{unstable}}]) \cdot \epsilon_{\mathsf{DiffSD}}$. It follows that $\epsilon_{\mathsf{QCSD}} \geq (1 - P[\mathbf{c}_1] - P[\mathbf{c}_{\mathsf{unstable}}]) \cdot \epsilon_{\mathsf{DiffSD}}$.

Working modulo $x^n - 1$ and writing $\mathbf{c}$ as $c(x) = \sum_{i=0}^{n-1} c_i x^i$ being stable by rotation of order j implies $x^j c(x) = c(x) \mod x^n - 1$ hence $(x^j + 1)c(x) = 0 \mod x^n - 1$. In our case where 2 is primitive modulo n, one has $x^n - 1 = (x-1)(1 + x + x^2 + \cdots + x^{n-1})$ where $(1 + x + x^2 + \cdots + x^{n-1})$ is an irreducible polynomial [GZ08]. Since $c(x)$ divides $x^n - 1$ and since $(x - 1)$ is not compatible with $\mathbf{c}$ being stable by rotation, the only non zero possibility is $\mathbf{c} = (1, \cdots, 1)$.

Hereafter, we compute $P[\mathbf{c}_1]$ and $P[\mathbf{c}_{\texttt{unstable}}]$. The probability that the DiffSD problem admits another solution than the one of its underlying QCSD instance where $\mathbf{c} = (1, \cdots, 1)$ is the same as the probability that the vector $\mathbf{y}_{\mu_j} - \mathbf{c}$ has a preimage by $\mathbf{H}$ of weight w namely p. As M vectors $(\mathbf{y}_{\mu_j})_{j \in [1,M]}$ can be considered, it follows that $P[\mathbf{c}_1] = M \times p = M \times \binom{n}{\omega}/2^{(n-k)}$.

In the case where $\mathbf{c}$ is not stable by rotation, one cannot use cyclicity to find several valid DiffSD equations from a unique one as in the previous case. Therefore, to compute the probability that the DiffSD admits another solution than the one of its underlying QCSD instance when $\mathbf{c}$ is unstable by rotation, one has to consider the probability that all the Δ vectors $\mathbf{rot}_{\kappa_j}(\mathbf{y}_{\mu_j}) - \mathbf{c}$ have a preimage by $\mathbf{H}$ of weight w. Each pre-image may exist with probability p thus there exists Δ pre-images with probability $p^\Delta = \left(\binom{n}{\omega}/2^{(n-k)}\right)^\Delta$. As $2^{(n-k)} - 2$ possible values can be considered for $\mathbf{c}$ (all possible values except $\mathbf{0}$ and $\mathbf{1}$), it follows that $P[\mathbf{c}_{\texttt{unstable}}] = (2^{(n-k)} - 2) \times \left(\binom{n}{\omega}/2^{(n-k)}\right)^\Delta$.

Theorem 3. *If the hash function used is collision-resistant and if the commitment scheme used is binding and hiding, then the protocol depicted in Fig. 4 is an honest-verifier zero-knowledge PoK for the QCSD(n, k, w, M) problem with soundness error equal to $\frac{1}{N} + \frac{(N-1)(\Delta-1)}{N \cdot M \cdot k}$ for some parameter Δ.*

Proof. The proofs of the correctness and special honest-verifier zero-knowledge properties follow the same arguments as the proofs given in Appendix A. Hereafter, we provide a proof for the (Mk, N)-special soundness property.

(Mk, N)-**Special Soundness.** To prove the (Mk, N)-special soundness, one need to build an efficient knowledge extractor Ext which returns a solution of the QCSD instance defined by $(\mathbf{H}, (\mathbf{y}_i)_{i \in [1,M]})$ with high probability given a (Mk, N)-tree of accepting transcripts. In our case, we build Ext as a knowledge extractor for the DiffSD problem and use it as extractor for the QCSD problem thanks to Theorem 5. One only need a subset of the tree of accepting transcripts to complete the proof namely 2Δ leafs corresponding to challenges $(\mu_j, \kappa_j, \alpha_i)_{i \in [1,2]}^{j \in [1,\Delta]}$. The knowledge extractor Ext computes the solution as:

1. Compute $(\bar{\pi}_i)_{i \in [1,n]}$ from $z_2^{(\mu_1, \kappa_1, \alpha_1)}$ and $z_2^{(\mu_1, \kappa_1, \alpha_2)}$
2. Compute $\mathbf{c}_1 = \mathbf{H}\mathbf{z}_1^{(\mu_1, \kappa_1)} - \mathbf{rot}_{\kappa_1}(\mathbf{y}_{\mu_1}) = \cdots = \mathbf{H}\mathbf{z}_1^{(\mu_\Delta, \kappa_\Delta)} - \mathbf{rot}_{\kappa_\Delta}(\mathbf{y}_{\mu_\Delta})$
3. Compute $\mathbf{c}_2 = \bar{\pi}_{\alpha_1} \circ \cdots \circ \bar{\pi}_1[\mathbf{z}_1^{(\mu_1, \kappa_1)}] - \mathbf{z}_4^{(\mu_1, \kappa_1, \alpha_1)} = \cdots = \bar{\pi}_{\alpha_1} \circ \cdots \circ \bar{\pi}_1[\mathbf{z}_1^{(\mu_\Delta, \kappa_\Delta)}]$
   $- \mathbf{z}_4^{(\mu_\Delta, \kappa_\Delta, \alpha_\Delta)}$
4. Compute $\mathbf{c}_3 = \mathbf{H}(\bar{\pi}_1^{-1} \circ \cdots \circ \bar{\pi}_{\alpha_1}^{-1}[\mathbf{c}_2]) - \mathbf{c}_1$
5. Compute $\mathbf{d}_j = \bar{\pi}_1^{-1} \circ \cdots \circ \bar{\pi}_{\alpha_1}^{-1}[\mathbf{z}_4^{(\mu_j, \kappa_j, \alpha_j)}]$ for all $j \in [1, \Delta]$
6. Output $(\mathbf{c}_3, (\mathbf{d}_j, \kappa_j, \mu_j)_{j \in [1,\Delta]})$

One can compute $\left(\bar{\pi}_i^{(\mu_j, \kappa_j)}, \bar{\mathbf{v}}_i^{(\mu_j, \kappa_j)}\right)_{i \in [1,N]}^{j \in [1,\Delta]}$ from $\left(z_2^{(\mu_j, \kappa_j, \alpha_i)}\right)_{i \in [1,2]}^{j \in [1,\Delta]}$. From the binding property of the commitments $(\texttt{com}_{1,i})_{i \in [1,N]}$, one can see that $(\pi_i, \mathbf{v}_i)_{i \in [1,N]} = (\bar{\pi}_i^{(\mu_1, \kappa_1)}, \bar{\mathbf{v}}_i^{(\mu_1, \kappa_1)})_{i \in [1,N]} = \cdots = (\bar{\pi}_i^{(\mu_\Delta, \kappa_\Delta)}, \bar{\mathbf{v}}_i^{(\mu_\Delta, \kappa_\Delta)})_{i \in [1,N]}$.

From the binding property of commitment com_2, one has $\bar{\mathsf{s}}_0^{(\mu_j,\kappa_j,\alpha_1)} = \bar{\mathsf{s}}_0^{(\mu_j,\kappa_j,\alpha_2)} = \mathbf{z}_1^{(\mu_j,\kappa_j)}$ for all $j \in [1,\Delta]$. In addition, one has $\bar{\mathsf{s}}_i^{(\mu_j,\kappa_j,\alpha_1)} = \bar{\pi}_i[\bar{\mathsf{s}}_{i-1}^{(\mu_j,\kappa_j,\alpha_1)}] + \bar{\mathbf{v}}_i$ for all $i \in [1,N] \setminus \alpha_1$ and all $j \in [1,\Delta]$ as well as $\bar{\mathsf{s}}_i^{(\mu_j,\kappa_j,\alpha_2)} = \bar{\pi}_i[\bar{\mathsf{s}}_{i-1}^{(\mu_j,\kappa_j,\alpha_2)}] + \bar{\mathbf{v}}_i$ for all $i \in [1,N] \setminus \alpha_2$ and all $j \in [1,\Delta]$. Using the binding property of commitment com_2 once again, one can deduce that $\bar{\mathsf{s}}_i^{(\mu_j,\kappa_j)} = \bar{\pi}_i[\bar{\mathsf{s}}_{i-1}^{(\mu_j,\kappa_j)}] + \bar{\mathbf{v}}_i$ for all $i \in [1,N]$ and $j \in [1,\Delta]$ hence $\bar{\mathsf{s}}_{\alpha_1}^{(\mu_j,\kappa_j)} = \bar{\pi}_{\alpha_1} \circ \cdots \circ \bar{\pi}_1[\mathbf{z}_1^{(\mu_j,\kappa_j)}] + \mathbf{v}_{\alpha_1} + \sum_{i\in[1,\alpha_1-1]} \bar{\pi}_{\alpha_1} \circ \cdots \circ \bar{\pi}_{i+1}[\mathbf{v}_i]$ for all $j \in [1,\Delta]$. From the binding property of commitment com_1, one has $\mathbf{c}_1 = \mathbf{Hz}_1^{(\mu_1,\kappa_1)} - \mathrm{rot}_{\kappa_1}(\mathbf{y}_{\mu_1}) = \cdots = \mathbf{Hz}_1^{(\mu_\Delta,\kappa_\Delta)} - \mathrm{rot}_{\kappa_\Delta}(\mathbf{y}_{\mu_\Delta})$. In addition, one has $\bar{\mathbf{r}}^{(\mu_1,\kappa_1)} = \cdots = \bar{\mathbf{r}}^{(\mu_\Delta,\kappa_\Delta)}$ which implies that $\bar{\mathbf{t}}_{\alpha_1} = \bar{\mathbf{t}}_{\alpha_1}^{(\mu_\Delta,\kappa_\Delta)} = \cdots = \bar{\mathbf{t}}_{\alpha_1}^{(\mu_\Delta,\kappa_\Delta)}$. From the binding property of commitment com_2, one has $\bar{\mathsf{s}}_{\alpha_1}^{(\mu_j,\kappa_j)} = \bar{\mathbf{t}}_{\alpha_1}^{(\mu_j,\kappa_j)} + \bar{\mathbf{z}}_4^{(\mu_j,\kappa_j)}$ for all $j \in [1,\Delta]$. Using $\bar{\mathbf{t}}_{\alpha_1} = \bar{\mathbf{t}}_{\alpha_1}^{(\mu_1,\kappa_1)} = \cdots = \bar{\mathbf{t}}_{\alpha_1}^{(\mu_\Delta,\kappa_\Delta)}$, one can deduce that $\mathbf{c}_2 = \bar{\mathbf{t}}_{\alpha_1} - \mathbf{v}_{\alpha_1} - \sum_{i\in[1,\alpha_1-1]} \bar{\pi}_{\alpha_1} \circ \cdots \circ \bar{\pi}_{i+1}[\mathbf{v}_i] = \bar{\pi}_{\alpha_1} \circ \cdots \circ \bar{\pi}_1[\mathbf{z}_1^{(\mu_1,\kappa_1)}] - \mathbf{z}_4^{(\mu_1,\kappa_1,\alpha_1)} = \cdots = \bar{\pi}_{\alpha_1} \circ \cdots \circ \bar{\pi}_1[\mathbf{z}_1^{(\mu_\Delta,\kappa_\Delta)}] - \mathbf{z}_4^{(\mu_\Delta,\kappa_\Delta,\alpha_\Delta)}$. It follows that $\mathbf{z}_1^{(\mu_j,\kappa_j)} = \bar{\pi}_1^{-1} \circ \cdots \circ \bar{\pi}_{\alpha_1}^{-1}[\mathbf{c}_2 + \mathbf{z}_4^{(\mu_j,\kappa_j,\alpha_j)}]$ for all $j \in [1,\Delta]$. As $\mathbf{c}_1 = \mathbf{Hz}_1^{(\mu_j,\kappa_j)} - \mathrm{rot}_{\kappa_j}(\mathbf{y}_{\mu_j})$, one has $\mathbf{c}_1 = \mathbf{H}(\bar{\pi}_1^{-1} \circ \cdots \circ \bar{\pi}_{\alpha_1}^{-1}[\mathbf{c}_2 + \mathbf{z}_4^{(\mu_j,\kappa_j,\alpha_j)}]) - \mathrm{rot}_{\kappa_j}(\mathbf{y}_{\mu_j})$ hence $\mathbf{H}(\bar{\pi}_1^{-1} \circ \cdots \circ \bar{\pi}_{\alpha_1}^{-1}[\mathbf{z}_4^{(\mu_j,\kappa_j,\alpha_j)}]) + \mathbf{c}_3 = \mathrm{rot}_{\kappa_j}(\mathbf{y}_{\mu_j})$ for all $j \in [1,\Delta]$. Given that $w_H(\mathbf{z}_4^{(\mu_j,\kappa_j,\alpha_j)}) = \omega$ for all $j \in [1,\Delta]$, one can conclude that $(\mathbf{c}_3, (\mathbf{d}_j, \kappa_j, \mu_j)_{j\in[1,\Delta]})$ is a solution of the considered DiffSD problem instance. One completes the proof by using Theorem 5.

D   Proof of Theorem 4

Theorem 4. *If the hash function used is collision-resistant and if the commitment scheme used is binding and hiding, then the protocol depicted in Fig. 5 is an honest-verifier zero-knowledge PoK for the* IRSL *problem with soundness error equal to* $\frac{1}{N} + \frac{(N-1)(\Delta-1)}{N(q^{Mk}-1)}$ *for some parameter* Δ.

Proof. The proof of our protocol in the rank metric (Theorem 4) is similar to the proof of our protocol in Hamming metric (Theorem 3) presented in Appendix C. It relies on the introduction of the intermediary DiffIRSL problem (Definition 24) along with a reduction from the IRSL problem to the DiffIRSL problem (Theorem 6).

Definition 24 (DiffIRSL problem). *Let* $(q, m, n = 2k, k, w, M, \Delta)$ *be positive integers,* $P \in \mathbb{F}_q[X]$ *be an irreducible polynomial of degree* k, $\mathbf{H} \in \mathcal{ID}(\mathbb{F}_{q^m}^{(n-k)\times n})$

be a random parity-check matrix of an ideal code of index 2, E be a random subspace of $\mathbb{F}_{q^m}$ of dimension ω, $(\mathbf{x}_i)_{i \in [1,M]} \in (\mathbb{F}_{q^m}^n)^M$ be random vectors such that $\mathrm{Supp}(\mathbf{x}_i) = E$ and $(\mathbf{y}_i)_{i \in [1,M]} \in (\mathbb{F}_{q^m}^{(n-k)})^M$ be vectors such that $\mathbf{H}\mathbf{x}_i^\top = \mathbf{y}_i^\top$. Given $(\mathbf{H}, (\mathbf{y}_i)_{i \in [1,M]})$, the Differential Ideal Rank Support Learning problem $\mathsf{IRSL}(q, m, n, k, w, M, \Delta)$ *asks to find* $(\mathbf{c}, (\mathbf{d}_\delta, (\gamma_{i,j}^\delta)_{i \in [1,M], j \in [1,k]})_{\delta \in [1,\Delta]}) \in \mathbb{F}_2^{(n-k)} \times (\mathbb{F}_2^n \times (\mathbb{F}_q^{Mk} \setminus (0, \cdots, 0))^\Delta)$ *such that* $\mathbf{H}\mathbf{d}_\delta^\top + \mathbf{c} = \sum_{(i,j) \in [1,M] \times [1,k]} \gamma_{i,j}^\delta \cdot \mathrm{rot}_j(\mathbf{y}_i^\top)$ *with* $\mathrm{Supp}(\mathbf{d}_\delta) = F$ *and* $|F| = \omega$ *for each* $\delta \in [1, \Delta]$.

Theorem 6. *If there exists a* PPT *algorithm solving the* $\mathsf{DiffIRSL}(q, m, n, k, w, M, \Delta)$ *with probability* $\epsilon_{\mathsf{DiffIRSL}}$, *then there exists a* PPT *algorithm solving the* $\mathsf{IRSL}(q, m, n, k, w, M)$ *problem with probability* $\epsilon_{\mathsf{IRSL}} \geq (1 - (q^{m(n-k)} - 1) \times (q^{\omega(m-\omega)+n\omega-m(n-k)})^\Delta) \cdot \epsilon_{\mathsf{DiffIRSL}}$.

Sketch of Proof. The proof of Theorem 6 in the rank metric setting is similar to the proof of Theorem 5 in the Hamming metric setting. A noticeable difference in the rank metric setting is related to the use of the irreducible polynomial $P \in \mathbb{F}_q[X]$ of degree k. Indeed, the later implies that $P[\mathbf{c}_{\mathtt{stable}}] = 0$ namely there is no solution where both $\mathbf{c}$ is stable by rotation and $\mathbf{c} \neq (0, \cdots, 0)$.

Given an $[n, k]$ ideal code $\mathcal{C}$, we restrict our analysis to the case where the weight ω is lower than the rank Gilber-Varshamov bound associated to $\mathcal{C}$ *i.e.* the value for which the number of words of weight less or equal w corresponds to the number of syndromes. As a consequence, given a syndrome $\mathbf{y}$, the probability that there exists a pre-image $\mathbf{x}$ of $\mathbf{y}$ such that $\mathbf{H}\mathbf{x}^\top = \mathbf{y}^\top$ and $w_R(\mathbf{x}) = \omega$ is $q^{\omega(m-\omega)+n\omega-m(n-k)}$ where $q^{\omega(m-\omega)}$ is an approximation of the Gaussian binomial which counts the number of vector spaces of dimension ω in $\mathbb{F}_{q^m}$, $q^{n\omega}$ is the number of words in a basis of dimension ω and $q^{m(n-k)}$ is the number of syndromes. As such, this probability describes the number of codewords of rank weight ω divided by the number of possible syndromes. Following the same steps than the proof of Theorem 5 (with $\sum_{(i,j) \in [1,M] \times [1,k]} \gamma_{i,j}^\delta \cdot \mathrm{rot}_j(\mathbf{y}_i^\top) - \mathbf{c}$ playing the role of $\mathrm{rot}_{\kappa_j}(\mathbf{y}_{\mu_j}) - \mathbf{c}$) and taking into account that $P[\mathbf{c}_{\mathtt{stable}}] = 0$, one get $\epsilon_{\mathsf{IRSL}} \geq (1 - (q^{m(n-k)} - 1) \times (q^{\omega(m-\omega)+n\omega-m(n-k)})^\Delta) \cdot \epsilon_{\mathsf{DiffIRSL}}$.

E   PoK Leveraging Structure Related to the $\mathcal{MQ}$ Problem

(See Fig. 6).

Inputs & Public Data

$w = (\mathbf{x}_i)_{i \in [1,M]}$, $x = (\mathcal{F}, (\mathbf{y}_i)_{i \in [1,M]})$, $\mathcal{C}_{\text{struct}} = [1, M] \times \mathbb{F}_q^*$, $\text{ch}_{\text{struct}} = (\mu, \kappa)$

$\underline{\mathsf{P}_1(w, x)}$

$\theta \xleftarrow{\$} \{0,1\}^\lambda$

for $i \in [1, N-1]$ **do**

$\quad \theta_i \xleftarrow{\$, \theta} \{0,1\}^\lambda$, $\phi_i \xleftarrow{\$, \theta_i} \{0,1\}^\lambda$, $\mathbf{u}_i \xleftarrow{\$, \phi_i} \mathbb{F}_q^n$, $\mathbf{v}_i \xleftarrow{\$, \phi_i} \mathbb{F}_q^m$, $r_{1,i} \xleftarrow{\$, \theta_i} \{0,1\}^\lambda$, $\text{com}_{1,i} = \text{Com}(r_{1,i}, \phi_i)$

end

$\theta_N \xleftarrow{\$, \theta} \{0,1\}^\lambda$, $\phi_N \xleftarrow{\$, \theta_N} \{0,1\}^\lambda$, $\mathbf{u}_N \xleftarrow{\$, \phi_N} \mathbb{F}_q^n$, $\mathbf{u} = \sum_{i \in [1,N]} \mathbf{u}_i$, $\mathbf{v}_N = \mathcal{F}(\mathbf{u}) - \sum_{i \in [1, N-1]} \mathbf{v}_i$

$r_{1,N} \xleftarrow{\$, \theta_N} \{0,1\}^\lambda$, $\text{com}_{1,N} = \text{Com}(r_{1,N}, \mathbf{v}_N \,\|\, \phi_N)$

$\text{com}_1 = \text{Hash}\big((\text{com}_{1,i})_{i \in [1,N]}\big)$

$\underline{\mathsf{P}_2(w, x, \mu, \kappa)}$

$\mathbf{s}_0 = \kappa \cdot \mathbf{x}_\mu - \mathbf{u}$

for $i \in [1, N]$ **do**

$\quad \mathbf{s}_i = \mathcal{G}(\mathbf{u}_i, \mathbf{s}_0) + \mathbf{v}_i$

end

$\text{com}_2 = \text{Hash}\big(\mathbf{s}_0 \,\|\, (\mathbf{s}_i)_{i \in [1,N]}\big)$

$\underline{\mathsf{P}_3(w, x, \mu, \kappa, \alpha)}$

$\mathbf{z}_1 = \kappa \cdot \mathbf{x}_\mu - \mathbf{u}$

if $\alpha \neq N$ **do**

$\quad z_2 = \mathbf{v}_N \,\|\, (\theta_i)_{i \in [1,N] \setminus \alpha}$

else

$\quad z_2 = (\theta_i)_{i \in [1,N] \setminus \alpha}$

end

$\text{rsp} = (\mathbf{z}_1, z_2, \text{com}_{1,\alpha})$

$\underline{\mathsf{V}(x, \text{com}_1, (\mu, \kappa), \text{com}_2, \alpha, \text{rsp})}$

Compute $(\bar{\phi}_i, \bar{r}_{1,i}, \bar{\mathbf{u}}_i, \bar{\mathbf{v}}_i)_{i \in [1,N] \setminus \alpha}$ from z_2

$\bar{\mathbf{s}}_0 = \mathbf{z}_1$

for $i \in [1, N] \setminus \alpha$ **do**

$\quad \bar{\mathbf{s}}_i = \mathcal{G}(\bar{\mathbf{u}}_i, \bar{\mathbf{s}}_0) + \bar{\mathbf{v}}_i$

end

$\bar{\mathbf{s}}_\alpha = \kappa^2 \cdot \mathbf{y}_\mu - \mathcal{F}(\mathbf{z}_1) - \sum_{i \in [1,N] \setminus \alpha} \bar{\mathbf{s}}_i$, $\bar{\text{com}}_{1,\alpha} = \text{com}_{1,\alpha}$

for $i \in [1, N] \setminus \alpha$ **do**

$\quad$ **if** $i \neq N$ **do**

$\quad\quad \bar{\text{com}}_{1,i} = \text{Com}(\bar{r}_{1,i}, \bar{\phi}_i)$

$\quad$ **else**

$\quad\quad \bar{\text{com}}_{1,N} = \text{Com}(\bar{r}_{1,N}, \bar{\mathbf{v}}_N \,\|\, \bar{\phi}_N)$

$\quad$ **end**

end

$b_1 \longleftarrow \big(\text{com}_1 = \text{Hash}((\text{com}_{1,i})_{i \in [1,N]})\big)$, $b_2 \longleftarrow \big(\text{com}_2 = \text{Hash}(\mathbf{z}_1 \,\|\, (\bar{\mathbf{s}}_i)_{i \in [1,N]})\big)$

return $b_1 \wedge b_2$

Fig. 6. PoK leveraging structure for the $\mathcal{MQ}_{\mathcal{H}}^+$ problem

F PoK Leveraging Structure Related to SD over $\mathbb{F}_q$

(See Fig. 7).

Inputs & Public Data

$w = \mathbf{x}$, $x = (\mathbf{H}, \mathbf{y})$

$\mathcal{C}_{\text{struct}} = \mathbb{F}_q^*$, $\text{ch}_{\text{struct}} = \kappa$

$\underline{\mathsf{P}_1(w, x)}$

$\theta \xleftarrow{\$} \{0,1\}^\lambda$, $\xi \xleftarrow{\$} \{0,1\}^\lambda$

for $i \in [1, N]$ **do**

$\quad \theta_i \xleftarrow{\$,\theta} \{0,1\}^\lambda$, $\phi_i \xleftarrow{\$,\theta_i} \{0,1\}^\lambda$, $,\pi_i \xleftarrow{\$,\phi_i} S_n$, $\mathbf{v}_i \xleftarrow{\$,\phi_i} \mathbb{F}_q^n$, $,r_{1,i} \xleftarrow{\$,\theta_i} \{0,1\}^\lambda$, $\text{com}_{1,i} = \text{Com}(r_{1,i}, \phi_i)$

end

$\pi = \pi_N \circ \cdots \circ \pi_1$, $\mathbf{v} = \mathbf{v}_N + \sum_{i \in [1, N-1]} \pi_N \circ \cdots \circ \pi_{i+1}[\mathbf{v}_i]$, $\mathbf{r} \xleftarrow{\$,\xi} \mathbb{F}_q^n$, $\mathbf{u} = \pi^{-1}[\mathbf{r} - \mathbf{v}]$

$\text{com}_1 = \text{Hash}(\mathbf{Hu} \,\|\, \pi[\mathbf{u}] + \mathbf{v} \,\|\, \pi[\mathbf{x}] \,\|\, (\text{com}_{1,i})_{i \in [1,N]})$

$\underline{\mathsf{P}_2(w, x, \kappa)}$

$\mathbf{s}_0 = \mathbf{u} + \kappa \cdot \mathbf{x}$

for $i \in [1, N]$ **do**

$\quad \mathbf{s}_i = \pi_i[\mathbf{s}_{i-1}] + \mathbf{v}_i$

end

$\text{com}_2 = \text{Hash}(\mathbf{u} + \kappa \cdot \mathbf{x} \,\|\, (\mathbf{s}_i)_{i \in [1,N]})$

$\underline{\mathsf{P}_3(w, x, \kappa, \alpha)}$

$\mathbf{z}_1 = \mathbf{u} + \kappa \cdot \mathbf{x}$, $z_2 = (\theta_i)_{i \in [1,N] \setminus \alpha}$, $z_3 = \xi$, $\mathbf{z}_4 = \pi[\mathbf{x}]$

$\text{rsp} = (\mathbf{z}_1, z_2, z_3, \mathbf{z}_4, \text{com}_{1,\alpha})$

$\underline{\mathsf{V}(x, \text{com}_1, \kappa, \text{com}_2, \alpha, \text{rsp})}$

Compute $(\bar{\phi}_i, \bar{r}_{1,i}, \bar{\pi}_i, \bar{\mathbf{v}}_i)_{i \in [1,N] \setminus \alpha}$ from z_2 and $\bar{\mathbf{r}}$ from z_3

$\bar{\mathbf{t}}_N = \bar{\mathbf{r}}$, $\bar{\mathbf{b}}_N = \mathbf{z}_4$

for $i \in \{N, \ldots, \alpha + 1\}$ **do**

$\quad \bar{\mathbf{t}}_{i-1} = \bar{\pi}_i^{-1}[\bar{\mathbf{t}}_i - \bar{\mathbf{v}}_i]$, $\bar{\mathbf{b}}_{i-1} = \bar{\pi}_i^{-1}[\bar{\mathbf{b}}_i]$

end

$\bar{\mathbf{s}}_0 = \mathbf{z}_1$, $\bar{\mathbf{s}}_\alpha = \bar{\mathbf{t}}_\alpha + \kappa \cdot \bar{\mathbf{b}}_\alpha$, $\text{c\={o}m}_{1,\alpha} = \text{com}_{1,\alpha}$

for $i \in [1, N] \setminus \alpha$ **do**

$\quad \bar{\mathbf{s}}_i = \bar{\pi}_i[\bar{\mathbf{s}}_{i-1}] + \bar{\mathbf{v}}_i$, $\text{c\={o}m}_{1,i} = \text{Com}(\bar{r}_{1,i}, \bar{\phi}_i)$

end

$b_1 \longleftarrow (\text{com}_1 = \text{Hash}(\mathbf{Hz}_1 - \kappa \cdot \mathbf{y} \,\|\, \bar{\mathbf{r}} \,\|\, \mathbf{z}_4 \,\|\, (\text{c\={o}m}_{1,i})_{i \in [1,N]}))$

$b_2 \longleftarrow (\text{com}_2 = \text{Hash}(\mathbf{z}_1 \,\|\, (\bar{\mathbf{s}}_i)_{i \in [1,N]}))$

$b_3 \longleftarrow (w_H(\mathbf{z}_4) = \omega)$

return $b_1 \wedge b_2 \wedge b_3$

Fig. 7. PoK leveraging structure for the SD problem over $\mathbb{F}_q$

References

[ABG+19] Aragon, N., Blazy, O., Gaborit, P., Hauteville, A., Zémor, G.: Durandal: a rank metric based signature scheme. In: Ishai, Y., Rijmen, V. (eds.) EUROCRYPT 2019. LNCS, vol. 11478, pp. 728–758. Springer, Cham (2019). https://doi.org/10.1007/978-3-030-17659-4_25

[AFK21] Attema, T., Fehr, S., Klooß, M.: Fiat-Shamir transformation of multi-round interactive proofs. Cryptology ePrint Archive, Report 2021/1377 (2021)

[AGS11] Melchor, C.A., Gaborit, P., Schrek, J.: A new zero-knowledge code based identification scheme with reduced communication. In: IEEE Information Theory Workshop (2011)

[BB21] Bardet, M., Briaud, P.: An algebraic approach to the rank support learning problem. In: Cheon, J.H., Tillich, J.-P. (eds.) PQCrypto 2021 2021. LNCS, vol. 12841, pp. 442–462. Springer, Cham (2021). https://doi.org/10.1007/978-3-030-81293-5_23

[BBBG21] Bettaieb, S., Bidoux, L., Blazy, O., Gaborit, P.: Zero-knowledge reparation of the Véron and AGS code-based identification schemes. In: IEEE International Symposium on Information Theory (ISIT) (2021)

[BBC+20] Bardet, M., et al.: Improvements of algebraic attacks for solving the rank decoding and MinRank problems. In: Moriai, S., Wang, H. (eds.) ASIACRYPT 2020. LNCS, vol. 12491, pp. 507–536. Springer, Cham (2020). https://doi.org/10.1007/978-3-030-64837-4_17

[BBPS21] Barenghi, A., Biasse, J.-F., Persichetti, E., Santini, P.: LESS-FM: fine-tuning signatures from a code-based cryptographic group action. In: International Workshop on Post-Quantum Cryptography (PQCrypto) (2021)

[BCG+19] Bellini, E., Caullery, F., Gaborit, P., Manzano, M., Mateu, V.: Improved véron identification and signature schemes in the rank metric. In: IEEE International Symposium on Information Theory (ISIT) (2019)

[Beu20] Beullens, W.: Sigma protocols for MQ, PKP and SIS, and fishy signature schemes. In: Canteaut, A., Ishai, Y. (eds.) EUROCRYPT 2020. LNCS, vol. 12107, pp. 183–211. Springer, Cham (2020). https://doi.org/10.1007/978-3-030-45727-3_7

[BGKM22] Bidoux, L., Gaborit, P., Kulkarni, M., Mateu, V.: Code-based signatures from new proofs of knowledge for the syndrome decoding problem. arXiv preprint arXiv:2201.05403 (2022)

[BGKS21] Bidoux, L., Gaborit, P., Kulkarni, M., Sendrier, N.: Quasi-cyclic stern proof of knowledge. arXiv preprint arXiv:2110.05005 (2021)

[BHK+19] Daniel J Bernstein, Andreas Hülsing, Stefan Kölbl, Ruben Niederhagen, Joost Rijneveld, and Peter Schwabe. The sphincs+ signature framework. In ACM SIGSAC Conference on Computer and Communications Security, 2019

[BJMM12] Becker, A., Joux, A., May, A., Meurer, A.: Decoding random binary linear codes in $2^{n/20}$: how $1 + 1 = 0$ improves information set decoding. In: Pointcheval, D., Johansson, T. (eds.) EUROCRYPT 2012. LNCS, vol. 7237, pp. 520–536. Springer, Heidelberg (2012). https://doi.org/10.1007/978-3-642-29011-4_31

[CDG+20] Chase, M., et al.: The picnic signature algorithm. NIST Post-Quantum Cryptography Standardization Project (Round 3) (2020). https://microsoft.github.io/Picnic/

[CHR+20] Chen, M.-S., Hülsing, A., Rijneveld, J., Samardjiska, S., Schwabe, P.: MQDSS specifications. NIST Post-Quantum Cryptography Standardization Project (Round 2) (2020). https://mqdss.org/

[CVE11] Cayrel, P.-L., Véron, P., El Yousfi Alaoui, S.M.: A zero-knowledge identification scheme based on the q-ary syndrome decoding problem. In: Biryukov, A., Gong, G., Stinson, D.R. (eds.) SAC 2010. LNCS, vol. 6544, pp. 171–186. Springer, Heidelberg (2011). https://doi.org/10.1007/978-3-642-19574-7_12

[DAST19] Debris-Alazard, T., Sendrier, N., Tillich, J.-P.: Wave: a new family of trapdoor one-way preimage sampleable functions based on codes. In: Galbraith, S.D., Moriai, S. (eds.) ASIACRYPT 2019. LNCS, vol. 11921, pp. 21–51. Springer, Cham (2019). https://doi.org/10.1007/978-3-030-34578-5_2

[DAT18] Debris-Alazard, T., Tillich, J.-P.: Two attacks on rank metric code-based schemes: RankSign and an IBE scheme. In: Peyrin, T., Galbraith, S. (eds.) ASIACRYPT 2018. LNCS, vol. 11272, pp. 62–92. Springer, Cham (2018). https://doi.org/10.1007/978-3-030-03326-2_3

[Fen22] Feneuil, T.: Building MPCitH-based signatures from MQ, MinRank, Rank SD and PKP. Cryptology ePrint Archive, Report 2022/1512 (2022)

[FJR21] Feneuil, T., Joux, A., Rivain, M.: Shared permutation for syndrome decoding: new zero-knowledge protocol and code-based signature. Cryptology ePrint Archive, Report 2021/1576 (2021)

[FJR22] Feneuil, T., Joux, A., Rivain, M.: Syndrome decoding in the head: shorter signatures from zero-knowledge proofs. Cryptology ePrint Archive, Report 2022/188 (2022)

[FS86] Fiat, A., Shamir, A.: How to prove yourself: practical solutions to identification and signature problems. In: Odlyzko, A.M. (ed.) CRYPTO 1986. LNCS, vol. 263, pp. 186–194. Springer, Heidelberg (1987). https://doi.org/10.1007/3-540-47721-7_12

[GHPT17] Gaborit, P., Hauteville, A., Phan, D.H., Tillich, J.-P.: Identity-based encryption from codes with rank metric. In: Katz, J., Shacham, H. (eds.) CRYPTO 2017. LNCS, vol. 10403, pp. 194–224. Springer, Cham (2017). https://doi.org/10.1007/978-3-319-63697-9_7

[GPS21] Gueron, S., Persichetti, E., Santini, P.: Designing a practical code-based signature scheme from zero-knowledge proofs with trusted setup. Cryptology ePrint Archive, Report 2021/1020 (2021)

[GRS15] Gaborit, P., Ruatta, O., Schrek, J.: On the complexity of the rank syndrome decoding problem. IEEE Trans. Inf. Theory 62, 1006–1019 (2015)

[GZ08] Gaborit, P., Zemor, G.: Asymptotic improvement of the Gilbert-Varshamov bound for linear codes. IEEE Trans. Inf. Theory 54(9), 3865–3872 (2008)

[IKOS07] Ishai, Y., Kushilevitz, E., Ostrovsky, R., Sahai, A.: Zero-knowledge from secure multiparty computation. In: Proceedings of the 39th Annual ACM Symposium on Theory of Computing (STOC) (2007)

[KKW18] Katz, J., Kolesnikov, V., Wang, X.: Improved non-interactive zero knowledge with applications to post-quantum signatures. In: Proceedings of the 2018 ACM Conference on Computer and Communications Security (CCS) (2018)

[KMRP19] Koussa, E., Macario-Rat, G., Patarin, J.: On the complexity of the permuted kernel problem. Cryptology ePrint Archive, Report 2019/412 (2019)

[KZ20]   Kales, D., Zaverucha, G.: An attack on some signature schemes constructed from five-pass identification schemes. In: Krenn, S., Shulman, H., Vaudenay, S. (eds.) CANS 2020. LNCS, vol. 12579, pp. 3–22. Springer, Cham (2020). https://doi.org/10.1007/978-3-030-65411-5_1

[PS96]   Pointcheval, D., Stern, J.: Security proofs for signature schemes. In: Maurer, U. (ed.) EUROCRYPT 1996. LNCS, vol. 1070, pp. 387–398. Springer, Heidelberg (1996). https://doi.org/10.1007/3-540-68339-9_33

[Sen11]   Sendrier, N.: Decoding one out of many. In: Yang, B.-Y. (ed.) PQCrypto 2011. LNCS, vol. 7071, pp. 51–67. Springer, Heidelberg (2011). https://doi.org/10.1007/978-3-642-25405-5_4

[Sha89]   Shamir, A.: An efficient identification scheme based on permuted kernels (extended abstract). In: Brassard, G. (ed.) CRYPTO 1989. LNCS, vol. 435, pp. 606–609. Springer, New York (1990). https://doi.org/10.1007/0-387-34805-0_54

[SSH11]   Sakumoto, K., Shirai, T., Hiwatari, H.: Public-key identification schemes based on multivariate quadratic polynomials. In: Rogaway, P. (ed.) CRYPTO 2011. LNCS, vol. 6841, pp. 706–723. Springer, Heidelberg (2011). https://doi.org/10.1007/978-3-642-22792-9_40

[Ste93]   Stern, J.: A new identification scheme based on syndrome decoding. In: Stinson, D.R. (ed.) CRYPTO 1993. LNCS, vol. 773, pp. 13–21. Springer, Heidelberg (1994). https://doi.org/10.1007/3-540-48329-2_2

[Unr15]   Unruh, D.: Non-interactive zero-knowledge proofs in the quantum random oracle model. In: Oswald, E., Fischlin, M. (eds.) EUROCRYPT 2015. LNCS, vol. 9057, pp. 755–784. Springer, Heidelberg (2015). https://doi.org/10.1007/978-3-662-46803-6_25

[Vér97]   Véron, P.: Improved identification schemes based on error-correcting codes. Appl. Algebra Eng. Commun. Comput. 8, 57–69 (1997)

[Wan22]   Wang, W.: Shorter signatures from MQ. Cryptology ePrint Archive, Report 2022/344 (2022)

On Catalan Constant Continued Fractions

David Naccache[(✉)] and Ofer Yifrach-Stav

DIÉNS, ÉNS, CNRS, PSL University, 45 rue d'Ulm, 75230 Paris Cedex 05, France
{david.naccache,ofer.friedman}@ens.fr

Abstract. The Ramanujan Machine project detects new expressions related to constants of interest, such as ζ function values, γ and algebraic numbers (to name a few).

In particular the project lists a number of conjectures concerning the Catalan constant $G = 0.91596559\ldots$

We show how to generate infinitely many.

We used an ad hoc software toolchain and rather tedious mathematical developments.

Because we do not provide a proper peer-reviewed proof of the relations given here we do not claim them to be theorems.

1 Introduction

The Ramanujan Machine project [2–4] detects new expressions related to constants of interests, such as ζ function values, γ and various algebraic numbers (to name a few).

In particular the project lists several of conjectures[1] concerning the Catalan constant $G = 0.91596559\ldots$

We show how to generate infinitely many.

We used an ad hoc software toolchain and rather tedious mathematical developments.

Because we do not provide a proper peer-reviewed proof of the relations given here we do not claim them to be theorems.

2 The Initial Conjectures

Let $a_n = 3n^2 + (3 + 4\kappa)n + 2\kappa + 1$ and $b_n = -2n^2(n + 2\kappa)(n + c)$ and consider the continued fraction:

$$Q_{c,\kappa} = a_0 + \cfrac{b_1}{a_1 + \cfrac{b_2}{a_2 + \cfrac{b_3}{a_3 + \cfrac{b_4}{a_4 + \cdots}}}}$$

---

[1] http://www.ramanujanmachine.com/wp-content/uploads/2020/06/catalan.pdf.

© The Author(s), under exclusive license to Springer Nature Switzerland AG 2023
S. El Hajji et al. (Eds.): C2SI 2023, LNCS 13874, pp. 43–54, 2023.
https://doi.org/10.1007/978-3-031-33017-9_3

The Ramanujan Project conjectures that:

c	$Q_{c,0}$	$Q_{c,1}$	$Q_{c,2}$
0	$\frac{1}{2G}$	$\frac{2}{2G-1}$	$\frac{24}{18G-11}$
1	$\frac{2}{2G-1}$	$\frac{4}{2G+1}$	$\frac{16}{6G-1}$
2	$\frac{24}{18G-11}$	$\frac{16}{6G-1}$	$\frac{64}{18G+13}$
3	$\frac{720}{450G-299}$	$\frac{288}{90G-31}$	?

3   Notations

We denote by $n!!$ the semifactorial of, i.e. the product of all the integers from 1 up to n having the same parity as n:

$$n!! = \prod_{k=0}^{\lceil \frac{n}{2} \rceil - 1} (n - 2k) = n(n-2)(n-4)\cdots$$

Because in all the following we will only apply semifactorials to odd numbers, this can simplified as:

$$n!! = \prod_{k=1}^{\frac{n+1}{2}} (2k-1) = n(n-2)(n-4)\cdots 3 \cdot 1$$

4   The Generalized Formulae

For $\kappa \in \{0, \ldots, 6\}$ we have:

$$\lim_{c \to \infty} Q_{c,\kappa} - Q_{c-1,\kappa} = 2$$

In the following sections we crunch very smooth constants into factorials and semifactorials. This is done for the sole purpose of saving space and does not imply any specific property.

4.1 $\kappa = 0$

The generalized form for $\kappa = 0$ is:

$$Q_{c,0} = \frac{(2c)!}{2(2c-1)!!^2 \, G - \Delta_{c-1,0}}$$

where:

$$\Delta_{c,0} = \begin{cases} 1 + 10c & \text{if } c < 2 \\ -2c(2c-1)^3 \Delta_{c-2,0} + (1 + 2c + 8c^2)\Delta_{c-1,0} & \text{if } c \geq 2 \end{cases}$$

or under an equivalent more compact form:

$$\Delta_{c,0} = \begin{cases} 1 & \text{if } c = 0 \\ (2c)! + (2c+1)^2 \Delta_{c-1,0} & \text{if } c > 0 \end{cases}$$

This is easy to check up to any practical rank using the Mathematica code:

```
1 f[x_, {m_, d_}] := m/(d + x);
2 F1[x_] := (2 x)!;
3 F2[x_] := 2 (2 x  1)!!^2;
4 (*F3[x_]:=If[x==0,1,(2x)!+(2x+1)^2 *F3[x1]]; or the unfolded form:*)
5 F3[x_] :=
6  If[x < 2,
7    1 + 10 x, (1 + 2 x + 8 x^2) F3[x  1]  2 x (2 x  1)^3 F3[x  2]];
8 den = Table[3 n^2 + 3 n + 1, {n, 1, 12000}];
9 For[c = 1, c < 20,
10   num = Table[2 n^3 (n + c), {n, 1, 12000}];
11   r = 1 + N[(Fold[f, Last@num/Last@den,
12       Reverse@Most@Transpose@{num, den}]), 200];
13 e=F1[c]/(Catalan F2[c]  F3[c  1]);
14 Print["Comparison: ", N[{r, e}, 200]];
15 c++]
```

Remark 1. At times $\gcd(\gcd(\alpha, \beta), \gcd(\alpha, \gamma)) \neq 1$ and Q can be simplified[2]. Because $(2c)!$ and $2((2c-1)!!)^2$ are both smooth, this happens quite frequently.

4.2 $\kappa = 1$

The generalized form for $\kappa = 1$ is:

$$Q_{c,1} = \frac{2(2c)!}{2(2c-1)!!^2 \, G + (2c-1)\Delta_{c-1,1}}$$

where:

$$\Delta_{c,1} = \begin{cases} 1 - 2c & \text{if } c < 2 \\ -2c(2c-1)(2c-3)^2 \Delta_{c-2,1} + (-1 - 6c + 8c^2)\Delta_{c-1,1} & \text{if } c \geq 2 \end{cases}$$

As is checked by the following code:

```
1 f[x_, {m_, d_}] := m/(d + x);
2 F1[x_] := 2 (2 x)!;
3 F2[x_] := 2 (2 x  1)!!^2;
4 F3[x_] :=
5  If[x < 2,
6   1  2 x, 2 (3  2 x)^2 x (1 + 2 x) F3[
7      x  2] + (1  6 x + 8 x^2) F3[x  1]];
```

[2] A typical example is $\kappa = 0$ and $c = 5$ where our formulae predict $3628800/(1285371 - 1786050G)$, which, after division by 9, yields the reduced value $403200/(142819 - 198450G)$.

```
 8  den = Table[3 n^2 + 7 n + 3, {n, 1, 12000}];
 9  For[c = 1, c < 20,
10   num = Table[2 n^2 (n + 2) (n + c), {n, 1, 12000}];
11   r = 3 + N[(Fold[f, Last@num/Last@den,
12      Reverse@Most@Transpose@{num, den}]), 200];
13   e=F1[c]/(Catalan F2[c] + (2 c  1) F3[c  1]);
14   Print["Comparison: ",
15    N[{r, e}, 200]];
16   c++]
```

4.3 $\kappa = 2$

The generalized form for $\kappa = 2$ is:

$$Q_{c,2} = \frac{8(2c)!}{6(2c-1)!!^2\, G + (2c-1)(2c-3)\Delta_{c-1,2}}$$

where:

$$\Delta_{c,2} = \begin{cases} 1 + 12c & \text{if } c < 2 \\ -2c(2c-5)^2(-1+2c)\Delta_{c-2,2} + (-3-14c+8c^2)\Delta_{c-1,2} & \text{if } c \geq 2 \end{cases}$$

```
 1  F1[x_] := 8 (2 x)!;
 2  F2[x_] := 6 (2 x  1)!!^2;
 3  F3[x_] :=
 4   If[x < 2, 1+12x, (3  14 x + 8 x^2) F3[x  1]
 5     2 (5  2 x)^2 x (1 + 2 x) F3[x  2]];
 6  den = Table[3 n^2 + 11 n + 5, {n, 1, 12000}];
 7  f[x_, {m_, d_}] := m/(d + x);
 8  For[c = 1, c <= 30, num = Table[2 n^2 (n + 4) (n + c), {n, 1, 12000}];
 9   r = 5 + N[(Fold[f, Last@num/Last@den,
10      Reverse@Most@Transpose@{num, den}]), 200];
11   e = F1[c]/(F2[c] Catalan + (2 c  1) (2 c  3) F3[c  1]);
12   Print["Comparison: ", N[{r, e}, 200]];
13   c++]
```

4.4 $\kappa = 3$

The generalized form for $\kappa = 3$ is:

$$Q_{c,3} = \frac{(3^3 + 4^3 + 5^3 + 6^3)(2c)!}{270(2c-1)!!^2\, G + (2c-1)(2c-3)(2c-5)\Delta_{c-1,3}}$$

where:

$$\Delta_{c,3} = \begin{cases} 22c - 31 & \text{if } c \leq 2 \\ -2c(2c-1)(2c-7)^2\Delta_{c-2,3} + (-5-22c+8c^2)\Delta_{c-1,3} & \text{if } c > 2 \end{cases}$$

```
1  F1[x_] := 432 (2 x)!;
2  F2[x_] := 270 (2 x   1)!!^2;
3  F3[x_] :=
4    If[x < 2,
5      22 x   31 , 2 x (2 x   7)^2 (2 x   1) F3[
6        x   2] + (8 x^2   22 x   5) F3[x   1]];
7  f[x_, {m_, d_}] := m/(d + x);
8  For[c = 1, c <= 30,
9    den = Table[3 n^2 + 15 n + 7, {n, 1, 10000}];
10   num = Table[2 n^2 (n + 6) (n + c), {n, 1, 10000}];
11   r = 7 + (Fold[f, Last@num/Last@den,
12       Reverse@Most@Transpose@{num, den}]);
13   e = F1[c]/(F2[c] Catalan + (2 c   1) (2 c   3) (2 c   5) F3[c   1]);
14   Print["Comparison: ",N[{r, e}, 200]];
15   c++];
```

4.5 $\kappa = 4$

The generalized form for $\kappa = 4$ is:

$$Q_{c,4} = \frac{5!\,6!\,(2c)!}{14 \times 15^3 (2c-1)!!^2\,G + (2c-1)(2c-3)(2c-5)(2c-7)\Delta_{c-1,4}}$$

where:

$$\Delta_{c,4} = \begin{cases} 1327 - 10448c & \text{if } c < 2 \\ -2c(2c-1)(2c-9)^2\Delta_{c-2,4} + (-7 - 30c + 8c^2)\Delta_{c-1,4} & \text{if } c \geq 2 \end{cases}$$

```
1  f[x_, {m_, d_}] := m/(d + x);
2  F1[x_] := 5! 6! (2 x)!;
3  F2[x_] := 14*15^3 (2 x   1)!!^2;
4  F3[x_] :=
5    If[x < 2,
6      1327   10448 x, 2 x (9 + 2 x)^2 (1 + 2 x) F3[
7        x   2] + (7   30 x + 8 x^2) F3[x   1]];
8  For[c = 1, c <= 20,
9    den = Table[3 n^2 + 19 n + 9, {n, 1, 10000}];
10   num = Table[2 n^2 (n + 8) (n + c), {n, 1, 10000}];
11   r = 9 + (Fold[f, Last@num/Last@den,
12       Reverse@Most@Transpose@{num, den}]);
13   e = F1[c]/(F2[
14       c] Catalan + (2 c   1) (2 c   3) (2 c   5) (2 c   7) F3[
15       c   1]);
16   Print["Comparison: ",N[{r, e}, 200]];
17   c++];
```

4.6 $\kappa = 5$

The generalized form for $\kappa = 5$ is:

$$Q_{c,5} = \frac{2 \times 140^2 \times 5! \times (2c)!}{2 \times 105^3 (2c-1)!!^2 \, G + (2c-1) \times \cdots \times (2c-9) \Delta_{c-1,5}}$$

where:

$$\Delta_{c,5} = \begin{cases} -10891 + 150002c & \text{if } c < 2 \\ -2c(2c-1)(2c-11)^2 \Delta_{c-2,5} + (-9 - 38c + 8c^2) \Delta_{c-1,5} & \text{if } c \geq 2 \end{cases}$$

```
1  f[x_, {m_, d_}] := m/(d + x);
2  F1[x_] := 2*140^2* 5! (2 x)!;
3  F2[x_] := 2*105^3 (2 x  1)!!^2;
4  F3[x_] :=
5   If[x < 2, 10891 +
6     150002 x, 2 x (11 + 2 x)^2 (1 + 2 x) F3[
7       x  2] + (9  38 x + 8 x^2) F3[x  1]];
8  For[c = 1, c <= 20,
9    den = Table[3 n^2 + 23 n + 11, {n, 1, 10000}];
10   num = Table[2 n^2 (n + 10) (n + c), {n, 1, 10000}];
11   r = 11 + (Fold[f, Last@num/Last@den,
12     Reverse@Most@Transpose@{num, den}]);
13   e = F1[c]/(F2[
14     c] Catalan + (2 c  1) (2 c  3) (2 c  5) (2 c  7) (2 c
15       9) F3[c  1]);
16   Print["Comparison: ",N[{r, e}, 200]];
17   c++];
```

4.7 $\kappa = 6$

The generalized form for $\kappa = 6$ is:

$$Q_{c,6} = \frac{12 \times 7!! \times 10! \times (2c)!}{2 \times 7!! \times 9!! \times 11!! \, (2c-1)!!^2 \, G + (2c-1) \times \cdots \times (2c-11) \Delta_{c-1,6}}$$

where:

$$\Delta_{c,6} = \begin{cases} 1167809 - 23021852c & \text{if } c < 2 \\ -2c(2c-1)(2c-13)^2 \Delta_{c-2,6} + (-11 - 46c + 8c^2) \Delta_{c-1,6} & \text{if } c \geq 2 \end{cases}$$

```
 1  f[x_, {m_, d_}] := m/(d + x);
 2  F1[x_] := 12*7!!*10! (2 x)!;
 3  F2[x_] := 2*11!!*9!!*7!! (2 x  1)!!^2;
 4  F3[x_] :=
 5   If[x < 2,
 6    1167809
 7     23021852 x, 2 x (13 + 2 x)^2 (1 + 2 x) F3[
 8       x  2] + (11  46 x + 8 x^2) F3[x  1]];
 9  For[c = 1, c <= 20,
10    den = Table[3 n^2 + 27 n + 13, {n, 1, 10000}];
11    num = Table[2 n^2 (n + 12) (n + c), {n, 1, 10000}];
12    r = 13 + (Fold[f, Last@num/Last@den,
13      Reverse@Most@Transpose@{num, den}]);
14    e = F1[c]/(F2[
15       c] Catalan + (2 c  1) (2 c  3) (2 c  5) (2 c  7) (2 c
16         9) (2 c  11) F3[c  1]);
17    Print["Comparison: ",N[{r, e}, 200]];
18    c++];
```

4.8 $\kappa = 7$ and Beyond

Nothing fundamentally different is expected happen as we increase κ. In other words we should keep getting limits of the form:

$$Q_{c,\kappa} = \frac{\sigma_{\mathrm{num},\kappa} \times (2c)!}{\sigma_{\mathrm{den},\kappa} \times (2c-1)!!^2\, G + (2c-1) \times \cdots \times (2(c-\kappa)+1))\Delta_{c-1,\kappa}}$$

where $\sigma_{\mathrm{num},\kappa}, \sigma_{\mathrm{den},\kappa}$ are composed of a (very) smooth sub-factor times a few potentially larger primes. The polynomials that intervene in the definition of $\Delta_{c,\kappa}$ are:

$$8c^2 + (2 - 8\kappa)c - 2\kappa + 1 \quad \text{and} \quad -2c(2c-1)(2(c-\kappa)-1)^2$$

For instance we have: $\sigma_{\mathrm{num},7} = 1024$, $\sigma_{\mathrm{den},7} = 429$ and in $\Delta_{c,7}$ the $c < 2$ case is defined by:

$$\frac{2258335679c}{35 \times 11!!^2} - \frac{176673487}{70 \times 11!!^2}$$

We have good reasons to conjecture that the ratios of the coefficients $\sigma_{\mathrm{num},\kappa}, \sigma_{\mathrm{den},\kappa}$ appearing in front of F1 and F2 in our code, i.e. $2/2, 8/6, 432/270, \ldots$ satisfy[3]:

$$\frac{\sigma_{\mathrm{num},\kappa}}{\sigma_{\mathrm{den},\kappa}} = \frac{4^{\kappa-1}}{(2\kappa-1)C_{\kappa-1}} \quad \text{where } C_\ell \text{ is the } \ell\text{-th Catalan number.}$$

That is:

$$\frac{\sigma_{\mathrm{num},\kappa}}{\sigma_{\mathrm{den},\kappa}} = \left\{ \frac{1}{2}, 1, \frac{4}{3}, \frac{8}{5}, \frac{64}{35}, \frac{128}{63}, \frac{512}{231}, \frac{1024}{429}, \ldots \right\}$$

---

[3] With $\kappa = 0$ being an exception that does not fit this general rule.

The conjecture that the $\sigma_{\text{den},\kappa}$ and $\sigma_{\text{num},\kappa}$ are given by the function $1/T_s^k$ of [1] (cf. Table 1 of [1]) is backed by the fact that the same type of ratios between α and γ in $Q = \alpha/(\beta + \gamma G)$ can also be observed for polynomials that do not belong to the κ family. For instance[4] (Table 1):

Table 1. Ratios between α and γ for various example continued fractions.

δ	ϵ	η	τ	relation
15	15	2	4	$2^{2c+2}\gamma = 3\alpha(2c-5)C_{c-1}$
19	21	2	6	$2^{2c+3}\gamma = 5\alpha(2c-7)C_{c-1}$
19	25	4	4	$2^{2c+4}(2c-3)\gamma = 9\alpha(2c-7)(2c-5)C_{c-1}$
23	35	4	6	$2^{2c+5}(2c-3)\gamma = 15\alpha(2c-7)(2c-9)C_{c-1}$

The above provides an algorithmic way to compute generalized relations.

Step 1. For a given κ, generate[5] 2 limits, e.g. for $c = 1$ and $c = 2$.

Step 2. We have four unknowns to determine: the coefficients $\sigma_{\text{num},\kappa}, \sigma_{\text{den},\kappa}$ in front of F1 and F2 and the parameters A, B in the equation $Ac + B$ at the "if $c < 2$" part of Δ. The ratio of $\sigma_{\text{num},\kappa}$ and $\sigma_{\text{den},\kappa}$ being known, this reduces the number of unknowns to three.

Step 3. Arbitrarily set $\sigma_{\text{num},\kappa} = 1$ and push $\sigma_{\text{den},\kappa}$ into A and B. We are hence left with two rational unknowns which can be found by solving a system of two linear equations given by the two limits we started with.

Once this "bootstraping" achieved, we can keep generating limits using the generalized formula for that specific κ but for any desired rank c.

4.9   Other G Relations of the Ramanujan Machine Project

The same techniques generate many relations unlisted by the Ramanjuan Project. We give a few examples that we computed (or re-computed) up to rank 6^6 in the following tables where:

$$Q = \frac{\alpha}{\beta + \gamma G}, \quad a_n = 3n^2 + \delta n + \epsilon, \quad \text{and} \quad b_n = -2n(n+\tau)(n+\eta)(n+\mu)$$

---

[4] Modulo a possible sign flip for the very first values.

[5] By any analytic or computational manner.

[6] There is no intrinsic difficulty to keep computing those constants, we limit ourselves to 7 per category for space reasons.

μ	α	β	γ
0	1	0	2
1	2	-1	2
2	24	-11	18
3	720	-299	450
4	40320	-15371	22050
5	403200	-142819	198450
6	53222400	-17684299	24012450

(a) $\delta = 3$, $\epsilon = 1$, $\tau = 0$, $\eta = 0$

μ	α	β	γ
0	2	-1	2
1	4	1	2
2	16	-1	6
3	288	-31	90
4	11520	-1373	3150
5	89600	-10891	22050
6	9676800	-1167809	2182950

(b) $\delta = 7$, $\epsilon = 3$, $\tau = 0$, $\eta = 2$

μ	α	β	γ
0	24	-11	18
1	16	-1	6
2	64	13	18
3	384	1	90
4	3072	-121	630
5	51200	-2839	9450
6	4300800	-269803	727650

(c) $\delta = 11$, $\epsilon = 5$, $\tau = 0$, $\eta = 4$

μ	α	β	γ
0	4	-5	6
1	8	3	-2
2	32	5	2
3	192	13	18
4	4608	133	450
5	230400	1909	22050
6	2150400	-8419	198450

(d) $\delta = 11$, $\epsilon = 9$, $\tau = 2$, $\eta = 2$

μ	α	β	γ
0	720	-299	450
1	288	-31	90
2	384	1	90
3	2304	389	450
4	18432	419	3150
5	61440	-791	9450
6	737280	-20989	103950

(e) $\delta = 15$, $\epsilon = 7$, $\tau = 0$, $\eta = 6$

μ	α	β	γ
0	48	-79	90
1	32	19	-18
2	128	17	-6
3	768	77	18
4	2048	129	90
5	61440	2467	3150
6	1228800	31327	66150

(f) $\delta = 15$, $\epsilon = 15$, $\tau = 4$, $\eta = 2$

μ	α	β	γ
0	1440	-2813	3150
1	576	443	-450
2	768	127	-90
3	4608	383	-90
4	36864	2693	450
5	122880	6563	3150
6	294912	11497	9450

(g) $\delta = 19$, $\epsilon = 21$, $\tau = 2$, $\eta = 6$

μ	α	β	γ
0	192	-569	630
1	128	253	-270
2	512	-25	54
3	3072	179	-18
4	8192	487	54
5	81920	3983	1350
6	327680	12583	7350

(h) $\delta = 19$, $\epsilon = 25$, $\tau = 4$, $\eta = 4$

μ	α	β	γ
0	1920	-8599	9450
1	768	2909	-3150
2	1024	-379	450
3	2048	43	30
4	49152	1919	-90
5	163840	6789	450
6	393216	14755	3150

(i) $\delta = 23$, $\epsilon = 35$, $\tau = 4$, $\eta = 6$

To keep generating such examples fix an integer bound ℓ, set μ to any arbitrary positive integer, run $i = 3, \ldots, \ell$, $j = 0, \ldots, \lfloor i/2 \rfloor + 1$. Then the polynomials $a_n = j(2i - j + 2) + (4i + 3)n + 3n^2$ and $b_n = -2n(n + j - 1)(n + 2i - j + 1)(n + \mu)$ will result in Q values of the form $\alpha/(\beta + G\gamma)$. Increments of i by rational steps (e.g. $\frac{1}{2}$ instead of 1) generate additional relations. Table 6 gives a few examples for $\mu = 3$ (chosen arbitrarily as an example). For $0 \leq i \leq 2$ we have $Q = 0$ (Table 3).

This is one example, as there are other similar families: amongst the converging examples over a running variable μ and $i = 0, 1, \ldots$, three are given in Table 4 where $\epsilon = (\eta + 1)(\tau + 1)$.

Table 2. Sporadic case examples

δ	ϵ	τ	η	μ	α	β	γ
9	7	1	1	1	1	2	-2
13	13	1	1	3	6	17	-18
15	19	2	2	2	8	-49	54
17	19	1	1	5	120	419	-450
17	23	1	3	3	12	83	-90
19	29	2	2	4	32	-411	450
21	33	1	3	5	240	2893	-3150

Table 3. Other sporadic convergence examples, entries are given in the following order: $\delta,\ \epsilon,\ \tau,\ \eta,\ \mu$.

23,39,2,2,6	23,43,2,4,4	25,31,1,1,9	25,43,1,3,7	25,47,1,5,5
25,51,3,3,5	21,25,1,1,7	21,37,3,3,3	27,57,2,4,6	27,61,4,4,4
29,37,1,1,11	29,53,1,3,9	31,59,2,2,10	33,43,1,1,13	37,49,1,1,15

Table 4. Examples of families. Running μ, $i = 0, 1, \ldots$, $\epsilon = (\eta + 1)(\tau + 1)$.

δ	η	τ
$4i + 7$	0	$2i + 2$
$4i + 11$	2	$2i + 2$
$4i + 19$	4	$4i + 4$
$4i + 27$	6	$2i + 6$
$4i + 35$	8	$2i + 8$

Table 5. Examples not involving G

$\phi(n)$	converges to Q
$(n - 1)(n + i)$	15
$(n - 2)(n + i)$	$\frac{10i + 505}{33}$
$(n - 3)(n + 2i + 1)$	$\frac{25(421 + 40i)}{651 + 16i}$
$(n - 3)(n + 2i)$	$\frac{25(401 + 40i)}{643 + 16i}$
$(1 + n/2)(2n + 2j - 1)$	$\begin{cases} 12 & \text{for } j = 2 \\ 10 & \text{for } j = 3 \\ 0 & \text{for } j \geq 4 \end{cases}$

Some relations do not belong to families and are sporadic (e.g. Table 2).

Note: The same polynomials also yield relations not involving G, those are provable by standard techniques. For instance for $\delta = \eta = 15$ and denoting $b_n = -2n(n + 4)\phi(n)$ we get for all i the results in Table 5.

Table 6. Examples converging to Q values involving G. Polynomials are $a_n = j(2i - j+2) + (4i+3)n + 3n^2$ and $b_n = -2n(n+j-1)(n+2i-j+1)(n+\mu)$. $\mu = 3$ was chosen arbitrarily for the sake of the example. $\forall i, j = 0 \Rightarrow (\alpha, \beta, \gamma) = (0, 0, 1)$ (omitted).

i	j	α	β	γ
0	1	-720	-299	450
1	1	288	31	-90
2	1	-384	1	90
2	2	-6	1	0
3	1	-2304	389	450
3	2	-6	1	0
4	1	18432	-419	-3150
4	2	210	-19	0
4	3	-4608	383	-90
5	1	61440	791	-9450
5	2	630	-41	0
5	3	-12288	1145	-630
6	1	737280	20989	-103950
6	2	1386	-71	0
6	3	122880	-13079	9450
6	4	378	-11	0
7	1	-72253440	-2647279	9459450
7	2	-2574	109	0
7	3	7372800	-884203	727650
7	4	297	-7	0
8	1	231211008	9547469	-28378350
8	2	-858	31	0
8	3	80281600	-10675439	9459450
8	4	858	-17	0
8	5	-9830400	-1833409	2182950
9	1	-45779779584	-2016587711	5306751450
9	2	-6630	209	0
9	3	2312110080	-336233167	312161850
9	4	-117	2	0
9	5	-963379200	-272007887	312161850
10	1	11902742691840	543876944201	-1310767608150
10	2	9690	-271	0
10	3	457797795840	-71995419827	68987768850
10	4	1530	-23	0
10	5	-9248440320	-3600327811	4058104050
10	6	90	-1	0
11	1	12469539962880	581663428937	-1310767608150
11	2	-13566	341	0
11	3	-7935161794560	1337393123657	-1310767608150
11	4	969	-13	0
11	5	-122079412224	-61822135475	68987768850
11	6	-102	1	0
12	1	-5087572304855040	-239899940677247	512510134786650
12	2	18354	-419	0
12	3	124695399628800	-22357818254809	2228304933855
12	4	2394	-29	0
12	5	31740647178240	20090629170649	-22283049338550
12	6	-114	1	0
12	7	-732476473344	5376960927599	-5863960352250
13	1	502652143719677952	23380008825309473	-48688462804731750
13	2	-4830	101	0
13	3	50875723048550400	-9645671177722733	9737692560946350
13	4	-1449	16	0
13	5	-498781598515200	-383233413631771	423377937432450
13	6	126	-1	0
13	7	-38088776613888	388070083677979	-423377937432450

4.10   Further Extensions

Unless we missed something fundamental in the other relations involving G of the Ramanujan Machine project, the same type of generalization should *in principle* apply to the other G relations (given online as of October 2022).

References

1. Cação, I., Falcão, M., Malonek, H.: Hypercomplex polynomials, Vietoris' rational numbers and a related integer numbers sequence. Complex Anal. Oper. Theory **11**, 06 (2017)
2. David, N.B., Nimri, G., Mendlovic, U., Manor, Y., Kaminer, I.: On the Connection Between Irrationality Measures and Polynomial Continued Fractions (2021)
3. Raayoni, G., et al.: Generating conjectures on fundamental constants with the Ramanujan machine. Nature **590**(7844), 67–73 (2021)
4. Raayoni, G., et al.: The Ramanujan Machine: Automatically Generated Conjectures on Fundamental Constants. CoRR, abs/1907.00205 (2019)

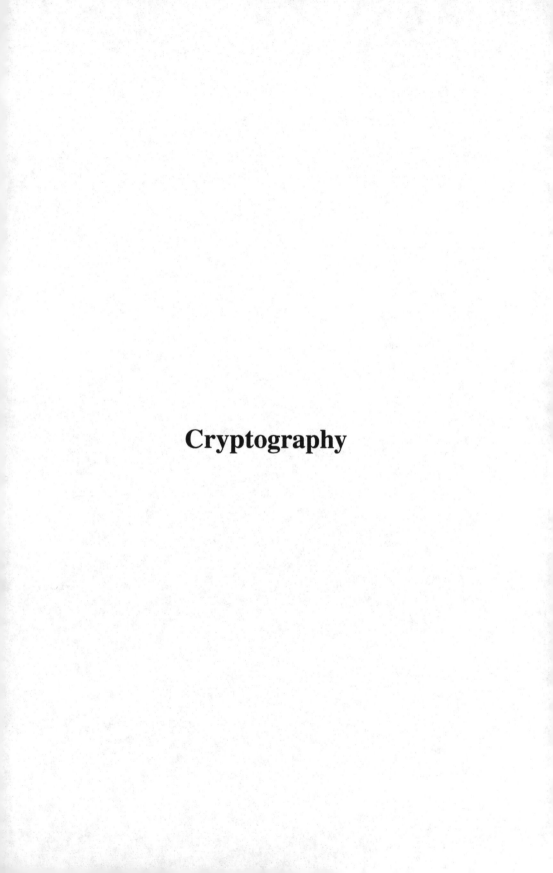

Cryptography

Full Post-Quantum Datagram TLS Handshake in the Internet of Things

Callum McLoughlin, Clémentine Gritti⬥, and Juliet Samandari(✉)⬥

University of Canterbury, Christchurch, New Zealand
cwm62@uclive.ac.nz, clementine.gritti@canterbury.ac.nz,
juliet.samandari@pg.canterbury.ac.nz

Abstract. Quantum computers are a threat to the current standards for secure communication. The Datagram Transport Layer Security (DTLS) protocol is a common protocol used by Internet of Things (IoT) devices that will be broken by such computers. Although quantum computers are yet to become commercially available, IoT devices are generally long-lived. Thus the transition to quantum secure cryptography, as soon as possible, is necessary. IoT devices are generally resource-constrained and Post-Quantum (PQ) cryptography is often more resource intensive computationally compared to current cryptographic standards, adding to the complexity of the transition. In this paper, we propose a PQ version of DTLS 1.3 in IoT, at some additional costs. We first identify a suitable PQ digital signature scheme and Key Encapsulation Mechanism (KEM) to be used in a PQ version of the DTLS protocol. Using the selected PQ algorithms, we implement and evaluate a full PQ DTLS 1.3 handshake on a Raspberry Pi 4B. We find that CPU usage is actually lower compared to current cryptographic schemes used in DTLS 1.3. We notice a significant increase of up to 6x as many packets sent when establishing a connection, depending on the security level. Moreover, memory usage is significantly greater, requiring at least an extra 800 KiB of memory to connect 100 devices.

Keywords: Datagram Transport Layer Security · Post-Quantum Implementation · Internet of Things

1 Introduction

Quantum computers are a new type of computers that use qubits rather than bits. These computers use quantum algorithms that can break our current security communication standards. In 2019, Google introduced a 53-qubit quantum computer [2], and more recently, IBM introduced an 127-qubit quantum computer[1]. Quantum computers today are not capable of breaking current asymmetric cryptosystems like RSA and Elliptic Curve Cryptography (ECC), but they

---

[1] https://research.ibm.com/blog/eagle-quantum-processor-performance (accessed on 29/11/22).

© The Author(s), under exclusive license to Springer Nature Switzerland AG 2023
S. El Hajji et al. (Eds.): C2SI 2023, LNCS 13874, pp. 57–76, 2023.
https://doi.org/10.1007/978-3-031-33017-9_4

will according to Shor's algorithm [33]. It can be seen that there is real progress being made, and quickly; quantum computers are projected to become generally available in approximately two or three decades [12].

It has been identified that it usually takes around 20 years for the framework of new cryptographic standards to be rolled out. This makes it imperative to begin considering possibilities for such standards now, to be prepared for when quantum computers are available. Here, the cryptosystems are referred to as Post-Quantum (PQ) cryptosystems because they will provide our current computers, that rely on classical computing mechanisms for their operation, with security that is robust in the face of future attacks from quantum computers. This process of standardization has already been set in motion by the National Institute of Standards and Technology (NIST)[2].

Internet of Things (IoT) is a concept outlining there being a system consisting of a number of objects with communication capabilities that are interconnected. The connection is usually over the Internet [34]. IoT commonly uses cryptographic protocols to secure unicast communication to a central server. IoT devices are generally cheap and cryptographically weak [37]. As a result, the underlying algorithms have to be carefully selected. It is predicted that the number of connected IoT devices will increase to 27 billion by 2025[3] making it imperative to consider IoT devices when looking at communication standards.

PQ schemes proposed to NIST so far have shown considerably larger component sizes, or more computations compared to the current cryptographic schemes [29]. They can feasibly be run on machines such as computers and laptops, and some smart devices. However, many IoT devices have become popular because they are inexpensive so the cost of production is minimized. As a consequence, such devices are noticeably resource-constrained, and thus deploying proposed PQ schemes in these devices is not straightforward.

One specific protocol commonly used in IoT is the Datagram Transport Layer Security (DTLS) protocol [32]. This protocol is one of many that will be easily broken through the use of quantum computers. It is important that existing devices and future devices running this protocol are able to transition to a quantum secure version of DTLS. Therefore, we must carefully consider suitable PQ algorithms for IoT and better understand the potential costs (in terms of computation, storage, and communication) that a transition to a PQ version of the DTLS protocol will bring.

Contributions. This paper outlines how existing PQ cryptography fits with the existing communication protocol DTLS being widely used in IoT networks. We first analyse the current cryptographic algorithms used by version 1.3 of DTLS (denoted as DTLS 1.3), and find their computation, storage, and communication costs on IoT devices. Those costs will help us understand the feasibility of a PQ version of DTLS 1.3 for IoT, by comparing them with the ones we will obtain by running selected PQ cryptographic algorithms.

---

[2] https://csrc.nist.gov/projects/post-quantum-cryptography (accessed on 28/11/22).
[3] https://iot-analytics.com/number-connected-iot-devices/ (accessed on 29/11/22).

Potential PQ algorithms have been identified previously, but it is not well understood how realistic implementing these are in DTLS. This is particularly challenging as NIST's standardization process has shown that larger computational, storage, and communication costs are generally induced by PQ algorithms [13].

The contributions in this paper are as follows:

Select a suitable PQ Digital Signature Algorithm for DTLS 1.3. DTLS uses digital signatures as a means of authenticating when establishing connections between servers and clients. We look at how PQ digital signature algorithms differ from current digital signature ones when used by the DTLS protocol.

Select a suitable PQ KEM Algorithm for DTLS 1.3. Classical DTLS 1.3 requires parties to exchange key information in order to agree upon shared keys. The transition to PQ key agreement will use a KEM. We aim to understand the effect that PQ KEMs have on DTLS during connection establishment.

Implement and Evaluate the Full PQ DTLS 1.3 Handshake in IoT. From the above results, we will implement and evaluate a full DTLS 1.3 handshake, using the selected PQ digital signature and KEM algorithms, CRYSTALS-Dilithium and CRYSTALS-Kyber respectively, in a designed IoT environment.

IoT devices are generally cryptographically weak due to cryptography requiring a significant amount of resources. Because it is already clear that classical cryptography can be problematic in cases requiring strong security, it is possible that the costs are too great for a PQ DTLS protocol in practice. It is essential to understand if it is feasible for an IoT device to run a PQ version of DTLS 1.3 in practice.

Road Map. In the next section, we introduce the building blocks needed to develop and analyse our full PQ handshake in DTLS 1.3. In Sect. 3, we review works on PQ cryptography, including where it is applied to IoT. In Sect. 4, we first work on selecting the appropriate PQ digital signature and KEM algorithms, and then deploy the full DTLS 1.3 handshake based on this selection. In Sect. 5, we discuss the implementation and evaluation results from the previous section. We conclude the paper in the final section.

2   Building Blocks

In this section, we introduce the various building blocks that will help build and evaluate our PQ DTLS handshake.

2.1   Digital Signatures and Certification

In the context where a sender sends a message to a receiver, a digital signature is used to verify the sender's identity and/or to check the integrity of the received message [22]. Two actions have to be carried out: to sign a message using the secret key and to verify if a received signature is valid using the public key [10,20].

The current standards are the RSA-based Digital Signature Algorithm (DSA) and the Elliptic Curve Digital Signature Algorithm (ECDSA) and are available in the DTLS protocol [5].

Digital certificates are the backbone to authenticating and establishing the initial connection between servers and clients using digital signature schemes in DTLS. Digital certificates are used to bind a public key to a party, either the server or the client, by having a trusted Certificate Authority (CA) sign the associated certificate [7]. Certificates are often chained together, with each certificate in the chain signed by an intermediate certificate authority, resulting in a chain of trust. Certificate chains found on the Internet often consist of two to four certificates, resulting in sizes in the order of a few kilobytes using current digital signature schemes [17].

2.2 Key Encapsulation Mechanisms

The DTLS protocol allows the server and client to exchange key information to derive an agreed upon symmetric secret key. More specifically, each party generates their own public and secret key pair, shares the public part with each other and then computes the shared secret key using their own secret key and the public information of the other party. This shared key is then used to secure communication between both parties. The underlying algorithm is, in general, from the Diffie-Hellman family of algorithms [25].

PQ key agreement works slightly differently, through a Key Encapsulation Mechanism (KEM). KEM involves the generation of a random key, which an agreed upon key encapsulates (akin to encryption). The random key is then sent to the other party, which decapsulates (akin to decryption) [8]. The end result is the same as a classical key exchange, having an agreed upon shared symmetric key, but different intermediate steps are performed.

2.3 NIST Post-Quantum Standardization

The National Institute of Standards and Technology (NIST), from the U.S. Department of Commerce, provides standards and support for technological advancements in the U.S. and around the world. In 2016, NIST called for submissions for PQ algorithms for both digital signature schemes and KEMs [13]. Submitted algorithms were evaluated, and unacceptable candidates removed throughout several rounds of the competition. Currently, some of these algorithms are set to be standardized, while an additional round of changes are needed for others. A call for additional digital signature schemes has also been made[4]. PQ cryptography comprises five types: lattice-based cryptography, multivariate cryptography, hash-based cryptography, code-based cryptography, and isogeny cryptography. Note that in this paper, we only consider asymmetric PQ

---

[4] https://csrc.nist.gov/News/2022/pqc-candidates-to-be-standardized-and-round-4 (accessed on 29/11/22).

cryptography. Symmetric cryptography is made quantum resistant by doubling the size of the secret key according to the Grover algorithm [16].

Table 1 is a summary of each algorithm included within Round 3 [13], along with their PQ cryptographic type. Alternative candidates, which are not NIST's ideal candidates, are denoted by ⋆. Candidates that have subsequently been proven broken [4,6,11] have been denoted by † and are included for reference.

Table 1. NIST Round 3 Post-Quantum Candidates [13]

Digital Signature Algorithms	Cryptographic Type
CRYSTALS-Dilithium	Lattice-based cryptography
Falcon	Lattice-based cryptography
Rainbow†	Multivariate cryptography
Picnic⋆	Symmetric cryptography
SPHINCS+⋆	Hash-based cryptography
GeMSS⋆†	Multivariate cryptography
KEM Algorithms	Cryptographic Type
CRYSTALS-Kyber	Lattice-based cryptography
Saber	Lattice-based cryptography
NTRU	Lattice-based cryptography
Classic McEliece	Code-based cryptography
Bike⋆	Code-based cryptography
FrodoKEM⋆	Lattice-based cryptography
HQC⋆	Code-based cryptography
NTRU-Prime⋆	Lattice-based cryptography
SIKE⋆†	Isogeny cryptography

Additionally, these candidates have varying security categories[5], as shown in Table 2. When analysing our testing results, we list the candidates in order of increasing strength. Henceforth, we define the following notation of either *(PQ scheme)(security level)* or *(PQ scheme)(key bit size)* in further discussion. For clarity, Fig. 2 and Fig. 4 show the correspondence between the name and security level of each algorithm tested. Furthermore, we drop the CRYSTALS part of CRYSTALS-Dilithium and CRYSTALS-Kyber for readability. As a result, the implementation of the CRYSTALS-Dilithium digital signature scheme at security level 3 will be notated as Dilithium3.

---

[5] https://csrc.nist.gov/projects/post-quantum-cryptography/post-quantum-cryptogr
aphy-standardization/evaluation-criteria/security-(evaluation-criteria) (accessed on 29/11/22).

Table 2. NIST Post-Quantum Security Categories

Security Level	Computational Resources Required
1	Key search on block cipher with 128-bit key (e.g. AES128)
2	Collision search on 256-bit hash function (e.g. SHA256)
3	Key search on block cipher with 192-bit key (e.g. AES192)
4	Collision search on 384-bit hash function (e.g. SHA384)
5	Key search on block cipher with 256-bit key (e.g. AES256)

2.4 Datagram Transport Layer Security

Datagram Transport Layer Security (DTLS) operates on top of datagram transport mechanisms that do not require or provide reliable or in-order delivery of data. In addition, DTLS aims to provide the same security guarantees for confidentiality, integrity, and authenticity as Transport Layer Security (TLS) through datagram transport.

The main aim of DTLS is thus to allow for "TLS over datagram transport" [26]. Datagram transport is a popular choice for securing communication in cases such as video streaming, online gaming, or any application that requires low latency and is not sensitive to unreliable delivery. We focus on the User Datagram Protocol (UDP) within DTLS, which is a "fire and forget" communication protocol intended to be used when low latency, simplicity, and efficiency is required [1].

DTLS exists since TLS cannot be used directly over datagram transport for several reasons. One reason is that TLS relies on implicit sequence numbers on records due to reliable in-order delivery. If an encrypted record were to arrive out of order, as is possible with UDP, then the wrong sequence number will be used to decrypt it. Secondly, fragmentation of large handshake messages over multiple datagrams is possible with datagram transport, which requires detection and reassembly [26].

One important part of the DTLS protocol is handshakes, which are used to establish connections between a server and client, with several packets being exchanged during this phase. The fewer packets sent during the handshake, the less likely a packet is to be lost or delivered out of order. Hence, the handshake requires less transmission time.

Figure 1 depicts the exchange of data during a handshake between two parties.

During the handshake, the server sends its signed certificate to authenticate to the client, and optionally (as marked by an *) the client can send their own certificate. With the client sending their certificate, both parties mutually authenticate each other, which is common in IoT [3]. During this, both the client and server agree upon a shared symmetric key from additional key share data sent between them. This shared secret key is then used to provide secure communication between both parties. As a result, the DTLS protocol requires both

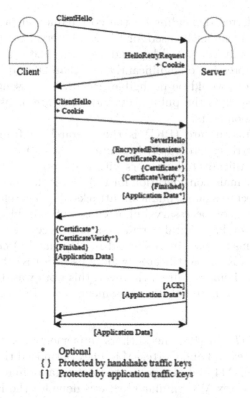

Fig. 1. DTLS Handshake Adapted From [26]

a digital signature scheme for authentication, and a KEM for confidentiality. In our PQ implementation, we use the latest 1.3 version of DTLS, commonly named as DTLS 1.3.

3   Related Work

Post-Quantum Digital Certification. Digital signatures are embedded in X.509 digital certificates to authenticate servers over the Internet. PQ X.509 certificates have been explored previously in [17], showing significant public key and signature sizes in the order of hundreds of kilobytes for the NIST Round one candidates. It was shown, for both TLS and DTLS, that significantly more fragmentation of packets is necessary to transmit these certificates. Furthermore, transmitting more packets was viable, but not negligible in terms of connection overhead. It was claimed that this is acceptable for most modern use cases. However, the paper did not look at the signature processing overhead due to the overhead being calculated on a per algorithm basis, nor did it describe the claimed modern use hardware or computing power necessary. Additionally, this overhead varies depending on the combination of schemes used, with certain schemes being preferred depending on the cost reduction priorities [23]. Additionally, compression cannot be used for PQ X.509 certificates since they consist of up to 90% randomly generated key and signature data, as suggested in [17]. This results in compression of significantly less than 20% and improvements in transmission overhead would be negligible. Hence, it is essential that data in a digital certificate, such as the public key and signature, is as small as possible to reduce transmission costs.

Public-Key Infrastructure (PKI) is the overarching framework needed to implement asymmetric cryptography in communication. PKI is used in conjunction with digital certificates to link users with keys and provide trust throughout the interaction. The main consideration for PQ PKI is the need for cryptographic algorithms to be secure against quantum attacks [36]. Therefore, organizational changes to PKI are not necessary but a choice of suitable PQ algorithms is needed. Similarly, for PQ digital certificates it is necessary to identify appropriate PQ algorithms for use. It was found in [24] that PQ cryptosystems were feasible for use with X.509 certificates, widely used in PKI, but would result in increased processing being required. However, this work was done specifically for X.509 certificates, so a more holistic assessment of the PQ algorithms would be beneficial.

Quantum Secure IoT. In [15], the authors implemented a compact version of Dilithium on a Cortex-M3 and Cortex-M4. They optimized the NIST implementation on the Cortex-M4 and also presented a constant-time implementation of Dilithium on the Cortex-M3. Similar work was done for the KEM Kyber in [9]. In [35], Kyber was optimized for a Field Programmable Gate Array (FPGA), which are semiconductor devices that have an array of different uses, one of then being for IoT. In [30], the authors optimized Dilithium for FPGA and found that all security levels were possible but that Dilithium3 is the best option in terms of the security provided compared to the processing overhead.

It can be seen that much of the work that has taken place was very specific to certain devices, meaning that it does not consider the variety of IoT devices and the varying resources these devices may have. It can also be seen that these papers have not taken into account the communication protocol to be used.

Post-Quantum Datagram Transport Layer Security. A PQ DTLS protocol has been proposed in [14]. However, it was based on DTLS 1.2 rather than DTLS 1.3. The latter offers noticeable improvements over earlier versions, in particular a faster handshake, and simpler and more secure combinations of algorithms for authentication and confidentiality. In addition, many changes have been made to PQ cryptography since, and the proposed PQ DTLS 1.2 protocol is no longer considered quantum secure, as discussed in [19]. In [28], a PQ version of DTLS 1.2 is proposed for cyber physical systSpringer Template for Callums Research (Copy)ems. Nevertheless, NTRU is the only considered PQ algorithm, although it is not one of the selected algorithms for standardization by NIST. In [27], a TLS Cached Information Extension could potentially be used for the PQ version of DTLS 1.3, as a mechanism to reduce the amount of information exchanged during handshake. However, it is not a general solution, since in some cases the cache will either be empty or invalid, thus requiring the full certificate to be both stored and transmitted. In addition, security concerns regarding caching from trusted sources and Man-In-The-Middle attacks all prevent this from being a possibility for PQ certificates. Therefore, it can be seen that further work on finding a PQ DTLS protocol, based on the current version 1.3 and assuring security against quantum computers, is needed.

4   Full Post-Quantum DTLS Handshake in IoT

In this section, we first detail our testing framework. We then present our PQ algorithm evaluations for selecting an adequate digital signature scheme and KEM for IoT. We finally propose the implementation of our full PQ DTLS 1.3 handshake in an IoT environment.

4.1   Design and Environment Considerations

Our IoT device, acting as a client, is a Raspberry Pi 4B, with a Quad Core ARM64 Cortex-A72 CPU running at 1.5 GHz with 8 GB of 3200 MHz SDRAM. The Raspberry Pi is a low cost, ubiquitous device, and hence is a realistic assumption of the type of computational power IoT devices will have for applications such as in factories, businesses, and homes in the future, when a sufficient quantum computer architecture becomes available. The server, unless otherwise specified, is a Dell XPS 9305 with 8 GB of RAM running an 11th Generation Intel Core i5-1135G7.

Our implementation was done using the Open Quantum Safe's OpenSSL library[6], the IoT-oriented WolfSSL cryptographic library[7]. OpenSSL and WolfSSL are open source, general purpose cryptographic libraries. Additionally, the reference implementations of NIST's Round 3 PQ candidates [13] can be used alongside OpenSSL and WolfSSL thanks to the Open Quantum Safe project[8]. The code we used to run these experiments can be found in a GitHub repository[9].

At the time of writing, WolfSSL has the first and only implementation of DTLS 1.3 so WolfSSL's compatibility with external systems for validation is limited. This is further exacerbated by the fact that the implementation includes PQ additions. Additionally, research has been conducted into each of the NIST PQ Round 3 submissions. The following results were compiled from the Open Quantum Safe's implementation of quantum resistant algorithms. Compiler settings to optimize for specific hardware were disabled, as the results are intended to be a generalization for all types of IoT devices that may or may not have certain hardware acceleration. Comparisons are therefore meant to be relative between algorithms, rather than specific values.

---

[6] https://github.com/open-quantum-safe/openssl (accessed on 29/11/22).
[7] https://github.com/wolfSSL/wolfssl (accessed on 29/11/22).
[8] https://github.com/open-quantum-safe/liboqs (accessed on 29/11/22).
[9] https://github.com/Juliet-S/Post-Quantum_DTLS (accessed on 28/02/23).

4.2   PQ Digital Signature Scheme Selection

The DTLS 1.3 handshake uses digital signatures embedded into certificates to provide authentication between the server and client. The certificates have to be transmitted from the server to the client, and optionally from the client back to the server.

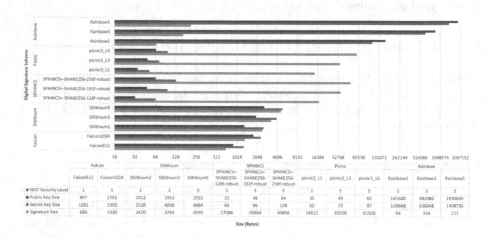

Fig. 2. Post-Quantum Public Key, Secret Key and Signature Sizes

Significant variance exists between the PQ digital signature candidates[10], as seen in Fig. 2. For most algorithms, at least one of the public key, secret key, or signature sizes is extremely large. Figure 2 demonstrates that algorithms such as SPHINCS+ have small public and secret keys, but comparatively large signature sizes. Additionally, algorithms such as Dilithium and Falcon have overall larger sizes in all three, but are more consistent and signatures are smaller than SPHINCS+'s large ones.

Not only is the raw size of the elements that make up a digital certificate important, but also the performance of signature generation and verification when in use. Setting up a DTLS 1.3 connection requires transmission of the certificate itself, signing of data, and verification of that signed data. Figure 3 shows Dilithium is fast in both signing and verification, with Falcon being as fast as Dilithium in verifying but not when signing. Furthermore, compared to traditional digital signature schemes such as RSA and ECDSA, we see comparable or even better performance in both signature generation and verification. Results found in [24] also concluded Dilithium and Falcon outperform classical algorithms in signing. Other algorithms such as SPHINCS+ and Picnic perform significantly worse. Taking into account the logarithmic scale of the graph, they have less than 100 operations per second with most variants.

---

[10] https://openquantumsafe.org/liboqs/algorithms (accessed on 29/11/22).

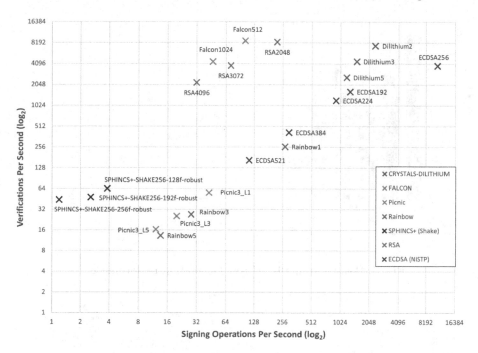

Fig. 3. Post-Quantum Signing and Verification Performance

We decided Dilithium is the best digital signature candidate since its performance was best, even compared to Falcon, as shown in Fig. 3. Dilithium is a lattice-based digital signature and is based on the LWE and Short Integer Solution (SIS) problems. Dilithium uses ring operations to compute its values and can be either random or deterministic. NIST also concluded that Dilithium was well suited for most applications [13]. Additionally, Falcon uses floating point arithmetic, which is undesirable for IoT devices due to the greater computational costs required and potential side-channel attacks as a result [18].

4.3 PQ Key Encapsulation Mechanism Selection

The other half of the DTLS 1.3 handshake uses KEMs to allow both the server and client to generate and use a more efficient symmetric key for further secure communication. This key is used to guarantee confidentiality between the two parties. We use PQ KEM as a way to exchange key information between parties and to build the shared secret key.

The performance of the PQ KEMs can be seen in Fig. 4. Sorting based on keys generated per second has all variants of Kyber and Saber being significantly faster than other algorithms such as NTRU and McEliece. Depending on the algorithms selected, there is a speed difference of up to 16,000 times (e.g. Kyber1 and McEliece-460896). Figure 4 also shows the general trend that variants which

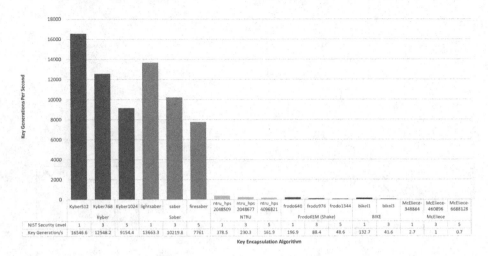

Fig. 4. Post-Quantum KEM Key Generation Performance

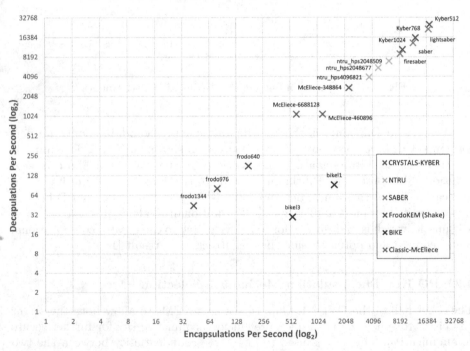

Fig. 5. Post-Quantum Key Encapsulation and Decapsulation Performance

target a lower security level such as Kyber1 perform better than higher level security variants such as Kyber5.

In addition to key generation, the relative performance of encapsulating and decapsulating the shared keys is also important. DTLS 1.3 uses key agreement algorithms within the handshake to establish a connection [26], with encapsulation and decapsulation being comparable to encrypting and decrypting respectively. It is evident within Fig. 5 that all Kyber and Saber variants perform well compared to other KEMs, taking into account the logarithmic scales on both the X and Y axes. Kyber and Saber performing similarly is unsurprising due to both KEMs being lattice-based [21].

Figure 4 demonstrates that most PQ KEMs are time consuming, with only two candidates, namely Kyber and Saber, being high in performance on the device. Kyber and Saber have over of 16,000 times more key generations than other schemes such as McEliece. Further solidifying Kyber and Saber as the best candidates, Fig. 5 demonstrates that both are high in performance when encapsulating and decapsulating the key generated. This is important as the server encapsulates the key, while the client, as the IoT device, decapsulates it, hence requiring both encapsulation and decapsulation to be fast.

Kyber was selected due to being the best performing KEM, but also because it is currently the only KEM algorithm to be standardized. NIST has concluded that the security of the lattice problem on which Kyber is based is more convincing than of the lattice problem on which Saber is based. Kyber is based on the LWE problem over module lattices.

4.4   Full PQ DTLS 1.3 Handshake Implementation

As a result of the previous testing, Dilithium and Kyber were selected and implemented in the DTLS 1.3 protocol, making a full PQ handshake implementation. This implementation was then tested against DTLS 1.3 with current algorithms, namely RSA for digital signatures (RSA2048 and RSA4096) and ECC-based Diffie-Hellman scheme for key exchange (SECP256R1 and SECP521R1), to see and compare the effect of PQ algorithms within DTLS 1.3 in practice.

We select the variants of Dilithium and Kyber as follows. Security level 3 is the recommended level by the authors for both Dilithium and Kyber in general use cases [8]. The combination of Dilithium5 and Kyber5 offers a more secure option. The use of RSA2048 and SECP256R1 is suggested for standard applications, hence we match this combination with Dilithium3/Kyber3. The use of RSA4096/SECP521R1 enables the assurance of higher security, thus we match this combination with Dilithium5/Kyber5. However, the aforementioned combinations of RSA and SECP algorithms could be considered slightly less secure than their PQ alternatives. RSA2048 has 112-bit security, so it is slightly lower than PQ security level 1, while RSA4096 would be somewhere between security levels 1 and 3. SECP256R1's security would be security level 2 and SECP521R1's security would be between security levels 4 and 5. The server and client use the ciphersuite *TLS_AES_256_GCM_SHA384*, with 256-bit AES symmetric encryption in authenticated encryption Galois Counter Mode (GCM) and hash function SHA384 in all tests unless otherwise specified. These algorithms were chosen as this is closer to the requirements of PQ schemes.

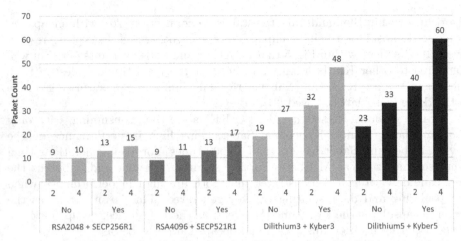

Fig. 6. DTLS 1.3 Packet Count

Figure 6 shows the number of packets sent for algorithms used within DTLS 1.3. The figure shows the packet counts for digital signature schemes and their corresponding KEMs, whether client authentication was enabled, and based on the number of digital certificates in the certificate chain (2 and 4).

A general trend upward can be seen in Fig. 6, when using a longer certificate chain, enabling client authentication, and using more computationally intensive and stronger algorithms such as RSA4096 or Dilithium5. Dilithium3 and Kyber3 require more packets than higher security level traditional algorithms RSA4096 (digital signatures) and SECP521R1 (key exchange). Since more packets are being sent and DTLS 1.3 operates over UDP, this could be of significant concern. DTLS 1.3 does have mechanisms in place to establish connections in the event of a packet loss, so the ability to connect could remain unaffected. However, this can affect the connection time between the server and client.

Figure 7 shows connection times when using traditional DTLS and the fully post-quantum implementation of DTLS 1.3 without client authentication. The connection was wireless with one hop between the client and server. Additionally during this test, no packet loss or alteration was introduced and so represents a best-case scenario for connection establishment. Connection times were averaged over 100 connection establishments.

Figure 7 shows that connection times increased when going from RSA2048/ SECP256R1 to Dilithium/Kyber at level 3. However, in the case of going from RSA4096/SECP521R1 to Dilithium/Kyber at level 5, the opposite is true, connection times decreased. This demonstrates that increasing the security level of classical cryptography results in a greater increase in connection time than that seen for Dilithium and Kyber.

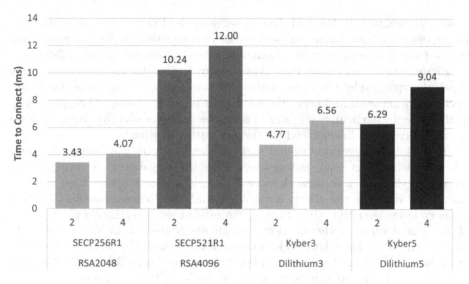

Fig. 7. DTLS 1.3 Connection Time without Client Authentication

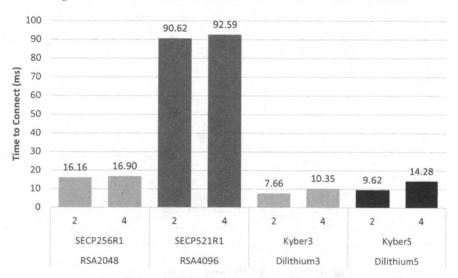

Fig. 8. DTLS 1.3 Connection Time with Client Authentication

Figure 8 shows the connection times with client authentication enabled within the connection, using the same setup as in Fig. 7. An exponential jump in the time to connect from the RSA2048/SECP256R1 combination to the RSA4096/SECP521R1 combination can be seen. This increase in connection time is approximately five-fold. In comparison, the PQ combinations of DTLS 1.3 experience a more linear, subtle increase in connection time when going from level 3 to level 5, with a more reasonable increase of approximately 1.3-fold.

Figure 8 also shows that PQ cryptography is not always more costly than classical cryptography. Client authentication is commonplace to authenticate IoT devices on a network, and hence there is a clear benefit to using PQ cryptography in this case. In particular, if the need arises for a higher security level, we see a considerably better linear trend for the PQ authentication.

To examine the computational and memory costs on the device, the same setup as before was used, but reversed with the Raspberry Pi acting as the server. We chose such framework since if a single connection were used with the Raspberry Pi being the client, it would be difficult to measure the CPU and memory usage over time. In addition, the setup used a certificate chain length of 4, without client authentication. 100 clients connected in 100ms intervals, transmitting 1200 byte data packets every second which the server echoed back immediately. With the Raspberry Pi being the server, we could see all 100 clients connecting, and thus obtain more accurate results of the general trend.

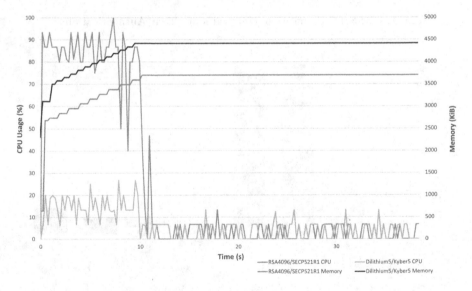

Fig. 9. DTLS 1.3 CPU and Memory Usage

In Fig. 9, the trend for each implementation is similar, with an initial spike for both while the clients connect, then dropping significantly after 10 s when all the clients have established a connection to the server and are just exchanging encrypted packets back and forth.

Within the same figure, it is evident that the RSA4096/SECP521R1 combination in DTLS requires a significant amount of computational resources to establish connections with all 100 clients, reaching around 80–100% of the CPU usage. However, the CPU cost for the PQ Dilithium5/Kyber5 combination when establishing the same amount of connections is lower, being anywhere from 10–30% of the CPU usage. After all 100 connections had been established, the computational cost to send and receive messages is similar for both traditional and PQ combinations.

In Fig. 9, a clear memory-time trade-off can be seen where the PQ implementation of DTLS 1.3 performs significantly better in terms of computational cost, with the downside of significantly more memory being used, on the order of 800–900 KiB when all 100 clients are connected. The larger memory usage can mainly be attributed to the larger certificate sizes from the usage of Dilithium5 as noted in Fig. 2 and the size differences of the shared keys in SECP521R1 and Kyber5. This can be problematic in the case of lower-end IoT devices that only have kilobytes of memory. Nevertheless, as mentioned previously, we can assume that, in a world with quantum computers, IoT devices will have computing power similar to our Raspberry Pi 4B [31].

5 Discussion

Initial results on the individual PQ candidate schemes showed significant variance, with most algorithms performing well with regard to computational, memory, or communication costs but not all. This reaffirms prior research that PQ schemes have considerably larger component sizes or computations required. This is problematic in the case of IoT devices with limited processing power.

Regarding the PQ Algorithm Selections. As DTLS 1.3 requires both a digital signature scheme and a KEM, research was conducted to find suitable schemes for both. Dilithium was selected as the best digital signature scheme as it performed the best in both signing and verification performance tests, in addition to being one of the smallest in component size.

For the second half of DTLS 1.3, namely the KEM, we identified Kyber as the most suitable algorithm. Kyber outperformed every other scheme in every metric shown, barring Saber. Saber was unsurprisingly a close candidate due to both Kyber and Saber being based off lattices. However, NIST has dismissed Saber because the lattice problem it is based on has been less studied than the problem Kyber is based on. Hence, we decided on the use of Kyber.

Regarding the PQ DTLS 1.3 Handshake Implementation. Results for the implementation within DTLS 1.3 showed that a PQ DTLS implementation increases the connection time when client authentication is not involved at lower security levels. Increased connection times were experienced from RSA2048/SECP256R1 to Dilithium3/Kyber3, and better connection times from RSA4096/SECP521R1 to Dilithium5/Kyber5. Large benefits were experienced when it came to using client authentication, which IoT uses commonly. A linear growth trend was experienced when increasing security levels within PQ DTLS 1.3, compared to an exponential growth increase from traditional cryptography in DTLS.

Communication costs on devices are exceptionally high when using the security level 5 implementation of DTLS 1.3, with up to a 6-fold increase in packets sent during the handshake. It was shown that even a lower security level of 3, using Dilithium3 and Kyber3 without client authentication and with a certificate chain length of two, resulted in more packets than a 4-chain RSA4096 certificate with client authentication on. This can be a significant problem in areas with large packet loss, resulting in issues establishing a connection properly. If a packet is lost, DTLS 1.3 does resend it; however, this can severely affect the connection times.

Computational costs are considerably less with the PQ implementation of DTLS 1.3 compared to that of classical DTLS 1.3. The trend of high initial computation during the client connection phase, and then leveling out once the client is only exchanging data, is exhibited in both traditional and PQ DTLS, albeit to a lesser extent with PQ DTLS 1.3.

Memory usage is significantly higher in the context of IoT devices. However, it was exhibited that there is up to 800–900 KiB of additional memory needed to connect all the clients when using PQ DTLS 1.3. This can mainly be attributed to the larger certificate sizes when using Dilithium and differences between key exchange with Diffie-Hellman and key exchange with Kyber.

6 Conclusion

In conclusion, a PQ version of DTLS 1.3 using Dilithium and Kyber is feasible for IoT. Increases in communication and memory costs are evident, but not significant enough to stop a PQ implementation being used. Computational costs are significantly less however, with less processing power needed compared to traditional DTLS 1.3 using RSA signatures and ECC-based key exchange.

PQ algorithms are still being evaluated by NIST, with candidates being broken, introduced, and standardized. It is quite possible that, in the future, new algorithms more suited for a PQ version of DTLS 1.3 will be introduced. More specifically, to-be-invented algorithms with smaller component sizes and/or processing costs than Dilithium or Kyber may be proposed. Additionally, our implementation only looked at Dilithium and Kyber. It is possible that one of the algorithms tested but not selected could perform better in some metrics and scenarios. For example, when the certificates are cached and do not require to be sent, an algorithm with a larger signature size but smaller key sizes could be possibly used.

Future research could also evaluate the real effect of compression with the usage of Dilithium and Kyber. Compression of their components could reach up to 20% as claimed in [17], which implies that up to 12 out of 60 packets would no longer need to be sent when establishing a connection using Dilithium and Kyber at security level 5. Nevertheless, implementing PQ DTLS may show this value to differ.

References

1. Al-Dhief, F.T., et al.: Performance comparison between TCP and UDP protocols in different simulation scenarios. Int. J. Eng. Technol. **7**(4.36), 172–176 (2018)
2. Arute, F., et al.: Quantum supremacy using a programmable superconducting processor. Nature **574**(7779), 505–510 (2019)
3. Atwady, Y., Hammoudeh, M.: A survey on authentication techniques for the internet of things. In: International Conference on Future Networks and Distributed Systems, pp. 1–5 (2017)
4. Baena, J., Briaud, P., Cabarcas, D., Perlner, R., Smith-Tone, D., Verbel, J.: Improving support-minors rank attacks: applications to gemss and rainbow. In: Dodis, Y., Shrimpton, T. (eds.) CRYPTO 2022. LNCS, vol. 13509, pp. 376–405. Springer, Cham (2022). https://doi.org/10.1007/978-3-031-15982-4_13
5. Barker, E.: Digital signature standard (DSS). NIST FIPS (2013)
6. Beullens, W.: Breaking rainbow takes a weekend on a laptop. Cryptology ePrint Archive, Paper 2022/214 (2022)
7. Boeyen, S., Santesson, S., Polk, T., Housley, R., Farrell, S., Cooper, D.: Internet X.509 public key infrastructure certificate and certificate revocation list (CRL) profile. RFC 5280 (2008)
8. Bos, J., et al.: CRYSTALS-Kyber: a CCA-secure module-lattice-based KEM. In: 2018 IEEE European Symposium on Security and Privacy, pp. 353–367 (2018)
9. Botros, L., Kannwischer, M.J., Schwabe, P.: Memory-efficient high-speed implementation of kyber on Cortex-M4. In: Buchmann, J., Nitaj, A., Rachidi, T. (eds.) AFRICACRYPT 2019. LNCS, vol. 11627, pp. 209–228. Springer, Cham (2019). https://doi.org/10.1007/978-3-030-23696-0_11
10. Buchmann, J., Dahmen, E., Szydlo, M.: Hash-based digital signature schemes. In: Bernstein, D.J., Buchmann, J., Dahmen, E. (eds.) Post-Quantum Cryptography, pp. 35–93. Springer, Heidelberg (2009). https://doi.org/10.1007/978-3-540-88702-7_3
11. Castryck, W., Decru, T.: An efficient key recovery attack on SIDH (preliminary version). Cryptology ePrint Archive, Paper 2022/975 (2022)
12. Company, M.: The next tech revolution: quantum computing (2020)
13. Computer Security Division Information Technology Laboratory: Post-quantum cryptography standardization - CSRC. NIST (2017)
14. Garcia-Morchon, O., Rietman, R., Sharma, S., Tolhuizen, L., Torre-Arce, J.L.: DTLS-HIMMO: efficiently securing a post-quantum world with a fully-collusion resistant KPS. Cryptology ePrint Archive (2014)
15. Greconici, D.O., Kannwischer, M.J., Sprenkels, D.: Compact Dilithium implementations on Cortex-M3 and Cortex-M4. IACR Trans. Cryptogr. Hardw. Embed. Syst. **2021**(1), 1–24 (2021)
16. Jozsa, R.: Searching in Grover's algorithm. arXiv preprint quant-ph/9901021 (1999)
17. Kampanakis, P., Panburana, P., Daw, E., Geest, D.V.: The viability of post-quantum X.509 certificates. Cryptology ePrint Archive, Paper 2018/063 (2018)
18. Karabulut, E., Aysu, A.: Falcon down: breaking Falcon post-quantum signature scheme through side-channel attacks. In: 58th ACM/IEEE Design Automation Conference, pp. 691–696 (2021)
19. Mariano, A., Laarhoven, T., Correia, F., Rodrigues, M., Falcao, G.: A practical view of the state-of-the-art of lattice-based cryptanalysis. IEEE Access **5**, 24184–24202 (2017)

20. Merkle, R.C.: A digital signature based on a conventional encryption function. In: Pomerance, C. (ed.) CRYPTO 1987. LNCS, vol. 293, pp. 369–378. Springer, Heidelberg (1988). https://doi.org/10.1007/3-540-48184-2_32
21. Moody, D.: Status report on the third round of the NIST post-quantum cryptography standardization process. NIST technical report (2022)
22. NIST: The digital signature standard. Commun. ACM **35**(7), 36–40 (1992)
23. Paul, S., Kuzovkova, Y., Lahr, N., Niederhagen, R.: Mixed certificate chains for the transition to post-quantum authentication in TLS 1.3. In: Asia Conference on Computer and Communications Security, pp. 727–740 (2022)
24. Raavi, M., Chandramouli, P., Wuthier, S., Zhou, X., Chang, S.Y.: Performance characterization of post-quantum digital certificates. In: International Conference on Computer Communications and Networks, pp. 1–9 (2021)
25. Rescorla, E.: The transport layer security (TLS) protocol version 1.3. RFC 8446 (2018)
26. Rescorla, E., Tschofenig, H., Modadugu, N.: The datagram transport layer security (DTLS) protocol version 1.3. RFC 9147 (2022)
27. Santesson, S., Tschofenig, H.: Transport layer security (TLS) cached information extension. RFC 7924 (2016)
28. Sepúlveda, J., Liu, S., Mera, J.M.B.: Post-quantum enabled cyber physical systems. IEEE Embed. Syst. Lett. **11**(4), 106–110 (2019)
29. Sikeridis, D., Kampanakis, P., Devetsikiotis, M.: Post-quantum authentication in TLS 1.3: a performance study. In: Network and Distributed System Security Symposium. Internet Society (2020)
30. Soni, D., Basu, K., Nabeel, M., Aaraj, N., Manzano, M., Karri, R.: CRYSTALS-dilithium. In: Hardware Architectures for Post-Quantum Digital Signature Schemes, pp. 13–30. Springer, Cham (2021). https://doi.org/10.1007/978-3-030-57682-0_2
31. Sun, Y., Agostini, N.B., Dong, S., Kaeli, D.: Summarizing CPU and GPU design trends with product data. arXiv preprint arXiv:1911.11313 (2019)
32. Tiloca, M., Nikitin, K., Raza, S.: Axiom: DTLS-based secure IoT group communication. ACM Trans. Embed. Comput. Syst. **16**(3), 1–29 (2017)
33. Van Meter, R., Horsman, D.: A blueprint for building a quantum computer. Commun. ACM **56**, 84–93 (2013)
34. Wortmann, F., Flüchter, K.: Internet of things. Bus. Inf. Syst. Eng. **57**(3), 221–224 (2015). https://doi.org/10.1007/s12599-015-0383-3
35. Xing, Y., Li, S.: A compact hardware implementation of CCA-secure key exchange mechanism CRYSTALS-KYBER on FPGA. IACR Trans. Cryptogr. Hardw. Embed. Syst. **2021**(2), 328–356 (2021)
36. Yunakovsky, S.E., et al.: Towards security recommendations for public-key infrastructures for production environments in the post-quantum era. EPJ Quantum Technol. **8**(1), 1–19 (2021). https://doi.org/10.1140/epjqt/s40507-021-00104-z
37. Zhang, Z.K., Cho, M.C.Y., Wang, C.W., Hsu, C.W., Chen, C.K., Shieh, S.: IoT security: ongoing challenges and research opportunities. In: IEEE 7th International Conference on Service-Oriented Computing and Applications, pp. 230–234 (2014)

Moderate Classical McEliece Keys from Quasi-Centrosymmetric Goppa Codes

Ousmane Ndiaye[(✉)]

Université Cheikh Anta Diop de Dakar, FST, DMI, LACGAA, Dakar, Senegal
ousmane3.ndiaye@ucad.edu.sn

Abstract. As the development of quantum machines is booming and would threaten our standard cryptography algorithms, a transition period is necessary for the protection of the data processed by our classical machines as well before the arrival of theses machines as after.

Recently, to get ahead of the curve, the National Institute of Standards and Technology (NIST) launched the Post Quantum Cryptography Standardization Project, started since late 2016. Among finalists, 3 promising code-theoretic finalist candidates, Classic McEliece, BIKE, and HQC are sent to the fourth round.

In this work, to reduce classical McEliece key size without loss of security, we present a new key generation algorithm by introducing new family of codes called quasi-centrosymmetric Goppa codes with a moderate key size for storage optimisation. We also have characterized these codes in the case where the parity matrix is in Cauchy form by giving an algorithm to build them. We ended up giving a detailed analysis of the security against the most known structural attacks by giving the new complexities.

Keywords: Post-quantum Cryptography · Coding-based Cryptography · Goppa Code · McEliece · Quasi-Centrosymmetric · Classic McEliece

1 Introduction

Today, a lot of confidential data is exchanged on the internet in a secure way thanks to asymmetric cryptographic algorithms designed with computationally difficult problems such as the factorization of large numbers or the discrete logarithm. Generally solving these problems on our classical computers is as difficult as finding a hidden atom somewhere in the universe because the complexities are exponential.

A new revolution is coming, the one that would allow us to solve these difficult problems in a few minutes with a new type of machines called quantum machines. This is why a transition period is necessary in the protection of the data processed by our classical machines as well before the arrival of these machines as after: We talk about post-quantum cryptography which is cryptography under the assumption that the attacker has a large quantum computer.

© The Author(s), under exclusive license to Springer Nature Switzerland AG 2023
S. El Hajji et al. (Eds.): C2SI 2023, LNCS 13874, pp. 77–90, 2023.
https://doi.org/10.1007/978-3-031-33017-9_5

Recently, to get ahead of the curve, the National Institute of Standards and Technology (NIST) launched the Post Quantum Cryptography Standardization Project, started since late 2016. Several candidates based on families supposed to be post-quantum such as lattice-based cryptography, isogeny-based cryptography, hash-based digital signatures, multivariate cryptography, and code-based cryptography, were proposed. 69 after the first round, only 7 finalists and 8 purported alternatives were selected for the third-round finalist public-key encryption and key-establishment algorithms. Now for this category only CRYSTALS-KYBER [14] which is lattice-based is standardized while the 3 promising code-theoretic finalist candidates, BIKE [2], Classic McEliece and HQC are sent to the fourth round.

Classic McEliece merger of Classic McEliece [13] and NTS-KEM [1], is a KEM designed for IND-CCA2 security at a very high long-term security, even against quantum computers and built conservatively Niederreiter's dual version of McEliece's PKE using binary Goppa codes.

This cryptosystem has many advantages such as the rapidity of its encryption defined by a vector-matrix product, the simplicity of its decryption using the extended euclidean algorithm but also not less important the exponential complexity of the best attack named ISD. During 40 years, since 1978, about ten attacks have been mounted without really a significant gain estimated at less than 1% if the security level is relatively high, while the lattice-based cryptography has lost almost 40% of its security. In spite of all these advantages, the McEliece cryptosystem has a major drawback which explains in part why it was sent to the fourth round: it is the large size of its public keys. Today, the security levels proposed by NIST for key sizes range from 255 KB to 1326 KB.

Related Work: As the public key is represented by a matrix, the rows form a base of a vector space, many have thought of using redundant matrices, some rows of which are obtained from permutations of others, therefore Goppa codes whose permutation group is not trivial, among others, we can quote quasi-cyclic [5,10], quasi-dyadic [3,4,23] or quasi-monoidic [8] Goppa codes with key sizes around a few tens of KB (first line of each block). Other filtration type attacks have also been proposed on the DAGS candidate which uses quasi-dyadic Srivastava codes [7] whose extension degree is equal to 2. Even if quasi-dyadic and quasi-cyclic binary alternant codes [4,5] remain inviolate, they were eliminated at the end of the first round.

However, the use of these codes makes algebraic attacks easier by allowing the number of unknowns to be reduced by a factor equal to the order of the permutation group through the folded code [7,20]. So this gain in size translates into a loss of security.

Our Contribution: In this paper, we propose to cut the pear in two by introducing quasi-centrosymmetric Goppa codes whose generating matrix (of parity) is represented by half of each block. These quasi-centrosymmetric Goppa codes contains the quasi-dyadic codes and admit a non-trivial permutation group of the smallest possible order equal to 2. Centrosymmetric matrices are square matrices that are symmetric about there center. The set of $n \times n$ centrosymmetric matrices of is a sub-algebra of the associative algebra of all $n \times n$ matrices which would keep the same structure after the Gauss-Jordan reduction applied to the secret matrix to obtain the systematic form. Our design will focus on the special case of quasi-centrosymmetric Goppa whose parity matrix is Cauchy form with an affine invariant alternating code.

Organization of the Paper: The document is organized as follows, we will start with Sect. 2 Coding Theory Background, to identify the generalities relating to centrosymmetric matrices, the bases of algebraic coding, Reed-Solomon codes and their derivatives. Section 3 will present the first results on Goppa codes in Cauchy and symmetric Centrosymmetric form and Sect. 4 will present the specifications of the protocol we propose. Section 5 will be dedicated to the schema Security.

2   Coding Theory Background

Definition 1. *A centrosymmetric matrix is a matrix which is symmetric about its center. More precisely, an $r \times n$-matrix $A = (a_{ij})$ is centrosymmetric when its entries satisfy:*

$$a_{ij} = a_{r-i-1,n-j-1} \ \ for \ \ 0 \le i \le r-1 \ \ 0 \le j \le n-1.$$

Lemma 1. *Let H be an $r \times r$ centrosymmetric matrix over a field K. If r is even, then H can be written as*

$$\begin{pmatrix} A & JCJ \\ C & JAJ \end{pmatrix}$$

where A, J and C are $\delta \times \delta$ matrices. If r is odd, then H can be written

$$\begin{pmatrix} A & x & JCJ \\ y^\top & q & y^\top J \\ C & Jx & JAJ \end{pmatrix}$$

where A, J and C are $\delta \times \delta$ matrices, x and y are $\delta \times 1$ vectors, and $q \in K$.

Definition 2. *A quasi-centrosymmetric matrix is a block matrix whose component blocks are centrosymmetric submatrices.*

The quasi-centrosymmetric codes form a generalization of the quasi-dyadic codes which are already used in cryptography whose signature is no longer the first of each block but half of the latter with respect to the center.

Definition 3 *(Linear Code). A linear code C of length n and dimension k on the finite field $\mathbb{F}_q$ ([n,k]-code), is a vector sub-space of dimension $k < n$ of $\mathbb{F}_q^n$. The elements of $\mathbb{F}_q^n$ are called words and those of C codewords. The transmission rate of the code R is defined by $R = \frac{k}{n}$.*

Definition 4 *(Parity-Check Matrix).* *Let $\mathcal{C}$ be a (n,k)-code over $\mathbb{F}_q$.*
Then there is a $(n-k) \times n$-matrix $\mathbf{H}$ over $\mathbb{F}_q$ of rank $n-k$ such that

$$\mathcal{C} = \{c \in \mathbb{F}_q^n | \mathbf{H} \cdot c^\top = 0\}$$

Theses matrix are called Parity-check matrices of the code $\mathcal{C}$.

Definition 5 *(Permutation group).* *Let $\mathcal{C}$ be a linear code of length n on $\mathbb{F}_q$.*
Let $\sigma \in S_n$ acting on $\mathcal{C}$ by $\forall c \in \mathcal{C}, \sigma(c) = (c_{\sigma^{-1}(0)}, ..., c_{\sigma^{-1}(n-1)})$. The code $\mathcal{C}$ is
said σ-invariant if $\sigma(\mathcal{C}) = \mathcal{C}$. The permutation group of $\mathcal{C}$ is:

$$Perm(\mathcal{C}) = \{\sigma \in S_n | \sigma(\mathcal{C}) = \mathcal{C}\}$$

More generally, if $q = p^m$, the group $(\mathbb{F}_q^*)^n \rtimes (S_n \times Gal_{\mathbb{F}_p}(F_q))$ defined by the
law $(e, \sigma, \gamma)(\epsilon, \tau, \pi) := (e \star \gamma(\sigma(\epsilon)), \sigma \circ \tau, \gamma \circ \pi,)$ with $\star$ the component product.
This group is called the isometric, in hamming sens, semi-linear automorphism
group $\mathbb{F}_q^n$.

Definition 6 *(Generelized Reed-Solomon code).* *Let $q = p^m$ for some positive*
integer m, k a power of prime number p, n be such that $1 \le k < n \le n$. Let a
and b be two n-tuples such that the entries of x are pairwise distinct elements
of $\mathbb{F}_q$ and those of y are nonzero elements in $\mathbb{F}_q$. The generalized Reed-Solomon
code, $GRS_k(a,b)$ on $\mathbb{F}_q$ of dimension k associated to (a,b) is defined as:

$$GRS_k(a,b) = \{(b_0 P(a_0), ..., b_{n-1} P(a_{n-1})) \mid P \in \mathbb{F}_q[z]_{<k}\}$$

Definition 7 *(Alternant code).* *Let $a, b \in \mathbb{F}_{p^m}^n$ be a support and multiplier as*
given in Definition 6. Let r be a positive integer, the p-arry alternant code of
order r $A_r(a,b)$ is defined as:

$$A_r(a,b) = GRS_r(a,b)^\perp \cap \mathbb{F}_p^n$$

r is defined as the degree of the alternant code, and the m as its extension degree.

Proposition 1 *([MS86, Chap. 12, §2]).* *Let a, b r be as in Definition 7.*

1. $\dim_{\mathbb{F}_2}(A_r(a,b)) > n - mr$;
2. $d_{min}(A_r(a,b)) > r + 1$;

where $d_{min}(.)$ denotes the minimum distance of a code.

Definition 8 *(Goppa codes).* *Let $a \in \mathbb{F}_q^n$ be support and $\Gamma \in \mathbb{F}_q[z]$ be a polino-*
mial such that $\Gamma(a_i) \ne 0$ for all $i \in \{0, ..., n-1\}$. The p-arry Goppa code $\mathcal{G}(a,\Gamma)$
associated to Γ and of support a es defined as:

$$\mathcal{G}(a,\Gamma) = A_{deg(\Gamma)}(a, \Gamma(a)^{-1})$$

The code $\mathcal{G}(a, \Gamma^{p-1})$ therefore has minimum distance at least $p \cdot deg(\Gamma) + 1$. The
case $p = 2$ has been used by McEliece to construct his cryptosystem to correct
$deg(\Gamma)$ errors unstead of $\frac{deg(\Gamma)}{2}$.

Operations on Quasi-centrosymmetric Codes

Definition 9. *Let r be a positive even integer and $\sigma : \mathbb{F}_q^r \to \mathbb{F}_q^r$ be a centrosymetric shift map:*

$$\sigma : \mathbb{F}_q^r \longrightarrow \mathbb{F}_q^r$$
$$(x_0, ..., x_{r-1}) \longmapsto (x_{r-1}, x_{r-2}, ..., x_1, x_0).$$

the r-th quasi-centrosymetric shift σ_r as the map obtained by applying σ blockwise on blocks of length r:

$$\sigma_r : (\mathbb{F}_q^r)^{\frac{n}{r}} \longrightarrow (\mathbb{F}_q^r)^{\frac{n}{r}}$$
$$(\boldsymbol{y}_0 \mid ... \mid \boldsymbol{y}_{\frac{n}{r}-1}) \longmapsto (\sigma(\boldsymbol{y}_0) \mid ... \mid \sigma(\boldsymbol{y}_{\frac{n}{r}-1})).$$

We define also

$$S : \mathbb{F}_q^{r \times r} \longrightarrow \mathbb{F}_q^{\frac{r}{2} \times r}$$
$$(a_{ij})_{0 \leq i,j \leq r-1} \longmapsto (a_{ij})_{0 \leq i \leq \frac{r}{2}-1, 0 \leq j \leq r-1}.$$

and

$$S_r : (\mathbb{F}_q^{r \times r})^{\frac{n}{r}} \longrightarrow (\mathbb{F}_q^{\frac{r}{2} \times r})^{\frac{n}{r}}$$
$$(A_0, ..., A_{\frac{n}{r}-1}) \longmapsto (S(A_0), ..., S(A_{\frac{n}{r}-1})).$$

Definition 10. *A code $C \subset \mathbb{F}_q^n$ is said to be r-quasi-centrosymetric if the code is stable by the quasi-centrosymetric shift map σ_r.*
r is also called the order quasi-centrosymetricity of the code.

3   Goppa Codes in Cauchy and Symetric Centrosymmetric Form

if the Goppa polynomial is separable and has single roots then the associated Goppa code admits a parity-check matrix in Cauchy form.

Theorem 1 *([25]). The Goppa code generated by a monic polynomial $g(x) = (x - z_0)...(x - z_{r-1})$ without multiple zeros admits a parity-check matrix of the form $H = C(z, L)$, i.e. $H_{ij} = \frac{1}{z_i - L_j}$, $0 \leq i < r$, $0 \leq j < n$.*

These matrices constitute a central element in this proposal because the set of Goppa codes verifying this property is quite large as well as its intersection with the family of centrosymmetric codes.

3.1   Building a Binary Goppa Code in Centrosymmetric Form

There are several ways to construct centrosymmetric Goppa codes from its permutation group but here we limit ourselves only to centrosymmetric alternating codes having a parity check matrix in a Cauchy form. Those are induced by an affine map of the linear translation type in a field of characteristic 2.

Theorem 2. *Let $H \in \mathbb{F}_q^{r \times n}$ with $r > 1$, $q = 2^m$ be simultaneous a centrosymmetric and Cauchy matrix $H = C(z, L)$ for two disjoint sequences $z \in \mathbb{F}_q^r$ and $L \in \mathbb{F}_q^n$ of distinct elements. Then z and L satisfy:*

$$z_{r-1-i} = z_i + \alpha, \text{ and } L_{n-1-j} = L_j + \alpha$$

for some $\alpha \in \mathbb{F}_q^*$

Proof. These conditions verify simultaneously the Definition 1 and the Theorem 1.
$$H_{ij} = \frac{1}{z_i - L_j} = \frac{1}{z_i + 2\alpha - L_j} = \frac{1}{(z_i + \alpha) - (L_j + \alpha)} = \frac{1}{z_{r-1-i} - L_{n-1-j}} = H_{r-1-i, n-1-j},$$
$0 \leq i < r, 0 \leq j < n$.

Corollary 1. *The number of Goppa codes in simultaneous centrosymetric and Cauchy form is $N = \displaystyle\prod_{i=0}^{\lfloor \frac{n+r}{2} \rfloor - 1} (q - 2i)$.*

3.2   Constructing Quasi-Centrosymmetric Subfield Subcodes

Theorem 3. *Let $q = 2^m$, $n = n_0 r$, $s = s_0 r$ with r even number. Let $H \in \mathbb{F}_q^{s \times n}$ is simultaneous a (s_0, n_0) quasi-centrosymmetric of order r and Cauchy matrix $H = C(z, L)$ for two disjoint sequences $z \in \mathbb{F}_q^s$ and $L \in \mathbb{F}_q^n$ of distinct elements. Then z and L satisfy:*

$$z_{(c+1)r-1-i} = z_{cr+i} + \alpha_c, \text{ and } L_{(b+1)r-1-j} = L_{br+j} + \alpha_c$$

for some $\alpha_c \in \mathbb{F}_q$, $0 \leq i, j \leq r - 1$, $0 \leq c \leq s_0 - 1$ and $0 \leq b \leq n_0 - 1$

Corollary 2. *Let $H \in \mathbb{F}_q^{r \times n}$ with r an even number, $q = 2^m$, $n = n_0 r$ be simultaneous a $(1, n_0)$ quasi-centrosymmetric of order r and Cauchy matrix $H = C(z, L)$ for two disjoint sequences $z \in \mathbb{F}_q^r$ and $L \in \mathbb{F}_q^n$ of distinct elements. Then z and L satisfy:*

$$z_{r-1-i} = z_i + \alpha, \text{ and } L_{(b+1)r-1-j} = L_{br+j} + \alpha$$

for some $\alpha \in \mathbb{F}_q$, $0 \leq i, j \leq r - 1$ and $0 \leq b \leq n_0 - 1$

Algorithm 1: Constructing a Goppa code in quasi-Centrosymmetric form

---

Input;

Output: Support L, generator polynomial g, quasi-centrosymmetric parity-check matrix H for a binary Goppa code $\Gamma(L, g)$ of length $n = rn_0$ and design distance $2r + 1$ over $\mathbb{F}_q$.;

initialization;

$U \leftarrow \mathbb{F}_q^*$;

$\alpha \leftarrow \mathbb{F}_q^*$;

for $i=0$ to $\frac{r}{2} - 1$ do
$\quad$ | $z_i \leftarrow U$;
$\quad$ | $z_{r-1-i} \leftarrow z_i + \alpha$;
$\quad$ | $U \leftarrow U \setminus \{z_i, z_{r-1-i}\}$;
end

for $b=0$ To $\frac{n}{r} - 1$ do
$\quad$ | for $j=0$ To $\frac{r}{2} - 1$ do
$\quad\quad$ | $L_{br+j} \leftarrow U$;
$\quad\quad$ | $L_{br+r-1-j} \leftarrow L_{br+j} + \alpha$;
$\quad\quad$ | $U \leftarrow U \setminus \{L_{br+j}, L_{br+r-1-j}\}$;
$\quad$ | end
end

$g \leftarrow 1$;

for $i=0$ To $r\text{-}1$ do
$\quad$ | $g \leftarrow g * (x - z_i)$;
$\quad$ | for $j=0$ To $n\text{-}1$ do
$\quad\quad$ | $H_{ij} \leftarrow \frac{1}{z_i - L_j}$;
$\quad$ | end
end

return L, g, H

---

4 Protocol Specification

In this section we propose to use the McEliece framework for encryption using the generator matrix the corresponding Goppa code [22]. The difference will be only on the Key generation where we use the special quasi-Centrosymmetric Goppa code family. As the McEliece framework is IND-CPA, we focus on it for simplicity as it is possible to use Imai-Kobara type of conversion to put it into IND-CCA2.

As among NIST PQ-Crypto 4th round candidates only classic McEliece [13] is based Binary Goppa code, we choose this later protocol with a slightly modification by replacing the Binary classic Goppa code a Centrosymmetric Binary Goppa with the same parameters in order to reduce the key size by factor $\frac{1}{2}$.

4.1 Parameters

Some parameters must set:

- m the extension degree of $\mathbb{F}_{2^m}$
- r a positive even integer, the order of centro-symmetricity of codes which is also the degree of the binary Goppa code.
- k a positive even integer, the dimension of centro-symmetricity of codes.
- n the length of the code, denotes a positive even integer $n < 2^m - 1$ such that $r \mid n$ and $rm < n$.

4.2 New Key Generation

Key generation follows the process described below

1. call the Algorithm 1 to get L, g and $H = C(z, L)$.
2. Project H onto $\mathbb{F}_2$ using the co-trace function: call this H_{bin}.
3. Get systematic form of H_{bin} as $(I_{rm} \mid M)$. if $rm \neq n - k$ go back to step 1.
4. The public key is the half of the quasi-centrosymmetric matrix $S_r(M) \in \mathbb{F}_2^{\frac{rm}{2} \times (n-rm)}$.
5. The private key consists of (L, g)

5 Security

Hard Problems from Coding Theory. Most of the code-based cryptographic constructions are based on the hardness of the following the binary Syndrome Decoding Problem (SDP).

Problem 1. Given an $(n - k) \times n$ random full-rank binary matrix H and a vector $y \in \mathbb{F}_2^{n-k}$ and a non-negative integer w, find a vector $e \in \mathbb{F}_2^n$ of weight w such that $H \cdot e^{\perp} = y$.

The corresponding decision problem was proved to be NP-complete in 1978 [11] for binary codes and all schemes based on original McEliece framework (including the Niederreiter proposal [24]) require the following computational assumption.

Assumption 1. The SDP based on random full-rank binary quasi-centrosymmetric matrix is NP-complete.

Assumption 2. The public binary matrix output by the key generation algorithm is computationally indistinguishable from a uniformly chosen quasi-centrosymmetric matrix of the same size.

The above assumption is considered to be true for binary Goppa codes, except in very special cases called high-rate Goppa codes (like the CFS signature scheme [18]).

Generally, the McEliece cryptosystem is susceptible to two kinds of attacks: Decoding and Structural attacks.

5.1 Key Recovery Attacks

Decreasing the public-key size by focusing on sub-classes of alternant/Goppa codes which admit a very compact public matrix, typically quasi-cyclic (QC), quasi-dyadic (QD), or quasi-monoidic (QM) matrices was a very popular trend in code-based innovation. Faugère et al. [16] show that constructing a compact public-key in that way makes the key-recovery problem intrinsically much easier and the security of such schemes are not relying on the bigger compact public matrix but on the small folded code which can be efficiently broken in practice with an algebraic attack for a large set of parameters.

Invariant and Folded Codes

Definition 11. *Let C be a linear code and $\sigma \in Perm(C)$ of order l, we consider the following map:*

$$f_\sigma : C \longrightarrow C$$
$$c \longmapsto \sum_{i=0}^{l-1} \sigma^i(c)$$

The folded code of C is defined by
$Fold_\sigma(C) := Im(f_\sigma) = Im(Id + \sigma + ... + \sigma^{l-1})$. The invariant code of C is defined by $C^\sigma := ker(\sigma - Id)$.

Proposition 2 *([16]). Let C be a code of length n that has a permutation automorphism group $S = < \sigma >$ of order l and a generator matrix G such that if g_i is a row of G then $\sigma^j(g_i)$ is also a row of G for any $j \in \mathbb{Z}$.*
Denote by $\{g_0, ..., g_{k-1}\}$ the rows of G. Consider the group action of S on the set of rows of G.
Assume that the size of each orbit is equal to l. Then, the dimension of $Fold_\sigma(C)$ is equal to $\frac{dim(C)}{l}$.

Remark 1. We denote the r-quasi-centrosymmetric Puncturing by P_r, with r an even positive integer, the function :

$$P_r : \mathbb{F}_q^n \longrightarrow \mathbb{F}_q^{\frac{n}{2}}$$
$$(x_0, ..., x_{n-1}) \longmapsto (x_{jr}, ..., x_{jr+\frac{r}{2}-1})_{0 \le j < \frac{n}{r}-1}$$

The folded code is isomorphic to the shortened length and dimension code obtained by keeping only one position per orbit. In the following we will no longer make a difference between the folded code and its punctured in keeping in each orbit a single position, for example $Fold_{\sigma_r}(C) \simeq P_r(Fold_{\sigma_r}(C))$.

In [16], it has been proved that the security of permutation-induced code reduces to that of the invariant code. We note that $Fold_\sigma(C) \subseteq C^\sigma$, and equality is achieved if $p \nmid l$ where p is the characteristic of $\mathbb{F}_q$.

Key Recovery Attacks. Recovering a private matrix(or a support and a multiplier) from a public matrix can in general be a very difficult problem, the presence of an algebraic structure has a considerable effect in reducing this difficulty using the non-trivial permutation group.

In [17] A very effective structural attack was introduced by Faugère, Otmani, Perret and Tillich based quasi cyclic/dyadic codes. This attack aims to recover one couple $(a, b) \in (\mathbb{F}_{2^m}^n)^2$ support and multiplier of the public code based on Grobner basis technique after reducing the number of variables based on the linear equations and those that are 2-linear By Combining this attacks with the folding trick, the reduction is finest [16].

The attack was originally aimed at two variants of McEliece, introduced respectively in [10] and [23]. It has been proved that the security of σ-invariant Goppa codes reduces to that of the invariant code stipulated in the result below in the case of quasi-centrosymmetric Goppa code in Cauchy form.

Proposition 3. *Let $\Gamma \in \mathbb{F}_q[x]$ of even degree, for any quasi-centrosymmetric Goppa $\mathcal{G}(a, \Gamma(x))$ whose a parity check matrix is in Cauchy form, then the exists $\gamma \in \mathbb{F}_q[x]$ of degree $\frac{\deg(\Gamma)}{2}$ such that $\Gamma(x) = \gamma(x^2 + \alpha x)$ with $\alpha \in \mathbb{F}_q$.*

Proof. According to Theorem 2, $g(x) = (x - z_0)...(x - z_{r-1})$ without multiple zeros $z_{r-1-i} = z_i - \alpha$ with $\alpha \in \mathbb{F}_q^*$. Then $g(x) = \prod_{i=0}^{\frac{t}{2}}(x - z_i)(x - z_i + \alpha) = \prod_{i=0}^{\frac{t}{2}}(x^2 + \alpha x + z_i^2 + \alpha z_i) = \gamma(x^2 + \alpha x)$ with $\gamma(x) = \prod_{i=0}^{\frac{t}{2}}(x + z_i^2 + \alpha z_i)$

Theorem 4 (Th. 3, [16]). *Consider a Goppa code $C = \mathcal{G}(a, \Gamma)$ with an affine induced automorphism group G isomorphic to $(\mathbb{Z}/p\mathbb{Z})^\lambda$ where p is the characteristic of the field over which the Goppa code is defined, then the folding $Fold_G(C^\perp)$ is the dual of a Goppa code $G(P_G(x), \gamma(z))$ where the degree $\deg(\gamma)$ of γ is equal to $\frac{\deg(\Gamma)}{p^\lambda}$.*

Corollary 3. *Let $\mathcal{G}(a, \gamma(z^2 + \alpha z))$ be a r-quasi-centrosymmetric Goppa code induced by $\sigma = x + \alpha$ with $\alpha \in \mathbb{F}_q^*$. Then,*

$$P_r(\mathcal{G}(a, \gamma(z^2 + \alpha z))^\sigma) = \mathcal{G}(P_r(a^2 + \alpha a), \gamma(z))$$

where $a^2 + \alpha a = (a_0^2 + \alpha a_0, ..., a_{n-1}^2 + \alpha a_{n-1})$

One of the first idea of attack is the exhaustive search on Goppa Polynomials and supports whose complexity is asymptotically 2^{mrn} but there is another approach to get better complexity based on solving a system of algebraic equation.

Algebraic Cryptanalysis. According to the Subsect. 4.2, the attacker knows the public matrix $G_{pub} = (I_{n-rm}|^t M)$ and it just has to find a solution $(x, y) \in (\mathbb{F}_{2^m}^{\frac{n}{2}})^2$ support and multiplier of

$$\left\{ \sum_{j=0}^{\frac{n}{2}} g_{ij} Y_j X_j^l = 0 \mid 0 \le i < \frac{n-r}{2}, 0 \le l < \frac{r}{2} \right\} \tag{1}$$

where $g_{ij} \in \mathbb{F}_{2^m}$ are entries of G_{pub}. The security of quasi-centrosymmetric code is reduced now to the security of its folded code that is also Alternant code without centrosymmetric structure. From this new smaller alternant the well known FOPT [16,20] attack can be applied. The complexity of the FOPT attack combined with folding using the guess-and-solve strategy (guessing multipliers would be cf. [16], and finding support) is asymptotically, by exhaustive search,

$$2^{\frac{\deg(\Gamma)}{2}} m^2 \cdot poly(n)$$

After reduction, the system 1 may be resolved by finding a reduced Gröbner basis. The complexity of computing a Gröbner basis for the grevlex ordering with the F5 algorithm [6] applied on 1 is asymptotically bounded, when the number of independent variables grows to infinity, by

$$s \cdot d_{reg} \binom{v + d_{reg} - 1}{v}^w$$

where $s = \frac{r(r-n)}{2}$ the number of equations, $v = n - k - 2$ the number of independent variables, $2 \le w < 2.3727$ and d_{reg} the degree of regularity of the Ideal generated by the s polynomials.

5.2   Decoding Attacks

Generally, the McEliece cryptosystem may suffer from to General decoding attack that aims to retrieve the clear message from the ciphertext by using a general decoding algorithm(Message Recovery Attack:MRA). The best known attack is Set Information Decoding(ISD) introduced for the time in 1962 by Prange [25]. Despite several improvements: Meurer, and Thomae at Asiacrypt 2011, then by Becker, Joux, May, and Meurer at Eurocrypt 2012, May and Ozerov at Eurocrypt 2015, and Both and May in WCC 2017 and PQCrypto 2018, [9,15,21] the complexity of the ISD remains exponential in size of data. The main idea behind the ISD attack is find in a receive message a set of error-free positions called Information set to find, for a fixed error weight t, a part of the corresponding codeword and used instead linear algebra to recover the other part of the codeword. For Better defense against ISD, the length, dimension, and number of errors parameters of the public code need to be carefully chosen. The best asymptotic variant of ISD is due to Both and May [15] that has cost $\tilde{O}(2^{0.0885n})$. Torres and Sendrier has also shown in [27] that, asymptotically, if $k = (R + o(1))n$, the number of errors $r = O(n/\log n)$, the ISD complexity tends to $WF(n,k,r) = 2^{-log_2(1-R)r(1+o(1))}$ where $0 < R < 1$ and $r = (1 - R + o(1))n/\log n$ as in the case of Goppa binary codes.

The ISD attack could be applied to the obtained folded Goppa code of length $\frac{n}{2}$, dimension $\frac{k}{2}$ and distance asymptotically $t = \frac{r}{2}$ (see Proposition 3). As the permutation group is of order 2 then the information positions $(e_i \oplus e_{\sigma^{-1}(n-1-i)} = 0)$ on the folding correspond to the equality $(e_i = e_{\sigma^{-1}(n-1-i)})$ of the bits per orbit on the unfolded code, so we just need to predict $\frac{n}{2}$ bits (one bit per orbit) which corresponds to the complexity $2^{\frac{n}{2}}$. Therefore the total complexity of the ISD attack through the folding is $2^{\frac{n}{2}} + WF(\frac{n}{2}, \frac{k}{2}, \frac{r}{2})$.

The centrosymmetry of the code may be used to improve the efficiency of the decoding using Sendrier's Decoding One out Of Many (DOOM, [26]). Such approach permits to improve the efficiency by a factor $\sqrt{2}$. So the use of DOOM may in the best case provide a less than 2 bits reduction of the work factor

The complexity of these algorithms using a quantum computer was studied in [12] and provides for Known quantum attacks multiply the security level of ISD by an asymptotic factor $0.5 + o(1)$.

5.3   Parameter Selection

The parameters will be chosen so as to the **Classic McEliece NIST proposal** [13] to relate to the targeted security levels $b \in \mathbb{N}$ while avoiding the Goppa code being indistinguishable from a random code with the same parameters as discussed in [5,19] where $n \leq \max_{2 \leq s \leq r} \frac{ms}{2}(s(m - 2e - 1) + 2^e + 2)$, $e = \lceil \log_2 s \rceil + 1$ and $n = cmr < 2^m$ with c constant $(c > 1)$.

m should be large enough to have a large enough code length and avoid filtration attack $(\neq 2, 3)$. As the ISD attack gives better complexity than the other attack, the parameters size will be fixed according its complexity and the targeted level of security b. According to **Classic McEliece NIST proposal** [13] the ciphertext size is $n - k = (1 - R + o(1))n$ bits, and the public key size is $(c_0 - o(1))b^2(\log_2 b)^2$ where $c_0 = R/(1-R)(\log_2(1-R))^2$ with $c_0 = 0.7418860694$ and $R = 0.7968121300$. Because of centrosymmetricity, the half of each block of the Public matrix os size $\frac{k(n-k)}{2}$ bits instead of $k(n - k)$ in [13] will be stored as well as half of the hidden Goppa parameters as private key whose size is $(\frac{n}{2} + \frac{r}{2} + 1)m$ bits (Fig. 1).

	m	n	r	public key ($\frac{k(n-k)}{2}$)	private key	w_{msg}
mceliece348864	12	3488	64	130560	2666	113
mceliece460896	13	4608	96	262080	3824	151
mceliece6688128	13	6688	128	522496	5540	213
mceliece6960119	13	6960	119	523370	5754	212
mceliece8192128	13	8192	128	678912	6762	240

Fig. 1. Quasi-centrosymmetric Classic McEliece. All sizes are expressed in bytes

References

1. Albrecht, M., Cid, C., Paterson, K.G., Tjhai, C.J., Tomlinson, M.: NTS-KEM. NIST PQC Round **2**, 4–13 (2019)
2. Aragon, N., et al.: Bike: it flipping key encapsulation. NIST PQC Round (2017)

3. Banegas, G., et al.: DAGS: key encapsulation using dyadic GS codes. J. Math. Cryptol. **12**(4), 221–239 (2018)
4. Banegas, G., et al.: DAGS: reloaded revisiting dyadic key encapsulation. In: Baldi, M., Persichetti, E., Santini, P. (eds.) CBC 2019. LNCS, vol. 11666, pp. 69–85. Springer, Cham (2019). https://doi.org/10.1007/978-3-030-25922-8_4
5. Bardet, M., et al.: BIG QUAKE BInary Goppa QUAsi-cyclic Key Encapsulation (2017). Submission to the NIST post quantum cryptography standardization process
6. Bardet, M., Faugere, J.-C., Salvy, B.: On the complexity of the F5 Gröbner basis algorithm. J. Symb. Comput. **70**, 49–70 (2015)
7. Barelli, É., Couvreur, A.: An efficient structural attack on NIST submission DAGS. In: Peyrin, T., Galbraith, S. (eds.) ASIACRYPT 2018. LNCS, vol. 11272, pp. 93–118. Springer, Cham (2018). https://doi.org/10.1007/978-3-030-03326-2_4
8. Barreto, P.S.L.M., Lindner, R., Misoczki, R.: Monoidic codes in cryptography. In: Yang, B.-Y. (ed.) PQCrypto 2011. LNCS, vol. 7071, pp. 179–199. Springer, Heidelberg (2011). https://doi.org/10.1007/978-3-642-25405-5_12
9. Becker, A., Joux, A., May, A., Meurer, A.: Decoding random binary linear codes in $2^{n/20}$: how $1 + 1 = 0$ improves information set decoding. In: Pointcheval, D., Johansson, T. (eds.) EUROCRYPT 2012. LNCS, vol. 7237, pp. 520–536. Springer, Heidelberg (2012). https://doi.org/10.1007/978-3-642-29011-4_31
10. Berger, T.P., Cayrel, P.-L., Gaborit, P., Otmani, A.: Reducing key length of the McEliece cryptosystem. In: Preneel, B. (ed.) AFRICACRYPT 2009. LNCS, vol. 5580, pp. 77–97. Springer, Heidelberg (2009). https://doi.org/10.1007/978-3-642-02384-2_6
11. Berlekamp, E., McEliece, R., van Tilborg, H.: On the inherent intractability of certain coding problems. IEEE Trans. Inform. Theory **24**(3), 384–386 (1978)
12. Bernstein, D.J.: Grover vs. McEliece. In: Sendrier, N. (ed.) PQCrypto 2010. LNCS, vol. 6061, pp. 73–80. Springer, Heidelberg (2010). https://doi.org/10.1007/978-3-642-12929-2_6
13. Bernstein, D.J., et al.: Classic McEliece: conservative code-based cryptography. NIST submissions (2017)
14. Bos, J., et al.: CRYSTALS - Kyber: a CCA-secure module-lattice-based KEM. In: 2018 IEEE European Symposium on Security and Privacy (EuroS&P), pp. 353–367 (2018)
15. Both, L., May, A.: Decoding linear codes with high error rate and its impact for LPN security. In: Lange, T., Steinwandt, R. (eds.) PQCrypto 2018. LNCS, vol. 10786, pp. 25–46. Springer, Cham (2018). https://doi.org/10.1007/978-3-319-79063-3_2
16. Faugère, J.-C., Otmani, A., Perret, L., de Portzamparc, F., Tillich, J.-P.: Folding alternant and Goppa codes with non-trivial automorphism groups. IEEE Trans. Inf. Theory **62**(1), 184–198 (2016)
17. Faugère, J.-C., Otmani, A., Perret, L., Tillich, J.-P.: Algebraic cryptanalysis of McEliece variants with compact keys. In: Gilbert, H. (ed.) EUROCRYPT 2010. LNCS, vol. 6110, pp. 279–298. Springer, Heidelberg (2010). https://doi.org/10.1007/978-3-642-13190-5_14
18. Faugère, J.-C., Gauthier-Umanã, V., Otmani, A., Perret, L., Tillich, J.-P.: A distinguisher for high rate McEliece cryptosystems. In: 2011 IEEE Information Theory Workshop, pp. 282–286 (2011)
19. Faugere, J.-C., Gauthier-Umana, V., Otmani, A., Perret, L., Tillich, J.-P.: A distinguisher for high-rate McEliece cryptosystems. IEEE Trans. Inf. Theory **59**(10), 6830–6844 (2013)

20. Faugère, J.-C., Otmani, A., Perret, L., De Portzamparc, F., Tillich, J.-P.: Structural cryptanalysis of McEliece schemes with compact keys. Des. Codes Crypt. **79**(1), 87–112 (2016)
21. May, A., Ozerov, I.: On computing nearest neighbors with applications to decoding of binary linear codes. In: Oswald, E., Fischlin, M. (eds.) EUROCRYPT 2015. LNCS, vol. 9056, pp. 203–228. Springer, Heidelberg (2015). https://doi.org/10.1007/978-3-662-46800-5_9
22. McEliece, R.J.: A public-key cryptosystem based on algebraic. Coding Thv **4244**, 114–116 (1978)
23. Misoczki, R., Barreto, P.S.L.M.: Compact McEliece keys from Goppa codes. In: Jacobson, M.J., Rijmen, V., Safavi-Naini, R. (eds.) SAC 2009. LNCS, vol. 5867, pp. 376–392. Springer, Heidelberg (2009). https://doi.org/10.1007/978-3-642-05445-7_24
24. Niederreiter, H.: Knapsack-type cryptosystems and algebraic coding theory. Probl. Control Inf. Theory (Problemy Upravlenija i Teorii Informacii) **15**, 159–166 (1986)
25. Prange, E.: The use of information sets in decoding cyclic codes. IRE Trans. Inf. Theory **8**(5), 5–9 (1962)
26. Sendrier, N.: Decoding one out of many. In: Yang, B.-Y. (ed.) PQCrypto 2011. LNCS, vol. 7071, pp. 51–67. Springer, Heidelberg (2011). https://doi.org/10.1007/978-3-642-25405-5_4
27. Canto Torres, R., Sendrier, N.: Analysis of information set decoding for a sub-linear error weight. In: Takagi, T. (ed.) PQCrypto 2016. LNCS, vol. 9606, pp. 144–161. Springer, Cham (2016). https://doi.org/10.1007/978-3-319-29360-8_10

QCB is Blindly Unforgeable

Jannis Leuther$^{(\boxtimes)}$ and Stefan Lucks

Bauhaus-Universität Weimar, Weimar, Germany
{jannis.leuther,stefan.lucks}@uni-weimar.de

Abstract. QCB is a proposal for a post-quantum secure, rate-one authenticated encryption with associated data scheme (AEAD) based on classical OCB3 and ΘCB, which are vulnerable against a quantum adversary in the Q2 setting. The authors of QCB prove integrity under plusone unforgeability, whereas the proof of the stronger definition of blind unforgeability has been left as an open problem. After a short overview of QCB and the current state of security definitions for authentication, this work proves blind unforgeability of QCB. Finally, the strategy of using tweakable block ciphers in authenticated encryption is generalised to a generic blindly unforgeable AEAD model.

Keywords: Post-Quantum Cryptography · QCB · Blind Unforgeability · AEAD · Symmetric Cryptography

1 Introduction

Motivation. As it stands, many cryptographic algorithms currently in use are weak or outright broken when challenged by an adversary using a quantum computer [20, 22]. The security of asymmetric cryptography is especially affected, as mathematical problems like integer factorization or the discrete logarithm are hardly a challenge for quantum computers. For example, integer factorization can be solved using Shor's algorithm [26, 27] with an almost exponential speedup compared to a classical computer. While many asymmetric cryptographic algorithms are broken by design, the impact on *post-quantum security* of most symmetric cryptographic schemes is expected to be less dramatic. However, there are symmetric-key constructions that are also vulnerable to certain quantum algorithms. Simon's algorithm can render many symmetric cryptographic modes that are secure in the classical sense broken in the quantum scenario [5, 16].

The authors in [16] are able to show that, additionally to the *Even-Mansour* and 3-Round Feistel construction, the *Liskov-Rivest-Wagner* (LRW) construction is also insecure against a quantum adversary. Furthermore, they describe forgery attacks against currently standardized classical encryption modes like *CBC-MAC, PMAC, GMAC, GCM* and *OCB* and imply that some authentication and authenticated encryption schemes are quantumly insecure even with an underlying post-quantum secure block cipher [16, pp. 2-3].

© The Author(s), under exclusive license to Springer Nature Switzerland AG 2023
S. El Hajji et al. (Eds.): C2SI 2023, LNCS 13874, pp. 91–108, 2023.
https://doi.org/10.1007/978-3-031-33017-9_6

Outline. After introducing the topic and defining notations, Sect. 3 goes into detail about QCB, a recent proposal for a post-quantum secure AEAD mode based on the quantumly broken OCB. Next, Sect. 2 briefly discusses the evolution and difference of unforgeability notions *plus-one unforgeability* and *blind unforgeability*. Section 4 follows up with a proof that blind unforgeability holds for QCB. Afterwards, a generic construction for blindly unforgeable AEAD schemes is given in Sect. 5. Section 6 concludes.

Preliminaries. Note that there exist symmetric and asymmetric encryption algorithms for privacy, and message authentication codes (MACs) to guarantee authenticity and integrity of communication. The combination of symmetric encryption algorithms and message authentication codes form combined algorithms for authenticated encryption (AE). The term AEAD refers to an AE scheme with support for associated data that can be used to strengthen security. In this work, security schemes and algorithms employed in current digital computers will be referred to as *classical* schemes or algorithms (*e.g.*, RSA [15], AES-128 [23], OCB3 [6]). Security schemes that are designed for providing security against an adversary with a quantum computer will be called *post-quantum* (*e.g.*, QCB [5], Saturnin [12]). Importantly, post-quantum secure security algorithms have to be designed such that they are still secure and viable when used in classical computers.

A common distinction of quantum adversary types is between a Q1 and Q2 adversary. A Q1 adversary may use a quantum computer for offline computations but is limited to classical queries to any oracle function. The stronger Q2 adversary is additionally allowed to perform superposition queries to the oracle functions. Unless mentioned otherwise, the following results assume an adversary in the Q2 model.

Notation. Addition in $\mathbb{GF}(2^n)$, XOR, is denoted as $\oplus$. The set of all possible binary strings of length n will be described as $\{0,1\}^n$.

A block cipher accepts as inputs a secret key $K \in \{0,1\}^k$ and a message block $M \in \{0,1\}^n$ to compute a ciphertext block $C \in \{0,1\}^n$:

$$E : \{0,1\}^k \times \{0,1\}^n \to \{0,1\}^n.$$

A block cipher E encrypting message M under key K into ciphertext C is signalled with $E_K(M) = C$ while the decryption $E_K^{-1}(C) = M$ acts as the inverse of the encryption under the same key K.

A *tweakable block cipher* (TBC) additionally accepts a *tweak* $T \in \{0,1\}^t$ as input. Tweaks can be used to define distinct families of block ciphers under the same key. It is a tool to introduce variability to many calls of a block cipher where the key does not change throughout [18,19]. Consequently, the signature of a TBC can be described as:

$$\widetilde{E} : \{0,1\}^k \times \{0,1\}^t \times \{0,1\}^n \to \{0,1\}^n.$$

The length of a message or ciphertext X measured as the amount of bits will be described with $|X| \in \mathbb{N}_0$.

For brevity, we will abbreviate *authenticated encryption with associated data* to AEAD, *plus-one unforgeability* to PO and *blind unforgeability* to BU.

2   Evolution of Unforgeability Notions

Authentication. In classical computing, the notions of *existential unforgeability under chosen-message attacks* (EUF-CMA) and *strong existential unforgeability under chosen-message attacks* (SUF-CMA) are prevalent to describe the security of MACs. However, these notions are not applicable in the quantum setting due to the properties of a quantum system [1, pp. 1-2] [9]. *E.g.,* the adversary may query in superposition and due to *no-cloning* and measurement behaviour, it is not possible to identify a correct prediction of the adversary in the superposition state [2, p. 1]. To combat the lack of a notion like UF-CMA for unforgeability in quantum computers, Boneh and Zhandry introduced *plus-one unforgeability* [8,9]. Alagic et al. followed up with the idea of *blind unforgeability* [2].

Plus-One Unforgeability. Plus-one unforgeability (PO) was proposed as a candidate to classify unforgeability on quantum computers [8, p. 598]. An adversary $\mathcal{A}$ makes $q < |\mathcal{X}|$ queries to an oracle $\mathcal{O} : \mathcal{X} \to \mathcal{Y}$. If $\mathcal{A}$ can produce $q+1$ valid input-output pairs with non-negligible probability, the plus-one unforgeability of the underlying algorithm is violated, and it is not post-quantum secure [8, p. 593]. By utilizing the *rank method*, the authors in [8, p. 602] show that if the size of $\mathcal{Y}$ is large enough, no (quantum) algorithm can produce $k + 1$ input-output pairs when given k queries. Furthermore, they prove that a post-quantum secure pseudorandom function (qPRF) [31] is plus-one unforgeable when used as a MAC [8, p. 604].

However, Alagic et al. show that PO suffers from a weakness in its definition that allows for efficient quantum attacks on MACs that are plus-one unforgeable [2, pp. 24-32]. They describe that one of the issues of the PO definition is the inability to include adversaries which need to measure states after the query phase to produce a forgery. Measuring a state would collapse the register during the security game which the PO definition does not account for. In the counterexample of Alagic et al., an adversary may perform a forgery with a single query by utilizing quantum period-finding. Importantly, due to quantum period-finding algorithms not collapsing the entire state, the adversary is able to learn the period *and* a random input-output pair of the MAC at the same time [2, p. 24].

Blind Unforgeability. Introduced in [2], blind unforgeability (BU) aims to describe an improved notion to characterize (strong) existential unforgeability of MACs when faced by a quantum adversary [2, pp. 8-10] by eliminating the weaknesses of plus-one unforgeability. Blind unforgeability of a MAC is defined through the *blind forgery game* [2, p. 3] which will also be revisited during the proof in Sect. 4.

Before the game starts, a random *blind set* is constructed. *I.e.*, for some fraction of messages in the MAC's message space, the oracle $\mathcal{O}_{\mathrm{MAC}}$ will not return a corresponding authentication tag $\tau = \mathcal{O}_{\mathrm{MAC}}(M)$ when queried but rather signal to the adversary $\mathcal{A}$ that this message M is in the blind set by returning $\perp$. $\mathcal{A}$ wins if they can create a message-tag pair (m, t) with t being a valid tag for the message m and m being a member of the blind set. In other words, if $\mathcal{A}$ succeeds, they forged a tag for a message that they were not able to get any relevant information on by querying $\mathcal{O}_{\mathrm{MAC}}$. Therefore, $\mathcal{A}$ was able to generate an *existential* forgery.

In classical computation, blind unforgeability is equal to EUF-CMA and *strong* blind unforgeability is equal to SUF-CMA [2, pp. 11-12]. Furthermore, against classical adversaries, BU implies plus-one unforgeability [2, p. 3]. Quantumly, however, BU is at least as strong as PO [2, p. 11] and due to solving unresolved issues with the PO notion, it can be considered a stronger security definition against quantum adversaries. A (pseudo)random function $R : X \to Y$ is considered a blindly unforgeable MAC if $1/|Y|$ is negligible in n [2, p. 15]. Furthermore, as with PO, post-quantum secure pseudorandom functions (qPRFs) are blindly unforgeable MACs [2, p. 4].

Blind unforgeability is equivalent to *generalised existential unforgeability* (μ-qGEU) where $\mu = 1$ [13, p. 18].

3   QCB: Post-Quantum Secure Authenticated Encryption

QCB, as introduced in [5], is a proposal for an authenticated encryption scheme with associated data (AEAD). The authors describe it as a post-quantum secure successor to the classically secure AEAD family OCB. Apart from being parallelizable, OCB [6] is a *rate-one* authenticated encryption scheme. For each message block being encrypted, approximately one call to the secure block cipher is carried out. These properties make OCB a highly efficient classical AEAD mode and mark the motivation for the creation of QCB: Defining a post-quantum secure, rate-one, parallelizable AEAD scheme on the basis of OCB [5, p. 2]. The authors acknowledge the similarity of the scheme to ΘCB [25] and the tweakable authenticated encryption (TAE) mode [18, pp. 39-41].

As shown by Kaplan et al. [16] and being revisited in Appendix A, the OCB family of authenticated encryption algorithms is not post-quantum secure. Importantly, the underlying construction using offsets is structurally broken by applying Simon's algorithm and increasing key sizes does not act as an easy remedy to this problem. As [5, pp. 9-11] point out, this does not only affect OCB but a large family of OCB-like schemes.

Tweakable Block Ciphers in QCB. To instantiate QCB, Bhaumik et al. define a family of tweakable block ciphers (TBC) that is post-quantum secure under the condition that tweaks may not be queried in superposition by the adversary [5, pp. 11-15].

Note that there are TBCs which are considered secure even when $\mathcal{A}$ has the ability to query tweaks in superposition, like LRWQ [14]. However, these TBCs can be broken by decryption queries and have a rate of $1/3$ as they use three block cipher calls for each TBC call. This renders them unattractive for QCB, as QCB tries to achieve rate-one efficiency similar to OCB [5, p. 15].

In [5, pp. 16-17], QCB is proposed to be instantiated with the key-tweak insertion TBC SATURNIN [12]. The design of this block cipher was originally motivated by the *NIST Lightweight Cryptography Standardization Process* [21,29,30] and is the only candidate where its designers tried to achieve post-quantum security while remaining in the lightweight domain. Alternatives for SATURNIN are discussed briefly in Appendix B. SATURNIN uses 256-bit blocks and keys which renders it as a potential candidate for usage as a post-quantum secure block cipher. The authors borrow internal design ideas from AES which is heavily researched with tight security bounds already in place. There exists a variant of SATURNIN denoted as SATURNIN$_{16}$ using 16 *super-rounds* increasing the resistance of the underlying compression function against related-key attacks [12, p. 7] [24].

The TBC used in [5] for QCB is defined as:

$$\widetilde{E}_{k,(d,IV,i)}(m) = \text{SATURNIN}_{16}^d(k \oplus (IV||i), m)$$

with

$$\widetilde{E} : \mathcal{K} \times \mathcal{D} \times \mathcal{IV} \times \mathcal{I} \times \mathcal{M} \to \mathcal{C},$$

$$\widetilde{E} : \{0,1\}^{256} \times \{0,1\}^4 \times \{0,1\}^{160} \times \{0,1\}^{96} \times \{0,1\}^{256} \to \{0,1\}^{256}.$$

Here, the tweak is denoted as the triple (d, IV, i), whereas $IV \in \mathcal{IV}$ is an initialization vector or nonce of at most 160 bits which is concatenated with $i \in \mathcal{I}$ describing the block number of the current block being encrypted (at most 2^{96} blocks are allowed). Parameter $d \in \mathcal{D}$ is the *domain separator* that can theoretically take 4 bits at maximum when SATURNIN is used. For QCB, however, only 5 values in total are required [5, pp. 15-17]. $k \in \mathcal{K}$ denotes the secret key while $m \in \mathcal{M}$ denotes the data block to be encrypted with $\mathcal{C}$ representing the ciphertext space.

Structure of QCB. QCB is an AEAD mode that is instantiated with a post-quantum secure TBC. In the following, the usage of the TBC SATURNIN is assumed. Figure 1 shows the encryption of ℓ plaintext blocks $M_i \in \{0,1\}^n$ into $\ell+1$ ciphertext blocks $C_i \in \{0,1\}^n$. If the last block M_* is of length $0 \leq c < n$, it will get padded with bitstring 10^{n-c-1} producing ciphertext block $C_* \in \{0,1\}^n$. Note that M_* will also be padded if it is empty ($c = 0$), which always leads to a ciphertext that will be longer than the plaintext input by at least 1 and at most n bits.

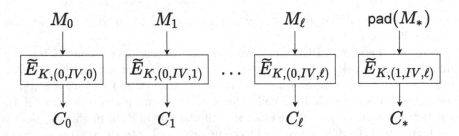

Fig. 1. Encryption of messages in QCB [5, Fig. 2].

Figure 2 illustrates how QCB uses all message blocks $M_0, \ldots, M_\ell$, all associated data blocks $A_0, \ldots, A_j$ and corresponding padding to calculate the authentication tag T. Padding of A_* behaves identically to the padding of M_* during the encryption procedure described above. Combining encryption and generation of the authentication tag leads to the full algorithm. Given a message M, associated data A, an initialization vector IV and a secret key K, QCB returns a ciphertext-tag pair C, T with $C = (C_0||C_1||\ldots||C_\ell||C_*)$.

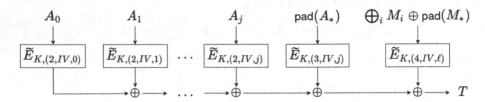

Fig. 2. Generation of the authentication tag and handling of associated data in QCB [5, Fig. 3].

QCB is Plus-One Unforgeable. Adversary $\mathcal{A}$ makes q superposition queries to QCB instantiated with the key-tweak insertion TBC $\widetilde{E}$ with ℓ blocks of messages or associated data at maximum. Furthermore, $\mathcal{A}$ makes q' encryption or decryption queries to the underlying block cipher E of the TBC $\widetilde{E}$. $\mathcal{A}$ succeeds in the plus-one unforgeability scenario if they output $q + 1$ valid quadruples (A, IV, C, T) with associated data A, initialization vector IV, ciphertext C and tag T. Importantly, IVs are classical and cannot be queried in superposition. Consequently, the advantage of $\mathcal{A}$ over QCB in the definition of plus-one unforgeability (see also Sect. 2) is upper bounded by

$$\Pr[\mathcal{A} \text{ succeeds}] \leq 8\sqrt{\frac{5\ell q q'^2}{2^n}} + \frac{3 + c}{2^n}. \tag{1}$$

The constant c relates from the PRP-PRF distinguishing advantage and the probability $c\frac{q^3}{2^n}$ which describes an upper bound of $\mathcal{A}$ succeeding to produce $q+1$

valid input-output pairs when quantumly attacking an ideal random permutation with q queries [5, p. 8].

Evidently, in each call to the TBC, the initialization vector IV is provided as input. This fact and the requirement that no IV shall be used more than once is critical for security. QCB is secure against period-finding attacks as described in the attack on OCB in Appendix A. QCB is also secure against *quantum linearization attacks* [10] due to the continuous usage of the initialization vector in tweaks of the TBC [5, p. 15]. Consider a weakened version of QCB where the IV is not used during the processing of associated data. This algorithm can be broken with application of Deutsch's algorithm as shown in [5, Appendix B]. After n queries, an adversary is able to fully recover certain values which allow them to perform forgeries. More specifically, they are able to compute a valid tag for any message with associated data $A = 1$ if they are provided the tag of the same message with associated data $A = 0$. This attack is made possible since in the weakened version of QCB, the associated data is encrypted independently of the IV allowing an adversary to repeatedly use the encryption of blocks of associated data made in prior queries. The full specification of QCB, however, denies this vulnerability by using the IV in each block as part of the tweak for the TBC [5, Appendix B].

4   QCB is Blindly Unforgeable

On the following pages, blind unforgeability of QCB will be proven by employing a similar technique to the proof about QCB's plus-one unforgeability in [5, pp. 21-22]. The authors of QCB acknowledged the existence of blind unforgeability and left the proof for QCB as an open problem [5, pp. 27-28].

BU Game. The blind forgery experiment or blind unforgeability (BU) game as presented in [2, p. 3] can be adjusted to work with QCB (or any authenticated encryption scheme).

To generate a random blinding B_ϵ, start with the empty set $B_\epsilon = \varnothing$ and place each triple (IV, A, M) into the set with probability ϵ. Here, IV represents the initialization vector, A the associated data and M the message. The encryption oracle blinded on B_ϵ is subsequently defined as:

$$B_\epsilon \mathrm{QCB}_K(IV, A, M) \begin{cases} \bot & \text{if } (IV, A, M) \in B_\epsilon, \\ (C, T) & \text{otherwise.} \end{cases}$$

The decryption under key K will be denoted as $\mathrm{QCB}_K^{-1}(\cdot)$.
The BU game is then carried out as follows:

1. Adversary $\mathcal{A}$ selects $0 < \epsilon < 1$.
2. Key K is generated uniformly at random. A random blinding B_ϵ is generated, whereas each triple (IV, A, M) is put into the blind set with probability ϵ.

3. $\mathcal{A}$ asks q queries with messages $\{M^1, \ldots, M^q\} = \mathcal{M}_q$ to the encryption oracle blinded on B_ϵ.
4. $\mathcal{A}$ produces a candidate forgery (IV, A, C, T), where C represents the ciphertext and T the authentication tag.
5. Output **win** if $\text{QCB}_K^{-1}(IV, A, C, T) \notin \{\bot\} \cup \mathcal{M}_q$ and corresponding M is such that $(IV, A, M) \in B_\epsilon$.

Definition 1 ([2], Definition 1). *QCB is blindly unforgeable if for every adversary $(\mathcal{A}, \epsilon)$, the probability of winning the blind unforgeability game is negligible.*

Theorem 1. *Let $(\mathcal{A}, \epsilon)$ be a Q2 adversary making q superposition queries to QCB with at most ℓ blocks of message and associated data combined and making q' queries to the block cipher E. Then QCB is blindly unforgeable on blind set B_ϵ with the success probability of $(\mathcal{A}, \epsilon)$ being bounded as:*

$$Pr[\mathcal{A} \ succeeds] \leq \frac{\epsilon}{2^n - q} + 8\sqrt{\frac{5\ell q q'^2}{2^n}}. \tag{2}$$

Proof. Consider two BU games G_0, G_1. In G_0, adversary $\mathcal{A}$ queries QCB constructed with TBC $\widetilde{E}$ and key K selected uniformly at random. G_1 is the modification of game G_0 where the TBC $\widetilde{E}$ is replaced by a family of ideal independent random permutations for all tweaks [5, p. 21]. We make use of Lemma 3 from the PO-proof in the original QCB publication.

Lemma 1 ([5], Lemma 3).

$$Pr_{G_0}[\mathcal{A} \ succeeds] \leq Pr_{G_1}[\mathcal{A} \ succeeds] + Adv_{\widetilde{E}^\pm(\$,\odot)}^{TPRP}(5q\ell, q')$$

Next, identify a bound for $Pr_{G_1}[\mathcal{A} \ succeeds]$ to get a bound on $\mathcal{A}$'s advantage against QCB as represented by $Pr_{G_0}[\mathcal{A} \ succeeds]$ on the left side of the inequation in Lemma 1.

For clarity, the BU game will be split up. For $\mathcal{A}$ to be successful in the full *BU game*, they need to be successful in both of the following events E_i:

E_1: $\mathcal{A}$ generates (IV, A, C, T) with $\text{QCB}_K^{-1}(IV, A, C, T) \notin \{\bot\} \cup \mathcal{M}_q$.
E_2: The corresponding (IV, A, M) is in the blind set.

Remember that, as game G_1 is being investigated, the underlying block cipher is an ideal random permutation.

After q queries to the oracle, the probability to generate a pair (C, T) which is valid, *i.e.*, the decryption of (C, T) does not return $\bot$ or any M which was already queried in the query phase, is

$$Pr_{G_1}[\mathcal{A} \ succeeds \ in \ E_1] = \frac{1}{2^{|T|} - q}, \tag{3}$$

where $|T|$ denotes the bit-length of authentication tag T. While ciphtertext C can be of variable size for different queries in an instance of QCB, the tag T is required to be of fixed size for each query [5, p. 4].

The blind set B_ϵ is of expected size $\epsilon \cdot 2^m$ with $m = |IV| + |A| + |M|$. The probability of randomly selecting any triple (IV, A, M) from the set of all possible triples is $\frac{1}{2^m}$. The expected probability of randomly hitting any item in the blind set B_ϵ is therefore

$$Pr_{G_1}[\mathcal{A}\ succeeds\ in\ \mathrm{E}_2] = \frac{|B_\epsilon|}{2^m} = \frac{\epsilon \cdot 2^m}{2^m} = \epsilon. \qquad (4)$$

The probabilities for E_1 and E_2 can be treated as being independent as the blind set had been generated independently of the encryption algorithm. Thus, the expected probability that $\mathcal{A}$ successfully generates a valid forgery with the corresponding triple (IV, A, M) being in the blind set is

$$Pr_{G_1}[\mathcal{A}\ succeeds] = Pr_{G_1}[\mathcal{A}\ succeeds\ in\ \mathrm{E}_1] \cdot Pr_{G_1}[\mathcal{A}\ succeeds\ in\ \mathrm{E}_2].$$

Substituting observations from Eqs. 3 and 4 leads to

$$Pr_{G_1}[\mathcal{A}\ succeeds] = \frac{1}{2^{|T|} - q} \cdot \epsilon = \frac{\epsilon}{2^{|T|} - q} = \frac{\epsilon}{2^n - q}. \qquad (5)$$

Length $|T|$ of the final tag T is equal to the block size n of message or associated data blocks. Subsequently, substituting Eq. 5 into Lemma 1 yields

$$Pr_{G_0}[\mathcal{A}\ succeeds] \leq \frac{\epsilon}{2^n - q} + \mathrm{Adv}_{\widetilde{E}^{\pm}(\$, \circleddash)}^{\mathrm{TPRP}}(5q\ell, q'). \qquad (6)$$

The advantage $\mathrm{Adv}_{\widetilde{E}^{\pm}(\$, \circleddash)}^{\mathrm{TPRP}}(5q\ell, q')$ of $\mathcal{A}$ against the tweakable pseudorandom permutation (TPRP) security of $\widetilde{E}$ is defined in [5, pp. 12-14, 20]. Quantum adversary $\mathcal{A}$ makes q queries with blocks of length $\leq \ell$ and q' queries to the block cipher E that is the main building block of the TBC $\widetilde{E}$. The set of tweaks that may be queried has to be pre-declared (see also [5]) and may at most be of size $5\ell q$. Furthermore, tweaks are not allowed to be queried in superposition. As described in [5, p. 20], this advantage is upper bounded by

$$\mathrm{Adv}_{\widetilde{E}^{\pm}(\$, \circleddash)}^{\mathrm{TPRP}}(5q\ell, q') \leq 8\sqrt{\frac{5\ell q q'^2}{2^n}}. \qquad (7)$$

Finally, Eqs. 6 and 7 produce

$$Pr_{G_0}[\mathcal{A}\ succeeds] \leq \frac{\epsilon}{2^n - q} + 8\sqrt{\frac{5\ell q q'^2}{2^n}}, \qquad (8)$$

which gives an upper bound for the probability of $\mathcal{A}$ to succeed in a forgery on QCB. This bound depends on the size ϵ of the blind set, block size $n = |T|$, the amount $5\ell q$ of pre-declared tweaks and the amount q, q' of queries made by $\mathcal{A}$ to $\widetilde{E}$ or E respectively.

□

In the case of using SATURNIN as the TBC $\widetilde{E}$ for QCB, a message block or associated data block consists of 256 bits. As QCB generates the tag by XOR of these blocks (see Fig. 2), the resulting tag T is also of size $|T| = 256$ bits. For reasonable parameters q, q', this renders the advantage of $\mathcal{A}$ to succeed in the blind unforgeability game G_0 on QCB with SATURNIN negligible. For an example, consider $\mathcal{A}$ making $q = q' = 2^{32}$ queries to $\widetilde{E}, E$ respectively with $\ell = n = 256$. The probability that $\mathcal{A}$ succeeds in creating a blind forgery is therefore

$$Pr_{G_0}[\mathcal{A}\ succeeds] \leq \frac{\epsilon}{2^{256} - 2^{32}} + 8\sqrt{\frac{5 \cdot 256 \cdot 2^{32^2}}{2^{256}}}$$

$$\leq \frac{\epsilon}{2^{224}} + 8\sqrt{\frac{1}{2^{149}}},$$

which is negligible for any ϵ with $0 < \epsilon < 1$.

5   General Blindly Unforgeable Authenticated Encryption

In QCB, the authentication procedure (Fig. 2) makes use of a TBC $\widetilde{E}_{K,T}$ whereas for each block cipher call, the tweak T_i is ensured to be different to the tweaks T_j with $j < i$. Similar to PMAC, this construction is parallelizable.

This idea can be generalised to describe a generic AEAD construction that is blindly unforgeable. For the security proof of blind unforgeability to hold, a set of tweaks has to be pre-declared and each tweak used throughout the BU-game needs to be inside the tweak set.

Initially, tweak space $\mathcal{T}$ and initialisation vector space $\mathcal{IV}$ are generated. Let $T \xleftarrow{gen} \mathcal{T}(X)$ denote tweak T being picked through some black box function $f(X)$ from $\mathcal{T}$. Importantly, the initialisation vector needs to be included in the (derivation of the) tweak of each TBC call to be secure against a quantum forgery attack based on Deutsch's algorithm [10]. In other words, one input to f needs to be but is not limited to an IV or *nonce* which is then used to generate a tweak. Algorithm 1 describes an authenticated encryption scheme. Algorithms 2 and 3 denote the encryption and tag generation procedures respectively. Algorithm 4 chooses and returns a tweak from $\mathcal{T}$. Importantly, the chosen tweak is removed from $\mathcal{T}$ to ensure that no tweak is used more than once. Algorithm 5 performs 10* padding to pad a block to size n. If $|M|$ or $|A|$ respectively are a multiple of n, the blocks M_* or A_* will be of length 0. Nevertheless, they are still needed for further calculation and will be padded to length n. The Ciphertext C is therefore always at least 1 bit longer than M.

Algorithm 1: AUTHENTICATEDENCRYPTION(M, A, IV, K)

Input: Message M, associated data A, initialisation vector IV, key K
1 **Requirements:** Initialisation vectors should not be reused;
  Output: Ciphertext C, tag τ
2 $C \leftarrow$ ENCRYPTION(M, IV, K);
3 $\tau \leftarrow$ GENERATETAG(M, A, IV, K);
4 **return** (C, τ)

Algorithm 2: ENCRYPTION(M, IV, K)

Input: Message M, initialisation vector IV, key K
1 $(M_1, \ldots, M_\ell, M_*) \leftarrow M$ with $|M_i| = n$;   // $|M_*|$ can be 0.
2 **for** $i = 1$ *to* ℓ **do**
3     $T_i \leftarrow$ GENTWEAK(IV);
4     $C_i \leftarrow \widetilde{E}_{K, T_i}(M_i)$;
5 **end**
6 $T_{\ell+1} \leftarrow$ GENTWEAK(IV);
7 $C_* \leftarrow \widetilde{E}_{K, T_{\ell+1}}(\text{PAD}(M_*, n))$;
8 $C \leftarrow (C_1, \ldots, C_\ell, C_*)$;
9 **return** C

Algorithm 3: GENERATETAG(M, A, IV, K)

Input: Message M, associated data A, initialisation vector IV, key K
1 $(A_1, \ldots, A_j, A_*) \leftarrow A$ with $|A_i| = n$;   // $|A_*|$ can be 0.
2 $X_0 \leftarrow 0^n$;
3 **for** $i = 1$ *to* j **do**
4     $T_i \leftarrow$ GENTWEAK(IV);
5     $X_i \leftarrow X_{i-1} \oplus \widetilde{E}_{K, T_i}(A_i)$;
6 **end**
7 $T_{j+1} \rightarrow$ GENTWEAK(IV);
8 $X_{j+1} \leftarrow X_j \oplus \widetilde{E}_{K, T_{j+1}}(\text{PAD}(A_*, n))$;
9 $M' \leftarrow \bigoplus_i M_i \oplus \text{PAD}(M_*, n)$;
10 $T_{j+2} \leftarrow$ GENTWEAK(IV);
11 $\tau \leftarrow X_{j+1} \oplus \widetilde{E}_{K, T_{j+2}}(M')$;
12 **return** τ

Algorithm 4: GENTWEAK(IV)

Input: Initialisation vector IV
1 $T \xleftarrow{gen} \mathcal{T}(IV)$;
2 $\mathcal{T} = \mathcal{T} \setminus \{T\}$;
3 **return** T

Algorithm 5: PAD(X, n)

Input: Block $X \in \{0,1\}^m$, block size n

1 $X' \leftarrow X\|1$;

2 **while** $|X'| < n$ **do** $X' \leftarrow X'\|0$ **return** X'

---

6   Conclusion and Future Work

It is apparent that there are popular classical AEAD constructions that are structurally insecure when challenged by a quantum adversary. This means that new techniques need to be established which can substitute or repair the broken building blocks of the affected schemes and algorithms. The usage of a TBC where each tweak contains the initialization vector provides a defence strategy against quantum period finding and quantum linearization attacks. This strategy can fix vulnerabilities in known MACs and AEAD schemes like PMAC or OCB, which provide parallelizable, efficient authentication or authenticated encryption. QCB, a proposed post-quantum successor of the OCB-family, utilizes the TBC-strategy and seems to provide a post-quantum secure rate-one AEAD scheme. This recipe for security under blind unforgeability can be generalized to a more generic AEAD scheme.

Other classical schemes suffer from the same vulnerabilities against a quantum adversary like OCB. Enhancing those schemes with the aforementioned structure may prove to be a viable method to eliminate attack vectors in the quantum scenario.

A   Quantum Attacks Against Symmetric Cryptography

Simon's Algorithm for Period-Finding. Given a black-box function $f : \{0,1\}^n \rightarrow \{0,1\}^n$ with some unknown period $s \in \{0,1\}^n$ and $f(x) = f(y) \Leftrightarrow ((x = y) \vee (x = y \oplus s))$ for all $x, y \in \{0,1\}^n$. *I.e.*, there exist two distinct values x, y for which f produces the same result. The difference $x \oplus y$ between these values is s. In the context of this chapter, a function that satisfies this property is also described as satisfying *Simon's promise*. Finding s on a classical computer takes $\Theta(2^{n/2})$ queries to f. Simon's algorithm [28] can find s with $\mathcal{O}(n)$ queries to the black-box function on a quantum computer. The following paragraphs highlight some of the impactful attacks presented from Kaplan et al. against CBC-MAC, LRW, PMAC and OCB [16].

CBC-MAC. Consider some adversary $\mathcal{A}$ who has access to the encryption oracle $E_k : \{0,1\}^n \rightarrow \{0,1\}^n$ and a function f satisfying Simon's promise. Furthermore, $\mathcal{A}$ can query f in superposition if they have quantum oracle access to E_k. If $\mathcal{A}$ can find the hidden difference s, it is sufficient to break the cryptographic scheme. In this attack, $s = E(M_1) \oplus E(M_2)$ for two distinct messages M_1, M_2.

$$x_0 = 0 \qquad x_i = E_k(x_{i-1} \oplus m) \qquad \text{CBC-MAC}(M) = E'_k(x_\ell)$$

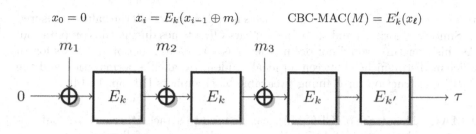

Fig. 3. Encrypted CBC-MAC [16, Fig. 9]. Here, k, k' denote two independent keys, $M = m_1 || \ldots || m_\ell$ is the message divided into ℓ blocks and τ the resulting authentication tag.

Figure 3 shows the standardized encrypted CBC-MAC. Classically, it is considered secure (up to the birthday bound) [4]. According to the attack strategy described above, f is defined as

$$f : \{0,1\} \times \{0,1\}^n \to \{0,1\}^n$$
$$b, x \mapsto \text{CBC-MAC}(\alpha_b || x) = E'_k(E_k(x \oplus E_k(\alpha_b)))$$

with α_0, α_1 representing two distinct message blocks [16, p. 15]. This function f satisfies Simon's promise with $s = 1 || E_k(\alpha_0) \oplus E_k(\alpha_1)$. Consequently, applying Simon's algorithm will return $E_k(\alpha_0) \oplus E_k(\alpha_1)$ which allows for the forgery of messages. Query the oracle to receive tag $\tau_0 = \text{CBC-MAC}(\alpha_0 || m_1)$ for an arbitrary m_1. Next, query the oracle for tag $\tau_1 = \text{CBC-MAC}(\alpha_1 || m_1 \oplus E_k(\alpha_0) \oplus E_k(\alpha_1))$. It holds that $\tau_1 = \tau_2$ and a valid tag has been forged successfully [16, pp. 15-16]. This attack directly violates *plus-one unforgeability* as well as *blind unforgeability*, which are examined in Sect. 2. If adversary $\mathcal{A}$ repeats the forgery step $q + 1$ times making $2q + 1$ classical and quantum queries to the oracle, they can produce $2(q + 1)$ messages with valid tags.

Liskov-Rivest-Wagner (LRW) Construction. By employing the *LRW* construction, a block cipher E is transformed into a tweakable block cipher E^*, whereas E^* is a family of unrelated block ciphers. The construction is defined as

$$E^*_{t,k}(x) = E_k(x \oplus h(t)) \oplus h(t)$$

with h being an (almost) universal hash function [18,19]. Here, h and k are both part of the joint key. Furthermore, for two arbitrary tweaks $t_0 \neq t_1$, the function f is defined as [16, p. 13]

$$f : \{0,1\}^n \to \{0,1\}^n$$
$$x \mapsto E^*_{t_0,k}(x) \oplus E^*_{t_1,k}(x)$$
$$f(x) = E_k(x \oplus h(t_0)) \oplus h(t_0) \oplus E_k(x \oplus h(t_1)) \oplus h(t_1).$$

This function satisfies Simon's promise with $f(x) = f(x \oplus s) = f(x \oplus h(t_0) \oplus h(t_1))$. Therefore, by running Simon's algorithm $\mathcal{O}(n)$ times, an attacker can recover $s = h(t_0 \oplus h(t_1))$. The difference s is orthogonal to all the values measured in Simon's algorithm and therefore appears $\mathcal{O}(n)$ times during the computation. As this structure would not occur when f is a random function, it allows for an efficient distinguisher between an ideal random tweakable permutation and the *LRW* construction for defining tweakable block ciphers [16, pp. 13-14].

PMAC. The attack on CBC-MAC can be used to attack other message authentication codes as well. PMAC [25], for example, works as follows:

$$c_i = E_k(m_i \oplus \Delta_i) \qquad \text{PMAC}(M) = E_k^*(m_\ell \oplus \sum_i c_i)$$

with E^* being a tweakable block cipher derived from E. PMAC has the same internal structure as CBC-MAC when only messages consisting of two blocks are considered: $\text{PMAC}(m_1 || m_2) = E_k^*(m_2 \oplus E_k(m_1 \oplus \Delta_0))$. $\mathcal{A}$ can therefore execute the identical attack as used to break CBC-MAC. Query the tag $\tau_0 = \text{PMAC}(\alpha_0 || m_1 || m_2)$ for arbitrary message blocks m_1, m_2. Consequently, $\tau_1 = \text{PMAC}(\alpha_1 || m_1 || m_2 \oplus E_k(\alpha_0) \oplus E_k(\alpha_1)) = \tau_0$ and a valid forgery has been achieved [16, pp. 16-17].

A different attack can be carried out by utilizing the vulnerabilities of *LRW* to gain knowledge of the differences Δ_i. First, the function fulfilling Simon's promise is defined as

$$f : \{0,1\}^n \rightarrow \{0,1\}^n$$
$$m \mapsto \text{PMAC}(m || m || 0^n) = E_k^*(E_k(m \oplus \Delta_0) \oplus E_k(m \oplus \Delta_1)).$$

The hidden difference s is given with $f(m) = f(m \oplus s) = f(m \oplus \Delta_0 \oplus \Delta_1)$. Therefore, $s = \Delta_0 \oplus \Delta_1$ can be recovered by an adversary efficiently using Simon's Algorithm in $\mathcal{O}(n)$ iterations. The adversary queries tag $\tau_1 = \text{PMAC}(m_1 || m_1)$ for an arbitrary message block m_1. It holds that τ_1 is equal to $\tau_2 = \text{PMAC}(m_1 \oplus \Delta_0 \oplus \Delta_1 || m_1 \oplus \Delta_0 \oplus \Delta_1)$ and therefore a valid forgery was generated.

PMAC is based on the *XE* construction, which is an instantiation of *LRW*. In PMAC, the offsets are calculated with $\Delta_i = \gamma(i) \cdot L$ with $\gamma(i)$ being the *Gray encoding* of i and $L = E_k(0)$ [25, p. 21]. This leads to an adversary being able to learn L from the hidden period $s = \Delta_0 \oplus \Delta_1$ with $L = (\Delta_0 \oplus \Delta_1) \cdot (\gamma(0) \oplus \gamma(1))^{-1}$. With this knowledge, the adversary can compute each Δ_i and forge any arbitrary message.

OCB. Finally, to attack the authenticated encryption mode OCB, it can be observed that OCB reduces to a randomized variant of PMAC when the message is empty [16, p. 20]. Encrypted ciphertexts c_i and authentication tag τ are generated by OCB as

$$c_i = E_k(m_i \oplus \Delta_i^N) \oplus \Delta_i^N,$$

$$\tau = E_k\left(\Delta_\ell'^N \oplus \sum_i m_i\right) \oplus \sum_i E_k(a_i \oplus \Delta_i)$$

with nonce N, message $M = m_1 || \ldots || m_\ell$ and associated data $A = a_i || \ldots || a_\ell$. Using an empty message ϵ, OCB generates the tag τ with

$$\text{PMAC}_k(N, \varepsilon, A) = \phi_k(N) \oplus \sum_i E_k(a_i \oplus \Delta_i).$$

Note that $\phi_k(N)$ denotes a permutation under key k whose specific description is of no interest to us. This construction can be attacked as described by the second attack on PMAC based on the LRW vulnerabilities. Consider a family of functions f_N with

$$f_N : \{0,1\}^n \rightarrow \{0,1\}^n$$
$$x \mapsto \text{PMAC}_k(N, \epsilon, x||x)$$
$$f_N(x) = E_k(x \oplus \Delta_0) \oplus E_k(x \oplus \Delta_1) \oplus \phi_k(N).$$

Each function f_N for any N satisfies Simon's promise: $f_N(a) = f_N(a \oplus s) = f_N(a \oplus \Delta_0 \oplus \Delta_1)$. This allows for the recovery of the hidden period $s = \Delta_0 \oplus \Delta_1$. An adversary can now query the authenticated encryption with ciphertext and tag pair $C_1, \tau_1 = \text{OCB}(N, M, a||a)$ for arbitrary message M, an arbitrary block a and random Nonce N. C_1, τ_1 is also a valid authenticated encryption of $\text{OCB}(N, M, a \oplus \Delta_0 \oplus \Delta_1 || a \oplus \Delta_0 \oplus \Delta_1)$ with the same nonce N [16, p. 20].

B   Instantiation of QCB with TRAX and Pholkos

When using SATURNIN as the TBC for QCB, due to the *key-tweak-insertion* construction, each message or associated data block is encrypted with a separate block-key based on the key k which is modified by a distinct tweak for each block cipher call. For an adversary $\mathcal{A}$, it is therefore sufficient to find only one of these block-keys to break the TBC and thus QCB. Consequently, there are more chances of $\mathcal{A}$ breaking one of the TBC iterations than there would be for a block cipher that uses the same key for each block. Keep in mind that the latter construction would then be structurally vulnerable to quantum attacks like quantum linearization.

However, the authors of QCB mention the scarcity of usable 256-bit block ciphers. They do suggest to alternatively use the dedicated TBC TRAX-L-17 [3] which is based on 256-bit message blocks and keys but a smaller tweak than SATURNIN with 128 bits. This would allow for IVs of 80 bits and at most $2^{45} - 1$ blocks of plaintext and associated data [5, p. 17]. An alternative that may provide a better trade-off between security and efficiency is the TBC PHOLKOS [11]. PHOLKOS is a recent proposal for a post-quantum-secure TBC with a tweak size of 128 bits, block sizes of 256 or 512 bits and keys of size 256 bit. It is a substitution-permutation network (SPN) inspired by AESQ [7] and Haraka [17]. Any input plaintext block is encrypted in 8–14 steps depending on the configuration of block and key size. Initially, the n-bit plaintext block is split into $\frac{n}{128}$ 128-bit blocks which are then split into four 32-bit words each. Subsequently, each step performs the similar rounds as found in the classical block cipher

AES [23]. A *tweakey* is used for the ADDROUNDKEY step of AES, whereas a round tweakey is generated by a schedule from the secret key and the tweak. An advantage of PHOLKOS is that the block cipher AES is well researched in terms of cryptanalysis and security. Furthermore, efficient implementations in soft- and hardware already exist. PHOLKOS-QCB provides a larger security margin than SATURNIN-QCB due to the larger tweak space.

References

1. Alagic, G., Gagliardoni, T., Majenz, C.: Unforgeable quantum encryption. In: Nielsen, J.B., Rijmen, V. (eds.) EUROCRYPT 2018. LNCS, vol. 10822, pp. 489–519. Springer, Cham (2018). https://doi.org/10.1007/978-3-319-78372-7_16
2. Alagic, G., Majenz, C., Russell, A., Song, F.: Quantum-access-secure message authentication via blind-unforgeability. In: Canteaut, A., Ishai, Y. (eds.) EUROCRYPT 2020. LNCS, vol. 12107, pp. 788–817. Springer, Cham (2020). https://doi.org/10.1007/978-3-030-45727-3_27
3. Beierle, C., et al.: Alzette: a 64-bit ARX-box. In: Micciancio, D., Ristenpart, T. (eds.) CRYPTO 2020. LNCS, vol. 12172, pp. 419–448. Springer, Cham (2020). https://doi.org/10.1007/978-3-030-56877-1_15
4. Bellare, M., Kilian, J., Rogaway, P.: The security of the cipher block chaining message authentication code. J. Comput. Syst. Sci. **61**(3), 362–399 (2000)
5. Bhaumik, R., Bonnetain, X., Chailloux, A., Leurent, G., Naya-Plasencia, M., Schrottenloher, A., Seurin, Y.: Qcb: Efficient quantum-secure authenticated encryption. IACR Cryptol. ePrint Arch. **2020**, 1304 (2020)
6. Bhaumik, R., Nandi, M.: Improved security for OCB3, November 2017. https://doi.org/10.1007/978-3-319-70697-9_22, https://eprint.iacr.org/2017/845.pdf
7. Biryukov, A., Khovratovich, D.: PAEQ: parallelizable permutation-based authenticated encryption. In: Chow, S.S.M., Camenisch, J., Hui, L.C.K., Yiu, S.M. (eds.) ISC 2014. LNCS, vol. 8783, pp. 72–89. Springer, Cham (2014). https://doi.org/10.1007/978-3-319-13257-0_5
8. Boneh, D., Zhandry, M.: Quantum-secure message authentication codes. In: Johansson, T., Nguyen, P.Q. (eds.) EUROCRYPT 2013. LNCS, vol. 7881, pp. 592–608. Springer, Heidelberg (2013). https://doi.org/10.1007/978-3-642-38348-9_35
9. Boneh, D., Zhandry, M.: Secure signatures and chosen ciphertext security in a quantum computing world. In: Canetti, R., Garay, J.A. (eds.) CRYPTO 2013. LNCS, vol. 8043, pp. 361–379. Springer, Heidelberg (2013). https://doi.org/10.1007/978-3-642-40084-1_21
10. Bonnetain, X., Leurent, G., Naya-Plasencia, M., Schrottenloher, A.: Quantum linearization attacks. Cryptology ePrint Archive, Report 2021/1239 (2021)
11. Bossert, J., List, E., Lucks, S., Schmitz, S.: Pholkos – efficient large-state tweakable block ciphers from the AES round function. In: Galbraith, S.D. (ed.) CT-RSA 2022. LNCS, vol. 13161, pp. 511–536. Springer, Cham (2022). https://doi.org/10.1007/978-3-030-95312-6_21
12. Canteaut, A., et al.: Saturnin: a suite of lightweight symmetric algorithms for post-quantum security. IACR Trans. Symmetric Cryptol. **2020**(S1), 160–207 (2020). https://doi.org/10.13154/tosc.v2020.iS1.160-207, https://tosc.iacr.org/index.php/ToSC/article/view/8621

13. Doosti, M., Delavar, M., Kashefi, E., Arapinis, M.: A unified framework for quantum unforgeability (2021). https://doi.org/10.48550/ARXIV.2103.13994, https://arxiv.org/abs/2103.13994
14. Hosoyamada, A., Iwata, T.: Provably quantum-secure tweakable block ciphers. IACR Transactions on Symmetric Cryptology, pp. 337–377 (2021)
15. IEEE: IEEE standard specifications for public-key cryptography. IEEE Std. 1363-2000, pp. 1–228 (2000). https://doi.org/10.1109/IEEESTD.2000.92292
16. Kaplan, M., Leurent, G., Leverrier, A., Naya-Plasencia, M.: Breaking symmetric cryptosystems using quantum period finding (2016). https://arxiv.org/pdf/1602.05973.pdf
17. Kölbl, S., Lauridsen, M.M., Mendel, F., Rechberger, C.: Haraka v2-efficient short-input hashing for post-quantum applications. IACR Transactions on Symmetric Cryptology, pp. 1–29 (2016)
18. Liskov, M., Rivest, R.L., Wagner, D.: Tweakable block ciphers. In: Yung, M. (ed.) CRYPTO 2002. LNCS, vol. 2442, pp. 31–46. Springer, Heidelberg (2002). https://doi.org/10.1007/3-540-45708-9_3
19. Liskov, M., Rivest, R.L., Wagner, D.: Tweakable block ciphers. J. Cryptol. **24**(3), 588–613 (2011)
20. Mavroeidis, V., Vishi, K., Zych, M.D., Jøsang, A.: The impact of quantum computing on present cryptography. Int. J. Adv. Comput. Sci. Appl. **9**(3) (2018). https://doi.org/10.14569/ijacsa.2018.090354, http://dx.doi.org/10.14569/IJACSA.2018.090354
21. McKay, K., Bassham, L., Sönmez Turan, M., Mouha, N.: Report on lightweight cryptography. Technical report, National Institute of Standards and Technology (2016)
22. Moody, D., et al.: Nist report on post-quantum cryptography, April 2016. https://doi.org/10.6028/NIST.IR.8105
23. National Institute of Standards and Technology (NIST): Announcing the advanced encryption standard (AES), November 2001
24. Roetteler, M., Steinwandt, R.: A note on quantum related-key attacks. Inf. Process. Lett. **115**(1), 40–44 (2015)
25. Rogaway, P.: Efficient instantiations of tweakable blockciphers and refinements to modes OCB and PMAC. In: Lee, P.J. (ed.) ASIACRYPT 2004. LNCS, vol. 3329, pp. 16–31. Springer, Heidelberg (2004). https://doi.org/10.1007/978-3-540-30539-2_2
26. Shor, P.W.: Algorithms for quantum computation: discrete logarithms and factoring. In: Proceedings 35th Annual Symposium on Foundations of Computer Science, pp. 124–134 (1994). https://doi.org/10.1109/SFCS.1994.365700
27. Shor, P.W.: Polynomial-time algorithms for prime factorization and discrete logarithms on a quantum computer. SIAM J. Comput. **26**(5), 1484–1509 (Oct 1997). https://doi.org/10.1137/s0097539795293172, http://dx.doi.org/10.1137/S0097539795293172
28. Simon, D.: On the power of quantum computation. In: Proceedings 35th Annual Symposium on Foundations of Computer Science, pp. 116–123 (1994). https://doi.org/10.1109/SFCS.1994.365701
29. Sönmez Turan, M., et al.: Status report on the second round of the nist lightweight cryptography standardization process. Technical report, National Institute of Standards and Technology (2021)

30. Turan, M.S., McKay, K.A., Çalik, Ç., Chang, D., Bassham, L., et al.: Status report on the first round of the NIST lightweight cryptography standardization process. National Institute of Standards and Technology, Gaithersburg, MD, NIST Interagency/Internal Rep. (NISTIR) (2019)
31. Zhandry, M.: How to construct quantum random functions. Cryptology ePrint Archive, Report 2012/182 (2012)

A Side-Channel Secret Key Recovery Attack on CRYSTALS-Kyber Using k Chosen Ciphertexts

Ruize Wang[✉] and Elena Dubrova

KTH Royal Institute of Technology, Stockholm, Sweden
{ruize,dubrova}@kth.se

Abstract. At CHES'2021, a chosen ciphertext attack combined with belief propagation which can recover the long-term secret key of CRYSTALS-Kyber from side-channel information of the number theoretic transform (NTT) computations was presented. The attack requires k traces from the inverse NTT step of decryption, where k is the module rank, for a noise tolerance $\sigma \leq 1.2$ in the Hamming weight (HW) leakage on simulated data. In this paper, we present an attack which can recover the secret key of CRYSTALS-Kyber from k chosen ciphertexts using side-channel information of the Barret reduction and message decoding steps of decryption, for $k \in \{3, 4\}$. The key novel idea is to create a unique mapping between the secret key coefficients and multiple intermediate variables of these procedures. The redundancy in the mapping patterns enables us to detect errors in the secret key coefficients recovered from side-channel information. We demonstrate the attack on the example of a software implementation of Kyber-768 in ARM Cortex-M4 CPU using deep learning-based power analysis.

Keywords: Public-key cryptography · CRYSTALS-Kyber · post-quantum cryptography · side-channel attack

1 Introduction

CRYSTALS-Kyber is an IND-CCA2 secure public key encryption (PKE) and key encapsulation mechanism (KEM) whose security relies on the hardness of the module learning with errors (M-LWE) problem [23]. IND-CCA2 means indistinguishablity under adaptive chosen ciphertext attack (CCA).

However, it has been shown that the theoretical resistance of CRYSTALS-Kyber to CCAs can be bypassed using side channels. Many different side-channel attacks on software [3,4,17,20,21,24,25,28–30,32,33] and hardware [13,22] implementations of CRYSTALS-Kyber have been presented. The discovered vulnerabilities helped improve the subsequently released implementations of CRYSTALS-Kyber [5,8] as well as promoted stronger mitigation techniques against side-channel attacks such as [2,12,27].

Given that CRYSTALS-Kyber has been selected by the National Institute of Standards and Technology (NIST) for standardization [15] and included in the

© The Author(s), under exclusive license to Springer Nature Switzerland AG 2023
S. El Hajji et al. (Eds.): C2SI 2023, LNCS 13874, pp. 109–128, 2023.
https://doi.org/10.1007/978-3-031-33017-9_7

Table 1. The number of chosen ciphertexts (CCTs) required for Kyber-768 secret key recovery in different side-channel attacks.

Paper	Attack target	Attack method	#CCT	Detect errors	Protected implem.	Real
Xu et al. [32]	Message encoding	Template	4×3	No	No	Yes
Ravi et al. [21]	Message decoding		3×3	No	No	Yes
Mu et al. [16]	Barrett reduction		11	No	No	Yes
Sim et al. [26]		Clustering	3×3	No	No	Yes
Hamburg et al. [10]	NTT	Template	$1 \times 3^*$	No	Yes	No
Backlund et al. [3]	Message decoding	MLP	$4 \times 3^{**}$	Yes	Yes	Yes
This work	Message decoding & Barrett reduction		1×3	Yes	No	Yes

*For noise tolerance level $\sigma \leq 1.2$ in the Hamming weight (HW) leakage.
**If a linear code with the code distance two is used for constructing CCT.
"Real" means that the attack uses side-channel information acquired from a real physical device, rather than simulated data.

National Security Agency (NSA) suite of cryptographic algorithms recommended for national security systems [1], it is important to continue looking for potential new attack vectors.

Our Contributions: In this paper, we present a chosen chipertext side-channel attack method which requires a single ciphertext per module rank to recover the secret key of CRYSTALS-Kyber. This is an improvement over all previous chosen chipertext side-channel attacks which rely purely on side-channel information for secret key recovery, see Table 1 for a summary.

Only the attack of Hamburg et al. [10], which combines side-channel information of the number theoretic transform (NTT) computations with belief propagation [20], requires the same number of chipertexts as the presented attack[1]. The attack in [10] is carried out on simulated data from a first-order masked software implementation of CRYSTALS-Kyber. The presented attack is carried out on real power traces captured from an unprotected software implementation of Kyber-768 from [14] in ARM Cortex-M4 CPU.

The key novel idea of the presented method is to create a unique mapping between the secret key coefficients and multiple intermediate variables of within the same execution of an algorithm. In this paper, we use intermediate variables of the Barret reduction and message decoding steps of decryption. The redundancy in the mapping patterns enables us to detect errors in the secret key coefficients recovered from the side-channel information.

The rest of this paper is organized as follows. Section 2 reviews previous work on side-channel analysis of CRYSTALS-Kyber implementations. Section 3 gives a background on CRYSTALS-Kyber algorithm. Section 4 presents the new

---

[1] For noise tolerance levels ranging from $\sigma \leq 0.5$ to $\sigma \leq 0.7$ depending on the CRYSTALS-Kyber parameter set, the attack of Hamburg et al. [10] requires a single ciphertext in total.

chosen chipertext side-channel attack method. Sections 5 and 6 describe the profiling and attack stages, respectively. Section 7 summarizes experimental results. Section 8 concludes the paper and discusses future work.

2 Previous Work

Since the beginning of the NIST post-quantum cryptography (PQC) standardization process in 2016, many different side-channel attacks on CRYSTALS-Kyber have been presented, on both software [4,17,20,25,28,29] and hardware implementations [13,22]. In this section, we describe chosen ciphertext attacks from [3,10,16,21,24,26,32] which are the closest related work to the attack presented in this paper.

In [21], near field EM side-channel based secret key recovery attacks on unprotected and protected implementations of CRYSTALS-Kyber are described. In these attacks, at least three queries are required to identify each secret key coefficient uniquely. Thus, in total, $3 \times k$ chosen ciphertexts are required for the secret key recovery, were k is the rank of the module. It is also shown how a masked implementation can be broken in two steps, by attacking each share individually.

In [32] another EM-based chosen ciphertext side-channel attack on an unprotected software implementation of CRYSTALS-Kyber is demonstrated. One-versus-the-rest classifier and templates, constructed at the profiling stage for the message encoding procedure, are used to distinguish one of five coefficients from the rest. This results in four different chosen ciphertexts for all five different secret key coefficients, i.e. $4 \times k$ in total to recover the full secret key, for the module's ranks $k = 3$ and 4.

In [10], a chosen ciphertext side-channel attack on a first-order masked software implementation CRYSTALS-Kyber combined with belief propagation is presented. The attack can recover the secret key from k traces from the inverse NTT step of decryption, where k is the module rank, for a noise tolerance level $\sigma \leq 1.2$ in the HW leakage on simulated data. Furthermore, the attack can recover the secret key from a single trace if the noise in the range $\sigma \leq 0.5$ to $\sigma \leq 0.7$, depending on the CRYSTALS-Kyber parameter set.

In [16], a power-based chosen ciphertext template attack on an unprotected software implementation of CRYSTALS-Kyber is presented. It exploits the vulnerability of modular polynomial subtraction and uses templates constructed at the profiling stage for the Barrett reduce procedure. To enhance the classification accuracy of the template, 11 different chosen ciphertexts are used to extract the secret key.

In [26], a power-based chosen ciphertext clustering attack on an unprotected software implementation CRYSTALS-Kyber is described. The intermediate value tmp of the Barrett reduce procedure is used to represent a secret key coefficient. The attack requires $3 \times k$ chosen ciphertexts to recover the secret key.

Table 2. Parameters of different versions of CRYSTALS-Kyber.

Version	n	k	q	η_1	η_2	(d_u, d_v)
Kyber-512	256	2	3329	3	2	(10, 4)
Kyber-768	256	3	3329	2	2	(10, 4)
Kyber-1024	256	4	3329	2	2	(11, 5)

In [24] a chosen-ciphertext side-channel attack is presented which uses codes to detect faulty positions in the initially recovered secret key. These positions are further corrected with additional traces. An EM-based template attack on an unprotected software implementation of Kyber-512 is demonstrated which can recover a full secret key using 1619 traces on average with the 0.4 out of 512 faulty coefficients on average.

In [3], a chosen ciphertext side-channel attack on a first-order masked and shuffled software implementation of Kyber-768 on an ARM Cortex-M4 is demonstrated which which can extract the secret key from 38,016 power traces. The main idea is to recover shuffling indexes 0 and 255, extract the corresponding two message bits, and then cyclically rotate the message by modifying the ciphertext. In this way, all message bits are extracted using 128 rotations. The attack uses message decoding procedure as the attack point.

3   CRYSTALS-Kyber Algorithm

CRYSTALS-Kyber [23] contains a chosen plaintext attack (CPA)-secure PKE scheme, KYBER.CPAPKE, and a CCA-secure KEM scheme, KYBER. CCAKEM, based on a post-quantum version of the Fujisaki-Okamoto (FO) transform [9]. These algorithms are described in Fig. 1 and Fig. 2 respectively. We follow the notation of [13].

Let $\mathbb{Z}_q$ denote the ring of integers modulo a prime q, and R_q be the quotient ring $\mathbb{Z}_q[X]/(X^n + 1)$. CRYSTALS-Kyber works with vectors of ring elements in R_q^k, where k is the rank of the module defining the security level. There are three versions of CRYSTALS-Kyber, Kyber-512, Kyber-768 and Kyber-1024, for $k = 2, 3$ and 4, respectively, see Table 2 for details. In this paper, we focus on Kyber-768.

The term $x \leftarrow \chi(S; r)$ denotes sampling x from a distribution χ over a set S using seed r. The uniform distribution is denoted by $\mathcal{U}$. The centered binomial distribution with parameter μ is denoted by β_μ.

The Decode$_l$ function deserializes an array of $32l$ bytes into a polynomial with n coefficients in the range $\{0, 1, \cdots, 2^l - 1\}$. The Encode$_l$ function is the inverse of Decode$_l$, which converts a polynomial into a byte array. The polynomial multiplication is denoted by the sign "$\cdot$".

KYBER.CPAPKE.KeyGen()
1: $(\rho, \sigma) \leftarrow \mathcal{U}(\{0,1\}^{256})$
2: $\boldsymbol{A} \leftarrow \mathcal{U}(R_q^{k \times k}; \rho)$
3: $\boldsymbol{s}, \boldsymbol{e} \leftarrow \beta_{\eta_1}(R_q^{k \times 1}; \sigma)$
4: $\boldsymbol{t} = \mathsf{Encode}_{12}(\boldsymbol{A}\boldsymbol{s} + \boldsymbol{e})$
5: $\boldsymbol{s} = \mathsf{Encode}_{12}(\boldsymbol{s})$
6: return $(pk = (\boldsymbol{t}, \rho), sk = \boldsymbol{s})$

KYBER.CPAPKE.Dec($\boldsymbol{s}, c$)
1: $\boldsymbol{u} = \mathsf{Decompress}_q(\mathsf{Decode}_{d_u}(c_1), d_u)$
2: $v = \mathsf{Decompress}_q(\mathsf{Decode}_{d_v}(c_2), d_v)$
3: $\boldsymbol{s} = \mathsf{Decode}_{12}(\boldsymbol{s})$
4: $m = \mathsf{Encode}_1(\mathsf{Compress}_q(v - \boldsymbol{s} \cdot \boldsymbol{u}, 1))$

5: return m

KYBER.CPAPKE.Enc($pk = (\boldsymbol{t}, \rho), m, r$)
1: $\boldsymbol{t} = \mathsf{Decode}_{12}(\boldsymbol{t})$
2: $\boldsymbol{A} \leftarrow \mathcal{U}(R_q^{k \times k}; \rho)$
3: $\boldsymbol{r} \leftarrow \beta_{\eta_1}(R_q^{k \times 1}; r)$
4: $\boldsymbol{e}_1 \leftarrow \beta_{\eta_2}(R_q^{k \times 1}; r)$
5: $e_2 \leftarrow \beta_{\eta_2}(R_q^{1 \times 1}; r)$
6: $\boldsymbol{u} = \boldsymbol{A}^T \boldsymbol{r} + \boldsymbol{e}_1$
7: $v = \boldsymbol{t}^T \boldsymbol{r} + e_2 + \mathsf{Decompress}_q(m, 1)$
8: $c_1 = \mathsf{Encode}_{d_u}(\mathsf{Compress}_q(\boldsymbol{u}, d_u))$
9: $c_2 = \mathsf{Encode}_{d_v}(\mathsf{Compress}_q(v, d_v))$
10: return $c = (c_1, c_2)$

Fig. 1. Description of KYBER.CPAPKE algorithms from [23].

KYBER.CCAKEM.KeyGen()
1: $z \leftarrow \mathcal{U}(\{0,1\}^{256})$
2: $(pk, \boldsymbol{s}) =$
   KYBER.CPAPKE.KeyGen()
3: $sk = (\boldsymbol{s}, pk, \mathcal{H}(pk), z)$
4: return (pk, sk)

KYBER.CCAKEM.Encaps(pk)
1: $m \leftarrow \mathcal{U}(\{0,1\}^{256})$
2: $m = \mathcal{H}(m)$
3: $(\hat{K}, r) = \mathcal{G}(m, \mathcal{H}(pk))$
4: $c = $ KYBER.CPAPKE.Enc(pk, m, r)
5: $K = \mathsf{KDF}(\hat{K}, \mathcal{H}(c))$
6: return (c, K)

KYBER.CCAKEM.Decaps(sk,c)
1: $m' = $ KYBER.CPAPKE.Dec($\boldsymbol{s}, c$)
2: $(\hat{K}', r') = \mathcal{G}(m', \mathcal{H}(pk))$
3: $c' = $ KYBER.CPAPKE.Enc(pk, m', r')
4: if $c = c'$ then
5:     return $K = \mathsf{KDF}(\hat{K}, \mathcal{H}(c))$
6: else
7:     return $K = \mathsf{KDF}(z, \mathcal{H}(c))$
8: end if

Fig. 2. Description of KYBER.CCAKEM algorithms from [23].

The $\mathsf{Compress}_q(x, d)$ and $\mathsf{Decompress}_q(x, d)$ functions are defined by:

$$\mathsf{Compress}_q(x, d) = \lceil (2^d/q) \cdot x \rfloor \bmod^+ 2^d,$$

$$\mathsf{Decompress}_q(x, d) = \lceil (q/2^d) \cdot x \rfloor.$$

The functions $\mathcal{G}$ and $\mathcal{H}$ represent the SHA3-512 and SHA3-256 hash functions, respectively. The KDF represents key derivation function. It is realized by SHAKE-256.

4   Single Chosen Ciphertext Attack Method

In this section, we present the new side-channel attack method which requires only a single ciphertext per rank k of the module to recover the secret key of CRYSTALS-Kyber.

4.1   Intuitive Idea

In the decapsulation algorithm of CRYSTALS-Kyber KEM, KYBER.CCAKEM. Decaps(), the FO transform re-encrypts the decrypted message, m', and checks if the resulting ciphertext, c', is equal to the received one, c. If $c = c'$, the algorithm returns the shared session key K. Otherwise, it outputs a random sequence (see lines 3–7 of KYBER.CCAKEM.Decaps() in Fig. 2). So, in theory, an attacker cannot use chosen cihpertexts to deduce the secret key from the output results of KYBER.CCAKEM.Decaps().

However, in practice it is possible to use chosen ciphertexts to extract secret key-related intermediate variables of CRYSTALS-Kyber from the side-channel emissions captured during the execution of the decryption algorithm KYBER.CPAPKE.Dec(), which runs before the FO transform (see line 1 of KYBER.CCAKEM.Decaps() in Fig. 2). The secret key coefficients can then be deduced from the intermediate variables.

First we describe which secret key-related intermediate variables are used in the presented attack, and then explain the new chosen ciphertext construction method.

4.2   Selecting Secret Key-Related Intermediate Variables

During the decryption, the secret key s is used to compute $v - s \cdot u$, resulting in a polynomial with n coefficients. Modulo q operation is first performed on each polynomial coefficient before it is compressed by the Compress() function. Then, the message decoding operation (see line 4 of KYBER.CPAKEM.Dec() in Fig. 1) converts the corresponding polynomial in R_q to a byte array. In the implementation of CRYSTALS-Kyber from [14], which we use in our experiments, the modulo q operation and the message decoding operation are realized by poly_reduce() and poly_tomsg() procedures, respectively. Figure 3 and Fig. 4 show the C and assembly codes. The red lines mark the points exploited in the presented attack.

The vulnerability in poly_tomsg() procedure (line 5 of poly_tomsg() in Fig. 3) is known as the *incremental storage* in previous work [21]. Since each individual polynomial coefficient is converted to a single message bit, the secret key can be recovered from chosen ciphertexts in which different coefficients correspond to different unique message bit sequences [21, 32].

Sim et al. [26] found that it is also possible to recover the secret key using the intermediate variable tmp of doublebarrett procedure (line 5–6 of doublebarrett in Fig. 4). In the attacks presented in [16, 26], the secret key is

```
void indcpa_dec(char *m, char *c, char *sk)
poly mp, bp;
poly *v = &bp;
int i;
 1: poly_unpackdecompress(&mp,c,0);
 2: poly_ntt(&mp);
 3: poly_frombytes_mul(&mp,sk);
 4: SABER_un_pack(&ct, v);
 5: for  (i = 1; i < KYBER_K; i++) do
 6:    poly_unpackdecompress(&bp,c,i);
 7:    poly_ntt(&bp);
 8:    poly_frombytes_mul(&bp,sk+i*KYBER_POLYBYTES);
 9:    poly_add(&mp,&mp,&bp);
10: end for
11: poly_invntt(&mp);
12: poly_decompress(v,c+KYBER_POLYVECCOMPRESSEDBYTES);
13: poly_sub(&mp,v,&mp);
14: poly_reduce(&mp);
15: poly_tomsg(m,&mp);

void poly_tomsg(char *msg, poly *a)
 1: for (i = 0; i < BYTES; i++) do
 2:    msg[i] = 0;
 3:    for (j = 0; j < 8; j++) do
 4:       t=(((a->coeffs[8*i+j]<<1) +KYBER_Q/2)/KYBER_Q)&1;
 5:       msg[i] |= t<<j;
 6:    end for
 7: end for

void poly_reduce(poly *r)
 1: asm_barrett_reduce(r->coeffs); /*In assembly*/
```

Fig. 3. The C code of KYBER.CPAPKE.Dec() implementation from [14]. The attack points are marked in red. (Color figure online)

recovered from chosen ciphertexts in which different key coefficients correspond to different unique combinations of values of tmp.

However, since message bits values are either 0 or 1, and tmp values of are $-q$, 0 or q, while the secret key coefficients are in the range $\{-2, -1, 0, 1, 2\}$ (for $k = 3$ and 4), if only poly_tomsg(), or only poly_reduce() attack point is used, then more than one chosen ciphertext is required to recover each secret key coefficient. More specifically, at least three different ciphertexts are required to represent the key coefficients by message bits, since $\lceil \log_2 5 \rceil = 3$. If tmp is used, then at least two different ciphertexts are required, since $\lceil log_3 5 \rceil = 2$. In the attack of Sim et al. [26], only $tmp = 0$ and $tmp = -q$ values are used in order to maximize the Hamming distance (and hence increase chances to recover the values). In this case, three different ciphertexts are required.

```
asm_barrett_reduce:
 1: ... /* assign registers to variables */
 2: movw barrettconst, #20159
 3: movw q, #3329
 4: movw loop, #16
 5: 1:
 6:   ldm poly, {poly0-poly7}
 7:   doublebarrett poly0,tmp,tmp2, q, barrettconst
 8:   doublebarrett poly1,tmp,tmp2, q, barrettconst
 9:   doublebarrett poly2,tmp,tmp2, q, barrettconst
10:   doublebarrett poly3,tmp,tmp2, q, barrettconst
11:   doublebarrett poly4,tmp,tmp2, q, barrettconst
12:   doublebarrett poly5,tmp,tmp2, q, barrettconst
13:   doublebarrett poly6,tmp,tmp2, q, barrettconst
14:   doublebarrett poly7,tmp,tmp2, q, barrettconst
15:   stm poly!, {poly0-poly7}
16:   subs.w loop, #1
17: bne.w 1b

.marco doublebarrett a, tmp,tmp2, q, barrettconst
 1: smulbb \tmp, \a, \barrettconst
 2: smulbb \tmp2, \a, \barrettconst
 3: asr \tmp, \tmp, #26
 4: asr \tmp2, \tmp2, #26
 5: smulbb \tmp, \tmp, \q
 6: smulbb \tmp2, \tmp2, \q
 7: pkhbt \tmp, \tmp, \tmp2, lsl#16
 8: usub16 \a, \a, \tmp
.endm
```

Fig. 4. The assembly code of `poly_reduce()` [14]. The lines corresponding to the computation of tmp are marked in red. (Color figure online)

We discovered that it is possible to uniquely represent five secret key coefficients using a single chosen ciphertext if both, message bits of `poly_tomsg()` and tmp of `poly_reduce()`, are used together with the input and output of `poly_reduce()`. The next subsection describes how this ciphertext is constructed.

4.3   Chosen Ciphertext Construction Method

In Kyber-768, the secret key s consists three polynomials $s = (s_0, s_1, s_2)$, and the ciphertext (u, v) consists of three polynomials $u = (u_0, u_1, u_2)$ and one polynomial v.

Following the chosen ciphertext construction method of [19], to recover n coefficients of s_i, we set one of the polynomials of $\boldsymbol{u}$ a non-zero constant k_1 and the other two polynomials of $\boldsymbol{u}$ to zero:

$$\boldsymbol{u} = \begin{cases} (k_1, 0, 0) \in R_q^{3\times 1} & \text{for } i = 0, \\ (0, k_1, 0) \in R_q^{3\times 1} & \text{for } i = 1, \\ (0, 0, k_1) \in R_q^{3\times 1} & \text{for } i = 2. \end{cases} \tag{1}$$

All n coefficients of v are set to the same constant k_0:

$$v = k_0 \sum_{j=0}^{255} x^j \in R_q^{1\times 1}. \tag{2}$$

Then, for $i \in \{0, 1, 2\}$, we get:

$$v - \boldsymbol{s} \cdot \boldsymbol{u} = \sum_{j=0}^{255} (k_0 - k_1 s_{i,j}) x^j. \tag{3}$$

where $s_{i,j}$ is the jth coefficient of the polynomial s_i. Since $s_{i,j} \in \{-2, -1, 0, 1, 2\}$, we can search through all possible values of k_0 and k_1 in $\mathbb{Z}_q$ to construct a ciphertext such that the intermediate values during the computation of $m = \mathsf{Encode}_1(\mathsf{Compress}_q(v - \boldsymbol{s} \cdot \boldsymbol{u}, 1))$ (line 4 of KYBER.CPAKEM.Dec() in Fig. 1) satisfy the following criteria:

1. The number of different HW values of `poly_reduce()` intermediate variables is minimized.
2. The Hamming distances between different values of `poly_reduce()` intermediate variables are maximized.
3. There are both 0 and 1 values of message bits in `poly_tomsg()`.
4. Given 1–3, all five key coefficients are distinguishable.

We found that $k_0 = 0$ and $k_1 = 1369$ satisfy these criteria (the solution is not unique, there are others). Table 3 defines the mapping between the secret key coefficients and the intermediate values of `poly_reduce()` and `poly_tomsg()` for the chosen ciphertext with $k_0 = 0$ and $k_1 = 1369$ constructed according to Eqs. (1) and (2). The numbers in brackets are the HW of the intermediate values. The input value of `poly_reduce()` is the result of Eq. (3).

The presented chosen ciphertext construction method is applicable to the versions of CRYSTALS-Kyber which use five secret key coefficients, i.e. Kyber-768 and Kyber-1024.

5 Profiling Stage

This section describes our profiling strategy.

Table 3. Mapping of intermediate values of `poly_reduce()` and `poly_tomsg()` to secret key coefficients for the chosen ciphertext with $k_0 = 0$ and $k_1 = 1369$. The HW of the values is given in brackets.

Procedure	Variable	−2	−1	0	1	2
`poly_reduce`	input	−591 (11)	1369 (6)	0 (0)	−1369 (11)	591 (6)
	tmp	−3329 (13)	0 (0)	0 (0)	−3329 (13)	0 (0)
	output	2738 (6)	1369 (6)	0 (0)	1960 (6)	591 (6)
`poly_tomsg`	message bit	0	1	0	1	0

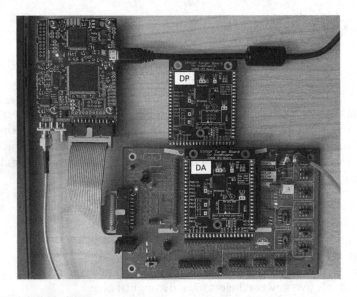

Fig. 5. The equipment used in the experiments. Two different devices, D_P and D_A, are used for the profiling and attack stages, respectively.

5.1 Equipment

The equipment used in the experiments is shown in Fig. 5. It consists of the ChipWhisperer-Lite [18], the CW308 UFO main board [6] and two CW308T-STM32F4 target boards [7]. Each target board contains a 32-bit ARM Cortex-M4 CPU running at 24Mhz.

The C implementation of CRYSTALS-Kyber from [14] is compiled using `arm-none-eabi-gcc` with the highest optimization level -O3.

The traces are acquired using the sampling rate of 96MS/s to have $96/24 = 4$ points per clock cycle.

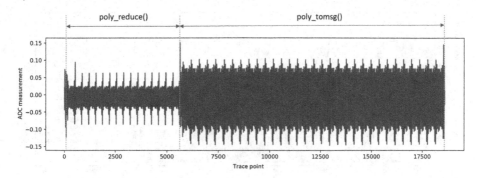

Fig. 6. An average power trace representing the execution of `poly_reduce()` and `poly_tomsg()` procedures of KYBER.CCAKEM.Decap().

5.2 Trace Acquisition

We generate 80K different secret and private key pairs using the key generation algorithm KYBER.CCAKEM.KeyGen(). Then, using the equipment described above, we capture from the profiling device D_P 80K power traces, one per each secret key, during the execution of KYBER.CCAKEM.Decap() with the fixed ciphertext $u = (1369, 0, 0)$ and $v = 0$ as input.

Figure 6 shows the trace segment which we record. It contains `poly_reduce()` and `poly_tomsg()` procedures. From the assembly code in Fig. 4, we can see that there are eight executions of `doublebarrett()` procedure in one loop of `poly_reduce()`. Doublebarrett() computes two secret key coefficients at the same time. Thus, in the beginning of a trace we expect to see $\frac{256}{8 \times 2} = 16$ repeated patterns, where each pattern represents the computation of 16 secret key coefficients by `poly_reduce()`. The 16 patterns are easy to distinguish in Fig. 4.

The trace segment after `poly_reduce()` is the execution of `poly_tomsg()`. It contains 32 similarly looking patterns representing the computation of each message bit and packing of groups of eight bits into a byte by `poly_tomsg()`.

Since the patterns in `poly_reduce()` and `poly_tomsg()` are identical, it is possible to apply the cut-and-join technique of [19] to the training set and expand it to 80K $\times$ 16 = 1.28M for `poly_reduce()` and 80K $\times$ 32 = 2.56M for `poly_tomsg()`.

We also apply standardization to traces. Given a set of traces T with elements $T = (t_1, \ldots, t_{|T|})$, each $T \in T$ is standardized to $T' = (t'_1, \ldots, t'_{|T|})$ such as:

$$t'_i = \frac{t_i - \mu_i}{\sigma_i},$$

where and μ_i and σ_i are the mean and the standard deviation of the elements of T at the ith data point, $i \in \{1, \ldots, |T|\}$.

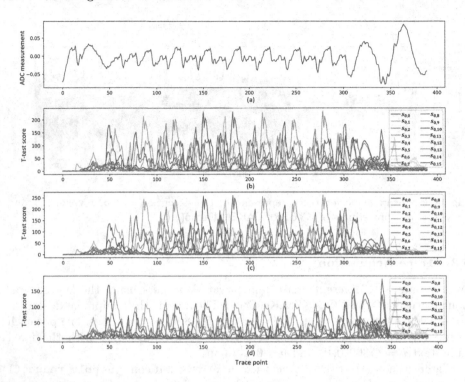

Fig. 7. (a) An average power trace of `poly_reduce()`; (b, c, d) t-test results for the first 16 secret key coefficients for input, tmp, and output variables, respectively. (Color figure online)

5.3   Leakage Analysis

To analyze side-channel information, we use Welch's t-test [31]. The Welch's t-test determines if there is a noticeable difference in the means of T_0 and T_1 by computing:

$$t = \frac{\mu_0 - \mu_1}{\sqrt{\frac{\sigma_0^2}{|T_0|} + \frac{\sigma_1^2}{|T_1|}}},$$

where μ_i and σ_i are the mean and the standard deviation of the set T_i, for $i \in \{0, 1\}$.

Figure 7 shows an average power trace of `poly_reduce()` for $|T| = 100K$ traces and t-test results for the first 16 secret key coefficients for the input, tmp, and output intermediate variables. For a given secret key coefficient $s_{i,j}$, $i \in \{0, 1, 2\}$, $j \in \{0, 1, \ldots, 255\}$, we partition T into two subsets, T_0 and T_1,

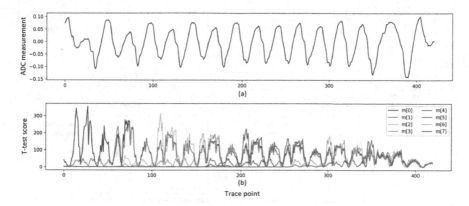

Fig. 8. (a) An average power trace of `poly_tomsg()`; (b) t-test results for the first eight message bits. (Color figure online)

according to the value of the intermediate variables in Table 3. For the input variable, Fig. 7(b) shows the t-test results for the partitioning:

$$T_0 = \{T \in \boldsymbol{T} \mid HW(\text{input}) = 0\},$$
$$T_1 = \{T \in \boldsymbol{T} \mid HW(\text{input}) = 11\}.$$

Since the input variable takes three different values, two other partitionings can be considered: $HW(\text{input}) = 0$ vs $HW(\text{input}) = 6$ and $HW(\text{input}) = 6$ vs $HW(\text{input}) = 11$. The t-tests for these cases look similarly to the one in Fig. 7(b).

Figure 7(c) and (d) show the t-test results for the partitionings $HW(tmp) = 0$ vs $HW(tmp) = 13$ and $HW(\text{output}) = 0$ vs $HW(\text{output}) = 6$ for tmp and output variables, respectively.

Figure 8 shows an average power trace of `poly_tomsg()` on $|\boldsymbol{T}| = 100\text{K}$ traces and t-test results for the first eight message bits. We partition $\boldsymbol{T}$ into two subsets, T_0 and T_1, according to the value of the message bit computed by `poly_tomsg()`:

$$T_0 = \{T \in \boldsymbol{T} \mid m[i] = 0\},$$
$$T_1 = \{T \in \boldsymbol{T} \mid m[i] = 1\}.$$

where $m[i]$ is the ith bit of the message m.

We can see that, for the three intermediate variables of `poly_reduce()` in Fig. 7(b, c, d), the leakage is quite strong. We can also see that the key coefficients are processed in pairs, which is consistent with the assembly code in Fig. 4. For the pairs, the leakage patterns look similarly, except for the corner cases, $s_{0,0}$ and $s_{0,16}$. The corner cases typically differ from the rest.

On the contrary, the leakage patterns in `poly_tomsg()` procedure in Fig. 8(b) are different for all eight message bits. This is becuase in the implementation of `poly_tomsg()` from [14] the message bits are accumulated into a byte array in memory during their processing by poly_tomsg(). As a result, within each byte,

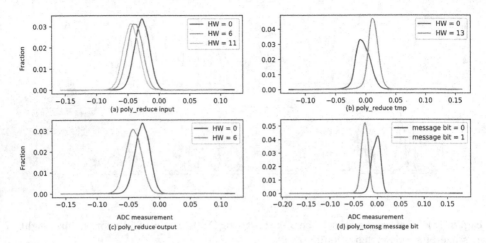

Fig. 9. Distributions of power consumption during the computation of different intermediate variables at trace points with the maximum absolute t-test score. (Color figure online)

the bit which is accumulated first leaks stronger than the bit which is accumulated last. As we mentioned earlier, such type of leakage is called *incremental leakage* in previous work [21].

Figure 9 shows the distributions of power consumption during the computation of four intermediate variables at trace points with the maximum absolute t-test score. The overlap in the distributions determines the difficulty of distinguishing among different values of these variables. We can see that the distributions do not overlap completely, so different values can be distinguished in all four cases.

5.4 MLP Model Training

This section describes how we create four types of neural network models which distinguish secret key coefficients based on the values of four types of intermediate variables in Table 3.

For `poly_reduce()` we assign labels to traces based on the HW of the values in each row of Table 3. For `poly_tomsg()` the message bit values are used as labels. We use four types of multilayer perceptron (MLP) neural networks: $\mathcal{M}^{in}, \mathcal{M}^{tmp}, \mathcal{M}^{out}$ and $\mathcal{M}^{p2m}$, one for each intermediate variable in Table 4.

Note that, in Table 4, the sequences defining the secret key coefficients are not minimal. Any combination of two out of three intermediate variables of `poly_reduce()` together with the message bit of `poly_tomsg()` is sufficient to uniquely define the key coefficients. However, we allow for redundancy in order to detect errors during secret key recovery.

The idea of incorporating redundancy in the construction of chosen ciphertexts is introduced in [19] where the secret key coefficients are mapped into

Table 4. Mapping of MLP's labels to secret key coefficients. The columns define a unique sequence for each coefficient.

Procedure	MLP models	-2	-1	0	1	2
poly_reduce	$\{\mathcal{M}_0^{in}, \cdots, \mathcal{M}_{15}^{in}\}$	1	2	0	1	2
	$\{\mathcal{M}_0^{tmp}, \cdots, \mathcal{M}_{15}^{tmp}\}$	1	0	0	1	0
	$\{\mathcal{M}_0^{out}, \cdots, \mathcal{M}_{15}^{out}\}$	1	1	0	1	1
poly_tomsg	$\{\mathcal{M}_0^{p2m}, \cdots, \mathcal{M}_7^{p2m}\}$	0	1	0	1	0

Table 5. MLP architecture used for four types of models.

Layer type	Output shape
Batch Normalization 1	A
Dense 1 (ReLU)	512
Dense 2 (ReLU)	256
Dense 3 (ReLU)	32
Dense 4 (ReLU)	16
Softmax	B

$\mathcal{M}^{in}$: A = 390, B = 3. $\mathcal{M}^{tmp}$: A = 390, B = 2.
$\mathcal{M}^{out}$: A = 390, B = 2. $\mathcal{M}^{p2m}$: A = 420, B = 2.

the codewords of an $[8, 4, 4]$-extended Hamming code composed from the bits of eight messages (for Saber KEM). This method is further extended in [3] to more powerful codes with code distances up to six for Saber and up to eight for CRYSTALS-Kyber. Another unteresting code-based chosen ciphertext construction method for CRYSTALS-Kyber is presented in [24].

In the code-based methods [3,19,24] the redundancy is added by using more ciphertexts than the minimal number required to obtain a unique mapping pattern between the message bits and the secret key coefficients. In our case, the redundancy is added by employing more intermediate variables as attack points. This allows us to minimize the total number of chosen chipertexts required for the attack to one per module's rank.

Since there are 16 repeated patterns in poly_reduce() and 32 repeated patterns in poly_tomsg(), there is no need to train a model for each secret key coefficient $s_{i,j}$ separately. Instead, we train 16 models for poly_reduce() and 32 models for poly_tomsg() on the cut-and-joined trace sets.

The neural networks with the architecture listed in Table 5 are trained with a batch size of 256 for a maximum of 100 epochs using early stopping with patience 5. We use Nadam optimizer with a learning rate of 0.001 and a numerical stability constant $epsilon$ = 1e-08. Categorical cross-entropy is used as a loss function to evaluate the network classification error. 70% of the training set is used for training and 30% is left for validation. Only the model with the highest validation accuracy is saved.

Table 6. Empirical probability (mean for 100 different secret keys) to recover the secret key from $N \times k$ traces captured from the device under attack D_A for the chosen ciphertext with $k_0 = 0$ and $k_1 = 1369$.

$N \times k$	Single coefficient	Full secret key	Max. # enumerations
1×3	0.9940	0.02	5^{16}
10×3	0.9990	0.43	5^4
20×3	0.9991	0.45	5^3
50×3	0.9994	0.53	5^2
100×3	0.9994	0.53	5^2

Table 7. Empirical probability (mean for 100 different secret keys) to recover the secret key from $N \times k$ traces captured from the profiling device D_P for the chosen ciphertext with $k_0 = 0$ and $k_1 = 1369$.

$N \times k$	Single coefficient	Full secret key	Max. # enumerations
1×3	0.9990	0.47	5^8
10×3	0.9997	0.81	5^3
20×3	0.9997	0.81	5^3
50×3	0.9997	0.81	5^2
100×3	0.9997	0.81	5^2

6   Attack Stage

At the attack stage, we acquire from the device under attack D_A power traces captured during the execution of KYBER.CCAKEM.Decaps() for three chosen ciphertexts constructed using Eqs. (1) and (2) with $k_1 = 1369$ and $k_0 = 0$. Each secret key coefficient $s_{i,j}$ is recovered from the labels predicted by the models ($\mathcal{M}_{j \bmod 16}^{in}, \mathcal{M}_{j \bmod 16}^{tmp}, \mathcal{M}_{j \bmod 16}^{out}, \mathcal{M}_{j \bmod 8}^{p2m}$) using the mapping in Table 4, for all $i \in \{0, 1, 2\}$ and $j \in \{0, 1, \cdots, 255\}$. If the sequence of predicted labels does not match any of the columns in Table 4, the coefficient $s_{i,j}$ is marked as faulty. If there are only a few detected faulty coefficients, they can be recovered by enumerating all possible values for each. To recover the secret key with i faulty coefficients, at most 5^i enumerations are required.

7   Experimental Results

To evaluate the presented side-channel attack method, we generate 100 different secret and private key pairs using KYBER.CCAKEM.KeyGen(). Then, we capture from the device under attack D_A 100 traces for each secret key during the execution of KYBER.CCAKEM.Decap() for the chosen ciphertexts constructed using Eqs. (1) and (2) with $k_1 = 1369$ and $k_0 = 0$.

Table 6 summarizes the results. It lists the empirical probability (mean over 100 tests for different secret keys) to recover a key coefficient and the full secret key from $N \times k$ traces, for module's rank $k = 3$ and the number of repetitions $N \in \{1, 10, 20, 50, 100\}$. Increasing N further does not bring any improvement.

The last column of Table 6 lists the maximum number of enumerations 5^i required to enumerate i coefficients which are marked as faulty. To demonstrate the importance of using a different from profiling device for evaluating full key recovery success rate, we also include the results of the attack on the profiling device D_p, see Table 7. One can see a significant difference in the probabilities of recovering the full secret key in Tables 6 and 7.

Note that the ability to extract a full secret key with 100% probability claimed in some previous works [16, 26] may be the result of using the same device for the profiling and attack, and/or using a small number of secret keys for tests. It is also worth mentioning that the attacks on simulated data, such as [10], may lead to an overestimation of the attack's success rate becuase simulated data typically do not reflect inter-device differences due to manufacturing process variation, aging, wear out, etc.

8   Conclusion

We presented a chosen chipertext side-channel attack which requires a single ciphertext per module rank k to recover the secret key of CRYSTALS-Kyber. We demonstrated the attack on the example of an unprotected software implementation of Kyber-768 from [14] in ARM Cortex-M4 CPU.

A main contribution of the paper is the idea to create a unique mapping between the secret key coefficients and multiple intermediate variables within the same execution of an algorithm. In this paper, we use intermediate variables of the Barret reduction and message decoding steps of decryption. However, other intermediate variables, e.g. from the re-encryption step of decapsulation, can potentially be used in the attack. By using multiple intermediate variables, we add redundancy which enables us to detect of errors in the recovered secret key coefficients while, at the same time, minimizing the total number of chosen chipertexts required for the attack.

We are currently working on extending the presented attack to the first-order masked implementation of CRYSTALS-Kyber from [11]. This is a challenging problem because the `poly_reduce` procedure's input is protected by the arithmetic masking. Note that the attack on the arithmetic masking presented in [10] only addresses the special case in which the secret key is masked during decryption, but not the input. In the implementation [11], the input of the inverse NTT is masked, it consists of two polynomials representing the shares. Since the assumption on a sparse input to the inverse NTT does not hold when the input is masked, the attack presented in [10] is not applicable to the general case. The general case remains an open problem.

Acknowledgments. This work was supported in part by the Swedish Civil Contingencies Agency (Grant No. 2020-11632) and the Swedish Research Council (Grant No. 2018-04482).

References

1. Announcing the commercial national security algorithm suite 2.0. National Security Agency, U.S Department of Defense, September 2022. https://media.defense.gov/2022/Sep/07/2003071834/-1/-1/0/CSA_CNSA_2.0_ALGORITHMS_.PDF
2. Azouaoui, M., Kuzovkova, Y., Schneider, T., van Vredendaal, C.: Post-quantum authenticated encryption against chosen-ciphertext side-channel attacks. Cryptology ePrint Archive, Paper 2022/916 (2022). https://eprint.iacr.org/2022/916
3. Backlund, L., Ngo, K., Gartner, J., Dubrova, E.: Secret key recovery attacks on masked and shuffled implementations of CRYSTALS-Kyber and Saber. Cryptology ePrint Archive, Paper 2022/1692 (2022). https://eprint.iacr.org/2022/1692
4. Bhasin, S., D'Anvers, J.P., Heinz, D., Pöppelmann, T., Beirendonck, M.V.: Attacking and defending masked polynomial comparison for lattice-based cryptography. Cryptology ePrint Archive, Paper 2021/104 (2021). https://eprint.iacr.org/2021/104
5. Bos, J.W., Gourjon, M., Renes, J., Schneider, T., van Vredendaal, C.: Masking kyber: first- and higher-order implementations. IACR Trans. Cryptogr. Hardw. Embed. Syst. **2021**(4), 173–214 (2021). https://doi.org/10.46586/tches.v2021.i4.173-214
6. CW308 UFO Board. https://rtfm.newae.com/Targets/CW308
7. CW308T-STM32F4 target board. https://rtfm.newae.com/Targets/UFO
8. D'Anvers, J.P., Beirendonck, M.V., Verbauwhede, I.: Revisiting higher-order masked comparison for lattice-based cryptography: algorithms and bit-sliced implementations. Cryptology ePrint Archive, Paper 2022/110 (2022). https://eprint.iacr.org/2022/110
9. Fujisaki, E., Okamoto, T.: Secure integration of asymmetric and symmetric encryption schemes. In: Wiener, M. (ed.) CRYPTO 1999. LNCS, vol. 1666, pp. 537–554. Springer, Heidelberg (1999). https://doi.org/10.1007/3-540-48405-1_34
10. Hamburg, M., et al.: Chosen ciphertext k-trace attacks on masked cca2 secure kyber. IACR Trans. Cryptogr. Hardw. Embed. Syst. **2021**(4), 88–113 (2021). https://doi.org/10.46586/tches.v2021.i4.88-113
11. Heinz, D., Kannwischer, M.J., Land, G., Pöppelmann, T., Schwabe, P., Sprenkels, D.: First-order masked Kyber on ARM Cortex-M4. Cryptology ePrint Archive, Paper 2022/058 (2022). https://eprint.iacr.org/2022/058
12. Hoffmann, C., Libert, B., Momin, C., Peters, T., Standaert, F.X.: Towards leakage-resistant post-quantum CCA-secure public key encryption. Cryptology ePrint Archive, Paper 2022/873 (2022). https://eprint.iacr.org/2022/873
13. Ji, Y., Wang, R., Ngo, K., Dubrova, E., Backlund, L.: A side-channel attack on a hardware implementation of CRYSTALS-Kyber. Cryptology ePrint Archive, Paper 2022/1452 (2022). https://eprint.iacr.org/2022/1452
14. Kannwischer, M.J., Petri, R., Rijneveld, J., Schwabe, P., Stoffelen, K.: PQM4: post-quantum crypto library for the ARM Cortex-M4. https://github.com/mupq/pqm4
15. Moody, D.: Status report on the third round of the NIST post-quantum cryptography standardization process. Nistir 8309, pp. 1–27 (2022). https://nvlpubs.nist.gov/nistpubs/ir/2022/NIST.IR.8413.pdf

16. Mu, J., et al.: A voltage template attack on the modular polynomial subtraction in Kyber. In: 2022 27th Asia and South Pacific Design Automation Conference (ASP-DAC), pp. 672–677. IEEE (2022)
17. Mujdei, C., Beckers, A., Mera, J.M.B., Karmakar, A., Wouters, L., Verbauwhede, I.: Side-channel analysis of lattice-based post-quantum cryptography: Exploiting polynomial multiplication. Cryptology ePrint Archive, Report 2022/474 (2022). https://eprint.iacr.org/2022/474
18. NewAE Technology Inc.: Chipwhisperer. https://newae.com/tools/chipwhisperer
19. Ngo, K., Dubrova, E., Guo, Q., Johansson, T.: A side-channel attack on a masked IND-CCA secure saber KEM implementation. IACR Trans. Cryptographic Hardware Embed. Syst. **2021**(4), 676–707 (2021). https://doi.org/10.46586/tches.v2021.i4.676-707
20. Pessl, P., Primas, R.: More practical single-trace attacks on the number theoretic transform. In: Schwabe, P., Thériault, N. (eds.) LATINCRYPT 2019. LNCS, vol. 11774, pp. 130–149. Springer, Cham (2019). https://doi.org/10.1007/978-3-030-30530-7_7
21. Ravi, P., Bhasin, S., Roy, S.S., Chattopadhyay, A.: On exploiting message leakage in (Few) NIST PQC candidates for practical message recovery attacks. IEEE Trans. Inf. Forensics Secur. **17**, 684–699 (2022). https://doi.org/10.1109/TIFS.2021.3139268
22. Rodriguez, R.C., Bruguier, F., Valea, E., Benoit, P.: Correlation electromagnetic analysis on an FPGA implementation of CRYSTALS-Kyber. Cryptology ePrint Archive, Paper 2022/1361 (2022). https://eprint.iacr.org/2022/1361, https://eprint.iacr.org/2022/1361
23. Schwabe, P., et al.: CRYSTALS-Kyber algorithm specifications and supporting documentation (2020). https://pq-crystals.org/kyber/data/kyber-specification-round3-20210131.pdf
24. Shen, M., Cheng, C., Zhang, X., Guo, Q., Jiang, T.: Find the bad apples: an efficient method for perfect key recovery under imperfect SCA oracles - a case study of Kyber. Cryptology ePrint Archive, Paper 2022/563 (2022). https://eprint.iacr.org/2022/563
25. Sim, B.Y., et al.: Single-trace attacks on message encoding in lattice-based KEMs. IEEE Access **8**, 183175–183191 (2020)
26. Sim, B.-Y., Park, A., Han, D.-G.: Chosen-ciphertext clustering attack on CRYSTALS-KYBER using the side-channel leakage of barrett reduction. IEEE Internet Things J. **9**(21), 21382–21397 (2022). https://doi.org/10.1109/JIOT.2022.3179683
27. Tsai, T.T., Huang, S.S., Tseng, Y.M., Chuang, Y.H., Hung, Y.H.: Leakage-resilient certificate-based authenticated key exchange protocol. IEEE Open J. Comput. Soc. **3**, 137–148 (2022). https://doi.org/10.1109/OJCS.2022.3198073
28. Ueno, R., Xagawa, K., Tanaka, Y., Ito, A., Takahashi, J., Homma, N.: Curse of re-encryption: a generic power/EM analysis on post-quantum KEMs. IACR Trans. Cryptogr. Hardw. Embed. Syst. **2022**(1), 296–322 (2021). https://doi.org/10.46586/tches.v2022.i1.296-322
29. Wang, J., Cao, W., Chen, H., Li, H.: Practical side-channel attack on masked message encoding in latticed-based KEM. Cryptology ePrint Archive, Paper 2022/859 (2022). https://eprint.iacr.org/2022/859
30. Wang, R., Ngo, K., Dubrova, E.: A message recovery attack on LWE/LWR-based PKE/KEMs using amplitude-modulated EM emanations. In: Proceedings of the 25th Annual International Conference on Information Security and Cryptology (2022). https://eprint.iacr.org/2022/852

31. Welch, B.L.: The generalization of 'Student's' problem when several different population variances are involved. Biometrika **34**(1–2), 28–35 (1947)
32. Xu, Z., Pemberton, O., Roy, S.S., Oswald, D., Yao, W., Zheng, Z.: Magnifying side-channel leakage of lattice-based cryptosystems with chosen ciphertexts: the case study of Kyber. IEEE Trans. Comput. **71**(9), 2163–2176 (2022). https://doi.org/10.1109/TC.2021.3122997
33. Chang, Y., Yan, Y., Zhu, C., Guo, P.: Template attack of LWE/LWR-based schemes with cyclic message rotation. Entropy **24**, 1489 (2022). https://doi.org/10.3390/e24101489

A New Keyed Hash Function Based on Latin Squares and Error-Correcting Codes to Authenticate Users in Smart Home Environments

Hussain Ahmad$^{(\boxtimes)}$ (ID) and Carolin Hannusch (ID)

Department of Computer Science, Faculty of Informatics, University of Debrecen,
Kassai út 26, Debrecen 4028, Hungary
{hussain.ahmad,hannusch.carolin}@inf.unideb.hu

Abstract. We introduce the scheme of a keyed hash function, also called message authentication code (MAC) based on previously given latin squares and binary linear error-correcting codes. We investigate the properties of the introduced scheme regarding its security and applicability. Further, we give a possible application in a smart home environment, especially for opening the entrance door to a house by using a mobile device.

Keywords: Keyed hash function · message authentication code · smart home · latin square · error-correcting codes

1 Introduction

1.1 Motivation

Smart homes have become more and more present in our lives. Parallel to the development of smart home environments, their security also needs to be considered [11]. The aim of the current paper is to introduce a keyed hash function (message authentication code MAC) based on a given latin square and a fixed binary linear error-correcting code. We want to apply the introduced hash function to authenticate users in a smart home environment.

1.2 Preliminaries

Latin squares have a wide literature, as well as error-correcting codes have. We direct the reader for some fundamental literature about latin squares to [12] and about linear codes to [18]. Recently, a program package named Torch was introduced [9]. This program package can be used for the fast generation of linear codes and it can be implemented in a software. Hash functions have played an important role in cryptography for the last decades. There exists a huge literature about hash functions. We direct the reader for some fundamental

S. El Hajji et al. (Eds.): C2SI 2023, LNCS 13874, pp. 129–135, 2023.
https://doi.org/10.1007/978-3-031-33017-9_8

literature about hash functions to [13,15]. An overview of cryptographic non-keyed hash functions is given in [23] and some literature about cryptographic keyed hash functions (message authentication codes) can be found in [19,20]. Several approaches for unkeyed hash functions have been made [6–8,24] as well as for keyed hash functions [10,21,25], for identification in small devices [1], using latin squares in hash functions [5,17], even regarding critical sets of latin squares [2] and applying error-correcting codes in hash functions [4]; to mention some results of the last years without claim of completeness.

2 Definitions and Notations

Latin Squares. A **latin square** L is an $n \times n$ square containing n distinct symbols exactly once in each row and each column. Then each row and each column of L determines a **permutation** of the **symmetric group** S_n. We denote the permutations determined by the rows by $\sigma_1, \ldots, \sigma_n$ and the permutations determined by the columns by $\tau_1, \ldots, \tau_n$. The cardinality of S_n is $n! = 1 \cdot 2 \cdot \ldots \cdot n$. The number of latin squares is known for $n \leq 11$ (A002860 in [16]).

Error-Correcting Codes. A **binary linear code** of length N is a subspace of the N-dimensional vector space over the finite field with two elements $\mathbb{F}_2$. A linear code is called **error-correcting code** if it can correct at least 1 error, which occurred in the communication channel. The distance of two codewords is the number of distinct coordinates. The **minimum distance** of a linear code is the minimum of all occurring distances between its codewords. It is well known, that if the minimum distance of a linear code is d, then the code can correct up to $\lfloor \frac{d-1}{2} \rfloor$ errors. The number of all k-dimensional subspaces of $\mathbb{F}_2$ is $\binom{N}{k}_2$, where $\binom{N}{k}_2$ denotes the Gaussian polynomial coefficient ([14], p. 698).

3 Protocol of the Hash Function

In this section, we give the protocol for a new hash function based on a given latin square and a given binary linear code.

Input. Let L be a latin square of order n. Let $m = (m_1, \ldots, m_k)$ be a binary string of length k. Then let C be a binary linear code of length N and dimension k and let G be a generator matrix for C.

Computing the Hash Value. Choose a set $I_1 \times I_2 \subseteq \{1, \ldots, n\} \times \{1, \ldots, n\}$ and compute

$$\rho := \prod_{i \in I_1} \sigma_i \prod_{j \in I_2} \tau_j.$$

Then compute $(mG)^\rho$ (which means multiply m with G and apply the permutation ρ on the columns of the product).

Output. Finally, determine its value in the binary number system. Thus

$$hash(m) = (mG)^\rho_{BINARY}.$$

4   Properties of the Hash Function

According to Sect. 9.2.2 in [15] a good hash function has to fulfill the following properties: deterministic, pre-image resistance, second pre-image resistance and strong collision resistance. In this section, we investigate our hash function introduced in Sect. 3 regarding these properties:

Deterministic. Since G and ρ are fixed in the protocol, it follows that $m_1 = m_2$ implies $hash(m_1) = hash(m_2)$.

Pre-image Resistance. Let us assume $y = hash(m)$ is given. In order to find m, we need to find ρ, for which we have $n!$ possibilities and G, for which there exist $\binom{N}{k}_2$ possibilities. Thus, if n is large enough, then it is computational infeasible to compute m from y.

Second Pre-image Resistance. Given m_1 and $hash(m_1)$, we want to find m_2, such that $hash(m_1) = hash(m_2)$. We denote $m_1 = (a_1, \ldots, a_k)$ and $m_2 = (b_1, \ldots, b_k)$ and

$$G = \begin{pmatrix} g_{1,1} & \cdots & g_{1,N} \\ g_{2,1} & \cdots & g_{2,N} \\ \vdots & & \\ g_{k,1} & \cdots & g_{k,N} \end{pmatrix}.$$

Thus we need to solve

$$(m_1 G)^\rho = (m_2 G)^\rho$$

and therefore we have to solve the following system of binary equations.

$$\sum_{i=1}^{k} a_i g_{i,j} = \sum_{i=1}^{k} b_i g_{i,j} \ \forall j = 1, \ldots, N \tag{1}$$

Since $g_{i,j}$ is fix and $g_{i,j} \in \{0, 1\}$ for each $1 \leq i \leq k$ and $1 \leq j \leq N$, there is no relation between a_i and b_i which is true for each $1 \leq i \leq k$. Thus it is computational infeasible to determine m_2 from m_1.

Strong Collision Resistance. In order to find a pair of messages m_1 and m_2, such that $hash(m_1) = hash(m_2)$, we need to solve the system of Eq. 1. Again, there is no relation between two distinct solutions of these equations, therefore it is computational infeasible to find such a pair if n is large enough.

5   Application in Smart Home Environment

Imagine, Bob arrives home, but he forgot his key at his workplace. Unfortunately, Alice is also out for the whole evening, so Bob cannot enter the house. Bob just grabs his smartphone in order to call Alice, when realizing that they built in a smart door system. Bob turns on the display, which will show a latin square.

Then Bob will open the corresponding software (app) on his mobile device and scan the latin square. The software knows the necessary keys, so it can compute Bob's hash value. Since Bob is an authorized person for entering the house, the hash value will be accepted by the smart door system and the system will finally open the door (see Fig. 1).

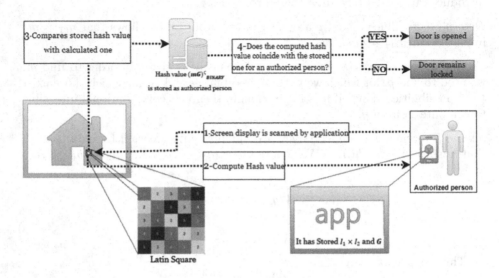

Fig. 1. Application in smart door system

Keysize. The matrix G contains $n \cdot k$ entries, the cardinality of the set $I_1 \times I_2$ is at most n^2, the permutation ρ can be stored as a product of cycles moving at most n elements.

Storage. For a message (identifier) m we have $1 \leq hash(m) \leq 2^N - 1$, which has to be stored for each authorized person t-times, if each authorized person has t identifiers. Furthermore, we need to store latin squares, sets $I_1 \times I_2$ and the generator matrices. How many we store of each of these, is actually due to the implementation and can be customized for individual needs.

Computational Capability. The mobile device has to compute ρ from the latin square, i.e. it must be able to compute the product of $2n$ permutations in acceptable time. Further, it has to compute mG, which is a vector-matrix multiplication, and apply the permutation ρ to mG, which means mixing up the coordinates of mG. Finally it has to compute the value of $(mG)^\rho$ in binary number system, which means it must be able to compute $\sum_{i=0}^{N-1} a_i \cdot 2^i$ in acceptable time, where $a_i \in \{0, 1\}$.

6   Security of the Smart Door System

Let us assume that each authorized person has $m_1, \ldots, m_t$ identifiers of length k. We denote the hash values of the identifiers by

$$H_1 = (m_1 G)^\rho_{BINARY}$$

$$\vdots$$

$$H_t = (m_t G)^\rho_{BINARY}.$$

We have

$$1 \leq H_i \leq 2^N - 1$$

for each H_i, where $i = 1, \ldots, t$. Then the security of the smart door system can be scaled by increasing t and k.

Every linear code has a minimum distance. Within the known bounds [3] we can choose the minimum distance d. Since we want C to be an error-correcting code, we need to choose $d \geq 4$. The used linear code C, as well as its generator matrix G should be kept as a secret, which implies that d is also kept as a secret. Therefore, an unauthorized person who wants to attack the hash function has to find the generator matrix G. The number of possible matrices G is $\binom{N}{k}_2 \cdot n! \cdot k!$, since $\binom{N}{k}_2$ is the number of all k-dimensional subspaces of $\mathbb{F}_2^N$ and in each generator matrix permuting the rows and columns changes the matrix.

Actually, the number of all possible latin squares is not known for $n > 11$. Therefore if $n > 11$ and the latin square L of order n is kept as a secret, then it is computational infeasible for an unauthorized person to find L. In fact, for the protocol of the hash function, we do not need to know L, but just the permutation ρ. A permutation can be tried in brute-force attack and since $\rho \in S_n$, we have $n!$ possibilities for ρ. Since the latin square L can be seen on the display also by unauthorized persons, $I_1 \times I_2$ has to be kept as a secret necessarily.

Note that the security of the introduced protocol can be customized according to computational capability of devices, since we can increase n and N theoretically to infinity.

7   Conclusion and Future Work

We introduced a protocol for a keyed hash function (message authentication code), whose security is based on well-known mathematical facts. The introduced hash function fulfills all required properties for a good and useful hash function. Its strength is its security, which can be customized to actual needs for protection against brute-force attacks in accordance with computational capability of mobile and small devices. It's the task of future work to create a software in order to realize an application for mobile devices in combination with a smart home environment. Using the Torch program package [9] we can create generator matrices for binary linear codes. The scanning of latin squares can work similarly to the scanning of QR codes [22]. It's up to further research work to combine these results efficiently and finalize a software of the introduced smart door system.

References

1. Ayebie, E.B., Assidi, H., Souidi, E.M.: An efficient identification scheme based on rank metric. In: Benzekri, A., Barbeau, M., Gong, G., Laborde, R., Garcia-Alfaro, J. (eds.) FPS 2019. LNCS, vol. 12056, pp. 273–289. Springer, Cham (2020). https://doi.org/10.1007/978-3-030-45371-8_17
2. Chum, C.S., Zhang, X.: Applying hash functions in the Latin square based secret sharing schemes. In: Security and Management, pp. 197–203 (2010)
3. Conway, J.H., Sloane, N.J.A.: A new upper bound on the minimal distance of self-dual codes. IEEE Trans. Inf. Theory **36**(6), 1319–1333 (1990)
4. Cramer, R., Damgård, I.B., Döttling, N., Fehr, S., Spini, G.: Linear secret sharing schemes from error correcting codes and universal hash functions. In: Oswald, E., Fischlin, M. (eds.) EUROCRYPT 2015. LNCS, vol. 9057, pp. 313–336. Springer, Heidelberg (2015). https://doi.org/10.1007/978-3-662-46803-6_11
5. Ghosh, R., Verma, S., Kumar, R., Kumar, S., Ram, S.: Design of hash algorithm using Latin square. Procedia Comput. Sci. **46**, 759–765 (2015)
6. Gnatyuk, S., Kinzeryavyy, V., Kyrychenko, K., Yubuzova, K., Aleksander, M., Odarchenko, R.: Secure hash function constructing for future communication systems and networks. In: Hu, Z., Petoukhov, S.V., He, M. (eds.) AIMEE2018 2018. AISC, vol. 902, pp. 561–569. Springer, Cham (2020). https://doi.org/10.1007/978-3-030-12082-5_51
7. Grassi, L., Khovratovich, D., Rechberger, C., Roy, A., Schofnegger, M.: Poseidon: a new hash function for zero-knowledge proof systems. In: 30th USENIX Security Symposium (USENIX Security 21), pp. 519–535 (2021)
8. Hannusch, C., Horváth, G.: Properties of hash functions based on Gluškov product of automata. J. Autom. Lang. Comb. **26**(1–2), 55–65 (2021)
9. Hannusch, C., Major, S. R.: Torch: software package for the search of linear binary codes. In: 2022 IEEE 2nd Conference on Information Technology and Data Science (CITDS), pp. 103–106, IEEE (2022)
10. Hussain, S.S., Farooq, S.M., Ustun, T.S.: Analysis and implementation of message authentication code (MAC) algorithms for GOOSE message security. IEEE Access **7**, 80980–80984 (2019)
11. Huszti, A., Kovács, S., Oláh, N.: Scalable, password-based and threshold authentication for smart homes. Int. J. Inf. Sec., 1–17 (2022)
12. Keedwell, A.D., Dénes, J.: Latin Squares and Their Applications. Elsevier, Amsterdam (2015)
13. Knuth, D.E.: The Art of Computer Programming, vol. 3. Sorting and Searching (1973)
14. MacWilliams, F.J., Sloane, N.J.A.: The Theory of Error Correcting Codes, vol. 16. Elsevier, Amsterdam (1977)
15. Menezes, A.J., Van Oorschot, P.C., Vanstone, S.A.: Handbook of Applied Cryptography. CRC Press, Boca Raton (2018)
16. OEIS Foundation Inc. (2022). The On-Line Encyclopedia of Integer Sequences, Published electronically at http://oeis.org
17. Pal, S.K., Kapoor, S., Arora, A., Chaudhary, R., Khurana, J.: Design of strong cryptographic schemes based on Latin squares. J. Discr. Math. Sci. Crypt. **13**(3), 233–256 (2010)
18. Pless, V., Brualdi, R.A., Huffman, W.C.: Handbook of Coding Theory. Elsevier Science Inc., Amsterdam (1998)

19. Preneel, B.: Cryptanalysis of message authentication codes. In: Okamoto, E., Davida, G., Mambo, M. (eds.) ISW 1997. LNCS, vol. 1396, pp. 55–65. Springer, Heidelberg (1998). https://doi.org/10.1007/BFb0030408
20. Preneel, B., Van Oorschot, P.C.: On the security of iterated message authentication codes. IEEE Trans. Inf. Theory **45**(1), 188–199 (1999)
21. Ramadhani, F., Ramadhani, U., Basit, L.: Combination of hybrid cryptography in one time pad (OTP) algorithm and keyed-hash message authentication code (HMAC) in securing the Whatsapp communication application. J. Comput. Sci. Inf. Technol. Telecommun. Eng. **1**(1), 31–36 (2020)
22. Rouillard, J.: Contextual QR codes. In: 2008 The Third International Multi-Conference on Computing in the Global Information Technology (ICCGI 2008), pp. 50–55. IEEE (2008)
23. Sobti, R., Geetha, G.: Cryptographic hash functions: a review. Int. J. Comput. Sci. Issues (IJCSI) **9**(2), 461 (2012)
24. Teh, J.S., Alawida, M., Ho, J.J.: Unkeyed hash function based on chaotic sponge construction and fixed-point arithmetic. Nonlinear Dyn. **100**(1), 713–729 (2020)
25. Wang, Y., Chen, L., Wang, X., Wu, G., Yu, K., Lu, T.: The design of keyed hash function based on CNN-MD structure. Chaos, Solitons Fractals **152**, 111443 (2021)

Attack on a Code-Based Signature Scheme from QC-LDPC Codes

Theo Fanuela Prabowo[✉][ID] and Chik How Tan[ID]

Temasek Laboratories, National University of Singapore, Singapore, Singapore
{tsltfp,tsltch}@nus.edu.sg

Abstract. Meneghetti, Picozzi, and Tognolini proposed a Hamming-metric code-based digital signature scheme from QC-LDPC codes in [10]. Using quasi cyclic codes enables the scheme to have small key sizes, while the structure of LDPC codes helps to achieve good overall performance. In this paper, we discuss the security of this code-based signature scheme. In particular, we present a partial key recovery attack that uses a statistical method to recover an important part of the secret key. Using a proof-of-concept Sagemath implementation, we are able to recover part of the secret key using as few as 25 signatures in less than 2 minutes for all proposed parameter sets. Furthermore, we follow up this partial key recovery attack by a forgery attack.

1 Introduction

Code-based cryptography is the study of cryptographic schemes whose security relies on the hardness of some coding-theoretic problems, such as the syndrome decoding problem and the codeword finding problem. Both of these problems have been shown to be NP-hard [4,14]. As such, solving these problems are believed to be hard even for quantum computers. Over the years, a number of code-based cryptographic schemes have been proposed. These include some promising key encapsulation mechanisms called BIKE [2], Classic McEliece [3] and HQC [1], which become fourth-round candidates in the NIST call for post-quantum cryptography standardization.

Unlike encryption and key encapsulation mechanisms, the construction of code-based digital signature schemes seems to be more challenging. This is indicated by the absence of code-based signature scheme in the second round onwards of the NIST PQC standardization. Many code-based signature schemes have been proposed in the literature, such as CFS [5], Wave [8] (which are constructed using the hash-and-sign framework) and Stern [13], CVA [6] (which are constructed using the Fiat-Shamir framework). However, most of them are inefficient or have large key or signature sizes. Some of the proposed code-based signatures were even found to be insecure. For example, the KKS signature [9] is shown to be insecure in [11]; and the signature proposed in [12] is shown to be insecure in [7].

S. El Hajji et al. (Eds.): C2SI 2023, LNCS 13874, pp. 136–149, 2023.
https://doi.org/10.1007/978-3-031-33017-9_9

Meneghetti, Picozzi, and Tognolini try to address this problem by proposing a digital signature scheme from QC-LDPC codes in [10]. Using 2-quasi-cyclic codes allows them to have relatively small key sizes, while the use of sparse matrices (low density parity check matrices) makes the computation more efficient. Three parameter sets were proposed in [10], targeting 128, 192, and 256-bit security level respectively.

It is noted in [10, Sect. 7] that the distribution of α (which is a part of the signature) is distinguishable from the distribution of random parameters. This calls for further security analysis of the signature scheme. In this paper, we discuss the security of the signature scheme. In particular, we propose a partial key recovery attack which uses statistical method to recover an important part y of the long term secret key. Moreover, we extend it into a forgery attack. The rest of this paper is organized as follows. In Sect. 2, we setup some notations and give a brief review of the signature scheme proposed in [10]. We then give some theoretical results which are helpful to analyze our attack in Sect. 3. The proposed partial key recovery and forgery attacks are described in Sect. 4. This is followed by a discussion on some simulation results from our Sagemath implementation of the attack in Sect. 5. Finally, the paper is concluded in Sect. 6.

2 Preliminaries

2.1 Notations

Let $\mathbb{F}_2$ be the finite field of two elements and let $\mathcal{R} := \mathbb{F}_2[X]/(X^n - 1)$ be the quotient ring of polynomials over $\mathbb{F}_2$ of degree less than n. Given $a = a_0 + a_1 X + \ldots + a_{n-1} X^{n-1} \in \mathcal{R}$, we denote $\overline{a} := (a_0, a_1, \ldots, a_{n-1}) \in \mathbb{F}_2^n$. We define $\mathrm{wt}(a)$ to be the Hamming weight of the vector $\overline{a}$, i.e. $\mathrm{wt}(a)$ denotes the number of nonzero coefficients in a. Denote $\mathcal{V}_{n,w} := \{a \in \mathcal{R} = \mathbb{F}_2[X]/(X^n - 1) \mid \mathrm{wt}(a) = w\}$.

Let $a, b \in \mathcal{R}$ and $c = ab$. Then $\overline{c} = (c_0, c_1, \ldots, c_{n-1})$ can be computed via the following matrix multiplication:

$$(c_0, c_1, \ldots, c_{n-1})^T = \mathrm{circ}(a) \cdot (b_0, b_1, \ldots, b_{n-1})^T,$$

where

$$\mathrm{circ}(a) := \begin{pmatrix} a_0 & a_{n-1} & \ldots & a_1 \\ a_1 & a_0 & \ldots & a_2 \\ \vdots & \vdots & \ddots & \vdots \\ a_{n-1} & a_{n-2} & \ldots & a_0 \end{pmatrix}.$$

For $0 \leq i \leq n - 1$, let $a^{(i)}$ denote the i-th row of $\mathrm{circ}(a)$. Then $c_i = a^{(i)} \cdot \overline{b}^T$.

2.2 MPT Signature Scheme

In this section, we present the Hamming-metric code-based digital signature scheme from QC-LDPC codes proposed by Meneghetti, Picozzi, and Tognolini in [10], which we shall refer to as the MPT signature scheme. Given the public parameters consisting of some integers $n, \omega, \omega_{pq}, \omega_r$ and two intervals I, I_t, the MPT signature scheme is as follows.

Algorithm 1: Key Generation of MPT Signature Scheme

    Input   : security parameter λ
    Output: $pk = (h, s)$ and $sk = (y, q)$
1 Choose $x, y \in \mathcal{V}_{n,\omega}$
2 Choose $p, q \in \mathcal{V}_{n,\omega_{pq}}$
3 Compute $h := pq^{-1}$ in $\mathcal{R}$
4 Compute $s := x + hy$ in $\mathcal{R}$
5 The public key is $pk = (h, s)$ and the secret key is $sk = (y, q)$

Algorithm 2: Signing of MPT Signature Scheme

    Input   : message m, $pk = (h, s)$ and $sk = (y, q)$
    Output: signature σ
1 Generate a random bitstring nonce
2 Compute $r := \mathcal{H}(m\|pk\|\text{nonce}) \in \mathcal{V}_{n,\omega_r}$
3 Choose $t \in R$ such that $\text{wt}(t) \in I_t$
4 Compute $\alpha := qt + ry$ and $\beta := \alpha h + sr$ in $\mathcal{R}$
5 **if** $\text{wt}(\alpha) \notin I$ *or* $\text{wt}(\beta) \notin I$ **then**
6 | repeat from Step 1
7 **else**
8 | the signature is $\sigma = (\alpha, \text{nonce})$
9 **end if**

Algorithm 3: Verification of MPT Signature Scheme

    Input   : message m, pk, signature $\sigma = (\alpha, \text{nonce})$
    Output: validity of the signature
1 Compute $r := \mathcal{H}(m\|pk\|\text{nonce}) \in \mathcal{V}_{n,\omega_r}$
2 Compute $\beta := \alpha h + sr$ in $\mathcal{R}$
3 **if** $\text{wt}(\alpha) \in I$ *and* $\text{wt}(\beta) \in I$ **then**
4 | the signature is valid
5 **else**
6 | the signature is invalid
7 **end if**

In [10], the parameter is chosen with the following guideline: ω, ω_{pq} are odd integers with $\omega, \omega_{pq} \approx \sqrt{n}$; ω_r is an even integer with $\omega_r \approx 3\log(n)$. The interval $I_t = [\lceil \frac{\sqrt{n}}{2} \rceil, \lceil \frac{2\sqrt{n}}{3} \rceil]$. The parameters for various security levels are given in the following Table 1.

Table 1. The parameters of the MPT signature

Name	λ	n	I	$\omega = \omega_{pq}$	ω_r	I_t
Para-1	128	14627	[5339, 6515]	121	42	[61, 81]
Para-2	192	18143	[6601, 7981]	135	42	[68, 90]
Para-3	256	21067	[7620, 9186]	145	44	[73, 97]

Remark 1. *The parameters are chosen in such a way that the condition in Step 4 of Algorithm 2 (namely that* wt(α) $\notin I$ *or* wt(β) $\notin I$) *happens only with probability about* 10^{-10} *(negligible). One may thus assume that no repetition is needed during the signing, which is true with overwhelming probability.*

3   Deciding Between Two Bernoulli Distributions

In our attack, we will need to distinguish between two Bernoulli distributions from a given set of samples (obtained from a collection of signatures). This can be done using the threshold criterion which will be discussed in this section.

Let $0 < p < 1$. We denote the Bernoulli probability distribution with parameter p by $\mathcal{B}(p)$. By definition, if x is sampled from $\mathcal{B}(p)$, then $x = 1$ with probability p and $x = 0$ with probability $1 - p$.

3.1   Deciding a Distribution via Threshold Criterion

Suppose we have a collection of numbers $x^{(1)}, x^{(2)}, \ldots, x^{(N)}$ sampled independently from a probability distribution $\mathcal{D}$. It is known that $\mathcal{D}$ is either $\mathcal{B}(p_0)$ or $\mathcal{B}(p_1)$ for some $0 < p_0 < p_1 < 1$. Given p_0, p_1, and the samples $x^{(1)}, x^{(2)}, \ldots, x^{(N)}$, one may decide whether $\mathcal{D} = \mathcal{B}(p_0)$ or $\mathcal{B}(p_1)$ using a simple threshold criterion as described in the following Algorithm 4.

Algorithm 4: Threshold criterion

---

1 fix δ satisfying $p_0 < \delta < p_1$
2 $x = x^{(1)} + x^{(2)} + \ldots + x^{(N)}$
3 **if** $x < \delta N$ *(or equivalently $x/N < \delta$)* **then**
4 $\quad$ | $\quad \mathcal{D} = \mathcal{B}(p_0)$
5 **else**
6 $\quad$ | $\quad \mathcal{D} = \mathcal{B}(p_1)$
7 **end if**

The threshold criterion intuitively will correctly identify the distribution $\mathcal{D}$ when the number of samples are sufficiently large except with some small error probability. In this subsection, we shall derive a bound for the error probability. We shall need the following result.

Theorem 1 (Chernoff Bound). *Let* $X = \sum_{u=1}^{M} x^{(u)}$, *where* $x^{(u)}$ *are independent and identically distributed random variables with* $x^{(u)} \sim \mathcal{B}(p)$. *Then*

(i) $\Pr[X \leq (1-\gamma)pM] \leq \exp(-\frac{\gamma^2}{2}pM)$ *for all* $0 < \gamma < 1$.

(ii) $\Pr[X \geq (1+\gamma)pM] \leq \exp(-\frac{\gamma^2}{2+\gamma}pM)$ *for all* $\gamma > 0$.

We now consider the probability that we incorrectly decide $\mathcal{D} = \mathcal{B}(p_1)$ (while actually $\mathcal{D} = \mathcal{B}(p_0)$). This decision is made if and only if $\sum_{u=1}^{N} x^{(u)} \geq \delta N$. We denote this probability by ε_0, i.e. set

$$\varepsilon_0 := \Pr\left[\sum_{u=1}^{N} x^{(u)} \geq \delta N \mid x^{(u)} \sim \mathcal{B}(p_0)\right].$$

As $x^{(u)} \sim \mathcal{B}(p_0)$ for each u, we have $x^{(u)} = 1$ (resp. $x^{(u)} = 0$) with probability p_0 (resp. $1 - p_0$). In order to have $\sum_{u=1}^{N} x^{(u)} \geq \delta N$, we must have at least $\lceil \delta N \rceil$ indices u with $x^{(u)} = 1$. Therefore,

$$\varepsilon_0 = \sum_{u=\lceil \delta N \rceil}^{N} \binom{N}{u} p_0^u (1-p_0)^{N-u}.$$

Similarly, denote the probability that we incorrectly decide that $\mathcal{D} = \mathcal{B}(p_0)$ (while actually $\mathcal{D} = \mathcal{B}(p_1)$) by ε_1. Then

$$\varepsilon_1 := \Pr\left[\sum_{u=1}^{N} x^{(u)} < \delta N \mid x^{(u)} \sim \mathcal{B}(p_1)\right]$$

$$= \sum_{u=0}^{\lfloor \delta N \rfloor} \binom{N}{u} p_1^u (1-p_1)^{N_u}.$$

We may apply the Chernoff Bound to get an upperbound for ε_1 and ε_2. Applying Theorem 1(ii) with $p = p_0$ and $\gamma = \frac{\delta}{p_0} - 1$ gives us

$$\varepsilon_0 \leq \exp\left(-\frac{(\delta - p_0)^2}{\delta + p_0} N\right).$$

Similarly, applying Theorem 1(i) with $p = p_1$ and $\gamma = 1 - \frac{\delta}{p_1}$, we have

$$\varepsilon_1 \leq \exp\left(-\frac{(p_1 - \delta)^2}{2p_1} N\right).$$

For convenience, denote $\varepsilon_0^* := \exp(-\frac{(\delta-p_0)^2}{\delta+p_0} N)$ and $\varepsilon_1^* := \exp(-\frac{(p_1-\delta)^2}{2p_1} N)$. The probability that the threshold criterion decides the distribution incorrectly is at most $\max\{\varepsilon_0^*, \varepsilon_1^*\}$.

3.2 Repeated Uses of the Threshold Criterion

We now consider n repetitions of the threshold criterion. For $1 \leq i \leq n$, we are given N samples $x_i^{(1)}, x_i^{(2)}, \ldots, x_i^{(N)}$ sampled independently from $\mathcal{D}_i$. As before each $\mathcal{D}_i$ is either $\mathcal{B}(p_0)$ or $\mathcal{B}(p_1)$. Given p_0, p_1 and the samples $x_i^{(1)}, \ldots, x_i^{(N)}$, we are to decide whether $\mathcal{D}_i$ is $\mathcal{B}(p_0)$ or $\mathcal{B}(p_1)$.

Instead of counting the probability of deciding just one of the n distributions $\mathcal{D}_i$'s correctly, we now give an estimate of the probability that (repeated uses of) the threshold criterion correctly decides all n of them.

Let N be the number of samples given for each distribution $\mathcal{D}_i$ and α_N be the probability that the threshold criterion decides the n distributions $\mathcal{D}_1, \ldots, \mathcal{D}_n$ correctly. Then α_N can be made as close as possible to 1 for sufficiently large N. Set $n_0 := |\{1 \leq i \leq n \mid \mathcal{D}_i = \mathcal{B}(p_0)\}|$ and $n_1 := |\{1 \leq i \leq n \mid \mathcal{D}_i = \mathcal{B}(p_1)\}| = n - n_0$.

Proposition 1. *Fix $0 < \alpha^* < 1$. If*

$$N \geq \max\left\{\frac{\delta + p_0}{(\delta - p_0)^2}\ln\frac{2n_0}{1 - \alpha^*}, \frac{2p_1}{(\delta - p_1)^2}\ln\frac{2n_1}{1 - \alpha^*}\right\},$$

then $\alpha_N > \alpha^*$, i.e. the probability that the threshold criterion decides the n distributions $\mathcal{D}_1, \ldots, \mathcal{D}_n$ correctly is strictly greater than α^*.

Proof. Note that

$$
\begin{aligned}
\alpha_N &= (1 - \varepsilon_0)^{n_0}(1 - \varepsilon_1)^{n_1} \\
&\geq (1 - \varepsilon_0^*)^{n_0}(1 - \varepsilon_1^*)^{n_1} \\
&\approx (1 - n_0\varepsilon_0^*)(1 - n_1\varepsilon_1^*) \\
&> 1 - n_0\varepsilon_0^* - n_1\varepsilon_1^*,
\end{aligned}
$$

where we use the well-known approximations $(1 - \varepsilon_0^*)^{n_0} \approx 1 - n_0\varepsilon_0^*$ and $(1 - \varepsilon_1^*)^{n_1} \approx 1 - n_1\varepsilon_1^*$ in the second last step.

As $N \geq \frac{\delta + p_0}{(\delta - p_0)^2}\ln\frac{2n_0}{1-\alpha^*}$, we have

$$\varepsilon_0^* = \exp\left(-\frac{(\delta - p_0)^2}{\delta + p_0}N\right) \leq \frac{1 - \alpha^*}{2n_0}.$$

Similarly, as $N \geq \frac{2p_1}{(\delta - p_1)^2}\ln\frac{2n_1}{1-\alpha^*}$, then

$$\varepsilon_1^* = \exp\left(-\frac{(p_1 - \delta)^2}{2p_1}N\right) \leq \frac{1 - \alpha^*}{2n_1}.$$

Hence,

$$\alpha_N > 1 - n_0\varepsilon_0^* - n_1\varepsilon_1^* \geq 1 - \frac{1 - \alpha^*}{2} - \frac{1 - \alpha^*}{2} = \alpha^*.$$

$\square$

4   The Proposed Attack on MPT Signature

4.1   Partial Key Recovery Attack

In this section, we shall describe a partial key recovery attack on the MPT signature. The attack uses statistical method to recover y, which is an important part of the signer's long term secret key.

In the MPT signature, we have $\alpha = qt + ry$, where $q \in \mathcal{V}_{n,pq}$ and $y \in \mathcal{V}_{n,\omega}$ are fixed secret key. We shall prove that $\Pr[\alpha_i = 1]$ is dependent on whether $y_j = 1$ or $y_j = 0$ (subject to the condition that $r_{(i-j) \bmod n} = 1$).

Let $P(n, w_u, w_v)$ denote the probability that $\overline{u} \cdot \overline{v}^T = 1$, where $u \in \mathcal{V}_{n,w_u}$ and v is sampled uniformly randomly from $\mathcal{V}_{n,w_v}$. Then

$$P(n, w_u, w_v) = \frac{1}{\binom{n}{w_v}} \sum_{\substack{1 \leq l \leq \min(w_u, w_v) \\ l \text{ odd}}} \binom{w_u}{l} \binom{n - w_u}{w_v - l}.$$

Note that for any $0 \leq i \leq n - 1$, if $\mathrm{wt}(t) = \omega_t$, then $\Pr[(qt)_i = 1] = P(n, \omega_{pq}, \omega_t)$. However, as ω_t is taken from an interval I_t, we have

$$p_{qt} := \Pr[(qt)_i = 1] = \frac{1}{|I_t|} \sum_{\omega_t \in I_t} P(n, \omega_{pq}, \omega_t).$$

Proposition 2. *Fix* $0 \leq j \leq n - 1$. *Suppose* $0 \leq i \leq n - 1$ *such that* $r_{(i-j) \bmod n} = 1$.

(i) If $y_j = 1$, *then*

$$\Pr[\alpha_i = 1] = p_{qt} p_{sum} + (1 - p_{qt})(1 - p_{sum}),$$

where $p_{sum} := P(n - 1, \omega - 1, \omega_r - 1)$.
In other words, if $y_j = 1$, *then* $\alpha_i \sim \mathcal{B}(p_1)$, *where* $p_1 := p_{qt} p_{sum} + (1 - p_{qt})(1 - p_{sum})$.
(ii) If $y_j = 0$, *then*

$$\Pr[\alpha_i = 1] = p_{qt}(1 - p'_{sum}) + (1 - p_{qt})p'_{sum},$$

where $p'_{sum} := P(n - 1, \omega, \omega_r - 1)$.
In other words, if $y_j = 1$, *then* $\alpha_i \sim \mathcal{B}(p_0)$, *where* $p_0 := p_{qt}(1 - p'_{sum}) + (1 - p_{qt})p'_{sum}$.

Proof. As $\alpha = qt + ry$, we have $\alpha_i = (qt)_i + r^{(i)} \overline{y}^T$. Therefore,

$$\alpha_i = y_j + (qt)_i + \sum_{\substack{0 \leq j \leq n-1 \\ l \neq j}} r_{(i-l) \bmod n} y_l.$$

Note that

$$
\Pr\left[\sum_{\substack{0\le j\le n-1\\ l\ne j}} r_{i-l}y_l = 1\right] = \begin{cases} P(n-1,\ w-1,\ w_r-1) & \text{if } y_j = 1, \\ P(n-1,\ w,\ w_r-1) & \text{if } y_j = 0, \end{cases}
$$

$$
= \begin{cases} p_{sum} & \text{if } y_j = 1, \\ p'_{sum} & \text{if } y_j = 0. \end{cases}
$$

Now suppose that $y_j = 1$. Then $\alpha_i = 1 + (qt)_i + \sum_{l\ne j} r_{i-l}y_l$, so that

$$
\Pr[\alpha_i = 1] = \Pr[(qt)_i + \sum_{l\ne i} r_l y_{i-l} = 0]
$$

$$
= p_{qt}p_{sum} + (1 - p_{qt})(1 - p_{sum}).
$$

On the other hand, if $y_j = 0$, then $\alpha_i = (qt)_i + \sum_{l\ne j} r_{i-l}y_l$. In this case,

$$
\Pr[\alpha_i = 1] = \Pr[(qt)_i + \sum_{l\ne i} r_l y_{i-l} = 1]
$$

$$
= p_{qt}(1 - p'_{sum}) + (1 - p_{qt})p'_{sum}.
$$

$\square$

We give the numerical values of these probabilities for the various parameter sets in the following Table 2.

Table 2. Numerical values of the probabilities, where $p_1 := p_{qt}p_{sum}+(1-p_{qt})(1-p_{sum})$ and $p_0 := p_{qt}(1 - p'_{sum}) + (1 - p_{qt})p'_{sum}$

Param	p_{qt}	p_{sum}	p'_{sum}	p_1	p_0
Para-1	0.347150	0.246754	0.248198	0.577417	0.423024
Para-2	0.347082	0.228746	0.229991	0.582959	0.417421
Para-3	0.346046	0.223700	0.224844	0.585075	0.415277

For any fixed $0 \le j \le n - 1$, according to Proposition 2, we may decide whether $y_j = 1$ or $y_j = 0$ by determining whether α_i follows $\mathcal{B}(p_1)$ or $\mathcal{B}(p_0)$ (where i is chosen such that $r_{(i-j) \bmod n} = 1$). This can be done using the threshold criterion explained in Sect. 3. We turn this idea into a partial key recovery attack, where the attacker collects a number of valid signatures and uses the threshold criterion to recover y_j as follows.

Remark 2. *In Algorithm 5,*

- *at the end of Step 10, S counts the number of times we have $\alpha_i = 1$ (under the condition that $r_{(i-j) \bmod n} = 1$);*

Algorithm 5: Recovering y_j for any fixed $0 \leq j \leq n-1$

---

1   Collect N^* signatures $(\alpha^u, \mathrm{nonce}^u)_{u=1}^{N^*}$ for messages $(m^u)_{u=1}^{N^*}$
2   Set $S = 0$
3   **for** $1 \leq u \leq N^*$ **do**
4 | Compute $r^u := \mathcal{H}(m^u \| pk \| \mathrm{nonce}^u)$
5 | **for** $0 \leq i \leq n-1$ **do**
6 | | **if** $r^u_{(i-j) \bmod n} = 1$ **then**
7 | | | $S = S + \alpha_i$
8 | | **end if**
9 | **end for**
10 **end for**
11 $S = S/(N^* \omega_r)$
12 **if** $S < \delta$ **then**
13 | $y_j = 0$
14 **else**
15 | $y_j = 1$
16 **end if**

- note that for a fixed r^u and j, we have $r^u_{(i-j) \bmod n} = 1$ exactly ω_r number of times as $\mathrm{wt}(r^u) = \omega_r$;
- at the end of Step 11, S estimates the probability that $\alpha_i = 1$;
- as can be seen from Table 2, $p_1 > 0.5$ and $p_0 < 0.5$ for all parameter sets. Therefore, we may take $\delta = 0.5$.

Algorithm 5 recovers one coordinate y_j of y. One may apply Algorithm 5 repeatedly with j running from 0 through $n-1$ in order to fully recover $y = (y_0, y_1, \ldots, y_{n-1})$. Note that some steps (e.g. Step 4 of Algorithm 5) need not be repeated n times. We present the algorithm to fully recover y in the following Algorithm 6.

We now estimate the cost needed to recover y using this attack.

Proposition 3. *Let N^* be the total number of signatures used in the attack. Then the partial key recovery attack (given in Algorithm 6) can recover y using $(2\omega_r + n + 1)N^* + n$ operations.*

Proof. We list the number of operations required to perform each step of Algorithm 6 as follows:

- Step 4: N^* hash function evaluations;
- Step 7: nN^* comparison operations;
- Step 8: $\omega_r N^*$ subtraction/re-indexing operations
  (note that for any fixed u, there are exactly ω_r indices k such that $r^u_k = 1$ since $\mathrm{wt}(r^u) = \omega_r$);
- Step 9: $\omega_r N^*$ additions;
- Step 14: n comparison operations.

Algorithm 6: Recovering $y = (y_0, y_1, \ldots, y_{n-1})$

---

1 Collect N^* signatures $(\alpha^u, \text{nonce}^u)_{u=1}^{N^*}$ for messages $(m^u)_{u=1}^{N^*}$
2 Set $S = (S_0, S_1, \ldots, S_{n-1}) = (0, 0, \ldots, 0)$
3 **for** $1 \leq u \leq N^*$ **do**
4 $\quad$ Compute $r^u := \mathcal{H}(m^u \| pk \| \text{nonce}^u)$
5 $\quad$ **for** $0 \leq k \leq n-1$ **do**
6 $\quad\quad$ /* the index k plays the role of (i-j) mod n   */
7 $\quad\quad$ **if** $r_k^u = 1$ **then**
8 $\quad\quad\quad$ $j = (i - k) \bmod n$
9 $\quad\quad\quad$ $S_j = S_j + \alpha_i$
10 $\quad\quad$ **end if**
11 $\quad$ **end for**
12 **end for**
13 **for** $0 \leq j \leq n-1$ **do**
14 $\quad$ **if** $S_j < \delta N^* \omega_r$ **then**
15 $\quad\quad$ $y_j = 0$
16 $\quad$ **else**
17 $\quad\quad$ $y_j = 1$
18 $\quad$ **end if**
19 **end for**

Summing the number of operations given above, we conclude that the total cost of the partial key recovery attack to recover y is $(2\omega_r + n + 1)N^* + n$ operations.

$\square$

4.2   Forgery Attack

In this section, we propose a forgery attack where an attacker may forge a valid signature for any message of his choice. This forgery attack uses the partial key recovery attack explained in Sect. 4.1 as a first step.

Suppose the adversary knows a valid signature $\sigma = (\alpha, \text{nonce})$ for a message m. Then the adversary may forge a signature $\sigma' = (\alpha', \text{nonce}')$ for a message m' of his choice as described in the following Algorithm 7.

Remark 3. *(i) Note that in Algorithm 7, qt is recovered from a valid signature and r' is obtained as an output of the hash function $\mathcal{H}$ just like in the actual signing algorithm. Thus, the distribution of $\alpha' = (qt) + r'y$ and $\beta' = \alpha'h + sr'$ is the same as that of α, β generated from the actual signing algorithm given in Algorithm 2. Consequently, just like in Remark 1, the condition in Step 8 of Algorithm 7 (namely that $\text{wt}(\alpha') \notin I$ or $\text{wt}(\beta') \notin I$) happens only with negligible probability.*

(ii) Steps 8–10 in Algorithm 7 ensure that the forged signature σ' for the new message m' satisfies the condition that $\text{wt}(\alpha') \in I$ and $\text{wt}(\alpha'h + sr') \in I$, where $r' = \mathcal{H}(m' \| pk \| \text{nonce}')$. This is precisely the condition that is being checked in the verification algorithm (Algorithm 3). Therefore, the forged signature σ' will verify correctly.

Algorithm 7: Forging a signature σ' for a message m'

Input   : some valid signatures $\sigma = (\alpha, \mathsf{nonce})$ for some message m
Output: signature $\sigma' = (\alpha', \mathsf{nonce}')$ for a new message m'
1 Perform partial key recovery attack (given in Sect. 4.1 and Algorithm 6) to recover y
2 Compute $r = \mathcal{H}(m\|pk\|\mathsf{nonce})$
3 Compute $(qt) := \alpha - ry$ in $\mathcal{R}$
4 Randomly generate nonce'
5 Compute $r' := \mathcal{H}(m'\|pk\|\mathsf{nonce}')$
6 Compute $\alpha' := (qt) + r'y$ in $\mathcal{R}$
7 Compute $\beta' := \alpha'h + sr'$ in $\mathcal{R}$
8 **if** $\mathrm{wt}(\alpha') \notin I$ or $\mathrm{wt}(\beta') \notin I$ **then**
9 | change nonce' and repeat from Step 4
10 **end if**
11 Output the forged signature $\sigma' := (\alpha', \mathsf{nonce}')$ for the new message m'

(iii) *In Step 6 of Algorithm 7, we may alternatively take $\alpha' := (qt)X^i + r'y$ for any $0 \leq i \leq n-1$, i.e. we may replace (qt) with any circular shift of (qt). Note that $\mathrm{wt}(qt) = \mathrm{wt}(qtX^i)$ for any $0 \leq i \leq n-1$.*

5   Experimental Results

We implement the partial key recovery attack described in Sect. 4.1 using Sagemath. We first use Proposition 1 to estimate the number of signatures required to accurately recover y. In our case, we take $n_1 = \mathrm{wt}(y) = \omega$ and $n_0 = n - n_1 = n - \omega$. The values of p_0 and p_1 has been presented in Table 2. We take $\delta = 0.5$ and $\alpha^* = 0.999$.

According to Proposition 1, the number of samples required to recover y with probability greater than 0.999 is

$$N := \max\left\{ \left\lceil \frac{\delta + p_0}{(\delta - p_0)^2} \ln \frac{2n_0}{1 - \alpha^*} \right\rceil, \left\lceil \frac{2p_1}{(\delta - p_1)^2} \ln \frac{2n_1}{1 - \alpha^*} \right\rceil \right\}.$$

We further note that in our attack (Algorithm 6), each collected signature contributes ω_r samples of α_i (i.e. one sample of α_i is obtained for any index $0 \leq k \leq n-1$ satisfying $r_k = r_{(i-j) \bmod n} = 1$). Thus, the total number of samples obtained from N^* signatures is $N^*\omega_r$. Therefore, the number N^* of signatures required to perform the attack is

$$N^* := \lceil N/\omega_r \rceil.$$

We tabulate the value of N^* for various parameter sets in the following Table 3.

Table 3. Number of signatures required to perform the attack

Parameter	n	n_0	n_1	p_0	p_1	N	$N^* = \lceil N/\omega_r \rceil$
Para-1	14627	14506	121	0.423024	0.577417	2677	64
Para-2	18143	18008	135	0.417421	0.582959	2341	56
Para-3	21067	20922	145	0.415277	0.585075	2238	51

We remark that the required number N^* of signatures given in Table 3 is computed according to the theoretical bound derived in Proposition 1. However, this theoretical bound is only a rough bound on the required number of samples (and signatures) to ensure very high probability of successfully recovering y. Through simulations in Sagemath, we empirically find that it is in fact enough to use 25 signatures in order to successfully apply the attack.

In the following Table 4, we list the timing results from our Sagemath implementation of the attack. We also present the complexity of the attack (computed using Proposition 3).

Table 4. Average timing (in seconds) and theoretical complexity (according to Proposition 3) of the partial key recovery attack to recover y

Parameter	No. of signatures	Avg. timing (sec)	Complexity
Para-1	25	64.955	$2^{18.5}$
	64	177.051	$2^{19.9}$
Para-2	25	83.294	$2^{18.9}$
	56	188.254	2^{20}
Para-3	25	100.804	$2^{19.1}$
	51	202.193	$2^{20.1}$

As can be seen in Table 4, using the proof-of-concept Sagemath implementation, we are able to recover an important part y of the secret key using as few as 25 signatures in under 2 minutes for any of the proposed parameter sets. The source code of our proof-of-concept Sagemath implementation is available at https://github.com/theofanuela/MPT.

6   Conclusion

Meneghetti, Picozzi, and Tognolini proposed a Hamming-metric code-based digital signature scheme from QC-LDPC codes in [10]. In this paper, we proposed a partial key recovery attack that uses statistical method to recover an important part y of the signer's long term secret key. We provided a proof-of-concept Sagemath implementation of this attack. Using the Sagemath implementation, we found that we are able to recover y (which is an important part of the signer's long term secret key) using as few as 25 signatures in under 2 minutes for any of the proposed parameter sets (which supposedly have 128, 192, 256-bit security respectively). Moreover, we followed up this partial key recovery attack by performing a forgery attack. As the attack has polynomial time complexity, it cannot be resolved by simply increasing the parameter sizes of the signature. We therefore conclude that the signature scheme proposed in [10] is insecure.

References

1. Aguilar-Melchor, C., et al.: Hamming quasi-cyclic (HQC). Submission to the NIST post quantum standardization process (2017). https://www.pqc-hqc.org/doc/hqc-specification_2021-06-06.pdf
2. Aragon, N., et al.: BIKE: bit flipping key encapsulation. Submission to the NIST post quantum standardization process (2017). https://bikesuite.org/files/v5.0/BIKE_Spec.2022.10.10.1.pdf
3. Bernstein, D.J., et al.: Classic McEliece: conservative code-based cryptography. Submission to the NIST post quantum standardization process (2017). https://classic.mceliece.org/mceliece-rationale-20221023.pdf
4. Berlekamp, E., McEliece, R., van Tilborg, H.: On the inherent intractability of certain coding problems (corresp.). IEEE Trans. Inf. Theory **24**(3), 384–386 (1978). https://doi.org/10.1109/TIT.1978.1055873
5. Courtois, N.T., Finiasz, M., Sendrier, N.: How to achieve a McEliece-based digital signature scheme. In: Boyd, C. (ed.) ASIACRYPT 2001. LNCS, vol. 2248, pp. 157–174. Springer, Heidelberg (2001). https://doi.org/10.1007/3-540-45682-1_10
6. Cayrel, P.-L., Véron, P., El Yousfi Alaoui, S.M.: A zero-knowledge identification scheme based on the q-ary syndrome decoding problem. In: Biryukov, A., Gong, G., Stinson, D.R. (eds.) SAC 2010. LNCS, vol. 6544, pp. 171–186. Springer, Heidelberg (2011). https://doi.org/10.1007/978-3-642-19574-7_12
7. D'Alconzo, G., Meneghetti, A., Piasenti, P.: Security issues of CFS-like digital signature algorithms. arXiv preprint arXiv:2112.00429 (2021)
8. Debris-Alazard, T., Sendrier, N., Tillich, J.-P.: Wave: a new family of trapdoor one-way preimage sampleable functions based on codes. In: Galbraith, S.D., Moriai, S. (eds.) ASIACRYPT 2019. LNCS, vol. 11921, pp. 21–51. Springer, Cham (2019). https://doi.org/10.1007/978-3-030-34578-5_2
9. Kabatianskii, G., Krouk, E., Smeets, B.: A digital signature scheme based on random error-correcting codes. In: Darnell, M. (ed.) Cryptography and Coding 1997. LNCS, vol. 1355, pp. 161–167. Springer, Heidelberg (1997). https://doi.org/10.1007/BFb0024461
10. Meneghetti, A., Picozzi, C., Tognolini, G.: A post-quantum digital signature scheme from QC-LDPC codes. IACR Cryptology ePrint Archive 2022/1477 (2022). https://eprint.iacr.org/2022/1477
11. Otmani, A., Tillich, J.-P.: An efficient attack on all concrete KKS proposals. In: Yang, B.-Y. (ed.) PQCrypto 2011. LNCS, vol. 7071, pp. 98–116. Springer, Heidelberg (2011). https://doi.org/10.1007/978-3-642-25405-5_7
12. Ren, F., Zheng, D., Wang, W.: An efficient code based digital signature algorithm. Int. J. Netw. Secur. **19**(6), 1072–1079 (2017). https://doi.org/10.6633/IJNS.201711.19(6).24

13. Stern, J.: A new identification scheme based on syndrome decoding. In: Stinson, D.R. (ed.) CRYPTO 1993. LNCS, vol. 773, pp. 13–21. Springer, Heidelberg (1994). https://doi.org/10.1007/3-540-48329-2_2
14. Vardy A.: Algorithmic complexity in coding theory and the minimum distance problem. In: STOC 1997, El Paso, TX, pp. 92–109. ACM, New York (1999). https://doi.org/10.1145/258533.258559

Computational Results on Gowers U_2 and U_3 Norms of Known S-Boxes

Vikas Kumar[1]([envelope]) [iD], Bimal Mandal[2], Aditi Kar Gangopadhyay[1],
and Sugata Gangopadhyay[3]

[1] Department of Mathematics, IIT Roorkee, Roorkee 247667, Uttarakhand, India
{v_kumar,aditi.gangopadhyay}@ma.iitr.ac.in
[2] Department of Mathematics, IIT Jodhpur, Karwar 342030, Rajasthan, India
bimalmandal@iitj.ac.in
[3] Department of Computer Science and Engineering, IIT Roorkee,
Roorkee 247667, Uttarakhand, India
sugata.gangopadhyay@cs.iitr.ac.in

Abstract. The $(r + 1)$th order Gowers norm of a Boolean function is
a measure of its resistance to rth order approximations. Gowers, Green,
and Tao presented the connection between Gowers uniformity norm
of a function and its correlation with polynomials of a certain degree.
Gowers U_2 and U_3 norms measure the resistance of a Boolean function
against linear and quadratic approximations, respectively. This paper
presents computational results on the Gowers U_2 and U_3 norms of some
known $4, 5$, and 6-bit S-Boxes used in the present-day block ciphers. It
is observed that there are S-Boxes having the same algebraic degree,
differential uniformity, and linearity, but their Gowers norms values are
different. Equivalently, they possess different strengths against linear and
quadratic cryptanalysis.

Keywords: (vectorial)Boolean function · Walsh–Hadamard
transform · Nonlinearity · differential uniformity · Gowers norm

1 Preliminaries

Let $\mathbb{F}_2$ be the prime field of two elements and $\mathbb{F}_2^n$ be an n-dimensional vector
space over $\mathbb{F}_2$. A function $F : \mathbb{F}_2^n \to \mathbb{F}_2^m$ is called an (n, m)-function or a vectorial
Boolean function or an S-Box. In particular, if $m = 1$, $(n, 1)$-function is said to
be a Boolean function. The set of all Boolean functions in n variables is denoted
by $\mathcal{B}_n$. Any $f \in \mathcal{B}_n$ can be uniquely written as a multivariate polynomial of the
form

$$f(x_1, x_2, \ldots, x_n) = \sum_{\mathbf{u} \in \mathbb{F}_2^n} \lambda_{\mathbf{u}} x_1^{u_1} x_2^{u_2} \cdots x_n^{u_n},$$

where $\lambda_{\mathbf{u}} \in \mathbb{F}_2$ for all $\mathbf{u} \in \mathbb{F}_2^n$. This polynomial form is called the algebraic
normal form (ANF) of f. The algebraic degree of $f \in \mathcal{B}_n$, denoted by $deg(f)$,
is defined as, $deg(f) = \max_{\mathbf{u} \in \mathbb{F}_2^n}\{wt(\mathbf{u}) : \lambda_{\mathbf{u}} \neq 0\}$. If $deg(f)$ is at most 1, then

S. El Hajji et al. (Eds.): C2SI 2023, LNCS 13874, pp. 150–157, 2023.
https://doi.org/10.1007/978-3-031-33017-9_10

f is called an affine function. An (n, m)-function F can be uniquely expressed using m Boolean functions in n variables as $F(\mathbf{x}) = (f_1(\mathbf{x}), f_2(\mathbf{x}), \ldots, f_m(\mathbf{x}))$, where $f_i \in \mathcal{B}_n$ is called the ith coordinate function of F. Any nonzero $\mathbb{F}_2$-linear combination of coordinate functions of F, i.e., $\mathbf{a} \cdot F$ for any nonzero $\mathbf{a} \in \mathbb{F}_2^m$, is called a component function. The associated character form of a Boolean function f is denoted by $\mathfrak{f}$, defined as $\mathfrak{f}(x) = (-1)^{f(x)}$ for all $\mathbf{x} \in \mathbb{F}_2^n$. The Fourier transform of f is defined as $\hat{f}(\mathbf{x}) = \frac{1}{2^n} \sum_{\mathbf{x} \in \mathbb{F}_2^n} \mathfrak{f}(\mathbf{x})(-1)^{\mathbf{a} \cdot \mathbf{x}}$. The nonlinearity of f, denoted by $nl(f)$, is defined as $nl(f) = 2^{n-1}(1 - \max_{\mathbf{x} \in \mathbb{F}_2^n} |\hat{f}(\mathbf{x})|)$, which is the minimum distance of f from the set of all affine functions in n variables. Linearity of f is defined as $\mathcal{L}(f) = 2^n \max_{\mathbf{x} \in \mathbb{F}_2^n} |\hat{f}(\mathbf{x})|$.

The general definition of kth order Gowers norm of a real valued function h defined on a finite set, denoted by $\|h\|_{U_k}$, can be found at [3, Definition 2.2.1]. Here, we consider the equivalent definitions of Gowers U_2 and U_3 norms of Boolean functions.

Definition 1 ([4]). *Let $f : \mathbb{F}_2^n \to \mathbb{F}_2$ be a Boolean function. Then Gowers U_2 and U_3 norms of f are denoted by $\quad \|\mathfrak{f}\|_{U_2}$ and $\quad \|\mathfrak{f}\|_{U_3}$, respectively, and are defined as*

$$\|\mathfrak{f}\|_{U_2}^4 = \sum_{\mathbf{x} \in \mathbb{F}_2^n} \hat{f}(\mathbf{x})^4 \quad and \quad \|\mathfrak{f}\|_{U_3}^8 = \frac{1}{2^{4n}} \sum_{\mathbf{h}_1, \mathbf{h}_2 \in \mathbb{F}_2^n} \left(\sum_{\mathbf{x} \in \mathbb{F}_2^n} (-1)^{D_{\mathbf{h}_1, \mathbf{h}_2} f(\mathbf{x})} \right)^2, \quad (1)$$

where $D_{\mathbf{h}_1, \mathbf{h}_2} f(\mathbf{x}) = f(\mathbf{x}) + f(\mathbf{x} + \mathbf{h}_1) + f(\mathbf{x} + \mathbf{h}_2) + f(\mathbf{x} + \mathbf{h}_1 + \mathbf{h}_2)$ is called the second order derivative of f.

Theorem 1. [3, Fact 2.2.1] *Let $k \in \mathbb{Z}^+$ and $\epsilon > 0$. Let $P : \mathbb{F}_2^n \longrightarrow \mathbb{F}_2$ be a polynomial of degree at most k, and $h : \mathbb{F}_2^n \longrightarrow \mathbb{R}$ such that $|\mathbb{E}_{\mathbf{x}}[h(\mathbf{x})(-1)^{P(\mathbf{x})}]| \geq \epsilon$. Then $\|h\|_{U_{k+1}} \geq \epsilon$.*

For $k = 1, 2$, the converse holds, i.e., if $\|h\|_{U_{k+1}} \geq \epsilon$ then there exist a polynomial P of degree at most k such that $|\mathbb{E}_{\mathbf{x}}[h(\mathbf{x})(-1)^{P(\mathbf{x})}]| \geq \epsilon$, where $\epsilon > 0$. Theorem 1 implies that if a Boolean function has a low Gowers U_{k+1} norm, then it has a low correlation with all the polynomials on $\mathbb{F}_2^n$ of degrees at most k, i.e., it has high kth order nonlinearity. An inverse theorem for Gowers U_3 norm is proved by Green and Tao [6]. Gangopadhyay et al. [4,5] derived some interesting results on Boolean functions using Gowers norm. Recently, Tang et al. [8] presented the Gowers U_3 norm of the multiplicative inverse functions. For a more detailed survey, we refer to [2,3]. The high Gowers norm value of an S-Box can be used to find a distinguisher.

For simplicity, the Gowers U_k norm of an S-Box F and its component function $\mathbf{v} \cdot F$ are denoted by $\|F\|_{U_k}$ and $\|\mathbf{v} \cdot F\|_{U_k}$, respectively.

Definition 2. [8, Definition 17] *Let* $F : \mathbb{F}_2^n \longrightarrow \mathbb{F}_2^m$ *be an* (n, m) *function. Then the Gowers* U_k *norm,* $k \geq 1$, *is defined as follows*

$$\|F\|_{U_k} = \max_{\mathbf{v} \in \mathbb{F}_2^m \setminus \{\mathbf{0}\}} \|\mathbf{v} \cdot F\|_{U_k},$$

where, $\mathbf{v} \cdot F$ *is the component function of* F *at a nonzero* $\mathbf{v} \in \mathbb{F}_2^m$. *And, we define the* k*th dimension Gowers uniformity norm spectrum of* F *as the set*

$$\mathcal{S}(\ \|F\|_{U_k}) = \{\ \|\mathbf{v} \cdot F\|_{U_k} : \mathbf{v} \in \mathbb{F}_2^m \setminus \{\mathbf{0}\}\}, \tag{2}$$

where $\mathbf{0}$ *denotes the all zero vector in* $\mathbb{F}_2^m$.

The invariance of kth order Gowers norm U_k of Boolean functions under extended affine equivalence is shown in [1], Theorem 7.3.6. It directly gives that the Gowers U_2 norm spectrum of a vectorial Boolean function is preserved under extended affine equivalence. The following theorem will show that the Gowers U_3 norm of a (n, n)-vectorial Boolean function is preserved under extended affine equivalence.

Theorem 2. *The Gowers* U_3 *norm spectrum is invariant under extended affine equivalence, i.e., if* $F : \mathbb{F}_2^n \to \mathbb{F}_2^n$ *and for all* $\mathbf{x} \in \mathbb{F}_2^n$, *we have,* $G(\mathbf{x}) = F(A\mathbf{x} + \mathbf{b}) + C\mathbf{x} + \mathbf{d}$ *where* A, C *are invertible* $n \times n$ *matrices over* $\mathbb{F}_2$ *and* $\mathbf{b}, \mathbf{d} \in \mathbb{F}_2^n$. *Then* $\mathcal{S}(\ \|F\|_{U_3}) = \mathcal{S}(\ \|G\|_{U_3})$.

Proof. We just need to show that for $f \in \mathcal{B}_n$, the multiset $[D_{\mathbf{u},\mathbf{v}} f : \mathbf{u}, \mathbf{v} \in \mathbb{F}_2^n]$ is invariant under extended affine equivalence. Let $g \in \mathcal{B}_n$ be extended affine equivalent to $f \in \mathcal{B}_n$, i.e., $g(\mathbf{x}) = f(A\mathbf{x} + \mathbf{b}) + C\mathbf{x} + \mathbf{d}$ where A, C are invertible $n \times n$ matrices over $\mathbb{F}_2$ and $\mathbf{b}, \mathbf{d} \in \mathbb{F}_2^n$. Then for any pair $(\mathbf{u}, \mathbf{v}) \in \mathbb{F}_2^n \times \mathbb{F}_2^n$

$$
\begin{aligned}
D_{\mathbf{u},\mathbf{v}} g(\mathbf{x}) &= g(\mathbf{x}) + g(\mathbf{x} + \mathbf{u}) + g(\mathbf{x} + \mathbf{v}) + g(\mathbf{x} + \mathbf{u} + \mathbf{v}) \\
&= f(A\mathbf{x} + \mathbf{b}) + C\mathbf{x} + \mathbf{d} + f(A\mathbf{x} + \mathbf{b} + A\mathbf{u}) + C\mathbf{x} + C\mathbf{u} + \mathbf{d} \\
&\quad + f(A\mathbf{x} + \mathbf{b} + A\mathbf{v}) + C\mathbf{x} + C\mathbf{v} + \mathbf{d} + f(A\mathbf{x} + \mathbf{b} + A\mathbf{u} + A\mathbf{v}) \\
&\quad + C\mathbf{x} + C\mathbf{u} + C\mathbf{v} + \mathbf{d} \\
&= f(A\mathbf{x} + \mathbf{b}) + f(A\mathbf{x} + \mathbf{b} + A\mathbf{u}) + f(A\mathbf{x} + \mathbf{b} + A\mathbf{v}) \\
&\quad + f(A\mathbf{x} + \mathbf{b} + A\mathbf{u} + A\mathbf{v}) \\
&= D_{A\mathbf{u},A\mathbf{v}} f(A\mathbf{x} + \mathbf{b})
\end{aligned}
$$

Now, suppose F, G are as discussed in the theorem. Then as above, one can show that for every pair $(\mathbf{h}_1, \mathbf{h}_2) \in \mathbb{F}_2^n \times \mathbb{F}_2^n$ and for every nonzero $\mathbf{v} \in \mathbb{F}_2^n \setminus \{\mathbf{0}\}$

$$D_{\mathbf{h}_1, \mathbf{h}_2} \mathbf{v} \cdot G(\mathbf{x}) = D_{A\mathbf{h}_1, A\mathbf{h}_2} \mathbf{v} \cdot F(A\mathbf{x} + \mathbf{b}).$$

Finally

$$\|\mathbf{v} \cdot G\|_{U_3}^8 = \frac{1}{2^{4n}} \left| \sum_{\mathbf{h}_1, \mathbf{h}_2 \in \mathbb{F}_2^n} \left(\sum_{\mathbf{x} \in \mathbb{F}_2^n} (-1)^{D_{\mathbf{h}_1, \mathbf{h}_2} \mathbf{v} \cdot G(\mathbf{x})} \right)^2 \right|$$

$$= \frac{1}{2^{4n}} \left| \sum_{\mathbf{h}_1, \mathbf{h}_2 \in \mathbb{F}_2^n} \left(\sum_{\mathbf{x} \in \mathbb{F}_2^n} (-1)^{D_{A\mathbf{h}_1, A\mathbf{h}_2} \mathbf{v} \cdot F(A\mathbf{x} + \mathbf{b})} \right)^2 \right|$$

$$= \frac{1}{2^{4n}} \left| \sum_{\mathbf{h}_1', \mathbf{h}_2' \in \mathbb{F}_2^n} \left(\sum_{\mathbf{y} \in \mathbb{F}_2^n} (-1)^{D_{\mathbf{h}_1', \mathbf{h}_2'} \mathbf{v} \cdot F(\mathbf{y})} \right)^2 \right|$$

$$= \|\mathbf{v} \cdot F\|_{U_3}^8$$

Since A is invertible, the map $(\mathbf{h}_1, \mathbf{h}_2) \to (A\mathbf{h}_1, A\mathbf{h}_2)$ is bijection on $\mathbb{F}_2^n \times \mathbb{F}_2^n$, and the same stands for the map $\mathbf{x} \to A\mathbf{x} + \mathbf{b}$ on $\mathbb{F}_2^n$.   □

2   Results and Observations

We first compute the Gowers U_2 and U_3 norms of the S-Boxes given by Leander et al. [7], then we consider most S-Boxes in $4, 5$ and 6-bits, given at [9]. In [7], Leander et al. classified all optimal 4-bit S-Boxes up to extended affine equivalence and observed that there are only 16 different classes of optimal S-Boxes, listed in Table 1, i.e., their differential uniformity is 4, and linearity is 8. Since, the Gowers norm spectrum is invariant under extended affine equivalence, we have computed the Gowers U_2 and U_3 norm spectra of all optimal 4-bit optimal S-Boxes. Table 3 first lists the Gowers U_2 and U_3 norms of these representative optimal S-Boxes. Then it contains Gowers U_2 and U_3 norms of some other known 4-bit and $5, 6$-bit S-Boxes given in Table 1, 2, which are taken from [9].

Table 1. 4-bit S-Boxes

Representatives of all 16 classes of optimal 4-bit S-Boxes in [7]			
G_0	$[0,1,2,13,4,7,15,6,8,11,12,9,3,14,10,5]$	G_1	$[0,1,2,13,4,7,15,6,8,11,14,3,5,9,10,12]$
G_2	$[0,1,2,13,4,7,15,6,8,11,14,3,10,12,5,9]$	G_3	$[0,1,2,13,4,7,15,6,8,12,5,3,10,14,11,9]$
G_4	$[0,1,2,13,4,7,15,6,8,12,9,11,10,14,5,3]$	G_5	$[0,1,2,13,4,7,15,6,8,12,11,9,10,14,3,5]$
G_6	$[0,1,2,13,4,7,15,6,8,12,11,9,10,14,5,3]$	G_7	$[0,1,2,13,4,7,15,6,8,12,14,11,10,9,3,5]$
G_8	$[0,1,2,13,4,7,15,6,8,14,9,5,10,11,3,12]$	G_9	$[0,1,2,13,4,7,15,6,8,14,11,3,5,9,10,12]$
G_{10}	$[0,1,2,13,4,7,15,6,8,14,11,5,10,9,3,12]$	G_{11}	$[0,1,2,13,4,7,15,6,8,14,11,10,5,9,12,3]$
G_{12}	$[0,1,2,13,4,7,15,6,8,14,11,10,9,3,12,5]$	G_{13}	$[0,1,2,13,4,7,15,6,8,14,12,9,5,11,10,3]$
G_{14}	$[0,1,2,13,4,7,15,6,8,14,12,11,3,9,5,10]$	G_{15}	$[0,1,2,13,4,7,15,6,8,14,12,11,9,3,10,5]$
Some other 4-bit S-Boxes from [9]			
Elephant	$[14,13,11,0,2,1,4,15,7,10,8,5,9,12,3,6]$	Knot	$[4,0,10,7,11,14,1,13,9,15,6,8,5,2,12,3]$
Pyjamask	$[2,13,3,9,7,11,10,6,14,0,15,4,8,5,1,12]$	Trifle	$[0,12,9,7,3,5,14,4,6,11,10,2,13,1,8,15]$
Present	$[12,5,6,11,9,0,10,13,3,14,15,8,4,7,1,2]$	Gift	$[1,10,4,12,6,15,3,9,2,13,11,7,5,0,8,14]$
Fountain$_1$	$[9,5,6,13,8,10,7,2,14,4,12,1,15,0,11,3]$	Fountain$_2$	$[9,13,14,5,8,10,15,2,6,12,4,1,7,0,11,3]$
Fountain$_3$	$[11,15,14,8,7,10,2,13,9,3,4,12,5,0,6,1]$	Qameleon	$[10,13,14,6,15,7,3,5,9,8,0,12,11,1,2,4]$
Rectangle	$[6,5,12,10,1,14,7,9,11,0,3,13,8,14,4,2]$	ForkSkinny	$[12,6,9,0,1,10,2,11,3,8,5,13,4,14,7,15]$
Whirlpool$_E$	$[1,11,9,12,13,6,15,3,14,8,7,4,10,2,5,0]$	Whirlpool$_R$	$[7,12,11,13,14,4,9,15,6,3,8,10,2,5,1,0]$
Noekeon	$[7,10,2,12,4,8,15,0,5,9,1,14,3,13,11,6]$	Piccolo	$[14,4,11,2,3,8,0,9,1,10,7,15,6,12,5,13]$
Midori64	$[12,10,13,3,14,11,15,7,8,9,1,5,0,2,4,6]$	Midori128	$[1,0,5,3,14,2,15,7,13,10,9,11,12,8,4,6]$
Klein	$[7,4,10,9,1,15,11,0,12,3,2,6,8,14,13,5]$	Twine	$[12,0,15,10,2,11,9,5,8,3,13,7,1,14,6,4]$
Pride	$[0,4,8,15,1,5,14,9,2,7,10,12,11,13,6,3]$	Prince	$[11,15,3,2,10,12,9,1,6,7,8,0,14,5,13,4]$
Iceberg$_{S0}$	$[13,7,3,2,9,10,12,1,15,4,5,14,6,0,11,8]$	Iceberg$_{S1}$	$[4,10,15,12,0,13,9,11,14,6,1,7,3,5,8,2]$
Spook	$[0,8,1,15,2,10,7,9,4,13,5,6,14,3,11,12]$	Saturn$_1$	$[0,6,14,1,15,4,7,13,9,8,12,5,2,10,3,11]$
Saturn$_2$	$[0,9,13,2,15,1,11,7,6,4,5,3,8,12,10,14]$	Yarara	$[4,7,1,12,2,8,15,3,13,10,14,9,11,6,5,0]$
Lucifer$_1$	$[12,15,7,10,14,13,11,0,2,6,3,1,9,4,5,8]$	Lucifer$_2$	$[7,2,14,9,3,11,0,4,12,13,1,10,6,15,8,5]$

Table 2. 5 and 6-bit S-Boxes

5-bit S-Boxes from [9]	
Sycon	$[8,19,30,7,6,25,16,13,22,15,3,24,17,12,4,27,11,0,29,20,1,14,23,26,28,21,9,2,31,18,10,5]$
Fides$_5$	$[1,0,25,26,17,29,21,27,20,5,4,23,14,18,2,28,15,8,6,3,13,7,24,16,30,9,31,10,22,12,11,19]$
Shamash	$[16,14,13,2,11,17,21,30,7,24,18,28,26,1,12,6,31,25,0,23,20,22,8,27,4,3,19,5,9,10,29,15]$
SC2000	$[20,26,7,31,19,12,10,15,22,30,13,14,4,24,9,18,27,11,1,21,6,16,2,28,23,5,8,3,0,17,29,25]$
DryGascon128	$[4,15,27,1,11,0,23,13,31,28,2,16,18,17,12,30,26,25,20,6,21,22,24,10,5,14,9,19,8,3,7,29]$
6-bits S-Boxes from [9]	
Fides$_6$	$[54,0,48,13,15,18,35,53,63,25,45,52,3,20,33,41,8,10,57,37,59,36,34,2,26,50,58,24,60,19,14,42,$ $46,61,5,49,31,11,28,4,12,30,55,22,9,6,32,23,27,39,21,17,16,29,62,1,40,47,51,56,7,43,38,44]$
SC2000$_6$	$[47,59,25,42,15,23,28,39,26,38,36,19,60,24,29,56,37,63,20,61,55,2,30,44,9,10,6,22,53,48,51,11,$ $62,52,35,18,14,46,0,54,17,40,27,4,31,8,5,12,3,16,41,34,33,7,45,49,50,58,1,21,43,57,32,13]$
APN	$[0,16,60,54,17,14,23,59,29,62,63,10,39,8,49,51,45,37,61,48,47,5,12,20,36,57,40,46,26,56,43,55,$ $11,31,24,6,27,13,53,19,15,30,1,4,33,34,28,35,21,52,58,3,9,7,18,32,25,22,41,50,44,2,38,42]$

In Table 3, the first coordinate of the ordered pairs in the column of algebraic degree, $\mathcal{S}(\|G\|_{U_2})$, and $\mathcal{S}(\|G\|_{U_3})$ represents the value attained and second coordinate represents its number of occurrences in the spectrum, i.e., the number of nonzero component functions attaining this value. For the sake of convenience, let us first clearly define some notations.

1. For 4-bit S-Boxes. Let $A_1 = 0.628716714$, $A_2 = 0.707106781$, $A_3 = 0.875044901$, $A_4 = 1$, $A_5 = 0.589902765$, $A_6 = 0.680817454$, $A_7 = 0.765703578$, and

Table 3. Computational results on the Gowers U_2 and U_3 norms of S-Boxes from Tables 1 and 2.

S-Box	Differential uniformity	Linearity	Algebraic degree	$\mathcal{S}(\|G\|_{U_2})$	$\|G\|_{U_2}$	$\mathcal{S}(\|G\|_{U_3})$	$\|G\|_{U_3}$
Gowers U_2 and U_3 norms of representatives of optimal 4-bit S-Boxes given in Table 1							
$G \in S_4^1$	4	8	$\{(2,3),(3,12)\}$	$\{(A_1,12),(A_2,3)\}$	A_2	$\{(A_3,12),(A_4,3)\}$	A_4
$G \in S_4^2$	4	8	$\{(2,1),(3,14)\}$	$\{(A_1,14),(A_2,1)\}$	A_2	$\{(A_3,14),(A_4,1)\}$	A_4
$G \in S_4^3$	4	8	$\{(3,15)\}$	$\{(A_1,15)\}$	A_1	$\{(A_3,15)\}$	A_3
Gowers U_2 and U_3 norms of other 4-bit S-Boxes given in Table 1							
$G \in S_4^4$	4	8	$\{(2,3),(3,12)\}$	$\{(A_1,12),(A_2,3)\}$	A_2	$\{(A_3,12),(A_4,3)\}$	A_4
$G \in S_4^5$	4	8	$\{(3,15)\}$	$\{(A_1,15)\}$	A_1	$\{(A_3,15)\}$	A_3
$G \in S_4^6$	6	8	$\{(2,3),(3,12)\}$	$\{(A_1,12),(A_2,3)\}$	A_2	$\{(A_3,12),(A_4,3)\}$	A_4
Yarara	4	8	$\{(3,14),(2,1)\}$	$\{(A_1,14),(A_2,1)\}$	A_2	$\{(A_3,14),(A_4,1)\}$	A_4
Lucifer$_1$	6	12	$\{(3,15)\}$	$\{(A_1,12),(A_7,3)\}$	A_7	$\{(A_3,15)\}$	A_3
Lucifer$_2$	6	8	$\{(3,15)\}$	$\{(A_1,15)\}$	A_1	$\{(A_3,15)\}$	A_3
Rectangle	6	10	$\{(2,1),(3,6),(4,8)\}$	$\{(A_1,6),(A_2,1)(A_5,2),(A_6,6)\}$	A_2	$\{(A_3,6),(A_4,1)(A_8,8)\}$	A_4
Gowers U_2 and U_3 norms of 5-bit S-Boxes given in Table 2							
$G \in S_5^1$	8	16	$\{(2,31)\}$	$\{(B_1,21),(B_2,10)\}$	B_2	$\{(B_4,31)\}$	B_4
$G \in S_5^2$	2	8	$\{(2,31)\}$	$\{(B_1,31)\}$	B_1	$\{(B_4,31)\}$	B_4
$G \in S_5^3$	2	8	$\{(3,31)\}$	$\{(B_1,31)\}$	B_1	$\{(B_3,31)\}$	B_3
Gowers U_2 and U_3 norms of 6-bit S-Boxes given in Table 2							
$G \in S_6^1$	2	16	$\{(4,56),(3,7)\}$	$\{(C_2,56),(C_1,7)\}$	C_1	$\{(C_3,56),(C_4,7)\}$	C_4
$G \in S_6^2$	4	16	$\{(5,63)\}$	$\{(C_5,63)\}$	C_5	$\{(C_6,63)\}$	C_6

$A_8 = 0.887461524$. Let $S_4^1 = \{G_i : i = 0, 1, 2, 8\}$, $S_4^2 = \{G_i : i = 9, 10, 14, 15\}$, and $S_4^3 = \{G_i : i = 3, 4, 5, 6, 7, 11, 12, 13\}$. Also, let $S_4^4 = \{$Elephant, Knot, Pyjamask, Present, ForkSkinny, Noekeon, Piccolo, Midori64, Pride, Spook$\}$, $S_4^5 = \{$Triffle, Qameleon, Whirlpool$_E$, Whirlpool$_R$, Midori128, Klein, Twine, Prince, Iceberg$_{S0}$, Iceberg$_{S1}$, Saturn$_1$, Saturn$_2\}$, and $S_4^6 = \{$Gift, Fountain$_1$, Fountain$_2$, Fountain$_3\}$.

2. For 5-bit S-Boxes. Let $B_1 = 0.5$, $B_2 = 0.707106781$, $B_3 = 0.806890743$, and $B_4 = 1$. Let $S_5^1 = \{$Sycon, DryGascon128$\}$, $S_5^2 = \{$Fides$_5$, Shamash$\}$, and $S_5^3 = \{$SC2000$\}$.

3. For 6-bit S-Boxes. Let $C_1 = 0.5$, $C_2 = 0.406644140$, $C_3 = 0.747674391$, $C_4 = 0.806890743$, $C_5 = 0.426869121$, and $C_6 = 0.742651235$. Let $S_6^1 = \{$Fides$_6$, APN$\}$ and $S_6^2 = \{$SC2000$_6\}$.

From experimental results in Table 3, we get some interesting observations that are given below. These observations can be used to find a weakness of an S-Box.

1. Although, all the optimal S-Boxes have the same linearity and differential uniformity. We obtained, for $G \in S_4^1$ there are 12 component functions of G with algebraic degree 3 and U_2 norm A_1, and 3 with algebraic degree 2 and U_2 norm A_2. While, for $G \in S_4^2$ there are 14 component functions of G with algebraic degree 3 and U_2 norm A_1, and 1 with algebraic degree 2 and U_2 norm A_2. Since $A_2 < A_1$, this means although their linearities are the

same, but the S-Boxes in S_4^2 are more resistant to linear approximations than the former ones. The same arguments tell that S-Boxes in S_4^3 are maximally resistant to linear attacks. And the same is true for their strength against quadratic approximations.

2. One more interesting observation is that S-Boxes in S_4^4 and S_4^5 are also optimal. Invariance of Gowers U_2 and U_3 norms spectra tells us that each S-Boxes in S_4^4 must be equivalent to one of the S-Boxes in S_4^1 and each S-Box in S_4^5 must be equivalent to one of the S-Boxes in S_4^3.

3. It is evident that there is a direct relationship between the algebraic degree of the component functions and their Gowers U_3 of the considered S-Boxes. If r component functions of some S-Box have equal algebraic degrees, then all those r functions have the same U_3 norm. More interestingly, component functions of different S-Boxes on an equal number of variables, with the same algebraic degree have equal U_3 norm. For example, if the algebraic degree of a component function of any 4-bit S-Box is 2 then it's U_3 norm is A_4; similarly, if its degree is 3 then U_3 norm is A_3. The same result holds for 5 and 6-bit S-Boxes.

4. However, a similar kind of result as above is not true for U_2 norm. For example, 8 component functions of Rectangle S-Box have algebraic degree 4, but 2 out of those 8 functions have U_2 norm A_5, and 6 functions have U_2 norm A_6. The same can be observed for Lucifer$_1$ and 5-bit S-Boxes in S_5^1.

5. Let $S(\mathbf{a}_1, \mathbf{a}_2; f) = \sum_{\mathbf{x} \in \mathbb{F}_2^n} (-1)^{D_{\mathbf{h}_1, \mathbf{h}_2} f(\mathbf{x})}$. Suppose G is a 4-bit S-Box and there is a component function $\mathbf{u} \cdot G$ with degree 2, then $\|\mathbf{u} \cdot G\|_{U_3} = 1$. Suppose degree of a component function $\mathbf{u} \cdot G$ is 3 then $\|\mathbf{u} \cdot G\|_{U_3} = A_3$. Since, $S(\mathbf{a}_1, \mathbf{a}_2; \mathbf{u} \cdot G) = 0, \pm 2^4$, for all $\mathbf{a}_1, \mathbf{a}_2 \in \mathbb{F}_2^4$. Let $|\{(\mathbf{a}_1, \mathbf{a}_2) \in \mathbb{F}_2^4 \times \mathbb{F}_2^4 : S(\mathbf{a}_1, \mathbf{a}_2; \mathbf{u} \cdot G) = \pm 2^4\}| = r$. Then

$$\|\mathbf{u} \cdot G\|_{U_3}^8 = A_3^8$$

$$\Leftrightarrow \quad \frac{1}{2^{16}} \left(r2^8 + 0 \right) = 0.343750$$

$$\Leftrightarrow \quad \frac{r}{2^8} = 0.343750$$

$$\Leftrightarrow \quad r = 88.$$

6. Algebraic degree of component functions of any 5-bit S-Box is also 2 or 3. For a component function $\mathbf{u} \cdot G$ of any 5-bit S-Box G with algebraic degree 3, there are exactly 184 pairs $(\mathbf{a}_1, \mathbf{a}_2)$ such that $S(\mathbf{a}_1, \mathbf{a}_2; \mathbf{u} \cdot G) = \pm 2^5$. Equivalently, for every nonzero component function, there are exactly 184 second order derivatives that are constant, and the remaining are non-constant affine functions.

3   Conclusion

It is clear from the computational results presented in this article that there are S-Boxes that display the same behavior when tested on the pre-existing set of distinguishers, like linearity, differential uniformity, and algebraic degree. However, they have different values of Gowers U_2 and U_3 norms. Thus, they have different resistance against linear and quadratic approximations. Therefore, it suggests that the Gowers norm should also be considered as a criterion for verifying S-Boxes' strength.

References

1. Mandal, B.: On Boolean bent functions and their generalizations. Ph.D. thesis, Indian Institute of Technology Roorkee (2018)
2. Gowers, T.: A new proof of Szemerédi's theorem. Geom. Funct. Anal. **11**(3), 465–588 (2001). https://doi.org/10.1007/s00039-001-0332-9
3. Chen, V.Y.-W.: The Gowers norm in the testing of Boolean functions. Ph.D. thesis, Massachusetts Institute of Technology (2009)
4. Gangopadhyay, S., Mandal, B., Stănică, P.: Gowers U_3 norm of some classes of bent Boolean functions. Des. Codes Crypt. **86**(5), 1131–1148 (2017). https://doi.org/10.1007/s10623-017-0383-z
5. Gangopadhyay, S., Riera, C., Stănică, P.: Gowers U_2 norm as a measure of nonlinearity for Boolean functions and their generalizations. Adv. Math. Commun. **15**(2), 241–256 (2021). https://doi.org/10.3934/amc.2020056
6. Green, B., Tao, T.: An inverse theorem for the Gowers $U^3(G)$ norm. Proc. Edinb. Math. Soc. **51**(1), 73–153 (2008). https://doi.org/10.1017/S0013091505000325
7. Leander, G., Poschmann, A.: On the classification of 4 bit S-boxes. In: Carlet, C., Sunar, B. (eds.) WAIFI 2007. LNCS, vol. 4547, pp. 159–176. Springer, Heidelberg (2007). https://doi.org/10.1007/978-3-540-73074-3_13
8. Tang, D., Mandal, B., Maitra, S.: Further cryptographic properties of the multiplicative inverse function. Discret. Appl. Math. **307**, 191–211 (2022). https://doi.org/10.1016/j.dam.2021.10.020
9. https://doc.sagemath.org/html/en/reference/cryptography/sage/crypto/sboxes.html

Multi-input Non-interactive Functional Encryption: Constructions and Applications

Grigor Artem[1], Vincenzo Iovino[1(✉)], and Răzvan Roşie[2]

[1] Aragon ZK Research, Zug, Switzerland
{artem,vincenzo}@aragon.org
[2] Lombard International, Miami, USA
razvan.rosie@lombardinternational.com

Abstract. We consider a non-interactive secure computation protocol that we call *multi-input non-interactive functional encryption* (MINI-FE). In a MINI-FE protocol for some class of functionalities F, N users independently and non-interactively setup their own pairs of public- and secret-keys. Each user $i \in \{1, \ldots, N\}$, with knowledge of the public-keys of all other participants, its own secret-key, an identifier id and a functionality F, can encode its own input x_i to produce a ciphertext Ct_i. There is a public evaluation function that, given N ciphertexts $\mathsf{Ct}_1, \ldots, \mathsf{Ct}_N$ for the same identifier and functionality F, outputs $F(x_1, \ldots, x_n)$. Moreover, the same public keys can be reused for an unbounded number of computations (for different identifiers). The security essentially guarantees that for any two tuples of inputs that map to the same value under a functionality, the corresponding tuples of ciphertexts are computationally indistinguishable to adversaries that can also corrupt a subset of the users.

MINI-FE shares some similarities with decentralized multi-client functional encryption (DMCFE) [Chotard *et al.* - Asiacrypt '18] but, unlike DMCFE and alike dynamic DMCFE (DDMCFE) [Chotard *et al.* - Crypto '20], in MINI-FE there is no interaction in the setup phase. Unlike DDMCFE and similarly to traditional secure computation, there is no concept of token and thus the leakage of information is limited to the execution of each computation for a given identifier.

In MINI-FE each user can completely work independently and the entire protocol can be executed over a broadcast channel (e.g., a distributed ledger) with just a single message from each user in both the setup and encoding phases.

We give an instantiation of a MINI-FE protocol for the Inner-Product functionality from bilinear groups; previous constructions were only known for the summation functionality. We show applications of our protocol to private stream aggregation and secure quadratic voting.

Keywords: functional encryption · bilinear maps · secure computation · e-voting

S. El Hajji et al. (Eds.): C2SI 2023, LNCS 13874, pp. 158–177, 2023.
https://doi.org/10.1007/978-3-031-33017-9_11

1 Introduction

Background. Functional Encryption (FE) [7,8,12,19,24] is a fine-grained form of public-key encryption in which users can learn specific functions of encrypted data rather than all the input. Specifically, there is a *central authority* (CA) that can issue tokens Tok_f for any function f in some class F and there is a decryption procedure that, on input a ciphertext Ct encrypting an input x and a token Tok_f, outputs $f(x)$. The security guarantees that no other information about x beyond $f(x)$ is leaked to an adversarial user.

Multi-Input FE (MIFE) [15], and in particular Multi-Client FE (MCFE), generalizes FE by allowing multi-variate functions and multiple encryptors. Specifically, the CA distributes to each user $i \in [N]$ an *encryption key* ek_i by means of which an encryption of the element x_i associated with an identifier (or label) id can be computed. The CA can compute the token Tok_f for the N-variate function f that can be used to compute $f(x_1, \ldots, x_N)$ from N cipher-texts $\mathsf{Ct}_1, \ldots, \mathsf{Ct}_N$ encrypting respectively the inputs $x_1, \ldots, x_N$ associated with the same identifier id.

Both FE and MCFE require the CA to be trusted for privacy. Indeed, the CA can always leak any encrypted input since it can compute a token for, e.g., the identity function that recovers the whole input.

For this reason, Decentralized Multi-Client FE (DMCFE) [11] has been proposed to the purpose of removing the authority. In DMCFE, after an initial *interactive* setup phase in which N users interact to compute their own secret-keys, the users can compute functions of encrypted data in a completely non-interactive way. Specifically, after the setup phase, each user keeps a secret-key by means of which a *share* DTok_f of a token for an N-variate function f can be computed. By combining all shares together it is possible to obtain the token Tok_f for the function f that in turn allows to compute the result $f(x_1, \ldots, x_N)$ from the N ciphertexts $\mathsf{Ct}_1, \ldots, \mathsf{Ct}_N$ encrypting respectively the inputs $x_1, \ldots, x_N$.

DMCFE has been generalized to dynamic DMCFE (DDMCFE) [10] removing the interaction in the setup phase and so easing the way of adding new users to the system and subsumes several other primitives like Ad-Hoc MIFE [3].

1.1 Fully Decentralization in Computing over Encrypted Data: MINI-FE

Unfortunately, DMCFE is not a fully decentralized protocol since the users must interact together in the initial setup phase.

A bit of thought reveals that complete non-interactive protocols are impossible to achieve. However, we envision the following cryptographic protocol that we call *Multi-Input Non-Interactive Functional Encryption* (MINI-FE).

A MINI-FE is a protocol among N users. Each user independently sets-up its own pair of public- and secret-keys by means of a KeyGen procedure. After this phase, we assume any public-key of any user to be publicly available to any other user. Notice that this implicitly requires a form of interaction: the public-keys need to be transmitted to any participant in the protocol. However, this interaction is *minimal* and indeed this can be implemented by making each user to send its own public-key to a distributed ledger (that serves as broadcast channel).

Each user $i \in [N]$ can *encode* (or encrypt) its input x_i to produce a ciphertext Ct_i. The encoding procedure Encode takes on input (1) all the public-keys, (2) an identifier (or label) id and (3) the secret-key of user i. There is a public *evaluation* procedure Eval that takes as input N ciphertexts $\mathsf{Ct}_1, \ldots, \mathsf{Ct}_N$ computed as before with respect to the same identifier and outputs $F(x_1, \ldots, x_N)$ where F is a given function supported by the protocol.[1] The evaluation procedure can be run by any party, not just from the N users. Therefore, once the ciphertexts are published on a distributed ledger (along the public-keys) the result of the computation is public. Observe that it is possible to run an unbounded number of computations for different identifiers using the same public-keys. Thus, m computations require just $m + 1$ messages over a distributed ledger.

For the security of MINI-FE, we require that for any two tuples of inputs that map to the same value under F, the corresponding tuples of ciphertexts are computationally indistinguishable to adversaries that can also corrupt an arbitrary subset of users.

Relation Between MINI-FE, DMCFE, DDMCFE, PSA and Secure Computation. MINI-FE shares similarities with DMCFE and DDMCFE. However, there are some technical differences. DMCFE requires an interaction between the users to setup the pairs of public- and secret-keys whereas in MINI-FE, like DDM-CFE, each user can run the KeyGen procedure independently from each other. The encoding procedure in MINI-FE may depend on all public-keys whereas in DMCFE/DDMCFE the encryption procedure depends only on the encryption key of the user. This is not a limitation of MINI-FE with respect to DMCFE/D-DMCFE since the encryption key of a DMCFE system can be seen as containing the list of public-keys of all users.

The main difference is that in both DMCFE and DDMCFE, a token can be used with any tuple of ciphertexts, independently from the associated identifier. Instead, in MINI-FE there is no concept of token: which function to be computed is decided at encoding time. Therefore, the leakage of information in MINI-FE is limited to a computation for a given identifier whereas in DMCFE/DDMCFE, a token can be *reused* over different tuples of ciphertexts.

Recently, Agrawal *et al.* [4] enriched the landscape of existing primitives with an "Uber"-FE scheme, dubbed multi-party functional encryption, which should capture most of the existing definitions. MINI-FE can be set in contraposition with such definition, given the lack of tokens required to be generated.

In this respect, MINI-FE is more similar to private stream aggregation (PSA) [25], a primitive in which an aggregator is able to compute the sum of the customers' inputs for each time period (corresponding to our concept of identifier). In PSA, however, there is a trusted setup phase among the users and the aggregator. Moreover, PSA does *directly* consider noise in the model (as in differential privacy) to preserve the users' privacy while we do consider noise only indirectly

---

[1] The protocol may be generalized so that the function F is chosen from some class and is given as input to the encoding procedure but to not overburden the notation we will not do that.

at the application layer. To our knowledge, PSA constructions are limited to the summation functionality whereas we will construct MINI-FE protocols for more general functionalities that have the summation as special case.

The setting of MINI-FE is similar to the one of general secure computation [14,27]. MINI-FE can be indeed seen as a non-interactive secure computation protocol in the public-key setting with an indistinguishability-based security notion.

Input-Indistinguishable Computation (IIC) proposed by Micali, Pass and Rosen [20] is a weakening of secure computation with an indistinguishability-based security (similarly to ours) proposed to deal with security under concurrent executions; the known constructions of ICC are for general functionalities and are not practical. Our MINI-FE for IP, seen as a secure computation protocol for the corresponding IP functionality, only requires $k + 1$ rounds when executing k secure evaluations, one for establishing the public-keys and one for each function evaluation.

1.2   Our Results: MINI-FE for the IP Functionality

In the context of e-voting, Giustolisi *et al.* [13] put forth protocols that are indeed MINI-FE for the sum and other related functionalities. In this work, we go beyond those basic functionalities and construct a MINI-FE protocol for the inner-product (IP) functionality. Specifically, we consider the following scenario.

There are two groups of N users and a known prime number p. Each user in the first group holds a *secret* input $x_i \in \mathbb{Z}_p$, and each user in the second group holds a *public* input $y_i \in \mathbb{Z}_p$, Each user in both groups encode its own input to produce $2N$ ciphertexts and the public evaluation function should output the inner-product of the vector $(x_1, \ldots, x_N)$ with the vector $(y_1, \ldots, y_N)$ in the field $\mathbb{Z}_p$.

Formally, given a positive integer N we build a MINI-FE protocol for the following functionality IP^N. The $\mathsf{IP}_N \triangleq \{\mathsf{IP}_{N,p_\lambda}\}_{\lambda > 0}$ functionality is a family of $2N$-variate functions indexed by a family of prime numbers $\{p_\lambda\}_{\lambda > 0}$ defined as follows:

$$\mathsf{IP}_{N,p}(x_1, \ldots, x_n, y_1, \ldots, y_N) \triangleq \left(\sum_{i \in [N]} x_i \cdot y_i \mod p, y_1, \ldots, y_N \right),$$

with all inputs being non-negative integers. For simplicity, when it is clear from the context we will write IP omitting the parameters.

Observe that, notwithstanding the inputs of the users in the second group are public, they are possibly unknown by the users in the first group. If this were not the case, the users in the first group could directly encode the inputs $x_i \cdot y_i \mod p$ but this would require interaction among the users in the two groups that we want to avoid. Therefore, the fact that the vector $(y_1, \ldots, y_N)$ is "public" must be interpreted in the sense that the users in the second group do not care about the privacy of their own inputs but, nonetheless, the vector is not known in advance to the users in the first group. This is similar to the setting of FE/MCFE/DMCFE for the IP functionality [1,2,11] in which the vector associated to the token can be likewise assumed to be public but is not known at encryption time. The users in the second group can be seen as *authenticators* providing a *one-time token* to being used only for a specific tuple of ciphertexts corresponding to the same identifier. Our MINI-FE protocol for the IP functionality is based on a standard assumption over bilinear groups, in particular we will prove the following theorem.

Theorem 1 (Informal). *If the Bilinear Decision Diffie-Hellman Assumption [9] defined in Sect. 3.2 holds, then in the Random Oracle model no non-uniform PPT adversary can break the privacy (see Definition 3) of the protocol of Sect. 4 with non-negligible probability.*

The proof is given in Sect. 5, allowing the adversary to corrupt up to N-2 users. Our protocol of Sect. 4 borrows similarities and in fact is inspired by the schemes in the works of Abdalla *et al.* [2] and Giustolisi *et al.* [13].

On-the-Fly Join. An important property of our protocol is that a ciphertext of a generic j-th user in the first group only depends on the public-key of the corresponding j-th user of the second group and *not* on all public-keys. This way, each user needs only to coordinate with the corresponding user of the second group and users can join in the system dynamically as in DDMCFE and Ad-Hoc MIFE. We call this property *on-the-fly join*. We will next see that this property turns to be useful in the applications.

2   Applications of MINI-FE for IP

Quadratic-Like Voting. Quadratic voting is a novel voting procedure proposed by Lalley and Weyl [18] to overcome several issues in social choice theory like the Condorcet paradox. In quadratic voting, each voter casts its preference along with a weight and is required to pay a cost that is quadratic in its weight; after the resulting of the election is announced, the collected revenue is shared, e.g., evenly among the voters. Quarfoot *et al.* [23] conducted an experiment that showed that when quadratic voting is employed in opinion polls, people tend to express less extreme preferences indicating that the preferences are closer to the actual ones.

Current solutions to secure quadratic voting [21,22] rely on election authorities that, colluding together, can break the privacy of individual voters; Pereira and Roenne's scheme [22] achieves everlasting privacy but recall that this property holds only assuming anonymous channels or that authorities are trusted in deleting their randomness. Our MINI-FE for IP can be used to build a system that has features similar (though not identical) to secure quadratic voting systems without trusted authorities in the following way.

Each voter j has a pair of public- and secret- keys for both user j in the first group and user j in the second group, that is a pair for user j and another for user $N+j$. Voter $j \in [N]$ casts its preference x_j computing MINI-FE's ciphertext as it were the user j of MINI-FE. The preferences are for instance in the domain $\{-1, 1\}$ with the meaning of "against" and "in favor".

Then the voter j chooses its weight y_j and pays for it the quantity y_j^2 and encodes a MINI-FE ciphertext as it were user $N+j$. The weight is for instance in the domain $\{1, \ldots, 10\}$. The ciphertexts are tallied according to the evaluation procedure of the MINI-FE protocol and thus the result is the inner-product $\sum_{i \in [N]} x_i \cdot y_i$ that measures how many voters are in favor or against a given proposal.

The capability to cast the weights in separate ciphertexts gives more flexibility with respect to solutions in which preferences and weights are cast together: a voter first *commits* to its own preference and later on can decide its weight. The choice of the voter's weight can be even done by means of a joint discussion with other voters without incurring the danger of affecting the preferences of each other. Indeed, having known how much the voters are going to pay for their preferences could affect the voter's preference. Our solution does not suffer this issue.

The flexibility of separating the cast of the preferences from the cast of the weights can be used to obtain a new *delegation* functionality. A subset of the users can delegate to a delegate their preferences and the choice of the weights of each user in the subset is left to the delegate. It is easy to see that the previous quadratic voting scheme can be adapted to provide this functionality: assign to the delegate the pairs of public- and secret-keys corresponding to the weights of the users in the subset.

In our quadratic voting solution, all the voters must cast their preferences and weights, otherwise the tally cannot be computed. While this is not a limitation in traditional political voting in which it is impossible to require that all eligible voters do actually vote, quadratic voting has been proposed for settings like corporate management voting or polls where this requirement is reasonable (e.g., the number of eligible voters is small and all of them need to participate in the voting procedure to validate some proposal).

The property of *on-the-fly join* outlined before turns to be useful in this context: it is possible that only a subset of the eligible voters submit preferences. Suppose indeed that only a subset S of the eligible voters cast preferences. Then, for the tally to be computed it is sufficient that for each voter $j \in S$ who cast its preference x_j, voter j later on will also cast its weight y_j. Thus, at time of submitting the preferences, each voter j may be agnostic of which voter in the set of the eligible voters will cast the preference or abstain. In this initial phase the voters could also submit their public-keys along with their preferences.

In private contexts (e.g., corporate voting) traditional e-voting solutions that require trusted election authorities can make a voter (e.g., a member of the board of directors of the company) to not indicate his actual preference due to the fear that someone, colluding with the election authorities, may discover his submitted preference. Our solution does not suffer from this issue since there is no authority at all.

Observe that a missing piece that we skipped is the verifiability: the voters should be able to cast only votes (the inputs x_j's) in the valid domain (e.g., $\{-1, 1\}$). This can be done via standard techniques (NIZK proofs in the RO model) and recent research [5, 16, 26] opens up the possibility of achieving even perfect verifiability.

Private Stream Aggregation. Like in the work of [11] we consider applications to variants of PSA [25].

A group of N companies want to compute statistics about their private data. The companies want to collaborate each other to compute the statistics but wish not to reveal their private data to each other or a third party. Moreover, the statistics to be computed on the private data are not known in advance to companies. Specifically, for any $i \in [N]$ the company i sets up two pairs of public- and secret-keys, one as user i and one as user $N+i$ and publishes such public-keys over a distributed ledger. On a daily (or hourly) basis, any company i *commits* to the distributed ledger an encoding of its private data x_i tagging it with an identifier id (e.g., the current day or an increasing counter). At any moment in the future the companies can decide *together* upon a statistic to compute, in particular a weighted sum in which the input of company i has to be weighted by the value y_i. Then, company i submits to the distributed ledger the encoding of weight y_i tagging it with id. Given the $2N$ so computed ciphertexts (N for the secret inputs x_i and N for the known inputs y_i) published on the ledger, it is possible to compute the statistic $\sum_{i \in [N]} x_i \cdot y_i \mod p$.

The weights are decided dynamically and collectively: the private data are made available daily (or hourly) while the weights for the statistics may be jointly decided by the companies only, e.g., at the end of each month. A solution in which each company waits until the end of each month to encode its private data directly in weighted form (i.e., like $x_i \cdot y_i$) is not satisfactory. In fact, in this case the company could change its actual private input x_i with a different value x_i' after knowing the weight y_i. For this reason, the companies are required to *commit* to their private data x_i's as soon as they are available (e.g., on a daily or hourly basis). Observe that company i does not know y_i when submitting an encoding of x_i.

We can also consider a variant of the previous scenario in which the weights are decided by N independent financial corporations that setup their own pairs of public- and secret-keys. The financial companies submit the encoding of their weights y_i's by means of which the statistics can be computed. In this case, if the financial firm i is malicious, it has the power of leaking x_i by encoding two ciphertexts, one for $y_i = 0$ and one for $y_i = 1$. This is unavoidable. To overcome this issue, it is possible to resort to differential privacy techniques like in traditional PSA constructions [25]. In particular, each company can add some noise to its respective secret input so that the financial firms have some degree of uncertainty about the companies' private data. This can be handled at the application layer and we skip details.

3   Definitions

Notations. A *negligible* function $\mathsf{negl}(\lambda)$ is a function that is smaller than the inverse of any polynomial in λ (from a certain point and on). We denote by $[n]$ the set of numbers $\{1, \ldots, n\}$, and we shorten *Probabilistic Polynomial-Time* as PPT. If g and A are elements of the same cyclic group, we denote by $\mathbf{dlog}_g A$ the discrete log of A in base g. If S is a finite set we denote by $S \rightarrow a$ the process of setting a equal to a uniformly chosen element of $S \overset{\triangle}{=}$ stands for definition.

3.1   MINI-FE

A multi-input non-interactive functional encryption protocol in the public-key setting (MINI-FE, in short) is associated with (1) a natural number $N > 0$, the *number of users*, (2) a family of sets $D \overset{\triangle}{=} \{D_\lambda\}_{\lambda>0}$, the *domain of valid individual inputs*, (3) a family of sets $I \overset{\triangle}{=} \{I_\lambda\}_{\lambda>0} \subset D^N$, the *domain of valid inputs*, (4) a family of sets $\Sigma \overset{\triangle}{=} \{\Sigma_\lambda\}_{\lambda>0}$, the *range of possible results*, and (5) a family of N-variate *functionalities* $F \overset{\triangle}{=} \{F_\lambda : D^N \rightarrow \Sigma\}_{\lambda>0}$ indexed by the security parameter λ. After that a *non-trusted* authority sets up the public parameters pp for security parameter λ, each user generates a pair of public and secret keys. By means of an algorithm Encode and of its own secret-key each user $i \in [N]$ can encode its input $x_i \in D$ generating a ciphertext Ct and, using the public-keys of all voters, the result $F(x_1, \ldots, x_N)$ can be publicly computed by means of an algorithm Eval.

Definition 1 (MINI-FE). *A* (N, D, I, Σ, F)-*multi-input non-interactive functional encryption scheme in the public-key setting MINI-FE for a number of users N, domain of valid individual inputs D and valid inputs I, range of possible results Σ and functionality F, is a tuple* MINI-FE $\overset{\triangle}{=}$ (Setup, KeyGen, Encode, Eval) *of four PPT algorithms with the following syntax:*

1. Setup(1^λ) $\rightarrow$ pp: *on input the security parameter in unary, outputs* public *parameters* pp.
2. KeyGen(pp, i) $\rightarrow$ (Pk$_i$, Sk$_i$): *on input the public parameters pp and some user index $i \in [N]$, outputs a* public-key Pk *and a* secret-key Sk.
3. Encode(pp, j, id, Sk$_j$, (Pk)$_{i \in [N] - \{j\}}$, x) $\rightarrow$ Ct: *on input the public parameters* pp, *the secret-key* Sk$_j$ *of user j, the identifier (or label)* id $\in \{0,1\}^\lambda$ *of the computation, the public keys* (Pk$_i$)$_{i \in [N] - \{j\}}$ *of the other users, and an input $x \in D$, outputs a ciphertext* Ct.
4. Eval(pp, Pk$_1$, \ldots, Pk$_N$, id, Ct$_1$, \ldots, Ct$_N$) $\rightarrow$ y: *on input the public parameters* pp, *the public-keys of all users, the identifier* id $\in \{0,1\}^\lambda$ *of the computation, and the ciphertexts encoded by all users, outputs $y \in \Sigma \cup \{\bot\}$.*

Definition 2 (Correctness.). *We require the following property for MINI-FE:* $\forall$ pp $\leftarrow$ Setup(1^λ), $\forall \{$(Pk$_1$, Sk$_1$), \ldots, (Pk$_N$, Sk$_N$)$\}$ *such that* $\forall i \in [N]$ KeyGen(pp) $\rightarrow$ (Pk$_i$, Sk$_i$), $\forall (x_1, \ldots, x_N) \in D^N$, $\forall$id $\in \{0,1\}^\lambda$, $\forall$Ct$_1$, \ldots, Ct$_N$, *such that for all* $i \in [N]$ $\mathsf{Encode}(\mathsf{pp}, j, \mathsf{id}, \mathsf{Sk}, (\mathsf{Pk})_{i \in [N] - \{j\}}, x_i) \to \mathsf{Ct}_i$, *we have that if* $(x_1, \ldots, x_N) \in I$ *then:*

$$\mathsf{Eval}(\mathsf{pp}, \mathsf{Pk}_1, \ldots, \mathsf{Pk}_N, \mathsf{id}, \mathsf{Ct}_1, \ldots, \mathsf{Ct}_N) = F_\lambda(x_1, \ldots, x_N).$$

Privacy. Now we state the notion of *privacy* in the style of indistinguishability-based security for encryption and related primitives. The privacy for a (N, D, I, Σ, F)-MINI-FE MINI-FE $\triangleq$ (Setup, KeyGen, Encode, Eval) is formalized by means of the following game $\mathsf{Priv}_{\mathcal{A}}^{N,D,I,\Sigma,F,\mathsf{MINI\text{-}FE}}$ between an adversary $\mathcal{A} \triangleq (\mathcal{A}_0, \mathcal{A}_1)$ (with access to an oracle) and a *challenger* $\mathcal{C}$.

$\mathsf{Priv}_{\mathcal{A}}^{N,D,I,\Sigma,F,\mathsf{MINI\text{-}FE}}(1^\lambda)$:

Setup phase. $\mathcal{C}$ generates $\mathsf{Setup}(1^\lambda) \to \mathsf{pp}$, samples uniformly $\{0,1\} \to b$ and runs $\mathcal{A}_0$ on input pp.

Corruption phase. $\mathcal{A}_0$, on input pp, outputs a set $\mathsf{SCU} \subset [N]$ of indices of users it wants to corrupt.

Key Generation Phase. For all $i \in [N]$ the challenger generates N pairs of public- and secret- keys $\mathsf{KeyGen}(\mathsf{pp}) \to (\mathsf{Pk}_i, \mathsf{Sk}_i)$, and runs $\mathcal{A}_1^{O(\cdot)}$ on input $(\mathsf{Pk}_i, \mathsf{Sk}_i)_{i \in \mathsf{SCU}}$ and $(\mathsf{Pk}_i)_{i \in [N] - \mathsf{SCU}}$, where O is an oracle defined next.

Query phase. The adversary $\mathcal{A}_1$ has access to an oracle O. The oracle O on input an identifier $\mathsf{id} \in \{0,1\}^\lambda$ and a pair of vectors $\vec{x}_0 \triangleq (x_{0,1}, \ldots, x_{0,n})$ and $\vec{x}_1 \triangleq (x_{1,1}, \ldots, x_{1,n})$ outputs the set of cipherexts $(\mathsf{Encode}(\mathsf{pp}, 1, \mathsf{id}, \mathsf{Sk}_1, (\mathsf{Pk}_i)_{i \in [N] - \{1\}}, x_{b,1}), \ldots, \mathsf{Encode}(\mathsf{pp}, N, \mathsf{id}, \mathsf{Sk}_N, (\mathsf{Pk}_i)_{i \in [N] - \{N\}}, x_{b,N}))$.

Output. At some point the adversary outputs its guess b'.

Winning conditions. The adversary wins the game if the following conditions hold:
1. $b' = b$.
2. $x_{0,i} = x_{1,i}$ for any $i \in \mathsf{SCU}$.
3. for any pair of vectors $(\vec{x}_0, \vec{x}_1)$ for which $\mathcal{A}$ asked a query to the oracle O it holds that: for any vector $\vec{x}$, $F_\lambda(\vec{x}_0') = F_\lambda(\vec{x}_1')$ where for $b \in \{0,1\}$, $\vec{x}_b'$ is the vector equal to $\vec{x}$ in all indices in SCU and equal to $\vec{x}_b$ elsewhere.
4. S has cardinality $< N$, $\vec{x}_0$ and $\vec{x}_1$ are vectors of dimension N over D and $\mathsf{id} \in \{0,1\}^\lambda$.
5. There is no pair of queries for the same identifier.

Fig. 1. The experiment $\mathsf{Priv}_{\mathcal{A}}^{N,D,\Sigma,F,\mathsf{MINI\text{-}FE}}$. The set SCU denotes the corrupted users.

The advantage of adversary $\mathcal{A}$ in the above game is defined as

$$\mathsf{Adv}_{\mathcal{A}}^{\mathsf{MINI\text{-}FE},\mathsf{Priv}}(1^\lambda) \triangleq \left| \mathrm{Prob}[\mathsf{Priv}_{\mathcal{A}}^{N,D,\Sigma,F,\mathsf{MINI\text{-}FE}}(1^\lambda) = 1] - 1/2 \right|$$

Definition 3 (Privacy). *We say that a MINI-FE protocol* MINI-FE *for parameters* (N, D, Σ, F) *is private if all PPT adversaries* $\mathcal{A} \triangleq (\mathcal{A}_0, \mathcal{A}_1)$ *have at most negligible advantage in the game defined in Fig. 1.*

Simulation-Based Privacy. In addition, we also present a stronger simulation-based definition.

Definition 4 (Simulation-based privacy). *We say that a MINI-FE protocol* MINI-FE *for parameters* (N, D, Σ, F) *is indistinguishably simulation-secure (SIM-Secure) if for all PPT (oracle) adversaries* $\mathcal{A} \triangleq (\mathcal{A}_0, \mathcal{A}_1)$, *there exists a probabilistic polynomial time simulator* Sim *such that the following two ensembles* $\{\mathsf{Real}_{\mathcal{A}}^{N,D,\Sigma,F,\mathsf{MINI\text{-}FE}}(1^\lambda)\}_{\lambda>0}$ *and* $\{\mathsf{Ideal}_{\mathcal{A},\mathsf{Sim}}^{N,D,\Sigma,F,\mathsf{MINI\text{-}FE}}(1^\lambda)\}_{\lambda>0}$ *defined in Fig. 2 are computationally indistinguishable.*

$\mathsf{Real}_{\mathcal{A}}^{N,D,\Sigma,F,\mathsf{MINI\text{-}FE}}(1^\lambda)$:

Setup phase. Generates $\mathsf{Setup}(1^\lambda) \to \mathsf{pp}$ and run $\mathcal{A}_0$ on input pp.

Corruption phase. $\mathcal{A}_0$, on input pp, outputs a set $\mathsf{SCU} \subset [N]$ of indices of users it wants to corrupt.

Key Generation Phase. For all $i \in [N]$ the challenger generates N pairs of public- and secret- keys $\mathsf{KeyGen}(\mathsf{pp}) \to (\mathsf{Pk}_i, \mathsf{Sk}_i)$, and runs $\mathcal{A}_1^{O(\cdot)}$ on input $(\mathsf{Pk}_i, \mathsf{Sk}_i)_{i \in \mathsf{SCU}}$ and $(\mathsf{Pk}_i)_{i \in [N]-\mathsf{SCU}}$.

Query phase. The adversary $\mathcal{A}_1$ has access to a stateful oracle O. The oracle O on input an identifier $\mathsf{id} \in \{0,1\}^\lambda$ and a vector $\vec{x} \triangleq (x_1, \ldots, x_n)$ outputs the set of cipherexts $(\mathsf{Encode}(\mathsf{pp}, 1, \mathsf{id}, \mathsf{Sk}_1, (\mathsf{Pk}_i)_{i \in [N]-\{1\}}, x_1), \ldots, \mathsf{Encode}(\mathsf{pp}, N, \mathsf{id}, \mathsf{Sk}_N, (\mathsf{Pk}_i)_{i \in [N]-\{N\}}, x_N))$.

Output. At some point the adversary outputs a string α.

$\mathsf{Ideal}_{\mathcal{A},\mathsf{Sim}}^{N,D,\Sigma,F,\mathsf{MINI\text{-}FE}}(1^\lambda)$:

Setup phase. Generates $\mathsf{Setup}(1^\lambda) \to \mathsf{pp}$ and run $\mathcal{A}_0$ on input pp.

Corruption phase. $\mathcal{A}_0$, on input pp, outputs a set $\mathsf{SCU} \subset [N]$ of indices of users it wants to corrupt.

Key Generation Phase. For all $i \in [N]$ the challenger generates N pairs of public- and secret- keys $\mathsf{KeyGen}(\mathsf{pp}) \to (\mathsf{Pk}_i, \mathsf{Sk}_i)$, and runs $\mathcal{A}_1^{O'(\cdot)}$ on input $(\mathsf{Pk}_i, \mathsf{Sk}_i)_{i \in \mathsf{SCU}}$ and $(\mathsf{Pk}_i)_{i \in [N]-\mathsf{SCU}}$, where O' is an oracle defined next.

Query phase. The adversary $\mathcal{A}_1$ has access to an oracle O'. The oracle O' on input an identifier $\mathsf{id} \in \{0,1\}^\lambda$, a vector $\vec{x} \triangleq (x_1, \ldots, x_n)$, the set of public-keys $(\mathsf{Pk}_i)_{i \in [N]-\mathsf{SCU}}$, the set of corrupted keys $(\mathsf{Pk}_i, \mathsf{Sk}_i)_{i \in \mathsf{SCU}}$, outputs $\mathsf{Sim}(F(\vec{x}), (\mathsf{Pk}_i)_{i \in [N]-\mathsf{SCU}}, (\mathsf{Pk}_i, \mathsf{Sk}_i)_{i \in \mathsf{SCU}})$.

Output. At some point the adversary outputs a string α.

Fig. 2. The experiments $\mathsf{Real}_{\mathcal{A}}^{N,D,\Sigma,F,\mathsf{MINI\text{-}FE}}$ and $\mathsf{Ideal}_{\mathcal{A},\mathsf{Sim}}^{N,D,\Sigma,F,\mathsf{MINI\text{-}FE}}$.

3.2 Bilinear Maps

In this section we describe the bilinear setting with groups of prime order and the assumption that we will use to prove the privacy of the MINI-FE of Sect. 4.

Prime Order Bilinear Groups. Prime order bilinear groups were first used in cryptography by Boneh and Franklin [6], and Joux [17]. We suppose the existence of an efficient group generator algorithm $\mathcal{G}$ which takes as input the security parameter λ and outputs a description $\mathcal{I} \stackrel{\triangle}{=} (p, \mathbb{G}, \mathbb{G}_T, \mathbf{e})$ of a bilinear instance of prime order, where $\mathbb{G}$ and $\mathbb{G}_T$ are cyclic groups of prime order p, and $\mathbf{e} : \mathbb{G} \times \mathbb{G} \to \mathbb{G}_T$ is a map with the following properties:

1. (Bilinearity): $\forall\ (g, h) \in \mathbb{G}^2$ and $(a, b) \in \mathbb{Z}_p^2$ it holds that $\mathbf{e}(g^a, h^b) = \mathbf{e}(g, h)^{ab}$.
2. (Non-degeneracy): $\exists\ g \in \mathbb{G}$ such that $\mathbf{e}(g, g)$ has order p in $\mathbb{G}_T$.

Bilinear Decision Diffie-Hellman Assumption [6]**.** More formally, we have the following definition. First pick a random bilinear instance $\mathcal{G}(1^\lambda) \to (p, \mathbb{G}, \mathbb{G}_T,$ $\mathbf{e}) \stackrel{\triangle}{=} \mathcal{I}$ and then pick $\mathbb{G} \to g$, $\mathbb{Z}_p^4 \to (a, b, c, z)$, and set $D \stackrel{\triangle}{=} (\mathcal{I}, g, g^a, g^b, g^c)$, $T_0 \stackrel{\triangle}{=} \mathbf{e}(g, g)^{abc}$ and $T_1 \stackrel{\triangle}{=} \mathbf{e}(g, g)^z$. We define the advantage of any $\mathcal{A}$ in breaking the BDDH Assumption (with respect to $\mathcal{G}$) to be

$$\mathsf{Adv}_{\mathsf{BDDH}}^{\mathcal{A}, \mathcal{G}}(\lambda) \stackrel{\triangle}{=} \Big| \mathrm{Prob}[\mathcal{A}(D, T_0) = 1] - \mathrm{Prob}[\mathcal{A}(D, T_1) = 1] \Big|.$$

We say that Assumption BDDH holds for generator $\mathcal{G}$ if for all non-uniform PPT algorithms $\mathcal{A}$, $\mathsf{Adv}_{\mathsf{BDDH}}^{\mathcal{A}(\lambda), \mathcal{G}}$ is a negligible function of λ.

4 MINI-FE for Inner Products

In this section we present our MINI-FE for the IP functionality (introduced in Sect. 1.2).

Definition 5 (MINI-FE for IP). *Let* RO *be a hash function[2] (that in the proof will be set to a random oracle), and let $\mathcal{G}$ be a generator for a bilinear map instance of prime order. Let $2N$ be the number of users, $D \stackrel{\triangle}{=} \mathbb{N}$ be the domain of valid inputs, $\Sigma \stackrel{\triangle}{=} \mathbb{N}$ and $\mathsf{IP}_{N,\mu}$ the IP functionality parameterized by N, and let $I \stackrel{\triangle}{=} \{I_\lambda\}_\lambda$ be such that for all $\lambda > 0$, I_λ is an element such that the discrete log of g^{I_λ} can be computed efficiently, where g is an element of the group $\mathbb{G}_T$ output by $\mathcal{G}$ with security parameter λ. Furthermore, the hash function RO takes as input a description of a bilinear instance $\mathcal{I} = (p, \mathbb{G}, \mathbb{G}_T, \mathbf{e})$ and maps strings from $\{0, 1\}^\lambda$ to $\mathbb{G}$. Our $(2N, D, I, \Sigma, \mathsf{IP}_N)$-MINI-FE in the random oracle model follows.*

- Setup(1^λ): *on input the security parameter in unary, it outputs* $\mathsf{pp} \stackrel{\triangle}{=} \mathcal{I}$ *where*

$$\mathcal{I} \stackrel{\triangle}{=} (p, \mathbb{G}, \mathbb{G}_T, \mathbf{e}) \leftarrow \mathcal{G}(1^\lambda).$$

- KeyGen(pp): *on input the public parameters* $\mathsf{pp} \stackrel{\triangle}{=} (g, p, \mathbb{G}, \mathbb{G}_T, \mathbf{e})$*, choose a random $x \leftarrow \mathbb{Z}_p$ and output the pair* ($\mathsf{Pk} \stackrel{\triangle}{=} g^x, \mathsf{Sk} \stackrel{\triangle}{=} x$)*. For notational convenience we will denote by*

$$\left\{ \mathsf{Pk}_i \stackrel{\triangle}{=} \mathsf{Pk}_i^{(1)} \stackrel{\triangle}{=} g^{z_i},\ \mathsf{Sk}_i \stackrel{\triangle}{=} \mathsf{Sk}_i^{(1)} \stackrel{\triangle}{=} z_i \right\}_{i \in [N]}$$

---

[2] For example SHA3.

the pairs of public- and secret-keys of users in the first *group, and by*

$$\left\{ \mathsf{Pk}_{N+i} \stackrel{\triangle}{=} \mathsf{Pk}_i^{(2)} \stackrel{\triangle}{=} g^{s_i}, \ \mathsf{Sk}_{N+i} \stackrel{\triangle}{=} \mathsf{Sk}_i^{(2)} \stackrel{\triangle}{=} s_i \right\}_{i \in [N]}$$

the pairs of users in the second *group.*

– $\mathsf{Encode}(\mathsf{pp}, j, \mathsf{id}, \mathsf{Sk}_j, (\mathsf{Pk})_{i \in [2N] - \{j\}}, x)$: *We consider two cases depending whether the user j is in the first ($j \in \{1, \ldots, N\}$) or second ($j \in \{N + 1, \ldots, 2N\}$) group. For each encoding session, a new and unique id of length λ is generated and shared between users.*

User j in the first group. *On input the public parameters pp, the secret-key $\mathsf{Sk}_j = \mathsf{Sk}_j^{(1)} = z_j$ of user j in the first group, the identifier id of the computation, the public keys $(\mathsf{Pk}_i)_{i \in [2N] - \{j\}}$ of the other users, and an input $x \stackrel{\triangle}{=} x_j \in D$, output the ciphertext $\mathsf{Ct}_j^{(1)}$ computed as follows:*

$$D_j \stackrel{\triangle}{=} \mathsf{e}(\mathsf{RO}(\mathcal{I}, \mathsf{id}), \mathsf{Pk}_j^{(2)})^{\mathsf{Sk}_j^{(1)}} \quad and \quad \mathsf{Ct}_j^{(1)} \stackrel{\triangle}{=} \mathsf{Ct}_j \stackrel{\triangle}{=} D_j \cdot \mathsf{e}(\mathsf{RO}(\mathcal{I}, \mathsf{id}), g)^{x_j}.$$

User $j + N$ in the second group. *On input the public parameters pp, the secret-key $\mathsf{Sk}_{j+N} = \mathsf{Sk}_j^{(2)} = s_j$ of user $j + N$ in the second group, the identifier id of the computation, the public keys $(\mathsf{Pk}_i)_{i \in [2N] - \{j\}}$ of the other users, and an input $x \stackrel{\triangle}{=} y_j \in D$, output the ciphertext $\left(y_j, \mathsf{Ct}_j^{(2)} \right)$, where $\mathsf{Ct}_j^{(2)}$ is computed below using the following notations: For any $i, j \in [N], i \neq j$, let*

$$S_{i,j} \stackrel{\triangle}{=} \left(\mathsf{Pk}_i^{(2)} \right)^{\mathsf{Sk}_j^{(2)}}. \tag{1}$$

For any $j \in [N]$, let

$$T_j \stackrel{\triangle}{=} \prod_{i<j} S_{i,j} / \prod_{i>j} S_{i,j} = g^{\mathsf{Sk}_j^{(2)} \cdot \left(\sum_{i<j} \mathsf{Sk}_i^{(2)} - \sum_{i>j} \mathsf{Sk}_i^{(2)} \right)}. \tag{2}$$

For any $j \in [N]$, let

$$E_j \stackrel{\triangle}{=} \mathsf{e} \left(\mathsf{RO}(\mathcal{I}, \mathsf{id}), \mathsf{Pk}_j^{(1)} \right)^{y_j \cdot \mathsf{Sk}_j^{(2)}} \tag{3}$$

Compute the ciphertext as

$$\mathsf{Ct}_j^{(2)} \stackrel{\triangle}{=} \mathsf{Ct}_{N+j} \stackrel{\triangle}{=} E_j \cdot \mathsf{e}(\mathsf{RO}(\mathcal{I}, \mathsf{id}), T_j). \tag{4}$$

Observe that the values T_j's have the property that their product is 1.

– $\mathsf{Eval}(\mathsf{pp}, \mathsf{Pk}_1, \ldots, \mathsf{Pk}_{2N}, \mathsf{id}, \mathsf{Ct}_1, \ldots, \mathsf{Ct}_{2N})$, *on input the public parameters pp, the public-keys of all users, the identifier $\mathsf{id} \in \{0, 1\}^\lambda$ of the computation, and the ciphertexts encrypted by all users, compute what follows.*

Recall that, for $i = 1, \ldots, N$, $\mathsf{Ct}_i = \mathsf{Ct}_i^{(1)}$ and $\mathsf{Ct}_{N+i} = (y_j, \mathsf{Ct}_i^{(2)})$. Then compute:

$$R_1 = \prod_{i \in [N]} \left(\mathsf{Ct}_i^{(1)} \right)^{y_i}, \qquad R_2 = \prod_{i \in [N]} \mathsf{Ct}_i^{(2)}, \qquad R = R_1/R_2. \tag{5}$$

By brute force compute $r = \mathbf{dlog}_{e(\mathsf{RO}(\mathcal{I},\mathsf{id}),g)} R$ and output r (this can be done efficiently if the inputs have the required norm).

Correctness. By definition of the values T_j's, we have that

$$
\begin{aligned}
R_2 &= \prod_{i \in [N]} \mathsf{Ct}_i^{(2)} = \prod_{i \in [N]} e(\mathsf{RO}(\mathcal{I},\mathsf{id}), \mathsf{Pk}_i^{(1)})^{y_i \cdot \mathsf{Sk}_i^{(2)}} \cdot e(\mathsf{RO}(\mathcal{I},\mathsf{id}), T_i) \\
&= \prod_{i \in [N]} e(\mathsf{RO}(\mathcal{I},\mathsf{id}), \mathsf{Pk}_i^{(1)})^{y_i \cdot \mathsf{Sk}_i^{(2)}}.
\end{aligned}
\tag{6}
$$

Moreover, we have that:

$$
\begin{aligned}
R_1 &= \prod_{i \in [N]} \mathsf{Ct}_{1,i}^{y_i} = \prod_{i \in [N]} e(\mathsf{RO}(\mathcal{I},\mathsf{id}), \mathsf{Pk}_i^{(2)})^{y_i \cdot \mathsf{Sk}_i^{(1)}} \cdot e(\mathsf{RO}(\mathcal{I},\mathsf{id}), g)^{y_i \cdot x_i} \\
&= \prod_{i \in [N]} e(\mathsf{RO}(\mathcal{I},\mathsf{id}), \mathsf{Pk}_i^{(1)})^{y_i \cdot \mathsf{Sk}_i^{(2)}} \cdot e(\mathsf{RO}(\mathcal{I},\mathsf{id}), g)^{y_i \cdot x_i} \text{(using e's bilinearity)} \\
&= R_2 \cdot e(\mathsf{RO}(\mathcal{I},\mathsf{id}), g)^{y_i \cdot x_i},
\end{aligned}
\tag{7}
$$

and thus $R_1/R_2 = e(\mathsf{RO}(\mathcal{I},\mathsf{id}), g)^{\sum_{i \in [N]} x_i \cdot y_i}$, as we had to show.

The security proof is provided in Sect. 5.

5   Security of the Protocol

Theorem 2 (Indistinguishability-based privacy). *The advantage of any PPT-bounded adversary $\mathcal{A}$ against the indistinguishability-based privacy notion (Fig. 1) for the MINIFE scheme defined in Definition 5 is negligible.*

Proof (Theorem 2). We prove Theorem 1 with respect to an SCU set of cardinality N-2 using a standard hybrid argument. Assume by contradiction that there exist a PPT adversary $\mathcal{A}$ with non-negligible advantage in the privacy game. To that aim, we define a sequence of hybrid experiments against a non-uniform PPT adversary $\mathcal{A}$ attacking the privacy game by asking at most q queries to its encryption oracle $\mathcal{O}$ and at most q_{RO} random oracle queries. We prove their computational indistinguishability.

To keep notation simple, we assume that whenever $\mathcal{A}$ corrupts a set of users SCU ($|\mathsf{SCU}| \leq N$-2), then: if $i \in \mathsf{SCU}$ and $i \in \{1, \ldots, N\}$ (respectively $i \in \{N+1, \ldots, 2N\}$), then also $i+N \in \mathsf{SCU}$ (respectively $i-N \in \mathsf{SCU}$). We assume that each query to the oracle O consists of two pairs of vectors

$(x_{0,1}, \ldots, x_{0,N}), (y_{0,1}, \ldots, y_{0,N})$ and $(x_{1,1}, \ldots, x_{1,N}), (y_{1,1}, \ldots, y_{1,N})$, where the first (respectively second) vector in each pair corresponds to the secret inputs of the users in the first (respectively second) group. It is important to note that $|\mathsf{SCU}| \leq N\text{-}2$. We provide an overview of the hybrids, and then motivate the transition between them:

$\underline{H^0}$: this hybrid game corresponds to the privacy experiment having the challenge bit set to 0.

$\underline{H^1_{i,j,k}}_{k \in [q], i, j \in [N], j > i}$: pictorially, we hybridize in the following way:

$$H^1_{1,2,1^+} \cdots \to H^1_{1,2,q} = H^1_{1,3,0^+} H^1_{1,3,1^+} \cdots \to H^1_{1,3,q} = H^1_{1,4,0^+} \qquad H^1_{1,4,1^+} \cdots \to H^1_{1,N,q} = H^1_{2,3,0}$$
$$H^1_{2,3,1^+} \cdots \to H^1_{2,3,q} = H^1_{2,4,0^+} \qquad H^1_{2,4,1^+} \cdots \to H^1_{2,N,q} = H^1_{3,4,0}$$

$$\vdots$$

$$H^1_{N-1,N,1^+} \cdots \to H^1_{N-1,N,q} = H^2$$

H_0 is identical to $H^1_{1,2,q}$, and let $H^1_{i+1,i+2,0}$ be identical to $H^1_{i,N,q}$ for any $i \in \{2, \ldots, N-1\}$. For any $i, j \in \{1, \ldots, N\}$ with $j > i+1$ let $H^1_{i,j,0}$ be identical to $H^1_{i,j-1,q}$.

The experiment $H^1_{i,j,k}$ for $k \in [q], i, j \in [N], j > i$ is identical to $H^1_{i,j,k-1}$ except that if $i, j \notin \mathsf{SCU}$ then the k-th query is answered in the following way: the elements $S_{i,j}$ used to compute the element $\mathsf{Ct}^{(2)}_i$ of the ciphertext is randomly and independently chosen[3].

$\underline{H^2}$: is identical to experiment $H^1_{N-1,N,q}$ except that for all queries $k \in [q]$, all $i \in [N], i \notin \mathsf{SCU}$, the product $\prod_{j \in [N], j > i, j \notin \mathsf{SCU}} S_{i,j}$ is replaced by a random element R_i subject to the constraint that the product of all R_i's is 1. That is, for all queries, all $i \in [N], i \notin \mathsf{SCU}$, the element T_i used to compute $\mathsf{Ct}^{(2)}_i$ is equal to $R_i \cdot \left(\left(\prod_{j \in \mathsf{SCU}, j < i} S_{i,j} \right) / \left(\prod_{j \in \mathsf{SCU}, j > i} S_{i,j} \right) \right)$.

$\underline{H^2_{j,k}}_{k \in [q], j \in [N]}$: let $H^2_{1,0}$ be identical to H^2. The experiment $H^2_{j,k}$ for $k \in [q], j \in [N]$ is identical to $H^2_{j,k-1}$ except that if $j \notin \mathsf{SCU}$ then the k-th query is answered in the following way: the element D_j used to compute $\mathsf{Ct}^{(1)}_j$ of the ciphertext is set to a random element Z_j and the element E_j used to compute the $\mathsf{Ct}^{(2)}_j$ is set to $Z_j^{y_{0,j}}$. The experiment $H^2_{j,0}$, for $j \in [N], j > 1$ is identical to $H^2_{j-1,q}$.

$\underline{H^3}$: Experiment H^3 is identical to experiment $H^2_{N,q}$ except that the queries are answered with respect to the pair of vectors $(x_{1,1}, \ldots, x_{1,N}), (y_{0,1}, \ldots, y_{0,N})$ rather than $(x_{0,1}, \ldots, x_{0,N}), (y_{0,1}, \ldots, y_{0,N})$ (observe that the vector of the inputs of the users in the second group is unchanged).

$\underline{H^4}$: Experiment H^4 is identical to experiment H^3 except that the queries are answered with respect to the pair of vectors $(x_{1,1}, \ldots, x_{1,N}), (y_{1,1}, \ldots, y_{1,N})$ rather than $(x_{1,1}, \ldots, x_{1,N}), (y_{0,1}, \ldots, y_{0,N})$.

We proceed with the transition between the hybrids.

---

[3] Rather than being computed as $(\mathsf{Pk}^{(2)}_i)^{\mathsf{Sk}^{(2)}_j}$.

Claim 1 (Indistinguishability of $H_{i,j,k-1}$ from $H_{i,j,k}$). The indistinguishability of $H^1_{i,j,k-1}$ from $H^1_{i,j,k}$ for $k \in [q], i, j \in [N], j > i$ follows from the BDDH assumption.

Proof (Claim 1). We construct a PPT adversary $\mathcal{B}$ against the BDDH (with respect to generator of the bilinear instance $\mathcal{G}$) as follows. We assume that $i, j \notin$ SCU (otherwise the experiments are identical by definition and the claim follows).

$\mathcal{B}$ receives as input a bilinear instance $\mathcal{I} = (p, \mathbb{G}, \mathbb{G}_T, \mathbf{e})$ and a tuple (g, A, B, C, Z) of group elements where $A \triangleq g^a, B \triangleq g^b, C \triangleq g^c$ are random group elements of $\mathbb{G}$ and Z is either $\mathbf{e}(g, g)^{abc}$ or a random element in $\mathbb{G}_T$. $\mathcal{B}$ can use $\mathcal{I}$ to generate the public parameters pp and executes the adversary $\mathcal{A}$ on it.

Care is needed in order to ensure the adversary $\mathcal{A}$ is given access to a correctly programmed random oracle RO. To this end, we assume the adversary is making q_{RO} queries to the random oracle, and out of these, at most q are ciphertext queries. Thus, we have that $q \leq q_{RO}$ is an upper bound on the random oracle queries. We must program RO such that $RO(\mathcal{I}, id^*) = C$, assuming that $\mathcal{A}$ queries for id in its kth step.

Since id^* is not known a priori, our reduction should guess the index of the random oracle query that will ask for id^*. Simply, the probability an adversary queries for id^* in its kth ciphertext query is $1/q_{RO}$. Easily, the probability to abort is $1 - \frac{1}{q_{RO}}$, which is fine as long as q_{RO} is polynomial.

Once the random oracle has been programmed, $\mathcal{A}$ outputs the set SCU of corrupted users, given access to these public parameters.

Setup's Simulation. $\mathcal{B}$ computes the public and secret-keys in the following way. $\mathcal{B}$ sets $Pk_i^{(2)} = A$ and $Pk_j^{(2)} = B$ and for any $l \in [N], l \neq i, j$ it chooses $s_l \leftarrow \mathbb{Z}_p$ and sets $Pk_l = g^{s_l}$. This implicitly defines $Sk_l \triangleq s_l$, for any $l \in [2N], l \neq i + N, j + N$, $Sk_i^{(1)} \triangleq a$ and $Sk_j^{(2)} \triangleq b$. Therefore, $\mathcal{B}$ executes $\mathcal{A}$ with input the PKs and the SKs corresponding to set SCU (and it can do that as it knows the secret-keys $Sk_l \triangleq s_l, l \in$ SCU).

Oracle Queries. $\mathcal{B}$ answers an oracle query id to O by setting $RO(\mathcal{I}, id) \triangleq g^{x_{id}}$ for $x_{id} \leftarrow \mathbb{Z}_p$ and by setting $RO(\mathcal{I}, id^*) = C$ where id^* is the identifier used by $\mathcal{A}$ in the kth query. With this setting, it is easy to see that $\mathcal{B}$ can simulate all queries $k' \neq k$ using the group elements A, B, the values s_i's and x_{id}'s.

For the k-th query, let us analyse how $\mathcal{B}$ can compute the elements $\{S_{i,j}\}_{i,j \in [N], j > i}$, in turn needed to compute the element T_j's in the ciphertexts $\{Ct_j^{(2)}\}_{j \in [N]}$.

$\mathcal{B}$ can symbolically set $S_{i',j'}$ for any $(i', j') \neq (i, j)$ by using A, B, C and the known values s_i's. Thus, it is left to be shown how $\mathcal{B}$ can compute $S_{i,j}$. $\mathcal{B}$ can simply set $\mathbf{e}(RO(\mathcal{I}, id^*), g)^{S_{i,j}} = Z$ and use it to directly compute Eq. (4).

Note that if $Z \triangleq \mathbf{e}(g, g)^{abc}$ then the elements $\{S_{i,j}\}_{i,j \in [N], j > i}$ are distributed like in experiment $H^1_{i,j,k-1}$ and so is the entire simulation.

On the other hand if Z is uniform in $\mathbb{G}_T$, then the element $S_{i,j}$ used to answer the k-th query is random as in experiment $H^1_{i,j,k}$. Therefore, we reach a contradiction. Furthermore, note that correct decryption is always possible on adversary's side, given that the random elements $S_{i,j}$ multiplied within the product T_j will cancel out during the aforementioned procedure.   □

It is easy to see that the previous proof can be easily adapted for the following claim:

Claim 2 (Indistinguishability of $H^1_{i,j,q}$ from $H^1_{i,j+1,1}$). The indistinguishability of the two experiments follow from the BDDH Assumption.

Then, the following two hybrids are identical:

Claim 3 (Indistinguishability of H^2 and $H^1_{N-1,N,q}$). Experiment H^2 is distributed identically to experiment $H_{N-1,N,q}$.

Observe that for each choice of i there will be at most $q \cdot (N - 1 - i)$ hybrid games. We also let q_{RO} denote the maximum of the number of queries to the random oracle (including the ciphertext generation queries). Henceforth we bound the winning probability of the adversary by:

$$
\begin{aligned}
\mathsf{Adv}_{\mathcal{B}}^{H^1 \to H^2} &\leq \sum_{i=1}^{N}(N - 1 - i) \cdot \left(\sum_{k=1}^{q} q_{\mathsf{RO}}\right) \cdot \mathsf{Adv}_{\mathsf{BDDH}}(\mathcal{I}, \mathsf{RO}) \\
&\leq \frac{N \cdot (N - 1)}{2} \cdot (q \cdot q_{\mathsf{RO}}) \cdot \mathsf{Adv}_{\mathsf{BDDH}}(\mathcal{I}, \mathsf{RO}) \\
&\leq N^2 \cdot q_{\mathsf{RO}}^2 \cdot \mathsf{Adv}_{\mathsf{BDDH}}(\mathcal{I}, \mathsf{RO}).
\end{aligned}
\tag{8}
$$

where the first two term denote a polynomial quantity, and thus the entire quantity is negligible.

The next hybrids can be proven to be computationally indistinguishable, down to the same assumption.

Claim 4 (Indistinguishability of $H^2_{j,k}$ from $H^2_{j,k-1}$). The indistinguishability of the two experiments follow from the BDDH assumption.

Proof (Claim 4). We construct a PPT adversary $\mathcal{B}$ against the BDDH experiment (with respect to the generator of the bilinear instance $\mathcal{G}$) as follows: we assume that $j \notin \mathsf{SCU}$ (otherwise the experiments are identical by definition and the claim follows).

$\mathcal{B}$ receives as input a bilinear instance $\mathcal{I} = (p, \mathbb{G}, \mathbb{G}_T, e)$ and a tuple (g, A, B, C, Z) of group elements where $A \overset{\triangle}{=} g^a$, $B \overset{\triangle}{=} g^b$, $C \overset{\triangle}{=} g^c$ are random group elements of $\mathbb{G}$ and Z is either $\mathbf{e}(g,g)^{abc}$ or a random element in $\mathbb{G}_T$. $\mathcal{B}$ can use $\mathcal{I}$ to generate the public parameters pp and executes the adversary $\mathcal{A}$ on it. Then $\mathcal{A}$ outputs the set SCU of corrupted users.

$\mathcal{B}$ computes the public- and secret-keys in the following way: $\mathcal{B}$ sets $\mathsf{Pk}_j^{(1)} = A$ and $\mathsf{Pk}_j^{(2)} = B$ and for any $l \in [2N], l \neq j$, it chooses $s_l \leftarrow \mathbb{Z}_p$ and sets $\mathsf{Pk}_l = g^{s_l}$. This implicitly defines $\mathsf{Sk}_l \overset{\triangle}{=} s_l$, for any $l \in [2N], l \neq j$, $\mathsf{Sk}_{1,j} \overset{\triangle}{=} a$ and $\mathsf{Sk}_{2,j} \overset{\triangle}{=} b$.

Therefore, $\mathcal{B}$ executes $\mathcal{A}$ with input the Pks and the Sks corresponding to set SCU (and it can do that as it knows the secret-keys $\mathsf{Sk}_l \stackrel{\triangle}{=} s_l, l \in \mathsf{SCU}$). $\mathcal{B}$ answers an oracle query id to O by programming $\mathsf{RO}(\mathcal{I}, \mathsf{id}) \stackrel{\triangle}{=} g^{x_{\mathsf{id}}}$ for $x_{\mathsf{id}} \leftarrow \mathbb{Z}_p$ and by setting $\mathsf{RO}(\mathcal{I}, \mathsf{id}^\star) = C$ where $\mathsf{id}^\star$ is the identifier used by $\mathcal{A}$ in the k-th query.

In this setting, it is easy to see that $\mathcal{B}$ can simulate all queries $k' \neq k$ using the group elements A, B, the values s_i's and x_{id}'s.

For the k-th query, let us analyze how $\mathcal{B}$ can compute the elements $\{D_j\}_{j \in [N]}$ (respectively $\{E_j\}_{j \in [N]}$), in turn needed to compute the ciphertexts $\{\mathsf{Ct}_j^{(1)}\}_{j \in [N]}$.

$\mathcal{B}$ can set $D_{j'}$ for any $j' \neq j$ by using A, B, C and the known values s_j's and thus can compute $E_{j'} = D_{j'}^{y_{0,j'}}$. So, what is left to show is how $\mathcal{B}$ can compute D_j and E_j. $\mathcal{B}$ can set $D_j = Z$ and $E_j = D_j^{y_{0,j}}$.

Note that if $Z \stackrel{\triangle}{=} \mathsf{e}(g,g)^{abc}$ then the elements $\{D_j, E_j\}_{j \in [N]}$ are distributed like in experiment $H_{j,k-1}^2$ and so the entire simulation follows.

On the other hand if Z is uniform over $\mathbb{G}_T$ then the element D_j used to answer the k-th query is random as in experiment $H_{j,k}^2$ and $E_j = D_j^{y_{0,j}}$ as in experiment $H_{j,k}^2$.

Therefore, we reach a contradiction, since distinguishing between hybrids implies breaking the hypothesis believed intractable.   □

Claim 5 H^3 is distributed identically to experiment $H_{N,q}^2$.

Proof (Claim 5). This follows from the following observations. For all $i \in [N], i \notin \mathsf{SCU}$, the element D_i used to compute (in experiment $H_{N,q}^2$) $\mathsf{Ct}_i^{(1)}$ can be rewritten by setting $D_i \stackrel{\triangle}{=} D_i' \cdot \mathsf{e}(\mathsf{RO}(\mathcal{I}, \mathsf{id}), g)^{-x_{0,i}+x_{1,i}}$ s.t. $\mathsf{Ct}_i^{(1)} \stackrel{\triangle}{=} D_i \cdot \mathsf{e}(\mathsf{RO}(\mathcal{I}, \mathsf{id}), g)^{x_{0,i}} = D_i' \cdot \mathsf{e}(\mathsf{RO}(\mathcal{I}, \mathsf{id}), g)^{x_{1,i}}$, as in H^3.

Moreover, since (in experiment $H_{N,q}^2$) for all $i \in [N], i \notin \mathsf{SCU}$, $E_i = D_i^{y_{0,i}}$, we have that:

$$E_i = D_i'^{y_{0,i}} \cdot \mathsf{e}(\mathsf{RO}(\mathcal{I}, \mathsf{id}), g)^{y_{0,i} \cdot (-x_{0,i}+x_{1,i})}. \tag{9}$$

By definition, the challenge vectors used in Fig. 1, we have that

$$\prod_{i \notin \mathsf{SCU}} \mathsf{e}(\mathsf{RO}(\mathcal{I}, \mathsf{id}), g)^{y_{0,i} \cdot (-x_{0,i}+x_{1,i})} = 1. \tag{10}$$

Recall that (in experiment $H_{N,q}^2$) for all $i \in [N]$, $\mathsf{Ct}_i^{(2)} \stackrel{\triangle}{=} E_i \cdot \mathsf{e}(\mathsf{RO}(\mathcal{I}, \mathsf{id}), T_i)$, where for all $i \notin \mathsf{SCU}$, the element T_i is equal to

$$R_i \cdot \frac{\prod_{j \in \mathsf{SCU}, j < i} S_{i,j}}{\prod_{j \in \mathsf{SCU}, j > i} S_{i,j}},$$

with R_i random in the group subject to the constraint that $\prod_{i \notin \mathsf{SCU}} R_i = 1$.

Then, from Eqs. (9) and (10) we can see that for all $i \notin \mathsf{SCU}$, $\mathsf{Ct}_i^{(2)}$ is distributed according to experiment H^3 by replacing R_i with $R_i' \stackrel{\triangle}{=} R_i \cdot$

$e(\mathsf{RO}(\mathcal{I}, \mathsf{id}), g)^{y_{0,i} \cdot (-x_{0,i} + x_{1,i})}$. In fact in this case the product of the R'_i's is still 1 and the distribution of $\mathsf{Ct}_i^{(2)}$ is unchanged.

Finally, observe that for all $i \in \mathsf{SCU}$, by the constraints on the winning condition we have that $x_{0,i} = x_{1,i}$ and thus for all $i \in \mathsf{SCU}$, the distribution of $\mathsf{Ct}_i^{(1)}, \mathsf{Ct}_i^{(2)}$ in the two experiments is identical as well.   □

Claim 6 (Final Game Hop). H^3 is indistinguishable from H^4.

Proof (Claim 6). This follows from the observation that, by definition of the functionality IP, $(y_{0,1}, \dots, y_{0,N}) = (y_{1,1}, \dots, y_{1,N})$.   □

Observe that experiment H^4 is the privacy experiment for bit $b = 1$; thus, if the BDDH assumption holds, then $\mathcal{A}$ has at most negligible advantage in the privacy game, as we had to prove.   □

Simulation-Based Security for IPFE. It can be easily shown the scheme above reaches a simulation based security notion. The proof follows the same steps.

5.1 Efficiency Analysis

Practicality is a crux aspect in the design of the primitive. Most of the modern, secure hash function are extremely fast, and the ciphertext generation consists of a few pairing operations on both groups.

Somewhat naturally, the evaluation is proportional to the number of users involved in the protocol. This step, however, is subject to massive parallelism. The last step, involves the computation of a discrete log, which is a common approach for Diffie-Hellman-inspired inner-product functional encryption schemes, and can be efficiently performed as long as the norm is bounded.

Acknowledgements. The authors are thankful to anonymous reviewers for valuable comments.

References

1. Abdalla, M., Benhamouda, F., Kohlweiss, M., Waldner, H.: Decentralizing inner-product functional encryption. In: Lin, D., Sako, K. (eds.) PKC 2019. LNCS, vol. 11443, pp. 128–157. Springer, Cham (2019). https://doi.org/10.1007/978-3-030-17259-6_5
2. Abdalla, M., Bourse, F., De Caro, A., Pointcheval, D.: Simple functional encryption schemes for inner products. In: Katz, J. (ed.) PKC 2015. LNCS, vol. 9020, pp. 733–751. Springer, Heidelberg (2015). https://doi.org/10.1007/978-3-662-46447-2_33
3. Agrawal, S., Clear, M., Frieder, O., Garg, S, O'Neill, A., Thaler, J.: Ad hoc multi-input functional encryption. In: Vidick, T. (ed.) 11th Innovations in Theoretical Computer Science Conference, ITCS 2020, Seattle, Washington, USA, 12–14 January 2020. LIPIcs, vol. 151, pp. 40:1–40:41. Schloss Dagstuhl - Leibniz-Zentrum für Informatik (2020)
4. Agrawal, S., Goyal, R., Tomida, J.: Multi-party functional encryption. Cryptology ePrint Archive, Report 2020/1266 (2020). https://eprint.iacr.org/2020/1266

5. Badrinarayanan, S., Goyal, V., Jain, A., Sahai, A.: Verifiable functional encryption. In: Cheon, J.H., Takagi, T. (eds.) ASIACRYPT 2016. LNCS, vol. 10032, pp. 557–587. Springer, Heidelberg (2016). https://doi.org/10.1007/978-3-662-53890-6_19
6. Boneh, D., Franklin, M.: Identity-based encryption from the Weil pairing. In: Kilian, J. (ed.) CRYPTO 2001. LNCS, vol. 2139, pp. 213–229. Springer, Heidelberg (2001). https://doi.org/10.1007/3-540-44647-8_13
7. Boneh, D., Sahai, A., Waters, B.: Functional encryption: definitions and challenges. In: Ishai, Y. (ed.) TCC 2011. LNCS, vol. 6597, pp. 253–273. Springer, Heidelberg (2011). https://doi.org/10.1007/978-3-642-19571-6_16
8. Boneh, D., Waters, B.: Conjunctive, subset, and range queries on encrypted data. In: Vadhan, S.P. (ed.) TCC 2007. LNCS, vol. 4392, pp. 535–554. Springer, Heidelberg (2007). https://doi.org/10.1007/978-3-540-70936-7_29
9. Boyen, X.: The uber-assumption family. In: Galbraith, S.D., Paterson, K.G. (eds.) Pairing 2008. LNCS, vol. 5209, pp. 39–56. Springer, Heidelberg (2008). https://doi.org/10.1007/978-3-540-85538-5_3
10. Chotard, J., Dufour-Sans, E., Gay, R., Phan, D.H., Pointcheval, D.: Dynamic decentralized functional encryption. In: Micciancio, D., Ristenpart, T. (eds.) CRYPTO 2020. LNCS, vol. 12170, pp. 747–775. Springer, Cham (2020). https://doi.org/10.1007/978-3-030-56784-2_25
11. Chotard, J., Dufour Sans, E., Gay, R., Phan, D.H., Pointcheval, D.: Decentralized multi-client functional encryption for inner product. In: Peyrin, T., Galbraith, S. (eds.) ASIACRYPT 2018. LNCS, vol. 11273, pp. 703–732. Springer, Cham (2018). https://doi.org/10.1007/978-3-030-03329-3_24
12. Garg, S., Gentry, C., Halevi, S., Raykova, M., Sahai, A., Waters, B.: Candidate indistinguishability obfuscation and functional encryption for all circuits. In: 54th Annual Symposium on Foundations of Computer Science, Berkeley, CA, USA, 26–29 October 2013, pp. 40–49. IEEE Computer Society Press (2013)
13. Giustolisi, R., Iovino, V., Rønne, P.B.: On the possibility of non-interactive e-voting in the public-key setting. In: Clark, J., Meiklejohn, S., Ryan, P.Y.A., Wallach, D., Brenner, M., Rohloff, K. (eds.) FC 2016. LNCS, vol. 9604, pp. 193–208. Springer, Heidelberg (2016). https://doi.org/10.1007/978-3-662-53357-4_13
14. Goldreich, O.: Foundations of Cryptography: Basic Applications, vol. 2. Cambridge University Press, Cambridge (2004)
15. Goldwasser, S., et al.: Multi-input functional encryption. In: Nguyen, P.Q., Oswald, E. (eds.) EUROCRYPT 2014. LNCS, vol. 8441, pp. 578–602. Springer, Heidelberg (2014). https://doi.org/10.1007/978-3-642-55220-5_32
16. Iovino, V., Rial, A., Rønne, P.B., Ryan, P.Y.A.: Universal unconditional verifiability in e-voting without trusted parties. In: 33rd IEEE Computer Security Foundations Symposium, CSF 2020, Boston, MA, USA, 22–26 June 2020, pp. 33–48. IEEE (2020)
17. Joux, A.: A one round protocol for tripartite Diffie-Hellman. J. Cryptol. 17(4), 263–276 (2004)
18. Lalley, S.P., Glen Weyl, E.: Nash equilibria for a quadratic voting game. CoRR, abs/1409.0264 (2014)
19. Mascia, C., Sala, M., Villa, I.: A survey on functional encryption. Adv. Math. Commun. (2021). https://doi.org/10.3934/amc.2021049
20. Micali, S., Pass, R., Rosen, A.: Input-indistinguishable computation. In: 47th Annual Symposium on Foundations of Computer Science, Berkeley, CA, USA, 21–24 October 2006, pp. 367–378. IEEE Computer Society Press (2006)
21. Park, S., Rivest, R.L.: Towards secure quadratic voting. IACR Cryptology ePrint Archive 2016:400 (2016)

22. Pereira, O., Rønne, P.B.: End-to-end verifiable quadratic voting with everlasting privacy. In: Bracciali, A., Clark, J., Pintore, F., Rønne, P.B., Sala, M. (eds.) FC 2019. LNCS, vol. 11599, pp. 314–329. Springer, Cham (2020). https://doi.org/10.1007/978-3-030-43725-1_22

23. Quarfoot, D., von Kohorn, D., Slavin, K., Sutherland, R., Goldstein, D., Konar, E.: Quadratic voting in the wild: real people, real votes. Public Choice **172**(1), 283–303 (2017)

24. Sahai, A., Waters, B.: Fuzzy identity-based encryption. In: Cramer, R. (ed.) EURO-CRYPT 2005. LNCS, vol. 3494, pp. 457–473. Springer, Heidelberg (2005). https://doi.org/10.1007/11426639_27

25. Shi, E., Hubert Chan, T.-H., Rieffel, E.G., Chow, R., Song, D.: Privacy-preserving aggregation of time-series data. In: ISOC Network and Distributed System Security Symposium, NDSS 2011, San Diego, California, USA, 6–9 February 2011. The Internet Society (2011)

26. Soroush, N., Iovino, V., Rial, A., Roenne, P.B., Ryan, P.Y.A.: Verifiable inner product encryption scheme. In: Kiayias, A., Kohlweiss, M., Wallden, P., Zikas, V. (eds.) PKC 2020. LNCS, vol. 12110, pp. 65–94. Springer, Cham (2020). https://doi.org/10.1007/978-3-030-45374-9_3

27. Yao, A.C.-C.: Protocols for secure computations (extended abstract). In: 23rd Annual Symposium on Foundations of Computer Science, Chicago, Illinois, 3–5 November 1982, pp. 160–164. IEEE Computer Society Press (1982)

Indifferentiability
of the Confusion-Diffusion Network
and the Cascade Block Cipher

Mridul Nandi[1,2], Sayantan Paul[1(✉)], and Abishanka Saha[1]

[1] Indian Statistical Institute, Kolkata, Kolkata, India
sayantan.paul89@gmail.com
[2] Institute for Advancing Intelligence, TCG-CREST, Kolkata, India

Abstract. Substitution Permutation Networks (SPNs) are widely used in the design of modern symmetric cryptographic building blocks. In their Eurocrypt 2016 paper titled 'Indifferentiability of Confusion-Diffusion Networks', Dodis et al. theorized such SPNs as *Confusion-Diffusion networks* and established their provable security in Maurer's indifferentiability framework. Guo et al. extended this work to *non-linear* Confusion-Diffusion networks (NLCDNs), i.e., networks using non-linear permutation layers, in weaker indifferentiability settings. The authors provided a security proof in the sequential indifferentiability model for the 3-round NLCDN and exhibited the tightness of the positive result by providing an (incorrect) attack on the 2-round NLCDN. In this paper, we provide a *corrected attack on the 2-round NLCDN*. Our attack on the 2-round CDN is primitive-construction-sequential, implying that the construction is not secure even in the weaker sequential indifferentiability setting of Mandal et al.

In their paper titled 'Revisiting Cascade Ciphers in Indifferentiability Setting', Guo et al. showed that four stages are necessary and sufficient to realize an ideal $(2\kappa, n)$-block cipher using the cascade of independent ideal (κ, n)-block ciphers with two alternated independent keys, in the indifferentiability paradigm (where a (k, n)-blockcipher has k-bit key space and n-bit message space). As part of their negative results, Guo et al. provided attacks for the 2-round and 3-round cascade constructions with two alternating keys. Further, they gave a heuristic outline of an attack on the 3-round cascade construction with (certain) stronger key schedules. As the second half of this paper, we formalize the attack explored by Guo et al. on the 3-round cascade construction with stronger key schedules and extend the same to *any 2n-bit to 3n-bit non-idealized key scheduling function*.

Keywords: Indifferentiability · Block Cipher · Permutation · Sequential indifferentiability · Distinguishing Advantage

Mathematics Subject Classification number 68P25

S. El Hajji et al. (Eds.): C2SI 2023, LNCS 13874, pp. 178–195, 2023.
https://doi.org/10.1007/978-3-031-33017-9_12

1   Introduction

INDIFFERENTIABILITY OF BLOCK CIPHER. The notion of indifferentiability was first introduced by Maurer et al. [13] and is the appropriate extension of indistinguishability security [12] in which the key of the construction is chosen by the distinguisher. Block ciphers account for the bulk of data encryption and data authentication occurring in cryptography and also play a critical role in the design of hash functions [2,8,9,14]. The "key complementary" property $(e(K, x) \oplus 1^n = e(K \oplus 1^n, x \oplus 1^n))$ of the previous U.S. block cipher standard DES was considered undesirable and, in fact, such properties should ideally be avoided by a "good" block cipher design. The Indifferentiability security notion for block ciphers captures such potentially compromising features. An n-bit ideal cipher $\mathbf{IC} \leftarrow_{\$} BC_n$, where BC_n denotes the set of all n-bit block ciphers with key space $\mathcal{K}$, is the ideal goal for a block cipher.

CONFUSION-DIFFUSION NETWORKS AND EXISTING RESULTS. Substitution Permutation Networks (SPNs) are a class of block ciphers that yield a wn-bit block cipher by iterating three steps, namely, *key addition* (XORing a round key with the wn-bit state), *substitution* (breaking the wn-bit state into w n-bit states and applying an n-bit permutation on each of them), and *permutation* (passing the entire wn-bit state through a key-less permutation). SPNs can be viewed as confusion-diffusion networks, where the "substitution" step is akin to "confusion", and the "permutation" step is viewed as "diffusion". Dodis et al. initiated the indifferentiability analysis of SPNs [5] and introduced the notion of *Confusion-Diffusion Networks* (CDNs). CDNs may be viewed as SPNs without the key addition step. Their CDN models are built upon public random (n-bit) primitives, typically called S-boxes, and non-cryptographic permutation layers, typically known as D-boxes. Other than showing an attack on the 2-round CDN construction with a non-idealized key schedule, they proved that, when the D-boxes are non-linear (and hence achieve more diffusion), five rounds are sufficient for indifferentiability, and that the security bounds improve with an increase in the number of rounds. They further showed that when the D-boxes are linear, nine rounds are sufficient for indifferentiability. These results go a long way in establishing that using non-linear diffusion layers leads to better security. Guo et al. continued the CDN exploration by analyzing their security in the sequential indifferentiability paradigm [13] - a weaker version of Maurer's indifferentiability setting. They proved the sequential indifferentiability of the 3-round CDN construction (under some moderate conditions on the D-boxes), and exhibit the tightness of their positive result by showing a primitive-construction-sequential attack on the 2-round construction.

BLOCK CASCADE CIPHERS AND EXISTING RESULTS. An ideal (κ, n)-block cipher $\mathbf{IC}[\kappa, n]$ is a collection of 2^κ independent, random, and efficiently invertible n-bit permutations, indexed by a κ-bit key k. A *Cascade cipher* is a concatenation of block cipher systems. A cascade of l block ciphers is called an l-cascade, and is of the form

$$E_l(k_l, E_{l-1}(k_{l-1}, \ldots, E_2(k_2, E_1(k_1, m)) \ldots)$$

for an input message m. In [15], Shannon showed that the cascade of l independent ideal (κ, n)-ciphers is a special case of product secrecy system, and is a set of $2^{l\kappa}$ n-bit permutations, but failed to provide additional insight on the nature and structure of the permutations. Even and Goldreich [6] proved that the set of permutations achieved by l-cascade are not independent and that their behavior could be modeled by conducting only $l \cdot 2^{\kappa}$ exhaustive experiments. These experiments, however, did not allow the adversary to query the underlying ciphers. Lampe and Seurin [10] observed that the cascade of two $\mathbf{IC}(\kappa, n)$ with two independent keys was not indifferentiable from $\mathbf{IC}(2\kappa, n)$.

Guo et al. addressed the question of the required conditions and sufficient value of l in the Ideal Cipher Model, under which an l-cascade of $\mathbf{IC}(\kappa, n)$ will be indifferentiable from $\mathbf{IC}(\kappa', n)$, where $\kappa' > \kappa$. They showed [7] that, for an alternating key schedule $KS(k_1, k_2) = (k_1, k_2, k_1, \ldots)$, the 4-cascade construction is indifferentiable from $\mathbf{IC}(2\kappa, n)$ with $n/6$-bit security, whereas the 2-cascade and 3-cascade constructions are not. The existence of the slide attack [1] rendered the authors incapable of considering using the same block cipher for an l-cascade under the alternating key schedule, irrespective of the value of l. The authors, on the request of the EUROCRYPT 2016 referees' panel, further explored the indifferentiability of 3-cascade with the key schedule $(k_1, k_2, k_1 \oplus k_2)$, which sidestepped the attack on 3-cascade with alternating key schedule given by Guo et al. They provided a 10-query distinguisher that succeeds against any simulator. They generalised this attack to cover all key schedules $KS(K) = (k_1, k_2, k_3)$ where $\pi_1(K) = (k_1, k_2)$, $\pi_2(K) = (k_2, k_3)$ and $\pi_3(K) = (k_3, k_1)$ are efficiently computable 2κ-bit permutations, for a 2κ-bit master key K.

1.1   Our Contribution

Our contribution to this paper is twofold:

1. The attack on 2-CDN provided by Dodis et al. [5] is not sequential (Their distinguisher may possibly make queries first to the construction, then to the primitive, and then to the construction again, depending on the primitive query outputs and the diffusion layer). The security proof by Guo et al. [4] establishes the sequential indifferentiability [11] of 3-CDN. However, the corresponding primitive-construction-sequential attack for 2-CDN given in [4] makes an *incorrect* assumption about the class of D-boxes, the non-cryptographic diffusion layer of the construction (explained in detail in Sect. 2.1). This begs the question if the sequential indifferentiability of 2-CDN is indeed a tight result, in terms of the number of rounds. We aim to answer this question by exhibiting a distinguisher making *at most 10 queries* which succeeds against *any* simulator with an advantage of at least $1 - \mathcal{O}(q_S^2/2^{2n})$, where q_S is the simulator query complexity. This shows that, even with respect to a weaker notion of indifferentiability (sequential), the 2-CDN construction is not secure. This implies that the other security guarantees that follows from sequential indifferentiability, e.g., correlation intractability [3], as shown by [11], also may not hold for 2-CDN.

2. With respect to the attack on 3-cascade, even though the generalization made on the key scheduling function by Guo et al. [7] cover a large range of possible key schedules, the question of indifferentiability is left unanswered for a much wider range of key schedules. To that end, we close the gap by showing an attack on the 3-cascade construction with a *generalized* $2n$-bit to $3n$-bit non-idealized key schedule. Our distinguisher makes *12 queries* and succeeds against *any* simulator with an advantage of at least $1/2 - \mathcal{O}(q_S/2^{2n})$, where q_S is the simulator query complexity.

1.2   Games for Indifferentiable Security

CLASSICAL INDIFFERENTIABILITY. A *distinguisher* $\mathcal{A}$ is an algorithm interacting with a game G consisting of one or more oracles denoted by $\mathcal{A}^{\mathsf{G}}$. The distinguishers considered in this paper are computationally unbounded and the games are independent of the distinguisher. So we assume $\mathcal{A}$ to be deterministic. We write $(\mathsf{Q}_i, \mathsf{R}_i)$ to denote the ith query-response pair and so

$$\tau_i := \tau_i(\mathcal{A}^{\mathsf{G}}) := \big((\mathsf{Q}_1, \mathsf{R}_1), \ldots, (\mathsf{Q}_i, \mathsf{R}_i)\big)$$

represents the *transcript of the interaction* $\mathcal{A}^{\mathsf{G}}$ (or simply transcript of $\mathcal{A}$) after i queries. After all queries have been made $\mathcal{A}$ returns a bit b (written as $\mathcal{A}^{\mathsf{G}} \to b$). Note that b is a deterministic function of $\tau_q := \tau(\mathcal{A}^{\mathsf{G}})$ where q is the number of queries made by $\mathcal{A}$. For two games $\mathsf{G}_0, \mathsf{G}_1$ of oracles, we define

$$\Delta_{\mathcal{A}}(\mathsf{G}_0 \; ; \; \mathsf{G}_1) := \big|\Pr[\mathcal{A}^{\mathsf{G}_0} \to 1] - \Pr[\mathcal{A}^{\mathsf{G}_1} \to 1]\big|.$$

Let E be an ideal oracle and P denote a collection of ideal primitives. We consider game $\mathsf{G} = (\mathsf{G.Cons}, \mathsf{G.Prim})$ where (i) G.Cons represents either a real stateless construction oracle C^{P} or the ideal oracle E, and (ii) G.Prim represents the collection of ideal primitives P or a stateful deterministic simulator $\mathsf{Sim}^{\mathsf{E}}$ (simulating primitive oracles).

Definition 1 (indifferentiability advantage). *The (classical) indifferentiability advantage of $\mathcal{A}$ against $\mathsf{C} := (\mathsf{C}^{\mathsf{P}}, \mathsf{P})$ for a simulator Sim is defined as*

$$\mathbf{Adv}^{\mathrm{indiff}}_{\mathsf{C},\mathsf{Sim}}(\mathcal{A}) := \Delta_{\mathcal{A}}((\mathsf{C}^{\mathsf{P}}, \mathsf{P}) \; ; \; (\mathsf{E}, \mathsf{Sim}^{\mathsf{E}})).$$

SEQUENTIAL INDIFFERENTIABILITY. In the classical indifferentiability setting, the distinguisher doesn't need to make its queries in any particular order with respect to when the construction is queried and when the primitive(s) is queried. A stricter version of the classical indifferentiability is the notion of *sequential indifferentiability*, introduced by Mandal et al. in [11]. A sequential distinguisher $\mathcal{D}$ is *primitive-construction-sequential* if it first makes all its primitive queries (without querying the construction), and then follows to make its construction queries (without querying the primitive), in that order. Formally, for a *wn*-bit random permutation $\mathcal{Z}$, if a sequential distinguisher $\mathcal{D}$ tries to distinguish between the real system $(\mathsf{CDN}^{\mathcal{P}}, \mathcal{P})$ and the ideal system $(\mathcal{Z}, \mathcal{S}^{\mathcal{Z}})$, its distinguishing advantage is defined as follows.

Definition 2 (sequential indifferentiability advantage). *The (sequential) indifferentiability advantage of a sequential distinguisher $\mathcal{A}$ against* $\mathsf{C} := (\mathsf{C}^\mathsf{P}, \mathsf{P})$ *for a simulator* Sim *is defined as*

$$\mathbf{Adv}_{\mathsf{C},\mathsf{Sim}}^{\mathrm{seq-indiff}}(\mathcal{A}) := \Delta_{\mathcal{A}}((\mathsf{C}^\mathsf{P}, \mathsf{P}) \; ; \; (\mathsf{E}, \mathsf{Sim}^\mathsf{E})).$$

Sequential indifferentiability is a weaker form of the classical indifferentiability notion of [13], in the sense that a sequential adversary acts in a restricted manner as compared to how an adversary might function in the classical indifferentiability setting. It is important to note that any sequential adversarial attack is also applicable in the classical paradigm. This directly implies that if a construction is not sequentially indifferentiable, then it is not differentiable in the classical sense, either.

2   Definition of CDN

NOTATIONS. We denote by $[w] := \{1, 2, \cdots, w\}$. We write any $x \in \{0,1\}^{wn}$, as $x =: (x[1], x[2], \cdots, x[w])$, with $x[i] \in \{0,1\}^n$ for $i \in [w]$, that is, by $x[i]$ we denote the i-th n-bit block of x.

CONFUSION DIFFUSION NETWORKS. Fix integers $w, r \in \mathbb{N}$. Consider a collection of rw permutations

$$\mathcal{P} = \{P_{ij} : \{0,1\}^n \to \{0,1\}^n \mid (i,j) \in [r] \times [w]\}$$

and a collection of $r - 1$ permutations,

$$\Pi = \{\pi_i : \{0,1\}^{wn} \to \{0,1\}^{wn} \mid i \in [r-1]\}$$

Given $\mathcal{P}$ we define the permutations $P_i : \{0,1\}^{wn} \to \{0,1\}^{wn}$, for $i \in [r]$, as follows:
$$P_i(x)[j] = P_{ij}(x[j]), \quad \forall j \in [w]$$

Then the confusion diffusion network based on the collections $\mathcal{P}$ and Π, is defined as

$$\mathsf{CDN}_{w,r}^{\mathcal{P},\Pi} := P_1 \circ \pi_1 \circ P_2 \circ \pi_2 \circ \cdots \circ \pi_{r-1} \circ P_r$$

We often refer to this construction as $\mathsf{CDN}_{w,r}$, whenever $\mathcal{P}, \Pi$ is clear from the context.

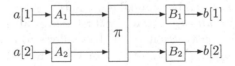

Fig. 1. The $\mathsf{CDN}_{2,2}$ construction.

NOTATIONS FOR $\mathsf{CDN}_{2,2}$. We give an indifferentiability attack against $\mathsf{CDN}_{2,2}$ and thus develop the following notations, which will be adapted henceforth. Consider the collection of four permutations from $\{0,1\}^n$ to $\{0,1\}^n$, $\mathcal{P} = \{A_1 := P_{1,1}, A_2 := P_{1,2}, B_1 := P_{2,1}, B_2 := P_{2,2}\}$ and a permutation $\pi : \{0,1\}^{2n} \to \{0,1\}^{2n}$, so that $\Pi = \{\pi\}$. These collections of permutations determine the construction $\mathsf{CDN}_{2,2}$, shown in the Fig. 1.

2.1   Attack Against $\mathsf{CDN}_{2,2}$

Consider the collection of four permutations from $\{0,1\}^n$ to $\{0,1\}^n$, $\mathcal{P} = \{A_1 := P_{1,1}, A_2 := P_{1,2}, B_1 := P_{2,1}, B_2 := P_{2,2}\}$ and a permutation $\pi : \{0,1\}^{2n} \to \{0,1\}^{2n}$, so that $\Pi = \{\pi\}$. These collections of permutations determine the construction $\mathsf{CDN}_{2,2}$.

ATTACKS ON 2-CDN. The attack against $\mathsf{CDN}_{2,2}$ proposed in [5] proves that this construction is not indifferentiable in the classical sense. Guo et al. proposed another attack in [4] that they claim proves that this construction is not even sequentially indifferentiable. The attack is as follows:

1. Find x and $x_1 \neq x_2$ such that $\pi(x||x_1)[1] = \pi(x||x_2)[1]$, where $\pi(x)[1]$ denotes the first n-bits of $\pi(x)$
2. Query the right oracles to get $A_1^{-1}(x) \to a$, $A_2^{-1}(x_1) \to a_1$, and $A_2^{-1}(x_2) \to a_2$
3. Query the left oracle to get $\mathcal{P}(a||a_1) \to b||b_1$ and $\mathcal{P}(a||a_2) \to b'||b_2$
4. Output 1 if and only if $b = b'$.

PROBLEM WITH THE ATTACK. Consider a function $\pi(x||x_1) = (x \oplus x_1||x_1)$. Clearly, $\pi(x||x_1) = \pi(x'||x_1') \implies x = x', x_1 = x_1'$. Hence, π is a permutation. It is pertinent to note that, for such a permutation π, there does not exist any x and $x_1 \neq x_2$ such that $\pi(x||x_1)[1] = \pi(x||x_2)[1]$ (Fig. 2).

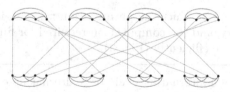

Fig. 2. The top and bottom vertices denote a pair of copies of $\{0,1\}^{2n} = A_1 \sqcup \cdots \sqcup A_{2^n}$, the blue edges are between 2n-bit numbers whose first n-bits match, the red edges denote input-output pairs under π restricted to the first n bits. (Color figure online)

In fact, there is an entire class of 2n-bit permutations for which the above assumption does not hold. Consider a partition of $\{0,1\}^{2n} = A_1 \sqcup A_2 \sqcup \cdots \sqcup A_{2^n}$ where the subset $A_i = \{x \in \{0,1\}^{2n} | x[1] = \langle i-1 \rangle_n\}$, where $\langle m \rangle_n$ is the n-bit representation of the integer m. Thus for any i, all elements of A_i have the same first n bits. Now suppose π sends distinct elements of A_i to elements of distinct subsets, i.e. for $x \neq x' \in A_i$, if $\pi(x) \in A_j$ and $\pi(x') \in A_k$, then $j \neq k$. There are exactly $[(2^n)!]^{2^n}$ such permutations π satisfying the above property. For all these permutations, there does not exist $x, x_1 \neq x_2 \in \{0,1\}^n$, such that $\pi(x\|x_1)[1] = \pi(x\|x_2)[1]$, and hence for which the above attack does not work.

2.2   Our Attack

For an easy understanding of our attack, we introduce the notion of a functional graph.

FUNCTIONAL GRAPH. Let $f : \{0,1\}^{2n} \to \{0,1\}^{2n}$ be a bijection. We define the functional graph $\mathcal{G}^f$ for the function f. Let X, Y be two disjoint copies of $\{0,1\}^{2n}$. Then the vertex set of $\mathcal{G}^f$ is $X \sqcup Y$, and the edges of $\mathcal{G}^f$ are as follows:

- For $x, x' \in X$, if $x[1] = x'[1]$, then the edge $\{x, x'\} \in \mathcal{G}^f$. For $y, y' \in Y$, if $y[1] = y'[1]$, then the edge $\{y, y'\} \in \mathcal{G}^f$. We call this kind of edges, *internal edges*.
- For $x \in X$ and $y \in Y$, if $f(x) = y$, then the edge $\{x, y\} \in \mathcal{G}^f$. We call this kind of edges *external edges*.

Definition 3. *Let f, $\mathcal{G}^f$ be defined as above. A cycle $C = (a_1, a_2, \ldots, a_k, a_1)$ in $\mathcal{G}^f$ is called an Alternating Cycle if, for every internal edge (a_i, a_{i+1}), the edges (a_{i-1}, a_i) and (a_{i+1}, a_{i+2}) are external.*

BASIC IDEA OF OUR ATTACK. Let $\mathcal{G}^{\text{cons}}$ be the functional graph of the construction permutation. Any alternating cycle in $\mathcal{G}^{\text{cons}}$ represents a constraint, that is a low probability event in the ideal world. Any alternating cycle in the functional graph, $\mathcal{G}^\pi$, of π, translates to an equivalent alternating cycle in $\mathcal{G}^{\text{cons}}$, with probability one in the real world. Hence finding an alternating cycle in $\mathcal{G}^\pi$ constitutes a valid attack on this construction.

THE DISTINGUISHER $\mathcal{D}_{\text{cdn}}$. Since the permutation π is non-idealized, it is available to $\mathcal{D}_{\text{cdn}}$ in totality, and the computation required for finding an alternating cycle in $\mathcal{G}^\pi$ can be done efficiently (Fig. 3).

1: Search for either a 4 alternating cycle or 8 alternating cycle in $\mathcal{G}^\pi$.
2: **if** the 4 alternating cycle (x_0, y_0, y_1, x_1) is found **then**
3:      Primitive queries to A_1^{-1}: $x_0[1]$.
           Let a_0 be the response received.
4:      Primitive queries to A_2^{-1}: $x_0[2]$ and $x_1[2]$.
           Let a_0' and a_1' be the respective responses received.
5:      Construction queries: (a_0, a_0') and (a_0, a_1').
           Let b_0 and b_1 be the respective responses received.
6:      **if** $b_0[1] = b_1[1]$ **then**
7:           return 0.
8:      **else**
9:           return 1.

10: **else if** the 8 alternating cycle $(x_0, y_0, y_1, x_1, x_2, y_2, y_3, x_3)$ is found **then**
11:      Primitive queries to A_1^{-1}: $x_0[1]$ and $x_1[1]$.
        Let a_0 and a_1 be the respective responses received.
12:      Primitive queries to A_2^{-1}: $x_0[2], x_1[2], x_2[2]$ and $x_3[2]$.
        Let a_0', a_1', a_2' and a_3' be the respective responses received.
13:      Construction queries: $(a_0, a_0'), (a_1, a_1'), (a_1, a_2')$ and (a_0, a_3').
        Let b_0, b_1, b_2 and b_3 be the respective responses received.
14:      **if** $b_0[1] = b_1[1]$ and $b_2[1] = b_3[1]$ **then**
15:          return 0.
16:      **else**
17:          return 1.

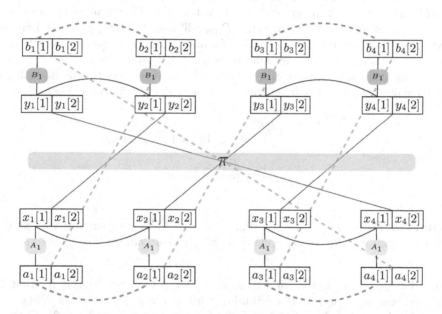

Fig. 3. Attack with an 8 alternating cycle in $\mathcal{G}^\pi$

In the real world, given that $\mathcal{D}_{\mathsf{cdn}}$ finds an alternating cycle, it returns 0 with probability 1. In the ideal world, even though the inputs of all construction queries are revealed to the simulator before $\mathcal{D}_{\mathsf{cdn}}$ queries the construction, finding a cycle in $\mathcal{G}^{\mathsf{cons}}$ is still necessary for the simulator to respond to the primitive queries appropriately in order to succeed against this attack. Any simulator making q queries finds a cycle in $\mathcal{G}^{\mathsf{cons}}$ with probability $\mathcal{O}(\frac{q^2}{2^{2n}})$. Thus, for any simulator making $\ll 2^n$ queries, the distinguisher $\mathcal{D}_{\mathsf{cdn}}$ can successfully differentiate between the two worlds, with probability negligibly close to 1, by just checking whether the alternating cycles of $\mathcal{G}^\pi$ has a corresponding isomorphic copy in $\mathcal{G}^{\mathsf{cons}}$.

2.3   Analysis of the Attack

Lemma 1. *For any simulator $\mathcal{S}$ which can make q many ideal cipher E-queries, the polynomial-time distinguisher $\mathcal{D}_{\text{cdn}}$ succeeds with advantage*

$$\mathbf{Adv}(\mathcal{D}_{\text{cdn}}) \geq 1 - \frac{q^2}{2^{2n}}$$

Proof. Let $p_1 := \Pr_{\text{re}}\left[\mathcal{D}_{\text{cdn}}^{\text{CDN}_{2,2}^{\Pi,\mathcal{P}},\mathcal{P}} \to 0\right]$ denote the probability that $\mathcal{D}_{\text{cdn}}$ returns 0 when interacting with the construction $\text{CDN}_{2,2}^{\Pi,\mathcal{P}}$ and primitives $\mathcal{P}$, in the real world. Let $p_2 := \Pr_{\text{id}}\left[\mathcal{D}_{\text{cdn}}^{\text{E},\mathcal{S}^{\text{E}}} \to 0\right]$ denote the probability that $\mathcal{D}_{\text{cdn}}$ returns 0 when interacting with ideal cipher E, and simulator $\mathcal{S}^{\text{E}}$, in the ideal world. Thus $\mathbf{Adv}(\mathcal{D}_{\text{cdn}}) = |p_1 - p_2|$. In Lemma 2 we show that $\mathcal{G}^\pi$ will contain either an alternating cycle of length 4 or 8 and hence $\mathcal{D}_{\text{cdn}}$ will find it. Thus $p_1 = 1$. In Lemma 3 we show that the probability of the simulator finding a cycle of any length in $\mathcal{G}^{\text{E}}$, by making q ideal cipher queries is $q^2/2^{2n}$. If and only if, $\mathcal{S}$ can find an alternating cycle of length 4 or 8 in $\mathcal{G}^{\text{cons}} = \mathcal{G}^{\text{E}}$, can it reply to the distinguisher's primitive queries such that it returns 0. Thus $p_2 \leq \Pr(\mathcal{S} \text{ finds a cycle in E})$.

$$\begin{aligned}\mathbf{Adv}(\mathcal{D}_{\text{cdn}}) &= |p_1 - p_2| \\ &\geq 1 - \Pr(\mathcal{S} \text{ finds a cycle in E}) \\ &= 1 - \frac{q^2}{2^{2n}}\end{aligned}$$

$\square$

Lemma 2. *For any bijection $\pi : \{0,1\}^{2n} \to \{0,1\}^{2n}$, the functional graph $\mathcal{G}^\pi$ either contains an alternating cycle of length 4, or an alternating cycle of length 8.*

Proof. Let $\mathcal{G}^\pi := \mathcal{G}[X,Y]$. For any $x \in X$, let $N_X(x) := N(x) \cap X$, that is the neighbourhood of x in $\mathcal{G}|_X$. Similarly for any $y \in Y$, we write $N_Y(y) := N(y) \cap Y$. We extend the definition of N_X for any subset $X' \subseteq X$, as $N_X(X') := \bigcup_{x \in X'} N_X(x)$. For any $Y' \subseteq Y$, we define $N_Y(Y')$ similarly. Note that for any $x \in X$ and $y \in Y$, $|N_X(x)| = |N_Y(y)| = 2^n - 1$.

We take any $x_0 \in X$, and let $y_0 := \pi(x_0)$. If $N_X(x_0) \cap \pi^{-1}(N_Y(y_0)) \neq \emptyset$, then let $x_1 \in N_X(x_0)$ and $y_1 \in N_Y(y_0)$ be such that $\pi(x_1) = y_1$, which implies that (x_0, y_0, y_1, x_1) is an alternating cycle in $\mathcal{G}^\pi$, and we are done. So we assume the contrary, that $N_X(x_0)$ and $\pi^{-1}(N_Y(y_0))$ are disjoint. Now if there is an internal edge between any two vertices $x_1, x_2 \in \pi^{-1}(N_Y(y_0))$, then there exists $y_1, y_2 \in N_Y(y_0)$ such that $\pi(x_1) = y_1$ and $\pi(x_2) = y_2$, which implies (x_1, y_1, y_2, x_2) is an alternating cycle in $\mathcal{G}^\pi$. Similarly, if there is an internal edge between any two points in $\pi(N_x(x_0))$, then also we end up with an alternating cycle of length 4. So we also assume that $\pi(N_X(x_0))$ and $\pi^{-1}(N_Y(y_0))$ are independent sets. In that case $|N_Y(\pi(N_X(x_0)))| = |N_X(\pi^{-1}(N_Y(y_0)))| = |\pi(N_X(\pi^{-1}(N_Y(y_0))))| = (2^n - 1)^2$. Since $N_Y(\pi(N_X(x_0))), \pi(N_X(\pi^{-1}(N_Y(y_0)))) \subseteq Y$ and $|Y| = 2^{2n}$, so

$N_Y(\pi(N_X(x_0))) \cap \pi(N_X(\pi^{-1}(N_Y(y_0)))) \neq \emptyset$. Let y_2 belong to this intersection. Since $y_2 \in \pi(N_X(\pi^{-1}(N_Y(y_0))))$ there exists $y_1 \in N_Y(y_0)$ and $x_2 \in N_X(x_1)$, with $x_1 := \pi^{-1}(y_1)$, such that $\pi(x_2) = y_2$. Since $y_2 \in N_Y(\pi(N_X(x_0)))$, there exists $x_3 \in N_X(x_0)$ with $y_3 = \pi(x_3)$, such that $y_2 \in N_Y(y_3)$. In this case $(x_0, y_0, y_1, x_1, x_2, y_2, y_3, x_3)$ form an alternating cycle in $\mathcal{G}^\pi$.   □

Lemma 3. *Let* E *be an ideal* $2n$-*bit permutation and let* $\mathcal{S}$ *be any algorithm making at most* q *oracle queries to* E. *Then,*

$$\Pr(\mathcal{S} \text{ finds an alternating cycle in } \mathcal{P}) \leq \frac{q^2}{2^{2n}}$$

Proof. We denote the transcript of $\mathcal{S}$ after i sessions as $\tau_i := \{(x,y)|\, \mathsf{E}(x) = y\}$. Let $\mathcal{G}_i$ be the functional graph of the transcript τ_i, which is a subgraph of $\mathcal{G}^{\mathsf{E}}$. Assuming that G_i is acyclic, $\Pr(\mathcal{S} \text{ finds a cycle after the } (i+1)^{th} \text{ session}) \leq \Pr(y_{i+1}[1] = y_j[1]|\, (\cdot, y_j) \in \tau_i) = \frac{i}{2^n}$. Then,

$$\Pr(\mathcal{S} \text{ finds a cycle in } \mathcal{P}) = \sum_{i \in [q]} \Pr(\mathcal{S} \text{ finds a cycle after the } i^{th} \text{ session})$$

$$\leq q \times \Pr(\mathcal{S} \text{ finds a cycle after the } q^{th} \text{ session})$$

$$\leq \frac{q^2}{2^n}$$

The second line of the inequality is obtained by applying the Union Bound.   □

3   Attacks on Three Round Cascade with Two Keys

(See Fig. 4).

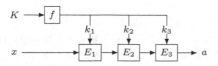

Fig. 4. The 3-Cascade construction for a key schedule f (taking $2n$-bit input K and providing a $3n$-bit output (k_1, k_2, k_3)), and n-bit block ciphers E_1, E_2, E_3.

3.1   Definitions

CASCADE BLOCK CIPHER. For $\ell \geq 2$, let $E_1, \cdots, E_\ell$ be ℓ independent ideal blockciphers, $E_i : \{0,1\}^k \times \{0,1\}^n \to \{0,1\}^n$, $i \in [\ell]$. Let $\mathcal{E}^\ell = (E_1, \cdots, E_\ell)$. Let KS $: \{0,1\}^{k'} \to \{0,1\}^{k\ell}$ be a function, called key-scheduling function, which basically derives ℓ round keys from a master key $K \in \{0,1\}^{k'}$. Then the ℓ-round cascade cipher construction based on E^ℓ and key-scheduling function KS is a blockcipher with key space $\{0,1\}^{k'}$ and message space $\{0,1\}^n$, defined as follows:

$$\mathsf{CC}^{\mathcal{E}^\ell}(K,x) := E_\ell(\kappa_\ell, \cdots E_2(\kappa_2, E_1(\kappa_1, x)) \cdots),$$

where $\mathsf{KS}(K) = \kappa^\ell = (\kappa_1, \kappa_2, \cdots, \kappa_\ell) \in (\{0,1\}^k)^\ell$ and $x \in \{0,1\}^n$. In the following sections, we discuss the security of cascade blockciphers for a few rounds with different sizes of the master key.

Definition 4. *A pair of distinct keys* $(K := (k_1, k_2, k_3), K' := (k_1', k_2', k_3'))$ *is said to be* left-colliding *if* $k_1 = k_1'$, *and are called* right-colliding *if* $k_3 = k_3'$. *We define the sets of left-colliding and right-colliding key pairs as* $\mathcal{C}_L$ *and* $\mathcal{C}_R$ *respectively.*

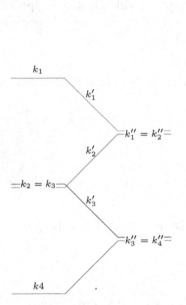

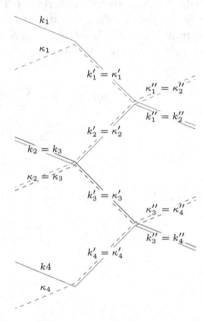

Fig. 5. 4 Chain at left: (K_1, K_2, K_3, K_4), where $K_i = (k_i, k_i', k_i'')$, satisfying the equalities in the figure.

Fig. 6. Double Intersecting 4 Chains: (K_1, K_2, K_3, K_4) and $(\varkappa_1, \varkappa_2, \varkappa_3, \varkappa_4)$, where $K_i = (k_i, k_i', k_i'')$ and $\varkappa_i = (\kappa_i, \kappa_i', \kappa_i'')$, satisfying the equalities in the figure.

Definition 5. *A 4-tuple* (K_1, K_2, K_3, K_4) *of keys is said to form* 4-chain at left *if*

- $(K_1, K_2), (K_3, K_4) \in \mathcal{C}_R$ *and*
- $(K_2, K_3) \in \mathcal{C}_L$

We can similarly define a 4-chain (K_1, K_2, K_3, K_4) at right in which (K_1, K_2), $(K_3, K_4) \in \mathcal{C}_L$ and $(K_2, K_3) \in \mathcal{C}_R$. See Fig. 5 for an illustration of 4-chains. We denote the set $\mathcal{C}_{4L} := \{(K_1, K_2, K_3, K_4) | K_1, K_2, K_3, K_4 \text{ form a 4-chain at left}\}$.

Definition 6. *A pair of distinct key tuples* (K_1, K_2, K_3, K_4) *and* (K'_1, K'_2, K'_3, K'_4) *from* C_{4L} *are said to be* intersecting *if* $K_{j,2} = K'_{j,2}, \forall j \in [4]$, *where* $K_j = (K_{j,1}, K_{j,2}, K_{j,3}) \in \{0, 1\}^{3n}$.

For an intersecting pair of 4-chains (K_1, K_2, K_3, K_4) *and* $(\kappa_1, \kappa_2, \kappa_3, \kappa_4)$, *we denote* (k'_1, κ'_1) *as the* starting pair *and call* (k'_4, κ'_4) *the* ending pair, *where* $K_1 = (k'_1, \cdot, \cdot)$, $\kappa_1 = (\kappa'_1, \cdot, \cdot)$, $K_4 = (k'_4, \cdot, \cdot)$, *and* $\kappa_4 = (\kappa'_4, \cdot, \cdot)$ *(See Fig. 6)*.

3.2 Our Distinguisher $\mathcal{D}$

We assume that $\mathcal{D}$ efficiently finds a starting pair (k'_1, κ'_1) and an ending pair (k'_4, κ''_4) such that there are $\mathcal{O}(2^{2n})$ intersecting 4-chains connecting them, the existence of which will be shown in the analysis section. From the above-mentioned set of paths, $\mathcal{D}$ selects a path uniformly and at random. Let (K_1, K_2, K_3, K_4) and $(\kappa_1, \kappa_2, \kappa_3, \kappa_4)$ be the randomly chosen intersecting 4-chains with $F(K_i) = (k'_i, k''_i, k'''_i)$ and $F(\kappa_i) = (\kappa'_i, \kappa''_i, \kappa'''_i)$, $i \in [4]$. $\mathcal{D}$ samples $y_1, y_2 \leftarrow_\$ \{0, 1\}^n$ and executes the following query routine:

1: Primitive queries to E_1^{-1}: (k'_1, y_1) and (κ'_1, y_1).
   Let x_1, x_2 be the respective responses received.
2: Construction queries to E: (K_1, x_1) and (κ_1, x_2).
   Let a_1, a_2 be the respective responses received.
3: Construction queries to E^{-1}: (K_2, a_1) and (κ_2, a_2).
   Let x'_1, x'_2 be the respective responses received.
4: Construction queries to E: (K_3, x'_1) and (κ_3, x'_2).
   Let a'_1, a'_2 be the respective responses received.
5: Construction queries to E^{-1}: (K_4, a'_1) and (κ_4, a'_2).
   Let x''_1, x''_2 be the respective responses received.
6: Primitive query to E_1: (k'_4, x''_1).
   Let y''_1 be the response received.
7: $b \leftarrow_\$ \{H, T\}$.
8: **if** $b = H$ **then**
9:     Primitive query to E_1: (κ'_4, x''_2).
10: **else**
11:     $x^* \leftarrow_\$ \{0, 1\}^n$ (If $x^* = x''_2$, sample again)
12:     Primitive query to E_1: (κ'_4, x^*).
   Let y''_1 be the response received in either case.
13: **if** $\left[b = H \text{ and } y''_1 = y''_2 \right]$ Or $\left[b = T \text{ and } y''_1 \neq y''_2 \right]$ **then**
14:     Return 0
15: **else**
16:     Return 1

In the Real World, if $b = H$, then $y''_1 = y''_2$ with probability 1, and if $b = T$, then $y''_1 \neq y''_2$ with overwhelming probability. Whereas in the Ideal World, these conditions are satisfied with negligible probability, which will be analyzed in detail in the following section (Fig. 7).

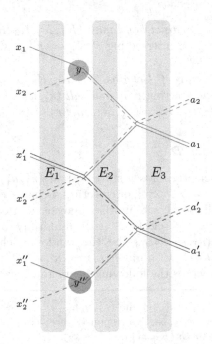

Fig. 7. The Distinguisher samples a pair of Double Intersecting 4-Chains as depicted above, and forces a collision in E_1 at y. Making forward and backward construction queries from x_1 and x_2 with appropriate keys, it obtains x_1'' and x_2'', which, in the real world, must exhibit a collision in E_1 at y''. (The corresponding keys for the primitive and construction queries are implied from the sampled pair of Double Intersecting 4-Chains)

3.3 Analysis of Attack

Let $f : A \to B$. A collision pair of f is a pair (a, a') of distinct elements such that $f(a) = f(a')$. Let $\mathcal{C}_f$ denote the set of collision pairs for the function f. We also write $C_f = |\mathcal{C}_f|$.

Lemma 4. *Let $f : A \to B$ be any function where $|A| = k \cdot |B|$, $k \geq 2$. Then,*

$$C_f \geq k(k-1) \cdot |B|$$

Proof. Fix a function f. There is no loss to assume that $B = \{1, 2, \ldots, b\}$ and $|A| = k \times b$. Let $(A_1^f, A_2^f, \ldots, A_b^f)$ be a partition of A such that $A_i^f = f^{-1}(i)$ (which may be the empty set). Let $|A_i^f| = a_i$, $i \in [b]$. Clearly, $\sum_{i \in [b]} a_i = k \times b$.

Thus,

$$C_f = \sum_{i \in [b]} a_i(a_i - 1)$$

$$= \left[\sum_{i \in [b]} (a_i)^2 - \sum_{i \in [b]} (a_i) \right]$$

$$\geq \left[\frac{1}{b} \times \left(\sum_{i \in [b]} a_i \right)^2 - \sum_{i \in [b]} (a_i) \right] \qquad \text{[Cauchy-Schwartz Inequality]}$$

$$= \left[\frac{(k \times b)^2}{b} - k \times b \right] = k(k - 1) \times |B|.$$

Note that the equality achieves if and only if $a_i = k \ \forall \ i \in [b]$ (i.e. f is a regular function).

Key Schedule Analysis. Let $F := \{0,1\}^{2n} \to \{0,1\}^{3n}$ be a key scheduling function for the 3-round Cascade cipher

$$E((k, k'), x) = E_3(k_3, E_2(k_2, E_1(k_1, x))), \quad F(k, k') = (k_1, k_2, k_3),$$

E_1, E_2, E_3 are independent n-bit block ciphers and $x \in \{0,1\}^n$. In order to explain how the attack works, we first take a detailed look at the key schedule F. Throughout the section, *keys* will mean the $3n$-bit outputs of the function F. We also assume that F is injective and hence there are exactly 2^{2n} many keys. When F is not injective (suppose $F(K) = F(K')$) a simple attack can be employed by querying the construction with the same input with the keys K and K'. In the ideal world, they yield the same output with negligible probability, whereas this is true with probability 1 in the real world.

Let $F_3 := \{0,1\}^{2n} \to \{0,1\}^n$ be a function defined as $F_3(k, k') = k_3$, where $F(k, k') = (k_1, k_2, k_3)$. Applying Lemma 4 to the function F_3, the number of right-colliding key pairs is at least $2^n(2^n - 1) \times 2^n$. A similar argument applies to right-colliding key pairs. Hence,

$$|\mathcal{C}_\mathsf{L}| \geq 2^{2n}(2^n - 1), \qquad\qquad |\mathcal{C}_\mathsf{R}| \geq 2^{2n}(2^n - 1). \qquad (1)$$

Lemma 5. *The number of 4-chains at left (and similarly at right) is at least $2^{5n}/4$ for all $n \geq 2$.*

Proof. Let $\pi_1 := \mathcal{C}_\mathsf{R} \to \{0,1\}^n$ be a function defined as $\pi_1(K := (k_1, k_2, k_3), K' := (k'_1, k'_2, k_3)) = k_1$. Now, consider any collision pair $((K_2, K_1), (K_3, K_4))$ of π_1. So, by definition of π_1, (K_2, K_3) is a left-colliding pair. Hence, (K_1, K_2, K_3, K_4) is a 4-chain. Thus, the number of 4-chains (using Lemma 4 once again, and the Eq. 1) is at least $2^n \times (2^{2n} - 2^n)(2^{2n} - 2^n - 1)$ which is more than 2^{5n-2} as $n \geq 2$.

So, the above result says that $|\mathcal{C}_{4L}| \geq 2^{5n}/4$. Once again due to the lower bound of the collision pairs, the number of intersecting 4-chains is at least $2^{6n}/8$.

Lemma 6. *The number of intersecting 4-chains is at least* $(2^{6n} - 2^{5n+3})/2^7$.

Proof. Let $F_{\circ\circ\circ} := \mathcal{C}_{LR} \to \{0,1\}^{4n}$ be a function defined as
$F_{\circ\circ\circ}(K_1, K_2, K_3, K_4) = (F_{|2}(K_1), F_{|2}(K_2), F_{|2}(K_3), F_{|2}(K_4))$, where $F_{|2}(K)$
is defined as above. For sufficiently large n, $|\mathcal{C}_{LR}| \geq 2^{5n-3}$ [from Lemma 5]. Using
Lemma 4 and noting that $|\mathrm{Dom}(F_{\circ\circ\circ})| \geq 2^{n-3} \times |\mathrm{Ran}(F_{\circ\circ\circ})|$, we get that the
number of intersecting 4-chains in $F \geq \frac{2^{n-3}(2^{n-3}-1)}{2} \times |\mathrm{Ran}(F_{\circ\circ\circ})| = \frac{2^{6n}-2^{5n+3}}{2^7} = \mathcal{O}(2^{6n})$.

Note that there can be a maximum of 2^{4n} combinations of starting and ending pairs. By applying the Pigeon Hole Principle, we get that there exists *at least one starting pair* (k, k') *and one ending pair* (k'', k''') such that there are 2^{2n-3} distinct intersecting 4-chains connecting them. It is this information that the distinguisher eventually leverages when executing the attack.

3.4   Probability Analysis

Let q_S be the number of queries allowed to the simulator $\mathcal{S}$. Recall that $\mathcal{D}$ randomly selects an intersecting pair of 4-chains from $\geq 2^{2n-7} - 2^{n-4}$ possible choices (from lemma 6). Let $\mathcal{I}_0$ be the event $[[b = H] \cap [y_1'' = y_2''] \cup [[b = T] \cap [y_1'' \neq y_2'']]$. Also, let $\mathcal{IW}$ be the event that $\mathcal{D}$ interacts with the Ideal World and $\mathcal{RW}$ be the event that $\mathcal{D}$ interacts with the Real World. Then,

$$\Pr(\mathcal{I}_0 | \mathcal{RW}) = \Pr([b = H] \cap [y_1'' = y_2''] | \mathcal{RW}) + \Pr([b = T] \cap [y_1'' \neq y_2''] | \mathcal{RW})$$
$$= \Pr(b = H) \cdot \Pr(E_1(k_4', x_1'') = E_1(\kappa_4', x_2'') | \mathcal{RW})$$
$$+ \Pr(b = T) \cdot [1 - \Pr(E_1(k_4', x_1'') = E_1(\kappa_4', x^*) | \mathcal{RW})]$$
$$= \frac{1}{2} + \frac{1}{2}[1 - 0] = 1$$

In the Ideal World, every intersecting 4-chains of keys connecting the starting pair (k_1', κ_1') and the ending pair (k_4', κ_4') is visible to $\mathcal{S}$. It is but a question of whether $\mathcal{S}$ is able to identify the exact path chosen by $\mathcal{D}$. Let $\mathcal{P} := \mathcal{P}_{(k_1', \kappa_1') \to (k_4', \kappa_4')} := \{(\overline{K}, \overline{K'}) | \overline{K}, \overline{K'} \in \mathcal{C}_{LR}\}$ be the set of all intersecting 4-chains with starting and ending pairs (k_1', κ_1') and (k_4', κ_4') respectively, and each $\overline{K}$ is a four-tuple of keys. For an element $(P, P') \in \mathcal{P}$, let $\mathsf{E}(P, x)$ denote the ideal cipher query sequence $E^{-1}(K_4, E(K_3, E^{-1}(K_2, E(K_1, x))))$, where $P = (K_1, K_2, K_3, K_4)$ and $P'[= (K_1', K_2', K_3', K_4')]$ are a pair of intersecting 4-chains. Let $(P_{\mathcal{D}}, P_{\mathcal{D}}') \in \mathcal{P}$ be the path randomly chosen by $\mathcal{D}$. For simplicity, when $\mathcal{S}$ makes any query of the form $\mathsf{E}(P, x)$ as described above, we will associate 1 query cost with it, instead of 4. Let $X^{\mathcal{S}}$ be a random variable that denotes the path $(P, P') \in \mathcal{P}$ chosen by $\mathcal{S}$. We will assume that if $\mathcal{S}$ observes, for some $(P, P') \in \mathcal{P}$, that $\mathsf{E}(P, x_1) = x_1''$ and $\mathsf{E}(P', x_2) = x_2''$ (or vice-versa), then $\mathcal{S}$ responds to the query $E_1(\kappa_4', x_2'')$ with the value y_1''. Then,

$[\mathsf{E}(P_\circ', x_2) = x_2'] \cap [(P_\circ, P_\circ') \neq (P_\mathcal{D}, P_\mathcal{D}')], \ (P_\circ, P_\circ') \in \mathcal{P}.$

$$\Pr(\mathcal{I}_0|\mathcal{IW}) = \Pr([b = H] \cap [y_1'' = y_2''] | \ \mathcal{IW}) + \Pr([b = T] \cap [y_1'' \neq y_2''] | \ \mathcal{IW})$$

$$\leq \Pr(b = H) \times \left[\Pr\left[\mathsf{E}(P_\mathcal{D}, x_1) = x_1'', \ \mathsf{E}(P_\mathcal{D}', x_2) = x_2'' | \ X^\mathcal{S} = (P_\mathcal{D}, P_\mathcal{D}')\right] \right.$$

$$\times \Pr\left[X^\mathcal{S} = (P_\mathcal{D}, P_\mathcal{D}')\right]$$

$$+ \Pr\left[\mathsf{E}(P, x_1) = x_1'', \ \mathsf{E}(P', x_2) = x_2'' | \ X^\mathcal{S} = (P, P')\right]$$

$$\left. \times \Pr\left[X^\mathcal{S} = (P, P') \neq (P_\mathcal{D}, P_\mathcal{D}')\right]\right]$$

$$+ \Pr(b = T)$$

$$\leq \frac{1}{2}\left[1 \times \frac{q_S}{2^{2n-7} - 2^{n-4}} + q_S \times \frac{1}{2^{2n}} \times \left[1 - \frac{1}{2^{2n-7} - 2^{n-4}}\right]\right] + \frac{1}{2}$$

$$= \frac{1}{2}\left[1 + \frac{q_S}{2^{2n-7} - 2^{n-4}}\left[1 - \frac{1}{2^{2n}}\right] + \frac{q_S}{2^{2n}}\right]$$

Hence, the indifferentiability advantage of the distinguisher $\mathcal{D}$ against any simulator $\mathcal{S}$ with query bound q_S is

$$\mathbf{Adv}_{\mathsf{E},\mathcal{S}}(\mathcal{D}) = |\Pr(\mathcal{I}_0|\mathcal{RW}) - \Pr(\mathcal{I}_0|\mathcal{IW})|$$

$$\geq 1 - \frac{1}{2}\left[1 + \frac{q_S}{2^{2n-7} - 2^{n-4}}\left[1 - \frac{1}{2^{2n}}\right] + \frac{q_S}{2^{2n}}\right]$$

$$= \frac{1}{2} - \left[\frac{q_S}{2^{2n-8} - 2^{n-5}}\left[1 - \frac{1}{2^{2n}}\right] + \frac{q_S}{2^{2n+1}}\right]$$

$$\geq \frac{1}{2} - \left[\frac{2^9 \times q_S}{2^{2n}}\left[1 - \frac{1}{2^{2n}}\right] + \frac{q_S}{2^{2n+1}}\right] \qquad [n \geq 5]$$

$$= \frac{1}{2} - \left[\frac{2^9 \times q_S}{2^{2n}} - \frac{2^9 \times q_S}{2^{4n}} + \frac{1}{2} \times \frac{q_S}{2^{2n}}\right]$$

$$= \frac{1}{2} - \left[\left(2^9 + \frac{1}{2}\right)\frac{q_S}{2^{2n}} - \frac{2^9 \times q_S}{2^{4n}}\right]$$

Theorem 1. *The indiffirentiability advantage of the distinguisher $\mathcal{D}$ against any simulator $\mathcal{S}$ with query bound q_S is given by*

$$\mathbf{Adv}_{\mathsf{E},\mathcal{S}}(\mathcal{D}) \geq \frac{1}{2} - \epsilon$$

Where $\epsilon = \left(2^9 + \frac{1}{2}\right)\frac{q_S}{2^{2n}} - \frac{2^9 \times q_S}{2^{4n}}.$

ILLUSTRATION OF THE ATTACK FOR A LINEAR KEY SCHEDULE. For the 3-round Cascade Cipher, consider the key schedule $f(k_1, k_2) = (k_1, k_2, k_1 \oplus k_2)$, $k_1, k_2 \in \{0,1\}^n$. Choose $(k_1, k_2), (k_1', k_2') \in \{0,1\}^{2n}$ such that $k_1 \neq k_1'$. Define the 3n-bit keys $K_1, K_2, K_3, K_4, K_1', K_2', K_3', K_4'$ as follows:

- $K_1 = f(k_1, k_2) = (k_1, k_2, k_1 \oplus k_2)$
- $K_2 = f(k_1 \oplus k_2 \oplus k_2', k_2') = (k_1 \oplus k_2 \oplus k_2', k_2', k_1 \oplus k_2)$
- $K_3 = f(k_1 \oplus k_2 \oplus k_2', k_2) = (k_1 \oplus k_2 \oplus k_2', k_2, k_1 \oplus k_2')$
- $K_4 = f(k_1, k_2') = (k_1, k_2', k_1 \oplus k_2')$
- $K_1' = f(k_1', k_2) = (k_1', k_2, k_1' \oplus k_2)$
- $K_2' = f(k_1' \oplus k_2 \oplus k_2', k_2') = (k_1' \oplus k_2 \oplus k_2', k_2', k_1' \oplus k_2)$
- $K_3' = f(k_1' \oplus k_2 \oplus k_2', k_2) = (k_1' \oplus k_2 \oplus k_2', k_2, k_1' \oplus k_2')$
- $K_4' = f(k_1', k_2') = (k_1', k_2', k_1' \oplus k_2')$

We note that both the four-tuples (K_1, K_2, K_3, K_4) and (K_1', K_2', K_3', K_4') form 4-chains, on top of which, the two 4-chains are intersecting. This means, for a fixed starting pair = ending pair = (k_1, k_1'), we have 2^{2n} choices for the pair (k_2, k_2'), giving us 2^{2n} intersecting 4-chains with the given starting and ending pair (k_1, k_1'). Thus, for a given (k_1, k_1'), a distinguisher D can select one of 2^{2n} choices of the pair (k_2, k_2'), define the keys K_i, K_i', $i \in [4]$, as described above and proceed in the same fashion as our attack approach for a generic 2n-bit to 3n-bit key schedule.

The 3-round Cascade construction with the linear key schedule given above has already been shown to not be indifferentiable with an Ideal Cipher by Guo et. al., in their 2011 paper 'Revisiting Cascade Ciphers in Indifferentiability Setting'. The two attacks for this key schedule are almost identical (barring the 'coin toss' modification), and the two distinguishers exploit the same limitation in the capabilities of a simulator.

4   Conclusion

Our attack on 2-CDN shows that the construction is not indifferentiable in the sequential setting, which is a weaker notion of security as compared to classical indifferentiability. This, combined with Guo et al.'s indifferentiability analysis on 3-CDN [4] solidifies the *exact* number of rounds required for the confusion-diffusion network to be sequentially indifferentiable as 3. This is better than the number of rounds required for full indifferentiability, as found by Dodis et al. [5].

Lampe and Seurin's results on the indifferentiability of the 2-Cascade construction [10] indicate that the use of underlying sub-keys is pertinent with respect to the question of a cascade of block ciphers being indifferentiable from an ideal block cipher of larger key space. In that regard, our attack on the 3-Cascade construction with a generalized 2n-bit to 3n-bit non-idealized key schedule shows that key reuse by considering domain extending bijections *do not* lead to a secure construction in the indifferentiability setting.

References

1. Biryukov, A., Wagner, D.: Slide attacks. In: Knudsen, L. (ed.) FSE 1999. LNCS, vol. 1636, pp. 245–259. Springer, Heidelberg (1999). https://doi.org/10.1007/3-540-48519-8_18

2. Brachtl, B.O., et al.: Data authentication using modification detection codes based on a public one way encryption function (1990). https://www.freepatentsonline.com/4908861.html

3. Canetti, R., Goldreich, O., Halevi, S.: The random oracle methodology, revisited. J. ACM **51**(4), 557–594 (2004). https://doi.org/10.1145/1008731.1008734

4. Da, Q., Xu, S., Guo, C.: Sequential indifferentiability of confusion-diffusion networks. In: Adhikari, A., Küsters, R., Preneel, B. (eds.) INDOCRYPT 2021. LNCS, vol. 13143, pp. 93–113. Springer, Cham (2021). https://doi.org/10.1007/978-3-030-92518-5_5

5. Dodis, Y., Stam, M., Steinberger, J., Liu, T.: Indifferentiability of confusion-diffusion networks. In: Fischlin, M., Coron, J.-S. (eds.) EUROCRYPT 2016, Part II. LNCS, vol. 9666, pp. 679–704. Springer, Heidelberg (2016). https://doi.org/10.1007/978-3-662-49896-5_24

6. Even, S., Goldreich, O.: On the power of cascade ciphers. ACM Trans. Comput. Syst. **3**(2), 108–116 (1985). https://doi.org/10.1145/214438.214442

7. Guo, C., Lin, D., Liu, M.: Revisiting cascade ciphers in indifferentiability setting. Cryptology ePrint Archive, Paper 2016/825 (2016). https://eprint.iacr.org/2016/825

8. Hirose, S.: Some plausible constructions of double-block-length hash functions. In: Robshaw, M. (ed.) FSE 2006. LNCS, vol. 4047, pp. 210–225. Springer, Heidelberg (2006). https://doi.org/10.1007/11799313_14

9. Lai, X., Massey, J.L.: Hash functions based on block ciphers. In: Rueppel, R.A. (ed.) EUROCRYPT 1992. LNCS, vol. 658, pp. 55–70. Springer, Heidelberg (1993). https://doi.org/10.1007/3-540-47555-9_5

10. Lampe, R., Seurin, Y.: How to construct an ideal cipher from a small set of public permutations. In: Sako, K., Sarkar, P. (eds.) ASIACRYPT 2013, Part I. LNCS, vol. 8269, pp. 444–463. Springer, Heidelberg (2013). https://doi.org/10.1007/978-3-642-42033-7_23

11. Mandal, A., Patarin, J., Seurin, Y.: On the public indifferentiability and correlation intractability of the 6-round feistel construction. In: Cramer, R. (ed.) TCC 2012. LNCS, vol. 7194, pp. 285–302. Springer, Heidelberg (2012). https://doi.org/10.1007/978-3-642-28914-9_16

12. Maurer, U.: Indistinguishability of random systems. In: Knudsen, L.R. (ed.) EUROCRYPT 2002. LNCS, vol. 2332, pp. 110–132. Springer, Heidelberg (2002). https://doi.org/10.1007/3-540-46035-7_8

13. Maurer, U., Renner, R., Holenstein, C.: Indifferentiability, impossibility results on reductions, and applications to the random oracle methodology. In: Naor, M. (ed.) TCC 2004. LNCS, vol. 2951, pp. 21–39. Springer, Heidelberg (2004). https://doi.org/10.1007/978-3-540-24638-1_2

14. Preneel, B., Govaerts, R., Vandewalle, J.: Hash functions based on block ciphers: a synthetic approach. In: Stinson, D.R. (ed.) CRYPTO 1993. LNCS, vol. 773, pp. 368–378. Springer, Heidelberg (1994). https://doi.org/10.1007/3-540-48329-2_31

15. Shannon, C.E.: Communication theory of secrecy systems. Bell Syst. Tech. J. **28**(4), 656–715 (1949). https://doi.org/10.1002/j.1538-7305.1949.tb00928.x

Quantum Cryptanalysis of 5 Rounds Feistel Schemes and Benes Schemes

Maya Chartouny[1,2]($\boxtimes$), Jacques Patarin[1,2], and Ambre Toulemonde[2]

[1] Thales DIS, Meudon, France
{maya.saab-chartouni,jacques.patarin}@thalesgroup.com
[2] Laboratoire de mathématiques de Versailles, Université Paris-Saclay, UVSQ, CNRS, 78000 Versailles, France
ambre.toulemonde@orange.fr

Abstract. In this paper, we provide new quantum cryptanalysis results on 5 rounds (balanced) Feistel schemes and on Benes schemes. More precisely, we give an attack on 5 rounds Feistel schemes in $\Theta(2^{2n/3})$ quantum complexity and an attack on Benes schemes in $\Theta(2^{2n/3})$ quantum complexity, where n is the number of bits of the internal random functions. This improves the best known attack in $\Theta(2^n)$ (before our attack).

Keywords: Feistel ciphers · Pseudo-random permutation · Quantum cryptanalysis · Luby-Rackoff block cipher · Benes network

1 Introduction

There exist several methods to build pseudo-random permutations and pseudo-random functions.

A random Feistel cipher also known as Luby-Rackoff block cipher is a symmetric structure used in the construction of block ciphers. The benefit of the Feistel network is that the same structure can be used for encryption and decryption, and both consist of iteratively running a function called a "round function" a fixed number of times. The most studied way to build pseudo-random permutations from random functions or random permutations is the r-round Feistel construction. The Feistel construction is important from a practical point of view since it is used to develop many block ciphers such as DES [2], 3DES [2]. We study generic attacks on Feistel schemes where we assume that the internal round functions $f_1, \ldots, f_r$ are randomly chosen.

The plaintext message of a Feistel scheme is denoted by $[L, R]$ that stands for *Left* and *Right*, and the ciphertext message after applying r rounds is denoted by $[S, T]$. A round of a Feistel scheme takes as input $[L, R]$ and it outputs $[R, L \oplus f(R)]$ with f a secret function from n bits to n bits.

A Benes scheme is a composition of two schemes called "Butterflies". It allows to construct, from random functions from n bits to n bits, a pseudorandom function from $2n$ bits to $2n$ bits. For many cryptographic primitives, e.g., hashing and pseudorandom functions, doubling the output length is useful even if the doubling transformation is not reversible.

S. El Hajji et al. (Eds.): C2SI 2023, LNCS 13874, pp. 196–203, 2023.
https://doi.org/10.1007/978-3-031-33017-9_13

The plaintext message of a Benes scheme is denoted by $[L, R]$ that stands for *Left* and *Right*, and the ciphertext message is denoted by $[S, T]$.

Our Contribution. In this paper, we describe a non-adaptive quantum chosen plaintext attack (QCPA) against 5-round balanced Feistel schemes. This attack allows to distinguish Feistel network from random permutations with quantum complexity of $\Theta(2^{2n/3})$ instead of $\Theta(2^n)$ for the best known attack (before our attack). We also describe a QCPA against the Benes schemes. This attack allows to distinguish a Benes scheme from random functions with quantum complexity of $\Theta(2^{2n/3})$ instead of $\Theta(2^n)$ for the best known attack (before our attack).

An originality of our results is the fact that we will use Zhandry's quantum algorithm (unlike the quantum attacks on the Feistel scheme with 3 and 4 rounds where Simon's algorithm [7] was used). In this way, we simply improve the exponent of the exponential complexity, unlike Simon's algorithm where a quantum polynomial attack was obtained. However, we will be able to attack Feistel with 5 rounds (unlike only 3 or 4 rounds).

Organization. Section 2 recalls the Feistel and Benes schemes. Section 3 gives an overview of previous works and the new results provided in this paper. Section 4 recall Zhandry's quantum algorithm. Finally, in Sect. 5 and Sect. 6, we present our QCPA against the Feistel shemes with 5 rounds and our QCPA against the Benes schemes.

2   Feistel and Benes Constructions

In this section, we recall the definition of a classical (aka balanced) Feistel scheme and the definition of a Benes scheme. Let $\mathcal{F}_{m,n}$ be the set of all functions from $\{0,1\}^m$ to $\{0,1\}^n$. When $m = n$, the set of all functions from $\{0,1\}^n$ to $\{0,1\}^n$ will be denoted by $\mathcal{F}_n$.

2.1   Feistel Scheme

First Round Feistel Scheme. Let $f \in \mathcal{F}_n$. The first round balanced Feistel scheme associated with f, denoted by $\Psi(f)$, is the function in $\mathcal{F}_{2n}$ defined by:

$$\forall (L, R) \in (\{0,1\}^n)^2, \ \Psi(f)\big([L, R]\big) = [S, T] \iff \begin{cases} S = R, \\ T = L \oplus f(R). \end{cases}$$

For any function f, $\Psi(f)$ is a permutation of $\{0,1\}^{2n}$.
The figure of the Feistel scheme for the first round is given in Figure 1.

r–round Feistel scheme. Let $f_1, f_2, \ldots, f_r$ be r functions in $\mathcal{F}_n$. The r–round balanced Fesitel network associated with $f_1, \ldots, f_r$, denoted by $\Psi^r(f_1, \ldots, f_r)$, is the function in $\mathcal{F}_{2n}$ defined by:

$$\Psi^r(f_1, \ldots, f_r) = \Psi^r(f_r) \circ \cdots \circ \Psi^1(f_1).$$

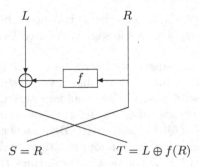

Fig. 1. First round of Feistel scheme

5−round Feistel scheme. We describe now in detail the equations of the Feistel network for the first five rounds.

1 round: $\begin{cases} S = R \\ T = L \oplus f_1(R) = X^1 \end{cases}$
4 rounds: $\begin{cases} S = X^3 \\ T = X^2 \oplus f_4(X^3) = X^4 \end{cases}$

2 rounds: $\begin{cases} S = X^1 \\ T = R \oplus f_2(X^1) = X^2 \end{cases}$
5 rounds: $\begin{cases} S = X^4 \\ T = X^3 \oplus f_5(X^4) = X^5 \end{cases}$

3 rounds: $\begin{cases} S = X^2 \\ T = X^1 \oplus f_3(X^2) = X^3 \end{cases}$

2.2   Benes Scheme

To give a definition of the Benes transformation, we need to recall first the definition of a butterfly transformation.

Butterfly Transformation. Let $f_1, \ldots, f_4$ be four functions in $\mathcal{F}_n$. A Butterfly transformation is the function in $\mathcal{F}_{2n}$ which takes as input $(L_i, R_i) \in (\{0,1\}^n)^2$ and gives as output (X_i, Y_i), where,

$$\begin{cases} X_i = f_1(L_i) \oplus f_2(R_i), \\ Y_i = f_3(L_i) \oplus f_4(R_i). \end{cases}$$

The figure of the Butterfly scheme is given in Figure 2.

Benes Transformation. Let $f_1, \ldots, f_8$ be functions in $\mathcal{F}_n$. A Benes transformation (back to back Butterfly) is the function in $\mathcal{F}_{2n}$ which takes as input $(L_i, R_i) \in (\{0,1\}^n)^2$ and gives as output (S_i, T_i), where,

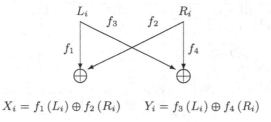

$$X_i = f_1(L_i) \oplus f_2(R_i) \qquad Y_i = f_3(L_i) \oplus f_4(R_i)$$

Fig. 2. Butterfly scheme

$$\begin{cases} S_i = f_5(\underbrace{f_1(L_i) \oplus f_2(R_i)}_{X_i}) \oplus f_6(\underbrace{f_3(L_i) \oplus f_4(R_i)}_{Y_i}) = f_5(X_i) \oplus f_6(Y_i), \\ T_i = f_7(f_1(L_i) \oplus f_2(R_i)) \oplus f_8(f_3(L_i) \oplus f_4(R_i)) = f_7(X_i) \oplus f_8(Y_i). \end{cases}$$

The figure of the Benes scheme is given in Fig. 3.

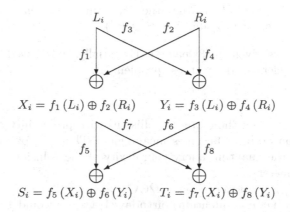

$$X_i = f_1(L_i) \oplus f_2(R_i) \qquad Y_i = f_3(L_i) \oplus f_4(R_i)$$

$$S_i = f_5(X_i) \oplus f_6(Y_i) \qquad T_i = f_7(X_i) \oplus f_8(Y_i)$$

Fig. 3. Benes scheme

3 Overview of Cryptanalysis on Feistel Schemes

In this section, we review the best known cryptanalysis results of the state of the art on the Feistel schemes and we point out the new results provided in this paper.

In Fig. 4, we summarize the cryptanalysis results on few rounds of Feistel schemes based on the distinguishing attacks presented in [3] and in [5] together with our new contributions.

We have not found a better attack for QCCA (quantum chosen ciphertext attack) than the one of the QCPA. Notice that any QCPA can also be seen as a special case of QCCA.

	KPA	CPA	CCA	QCPA	QCCA
Ψ^1	1	1	1	1	1
Ψ^2	$2^{n/2}$	2	2	2	2
Ψ^3	$2^{n/2}$	$2^{n/2}$	3	n	3
Ψ^4	2^n	$2^{n/2}$	$2^{n/2}$	$2^{n/2}$	n
Ψ^5	$2^{3n/2}$	2^n	2^n	This paper: $2^{2n/3}$	This paper: $2^{2n/3}$

Fig. 4. Number of computations to distinguish Feistel schemes (with 1, 2, 3, 4 and 5 rounds) from random permutations (best known attacks)

4   Quantum Collision

In this section, we recall the results of the quantum algorithm that we use in our quantum cryptanalysis. Theorem 1 below is Theorem 1.1 of [8] page 3.

Theorem 1. Let f be a random function with domain size M and codomain size N. Assume $M = \Omega(N^{1/2})$. Then the quantum query complexity of finding a collision with constant probability is $\Theta(N^{1/3})$.

Proof. The proof is given in [8] page 4. Essentially, it is based on a result of Ambainis on the element distinctness problem [1].

Notice that:

1. If $M = o(N^{1/2})$ then there are no collisions with probability approaching 1, so the collision problem becomes meaningless. Thus, Theorem 1 completely characterizes the quantum query complexity of the collision problem for all sensible parameters.
2. $M \geq \Omega(N^{1/2})$ is the same as $M = \Omega(N^{1/2})$.
3. For a classical (i.e. non-quantum) birthday attack, we would get a complexity of $\Theta(N^{1/2})$ instead of $\Theta(N^{1/3})$ in the Theorem 1.

5   Quantum Cryptanalysis on Feistel Network

In this section, we first describe a non quantum attack that distinguishes a 5-round Feistel scheme from a $2n$ bits random function with a complexity of 2^n presented in [5]. Then, we describe our quantum chosen plaintext attack that distinguishes a 5-round Feistel scheme from a $2n$ bits random function with a complexity of $2^{2n/3}$.

Classical Attack. We can choose messages $[L_i, R_i]$ and $[L_j, R_j]$ such that $R_i = R_j$, $\forall i, j$. Then, we can check whether S_i is equal to S_j and $L_i \oplus L_j$ is equal to $T_i \oplus T_j$, i.e., we count the number of (i, j) such that:

$$\begin{cases} S_i = S_j, \\ L_i \oplus L_j = T_i \oplus T_j. \end{cases}$$

For a 5-round Feistel scheme, we have two times more such collision than for truly random permutations. Indeed, for a truly random permutation if $R_i = R_j$, the numbers of (i, j), $1 \le i < j \le m$, where $m \simeq 2^n$, such that $S_i = S_j$ and $T_i \oplus T_j = L_i \oplus L_j$ is approximately $\dfrac{m(m-1)}{2} \dfrac{1}{2^{2n}}$.

However, for a 5-round Feistel scheme we have:

$$\begin{cases} T_i = L_i \oplus f_1(R_i) \oplus f_3\left(R_i \oplus f_2(L_i \oplus f_1(R_i))\right) \oplus f_5(S_i), \\ T_j = L_j \oplus f_1(R_j) \oplus f_3\left(R_j \oplus f_2(L_j \oplus f_1(R_j))\right) \oplus f_5(S_j). \end{cases}$$

Let us suppose that $R_i = R_j$ and $S_i = S_j$, hence, $T_i \oplus T_j = L_i \oplus L_j$ is equivalent to

$$f_3\left(R_i \oplus f_2(L_i \oplus f_1(R_i))\right) = f_3\left(R_j \oplus f_2(L_j \oplus f_1(R_j))\right),$$

which can occur either if $f_2\left(L_i \oplus f_1(R_i)\right) = f_2\left(L_j \oplus f_1(R_j)\right)$ with an approximate probability of $\dfrac{1}{2^n}$ or if these values are distinct but when XORed with R, they have the same images by f_3 with an approximate probability of $\dfrac{1}{2^n}$.

Hence, $\forall (i, j)$, $i < j$, the probability that $S_i = S_j$ and $T_i \oplus T_j = L_i \oplus L_j$ when $R_i = R_j$ is approximately $\dfrac{m(m-1)}{2} \dfrac{2}{2^{2n}}$.

Thus we have two times more such collision for a 5-round Feistel scheme compared to a truly random permutation. (This can also be demonstrated with the H-coefficient technique, see [4] page 148, value of h_5).

Therefore, we will be able to distinguish the 5-round Feistel scheme from truly random permutations when $\dfrac{m(m-1)}{2} \dfrac{2}{2^{2n}} \ge 1$, i.e. when m is about greater or equal to 2^n. We see that here the complexity is in 2^n by searching for collision of the form of $S_i \| L_i \oplus T_i$ (birthday paradox).

Note that there are several attacks on Ψ_5 with the same complexity but we choose this one to be able to detect collisions in quantum.

Quantum Attack. In quantum we detect collisions, when they exist, faster than on classical computers. In fact, we use the same attack in quantum to detect these collisions.

We apply Theorem 1 with $M = 2^n$ and $N = 2^{2n}$ ($M = \Omega(N^{1/2})$). Hence, the quantum complexity to detect such a collision is in $N^{1/3} = 2^{2n/3}$ (unlike 2^n as seen before). Therefore, we can distinguish 5-round Feistel schemes from truly random permutations with a quantum complexity of $2^{2n/3}$.

6   Quantum Distinguishing Attack on Benes Scheme

In this section, we first describe a non quantum attack that distinguishes a Benes scheme from a random function with a complexity of 2^n presented in [6]. Then, we describe a quantum chosen plaintext attack that distinguishes a Benes scheme from a random function with a complexity of $2^{2n/3}$.

Classical Attack. We can choose messages $[L_i, R_i]$, then, we check wether S_i is equal to S_j and T_i is equal to T_j.

For a truly random permuatation, the numbers (i, j), $1 \leq i < j \leq m$ such that $S_i = S_j$ and $T_i = T_j$ is approximately $\dfrac{m(m-1)}{2} \dfrac{1}{2^{2n}}$.

However, for Benes scheme we have

$$\begin{cases} S_i = f_5(X_i) \oplus f_6(Y_i), \\ T_i = f_7(X_i) \oplus f_8(Y_i). \end{cases}$$

Hence, $S_i = S_j$ and $T_i = T_j$ is equivalent to $f_5(X_i) \oplus f_6(Y_i) = f_5(X_j) \oplus f_6(Y_j)$ and $f_7(X_i) \oplus f_8(Y_i) = f_7(X_j) \oplus f_8(Y_j)$. This can occur either if $X_i = X_j$ and $Y_i = Y_j$ (probability $\dfrac{m(m-1)}{2} \dfrac{1}{2^{2n}}$) or if these values are distinct but $S_i = S_j$ and $T_i = T_j$ (probability $\dfrac{m(m-1)}{2} \dfrac{1}{2^{2n}}$).

Thus, $\forall (i, j)$, $i < j$, the probability that $S_i = S_j$ and $T_i = T_j$ is approximately $\dfrac{m(m-1)}{2} \dfrac{2}{2^{2n}}$ so we have two times more such collision for a Benes scheme compared to a random function. More details can be found in [6].

Therefore, we will be able to distinguish a Benes schemes from truly random functions when $\dfrac{m(m-1)}{2} \dfrac{2}{2^{2n}} \geq 1$, i.e. when $m \geq 2^n$. The number of computations needed for this attack is thus about 2^n from the birthday paradox.

Quantum Attack. We use the same attack in quantum to detect these collisions faster.

We apply Theorem 1 with $M = 2^{2n}$ and $N = 2^{2n}$ ($M = \Omega(N^{1/2})$). Hence, the quantum complexity to detect such a collision is in $N^{1/3} = 2^{2n/3}$ (unlike 2^n as seen before). Therefore, we can distinguish Benes schemes from truly random functions with a quantum complexity of $2^{2n/3}$.

References

1. Ambainis, A.: Quantum walk algorithm for element distinctness. In: 45th Symposium on Foundations of Computer Science (FOCS 2004), 17–19 October 2004, Rome, Italy, Proceedings, pp. 22–31. IEEE Computer Society (2004)

2. IBM: Data Encryption Standard. Federal Information Processing Standards Publication (1999)
3. Kuwakado, H., Morii, M.: Quantum distinguisher between the 3-round Feistel cipher and the random permutation. In: 2010 IEEE International Symposium on Information Theory, pp. 2682–2685 (2010)
4. Patarin, J.: Etude des generateurs de permutations pseudo-aleatoires bases sur le schema du d. E. S. Ph.D. thesis (1991). http://www.theses.fr/1991PA066601
5. Patarin, J.: Generic attacks on Feistel schemes. IACR Cryptol. ePrint Arch., p. 36 (2008)
6. Patarin, J., Montreuil, A.: Benes and butterfly schemes revisited. In: Won, D., Kim, S. (eds.) Information Security and Cryptology - ICISC 2005, 8th International Conference, Seoul, Korea, 1-2 December 2005, Revised Selected Papers. Lecture Notes in Computer Science, vol. 3935, pp. 92–116. Springer, Heidelberg (2005). https://doi.org/10.1007/11734727
7. Simon, D.R.: On the power of quantum computation. SIAM J. Comput. $26(5)$, 1474–1483 (1997)
8. Zhandry, M.: A note on the quantum collision and set equality problems. CoRR abs/1312.1027 (2013)

Lattice-Based Accumulator with Constant Time List Update and Constant Time Verification

Yuta Maeno[1], Hideaki Miyaji[1(✉)], and Atsuko Miyaji[1,2(✉)]

[1] Graduate School of Engineering, Osaka University, Suita, Japan
{maeno,hideaki}@cy2sec.comm.eng.osaka-u.ac.jp,
miyaji@comm.eng.osaka-u.ac.jp
[2] School of Information Science, Japan Advanced Institute of Science
and Technology, Nomi, Japan

Abstract. An accumulator is a cryptographic protocol that compresses a set of inputs into a short string of a certain size and can efficiently prove that the compressed set contains a particular input element. Accumulators have been actively studied in recent years and are used to streamline various protocols such as membership rosters, zero-knowledge proofs, group signatures, and blockchains. Libert et al. proposed a Merkle tree-based accumulator using lattice cryptography, one of the post-quantum cryptography. They proposed an accumulator with logarithmic time complexity for the verification algorithm. Ling et al. proposed an accumulator that satisfies logarithmic time updating lists. However, no algorithm has been proposed thus far that satisfies constant time updating lists and constant time verification based on the lattice-based accumulator. In this study, we propose an accumulator based on lattice that satisfies constant-time verification and constant-time updating lists for the first time. In our proposed accumulator, the bit length of the witness associated with each element is independent of the number of elements in the list. We developed techniques that use the Partial Fourier Recovery problem instead of the Merkle tree. We also prove that the proposed accumulator satisfies the security requirements of an accumulator scheme. Finally, to demonstrate that our proposed accumulator is more practical, we compared it with other lattice-based accumulators. The proposed accumulator scheme can be incorporated into membership list management, zero-knowledge proof, group signature, and blockchain to realize more efficient applications.

Keywords: accumulator · lattice-based accumulator · group signature · constant-time update · constant-time verify

1 Introduction

The accumulator is a cryptographic protocol that can compress data, like a hash function, and verify whether a set element is included in the list, like a digital signature. The accumulator was first proposed by Behaloh et al. [1] as a method

© The Author(s), under exclusive license to Springer Nature Switzerland AG 2023
S. El Hajji et al. (Eds.): C2SI 2023, LNCS 13874, pp. 204–222, 2023.
https://doi.org/10.1007/978-3-031-33017-9_14

for compressing the sizes of long lists. The accumulator compresses the list and verifies if an element is included in the list. The value obtained by compressing the list is called the accumulator value, and the certificate used for verification is called a witness. An accumulator is used in situations where a large amount of data is stored and used owing to its practical characteristics. In particular, it is widely used as a method to realize storage with less storage space and guaranteed authenticity. In fact, the accumulator is used in many applications, such as time stamps [1], membership list management [1], anonymous authentication [2–4], group signatures [5], ring signatures [6], and electronic money [7,8].

1.1 History of Accumulator

In 1993, Benaloh et al. [1] first constructed the concept of an accumulator, and Baric et al. [9] constructed an accumulator based on strong RSA assumption [9] in 1997. Since then, much research has been conducted to apply Baric et al.'s accumulator to various applications, and the following enhancements have been added. Camenisch et al. [2] proposed a function to efficiently add or remove elements from a list and update the accumulator value even after the list has been compressed once. This accumulator is known as a dynamic accumulator. However, this study did not satisfy the function of a non-membership witness, which guarantees that certain element is not included in the list. Li et al. [3] solved this problem in 2007 and constructed an accumulator with a non-membership witness, a feature that guarantees that certain element is not included in the list. An accumulator that satisfies the membership and non-membership witnesses is called a universal accumulator. Furthermore, Boneh et al. [10] proposed a function to update the accumulator value by adding and deleting multiple elements to and from the list simultaneously, as well as a function to verify multiple elements in the list simultaneously to make the blockchain with the accumulator more practical.

1.2 Accumulator Based on Lattice-Based Problem

Research on post-quantum accumulators has been conducted in preparation for the practical use and spread of quantum computers despite the construction of a strong RSA assumption-based accumulator. Various cryptographic protocols based on the lattice problem have been developed in recent years [11] because the lattice-based problem is currently one of the most promising post-quantum cryptography problems. A lattice-based accumulator was first constructed in 2015 by Jhanwar et al. [12], which is called JN in this paper. JN is based on the SIS problem [13,14], but it uses a trapdoor, and witnesses can only be created from the trapdoor [15] of the SIS problem owned by the manager (administrator). Due to this feature of using a trapdoor for the generation of a witness, no efficient updating function of listings has been proposed for this method. In other words, when the compressed list is updated, it must be compressed again from the beginning, and a witness must be generated for each element.

To address this problem, Libert et al. [6] constructed an accumulator without a trapdoor by using a Merkle tree with a hash function based on the SIS problem, and Ling et al. [16] proposed an efficient update algorithm for this accumulator. In this paper, the accumulator proposed by Libert et al. [6] is called LLNW, and the accumulator proposed by Ling et al. [16] is called LNWX.

In LNWX, using the structure of the Merkle Tree, it is no longer necessary to compress the entire list from the beginning when updating it, and the computational complexity of the update is reduced to the logarithmic order of the number of elements in the list. Consequently, efficient group updating can be performed by applying this scheme to the compression of the list of public keys of a signing group in group signatures.

In LNWX, on the other hand, due to the structure using the Merkle Tree, the witness length is of logarithmic order of the number of elements in the list, and the verification time is not of constant order. This makes the LNWX inefficient when the number of elements in the list is large. Consequently, it is important to propose a trapdoorless dynamic lattice-based accumulator without using the Merkle Tree.

1.3   Contribution

In this study, we propose the first lattice-based accumulator that satisfies the following:

- constant verification time (able to verify constant time, which is independent of the number of elements in the list),
- constant update time (able to update an element of the list with constant time, which is independent of the number of elements in the list), and
- the bit length of a witness is independent of the number of elements in the list.

We have developed techniques by using the Partial Fourier Recovery problem [17]. We achieve our accumulator by proposing an accumulator using the Partial Fourier Recovery problem without using a Merkle Tree. We also prove that our proposed accumulator satisfies the security of an accumulator scheme based on Vandermonde-$SIS_{q,t,N,\beta}^{\infty}$ problem. Furthermore, since our proposed accumulator uses the signature scheme of Hoffstein et al. [17] as a building block, as a preparation for proving the security of the accumulator, we prove that the signature scheme of Hoffstein et al. [17] satisfies unforgeability based on Vandermonde-$SIS_{q,t,N,k-b}^{\infty}$ problem. In addition, we compared the theoretical performance of our proposed accumulator and existing lattice-based accumulators.

1.4   Paper Organization

The remainder of this paper is organized as follows. Section 2 summarizes the notations and security assumptions used in this study. Section 3 describes the building blocks used in our proposal. The proposed accumulator is presented in detail in Sect. 4. We compare our proposed accumulator with existing lattice-based accumulators in Sect. 5. Finally, the paper is concluded in Sect. 6.

2 Preliminary

In this section, we present the notation used in this study and then describe the definitions.

- λ: security parameter
- N: a positive number
- q: a prime number $q = rN + 1$, with $r \geq 1$
- $\mathbb{Z}_q$: a set $\{0, \ldots, q-1\}$
- $\mathbb{R}_q$: $\mathbb{Z}_q[x]/\langle x^N + 1 \rangle$
- $[a|b]$: concatenation of a and b
- $*$: multiplication in $\mathbb{R}_q$, convolution product in $\mathbb{Z}_q^N$
- $\odot$: component-wise multiplication of vectors in $\mathbb{Z}_q^N$
- $\varepsilon(n)$: negligible function in n
- $poly(n)$: polynomial function in n
- pp: public parameter
- $||f||_\infty (= \max_i |f_i|)$: ℓ_∞-norm of $f = \Sigma_i f_i X^i$

- $||f||_2 = \left(\Sigma_i |f_i|^2 \right)^{1/2}$: ℓ_2-norm of $f = \Sigma_i f_i X^i$
- $\mathcal{B}^p(k)$: subset $\{a \in R_q|\ ||a||_p \leq k\}$ of R_q
- $T(d)$: {polynomials in R_q with d coefficients equal to 1, d coefficients equal to -1, and the rest $(N - 2d)$ coefficients equal to 0}
- d_c: parameter for hash function $Hash_1$
- $Hash_1$: $\{0,1\}^* \to T(d_c)$
- $Hash_2$: $\{0,1\}^* \to \{1, -1\}$
- $Hash_3$: $\mathbb{Z}_q^t \to \mathbb{Z}_q^m$

- $x \xleftarrow{\$} S$: uniform random choice of an element $x \in S$ from a set S
- Lattice L: set of linear integer combinations of linearly independent real vectors $\mathbf{b_1}, \ldots, \mathbf{b_d}$
- manager: a person who compresses the list, and generates and distributes witnesses
- f_i: The value that each user has and that is sent to the manager
- R: a list where the manager stores the f_i that each user has.
- acc_val: accumulator value made from $R = \{f_1, \ldots, f_K\}$ by the manager
- w_i: witness generated by the manager that f_i is stored in the list R
- update_info: update information for each user to update their witness w_i

Definition 1 (Shortest Independent Vectors Problem ($SIVP_\gamma$) [14]). *Given a full-rank basis B of an n-dimensional lattice B, the problem of finding a set of n linearly independent vectors $S \subset L(B)$ such that $||S||_2 \leq \gamma(n) \cdot \lambda_n(L(B))$, where $\lambda_n(L(B))$ is the n-th vector with the ℓ_2-norm of the lattice $L(B)$ consisting of B.*

Definition 2 (Short Integer Solutions ($\mathsf{SIS}^\infty_{n,m,q,\beta}$ problems) [13,14]). *Given a uniform random matrix $A \in \mathbb{Z}^{n \times m}_q$, the problem is to find a nonzero vector $x \in \mathbb{Z}^m$ such that $A \cdot x = 0 \pmod q$ and $||x||_\infty \leq \beta$.*

If $m, \beta = poly(n)$ and $q > \beta \cdot \tilde{O}(\sqrt{n})$, then $\mathsf{SIS}^\infty_{n,m,q,\beta}$ is at least as hard as SIVP_γ such that $\gamma = \beta \cdot \tilde{O}(\sqrt{mn})$ [14]. Next, we define cryptographic accumulators.

Definition 3 (Cryptographic Accumulators [16]). *An accumulator scheme is a tuple of polynomial-time algorithms defined as follows:*

- *TSetup(λ): On input security parameter n, output the public parameter pp.*
- *TAcc: On input pp and a set $R = \{f_1, \ldots, f_K\}$ of K data values, output an accumulator value u.*
- *TWitness: On input pp, a data set R, and a value f, output $\bot$ if $d \notin R$; otherwise output a witness ω for the fact that f is accumulated in TAcc(R).*
- *TVerify: On input pp, accumulator value u, and a value-witness pair (f, ω), output 1 (which indicates that (f, ω) is valid for the accumulator u) or 0.*

A natural security requirement for accumulators considered in [2,6,9,16] is that the accumulator scheme is known to be secure if the probability that an attacker can generate a witness w^* that passes TVerify for an element $f^* \notin R$ to be accumulated is negligible. This property is defined as follows:

Definition 4 (Security of accumulator scheme [6]). *An accumulator scheme (TSetup(λ), TAcc, TWitness, TVerify) is secure if for all PPT adversaries, $\mathcal{A}$: where $f^* \notin R$ and ω^* are witnesses for f^*.*

$$\Pr[pp \leftarrow Tsetup(n); (R, f^*, \omega^*) \leftarrow \mathcal{A}(pp) : f^* \notin R$$
$$\wedge\ Tverify(Tacc(R), f^*, \omega^*) = 1] < \varepsilon(n)$$

Next, we define the mapping in the Partial Fourier transform used in this study.

Definition 5 (Construction of the map $F(f)$ in the Partial Fourier transform [17]). *Choose each component of $\mathbb{Z}^N_q$ from $[-q/2, q/2]$ instead of $[0, q-1]$ and define the map $F : \mathbb{R}_q \to \mathbb{Z}^N_q$ as follows:*

$$F(f) = (f(1), f(g), f(g^2), \ldots, f(g^{N-1}))$$

In this study, we denote the map $F(f)$ by $\hat{f}$.

Definition 6 (Construction of the map F_Ω in the Partial Fourier Transform [17]). *For $t < N$, let Ω be $\Omega = \{\Omega_1, \ldots, \Omega_t\} \subset \{0, 1, \ldots, N-1\}$ and define the map $F_\Omega : \mathbb{R}_q \to \mathbb{Z}^t_q$ as follows:*

$$F_\Omega(f) = (f(g^{\Omega_1}), f(g^{\Omega_2}), \ldots, f(g^{\Omega_t}))$$

In this study, we denote map $F_\Omega(f)$ by $\hat{f}\,|_\Omega$.

Throughout the paper, we will work with these functions F and F_Ω.

Lemma 1 (Homomorphism of F and F_Ω [17]).
For F and F_Ω, the following homomorphic feature holds.

$$\begin{cases} F(a+b) = F(a) + F(b) \\ F(a*b) = F(a) \odot F(b) \end{cases}$$

$$\begin{cases} F_\Omega(a+b) = F_\Omega(a) + F_\Omega(b) \\ F_\Omega(a*b) = F_\Omega(a) \odot F_\Omega(b) \end{cases}$$

Hoffstein et al. [17] defined the $Partial Fourier Ricovery_{q,t,N,\beta}$ problem, which is a problem related to the Partial Fourier transform, as follows.

Definition 7 (*Partial Fourier Ricovery$_{q,t,N,\beta}$* **problem** [17]). *Given $\hat{f}\,|_\Omega \in \mathbb{Z}_q^t$, the problem is to find $x \in R_q$ such that $\hat{x}\,|_\Omega = \hat{f}\,|_\Omega$ (mod q) and $||x||_\infty \le \beta$.*

In the maps $F(f)$ and $F_\Omega(f)$ are in the Partial Fourier transform, the input f is a polynomial of R_q; however, if we consider it as an N-dimensional vector on $\mathbb{Z}_q^N$, the maps $F(f)$ and $F_\omega(f)$ can be regarded as products of a Vandermonde matrix generated from g and a vector f [17]. Based on this feature, they considered that there is a relationship between the Partial Fourier Recovery problem and SIS problem. For the security proof of the protocol using the Partial Fourier transform, we define the Vandermonde-$SIS_{q,t,N,\beta}^\kappa$ problem, which is a problem with Vandermonde matrix, as follows:

Definition 8 (Vandermonde-$SIS_{q,t,N,\beta}^\kappa$ problem). *Given a Vandermonde matrix $A \in \mathbb{Z}_q^{t \times N}$ available from a distribution κ, the problem is to find a nonzero vector $\mathbf{v} \in \mathbb{Z}_q^N$ such that $A\mathbf{v} = 0$ and $||\mathbf{v}||_\infty \le \beta$.*

3 Previous Research

In this section, we describe the previous research. Specifically, we describe the signatures in the signature schemes of Hoffstein et al. [17] and Doröz et al. [18], which are used in our proposed accumulator described in Sect. 4. In Subsect. 3.1, we describe the ideas in a signature scheme based on the Partial Fourier Recovery problem of Hoffstein et al. [17]. In Subsect. 3.2, we describe the ideas in an aggregate signature scheme based on the Partial Fourier Recovery problem of Doröz et al. [18].

3.1 A Signature Scheme Based on the Partial Fourier Recovery Problem [17]

A signature scheme [20] based on the Partial Fourier Recovery problem was proposed by Hoffstein et al. in 2000. However, the signature scheme had a problem that a secret key could be decrypted from a set of signatures by the same signer. Hoffstein et al. [17] solved the problem by adopting the aborting technique [21]. In this section, we explain their signature, which called HPSSW signature in this paper. HPSSW signature consists of the following four algorithms: {SigSetup, Keygen, Sign, SigVerify} described below.

- SigSetup(λ) → pp
  On input security parameter λ, output positive integers k and b, hash functions F_Ω, and $Hash_1$ as public parameters.
- Keygen(pp) → f, $\hat{f}$ $|_\Omega$
  On input public parameter pp, output the signer's private key f and public key $\hat{f}$ $|_\Omega$. The detailed algorithm is in Algorithm 1.
- Sign(pp, f, $\hat{f}$ $|_\Omega$, m) → σ
  The algorithm Sign is performed by the signer. On input pp, private key f, public key $\hat{f}$ $|_\Omega$, and message m, output signature σ. This algorithm allows a signer to sign a message m using his own secret key f. The detailed algorithm is in Algorithm 2.
- SigVerify(pp, $\sigma = \{\hat{y}$ $|_\Omega$, z$\}$, $\hat{f}$ $|_\Omega$, m) → 1 or 0
  The algorithm SigVerify is performed by the verifier. On input pp, signature σ, public key $\hat{f}$ $|_\Omega$, and message m, output 0 or 1. If σ is a valid signature for the message m and the secret key f, 1 is output, otherwise, 0 is output. The detailed algorithm is in Algorithm 3.

Algorithm 1. Keygen

Input: pp
1: $f \overset{\$}{\leftarrow} \mathcal{B}^\infty(1)$
2: $\hat{f}$ $|_\Omega \leftarrow F_\Omega(f)$
Output: $f, \hat{f}$ $|_\Omega$

Algorithm 2. Sign

Input: pp, $f, \hat{f}$ $|_\Omega, m$
1: **repeat**
2:     $y \overset{\$}{\leftarrow} \mathcal{B}^\infty(k)$
3:     $\hat{y}$ $|_\Omega \leftarrow F_\Omega(y)$
4:     $c \leftarrow Hash_1(\hat{y}$ $|_\Omega, \hat{f}$ $|_\Omega, m)$
5:     $z \leftarrow f * c + y$
6: **until** $z \in \mathcal{B}^\infty(k - b)$
7: $\sigma \leftarrow \{\hat{y}$ $|_\Omega, z\}$
Output: σ

Algorithm 3. SigVerify

Input: $pp, \sigma = \{\hat{y} \,|_{\Omega}, z\}, \hat{f} \,|_{\Omega}, m$
1: $c \leftarrow Hash_1(\hat{y} \,|_{\Omega}, \hat{f} \,|_{\Omega}, m)$
2: $\hat{c} \,|_{\Omega} \leftarrow F_{\Omega}(c)$
3: $Z \leftarrow \hat{f} \,|_{\Omega} \odot \hat{c} \,|_{\Omega} + \hat{y} \,|_{\Omega}$
4: $\hat{z} \,|_{\Omega} \leftarrow F_{\Omega}(z)$
5: **if** $z \in \mathcal{B}^{\infty}(k - b)$ **and** $Z == \hat{z} \,|_{\Omega}$ **then**
6:     $result \leftarrow 1$
7: **else**
8:     $result \leftarrow 0$
9: **end if**
Output: $result$

In Algorithm 2, they hide the secret key f and the hash value c by computing $f * c + y$. However, an attacker who obtains the distribution of $z(= f * c + y)$ from the set of signatures signed by the same private key can decrypt vector $f * c$ because the distributions of y and c are known to the attacker. They can decrypt the value of the secret key f using the attack technique of Gentry et al. against $f * c$ [22]. To solve this problem, we used the aborting technique [21] in line 5 of Algorithm 2. The value of z is sent to the verifier only when it is in a distribution $\mathcal{B}^{\infty}(k - b)$ that is different from the actual distribution, and the actual distribution of $z(= f * c + y)$ is hidden to prevent the secret key from being cracked. In HPSSW this signature, a valid signature generated in Sign is always accepted by a valid verifier in SigVerify. In other words, this signature scheme satisfies correctness. Lemma 2 confirms that Algorithm 3 is correctly verified.

Lemma 2 (Correctness of HPSSW signature)
In SigVerify, a signature created by a legitimate signer is always accepted by a legitimate verifier. That is, the following equation holds for any message m.

$$\Pr[pp \leftarrow \mathsf{SigSetup}(n); (f, \hat{f} \,|_{\Omega}) \leftarrow \mathsf{Keygen}(pp)$$

$$\wedge \, \mathsf{SigVerify}(pp, \mathsf{Sign}(pp, f, \hat{f} \,|_{\Omega}, m), \hat{f} \,|_{\Omega}, m) = 1] = 1$$

3.2 Aggregate Signature Scheme Based on Partial Fourier Recovery Problem [18]

Based on the signature scheme described in Sect. 3.1, Doröz et al. constructed an aggregate signature scheme based on the Partial Fourier Recovery problem [18]. Signatures generated by K signers using the Sign algorithm in Algorithm 2 clause for different messages are aggregated and verified simultaneously. They aggregated the K signatures from K people

$$\{\sigma_1 = \{z_1(= f_1 * c_1 + y_1), \hat{y}_1 \,|_{\Omega}\}), \ldots,$$
$$\sigma_K = \{z_K(= f_K * c_K + y_K), \hat{y}_K \,|_{\Omega}\}\}.$$

To realize the aggregate signature, they defined the hash function $Hash_4$: $\{0,1\}^* \rightarrow \{1,-1\}^K$ and aggregated all K signatures as

$$\{\beta_1, \ldots, \beta_K\} \leftarrow Hash_4(c_1, \ldots, c_K)$$
$$z = \beta_1 z_1 + \cdots + \beta_K z_K$$

and can realize an aggregate signature. In the batch verification of this signature scheme, the homomorphic feature of F_Ω in Lemma 1 is also used.

4 Proposed Constant Lattice-Based Accumulator

In this section, we propose the lattice-based accumulator, which satisfies three features:

1. verification time is constant to the size of the list;
2. update time is constant to the size of the list; and
3. bit length of the witness is independent of the size of the list.

The proposed accumulator is based on a Partial Fourier Recovery problem. In our accumulator, manager uses HPSSW signature as a tool to guarantee that an element is contained in the compressed list, and signature verification allows the authenticity of the element to be checked. HPSSW signature proved to satisfy unforgeability based on Information-theoretical security. In this paper, in order to propose an accumulator based on Vandermonde-$SIS^\infty_{q,t,N,k-b}$, we prove that HPSSW signature satisfies unforgeability based on Vandermonde-$SIS^\infty_{q,t,N,k-b}$ in Theorem 1. Furthermore, we use the idea of Sect. 3.2 to compress a list.

In this section, we first prove that HPSSW signature satisfies unforgeability based on Vandermonde-$SIS^\infty_{q,t,N,k-b}$. Next, we propose our accumulator, which consists of four algorithms, $\{\mathsf{Setup}, \mathsf{Acc}, \mathsf{Witness}, \mathsf{Verify}\}$. Verification time in Verify is constant to the size of a list, and the witness of the bit length in $\mathsf{Witness}$ is independent of the number of elements in the list. Then, we propose the update algorithm $\{\mathsf{Add}, \mathsf{Del}, \mathsf{WitUpdate}\}$, which can be executed at a constant time to the size of a list. Finally, we prove our proposed accumulator satisfies three features, and prove our accumulator satisfies the security requirements for an accumulator.

4.1 Unforgeability of HPSSW Signature

In this subsection, we prove that the HPSSW signature satisfies unforgeability based on Vandermonde-$SIS^\infty_{q,t,N,k-b}$ by Theorem 1.

Theorem 1 (Unforgeability of HPSSW signature)
HPSSW *signature scheme is unforgeable if Vandermonde-$SIS^\infty_{q,t,N,k-b}$ is hard. That is, for every polynomial-time forger $\mathcal{A}'$, the probability that after seeing the public key and* $\{(m_1, \mathsf{Sign}(\mathsf{pp}, \mathsf{f}, \hat{\mathsf{f}} |_\Omega, m_1)), \ldots, (m_\mathsf{l}, \mathsf{Sign}(\mathsf{pp}, \mathsf{f}, \hat{\mathsf{f}} |_\Omega, m_\mathsf{l}))\}$ *for any* l *messages* m_i *of its choosing (where l is polynomial in λ), $\mathcal{A}'$ can produce* $(m^* \neq m_i, \sigma^*)$ *such that* $\mathsf{SigVerify}(\mathsf{pp}, \sigma^*, \hat{\mathsf{f}} |_\Omega, m^*) = 1$, *is smaller than* $neg(\lambda)$.

Proof. We first assume there exists an adversary $\mathcal{A}$ that breaks the unforgeability of the signature scheme of [17]. We prove whether it is possible for another adversary $\mathcal{A}$ to break Vandermonde-$SIS^{\infty}_{q,t,N,k-b}$ problem using an adversary $\mathcal{A}'$.

Adversary $\mathcal{A}$ gains $f, \hat{f} \mid_{\Omega}, F_{\Omega}$ from the oracle. Subsequently, $\mathcal{A}$ sends $\hat{f} \mid_{\Omega}$, F_{Ω} to $\mathcal{A}'$. Because $\mathcal{A}'$ can break the signature scheme, it creates $m^*(\neq m_i)$ and its signature $\sigma^*(= \{\hat{y^*} \mid_{\Omega}, z^*\})$ satisfying Eq. (1).

$$\mathsf{SigVerify}(\mathsf{pp}, \sigma^*, \hat{f} \mid_{\Omega}, m^*) = 1 \tag{1}$$

From Algorithm 3, the signature $(m^* \neq m_i, \sigma^*)$ satisfies Eq. (2).

$$\hat{f} \mid_{\Omega} \odot F_{\Omega}(Hash_1(\hat{y} \mid_{\Omega}, \hat{f} \mid_{\Omega}, m)) + \hat{y^*} \mid_{\Omega} = \hat{z^*} \mid_{\Omega} \tag{2}$$

Because of Lemma 1, Eq. (2) is transformed to Eq. (3)

$$F_{\Omega}(f * Hash_1(\hat{y} \mid_{\Omega}, \hat{f} \mid_{\Omega}, m) + y^*) = F_{\Omega}(z^*) \tag{3}$$

Because of Lemma 1, Eq. (3) is transformed to Eq. (4)

$$F_{\Omega}(f * Hash_1(\hat{y} \mid_{\Omega}, \hat{f} \mid_{\Omega}, m) + y^* - z^*) = 0 \tag{4}$$

If $f * Hash_1(\hat{y} \mid_{\Omega}, \hat{f} \mid_{\Omega}, m) + y^* = z^*$ or $||f * Hash_1(\hat{y} \mid_{\Omega}, \hat{f} \mid_{\Omega}, m) + y^* - z^*||_{\infty} > k - b$, then we recompute $\sigma^*(= \{\hat{y^*} \mid_{\Omega}, z^*\})$. Otherwise, $f * Hash_1(\hat{y} \mid_{\Omega}, \hat{f} \mid_{\Omega}, m) + y^* - z^*$ is the solution to Vandermonde-$SIS^{\infty}_{q,t,N,k-b}$. Therefore, when $\mathcal{A}$ receive $\sigma^*(= \{\hat{y^*} \mid_{\Omega}, z^*\})$ from $\mathcal{A}'$, $\mathcal{A}$ can break Vandermonde-$SIS^{\infty}_{q,t,N,k-b}$. From the contraposition, the signature scheme satisfies unforgeability under the Vandermonde-$SIS^{\infty}_{q,t,N,k-b}$. ∎

4.2   Our Proposed Accumulator

Algorithms {Setup, Acc, Witness, Verify} are presented in this subsection. The entities consists of the manager, user, and verifier. The user means an owner of an element in the list. We consider a situation where each user i has value $f_i \in \mathbb{R}_q$. The manager constructs pp using Algorithm 4. Instead of storing the list $\{f_1, \ldots, f_K\}$ of K users' values, the manager compresses them using the algorithm Acc to store them as short values acc_val in Algorithm 5. The manager creates a witness for each owner of each value using Witness in Algorithm 6. The manager distributes witnesses to each user. Each user of value $f_i \in \{f_1, \ldots, f_K\}$ can claim to the verifier that f_i is a value in acc_val by Verify.

We show {Setup, Acc, Witness, Verify} and their corresponding algorithms as follows.

- Setup(λ) $\rightarrow$ pp
  On input security parameter λ, output public parameter pp. Setup is executed by the manager. The detailed algorithm is in Algorithm 4.

- $\mathsf{Acc}(\mathsf{pp}, \mathsf{R} = \{\mathsf{f}_1, \ldots, \mathsf{f}_\mathsf{K}\}) \to \{\mathsf{acc\_val}, \mathsf{Z}, \mathsf{y\_list}\}$
  On input public parameter pp and the list $R = \{\mathsf{f}_1, \ldots, \mathsf{f}_\mathsf{K}\}$, outputs the accumulator value $\mathsf{acc\_val}$. Here, $\mathsf{f}_i \in \mathbb{R}_q$ is the value each users own. Acc is executed by the manager. First, the value of f_i held by each user is sent to the manager, who creates $R = \{\mathsf{f}_1, \ldots, \mathsf{f}_\mathsf{K}\}$. Next, the manager compresses the list R into a single accumulator value $\mathsf{acc\_val}$, thereby reducing the number of values held by the manager. The values $\{Z, y\_list\}$ are generated in Acc to be used in $\mathsf{Witness}$. After the end of Acc, the manager publishes $\mathsf{acc\_val}$ and maintains $\{Z, y\_list\}$. The detailed algorithm is in Algorithm 5.
- $\mathsf{Witness}(\mathsf{pp}, sk, \mathsf{acc\_val}, Z, \mathsf{f}_i, y_i) \to \mathsf{w}_i$
  On input $\mathsf{pp}, sk, \mathsf{acc\_val}, Z, \mathsf{f}_i, \ y_i \in y\_list$, and outputs the witness w_i. $\mathsf{Witness}$ is executed by the manager. Manager generates witness w_i for f_i. In other words, witness w_i is generated by the manager as proof that the user is a valid owner of f_i in the list R. After the completion of this algorithm, the manager distributes w_i to the user who owns f_i. The detailed algorithm is in Algorithm 6.
- $\mathsf{Verify}(\mathsf{pp}, \mathsf{acc\_val}, \mathsf{f}_i, \mathsf{w}_i) \to 1 \text{ or } 0$
  On input $\mathsf{pp}, \mathsf{acc\_val}, \mathsf{f}_i, \mathsf{w}_i$, and outputs 0 or 1. Verify is executed by the verifier. In Verify, it is executed to verify whether the value f_i that a user has is really included in the list R. The detailed algorithm is in Algorithm 7.

Algorithm 4. Setup(λ) by manager

Input: λ

1: Construct the secret key of manager sk by $sk \xleftarrow{\$} \mathcal{B}^\infty(1)$.
2: Construct the public key of manager $\hat{sk} \mid_\Omega \leftarrow F_\Omega(sk)$, number of elements K, positive integer k, k', b, m, B_k, polynomial $c \xleftarrow{\$} T(d_c)$, and hash function $F_\Omega, Hash_1, Hash_2, Hash_3$
3: $\mathsf{pp} = \{\hat{sk} \mid_\Omega, K, k, k', b, m, B_k, c, F_\Omega, Hash_1, Hash_2, Hash_3\}$.

Output: pp

4.3   Update Method in the Proposed Accumulator

In this subsection, we propose an update method. Our update method consists from $\{\mathsf{Add}, \mathsf{Del}, \mathsf{WitUpdate}\}$. When an element f^* is added to the compressed list R, manager updates the accumulator value $\mathsf{acc\_val}$ using Algorithm Add. Then manager generates witness w^* and distributes it to the added user. When an element f_i is removed from the list R, manager uses the algorithm Del. When the list R is updated, the witness w_i possessed by each user must also be updated.

The witness w_i is updated by each user. WitUpdate is an algorithm for updating w_i by each user.

We show {Add, Del, WitUpdate} and their corresponding algorithms as follows.

Algorithm 5. $\mathsf{Acc}(pp, R = \{f_1, \ldots, f_K\})$ phase by manager

---

Input: $pp = \{\hat{sk}|_\Omega, K, k, k', b, m, B_k, c, F_\Omega, Hash_1, Hash_2, Hash_3\}, R = \{f_1, \ldots, f_K\}$
1: **repeat**
2:    **for** $i = 1$ to K step 1 do **do**
3:       **repeat**
4:          $y_i \leftarrow \mathcal{B}^\infty(k)$
5:          $z_i \leftarrow f_i * c + y_i$
6:       **until** $z_i \in \mathcal{B}^\infty(k - b)$
7:       $\hat{y}_i |_\Omega \leftarrow F_\Omega(y_i)$
8:       $\hat{f}_i |_\Omega \leftarrow F_\Omega(z_i)$
9:       $\beta_i \leftarrow Hash_2(\hat{y}_i |_\Omega, \hat{z}_i |_\Omega)$
10:   **end for**
11:   $Z \leftarrow \beta_1 z_1 + \cdots + \beta_K z_K$
12: **until** $\|Z\|_\infty \leq B_k \sqrt{K}(k - b)$
13: $\hat{Z} |_\Omega \leftarrow F_\Omega(Z)$
14: $acc\_val \leftarrow Hash_3(\hat{Z} |_\Omega)$
15: $y\_list = \{y_1, \ldots y_K\}$
Output: acc_val, Z, y_list

Algorithm 6. $\mathsf{Witness}(pp, sk, acc\_val, Z, f_i, y_i)$ phase by manager

---

Input: $pp, sk, acc\_val = \{\hat{sk} |_\Omega, h\}, Z, \hat{F} |_\Omega, \hat{Y} |_\Omega, f_i, y_i$
1: $\sigma \leftarrow \mathsf{Sign}(pp, sk, \hat{sk} |_\Omega, [f_i|y_i])$
2: $\hat{y} |_\Omega \leftarrow F_\Omega(y)$
3: $\hat{f} |_\Omega \leftarrow F_\Omega(f)$
4: $\beta_i \leftarrow Hash_2(\hat{y} |_\Omega, \hat{z} |_\Omega)$
5: $Z_i \leftarrow Z - \beta_i(f_i * c + y_i)$
6: $w_i \leftarrow \{\sigma, Z_i, y_i\}$
Output: w_i

Algorithm 7. Verify(pp, acc_val, f_i, w_i)

Input: $pp, acc\_val, f_i, w_i = \{\sigma, Z_i, y_i\}$

1:   $result \leftarrow$ SigVerify($pp, \sigma, \overset{\centerdot}{sk} |_{\Omega}, [f_i|y_i]$)
2:   **if** result==1 **then**
3:      $z' \leftarrow f_i * c + y_i$
4:      $\hat{y}_i |_{\Omega} \leftarrow F_{\Omega}(y_i)$
5:      $\hat{f}_i |_{\Omega} \leftarrow F_{\Omega}(f_i)$
6:      $\beta_i \leftarrow Hash_2(\hat{y}_i |_{\Omega}, \hat{f}_i |_{\Omega})$
7:      $\hat{Z} |_{\Omega} \leftarrow F_{\Omega}(Z_i + \beta_i z')$
8:      **if** $acc\_val \neq Hash_3(\hat{Z} |_{\Omega})$ **then**
9:        $result \leftarrow 0$
10:    **end if**
11: **end if**

Output: $result$

- Add(pp, sk, acc_val, f^*, Z) $\rightarrow \{acc\_val^*, w^*, update\_info\}$
  On input public parameter pp, secret key of manager sk, an accumulator value before being updated acc_val, an element newly added f^*, Z, and outputs $\{acc\_val^*, w^*, update\_info\}$. Add is executed by the manager. When f^* is added to the list, the manager updates acc_val^* and constructs a witness w^* for f^*. Manager open acc_val^* to all user. Then, manager outputs $update\_info$ for each user to enable to update their witness. Manager sends the $update\_info$ to each user. The detailed algorithm is in Algorithm 8.
- Del(pp, acc_val, f_i, w_i, Z) $\rightarrow \{acc\_val^*, update\_info, K', Z\}$
  On input public parameter pp, an accumulator value before being updated acc_val, f_i where an element deleted from the list R, Z, and outputs

$$\{acc\_val^*, update\_info, K', Z'\}.$$

  Del is executed by the manager. In Del, the manager updates the new accumulator value acc_val^* from which f_i has been removed. In addition, the manager creates $update\_info$ necessary for other users to update their own witness. The manager publishes the acc_val^* and sends the $update\_info$ to each user. The detailed algorithm is in Algorithm 9.
- WitUpdate($pp, update\_info, w_i$) $\rightarrow w_i^*$
  On input public parameter pp, update information send by manager $update\_info$, their original witness w_i, and outputs w_i^*. Witness is executed by each user. WitUpdate is executed when the algorithm Add or Del is executed. The detailed algorithm is in Algorithm 10.

4.4   Analysis of Our Proposed Accumulator

In this subsection, we first prove our proposed accumulator satisfies three features. We prove it in Theorem 2. Then, we prove our proposed accumulator satisfies the security of accumulator.

Algorithm 8. Add(pp, sk, acc_val, f*, Z) phase by manager

Input: pp, sk, acc_val, f*, Z
1: **repeat**
2:   **repeat**
3:     $y_i \leftarrow \mathcal{B}^\infty(k)$
4:     $z_i \leftarrow f^* * c + y_i$
5:   **until** $z_i \in \mathcal{B}^\infty(k - b)$
6:   $\hat{y}_i \mid_\Omega \leftarrow F_\Omega(y_i)$
7:   $\hat{f}^* \mid_\Omega \leftarrow F_\Omega(z_i)$
8:   $\beta_i \leftarrow Hash_2(\hat{y}_i \mid_\Omega, \hat{z}_i \mid_\Omega)$
9: **until** $||Z + \beta_i z_i||_\infty \leq B_k \sqrt{K + 1}(k - b)$
10: $Z \leftarrow Z + \beta_i z_i$
11: $K \leftarrow K + 1$
12: $\hat{Z} \mid_\Omega \leftarrow F_\Omega(Z)$
13: acc_val* $\leftarrow Hash_3(\hat{Z} \mid_\Omega)$
14: w* $\leftarrow$ Witness(pp, sk, acc_val*, Z, f*, y_i)
15: update_info $\leftarrow \{z_i, \beta_i\}$
Output: acc_val*, w*, update_info

Algorithm 9. Del(pp, acc_val, f_i, w_i, Z) phase by manager

Input: pp, acc_val, f_i, $w_i = \{\sigma, Z_i, y_i\}$, Z
1: **if** Verify(pp, acc_val, f_i, w_i) $== 1$ **then**
2:   **repeat**
3:     $\beta_i \xleftarrow{\$} \{-1, 1\}$
4:     $z_i \xleftarrow{\$} \mathcal{B}^\infty(k - b)$
5:   **until** $||Z - \beta_i z_i||_\infty \leq B_k \sqrt{K - 1}(k - b)$
6:   $Z' \leftarrow Z - \beta_i z_i$
7:   $K' \leftarrow K - 1$
8:   $\hat{Z} \mid_\Omega \leftarrow F_\Omega(Z)$
9:   acc_val* $\leftarrow Hash_3(\hat{Z} \mid_\Omega)$
10:   update_info $\leftarrow \{z_i, -\beta_i\}$
11: **end if**
Output: acc_val*, update_info, K', Z'

Algorithm 10. WitUpdate(pp, update_info, w_i)

Input: pp, update_info $= \{z', \beta'\}$, $w_i = \{\sigma, Z_i, y_i\}$
1: $Z_i \leftarrow Z_i + \beta' z'$
2: $w_i \leftarrow \{\sigma, Z_i, y_i\}$
Output: w_i^*

Theorem 2. *Our proposed accumulator satisfies three features:*

1. verification time is constant to the size of the list;

2. *update time is constant to the size of the list; and*
3. *bit length of the witness is independent of the size of the list.*

Proof:

– verification time is constant to the size of the list (Feature (1)):

In Algorithm 7, the verification of the witnesses w_i is composed by $\{\sigma, Z_i, y_i\}$. The bit length of $\{\sigma, Z_i, y_i\}$ is independent of the number of elements in the list. This shows that the verification time by the verifier is independent of the number of elements in the list. Indeed, if the SigVerify outputs 0, the execution time will be shorter than if it outputs 1. Consequently, verification time is constant to the size of the list.

– update time is constant to the size of the list (Feature (2)):

Algorithm 8 shows that the update time of acc_val when an element is added is independent of the number of elements in the list. Furthermore, Algorithm 9 shows that the update time of acc_val when an element is deleted is independent of the number of elements in the list. In addition, Algorithm 10 shows that the update time of a witness when an element is added or deleted is independent of the number of elements in the list. Consequently, update time is constant to the size of a list.

– bit length of the witness is independent of the size of the list (Feature (3)):

In Algorithm 6, the generation of witnesses w_i is composed by $\{\sigma, Z_i, y_i\}$. The bit length of $\{\sigma, Z_i, y_i\}$ is independent of the number of elements in the list. Consequently, the bit length of the witness is independent of the number of elements in the list. ∎

Next, we prove whether our accumulator satisfies the security requirements for an accumulator. In other words, we verify whether {Setup, Acc, Witness, Verify} satisfies Definition 4. By proving Theorem 3, we can demonstrate that the proposed accumulator satisfies Definition 4.

Theorem 3 (security of our proposed accumulator). *Given a Vandermonde matrix, $A \in \mathbb{Z}_q^{t \times N}$. Let $Hash_3$ be $Hash_3(x) := A \cdot x$ s.t. $x \in \mathbb{Z}_q^N$. We assume that the Vandermonde-$SIS_{q,t,N,\beta}^{\infty}$ problem (Definition 8) holds. Subsequently, the accumulator satisfies Definition 4 and is therefore secure.*

We first assume there exists an adversary $\mathcal{A}'$ that breaks the security of the accumulator scheme. That is, we assume $\mathcal{A}'$ can break Definition 4. We prove whether it is possible for another adversary $\mathcal{A}$ to break the Vandermonde-$SIS_{q,t,N,\beta}^{\infty}$ problem using an adversary $\mathcal{A}'$.

Adversary $\mathcal{A}$ gains $A \in \mathbb{Z}_q^{t \times N}$ from the oracle. Subsequently, $\mathcal{A}$ sends A to $\mathcal{A}'$. Because $\mathcal{A}'$ can break the accumulator scheme, it creates d^* and its witness $\omega^*(= \{\sigma^*, Z_i^*, y_i^*\})$, which are not included in the list R satisfying Eq. (5).

$$\Pr[pp \leftarrow \text{Tsetup}(n); (R, d^*, \omega^*) \leftarrow A(pp) : d^* \notin R \wedge \text{Tverify}(\text{Tacc}(R), d^*, \omega^*) = 1]$$
$$> \varepsilon(n).$$

$$(5)$$

Consider the case in which $\mathcal{A}'$ forges d^* instead of f_K where $f_K \in R$. From Algorithm 5, the accumulator value is acc_val, and acc_val satisfies Eq. (6).

$$\text{acc\_val} = Hash_3(F_\Omega(Hash_2(\hat{y}_K \,|_\Omega, \hat{f}_K \,|_\Omega) \cdot (f_K \cdot c + y_K) + Z_K))$$
$$= Hash_3(F_\Omega(Hash_2(\hat{y}_i^* \,|_\Omega, \hat{d}^* \,|_\Omega) \cdot (d^* \cdot c + y_i^*) + Z_i^*)) \qquad (6)$$

Let x_1 and x_2 as

$$x_1 = F_\Omega(Hash_2(\hat{y}_K \,|_\Omega, \hat{f}_K \,|_\Omega) \cdot (f_K \cdot c + y_K) + Z_K)$$
$$x_2 = F_\Omega(Hash_2(\hat{y}_i^* \,|_\Omega, \hat{d}^* \,|_\Omega) \cdot (d^* \cdot c + y_i^*) + Z_i^*)$$

From the above equation, we obtain $Hash_3(x_1) = Hash(x_2)$ and compute:

$$A \cdot x_1 = A \cdot x_2.$$

If $x_1 = x_2$ or $\|x_1 - x_2\|_\infty > \beta$, then we recompute (d^*, ω^*) using Eq. (5). Otherwise, we compute $A(x_1 - x_2) = 0$. Set v as $v = x_1 - x_2$, and v can satisfy $A \cdot v = 0 \wedge \|v\|_\infty \leq \beta$ which is the solution to the Vandermonde-$SIS_{q,t,N,\beta}^\infty$ oracle. Then, $\mathcal{A}$ can break the Vandermonde-$SIS_{q,t,N,\beta}^\infty$ problem. From the contraposition, our proposed accumulator satisfies the security of the accumulator scheme under the Vandermonde-$SIS_{q,t,N,\beta}^\infty$ problem. ∎

5 Comparison

In this section, we compare the existing accumulators with our proposed accumulator in Table 1. In this table, λ denotes the security parameters and K indicates the number of elements in the list to be compressed. In JN, the bit-length of the witness and the verification time can be achieved independently of the elements of the list, but they cannot be constructed without using a trapdoor. Furthermore, there is no algorithm for updating the list of elements.

Table 1. Comparison of lattice-based accumulator

Scheme	Security problem	Trapdoor	Bit-length of witness	Verification time	Update time
JN [12]	SIS	yes	$O(\lambda)$	$O(\lambda)$	no algorithm
LLNW [6]	SIS	no	$O(\lambda \log K)$	$O(\lambda \log K)$	no algorithm
LNWX [16]	SIS	no	$O(\lambda \log K)$	$O(\lambda \log K)$	$O(\lambda \log K)$
Our propose	Vandermonde-SIS	no	$O(\lambda)$	$O(\lambda)$	$O(\lambda)$

LLNW makes it possible to construct an accumulator without using a trapdoor. However, the bit-length of the witness and verification time depends on the logarithmic order of the list elements, and no algorithm exists for updating the list elements.

Conversely, LNWX constructed an algorithm that can update a list element in the logarithmic order of the number of list elements. However, the bit-length of the witness and verification time depends on the logarithmic order of the number of list elements.

In this proposal, the bit-length of witnesses, verification time, and update time can be constructed independently of the number of list elements. Furthermore, the proposed accumulator can be constructed without the use of a trapdoor.

Consequently, our proposed accumulator is the only lattice-based accumulator that does not use a trapdoor and whose bit-length of witnesses, verification time, and update time do not depend on the number of list elements.

6   Conclusion

In this study, we propose the first lattice-based accumulator that satisfies that verification time is constant to the size of the list, update time is constant to the size of the list, and bit length of the witness is independent of the size of the list. Our proposed accumulator does not require a trapdoor for construction. We prove our accumulator satisfies the security requirements for an accumulator. By Comparing with existing lattice-based accumulators, our proposed accumulator is more efficient from the point of view of verification and update time. Consequently, more efficient applications can be realized by incorporating the proposed accumulator scheme into membership list management, zero-knowledge proof, group signature, and blockchain.

Acknowledgment. This work is partially supported by JSPS KAKENHI Grant Number JP21H03443, and SECOM Science and Technology Foundation.

References

1. Benaloh, J., de Mare, M.: One-way accumulators: a decentralized alternative to digital signatures. In: Helleseth, T. (ed.) EUROCRYPT 1993. LNCS, vol. 765, pp. 274–285. Springer, Heidelberg (1994). https://doi.org/10.1007/3-540-48285-7_24
2. Camenisch, J., Lysyanskaya, A.: Dynamic accumulators and application to efficient revocation of anonymous credentials. In: Yung, M. (ed.) CRYPTO 2002. LNCS, vol. 2442, pp. 61–76. Springer, Heidelberg (2002). https://doi.org/10.1007/3-540-45708-9_5
3. Li, J., Li, N., Xue, R.: Universal accumulators with efficient nonmembership proofs. In: Katz, J., Yung, M. (eds.) ACNS 2007. LNCS, vol. 4521, pp. 253–269. Springer, Heidelberg (2007). https://doi.org/10.1007/978-3-540-72738-5_17
4. Lin, Z., Hopper, N.: Jack: scalable accumulator-based Nymble system. In: WPES, pp. 53–62 (2010)
5. Tsudik, G., Xu, S.: Accumulating composites and improved group signing. In: Laih, C.-S. (ed.) ASIACRYPT 2003. LNCS, vol. 2894, pp. 269–286. Springer, Heidelberg (2003). https://doi.org/10.1007/978-3-540-40061-5_16

6. Libert, B., Ling, S., Nguyen, K., Wang, H.: Zero-knowledge arguments for lattice-based accumulators: logarithmic-size ring signatures and group signatures without trapdoors. In: Fischlin, M., Coron, J.-S. (eds.) EUROCRYPT 2016. LNCS, vol. 9666, pp. 1–31. Springer, Heidelberg (2016). https://doi.org/10.1007/978-3-662-49896-5_1

7. Sander, T., Ta-Shma, A.: Flow control: a new approach for anonymity control in electronic cash systems. In: Franklin, M. (ed.) FC 1999. LNCS, vol. 1648, pp. 46–61. Springer, Heidelberg (1999). https://doi.org/10.1007/3-540-48390-X_4

8. Miers, I., Garman, C., Green, M., Rubin, A.D.: Zerocoin: anonymous distributed e-cash from bitcoin In: IEEE Symposium on Security and Privacy, pp. 397–411 (2013)

9. Barić, N., Pfitzmann, B.: Collision-free accumulators and fail-stop signature schemes without trees. In: Fumy, W. (ed.) EUROCRYPT 1997. LNCS, vol. 1233, pp. 480–494. Springer, Heidelberg (1997). https://doi.org/10.1007/3-540-69053-0_33

10. Boneh, D., Bünz, B., Fisch, B.: Batching techniques for accumulators with applications to IOPs and stateless blockchains. In: Boldyreva, A., Micciancio, D. (eds.) CRYPTO 2019. LNCS, vol. 11692, pp. 561–586. Springer, Cham (2019). https://doi.org/10.1007/978-3-030-26948-7_20

11. Baum, C., Damgård, I., Lyubashevsky, V., Oechsner, S., Peikert, C.: More efficient commitments from structured lattice assumptions. In: Catalano, D., De Prisco, R. (eds.) SCN 2018. LNCS, vol. 11035, pp. 368–385. Springer, Cham (2018). https://doi.org/10.1007/978-3-319-98113-0_20

12. Jhanwar, M.P., Safavi-Naini, R.: Compact accumulator using lattices. In: Chakraborty, R.S., Schwabe, P., Solworth, J. (eds.) SPACE 2015. LNCS, vol. 9354, pp. 347–358. Springer, Cham (2015). https://doi.org/10.1007/978-3-319-24126-5_20

13. Ajtai, M.: Generating hard instances of lattice problems (extended abstract). In: STOC, pp. 99–108 (1996)

14. Gentry, C., Peikert, C., Vaikuntanathan, V.: Trapdoors for hard lattices and new cryptographic constructions. In: STOC, pp. 197–206 (2008)

15. Micciancio, D., Peikert, C.: Trapdoors for lattices: simpler, tighter, faster, smaller. In: Pointcheval, D., Johansson, T. (eds.) EUROCRYPT 2012. LNCS, vol. 7237, pp. 700–718. Springer, Heidelberg (2012). https://doi.org/10.1007/978-3-642-29011-4_41

16. Ling, S., Nguyen, K., Wang, H., Yanhong, X.: Lattice-based group signatures: achieving full dynamicity (and deniability) with ease. Theor. Comput. Sci. **783**, 71–94 (2019)

17. Hoffstein, J., Pipher, J., Schanck, J.M., Silverman, J.H., Whyte, W.: Practical signatures from the partial Fourier recovery problem. In: Boureanu, I., Owesarski, P., Vaudenay, S. (eds.) ACNS 2014. LNCS, vol. 8479, pp. 476–493. Springer, Cham (2014). https://doi.org/10.1007/978-3-319-07536-5_28

18. Doröz, Y., Hoffstein, J., Silverman, J.H., Sunar, B.: MMSAT: a scheme for multi-message multiuser signature aggregation. IACR Cryptol. ePrint Arch. **2020**, 520 (2020)

19. Micciancio, D., Mol, P.: Pseudorandom knapsacks and the sample complexity of LWE search-to-decision reductions. In: Rogaway, P. (ed.) CRYPTO 2011. LNCS, vol. 6841, pp. 465–484. Springer, Heidelberg (2011). https://doi.org/10.1007/978-3-642-22792-9_26

20. Hoffstein, J., Kaliski Jr., B.S., Lieman, D.B., Robshaw, M.J.B., Yin, Y.L.. Secure user identification based on constrained polynomials. U.S. Classification (2000). 713/168; 380/28; 380/30; 713/170; 713/176 International Classification: H04L 932; H04L 928; H04L 930

21. Lyubashevsky, V.: Lattice-based identification schemes secure under active attacks. In: Cramer, R. (ed.) PKC 2008. LNCS, vol. 4939, pp. 162–179. Springer, Heidelberg (2008). https://doi.org/10.1007/978-3-540-78440-1_10

22. Gentry, C., Szydlo, M.: Cryptanalysis of the revised NTRU signature scheme. In: Knudsen, L.R. (ed.) EUROCRYPT 2002. LNCS, vol. 2332, pp. 299–320. Springer, Heidelberg (2002). https://doi.org/10.1007/3-540-46035-7_20

23. Lyubashevsky, V.: Fiat-Shamir with aborts: applications to lattice and factoring-based signatures. In: Matsui, M. (ed.) ASIACRYPT 2009. LNCS, vol. 5912, pp. 598–616. Springer, Heidelberg (2009). https://doi.org/10.1007/978-3-642-10366-7_35

Information Security

Malicious JavaScript Detection Based on AST Analysis and Key Feature Re-sampling in Realistic Environments

Ngoc Minh Phung[(✉)] and Mamoru Mimura

National defense academy of Japan, Kanagawa, Yokosuka, Japan
flamelion270796@gmail.com, mim@nda.ac.jp

Abstract. Malicious JavaScript detection using machine learning models has shown many great results over the years. However, real-world data only has a small fraction of malicious JavaScript, making it an imbalanced dataset. Many of the previous techniques ignore most of the benign samples and focus on training a machine learning model with a balanced dataset. This paper proposes a Doc2Vec-based filter model that can quickly classify JavaScript malware using Natural Language Processing (NLP) and feature re-sampling. The feature of the JavaScript file will be converted into vector form and used to train the classifiers. Doc2Vec, a NLP model used for documents is used to create feature vectors from the datasets. In this paper, the total features of the benign samples will be reduced using a combination of word vector and clustering model. Random seed oversampling will be used to generate new training malicious data based on the original training dataset. We evaluate our models with a dataset of over 30,000 samples obtained from top popular websites, PhishTank, and GitHub. The experimental result shows that the best f1-score achieves at 0.99 with the MLP classifier.

Keywords: malicious JavaScript · feature re-sampling · imbalance dataset

1 Introduction

JavaScript continues to be the most commonly used programming language for programming, scripting, and markup languages [22]. As of 2022, most websites use JavaScript for its simplicity and accessibility, mainly as the client-side programming language. For those reasons, the increasing threats of malicious JavaScript have been affecting users worldwide. A cybercriminal can use various types of attacks such as cryptominers, JavaScript downloaders, web skimmers, web scams and JavaScript redirectors. Malicious JavaScript downloaders are still commonly used to infect legitimate and popular webpages. These malicious scripts are often obfuscated and hard to detect. By simply accessing the infected website, the malicious JavaScript will be downloaded to the computer of the victim and redirect the system to the attacker-controlled domain to download

S. El Hajji et al. (Eds.): C2SI 2023, LNCS 13874, pp. 225–241, 2023.
https://doi.org/10.1007/978-3-031-33017-9_15

trojan malware. These so-called "Drive by download attacks" are hard to detect and can cause great damage to the infected system. It is important to be able to detect malicious JavaScript injected inside webpages. Therefore, studies about JavaScript classification have increased in recent years.

Previous study can be divided into static analysis and dynamic analysis. Static analysis evaluates the URLs or the source code of the file, mainly using Natural Language Processing (NLP) for feature extraction and machine learning for training the classifier. Dynamic analysis executes the code and detects malicious data by their action during runtime and can detect subtle malicious actions whose cause is often missed by static analysis methods. However, when dealing with a large amount of data, this can take a long runtime. This paper focuses on the static analysis method, using machine learning to learn the code pattern for the classification task.

Using a filter model that can quickly filter out most of the malicious data before passing the data to the dynamic analysis model can be more cost-effective. This approach requires training the filter model and testing it with unseen data. However, previous studies mostly validate their model with a balanced dataset [9,11,28]. Most classifier models trained with an imbalanced dataset will have low precision and recall scores [18]. Our experiment results show that recall scores for malicious detection varies from 0.1 to 0.56 for the model trained with an imbalanced dataset.

While different resampling methods were used in previous papers and increased detection score by a large margin, there is room for improvement with the data preprocessing. In [20], authors proposed methods that include AST parsing of JavaScript code for better representation of the function of the code. The experiment was done on a balanced dataset. It is unclear if this method is effective against imbalanced dataset. The low recall scores in [18] may also result from the simplicity when preprocessing code. In this paper, we propose a filter model that uses AST parsing using Esprima, key feature reduction using Word2vec and k-means clustering algorithm, randomseed oversampling for data augmentation and learns features from the JavaScript by converting them into vectors using Paragraph vector (Doc2Vec). The extracted data will then be used for training the classifier using supervised machine learning. Training with an imbalanced dataset also means that a dataset is biased towards a class in the dataset. If the dataset is biased towards one class, an algorithm trained on the same data will be biased towards the same class. The model learns more from biased samples and tends to ignore the samples in the minority class. As a result, the model trained this way will assume that any data fed to it belongs to the majority class. Despite achieving high accuracy scores, a model seems naive in its predictions.

The main purpose of the filter model is to quickly filter out most of the malicious JavaScript for dynamic analysis. When evaluating a machine learning model on an imbalanced dataset, precision and recall are better at showing the true performance of that model. High recall scoress mean that the model can be more effective in filtering out most of the malicious data. This study uses an imbalanced dataset with over 30,000 samples. The evaluation shows that the highest f1-score is 0.99.

The contributions in this paper are as follows:

1. Propose a feature reduction algorithm combined with oversampling that improves the recall scores and f1-score of a malware classifier, which is important to how well the classifier can detect malicious JavaScript. The algorithm helps to deal with the class imbalance problem.
2. Evaluate the performance of the feature reduction algorithm and random seed oversampling model on 2 different datasets.

The outline of this paper is as follows.

Section 2 discusses techniques that are used in this paper. Section 3 shows the previous studies that are related to this paper. Section 4 shows the proposed method. Section 5 shows the results of the evaluation experiments. Discussions about the results are described in Sect. 6. Section 7 shows the conclusion and future works.

2 Related Techniques

2.1 Feature Extraction Using Natural Language Processing

Using machine learning to detect malicious JavaScript can be difficult, as a machine cannot really understand the raw contents in the file without preprocessing. Natural Language Processing (NLP) is a branch of artificial intelligence created to deal with this problem and help improving the interaction between humans and machines using natural language. There are various techniques used in NLP such as syntax which refers to how the arrangement of words make sense in a sentence, and semantics which refer to the conveyed meaning of a text. These methods are essential in machine learning [23].

Word Embedding. Word embedding is a collection of NLP models that represent words in the form of low dimensional vectors called embedding, with the purpose of improving the performance of machine-learning-networks in textual analysis of the dataset [8,25]. If there are words that have the same meaning in a text document, they will have the same representation. In general, the unique words in the text data will be extracted and encoded in one-hot vector forms in the preprocessing process for easier computation. However, in large text data, computing thousands of one-hot vectors is very inefficient as most values in one-hot vectors are 0 and yield the results that have mostly 0 values.

Paragraph Vector. Word vector is a preprocessing step that is used to learn word embedding and represent a word from documents as a vector [17]. This vector describes the feature of its corresponding word so that if two words have the same meaning their feature vector converted from word vector model will be similar to each other. Two main models of word vector are Skip-gram and Continuous bag-of-words, which consist of two shallow layers of neural networks that are trained to reconstruct linguistic contexts of the words.

Paragraph vector is an extension of word vector model. Paragraph vector represents a text document from a group of input documents in the form of its fixed-length feature vector [14]. This model can apply to texts of any length and deals with two main weak points of the bag-of-words model: losing the ordering of words and ignoring the semantics of the words. Paragraph vector has two main methods inspired directly from Skip-gram and CBoW models: Distributed memory (PV-DM) and Distributed bag-of-words (PV-DBoW). This paper uses the PV-DBoW model to represent JavaScript snippets in the feature-vector forms. The PV-DM in [14] has a high performance in code analysis and can provide a better score than the PV-DBoW model used in this paper.

2.2 Representing JavaScript Code in AST Form

Abstract syntax tree, or AST for sort, is the representation of only the functional part of source code such as variables declarations of functions, variables. The parts of code that are not relate to functionality will be ignored in the AST after the parsing, such as comments and punctuation marks. Most techniques that use code pattern for detection are greatly affected by obfuscated JavaScript code, as most of the time the obfuscated file will have benign pattern and will be misclassified by the classifier. However, AST can be used to accurately represent the intended function of the code, therefore provides the solution to obfuscated JavaScript classification.

A parser, for example Esprima in Python, takes the tokenized source code as input, generates AST through syntax analysis and parses the result in JSON.

2.3 K-means Clustering Algorithm

This paper uses k-means clustering algorithm for clustering the benign words from the training dataset. K-Means clustering is an unsupervised learning algo-rithm. It groups the dataset into different clusters with K defines the number of pre-defined clusters that need to be created in the process. Each cluster is associated with a centroid. It can cluster the data into different groups and a convenient way to discover the categories of groups in the unlabeled dataset on its own without the need for any training. The main aim of this algorithm is to minimize the sum of distances between the data point and their corresponding clusters. The algorithm takes the unlabeled dataset as input, divides the dataset into k-number of clusters, and repeats the process until it does not find the best clusters. The k-means clustering algorithm mainly performs two tasks: Deter-mines the best value for K center points or centroids by an iterative process; Assigns each data point to its closest k-center, those data points which are near to the particular k-center, create a cluster.

3 Related Works

This section shows the notable studies that are related in the context of a comparison of the work presented in this paper.

3.1 Training Model with an Imbalanced Dataset

The machine learning model tends to ignore the minority class when trained with an imbalanced dataset. There are a few papers that attempt to deal with the class imbalance problem in malicious JavaScript classification.

In [19], the author attempts to generate fake text vectors with Paragraph Vector to enhance small training samples. These features allow users to directly vary each element of the vectors. The method adds random noise to the vectors to generate fake text vectors which represent the context and applies this technique to detect new malicious VBA (Visual Basic for Applications) macros to address the practical problem. This generic technique could be used for malware detection and any imbalanced and contextual data such as malicious JavaScript. In [18], the authors have proposed an undersampling method that reduces the size of the majority class while maintaining its feature and the imbalance of the dataset. For feature extraction, Word2Vec and Doc2Vec are used to extract feature vectors from the JavaScript snippet. In [1], the authors show that at least in the case of connection list systems, class imbalances hinder the performance of standard classifiers. It compared the performance of the previously proposed method to deal with the problem. In [15], the authors propose a minority over-sampling approach for fault detection with heterogeneous imbalanced data. In [6], the authors presented an experimental study of utilizing re-sampling methods for dealing with the class-imbalance problem. The conclusion shows that combining different expressions of the re-sampling approach is an effective solution to the tuning problem.

A clustering-based undersampling technique is used to reduce the size of benign JavaScript. A model using Attention for feature extraction also shows a high recall scores [21].

In the case of detecting malicious JavaScript, the number of benign samples that are available is far greater than the malicious ones. For good real-world representation, the experiment dataset has to be highly imbalanced, which will lead to inaccurate classification of the dataset. The goal of this paper is to create a model that can detect malicious JavaScript in real environment with high recall scores while being trained by an imbalanced dataset. It uses a combination of preprocessing and resampling methods that are not used before.

3.2 Analysis of Malicious JavaScript Detection

There are many studies that focus on detecting malicious JavaScript with machine learning [7,24]. However, the previous studies did not focus on improving the recall of the model trained with an imbalanced dataset. In the real world, the number of benign samples is always bigger than malicious samples, and the model tends to perform poorly. Training the model with too few samples [3] also has the risk of not having enough information and the model tends to perform poorly with new data. In addition, the previous paper did not focus into improving the recall scores. recall scores is important for building a filter model for dynamic analysis, as it determines how good the model is at filtering out as much malicious data as possible. This paper proposes a classification model to deal with the class imbalance problem and evaluate the prediction on an imbalanced dataset. In comparison with the baseline model that does not use oversampling, the proposed model trained with the imbalanced dataset has a better recall scores. Undersampling methods can be used to reduce the size of the benign dataset, which will decrease the actual number of the benign snippet or decrease the feature of the dataset [18]. This method can reduce run time and storage problems if the dataset is large, however it has the risk of potentially losing useful information for training the classifier.

There are two main categories of malicious JavaScript detection: static analysis and dynamic analysis. Most of these methods focus on learning features from malicious web pages.

Static analysis focuses on analyzing the source code of web pages [2, 26], host details, or URL [16] to extract features from malicious contents. These methods are able to extract the features of JavaScript snippets quickly without the needs of loading the web pages, and avoid the risk of being infected by malware as the code are not executed. The main drawback is that static analysis cannot detect attacks that exploit the execution phase of webpages. Using only the web page source code also makes it difficult to detect obfuscated JavaScript or the exploited browser plug-ins, in most cases these kind of malicious contents usually get ignored by a normal classifier.

In [2], authors proposed Prophiler, a static analysis method that quickly filters out malicious contents. This analysis takes into account features derived from the HTML contents of a page, from the associated JavaScript code, and from the corresponding URL. The detection models that use those features are automatically derived using machine-learning techniques applied to labeled dataset. In [20], the study adopts the Abstract Syntax Tree (AST) for code structure representation and a machine learning approach to conduct feature learning called Doc2Vec in order to deal with the evasion techniques of the malicious JavaScript. The experimental results show that the proposed AST features and Doc2Vec for feature learning provide better accuracy and fast classification in malicious JavaScript code detection compared to conventional approaches and can flag malicious JavaScript code previously identified as hard-to-detect.

Dynamic analysis is performed by executing JavaScript code in a real or virtual environment [13, 28]. As it observes the suitable data being propagated from source to output during execution, dynamic analysis is less prone to false positives. In [13], authors presented DbDHunter, a novel ensemble-based anomaly detection approach to detect drive-by-download attacks. It applies a binary particle swarm optimization algorithm on the one-class classifiers ensemble to find a near-optimal sub-ensemble for classifying web pages as benign or malicious. In

[4], the authors proposed ADSandbox, an analysis system for malicious websites that focusses on detecting attacks through JavaScript. Because JavaScript does not have any built-in sandbox concept, the idea is to execute any embedded JavaScript within an isolated environment and log every critical action. Using heuristics on these logs, ADSandbox decides whether the site is malicious or not. The model has great potential for a future version. These methods involve examining real-time actions of the JavaScript code and therefore, to cover all possible outputs, sufficient test inputs must be executed and a lot of resources for computing are required. There are also methods that combine both static analysis and dynamic analysis with high detection accuracy [9,27]. Using static analysis for preprocessing before dynamic analysis can often achieve greater results.

Most of the studies evaluate their models with a balanced dataset. However, as the data in the realistic environment is often times imbalanced, a model that can achieve high performance when trained with an imbalanced dataset can be more reliable in practical uses. The goal of this paper is to implement a machine learning model that can deal with the class imbalance problem with the usage of oversampling method and feature reduction technique and evaluate the model on an extremely imbalanced dataset.

4   Proposed Method

4.1   Outline

This section shows the proposed method for detection of malicious JavaScript using machine learning. Since the size of benign class is far greater than malicious class in realistic environment, the experimental dataset is also imbalanced, which will lead to the class imbalance problem in machine learning. To deal with the class imbalance problem, an oversampling method is applied to adjust the balance between the datasets. For data preprocessing, AST parser combined with feature reduction technique and pattern replacement are used. The dataset after preprocessing will be passed to the Doc2Vec model for feature extraction. The extracted feature will be used to train the classifiers for prediction. The outline of the proposed method is shown in Fig. 1.

The proposed method consists of 4 steps. Step 1 is to transform the original source code into their respective AST form using a parser, then split the snippets into separated words and unify some common word patterns. The preprocessed dataset will be divided equally into training data and test data. The malicious data is rearranged in time order, with previously detected data used for training data and new data for test data. In step 2, a feature reduction technique is used to reduce the total amount of unique words from the training benign samples. Paragraph vector is then used to extract feature vectors from the processed dataset. Step 3 includes the randomseed oversampling method to increase the number of training malicious samples to deal with the imbalance in the dataset. The oversampled dataset will be used to train the classifiers for prediction. The training data will be preprocessed in the same manner mentioned above and is

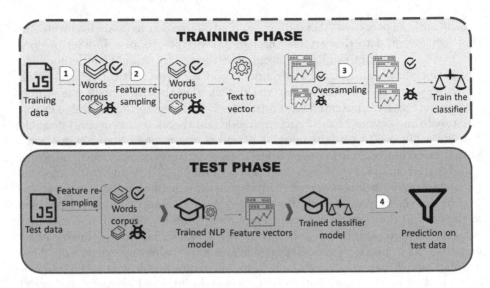

Fig. 1. Outline of the proposed method.

used as input for the trained classifiers to predict malicious JavaScript of the test data in step 4.

4.2 Feature Reduction and Pattern Replacement

The experiment in this paper uses Esprima port from Python for AST parsing, which is a line-by-line manual translation created by German Mendez Bravo (Kronuz). The original Esprima is created and maintained by Ariya Hidayat with the help of many contributors. It is a high performance, standard-compliant JavaScript parser and can be used for performing lexical analysis (tokenization) or syntactic analysis (parsing) of a JavaScript program. It takes a string representing a valid JavaScript program and produces a syntax tree, an ordered tree that describes the syntactic structure of the program. The resulting syntax tree is useful for static program analysis [5].

Pattern replacement is used to replace several common patterns in the JavaScript snippets with their representative words after step 1. This way the common patterns such as numbers and links will be converted into one single word to reduce unnecessary data. The replaced patterns are shown in Table 1. This can also reduce the size of the words dictionaries extracted from the raw JavaScript and lead to a better performance after passing those dictionaries to the Doc2Vec model. The data is split into training data and test data with labels. Words dictionaries will be created, which contain every unique word in the snippets.

Next, the total unique words of the training benign samples are reduced using feature reduction technique. This technique analyzes all extracted unique words using Word2Vec and clustering them in groups using k-means clustering

Table 1. List of replaced patterns in JavaScript snippets

Original patterns	Replaced patterns
URL in the source code	URL
comments in the source code	COMMENT
3–4 digits number	semiNUM
5 or more digits number	longNUM

algorithm in which the words have close relationship to each other. A fixed amount of words from each groups are removed and the remaining words are used to create new benign word corpus. In the experiment, the number of words that are kept is set to be the size of the smallest cluster. The new benign word corpus has total amount of features reduced and is used for preprocessing all the samples in the test dataset. The outline of this feature reduction technique is shown in Fig. 2. This is step 2 of the proposed method.

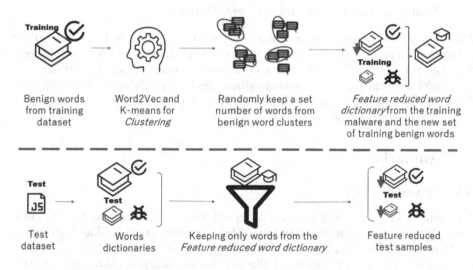

Fig. 2. Outline of the feature reduction technique.

4.3   Feature Extraction Using Doc2Vec

Step 3 of the proposed method is extracting features from words dictionaries. A feature vector model is constructed from the training dataset using Doc2Vec. The converted vectors are used in training the classifiers for evaluating the prediction of the model after training. Note that the proposed method only uses half of the dataset for training, therefore forces the classifier to detect unknown JavaScript snippets with the trained models. This means that the accuracy scores of the classifier have more reliability for practical uses.

4.4   Oversampling Malicious Data with Random Seed Oversampling

Step 3 of the proposed method is using Oversampling on malicious samples to rebalance the dataset. In this oversampling method, new data from the malicious data is generated. In this paper, random oversampling using random seed will be used. The samples are put in Python dictionary format that does not allow any duplicated data. The new data bear similar features as the pre-existed ones while still have their unique features to avoid duplication. The sampling process will randomly cycle through the pre-existed vectors extracted in the training data. In the experiment, malicious training data is generated until the malicious data and the benign data has the same number of samples. The augmented new dataset will be used to train the SVM model and random forest model for classification. In random seed oversampling, new training malicious data will be created by adjusting feature vectors extracted in Subsect. 4.3 for a small random value. The absolute value of the random seed is set at 0.1 for the Doc2Vec model to achieve optimal performance. These settings are determined by empirical methods.

4.5   Evaluate Trained Model on Test Dataset

This is step 4 of the proposed method. The words inside the test dataset will be reduced according to the word corpus created from training dataset in Subsect. 4.2. The trained Doc2vec model extracts feature vectors from the dataset and uses them as input for the trained classifiers model for validation. In this paper, SVM, random forest, XGBoost and Multi-layer Perceptron (MLP) are chosen as four main algorithms for classifier.

5   Evaluation

5.1   Dataset

The benign JavaScript snippets are collected using a web crawler, which crawls through normal popular websites from Alexa websites ranking. The legitimates URL are extracted from the top 50 URL from 178 countries and 762 categories respectively. The web crawler also collects malicious samples from almost 15,000 suspicious URL from PhishTank. To avoid duplicate samples, their hash values are compared and removed from the dataset. The collected suspicious snippets are uploaded to Virus Total for scanning. The snippets that are marked as malware will be used for malware samples. The unmarked ones are considered as benign in the dataset. To verify the reliability of the benign snippets, all samples are uploaded to Virus Total and scanned by anti-virus software. Both results show no malicious samples in the benign dataset. The snippets are then split into training data and test data based on the malware uploaded period on the Phish Tank website. Note that the dataset is imbalanced and that previously uploaded data is used for training. The second malicious dataset is collected from the GitHub source [12] which contains over 40,000 samples in time order. All the collected samples are split into dataset A and dataset B:

1. Dataset A has 21,745 benign samples from popular websites and 214 malicious samples from Phishtank.
2. Dataset B also has the same 21,745 benign samples from popular websites and 8000 malicious samples from GitHub.

5.2 Experiment

In this paper, the proposed method using randomseed oversampling algorithm and feature reduction is evaluated together with a baseline method. The baseline method shares the same settings as the proposed model without using oversampling and feature reduction. The malicious dataset is sorted in time series, the older one will be used to train the models. This is done to evaluate how good the baseline and the proposed model is at detecting unseen malicious JavaScript. The feature reduction technique and randomseed oversampling methods that use random seed are implemented in 2 different dataset A and dataset B. Comparison of the baseline method with the proposed method is used to evaluate the effectiveness of the feature reduction and oversampling methods. Five-fold cross validation is used to evaluate the generalizability of the model. We use 4 different classifiers for better comparison. SVM, random forest, XGBoost and MLP are used.

5.3 Implementation

The algorithms are implemented with Python-3.7 on Windows 10 system. The environment configuration and parameter settings are as follow:

1. System configuration: Window 10, with Intel Core i7-9700K (3.6 GHz) CPU, 64.0 GB RAM memory
2. Python Library: Gensim 3.8.3, Scikit-learn 0.23.2, tensorflow 2.5.0
3. SVM parameter: kernel : linear, c = 10, gamma = 0.1
4. Random foreset parameter: estimators = 100, max features : auto
5. Word2Vec parameter: iteration = 55, learning rate = 0.003, size = 200
6. Doc2Vec parameter: iteration = 55, learning rate = 0.003, size = 200
7. K-means clusters: 10

These setups will be used in both baseline and the proposed method to evaluate their effectiveness. The parameters are determined by empirical methods, in which we set up a range of parameters and pick the setup that improved the recall scores of the classifier.

5.4 Result

Figure 3 and Fig. 4 show the detection scores of the baseline model and proposed model respectively on dataset A. Figure 5 and Fig. 6 show the detection scores of the baseline model and proposed model respectively on dataset B.

Experiment results show that reducing benign words from both training and test benign samples can overall improve the detection scores of the classifier. It is

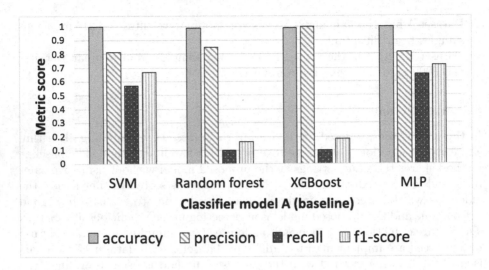

Fig. 3. Detection scores on dataset A of baseline model (no feature reduction and oversampling) with different classifiers.

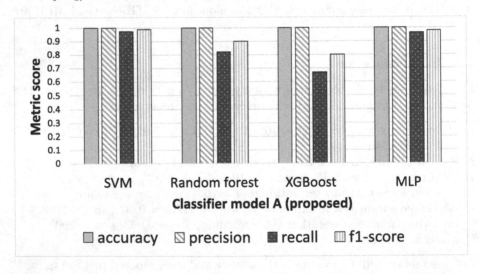

Fig. 4. Detection scores on dataset A of proposed model with different classifiers.

shown that the proposed method has higher positive effect on dataset A, which is very imbalanced with a ratio of benign to malicious is 100 to 1. Due to the ratio in dataset A, reducing benign feature makes the malicious feature to have higher impact to the machine learning process, therefore increasing the detection score of the trained classifier. Five-fold cross validation result shows that the model achieved scores higher than 0.9 on all the metric scores implemented in the experiments. The MLP model achieved highest recall scores on both dataset A and dataset B, with the SVM model comes in second.

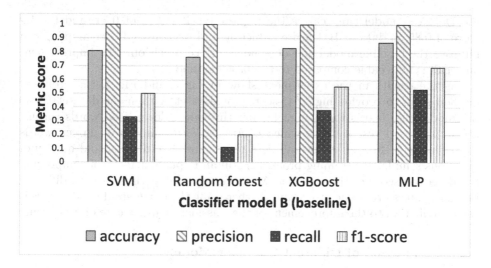

Fig. 5. Detection scores on dataset B of baseline model (no feature reduction and oversampling) with different classifiers.

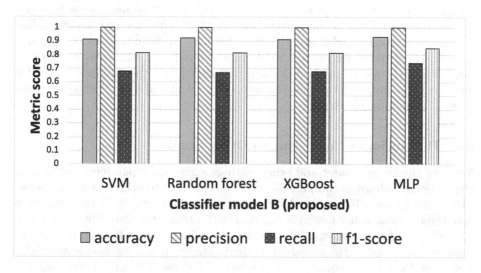

Fig. 6. Detection scores on dataset B of proposed model with different classifiers.

6   Discussion

6.1   The Effectiveness of the Feature Reduction Methods

In this experiment, the malware filtering method focuses on an oversampling-based algorithm to increase the total features and size of the malicious dataset. The resampled data is used to train the model to avoid the class imbalance problem. With the same setting and same random seed oversampling method, the Doc2Vec model can achieve the highest recall scores of 0.74, and the f1-score of 0.85 on dataset B. feature reduction and randomseed oversampling can improve the baseline model and does not sacrifice precision. The improvement on recall is noticeable compared to the baseline model.

As the results in the experiment show in Fig. 3 and Fig. 4, the proposed method seem to provide higher f1-scores for dataset A than the dataset B. As the model only learns the benign feature through a down-sized words corpus, the unprocessed test samples which contain a large number of unseen words can negatively affected the overall detection score. The number and quality of malicious samples for training process is still an important factor for improving the detection score of the classifier. Moreover, more experiments with different benign samples are needed to verify whether using the down-sized word corpus is the contribution to the improvement of the classifier or just a case of overfitting.

6.2   Comparison of Different Classifier Models

In this paper, we test the effectiveness of the proposed method on 4 different classifiers: SVM, random forest, XGBoost and MLP. As the experiment results shown, MLP achieved highest overall score. This might be due to the fact that unlike other classification algorithms like SVM or Naive Bayes Classifier, MLP classifier relies on an underlying Neural Network to perform the task of classification. However, old classifiers like SVM and random forest still perform relatively well with the proposed method. This further shows that the proposed method is effective in dealing with the class imbalanced problem and improves the detection score of malicious JavaScript.

6.3   Difficulties in Comparing to Other Studies

Without the same dataset and other settings such as the parameter settings of the model, it is hard to compare the proposed method to others. It is also necessary to implement different models in the same system setting. With obfuscation countermeasures, other methods can deal with obfuscated data but with a high cost of computing resources. It is also unknown how they will perform with the same dataset used in the proposed method. The proposed method is also lightweight and does not require too much time for detection. This is the required feature of a good filter model (Table 2).

6.4   Limitations

The datasets do not get under further inspection and are sorted in chronological order, which means the labeling of samples is not strict and can affect the result of the experiment. A dataset with a reliable label is necessary to evaluate a model. However, the samples taken from public source have their source code analyzed and processed before being shared with public. The parameters of the classifier model have a big influence in having a high recall scores.

Table 2. Comparison of malicious JavaScript detection methods

	AST [20]	JSForce [10]	proposed method
	static analysis	dynamic analysis	static analysis
Dataset	balanced	balanced	imbalanced (1 : 100 ratio)
Obfuscation contermeasures	yes	yes	yes
Performance	recall = 0.97	TP = 100%	recall = 0.68
	f-score = 0.96	FP = 0%	f-score = 0.81

6.5   Effectiveness of AST Parsing

Compared to the baseline model, the proposed method which utilize AST parsing to convert source code into a more structured form has better detection score, as shown in Subsect. 5.4. Parsing code into their AST form can also better represent the intended functions, even if the source code is obfuscated. It is speculated that AST parsing contribute to the improvement in training the classifier model, as obfuscated samples tend to be misclassified as bengin due to their raw source code contain very little malicious feature.

7   Conclusion

This paper proposes feature reduction and random seed oversampling-based methods to detect unseen malicious JavaScript. The practical performance of the proposed model is evaluated with an imbalanced dataset with over 30,000 samples. The evaluation results show a f1-score of 0.97 on a highly imbalanced dataset. This shows that the proposed method has greatly improved the detection score of the classifier, even when dealing with an imbalanced dataset. These scores show that this model is more efficient than the baseline method which does not use any resampling and feature reduction methods. To detect malicious JavaScript using the combination of static filter and dynamic analysis requires the filter model to quickly filter out as many malicious samples as possible while still being able to deal with the class imbalance problem. The experiment results show that the proposed model achieves a high recall scores on an imbalanced dataset, hence the model has practical results. The performance of the proposed models can be improved with a better preprocessing process and enough malicious samples, as shown in the experiment result. Future work will continue to collect different samples for the new dataset.

References

1. Aurelio, Y.S., de Almeida, G.M., de Castro, C.L., Braga, A.P.: Learning from imbalanced data sets with weighted cross-entropy function. Neural Process. Lett. **50**(2), 1937–1949 (2019). https://doi.org/10.1007/s11063-018-09977-1

2. Canali, D., Cova, M., Vigna, G., Kruegel, C.: Prophiler: a fast filter for the large-scale detection of malicious web pages. In: Proceedings of the 20th International Conference on World Wide Web, WWW 2011, Hyderabad, India, March 28–1 April 2011, pp. 197–206 (2011). https://doi.org/10.1145/1963405.1963436
3. Choi, J., Choi, C., You, I., Kim, P.: Polymorphic malicious JavaScript code detection for APT attack defence. J. Univers. Comput. Sci. **21**, 369–383 (2015)
4. Dewald, A., Holz, T., Freiling, F.: ADSandbox: sandboxing JavaScript to fight malicious websites. In: SAC 2010 (2010)
5. Esprima: Documentation on using esprima vol 4.0, December 2022. https://docs.esprima.org/en/4.0/
6. Estabrooks, A., Jo, T., Japkowicz, N.: A multiple resampling method for learning from imbalanced data sets. Comput. Intell. **20**(1), 18–36 (2004). https://doi.org/10.1111/j.0824-7935.2004.t01-1-00228.x
7. Fass, A., Backes, M., Stock, B.: JStap: a static pre-filter for malicious JavaScript detection. In: Balenson, D. (ed.) Proceedings of the 35th Annual Computer Security Applications Conference, ACSAC 2019, San Juan, PR, USA, 09–13 December 2019, pp. 257–269. ACM (2019). https://doi.org/10.1145/3359789.3359813
8. Ge, L., Moh, T.: Improving text classification with word embedding. In: 2017 IEEE International Conference on Big Data (Big Data), pp. 1796–1805 (2017). https://doi.org/10.1109/BigData.2017.8258123
9. He, X., Xu, L., Cha, C.: Malicious JavaScript code detection based on hybrid analysis. In: 25th Asia-Pacific Software Engineering Conference, APSEC 2018, Nara, Japan, 4–7 December 2018, pp. 365–374. IEEE (2018). https://doi.org/10.1109/APSEC.2018.00051
10. Hu, X., Cheng, Y., Duan, Y., Henderson, A., Yin, H.: JSForce: a forced execution engine for malicious JavaScript detection. In: Lin, X., Ghorbani, A., Ren, K., Zhu, S., Zhang, A. (eds.) SecureComm 2017. LNICST, vol. 238, pp. 704–720. Springer, Cham (2018). https://doi.org/10.1007/978-3-319-78813-5_37
11. Huang, Y., Li, T., Zhang, L., Li, B., Liu, X.: Jscontana: malicious JavaScript detection using adaptable context analysis and key feature extraction. Comput. Secur. **104**, 102218 (2021). https://doi.org/10.1016/j.cose.2021.102218, https://www.sciencedirect.com/science/article/pii/S0167404821000420
12. HynekPetrak: javascript-malware-collection, October 2019. https://github.com/HynekPetrak/javascript-malware-collection
13. Jodavi, M., Abadi, M., Parhizkar, E.: Dbdhunter: an ensemble-based anomaly detection approach to detect drive-by download attacks. In: 2015 5th International Conference on Computer and Knowledge Engineering (ICCKE), pp. 273–278 (2015)
14. Le, Q.V., Mikolov, T.: Distributed representations of sentences and documents. In: Proceedings of the 31th International Conference on Machine Learning, ICML 2014, Beijing, China, 21–26 June 2014, pp. 1188–1196 (2014). http://proceedings.mlr.press/v32/le14.html
15. Liu, J.: A minority oversampling approach for fault detection with heterogeneous imbalanced data. Expert Syst. Appl. **184**, 115492 (2021). https://doi.org/10.1016/j.eswa.2021.115492, https://www.sciencedirect.com/science/article/pii/S0957417421009027
16. Ma, J., Saul, L.K., Savage, S., Voelker, G.M.: Beyond blacklists: learning to detect malicious web sites from suspicious URLs. In: Proceedings of the 15th ACM SIGKDD International Conference on Knowledge Discovery and Data Mining, Paris, France, June 28–1 July 2009, pp. 1245–1254 (2009). https://doi.org/10.1145/1557019.1557153, https://doi.org/10.1145/1557019.1557153

17. Mikolov, T., Chen, K., Corrado, G., Dean, J.: Efficient estimation of word representations in vector space. In: 1st International Conference on Learning Representations, ICLR 2013, Scottsdale, Arizona, USA, 2–4 May 2013, Workshop Track Proceedings (2013). http://arxiv.org/abs/1301.3781
18. Mimura, M., Suga, Y.: Filtering malicious JavaScript code with doc2vec on an imbalanced dataset. In: 2019 14th Asia Joint Conference on Information Security (AsiaJCIS), pp. 24–31 (2019)
19. Mimura, M.: Using fake text vectors to improve the sensitivity of minority class for macro malware detection. J. Inf. Secur. Appl. **54**, 102600 (2020). https://doi.org/10.1016/j.jisa.2020.102600
20. Ndichu, S., Kim, S., Ozawa, S., Misu, T., Makishima, K.: A machine learning approach to detection of JavaScript-based attacks using AST features and paragraph vectors. Appl. Soft Comput. **84** (2019). https://doi.org/10.1016/j.asoc.2019.105721
21. Phung, N.M., Mimura, M.: Detection of malicious JavaScript on an imbalanced dataset. Internet Things **13**, 100357 (2021). https://doi.org/10.1016/j.iot.2021.100357, https://www.sciencedirect.com/science/article/pii/S2542660521000019
22. StackOverflow: Developer survey 2021, May 2021. https://insights.stackoverflow.com/survey/2021
23. Teufl, P., Payer, U., Lackner, G.: From NLP (Natural Language Processing) to MLP (Machine Language Processing). In: Kotenko, I., Skormin, V. (eds.) MMM-ACNS 2010. LNCS, vol. 6258, pp. 256–269. Springer, Heidelberg (2010). https://doi.org/10.1007/978-3-642-14706-7_20
24. Wang, Y., Cai, W., Wei, P.: A deep learning approach for detecting malicious JavaScript code. Secur. Commun. Netw. **9**(11), 1520–1534 (2016). https://doi.org/10.1002/sec.1441
25. Xu, H., Dong, M., Zhu, D., Kotov, A., Carcone, A.I., Naar-King, S.: Text classification with topic-based word embedding and convolutional neural networks. In: Proceedings of the 7th ACM International Conference on Bioinformatics, Computational Biology, and Health Informatics, BCB 2016, Seattle, WA, USA, 2–5 October 2016, pp. 88–97. ACM (2016). https://doi.org/10.1145/2975167.2975176
26. Xu, W., Zhang, F., Zhu, S.: The power of obfuscation techniques in malicious JavaScript code: a measurement study. In: 7th International Conference on Malicious and Unwanted Software, MALWARE 2012, Fajardo, PR, USA, 16–18 October 2012, pp. 9–16 (2012). https://doi.org/10.1109/MALWARE.2012.6461002
27. Xu, W., Zhang, F., Zhu, S.: Jstill: mostly static detection of obfuscated malicious JavaScript code. In: Third ACM Conference on Data and Application Security and Privacy, CODASPY'13, San Antonio, TX, USA, 18–20 February 2013, pp. 117–128 (2013). https://doi.org/10.1145/2435349.2435364
28. Xue, Y., Wang, J., Liu, Y., Xiao, H., Sun, J., Chandramohan, M.: Detection and classification of malicious JavaScript via attack behavior modelling. In: Young, M., Xie, T. (eds.) Proceedings of the 2015 International Symposium on Software Testing and Analysis, ISSTA 2015, Baltimore, MD, USA, 12–17 July 2015, pp. 48–59. ACM (2015). https://doi.org/10.1145/2771783.2771814

Searching for Gemstones: Flawed Stegosystems May Hide Promising Ideas

Evgnosia-Alexandra Kelesidis⬤, Diana Maimuţ(✉)⬤,
and Ilona Teodora Ciocan⬤

Advanced Technologies Institute, Bucharest, Romania
{alexandra.kelesidis,diana.maimut,ilona.ciocan}@dcti.ro

Abstract. The historical domain of information hiding is alternatively used nowadays for communication security. Maybe the oldest and certainly one of the most studied field that falls in this category is steganography. Within the current paper, we focus on image steganography techniques in the case of the JPEG format. We propose a corrected and optimized version of the J3 stegosystem which, to the best of our knowledge and as shown throughout the paper, may be considered a very good choice in terms of security and efficiency as compared to current solutions. We reconstruct the entire J3 algorithm (pre-processing, message insertion and extraction) and detail all the modifications. We also present implementation optimizations and cover all practical cases while still using the maximum image insertion capacity.

Keywords: Information hiding · steganography · stegosystem · image steganography · JPEG · steganalysis

1 Introduction

As communication methods have been constantly evolving together with the emerging technologies, the need of securing the transmitted data has grown exponentially. Closely related to this fact both cryptography and steganography have become undoubtable necessities for ensuring data protection. There is a clear difference between the goals of cryptography and steganography: cryptography's purpose is hiding the content of a message by means of various mathematical methods, while steganography's purpose consists of hiding the existence of a message or to minimize the probability of being discovered. Nonetheless, within the state-of-the-art digital stegosystems the message has to be either encrypted or at least randomized and then inserted into redundant areas of a particular file format.

Steganography [47] is used for hiding a secret message by means of an ordinary object seen as a cover. The goal is to keep the data secret even if the cover is analysed by means of various methods[1]. Thus, a steganographic system (stegosystem) has to ensure the transportation of a message by means of a cover object. These systems can be classified as classical or modern, where those considered modern take advantage of the vast existence and usage of digital files.

Modern steganography uses different digital carriers for message hiding from simple text to images, audio or video. Unusual covers can be adopted by means of using linguistic or natural language steganography for hiding secret messages into text corpuses. Vector objects, computer generated meshes and any other graph structured data, such as XML documents, relational databases, CAD documents can also be used successfully.

In this paper we mainly focus on images as cover objects, as they are considered very common [16] and also practical from the implementation point of view. Using digital images as carriers depends on the image encoding technique. Common types of image encodings are Graphics Interchange Format (GIF), which consists of a simple encoding in red, green and blue (RGB) colors for each pixel, and Joint Photographic Experts Group (JPEG) which is further detailed in Sect. 2 as it represents the type of encoding that interests us for the current paper.

One of the most common methods of digital steganography is the usage of the Least Significant Bit (LSB) from a particular piece of data. More exactly, we can use the LSB in order to transport bits from the secret message. This works due to the fact that this bit is considered redundant, and its modification does not visually alter the cover object. This is most common due to the ease of implementation and the fact that the changes that appear in the image by using this technique are too small to be noticed by the human eye, so the message actually becomes hidden. However, it also has major disadvantages such as the impossibility of using a lossy compression format (the information would change with compression) and the fact that it is not resistant to steganalysis [9]. Furthermore, applying error-correction codes can improve this technique as it can be detected and fixed on the fly by various visualization software, making it impossible to detect for the human eye. Various other techniques are specifically created for a certain file type.

Another steganographic technique is the frequency hiding technique which is suitable for JPEG images.

Related Work. According to [34], until 2010, among the best known steganographic algorithms that used the technique of inserting message bits into the Discrete Cosine Transformation (DCT) coefficients of an image were F5 [48], OutGuess [40] and Steghide [25]. However, their message insertion rate is too low for practical purposes and steganalysis methods[2] have been successfully applied to break them [22–24].

---

[1] even though the current good practice is to delete the original cover object after inserting the message and obtaining the resulting file.
[2] which allow the detection of the presence of embedded information.

Also, besides the previously discussed stegosystems, the nsF5 [21] version of F5 appeared before the scheme presented in [34]. Steganalysis methods for nsF5 are publicly available [2]. In addition, [2] is a tool that applies also to OutGuess, Steghide and J-UNIWARD.

After the publication of J3, other related steganographic algorithms such as HUGO [20], WOW [26], the initial UNIWARD family [27], J2-UNIWARD [15], and NS in JPEG [14] were published. Nonetheless, various steganalysis papers regarding these stegosystems were presented in the literature: [35] for HUGO, [43] for WOW, [33] for J-UNIWARD. Moreover, various characteristics and vulnerabilities of these stegosystems are studied in detail in [16].

Motivation. As already underlined before, a variety of steganographic algorithms have been proposed in the literature and used in practice. Most of them are vulnerable to steganalysis methods. We are particularly interested in the J3 algorithm [34].

We consider that given the lack of clarity in the presentation of J3 and the fact that its implementation is not publicly available, software engineers have turned their attention especially to other stegosystems when developing a steganographic application, even though these schemes may be weaker[3] and more inefficient[4]. We strongly believe that two of the characteristics of J3 are a must for the current design of secure stegosystems: histogram restoration[5] in order to resist steganalysis methods and high embedding capacity. However, we have observed various issues of the previously mentioned algorithm and, thus, we aimed at correcting and improving it.

Moreover, the current publicly available steganography software applications use either outdated steganographic algorithms or cryptographic schemes (as the first data protection layer). Among them we mention OpenStego [5] (which supports two steganographic plugins, LSB and randomized LSB and uses DES [39] for the initial encryption step), Hide'N'Send [6], in which data hiding is done using the standard LSB algorithm and StegoShare [3], where the cover file manipulation algorithm used is based on fixed location LSB insertion that makes its output pictures detectable to most steganalysis software. Given the previously mentioned facts, we believe that new steganographic software tools are a must. We provide the reader with a sketch of such an application within this paper in Appendix B.

Structure of the Paper. In Sect. 2, we introduce the notations and briefly describe image compression with a focus on JPEG and the J3 stegosystem. We also add pseudocode for the insertion and extraction algorithms of J3 in Appendix A. The main results are discussed in Sect. 3, namely corrections and enhancements of the J3 algorithm. Details regarding the implementation of the previously mentioned algorithm are presented in Sect. 4. We conclude and provide the reader with future work ideas in Sect. 5.

---

[3] in terms of security.

[4] when implemented in software.

[5] the distribution of bytes in the image is not affected.

2 Preliminaries

2.1 Notations

Throughout this paper, we denote by $Hist(x)$ the total number of coefficients x initially present in the cover image. Let W and H be the image width and height, respectively. We further consider that $C[i]$, $0 \le i < W \cdot H$ is the array of DCT coefficients of the image. We denote by $||m||$ the bit-length of m.

2.2 Image Compression

An image is a collection of numerical data that constitutes different intensities of light. This numerical representation forms a two-dimensional matrix with pixel elements. A pixel consists of one byte if the image is black and white or 3 bytes if the image is color, in RGB format.

As some images are too large to be transmitted in time, there have been proposed various algorithms that use mathematical formulas to reduce the size of files. We refer to these methods as compression techniques. In the case of images, there are two types of compression algorithms: lossless and lossy.

JPEG [28,37] is a lossy compression algorithm that consists in both types of components. The lossy stages include transformations to DCT [32] coefficients by applying the DCT transform followed by quantizations, and the actual compression is done without loss with the help of Huffmann encoding. Thus, steganography can be introduced between the two stages. Through the principles derived from LSB substitution, messages can be hidden in the least significant color bits of the coefficients resulting before Huffman encoding. The message becomes very difficult to detect, being inserted at this stage in the frequency range.

Lossless compression reduces image size by using approximations and partial data deletion as opposed to lossless compression that eliminates only redundant data. Thus, lossless compression ensures complete recovery of the original data while lossy compression allows an approximation to be reconstituted.

JPEG. JPEG has been subject to various patents and standardization processes for over 30 years now and it is widely adopted.

A JPEG file may be characterized by various encoding methods. The most common one in this case is JPEG File Interchange Format (JFIF) [4]. We further recall the steps of this encoding process.

When compressing an RGB image, the following steps are performed:

1. The preprocessing step consisting of converting the image from the RGB color space to the Y, C_r and C_b (*i.e.* luminance and chrominance) color space followed by decomposing the pixel matrices corresponding to each channel into 8×8 pixel blocks;
2. The lossy compression sub-algorithm that takes place in two steps and operates on the resulted pixel blocks:

- Applying the DCT transform [8] that maps the values of a pixel block into real numbers that represent essential information about the image. More precisely, 64 functions are applied to an 8 × 8 pixel block, each function offering information about different patterns present in the respective block;
- Applying the quantization algorithm that keeps the lower frequency information and discards[6] the higher frequency information. This takes place by dividing each coefficient resulted after the DCT transform to a value from a quantization matrix that is set beforehand and rounding to the nearest integer.

After performing this step, an 8 × 8 block contains integers whose absolute values are highest in the top left corner of the matrix, as they correspond to the lowest frequency information. Thus, at this point, each channel contains numbers that represent quantized information about lower frequency patterns present in the original image. These values are the DCT coefficients of the image. For an 8 × 8 block, the coefficient found at the top left corner is named the DC coefficient and the rest are the AC coefficients. If the process above is reversed, a visually accurate approximation of the image is obtained;

3. The lossless compression of the resulted values is performed using either Huffman or Arithmetic Encoding. This type of compression is optimal due to the high degree of redundancy of the DCT coefficients that are smallest in absolute value.

The decoding process consists in reversing the encoding steps.

Properties of the DCT Coefficients. We briefly discuss about the distribution of the DCT coefficients. When determining the histogram of the corresponding DCT coefficients for each of the Y, C_r and C_b channels, we observe that its values peak at -1 and 1 and decrease as the absolute value of the coefficients increase.

[42] shows that the AC coefficients for both luminance and chrominance follow a Laplacian distribution of mean 0 and standard deviation σ. Hence, the Probability Density Function is characterized by

$$p(x) = \lambda/2 \cdot e^{-\lambda \cdot |x|}, \lambda = \sqrt{2}/\sigma. \tag{1}$$

As estimated in [38], σ takes values around 10. Hence, $\lambda \sim 0.14$. More precisely, the array $C[\cdot]$ of DCT coefficients[7] follows the above mentioned distribution. As it is a discrete random variable, we have that $\forall k \in \mathbb{Z}$

$$\mathbb{P}(C = k) = \int_{k-\frac{1}{2}}^{k+\frac{1}{2}} p(x)dx. \tag{2}$$

---

[6] maps to 0.
[7] without the DC values.

We are interested in examining the speed at which the histogram values decrease as the coefficient's magnitude increases. It suffices to compute the ratio $Hist(n)/Hist(n+k)$ for $n, k > 0$.

Note that $Hist(n)/Hist(n+k) = \mathbb{P}(C = n)/\mathbb{P}(C = n+k)$.

Using the Mean Value Theorem, we know that there exist $c_1 \in [n - 1/2, n + 1/2]$ and $c_2 \in [n + k - 1/2, n + k + 1/2]$ such that $\mathbb{P}(C = n) = 2/2 \cdot p(c_1)$ and $\mathbb{P}(C = n + k) = 2/2 \cdot p(c_2)$.

Thus, $H = Hist(n)/Hist(n+k) = p(c_1)/p(c_2) = e^{\lambda \cdot (c_2 - c_1)}$ which is in the interval $[e^{\lambda \cdot (k-1)}, e^{\lambda \cdot (k+1)}]$, with $\lambda \sim 0.14$. When $k \geq 8$, $H > 2$ and, therefore, we can conclude that $Hist(n) > 2 \cdot Hist(n + 8)$ and, in particular, $Hist(1) > 2 \cdot Hist(9)$. The values in between are closer to each other.

2.3   The J3 Steganographic Algorithm

The J3 algorithm operates on the DCT coefficients of a JPEG image. For inserting or extracting data into or from such image, the first step that occurs is Huffman decoding for obtaining the coefficients array $C[\cdot]$. We will further consider that the array $C[\cdot]$ consists only in the AC coefficients, as the DC values represent the coefficients with zero frequency in both dimensions.

In the following we describe the J3 algorithm applied on the DCT coefficients array for any of the channels Y, C_r and C_b.

Remark 1. For more clarity, besides the following description of J3, we refer the reader to Algorithms 1 and 2 which represent the pseudocode for the insertion and the extraction methods.

Setup. The central technique used by the J3 Algorithm is LSB replacement of the DCT coefficients of an image. More specifically, a message bit b is inserted into a DCT coefficient i by replacing the LSB of i with b. The resulting coefficient is either in $\{i, i + 1\}$ if i is even or $\{i - 1, i\}$, if i is odd.

Let $THr \in \mathbb{N}^*$ be a threshold value chosen in advance and let $\mathscr{P} = \{-C_L, \ldots, C_L\} \setminus \{0\}$ be the set of coefficients used for data embedding, where C_L is the last odd coefficient with $\text{Hist}(C_L) > THr$. In order to perform the insertion, we use the set of ordered sets $\mathscr{C} = \{\{-C_L, -C_L + 1\}, \ldots, \{-3, -2\}, \{-1, 1\}, \{2, 3\}, \ldots, \{C_L - 1, C_L\}\}$.

The hidden component of J3 consists in embedding the message bits into DCT coefficients from $\mathscr{P}$ whose indices are determined by a Pseudorandom Number Generator (PRNG) which is initialised with a secret seed.

Remark 2 (Histogram Restoration). Data embedding is done under the condition that restoring the histogram of the resulting image is possible. Before inserting a bit into a pair of coefficients, the algorithm verifies if there are enough unused coefficients in the image from that pair in order to use them for restoring the original histogram.

Definition 1 (*Stop Point*). *Let $SP(x,y)$ be a* Stop Point *of the pair $\{x,y\}$. For each valid pair of coefficients, its corresponding* Stop Point *represents the first index (generated by the PRNG) such as bit insertion in the respective pair stops.*

Definition 2 (Notations). *To check if a generated index is a* Stop Point[8], *we define two counters in Table 1 for $\{x,y\} \in \mathscr{C}$ and $x \in \mathscr{P}$.*

Table 1. Definitions

Counter	Definition
$TC(x,y)$	The number of coefficients x changed to y.
$TR(x)$	The number of unused x coefficients

Remark 3 (Properties). Note that $TC(x,x)$ is the number of coefficients x that remained unchanged during the insertion of bits and $TR(x) = Hist(x) - TC(x,y) - TC(x,x)$. For each $x \in \mathscr{P}$, $TR(x)$ is initialised with $Hist(x)$ and it decreases at every insertion into x. For each pair $\{x,y\} \in \mathscr{C}$, both $TC(x,y)$ and $SP(x,y)$ are initialised with 0. $TC(x,y)$ increases for every bit insertion that maps x into y.

Both insertion and extraction start by computing C_L using the value THr and initialising the PRNG with the secret *seed*.

Insertion. For inserting a message bit b, a secret index i is generated using the PRNG such that $C[i] \in \mathscr{P}$. We map the obtained $C[i]$ into $\{x,y\} \in \mathscr{C}$. We further assume that $C[i] = x$.

First, it is verified whether there are enough coefficients with the value x that were not accessed in order to use them for restoring the histogram. $Hist(x)$ increases every time a coefficient y is mapped into x and decreases when x is mapped into y, so restoring the original histogram is only possible when $TR(x) > TC(y,x) - TC(x,y)$. In consequence, $SP(x,y)$ becomes i once the inequality

$$TR(x) \le TC(y,x) - TC(x,y) \tag{3}$$

occurs for the first time[9].

If $SP(x,y) \ne 0$, then the bit b is not inserted into any of the coefficients $\{x,y\}$ and another index i is generated. Else, we insert b into $x = C[i]$, decrease $TC(x)$, and if x becomes y, $TC(x,y)$ increases.

We consider $NSP = C_L$ as the number of *Stop Points* and $NbSP = \lfloor \log_2(W \cdot H) \rfloor + 1$ as the length in bits of a *Stop Point*. Before inserting any message bits,

---

[8] which is equivalent to checking if inserting a message bit into that pair is still possible or not.

[9] which means that we have reached the minimum number of untouched coefficients used for histogram restoration.

one must make space for inserting the *Stop Points* into the cover image, as they are necessary for extraction. In consequence, the PRNG is used for generating a set $\mathcal{D}$ of indices d, with $C[d] \in \mathscr{P}$ and $||\mathcal{D}|| = NSP \cdot NbSP$. We denote the set of indices for embedding the message bits by $\mathcal{M}$, with $\mathcal{M} \cap \mathcal{D} = \emptyset$ and $|\mathcal{M}| = ||m||$. Note that when constructing the $SP(\cdot, \cdot)$ array, one must allocate exactly $NbSP$ bits for each element.

The $SP(\cdot, \cdot)$ array is identified as the *Dynamic Header*. The actual first step of the embedding component of J3 is building a *Static Header* as follows: the message length is stored on the first 2 bytes of the array, and $NbSP$ and NSP on the last two bytes, respectively.

We further generate a set $\mathcal{S}$ of secret coefficients s, with $C[s] \in \mathscr{P}$ and $||\mathcal{S}|| = 32$, used for embedding the *Static Header* bits. Note that when generating the sets $\mathcal{D}$ and $\mathcal{M}$, the conditions $\mathcal{D} \cap \mathcal{S} = \emptyset$ and $\mathcal{S} \cap \mathcal{M} = \emptyset$ must also hold.

Given the previous notations and observations, the following steps take place during the insertion.

1. Build the *Static Header* and generate the set $\mathcal{S}$ as previously described. The *Static Header* bits are inserted into the coefficients $C[s]$, for $s \in \mathcal{S}$;
2. Generate the set $\mathcal{D}$ and store it separately;
3. Insert the message bits following the previously mentioned rules. Each index from the set $\mathcal{M}$ is generated once accessing a message bit b. The *Stop Points* array is built in the process;
4. Insert the *Dynamic Header* into the coefficients $C[d]$, for $d \in \mathcal{D}$;
5. Restore the original histogram by using coefficients from a set $\mathcal{R}$, with $\mathcal{R}[i] \in \mathscr{P}$ with the sets $\mathcal{R}, \mathcal{M}, \mathcal{D}$ and $\mathcal{S}$ being pairwise disjoint. For each set of coefficients $\{x, y\} \in \mathscr{C}$, proceed as follows: the value of $Hist(x)$ after insertion became $Hist(x) - TC(x, y) + TC(y, x)$, and $Hist(y)$ became $Hist(y) - TC(y, x) + TC(x, y)$. Without loss of generality, we suppose $TC(x, y) - TC(y, x) > 0$. Then, the $TC(x, y) - TC(y, x)$ additional y coefficients must become x. In consequence, we generate enough indices from $\mathcal{R}$ to restore the original histogram values for each $\{x, y\} \in \mathscr{C}$.

Note that when generating the sets $\mathcal{S}$ and $\mathcal{D}$, for each $i \in \mathcal{S} \cup \mathcal{D}$, the $TR(C[i])$ value decreases by 1. Moreover, the $TC(\cdot, \cdot)$ array is updated accordingly during any of the insertion steps.

Extraction. For extracting data bits from a cover image, one must know the secret *seed* in order to determine the indices used for insertion along with the *Stop Points*.

The following steps occur during the extraction algorithm.

1. Generate the indices from $\mathcal{S}$ and use them for extracting the *Static Header* and verify whether the last 2 bytes of the obtained header are equal to $NbSP$ and NSP, respectively. If one of the equalities doesn't hold, then either the values of the image coefficients where the static header bits were inserted are changed (the picture has been tampered with), either the seed entered is wrong or the picture has no message inserted.

2. Generate the indices from the set $\mathcal{D}$ and extract $SP(x, y)$, for $\{x, y\} \in \mathscr{C}$.
3. Generate the indices from $\mathcal{M}$ by taking into account the message length and the *Stop Points* found and use them to extract the message.

3   Main Results

Note that when recalling J3 in Sect. 2 we already presented some of the corrections we applied to the original algorithm. Next, we emphasize these modifications.

1. We have corrected the mechanism of finding *StopPoints*. In the original article [34], the *StopPoint* value was updated each time Eq. (3) was fulfilled. Therefore, the *StopPoint* became the last index of the coefficient with that value that was used when inserting, which led to the incorrect extraction of the message.
   Let $\{x, y\} \in \mathscr{C}$ be a pair of coefficients such that $SP(x, y) = i \neq 0$. We know i is not the first value for which Eq. (3) occurred. Let j be the first index for which Eq. (3) holds. Then, embedding in the pair $\{x, y\}$ has stopped once reaching j, but the $SP(x, y)$ value keeps changing until i is generated. During extraction, when generating j, a message bit is extracted automatically, which is incorrect, as no message bit was embedded into $C[j]$. Moreover, bit extraction occurs for each index k generated between i and j with $C[k] \in \{x, y\}$, which leads to obtaining a bit string that was not inserted in the first place.
2. Another fundamental observation that was omitted in [34] regarding the building blocks of the algorithm (*i.e.* bit insertion and extraction) is the fact that the sets $\mathcal{S}, \mathcal{D}$ and $\mathcal{R}$ must be pairwise disjoint.
   Supposing $i \in \mathcal{S} \cap \mathcal{M}$ such as the *Static Header* bit inserted into $C[i]$ was 0, and the message bit inserted was 1. Let $C[i] = x, \{x, y\} \in \mathscr{C}$. Then $C[i]$ becomes y after the two insertions. The first bit extracted is the *Static Header* bit, as i is firstly generated for this purpose. Simultaneously, the first bit extracted is the message bit, as the value of $C[i]$ corresponds to the last insertion made. In consequence, for both occurrences of i, the same bit is extracted which is a contradiction.
3. Within the extraction algorithm, we added the extracted header check. In the original version, the *Static Header* was built only for extracting the message length, the number of *Stop Points* and the number of bits on which a *Stop Point* is stored.
   The inadequacy of this approach resides in the fact that the *NbSP* and *NSP* obtained are used for further extraction, when they could be bogus values. Their use is only for verification as they depend only on the image and its histogram (which is preserved), so they are computed before any step of insertion/extraction and further compared to the extracted values.

In the following we detail other modifications and enhancements that we brought to the J3 stegosystem.

3.1 Adding a Pre-processing Step

A preprocessing step was added prior to each sub-algorithm of our proposed version of J3 (insertion and extraction). The outcomes of this component are obtaining an adequate C_L value that maximizes the embedding capacity depending on the distribution of the image histogram and determining a total embedding capacity of the image for assuring the robustness of the algorithm.

Setting THr and Computing C_L. In the original algorithm [34], C_L is computed using the value THr[10]. Note that the authors do not offer any optimal possible values for this threshold. More precisely, THr is hard-coded as a constant that intuitively determines a nonempty set $\mathscr{P}$ for images that have a histogram which takes smaller values. Usually, it is set somewhere near 300 for the luminance component and near 100 for the chrominance channels. Consequently, for higher quality images[11], the set of coefficients to be used for performing J3 is large.

In addition, the majority of images existing nowadays have a higher quality. E.g., for smartphone camera images even in the portrait mode, $Hist(1)$ and $Hist(-1)$ are surpassing 10000. Also, $Hist(2)$ and $Hist(3)$ exceed 7000 on the Y channel. Therefore, $\mathscr{P}$ is large: usually $C_L > 50$ on the Y channel and $C_L > 10$ on the Cr and Cb channels. What stands out about the distribution of the determined coefficients is the fact that the values closer to C_L have their $Hist(\cdot)$ values by definition near THr but disproportionately small compared to the $Hist(\cdot)$ values of the coefficients closer to 0. Even though apparently this implication has no impact on message insertion (the high frequency of the coefficients from $\mathscr{P}$ implies the possibility of inserting large messages), there are very often cases in which the algorithm loops as it is incapable of finding coefficients closer to C_L for restoring the histogram.

Moreover, before reaching this step of the J3 insertion, the algorithm speed is decreased compared to the case when we set a large THr (only for inserting into reasonable quality images) such as C_L is small. On the other hand, a large C_L implies a large *Stop Points* array, which means a big additional number of bits to be inserted into the image as the *Dynamic Header*. In most cases, $SP(x,y) = 0$ for all $\{x,y\} \in \mathscr{C}$ as $TR(\cdot)$ automatically contains large values, being initialised by $TR(i) = Hist(i)$. This means that for a large set of messages $||\mathcal{D}|| = C_L \cdot NbSP$ additional zeroes are inserted. For a common JPEG image of 1 MB and reasonable quality, there are $\mathcal{D} \approx 50 \cdot 20 = 1000$ null bits of *Dynamic Header*. As the image size increases, $||\mathcal{D}||$ increases, and this leads to the incapacity of embedding messages of reasonable length into the image because for coefficients closer to C_L, the corresponding *Stop Point* remains 0, but when inserting into the *Dynamic Header*, the coefficients that must remain untouched for restoring the histogram are used here for embedding the *Stop Points* array.

---

[10] set in advance.

[11] *i.e.* their histogram contains larger values.

To sum up, THr must be a value that depends on each image so it is computed according to the image histogram. The main property that THr must fulfill is to determine a C_L so as for an i with the absolute value close to C_L, $Hist(i)$ is proportional to $Hist(1)$ and $Hist(-1)$.

Remark 4 (Optimal THr). By taking into account the distribution of the DCT coefficients as exposed in 2, we concluded that $THr = Hist(1)/2$ is an optimal value for both performance and robustness. The choice was confirmed in practice, as both parameters substantially increased.

The Limit E_C. With the value C_L computed, one must know how many message bits can be safely embedded into an image (channel). The limit we propose is

$$E_C = \Sigma_{\{x,y\} \in \mathscr{C}} \min(Hist(x), Hist(y)) - ||\mathcal{S}|| - ||\mathcal{D}||.$$

The choice of E_C enables us to take advantage of the maximum embedding capacity of every pair $\{x,y\} \in \mathscr{C}$ while keeping exactly the minimum number of unused coefficients for restoring the histogram. This occurs in the worst case scenario which is for every pair $\{x,y\} \in \mathscr{C}, Hist(x) \geq Hist(y)$, every message bit to be inserted maps x into y.

Indeed, we start with $TR(x) = Hist(x), TR(y) = Hist(y), TC(x,y) = 0$ and $TC(y,x) = 0$. When insertion transforms x into y, $TR(x)$ becomes $Hist(x) - 1$ and $TC(x,y)$ becomes 1. After k successive identical steps, $TR(x)$ becomes $Hist(x) - k$ and $TC(x,y)$ becomes k. We know that in order to reach a *Stop Point* for the pair $\{x,y\}$, Eq. (3) must hold either for x or y. For y, we have $Hist(y) \leq k$. Thus, the number of steps needed for updating the value of $SP(x,y)$ is $k = Hist(y)$. In conclusion, the message piece to be inserted into $\{x,y\}$ must have the length at most $Hist(y)$ in order for the restoration of the histogram to occur.

If the message is constructed such that for each pair $\{x,y\} \in \mathscr{C}$ insertion occurs as above, then the longest message that can be inserted while keeping enough untouched coefficients for histogram restoration is $\Sigma_{\{x,y\} \in \mathscr{C}} \min(Hist(x), Hist(y))$. As the *Static* and *Dynamic* headers are also inserted, the maximum embedding capacity becomes E_C.

Remark 5 (Pre-processing Motivation). In conclusion, the pre-processing step is necessary for an accurate embedding process, as it reveals the optimal coefficient pairs for a correct and efficient insertion component and a safe upper bound for the size of the data to be inserted.

3.2   Taking Advantage of Each Channel's Embedding Capacity

In the original J3 algorithm, the embedding component is applied on all three channels Y, C_r and C_b: if the message length exceeds the total capacity of the Y channel[12], then the remaining bits are inserted into C_r. If message bits still remain, they are inserted into C_b.

---

[12] defined in [34] as $\Sigma_{\{x,y\} \in \mathscr{C}} Hist(x) + Hist(y)$.

Our proposal is to take advantage of each channel's embedding capacity (as defined in the previous paragraph) by splitting the message into pieces proportionate to the E_C of each channel.

We denote by $E_C(Y), E_C(C_r)$ and $E_C(C_b)$ the embedding capacities of Y, C_r and C_b respectively. We split the message into pieces of length

$$\left\lfloor \frac{E_C(Y)}{E_C(Y)+E_C(C_r)+E_C(C_b)} \cdot ||m|| \right\rfloor, \qquad \left\lfloor \frac{E_C(C_r)}{E_C(Y)+E_C(C_r)+E_C(C_b)} \cdot ||m|| \right\rfloor \qquad \text{and}$$

$$\left\lfloor \frac{E_C(C_b)}{E_C(Y)+E_C(C_r)+E_C(C_b)} \cdot ||m|| \right\rfloor.$$

Note that when adding the three lengths, we obtain a value in the set $\{||m||, ||m||+1, ||m||+2\}$. In consequence, if the sum is $||m||+1$, then one of the lengths is decreased by 1, and if it is $||m||+2$, then two of the lengths are decreased.

In summary, we maximize the relative embedding capacity of each channel. If a channel has a capacity much higher than the others, then the remaining channels will have the corresponding message lengths equal to 0 and no embedding will occur (only in their *Static Headers*, and each will have their first two bytes equal to 0). If a channel has a small capacity relatively to the other two channels, then its *Static Header* will begin with two null bytes.

3.3   Security Aspects

Cryptographic Security. A cryptographic component is necessary for a stegosystem for at least two reasons:

1. Given solely an image that hides the existence of a message m, if one knows beforehand the indices of the coefficients in which the bits of m were inserted, then recovering them can be done by simply applying the inverse of the LSB embedding. In consequence, the message insertion must be performed into coefficients of secret indices, known only by the sender and the receiver. A feasible method to ensure this is using a PRNG initialised with a secret seed (as currently done in most of the modern stegosystems).
2. If an adversary obtains a cover image both before and after insertion, then part of the message bits can be recovered by simply observing the DCT coefficients that differ. Thus, in general, half of the message bits can be obtained (the bit and the coefficient used for insertion must have different parities). Therefore, prior to insertion, the messages have to be encrypted with a key agreed between the sender and the recipient[13].

Steganographic Security. We further asssume that the cryptographic security requirements are fulfilled.

If an adversary has the two versions of an image (before and after insertion), recovering parts of the original message becomes infeasible due to the encryption step. Even so, by analyzing the differences in histograms in the case of various stegosystems using specific tools, it can be observed which of the two images hides information.

---

[13] Symmetric key cryptosystems are customarily used.

When the J3 stegosystem is used, both images have the same histogram due to the histogram compensation step. Therefore, an image that hides data is indistinguishable from an image that was not used for insertion. Thus, the security is theoretically assured by default.

We applied steganalysis techniques implemented in specific tools to our enhanced J3 algorithm (*e.g.* StegoHunt [7]) and obtained the expected result.

Remark 6. Regarding the cryptographic security, we propose the use of state-of-the-art cryptographic schemes (see Appendix B): the better the encryption scheme, the more secure the stegosystem. Nonetheless, without affecting the efficiency of the implementation.

4   Implementation

We ran the code for our algorithm on a standard laptop using both Windows 10 and Ubuntu 20.04.5 LTS OS[14], with the following specifications: Intel Core i7-10510U with 4 cores and 16 Gigabytes of RAM. The programming language we used for implementing our algorithms was C++.

To extract the DCT coefficients from an image and restore the image from them independently of the platform on which the application runs, it is necessary to use a library that implements the **ITU T.81 JPEG Compatible** standard. The main library that is used for encoding and decoding JPEG is libjpeg. It is written in the C programming language and distributed under the Custom BSD license (free software) for any platform (cross-platform) [45].

The latest released version is libjpeg 9e[15]. It underlies the OpenCv, torchjpeg, and JasPer libraries, implementing basic JPEG operations [45].

We refer the reader to [1] for the source code representing the implementation of our proposed results.

4.1   Implementation Results

Taking into account the fact that J3 was already compared to the other stegosystems mentioned in Sect. 1 and its performance and security were proven superior both theoretically and in practice, we directly compare our proposal to the original version of J3.

When given an image for extraction, the original J3 algorithm first obtains the *Static Header* and then uses it for further extracting data which leads to events such as obtaining bogus values or remaining stuck in a loop. By using our additional *Static Header* checkup, if an image has nothing embedded into it or if it was altered (for example by sending it through a channel that applies additional compression algorithms), then an exception is thrown that warns the user regarding the state of the image.

---

[14] The Ubuntu OS was installed on a virtual machine.
[15] as of January 16, 2022.

On the other hand, if the message inserted was long enough for at least a *Stop Point* to change its value, then the extraction using J3 is incorrect for the reasons previously exposed (in Sect. 3). Note that our proposal works with long messages, extraction taking place as expected.

For large images (especially for those taken with the camera of an Android/IOS phone, their size being over 1 MB), the original J3 algorithm loops even for very short messages (under 20 bytes), or lasts for an unreasonable amount of time (more than 5 minutes) as searching for indices for histogram restoring was time consuming (for pairs of the form $\{2k, 2k+1\}$, for $2k+1$ close to C_L). The reason of this occurrence is the fact that the search for indices such as the corresponding $C[i]$ is in $\{2k, 2k+1\}$ and i was not previously used takes too much time. This is caused by the fact that when generating i, $C[i]$ has a much higher probability to be closer to 0.

Remark 7. We present a set of results regarding the speed of our enhanced J3 algorithm in Table 2 for an image of $3, 4$ MB, taken with an Android camera having the quality 300×400. The metrics used were the average execution time (mean) and the standard deviation from the mean (std) of the obtained timings. We generated 50 random messages for each length. It can easily be observed that not only the average time of our proposal is considerably smaller, but also the execution times are closer to the average time than in the case of the original algorithm.

Table 2. Original vs. enhanced J3 implementation results

Message length (bytes)	Original J3 insertion (seconds)		Enhanced J3 insertion (seconds)	
	mean	std	mean	std
20	8.203	0.120	0.21	0.005
200	10.782	3.764	0.346	0.018
1000	21.740	6.036	2.615	0.126
5000	136.098	35.078	60.108	2.045
10000	234.663	49.002	139.67	6.008

For lower quality images, J3 not only has a very low embedding capacity, but it is also prone to being unable to completely insert a message of a reasonable length relatively to the total embedding capacity of the image.

Our approach performs well for very low quality images. For an image of 4.5 kB of a very small resolution (256×194, 96 dpi on 96 dpi), grayscale, with $Hist(1) = 1870$ on Y we could embed messages of 140 bytes in under $0.2\,\text{s}$.

In all the previously mentioned measurements, extraction was also performed and the message was correctly recovered in each case.

5   Conclusions and Future Work

We recalled the J3 algorithm, which differs from other stegosystems working with DCT coefficients both by its high ability to hide data and by keeping the histogram of the original image (and, thus, preventing statistical attacks). The main result of our work was the reconstruction of the entire J3 algorithm including all its sub-algorithms: pre-processing, message insertion and extraction. We also optimized the stegosystem and covered all practical cases while still using the maximum image insertion capacity.

Future Work. In the near future, a major goal of our research is building an application based on our short description in Appendix B that will enable the user to perform data insertion and extraction within different platforms, a feature not yet available in the case of current steganography applications.

A first step for continuing our research in this direction is to present a concrete comparison (especially in terms of efficiency) between our proposed software application and the publicly available applications.

Another idea is to apply more powerful steganalysis techniques in order to check the security of our proposed scheme.

A   Pseudocode

Algorithm 1. Insertion of message bits

$x \leftarrow PRNG(seed)$
if C_x is *even* and $b = 1$ **then**
    if $C_x > 0$ **then**
        $C_x \leftarrow C_x + 1$
        $TC(C_x, C_x + 1) \leftarrow TC(C_x, C_x + 1) + 1$
    else
        $C_x \leftarrow C_x - 1$
    end if
end if
if C_x is *odd* $\neq 1$ and $b = 0$ **then**
    if $C_x > 0$ **then**
        $C_x \leftarrow C_x - 1$
        $TC(C_x, C_x - 1) \leftarrow TC(C_x, C_x - 1) + 1$
    else
        $C_x \leftarrow C_x + 1$
    end if
end if
if $C_x = -1$ and $b = 1$ **then**
    $C_x \leftarrow 1$
    $TC(C_x, C_x + 1) \leftarrow TC(C_x, C_x + 1) + 1$
end if
if $C_x = 1$ and $b = 0$ **then**
    $C_x \leftarrow -1$
    $TC(C_x, C_x - 1) \leftarrow TC(C_x, C_x - 1) + 1$
end if

Algorithm 2. Extraction of message bits

$x \leftarrow PRNG(seed)$
if C_x is *even* **then**
    $b \leftarrow 1$
end if
if C_x is *odd* $\neq 1$ **then**
    $b \leftarrow 0$
end if
if $C_x = -1$ **then**
    $b \leftarrow 0$
end if
if $C_x = 1$ **then**
    $b \leftarrow 1$
end if

B   A Steganography Application Proposal

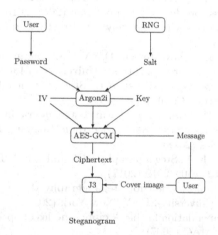

Fig. 1. The flow of our steganography application proposal

A natural continuation of our proposed results is putting them in practice. Thus, we briefly describe a steganography software application. The flow of the application is shortly presented in Fig. 1.

The user enters a password from which the secret key for AES-256 [18] is derived. AES is used in the GCM authenticated encryption mode of operation [17]. Thus, the plaintext (the message entered by the user) is encrypted and authenticated. Then, our proposed J3 variant is used to hide the cryptogram into a cover JPEG image.

Within the application, the Argon2i function [12] is used (as the winner of the Password Hashing Competition [10]) to derive both the key and the IV^{16}.

The keys should only be temporarily stored in the RAM of the smartphone/PC (while the cryptographic and steganographic operations are performed).

References

1. https://github.com/cryptocrew601
2. https://github.com/daniellerch/aletheia
3. https://stegoshare.soft112.com
4. https://www.iso.org/standard/54989.html
5. https://www.openstego.com
6. https://www.softpedia.com/get/Security/Encrypting/Hide-N-Send.shtml
7. https://www.wetstonetech.com/products/stegohunt-steganography-detection
8. Ahmed, N., Natarajan, T., Rao, K.: Discrete cosine transform. IEEE Trans. Comput. **C-23**(1), 90–93 (1974)
9. Singh, A.K., Singh, J., Singh, H.V.: Steganography in images using LSB technique. Int. J. Latest Trends Eng. Technol. **5**(1), 425–430 (2015)
10. Aumasson, J.P.: Password hashing competition (2013–2015)
11. Aumasson, J.P.: Serious Cryptography: A Practical Introduction to Modern Encryption. USA (2017)
12. Biryukov, A., Dinu, D., Khovratovich, D.: Argon2: the memory-hard function for password hashing and other applications. University of Luxembourg (2015)
13. Cormen, T.H., Leiserson, C.E., Rivest, R.L., Stein, C.: Introduction to Algorithms, 3rd edn. The MIT Press, Cambridge (2009)
14. Denemark, T., Bas, P., Fridrich, J.: Natural steganography in JPEG compressed images. In: Proceedings of the IS&T, Electronic Imaging, Media Watermarking, Security, and Forensics (2018)
15. Denemark, T., Fridrich, J.: Steganography with multiple JPEG images of the same scene. IEEE TIFS **12**, 2308–2319 (2017)
16. Denemark, T.: Side-information for steganography design and detection. Ph.D. thesis, Binghamton University-SUNY, New York (2018)
17. Dworkin, J.: Recommendation for block cipher modes of operation: Galois/counter mode (GCM) and GMAC (2007)
18. Dworkin, J., Barker, B., Foti, J., Bassham, E., Roback, E.: Announcing the Advanced Encryption Standard (AES). Computer Security Division, Information Technology Laboratory, National Institute of Standards and Technology Gaithersburg, MD (2001)
19. Petitcolas, F.A., Anderson, R.J., Kuhn, M.G.: Information hiding-a survey. Proc. IEEE **87**(7), 1062–1078 (1999)
20. Filler, T., Fridrich, J.: Gibbs construction in steganography. IEEE Trans. Inf. Forensics Secur. **5**(4), 705–720 (2010)
21. Fridrich, J., Pevný, T., Kodovský, J.: Statistically undetectable JPEG steganography: dead ends, challenges, and opportunities. In: Proceedings of the 9th ACM Multimedia & Security Workshop, Dallas, TX, pp. 3–14 (2007)

---

[16] of size 96 bits.

22. Fridrich, J., Goljan, M., Hogea, D.: Attacking the OutGuess. In: Proceedings of the ACM: Special Session on Multimedia Security and Watermarking (2002)
23. Fridrich, J., Goljan, M., Hogea, D.: Steganalysis of JPEG images: breaking the F5 algorithm. In: Petitcolas, F.A.P. (ed.) IH 2002. LNCS, vol. 2578, pp. 310–323. Springer, Heidelberg (2003). https://doi.org/10.1007/3-540-36415-3_20
24. Fridrich, J., Goljan, M., Hogea, D.: New methodology for breaking steganographic techniques for JPEGs. In: SPIE: Electronic Imaging 2003, Security and Watermarking of Multimedia Contents (2003)
25. Hetzl, S., Mutzel, P.: A graph–theoretic approach to steganography. In: Dittmann, J., Katzenbeisser, S., Uhl, A. (eds.) CMS 2005. LNCS, vol. 3677, pp. 119–128. Springer, Heidelberg (2005). https://doi.org/10.1007/11552055_12
26. Holub, V., Fridrich, J.: Designing steganographic distortion using directional filters. In: IEEE International Workshop on Information Forensics and Security (WIFS) (2012)
27. Holub, V., Fridrich, J., Denemark, T.: Universal distortion function for steganography in an arbitrary domain. EURASIP J. Inf. Secur. (2014). (Section: SI: Revised Selected Papers of ACM IH and MMS 2013)
28. International Organization for Standardization: Information Technology—Digital Compression and Coding of Continuous-Tone still Images: Requirements and Guidelines. ISO/IEC 10918-1 (1994)
29. Isnanto, R.R., Septiana, R., Hastawan, A.F.: Robustness of steganography image method using dynamic management position of least significant bit (LSB). In: 2018 International Seminar on Research of Information Technology and Intelligent Systems (ISRITI), pp. 131–135 (2018)
30. Jamil, T.: Steganography: the art of hiding information is plain sight. IEEE Potentials 18(01), 10–12 (1999)
31. Kaliski, B.: RFC2898: PKCS5: password-based cryptography specification version 2.0 (2000)
32. Kabeen, K., Gent, P.I.: Image compression and discrete cosine transform (2013)
33. Koshkina, N.V.: J-UNIWARD steganoanalysis. Cybern. Syst. Anal. 57(3), 501–508 (2021). https://doi.org/10.1007/s10559-021-00374-6
34. Kumar, M., Newman, R.: J3: high payload histogram neutral JPEG steganography. In: 2010 Eighth International Conference on Privacy, Security and Trust, pp. 46–53 (2010)
35. Luo, X., et al.: Steganalysis of HUGO steganography based on parameter recognition of syndrome-trellis-codes. Multimedia Tools Appl. 75(21), 13557–13583 (2015). https://doi.org/10.1007/s11042-015-2759-2
36. Morkel, T., Eloff, J.H.P., Olivier, M.S.: An overview of image steganography. In: ISSA (2005)
37. Al-Ani, M.S., Awad, F.H.: The JPEG image compression algorithm. Int. J. Adv. Eng. Technol. 6(3), 1055–1062 (2013)
38. Narayanan, G.: A study of probability distributions of DCT coefficients in JPEG compression (2010)
39. National Institute of Standards and Technology: Data Encryption Standard (DES) (1999)
40. Provos, N.: Defending against statistical steganalysis. In: Usenix Security Symposium, vol. 10, pp. 323–336 (2001)
41. Rif, D.: Re-encoding persistent video steganography (2018)
42. Smoot, S.R., Rowe, L.A.: DCT coefficient distributions. In: Human Vision and Electronic Imaging, vol. 2657, pp. 403–411. International Society for Optics and Photonics, SPIE (1996)

43. Tang, W., Li, H., Luo, W., Huang, J.: Adaptive steganalysis against WOW embedding algorithm. In: Proceedings of the 2nd ACM Workshop on Information Hiding and Multimedia Security, IH&MMSec 2014, pp. 91–96. Association for Computing Machinery, New York (2014)
44. Trithemius, J.: Steganographia: Hoc est: Ars Per Occultam Scripturam Animi Sui Voluntatem Absentibus aperiendi certa. Berner (1606)
45. Vollbeding, I.J.G.G.: Libjpeg (2022). http://ijg.org/
46. Wang, H., Wang, S.: Cyber warfare: steganography vs. steganalysis. Commun. ACM **47**(10), 73–83 (2004)
47. Wayner, P.: Disappearing Cryptography. Information Hiding: Steganography and Watermarking, 3rd edn. (2008)
48. Westfeld, A.: High capacity despite better steganalysis (F5—a steganographic algorithm). In: Moskowitz, I.S. (ed.) IH 2001. LNCS, vol. 2137, pp. 289–302. Springer, Heidelberg (2001). https://doi.org/10.1007/3-540-45496-9_21
49. Winarno, A., Arrasyid, A.A., Sari, C.A., Rachmawanto, E.H., et al.: Image watermarking using low wavelet subband based on 8×8 sub-block DCT. In: 2017 International Seminar on Application for Technology of Information and Communication (iSemantic), pp. 11–15. IEEE (2017)

A Study for Security of Visual Cryptography

Binh Le Thanh Thai$^{(\boxtimes)}$ (ID) and Hidema Tanaka

National Defense Academy of Japan, 1-10-20 Hashirimizu, Yokosuka,
Kanagawa 239-8686, Japan
binhbe603501@gmail.com, hidema@nda.ac.jp

Abstract. We verify the achievement of information-theoretic security of Visual Cryptography (VC) based on the detailed attack scenario. In addition, practical VCs use pseudo-random permutation (PRP) as a random shuffle, which we also verify in this case. As a result, practical VCs only have computational security and require true random number generators (TRNGs) to achieve information-theoretic security. We derive a rational evaluation standard for VC's security from the detailed attack scenario. Based on it, we consider an attack method using multiple shared images that is more effective than the brute-force search. In this study, we execute computer simulations of XOR differential attack on two shared images and observe the bias on the appearance frequency of the differential output. From these above results, we can conclude that it is necessary to generate the basis matrices with the same Hamming weight for all rows to guarantee the security of VCs.

Keywords: Visual Cryptography · security evaluation · security analysis · differential attack

1 Introduction

Visual Cryptography (VC) [15] is a type of secret sharing scheme (SSS) [17] in which secret information is encrypted in the form of digital images, referred to as "*shared images*". VCs do not require any PC or electric device to reconstruct the secret information, so various practical uses are possible. Especially, the application of anti-phishing [2,11] is paid attention to recently. Previous studies are well known for improving the quality of the reconstructed images [3,4,6], progressive type [8,12,16], applying to color images [5,13,21], and multiple secret information [10,19,20]. VCs have been evaluated based on the value of relative difference or by sight so far. These evaluation methods only focus on the quality of shared images or reconstructed images. That is, how hard we can see the secret information in the reconstructed images. Regarding security, Naor et al. [15] only implied information-theoretic security. Since the mechanism of VCs is simple, it is regarded that the implication of Naor et al. is applicable. Hence, the security evaluation has not been clearly shown in the previous developments. Eventually, VCs have been evaluated only by sight based on shared images and

S. El Hajji et al. (Eds.): C2SI 2023, LNCS 13874, pp. 261–277, 2023.
https://doi.org/10.1007/978-3-031-33017-9_17

reconstructed images, and have no standard security evaluation so far. On the other hand, some cheating methods have been proposed [7,14]. Thus, there is a gap between the implication of Naor et al. and the actual security. These facts motivated us to verify the information-theoretic security of VCs.

In this study, we verify the information-theoretic security of VCs by analyzing a detailed attack scenario. Notably, we consider that practical VCs use pseudo-random permutation (PRP) as a random shuffle for basis matrices; thus, we consider an attack algorithm when PRP and pseudo-random number generators (PRNGs) are used. As a result, practical VCs only have computational security and require true random number generators (TRNGs) to achieve information-theoretic security. Furthermore, we consider an attack scenario for specific basis matrices of practical VC and show how this scenario works in an example. Consequently, we derive a rational evaluation standard for VC's security. Our standard allows the attacker to use two or more and $t - 1$ or fewer shared images for the attack. In this study, we show that there exists a large bias in the output frequency of PRP from the XOR difference of multiple shared images by a computer simulation. From the results, we can conclude that it is necessary to generate the basis matrices with the same Hamming weight for all rows to guarantee the security of VCs.

2   Visual Cryptography

2.1   Outline [15]

In this section, we describe (t, n)-VC in the case where the secret image is a black-and-white binary image. In (t, n)-VC, the secret image can be reconstructed from any combination of (threshold) t shared images from n ones, whereas $t - 1$ or fewer shared images do not leak out any information about the secret image. In general, one pixel is expanded to ex [pixel], and we refer to ex as the "*pixel expansion*". We denote a white pixel as "0" and a black pixel as "1". According to the difference between the numbers of "0"s and "1"s, the difference between the expression of white and black in ex [pixel] becomes large owing to the stacking of shared images.

We use the "*basis matrix*" to realize such an expansion. Let B_0 and B_1 be the basis matrices for the white and black pixels, respectively. We define the basis matrix as follows: Let $G = \{1, 2, \ldots, n\}$ be a set of indices of the shared images.

Definition 1. *A pair (B_0, B_1) of $n \times ex$ Boolean matrices can be defined as the basis matrices of (t, n)-VC if it satisfies the following two conditions:*

Condition 1: *There exists a number $\alpha_k > 0$ such that for any $A \subset G$ and $|A| = k$ ($t \leq k \leq n$), the following two inequalities hold for some $d_A > 0$:*

$$H_w(B_0[A]) + \alpha_k \cdot ex \leq d_A,$$
$$H_w(B_1[A]) \geq d_A \tag{1}$$

where $B_i[A]$ ($i \in \{0,1\}$) denotes the $k \times ex$ matrix obtained by all the rows of B_i corresponding to A, and $H_w(\cdot)$ denotes the Hamming weight of the OR summation of each column in $B_i[A]$.

Condition 2: *For $A \subset G$ such that $|A| < t$, $B_1[A]$ can be made identical to $B_0[A]$ by an appropriate permutation with respect to the columns.*

Condition 1 ensures that the secret image can be reconstructed by stacking at least t ($t \leq n$) shared images. We can distinguish white pixels and black pixels in the reconstructed images due to the gap of at least $\alpha_k \cdot ex$ between the Hamming weights $H_w(B_0[A])$ and $H_w(B_1[A])$. The value of α_k in Eq. (1) is defined as the difference between the number of white and black pixels for the stacking of k shared images; this difference is called the *"relative difference"*.

$$\alpha_k = \min_{A:A\subset G,|A|=k} \frac{H_w(B_1[A]) - H_w(B_0[A])}{ex}, \quad t \leq k \leq n \tag{2}$$

In general, as the value of α increases or the value of ex decreases, we can perceive a secret image more clearly in the reconstructed image.

Condition 2 guarantees the security of VC. In a reconstructed image generated from fewer than t shared images, it is impossible to distinguish whether a pixel is black or white in the secret image because such a permuted $B_i[A]$ ($i \in \{0, 1\}$) occurs with the same probability, regardless of whether the pixel is black or white. According to [9] and [18], the following equation can be derived:

$$H_w(B_0[A]) = H_w(B_1[A]) \quad \forall A \subset G, |A| \leq t - 1 \tag{3}$$

Note that each column of B_0 and B_1 is shuffled at each time of pixel expansion. Figure 1 presents an example of the expansion process. If shuffle is not applied, the pixel expansion becomes a constant transformation, and such resultant will enable the prediction of whether the original pixel is black or white. Therefore, the security of VC relies on the shuffle. In this paper, we regard such shuffle as a "random permutation" with a secret initial value. If the random permutation is cryptographically secure, VC always achieves information-theoretic security [15]. We show a detailed analysis under such conditions in the following section.

2.2 Information-Theoretic Security of VC

In this section, we analyze the implication of Naor et al. that VC has information-theoretic security. Let $R(\cdot)$ denotes the random permutation. The i-th pixel expansion can be written as follow.

$$ex_i = R(B_{x_i}), \quad x_i \in \{0, 1\} \tag{4}$$

We consider the basic condition of the attacker as follows.

1. The secret image is unknown.
2. The random permutation is unknown.
3. The order to apply pixel expansion is known.
4. The basis matrices (B_0, B_1) and the value of ex are known.

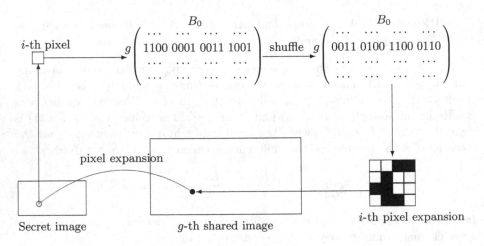

Fig. 1. Pixel expansion process ($ex = 16$, i-th pixel is white)

The Hamming weight of (B_0, B_1) can be any set within the condition that they satisfy Definition 1. To be easy to understand, we assume all the Hamming weights of rows are the same. This assumption is not a favorable condition for the attacker, and we show the reason later. The following two properties are obtained.

Property 1: There exists an equivalent transformation $e_1(\cdot)$ that satisfies the followings.

$$B_0 = e_1(B_1)$$
$$B_1 = e_1'(B_0) \tag{5}$$

where $e_1'(\cdot)$ denotes the inverse of $e_1(\cdot)$.

Property 2: For all users $g \in G$, there exists an equivalent transformation $e_2(\cdot)$ that satisfies the followings.

$$B_i^g = e_2(B_i^{g'})$$
$$B_i^{g'} = e_2'(B_i^g), \quad i \in \{0, 1\} \tag{6}$$

for all users $g' \in G \setminus \{g\}$ where B_i^g denotes the row of B_i corresponding to user g and $e_2'(\cdot)$ denotes the inverse of $e_2(\cdot)$.

Now, we consider the following three lemmas.

Lemma 1. *Even if an attacker satisfies the basic conditions, knows the procedure of generating and distributing all the shared images, and has infinite computing power, he/she cannot distinguish whether an original pixel in the secret image is black or white from one shared image.*

Proof. In this case, the attacker can identify the user g of the known shared image. From this condition, he/she can distinguish whether x_i is 0 or 1 with a significant probability from ex_i if the following holds.

$$\frac{1}{2} + \epsilon = \text{Prob}\{x_i = 0|ex_i \rightarrow x_i\}, \quad \epsilon > 0 \tag{7}$$

However, from **Property** 1 there exists an equivalent transformation; thus, $B_0^g = e_1(B_1^g)$ and $B_1^g = e_1'(B_0^g)$ occur with the same probability. Hence, it is impossible to distinguish the following two with a significant probability even when using infinite computing resources.

$$\begin{aligned} ex_i = R(B_0^g) = R(e_1(B_1^g)) \\ ex_i = R(B_1^g) = R(e_1'(B_0^g)) \end{aligned} \tag{8}$$

As a result, the attacker cannot hold Eq. (7). Therefore, **Lemma** 1 is proved.

Lemma 2. *Even if an attacker satisfies the basic conditions and has infinite computing power, he/she only can distinguish user $g \in G$ from one shared image with the probability less than or equal to $\frac{1}{n}$.*

Proof. As shown in **Lemma** 1, $ex_i = R(B_0^g)$ or $ex_i = R(B_1^g)$ holds for any ex_i; however, the attacker cannot distinguish these with a significant probability. From **Property** 2, $B_0^g = e_2(B_0^{g'})$ and $B_1^g = e_2(B_1^{g'})$ hold for all users $g' \in G\backslash\{g\}$. Therefore, the followings hold.

$$\begin{aligned} ex_i = R(B_0^g) = R(e_2(B_0^{g'})) = R(e_2'(B_1^{g'})) \\ ex_i = R(B_1^g) = R(e_2(B_1^{g'})) = R(e_2'(B_0^{g'})) \end{aligned} \tag{9}$$

The attacker also cannot distinguish these above from **Lemma** 1. Since all the above results hold for g' with the same probability, the attacker cannot distinguish g and g' even if an infinite number of trials is executed. Therefore, **Lemma** 2 is proved.

Lemma 3. *Even if an attacker satisfies the basic conditions, knows the procedure of generating and distributing all the shared images, and has infinite computing power, he/she cannot distinguish whether an original pixel in the secret image is black or white from k ($2 \leq k \leq t$) shared images.*

Proof. First, we consider the case the attacker gets two shared images. From these above conditions, the attacker can identify the users of these shared images. Let $g_a, g_b \in G$ be these users. For $ex_i^{g_a}$ and $ex_i^{g_b}$ (note that $ex_i^{g_a} \neq ex_i^{g_b}$), the followings hold under the assumption of $x_i = 0$.

$$\begin{aligned} ex_i^{g_a} = R_a(B_0^{g_a}) \\ ex_i^{g_b} = R_b(B_0^{g_b}) \end{aligned} \tag{10}$$

If the above assumption is correct, $R_a(\cdot)$ and $R_b(\cdot)$ will be the same permutation from **Definition** 1. It can be regarded that the attacker can distinguish whether x_i is 0 or 1 based on this result. However, from **Property** 1, the followings hold.

$$
\begin{aligned}
B_1^{g_a} = e_1'(B_0^{g_a}) \\
B_1^{g_b} = e_1'(B_0^{g_b})
\end{aligned}
\tag{11}
$$

Therefore, a permutation using B_1 can also satisfy the wrong assumption $x_1 = 0$.

$$
\begin{aligned}
ex_i^{g_a} = R_a(e_1'(B_0^{g_a})) = R_a(B_1^{g_a}) \\
ex_i^{g_b} = R_b(e_1'(B_0^{g_b})) = R_b(B_1^{g_b})
\end{aligned}
\tag{12}
$$

In the case $x_i = 1$, we have the followings using the equivalent transformation.

$$
\begin{aligned}
ex_i^{g_a} = R_a'(B_1^{g_a}) \\
ex_i^{g_b} = R_b'(B_1^{g_b})
\end{aligned}
\tag{13}
$$

It is obvious that $R_a'(\cdot)$ and $R_b'(\cdot)$ are the same permutations; thus, $R_a'(e_1'(\cdot))$ and $R_b'(e_1'(\cdot))$ are also the same permutations. Therefore, with the assumption $x_i = 0$, two pairs of the same permutation are determined. As shown in **Lemma** 1, the attacker cannot distinguish these pairs; thus, such distinguish attack is infeasible.

In the case the attacker gets three or more shared images, based on **Property** 2 there are more equivalent transformations are obtained; thus, the number of the pairs of the same permutation increases. In the case the attacker makes a reconstructed image from two shared images, based on the above results and **Definition** 1, the attacker also cannot distinguish whether an original pixel in the secret image is black or white. Therefore, **Lemma** 3 is proved.

Theorem 1. *VC has the information-theoretic security.*

Proof. The proof is trivial based on **Lemma** 1, 2 and 3.

3   Pseudo-random Permutation

In this section, we explain the pseudo-random permutation used in this paper. A random permutation $R(\cdot)$ is regarded as a random automaton that is executed sequentially in the proofs of **Lemmas** 1, 2, and 3 shown in Sect. 2.2. From the viewpoint of realizable implementation, it is difficult to use TRNG as an automaton. Therefore, it is feasible to apply PRP $P(\cdot)$ with the output sequences from a PRNG as the running variable as follow.

$$
ex_i = P(B_{x_i}, r_i)
\tag{14}
$$

where r_i is a running secret variable as follows.

$$
\begin{aligned}
\tilde{r} = r_0, r_1, \cdots, r_i, \cdots \\
= pseudorandom(seed)
\end{aligned}
\tag{15}
$$

where $\tilde{r}$ denotes the secret random number sequence with the size of $|r|$ and $pseudorandom(\cdot)$ is a random function with the initial value $seed$. The property of $R(\cdot)$ is realized by the sequence of $P(\cdot)$ based on the random number r_i. In addition, the unpredictability of $R(\cdot)$ can be equated to the condition that the initial value $seed$ is secret. From the viewpoint of the PRNG and its sequence, the secret image and shared images are also regarded as sequences as follows.

- Secret image sequence: $\tilde{x} = x_0, x_1, \cdots, x_i, \cdots, x_N$ $(x_i \in F_2)$
- Shared image sequence: $\tilde{ex} = ex_0, ex_1, \cdots, ex_i, \cdots, ex_N$ $(ex_i \in F_2^{ex})$

From these above viewpoints, we have the followings.

$$\begin{cases} \tilde{ex} = P(B_{\tilde{x}}, \tilde{r}) \\ ex_i = P(B_{x_i}, r_i) \end{cases} \tag{16}$$

From the security evaluation viewpoint, we assume that $P(\cdot)$ and $pseudorandom(\cdot)$ are open to the public; however, $seed$ and the random number sequence $\tilde{r}$ are unknown. Note that the random permutation $P(\cdot)$ is not equivalent to the sort of column numbers $(1, 2, \cdots, ex)$. Since B_0 and B_1 are binary matrices that are expanded from F_2 to F_2^{ex}, the result of the permutation takes only $\mathcal{H} = \dbinom{ex}{Hw(ex)}$ possibilities, not $ex!$. Notably, we assume $R(\cdot)$ is uniformly random on F_2^{ex} in the proofs of **Lemmas** 1, 2, and 3.

4   Attack Algorithm

In this section, we describe the attack algorithm for practical VCs. Let us consider the security of VC using PRP shown in Sect. 3. Since the PRNG has computational security depending on the size of the initial value, the security of PRP itself is also limited to computational security. As is shown in Sect. 2.2, the mechanism of VC can achieve information-theoretic security. Therefore, a VC scheme can be evaluated as "secure" if it requires a larger amount of calculation than the brute-force search for the initial value of the PRNG. And, if not, VC can only achieve conditional security, and the evaluation needs to be clarified.

In this section, we assume that the basis matrices are ideal, all rows have the same Hamming weight, $B_0^g \neq B_1^g$ holds for all $g \in G$, and $B_i^{g_a} \neq B_j^{g_b}$ $(i, j \in \{0, 1\})$ holds for at least one pair $(g_a, g_b) \in G^2$. Let N is the total pixel of the secret image; x_i and ex_i $(0 \leq i \leq N - 1)$, respectively, are the i-th pixel of the secret image and i-th pixel expansion of the shared image. Here, we have the total pixel of shared images is $height \cdot width = ex \cdot N$ [pixel].

Lemma 4. *If the period of the sequence $\tilde{r}$ is sufficiently larger than $2^N \cdot |r_i|^N$, where $|r_i|$ denotes the size of the i-th element r_i of $\tilde{r}$, there exists a sub-sequence $\tilde{r}'$ in $\tilde{r}$ satisfies $\tilde{ex}_{i+1} = P(\tilde{ex}_i, \tilde{r}')$ and the initial value $seed'$ can be determined.*

Proof. From **Properties** 1 and 2, there exists at least one permutation that changes $B_{x_i}^g$ to ex_{i+1} for all $B_{x_i}^g$. Let us consider N continuous sub-sequence

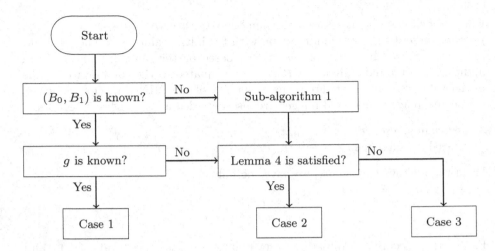

Fig. 2. Attack algorithm

$\tilde{r}_{\{N\}}$ in the sequence $\tilde{r}$. If there are all possible combinations in the set of this sub-sequence, the secret parameter of the permutation which can generate the sequence $\tilde{ex}_{i+1}$ from the sequence $\tilde{ex}_i$ is included. Since $x_i \in F_2$, there are 2^N possibilities of the sequence $\tilde{x}_i$ in total when $0 \leq i \leq N - 1$. In addition, since there are $|r|^N$ possibilities of the sequence $\tilde{r}_{\{N\}}$, we need $2^N \cdot |r|^N$ types of permutation. On the other hand, the period of the sequence $\tilde{r}$ is determined based on the size of the *seed*. Here, under the assumption that all *seed*s can output different series for a sub-sequence of length N, there exists an initial value *seed'* which can generate the sequence $\tilde{r}$ that satisfies $\tilde{ex}_{i+1} = P(\tilde{ex}_i, \tilde{r'})$, if $|seed| \geq 2^N \cdot |r|^N$ holds. Therefore, the **Lemma** 4 is proved.

Sub-algorithm 1 (Estimate the value of ex). Divide a shared image into $(m \times n)$ [pixel] blocks, with $m \mid height$ and $n \mid width$. Find the pair (m, n) that satisfies the following two conditions:

- The value of $m \cdot n$ is as small as possible
- The number of black pixels contained in all blocks is the same.

Then, we can obtain $ex = n \cdot m$ and $Hw(ex)$ is equal to the number of black pixels contained in a block.

Figure 2 presents the flowchart of our attack algorithm.

Case 1: Since the attacker knows (B_0, B_1) and g, he/she can identify (B_0^g, B_1^g). Here, the attacker knows the value of ex and gets the shared image of the user g; thus, he/she can use the following attack procedure.

Step 1: Search for the set S of *seed* that satisfies the following.

$$S = \{seed \mid ex_0 = P(B_0^g, r_0), \ r_0 = pseudorandom(seed)\} \qquad (17)$$

Step 2: Choose $c \in S$ as a candidate of true *seed* and generate $\tilde{r}_c = pseudorandom(c)$.

Step 3: Under the condition $\tilde{r}_c = r_{c_1}, r_{c_2}, \cdots, r_{c_i}$; if $ex_i = P(B_0^g, r_{c_i})$ holds then x_i will be 0 and if not, x_i will be 1. Then, convert the sequence $\tilde{ex}$ to the sequence $\tilde{x}$.

Step 4: If $\tilde{x}$ can be confirmed as an image by sight then this procedure ends and if not, back to Step 2 and choose another $c \in S$.

The calculation cost required is dominated by Step 1, which is a brute-force search for the *seed* of the $pseudorandom(\cdot)$.

Case 2: In this case, there are three situations as follows:

1. (B_0, B_1) is unknown but g is known.
2. Both (B_0, B_1) and g are unknown.
3. (B_0, B_1) is known but g is unknown.

In either situation, the attacker cannot identify B_0^g. However, from **Properties 1** and **2**, if the attacker executes the attack algorithm in **Case 1** with a change as follows, he/she can obtain the *seed'* that makes the secret image can be confirmed by sight.

$$S = \{seed' \mid ex_1 = P(ex_0, r_1), r_1 = pseudorandom(seed')\} \tag{18}$$

The required calculation cost is the same as **Case 1**. Note that the *seed'* obtained in this way is only effective for the attack target shared image.

Case 3: Similar to **Case 2**, the attacker needs to estimate B_0^g because he/she does not know B_0^g or B_1^g. However, the attacker cannot determine $B_0^g = ex_0$ because **Lemma 4** is not satisfied. Hence, he/she needs to execute **Case 1** with most $\mathcal{H} = \begin{pmatrix} ex \\ Hw(ex) \end{pmatrix}$ trials. Here, the candidate of B_0^g can be correctly found with a possibility as $\dfrac{2 \cdot |g|}{\mathcal{H}}$ and the needed calculation cost is $\mathcal{H}$ times of **Case 1** at most.

The computational cost required by **Cases 1** and **2** in our attack algorithm does not exceed the brute-force search for the *seed* of the PRNG. In **Case 3**, the required computational cost is $\mathcal{H}$ times of the brute-force search but in this case, **Lemma 4** is not satisfied. That is, the size of the *seed* that adapts to VC is not large enough or exists a bias in the applied PRP itself. Therefore, there is a possibility an attack method that requires a computational cost less than the brute-force search for *seed* can be applied. Hence, we can conclude that VC in **Case 3** is not secure.

Such a conclusion causes by the existence of a correlation between ex_i and ex_{i+1}. On the other hand, in the information-theoretic security evaluation shown in Sect. 2.2, the uncorrelation between them is an implicit premise. As is shown in Sect. 3, TRNGs are required to realize such uncorrelation. However, as is already shown, TRNGs are impractical, and practical VCs can be able to achieve only computational security. Therefore, we can conclude that we have to keep the value of the *seed* to be secret and the *seed* itself has to large size enough to guarantee computational security. From the viewpoint of the designer, these situations of the attack can be summarized as follows:

Fig. 3. Secret image

Case 1: The situation according to reasonable security evaluation.

Case 2: The situation that is difficult to implement because very large initial values and randomness are required for PRP and PRNG.

Case 3: The realistic situation because the attacker can have only ambiguous information if either (B_0, B_1) or g is unknown. There may exist weaknesses in PRP, and the initial values may be small, but such a situation enhances security.

In the following section, we consider a new attack scenario paying attention to the basis matrices.

5   Detailed Attack Scenario

In this section, we describe the detailed attack scenario using the attack algorithm shown in Sect. 4. In Sect. 4, we assume that the basis matrices are ideal; however, this condition is not always achieved. For example, a pair of basis matrices of $(3, 5)$-VC is as follows (Model A).

$$
B_0 = \begin{pmatrix}
0,0,0,0,0,0,1,0,1,1,0,0,1,0,0,1 \\
0,0,0,0,0,0,1,1,1,0,1,1,1,0,0,0 \\
0,0,0,0,0,0,0,1,1,0,0,1,1,0,0,1 \\
0,0,0,0,0,0,1,1,1,0,0,0,0,1,1,1 \\
0,0,0,0,0,0,0,0,0,1,1,1,1,1,1,1
\end{pmatrix}
$$
$$
B_1 = \begin{pmatrix}
1,1,0,0,0,0,0,0,0,0,0,0,0,1,1,1 \\
0,0,1,1,0,1,0,0,0,0,0,0,0,1,1,1 \\
0,0,0,0,1,1,0,0,0,0,0,0,0,1,1,1 \\
0,0,0,0,0,0,1,1,1,0,0,0,0,1,1,1 \\
0,0,0,0,0,0,0,0,0,1,1,1,1,1,1,1
\end{pmatrix}
$$

$$(19)$$

From here onwards, let S_i $(1 \leq i \leq 5)$ denotes i-th shared image and $R_{[i_1, i_2, \cdots, i_k]}$ $(2 \leq k \leq 5)$ denotes the reconstructed image generated from k shared images $S_{i_1}, S_{i_2}, \cdots, S_{i_k}$. We show the target image in Fig. 3 and Fig. 4 presents the shared and reconstructed images generated by using these basis matrices. From Eq. (19), we can find that $B_0^4 = B_1^4$ and $B_0^5 = B_1^5$. Therefore, if the attacker gets the shared image corresponding to $g = 4$ or 5, he/she can determine the *seed* in **Step 1** of **Case 1**; however, the secret image cannot be confirmed by sight in **Step 3**. Hence, he/she needs to use another shared image corresponding to g

which satisfies $B_0^g \neq B_1^g$ to confirm the secret image. Similarly, in **Cases 2** and **3**, if the attacker gets the shared image corresponding to $g = 4$ or 5, he/she can determine the $seed'$, but it cannot be adapted for other shared images to attack. In these situations, we can conclude that VC has sufficient security based on the practical point of view. However, the condition $B_0 = B_1$ is required to have such security, so VC cannot achieve it. The achievement of such security depends on the choice of g. Therefore, from the evaluation viewpoint, it is necessary to make it to be able to achieve with any g. The attack algorithm shown in Sect. 4 can be used with only one shared image. However, the aforementioned scenario is also necessary to the security evaluation; thus, it is necessary to allow the attacker to get any set of less than t shared images. From these above considerations, we summarize the conditions for rational security evaluation as follows.

– The value of $seed$ for PRNG must be secret and all VC configurations except it can be open.
– The attacker can get any set of less than t shared images.

As shown in Eq. (19), the Hamming weights of rows are different. Therefore, in the third situation of **Case 2**, the attacker can estimate the value of g with a high probability using the **Sub-algorithm 1**. In this situation, **Case 1** can be probabilistically executed. If the attacker successes to estimate g, he/she obtains $seed$; and obtains $seed'$ if not. In either situation, the secret image can be confirmed by sight. That is, our attack algorithm does not require the computational cost more than the brute-force for the size of the $seed$.

The following basis matrices also exist for the (3, 5)-VC (Model B).

$$B_0 = \begin{pmatrix} 0,0,0,0,0,0,1,1,1,1,1,1,1,1,0,0 \\ 0,0,0,0,0,0,1,1,1,1,1,1,0,0,1,1 \\ 0,0,0,0,0,0,1,1,1,1,0,0,1,1,1,1 \\ 0,0,0,0,0,0,1,1,0,0,1,1,1,1,1,1 \\ 0,0,0,0,0,0,0,0,1,1,1,1,1,1,1,1 \end{pmatrix}$$

$$B_1 = \begin{pmatrix} 1,1,0,0,0,0,0,0,0,0,1,1,1,1,1,1 \\ 0,0,1,1,0,0,0,0,0,0,1,1,1,1,1,1 \\ 0,0,0,0,1,1,0,0,0,0,1,1,1,1,1,1 \\ 0,0,0,0,0,0,1,1,0,0,1,1,1,1,1,1 \\ 0,0,0,0,0,0,0,0,1,1,1,1,1,1,1,1 \end{pmatrix}$$

(20)

Figure 5 shows the shared images generated by using them for the secret image in Fig. 3. Note that all rows have the same Hamming weight, so the attacker cannot estimate g. However, the computational cost required is the same as the case of Model A. Therefore, from the viewpoint of computational security, both Models A and B have the same security. On the other hand, the difference in Hamming weight greatly affects the number of output result $\mathcal{H}$ of PRP and its distribution. Such bias may cause a more favorable situation than the brute-force search in $seed$ estimation. We discuss such issues in the following section.

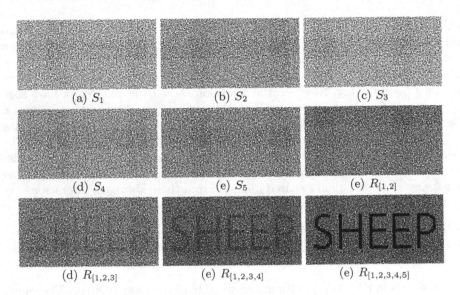

(a) S_1 (b) S_2 (c) S_3

(d) S_4 (e) S_5 (e) $R_{[1,2]}$

(d) $R_{[1,2,3]}$ (e) $R_{[1,2,3,4]}$ (e) $R_{[1,2,3,4,5]}$

Fig. 4. Model A

6 Statistical Property of PRP

6.1 Preliminary

According to the conditions of security evaluation shown in Sect. 5, we assume that the attacker can get any set of two shared images. Let $B_i^{g_a}$ and $B_i^{g_b}$ ($g_a, g_b \in G$, $i \in \{0, 1\}$) denote two rows of basis matrices corresponding to these shared images. We used the Random Sample function of Mathematica 12.0.0.0 [1] to generate shared images in this paper. The detailed information of this function is not found, but it is intended for general computer simulations and is not a security technology. Therefore, the results shown in this section are examples of observation regarding the bias of the output distribution and are not for the security evaluation with this function.

We use the differential input as follow.

$$\Delta x_{ij} = B^{S_i} \circ B^{S_j} \tag{21}$$

Since the PRP is used, we can have the differential output Δy for two shared images as follows.

$$
\begin{aligned}
P(B_i^{g_a}, \tilde{r}) \circ P(B_i^{g_b}, \tilde{r}) &= P(B_i^{g_a} \circ B_i^{g_b}, \tilde{r}) \\
&= P(\Delta x, \tilde{r}) \\
&= \Delta \tilde{y}
\end{aligned}
\tag{22}
$$

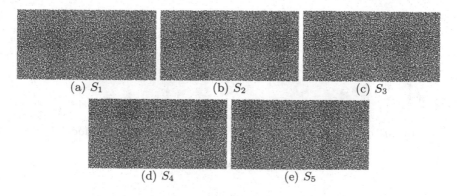

(a) S_1 (b) S_2 (c) S_3

(d) S_4 (e) S_5

Fig. 5. Model B

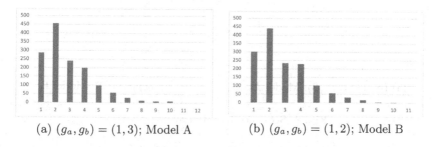

(a) $(g_a, g_b) = (1,3)$; Model A   (b) $(g_a, g_b) = (1,2)$; Model B

Fig. 6. Output-based observation - 1

The operation "◦" can be OR, AND, or XOR. Since OR operation is used in the reconstruction process, this case can be omitted. Now, we have the following result of Model A considering the case of AND.

$$Hw(\Delta y_A^\wedge) = Hw(B_0^{g_a} \wedge B_0^{g_b}) \text{ or } Hw(B_1^{g_a} \wedge B_1^{g_b}) \tag{23}$$

$$3 \le Hw(\Delta y_A^\wedge) \le 4 \tag{24}$$

Here, note that $Hw(B_0^g) = Hw(B_1^g)$ from **Definition 1**, so it is not necessary to consider $Hw(B_0^{g_a} \circ B_0^{g_b})$ or $Hw(B_1^{g_a} \circ B_1^{g_b})$ from the mechanism of generating shared images. The result for Model B is as follow.

$$Hw(\Delta y_B^\wedge) = Hw(B_0^{g_a} \wedge B_0^{g_b}) \text{ or } Hw(B_1^{g_a} \wedge B_1^{g_b}) \tag{25}$$

$$Hw(\Delta y_B^\wedge) = 6 \tag{26}$$

On the other hand, in considering the case of XOR, we have the following results.

$$4 \le Hw(\Delta y_A^\oplus) \le 7$$
$$Hw(\Delta y_B^\oplus) = 4 \tag{27}$$

Regarding that the larger range of Hamming weight brings more remarkable properties, we use XOR in this study.

We observe the output distribution Δy with two points of view.

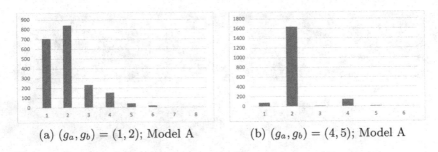

(a) $(g_a, g_b) = (1, 2)$; Model A   (b) $(g_a, g_b) = (4, 5)$; Model A

Fig. 7. Output-based observation - 2

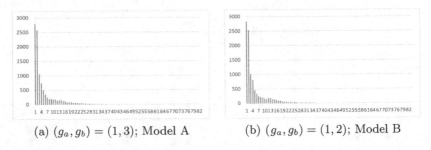

(a) $(g_a, g_b) = (1, 3)$; Model A   (b) $(g_a, g_b) = (1, 2)$; Model B

Fig. 8. Sequence-based observation - 1

Output-based observation (Observation with block (pixel expansion) unit): The bias in $Hw(\Delta x)$ affects directly to the differential output Δy.

Sequence-based observation (Observation with continuous l [bit] of the sub-sequence unit): The superiority and inferiority of randomness are clarified as sequences, and the weakness of PRP will be found.

From the viewpoint of symmetric-key ciphers, the output-based observation can be regarded as a differential property for block ciphers. On the other hand, sequence-based observation can be regarded as a chosen initial vector property for stream ciphers. If remarkable characteristics can be found in either, the *seed* can be more easily determined by adapting an effective attack method than the brute-force search. Such property can be observed by the following procedure.

Step 1: Create the XOR image from S_i and S_j. In other words, a stack of two black pixels changes to a white pixel.

Step 2: Observe the frequency of Δy in block unit or sequence length.

These observation results reveal the difference in Hamming weights of rows and the number of Δx's types. A small number of Δx's types reveals the differential output of the random permutation and increases the bias of Δy. Therefore, the *seed* may be easily distinguished.

6.2 Computer Experiment and Results

From Eq. (22), we have $Hw(\Delta x) = Hw(\Delta y)$, so $Hw(\Delta y)$ depends on the choice of (g_a, g_b). This difference affects the number of different values of output

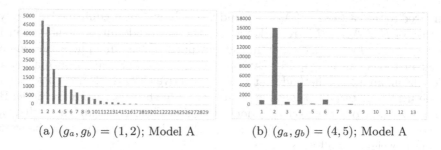

(a) $(g_a, g_b) = (1, 2)$; Model A   (b) $(g_a, g_b) = (4, 5)$; Model A

Fig. 9. Sequence-based observation - 2

$Hw(\Delta y)$. Therefore, It can be observed as a difference in the distribution of the frequency of Δy's types.

Output-Based Observation. From Eq. (27), we have $Hw(\Delta y_B^\oplus) = 4$, so we find the pairs (g_a, g_b) in both Models that satisfy $Hw(\Delta y_B^\oplus) = 4$ and observe the result. Figure 6 shows the results for $(g_a, g_b) = (1, 3)$ in Model A and $(1, 2)$ in Model B. The vertical axis represents the frequency of appearances, and the horizontal axis represents the label given to the value of Δy's types. Since $Hw(\Delta y) = 4$, the total possibilities of Δy are $\binom{16}{4} = 1,820$ ways, but the number of types that appear prominently is only 12 in both cases. However, the distribution of appearances is almost equal and is indistinguishable. From here onwards, we can evaluate that both Models have the same strength against differential attack in the case of $Hw(\Delta y) = 4$. However, Model A has a large range of possible values for $Hw(\Delta y)$. For $(g_a, g_b) = (1, 2)$ we have $Hw(\Delta y) = 5$, so the total possibilities of Δy is $4,368$ ways. This value is larger than the case of $Hw(\Delta y) = 4$, but the number of types that appear prominently is only 6. Similarly, for $(g_a, g_b) = (4, 5)$ we have $Hw(\Delta y) = 7$. The total possibilities of Δy increase to $11,440$ ways, but the number of types of appearing values is further decreased. We show these results in Fig. 7. Such a large bias generates an effective property for the differential attack. Therefore, in Model A, the Hamming weights of rows of basis matrices are different, so there exist some cases that are weak against differential attack. On the other hand, in Model B, all rows of basis matrices have the same Hamming weight. Hence, such weakness does not exist. From these above results, we can conclude that it is necessary to generate the basis matrices with the same Hamming weight for all rows for secure VC.

Sequence-Based Observation. In this study, we set $l = ex \ (= 16)$ and observe with continuous 16 [bit] of sub-sequence unit. Note that the Hamming weight of sub-sequence cannot be calculated definitively as in output-based observation. It can take the values in the range from 0 to $2 \cdot Hw(\Delta y)$. Figure 8 shows the results in the case of $Hw(\Delta y) = 4$. Similar to the output-based observation, both Models do not have a large difference, so they have the same security.

Figure 9 shows the results in the case of $Hw(\Delta y) = 5$ and $Hw(\Delta y) = 7$. Surprisingly, in both cases, the number of types of Δy is extremely limited compared to the case of $Hw(\Delta y) = 4$, and a very large bias is confirmed. Notably, the case of $Hw(\Delta y) = 7$ is remarkable and the low randomness is shown. Such a large bias is a fatal weakness from the viewpoint of stream ciphers, and many attack methods can be applied. By combining with the result of output-based observation, an attack method that is more effective than the brute-force search can be used to determine the value of the *seed*. On the other hand, in Model B, such a weakness of the choice of g does not exist. From these above results, we can conclude that it is necessary to configure the basis matrices with the same Hamming weight for all rows again.

7   Conclusion

We verified and confirmed the information-theoretic security of VC implied by Naor and Shamir in [15]. In this evaluation, we found the premise that random shuffle is ideal. Since the realizable implementation random shuffle is PRP, we evaluated the security of VC under the assumption PRP is used. We proposed an attack algorithm and verified it with a detailed scenario. As a result, we showed that practicable VCs only have computational security and require TRNGs to achieve information-theoretic security. We also showed reasonable conditions for security evaluation of VC in applying the proposed attack algorithm. These results contributed to solving the problem that the evaluation methods for VC are qualitative and have no clear standards. Based on our security evaluation standard, we verified the possibility of an attack using multiple shared images and considered the possibility of determining the *seed* of PRP with a more effective method than the brute-force search. We focused on the Hamming weight of rows of basis matrices and showed example experiments of the bias in the appearance frequency of XOR differential output of shared images. From these results, we conclude that all rows of basis matrices should have the same Hamming weight.

References

1. Mathematica. https://www.wolfram.com/mathematica/
2. Aravind, K., Krishnan, M.R.M.V.: Anti-phishing framework for banking based on visual cryptography. Int. J. Comput. Sci. Mob. Appl. **2**(1), 121–126 (2014)
3. Blundo, C., D'Arco, P., Santis, A.D., Stinson, D.R.: Contrast optimal threshold visual cryptography schemes. SIAM J. Discret. Math. **16**(2), 224–261 (2003)
4. D'Arco, P., Prisco, R.D., Santis, A.D.: Measure-independent characterization of contrast optimal visual cryptography schemes. J. Syst. Softw. **95**, 89–99 (2014)
5. Dutta, S., Adhikari, A., Ruj, S.: Maximal contrast color visual secret sharing schemes. Des. Codes Cryptogr. **87**(7), 1699–1711 (2019)
6. Hofmeister, T., Krause, M., Simon, H.U.: Contrast-optimal k out of n secret sharing schemes in visual cryptography. Theor. Comput. Sci. **240**(2), 471–485 (2000)
7. Horng, G., Chen, T., Tsai, D.: Cheating in visual cryptography. Des. Codes Cryptogr. **38**(2), 219–236 (2006)

8. Hou, Y., Quan, Z.: Progressive visual cryptography with unexpanded shares. IEEE Trans. Circuits Syst. Video Technol. **21**(11), 1760–1764 (2011)

9. Iwamoto, M.: A weak security notion for visual secret sharing schemes. IEEE Trans. Inf. Forensics Secur. **7**(2), 372–382 (2012)

10. Iwamoto, M., Yamamoto, H., Ogawa, H.: Optimal multiple assignments based on integer programming in secret sharing schemes with general access structures. IEICE Trans. Fundam. Electron. Commun. Comput. Sci. **90-A**(1), 101–112 (2007)

11. James, D., Philip, M.: A novel anti phishing framework based on visual cryptography. In: 2012 International Conference on Power, Signals, Controls and Computation, pp. 1–5. IEEE (2012)

12. Jin, D., Yan, W., Kankanhalli, M.S.: Progressive color visual cryptography. J. Electron. Imaging **14**(3), 033019 (2005)

13. Leung, B.W., Ng, F.Y., Wong, D.S.: On the security of a visual cryptography scheme for color images. Pattern Recogn. **42**(5), 929–940 (2009)

14. Liu, F., Wu, C.K., Lin, X.J.: Cheating immune visual cryptography scheme. IET Inf. Secur. **5**(1), 51–59 (2011)

15. Naor, M., Shamir, A.: Visual cryptography. In: De Santis, A. (ed.) EUROCRYPT 1994. LNCS, vol. 950, pp. 1–12. Springer, Heidelberg (1995). https://doi.org/10.1007/BFb0053419

16. Okada, K., Koga, H.: A construction of the progressive (3, n)-threshold visual cryptography using a BIBD and analysis of its optimality. In: 2017 IEEE Information Theory Workshop, ITW 2017, Kaohsiung, Taiwan, 6–10 November 2017, pp. 249–253. IEEE (2017)

17. Shamir, A.: How to share a secret. Commun. ACM **22**(11), 612–613 (1979)

18. Shyu, S.J., Chen, M.C.: Optimum pixel expansions for threshold visual secret sharing schemes. IEEE Trans. Inf. Forensics Secur. **6**(3-2), 960–969 (2011)

19. Weir, J., Yan, W.: Sharing multiple secrets using visual cryptography. In: International Symposium on Circuits and Systems (ISCAS 2009), Taipei, Taiwan, 24–17 May 2009, pp. 509–512. IEEE (2009)

20. Yamaguchi, Y.: Extended visual cryptography scheme for multiple-secrets continuous-tone images. Trans. Data Hiding Multim. Secur. **9**, 25–41 (2014)

21. Yang, C., Laih, C.: New colored visual secret sharing schemes. Des. Codes Cryptogr. **20**(3), 325–336 (2000)

Forecasting Click Fraud via Machine Learning Algorithms

Nadir Sahllal$^{(\boxtimes)}$ and El Mamoun Souidi

Faculty of Sciences, Laboratory of Mathematics, Computer Science,
Applications and Information Security, Mohammed V University in Rabat,
BP 1014 RP, 10000 Rabat, Morocco
sahllal.nadir@gmail.com

Abstract. Click fraud, the manipulation of online advertisement traffic figures, is becoming a major concern for businesses that advertise online. This can lead to financial losses and inaccurate click statistics. To address this problem, it is essential to have a reliable method for identifying click fraud. This includes distinguishing between legitimate clicks made by users and fraudulent clicks generated by bots or other software, which enables companies to advertise their products safely. The XGBoost model was trained on the TalkingData AdTracking Fraud Detection dataset from Kaggle, using binary classification to predict the likelihood of a click being fraudulent. The importance of data treatment was taken into consideration in the model training process, by carefully preprocessing and cleaning the data before feeding it into the model. This helped to improve the accuracy and performance of the model by reaching an AUC of 0.96 and $LogLoss$ of 0.15.

Keywords: Click Fraud · Machine Learning · Advertising · Classification

1 Introduction

Digital advertising on the internet has become a prevalent and effective marketing strategy for many organizations in recent years [2]. Website and mobile app owners monetize their traffic by displaying ads to their visitors, and earning revenue from clicks on those ads. This business model has become a major player in the internet economy, with the market size projected to reach 189.6 billion dollars in 2021 [1].

Click fraud refers to the practice of generating artificial clicks on an advertisement link with the intention of extracting revenue from the advertiser. The parties who benefit from click fraud can include the publishers who receive pay-per-click payments and third-party websites that host the ads. Thus, it is crucial to distinguish between legitimate clicks and those made by fraudulent scripts or sources that aim to benefit a certain party through illegitimate means [3,4].

There has been ongoing efforts to combat advertising fraud and specifically click fraud on the internet, with multiple works focused on this topic. various

S. El Hajji et al. (Eds.): C2SI 2023, LNCS 13874, pp. 278–289, 2023.
https://doi.org/10.1007/978-3-031-33017-9_18

statistical models were evaluated to identify Internet Protocol (IP) addresses involved in fraudulent clicks. In [7], statistical models were used to identify and flag suspicious activity on a Domain Network Server based on recurring patterns within a given time interval. In [6], feature extraction was applied to an Android app to perform machine learning and identify suspicious ads. Kantardzic et al. in [8] proposed a multi-modal real-time detection and prevention system based on the Collaborative Click Fraud Detection and Prevention (CCFDP) system [9], which utilizes client-server protocol communication.

One approach, proposed by Iqbal *et al.* [10] in their study, involves implementing a system called FCFraud that is integrated into the operating system to provide added security and save marketers billions of dollars. Another study by Thejas *et al.* [5] developed a time-series model with various scales to predict and identify click fraud behavior in real-time. These are just a few examples of the various methods that have been proposed to address the issue of click fraud in online advertising. As such, it is clear that there are various methods and models that have been proposed to detect and prevent click fraud, highlighting the need for continued research in this area.

The purpose of this research is to develop a scalable machine learning model with high performance for detecting fraudulent clicks in online advertising. With the increasing prevalence of click fraud and its negative impact on businesses, a reliable and efficient detection system is crucial. Our proposed model aims to address this problem by utilizing advanced techniques such as feature extraction and ensemble-based learning to accurately identify fraudulent clicks. Additionally, the scalability of the model ensures that it can handle large volumes of data and adapt to new types of click fraud as they emerge. Overall, the goal of this research is to provide businesses with a robust and effective tool for combating click fraud and protecting their advertising investments.

The remainder of this paper is structured as follows: In Sect. 2 the proposed approach is outlined, where we provide a detailed description of the techniques and methods used to develop our fraud detection model. Section 3 presents the results of our experimentation, and in Sect. 4 we discuss our findings and draw conclusions. Finally, Sect. 5, we conclude the paper and suggest areas for future work.

2 Methodology

In this section, we describe the various components of our proposed method and how they work together.

2.1 General Overview

The proposed method for detecting fraudulent clicks is composed of several key components, each of which plays an important role in achieving accurate and efficient results. In the first step, we focus on the data preprocessing and cleaning phase, where we carefully prepare the data for input into the model. This is a crucial step as it can greatly impact the performance of the model. Next, we move on to feature selection and extraction, where we carefully select and extract the features that are most relevant to the task of detecting fraudulent clicks. This step is also crucial as it can greatly affect the performance of the model.

After feature selection and extraction, we move on to the next step, which is the training of the model. In this step, we use XGBoost [15] as our primary machine learning algorithm. XGBoost is a powerful and efficient algorithm that is commonly used for classification and regression tasks. It is known for its ability to handle large datasets and high-dimensional feature spaces. Additionally, we use grid search [13] to find the optimal hyperparameters for our XGBoost model. Grid search is a method of systematically working through multiple combinations of hyperparameters to find the best set of hyperparameters that maximizes the performance of our model. By using grid search, we are able to fine-tune our model and achieve the best possible performance.

Finally, we evaluate the performance of the model using various metrics such as *AUC* and *LogLoss*. We pay particular attention to the performance of the model on the test set, as this is the most representative of a real-world scenario.

Not part of the methodology but to verify the worth of the current work, We also compare the results of the proposed method with other existing methods, and discuss the results in detail in the following section.

Overall, the proposed method is designed to be a scalable solution for detecting fraudulent clicks, with a focus on achieving high performance, while also being easy to implement and maintain.

2.2   Data Description

In this study, we utilize the TalkingData AdTracking Fraud Detection dataset from Kaggle [12] to train and evaluate our proposed model. The dataset includes records of 200 million clicks, spanning over four days, and contains eight features. TalkingData is a well-established big data service platform in China that serves a majority of active mobile devices in the country. They process a large volume of data, including 3 billion clicks per day, with a significant portion of those clicks potentially being fraudulent. Table 1 provides a detailed description of the features available in the used dataset. The dataset contains eight different features, including the IP, App, Device, OS, Channel, click time, attributed time, and is Attributed.

The dataset consisting of 179,903,890 lines for training and 25,000,000 lines for testing. The test set follows chronologically from the train set, allowing us to accurately simulate a real-world scenario and avoid data leakage. We paid particular attention to reproducing a realistic environment in our experiments to ensure the validity and reliability of our results.

2.3   Imbalanced Data

Unbalanced datasets are a common problem in Machine Learning classification, where the number of samples in one category is much higher than in other

Table 1. Features description

Features	Format	Description
IP	int32	IP address of click
App	int16	App ID for marketing
Device	int16	Device type ID of user mobile phone
OS	int16	OS Version ID of user mobile phone
Channel	int16	Channel ID of mobile ad publisher
Click_Time	int8	Time Stamp of click (UTC)
Attributed_Time	int8	If user download the app for after clicking an ad, this is the time of the app download
Is_Attributed	bool	the target that is to be predicted, indicating the presence of fraud

categories. This can lead to classification algorithms tending to classify minority class samples as majority class samples, which can result in lower accuracy. In the case of click fraud datasets, which are often extremely unbalanced with less than 1% of clicks resulting in a desired outcome, oversampling and undersampling are commonly used strategies to balance the dataset. We focus on using the Random Under-Sampling (RUS) [11] technique as a means of addressing the imbalance in the dataset. RUS is an effective technique for handling imbalanced datasets by randomly removing samples from the majority class in order to reduce the imbalance. By removing samples from the majority class, RUS aims to balance the distribution of samples in the dataset and prevent the classifier from being dominated by the majority class. This technique has been chosen following the experimental results provided by a different work of ours that is undergoing a different submission process, which showed that this technique was particularly effective in handling datasets with a similar imbalance as the TalkingData dataset.

2.4   XGBoost Model

XGBoost [15] is a gradient boosting algorithm that is primarily used for supervised learning tasks such as classification and regression. The algorithm works by building an ensemble of decision trees, where each tree is trained to correct the errors made by the previous tree. The training process begins by fitting an initial decision tree to the data, and then, in subsequent iterations, new trees are added to the ensemble and trained to correct the residual errors made by the previous trees. The final predictions are then made by taking the average of the predictions from all the trees in the ensemble. XGBoost has several key features that make it a popular choice for machine learning tasks. Firstly, it uses a technique called gradient boosting [14] which is efficient and can handle large datasets. Secondly, it uses a technique called regularization which helps to prevent overfitting. Thirdly, it has several built-in parallel processing capabilities, which makes it highly scalable.

Here is a step-by-step explanation of the XGBoost:

1. Initialize the model: The first step is to initialize the model with a set of parameters such as the number of trees, the maximum depth of the trees, the learning rate, etc.
2. Create the first tree: The algorithm starts by creating a decision tree model on a sub-sample of the data, known as the "negative gradient" of the loss function.
3. Add more trees: The algorithm continues to add more trees to the model, with each tree trying to correct the mistakes made by the previous tree. The new trees are created by fitting to the negative gradient of the loss function, which is calculated from the residuals of the previous tree.
4. Update the model: As new trees are added to the model, the algorithm updates the model by combining the predictions of all the trees in the ensemble.
5. Repeat steps 2–4: The algorithm continues to repeat steps 2–4 until the specified number of trees is reached or a stopping criterion is met.
6. Make predictions: Once the model is trained, it can be used to make predictions on new data by taking the average of the predictions of all the trees in the ensemble.

Algorithm 1 can be summarizes the XGBoost process:

Algorithm 1. XGBoost Algorithm

1: **procedure** XGBoost
   Input: Traning data and hyper parameter
   Output: A trained model
2:     Initialize the model with a set of parameters
3:     Create the first tree
4:     **while** stopping criterion not met **do**
5:         Add more trees
6:         Update the model
7:     **end while**
8:     Make predictions
9: **end procedure**

2.5   Evaluation Metrics

In this work, we use the Receiver Operating Characteristic (ROC) curve and the Area Under the Curve (AUC) metric to evaluate the performance of the XGBoost model for detecting click fraud. The ROC curve is a graphical representation of the performance of a binary classifier as the discrimination threshold is varied. It plots the true positive rate (TPR) against the false positive rate (FPR) at different threshold settings. The AUC is the area under the ROC curve, and it represents the probability that a classifier will rank a randomly chosen positive sample higher than a randomly chosen negative sample.

AUC has the advantage of being independent of the classification threshold, making it useful for imbalanced datasets where the threshold is often adjusted to achieve a desired balance between precision and recall. AUC ranges from 0 to 1, where a value of 1 represents a perfect classifier and a value of 0.5 represents a random classifier. In this work, we aim to achieve an AUC value as close to 1 as possible, indicating that our model is able to effectively distinguish between fraudulent and non-fraudulent clicks.

The formula for AUC is given by:

$$AUC = \frac{1}{m} \sum_{i=1}^{m} [y_i = 1] \sum_{j=1}^{n} [y_j \neq 1] \frac{1}{C_i^2} \tag{1}$$

where y_i is the true label of the ith instance, m is the number of positive instances and n is the number of negative instances, and C_i is the number of negative instances.

Additionally, we also use $LogLoss$ as a metric. $LogLoss$ is a measure of the performance of a classifier that is commonly used when classes are imbalanced or when the cost of misclassification is different. $LogLoss$ is calculated as the logarithm of the likelihood of the true labels given a predicted probability. $LogLoss$ ranges from 0 to infinity, where 0 represent perfect predictions and increasing values represent worse predictions.

$$LogLoss = -\frac{1}{N} \sum_{i=1}^{N} y_i * log(p_i) + (1 - y_i) * log(1 - p_i) \tag{2}$$

where N is the number of instances, y_i is the true label of the ith instance, and p_i is the predicted probability of the ith instance.

By using these two metrics AUC and $LogLoss$, we are able to evaluate the performance of our model in different aspects and gain a more comprehensive understanding of its ability to detect click fraud.

AUC and Logloss metrics were chosen as they are widely used in binary classification problems, and were deemed to be the most optimal for our specific problem of detecting fraudulent clicks. AUC measures the ability of the model to distinguish between positive and negative examples, while Logloss penalizes models that are overconfident in their predictions. We did not use metrics such as F1-score, precision, recall, or accuracy as they do not take into account the trade-off between false positives and false negatives, which is critical in click fraud detection. Additionally, these metrics do not provide a comprehensive view of the model's performance, especially in cases where the class distribution is highly imbalanced.

2.6   Normalization

In this study, the data normalization process is applied to adjust the feature values to a common scale. This is done to ensure that the features do not have an undue influence on the model due to their varying ranges. This is particularly important when the ranges of the features are vastly different. Normalizing the data can also help to improve the performance of many machine learning algorithms and can also speed up the training process.

The normalization process involves converting the values of numeric columns in the dataset to a common scale while preserving the relative differences between values. The formula used to normalize a specific feature X is as follows:

$$x' = (X - X_{mean})/(X_{max} - X_{min}) \tag{3}$$

where X_{mean} is the mean value of the feature, X_{max} is the maximum value of the feature, and X_{min} is the minimum value of the feature. This formula is used to calculate the normalized value of the feature, which is represented by x'.

2.7 Data-Split

In this study, we use Stratified KFold [16] cross-validation with $K = 5$ to split the dataset, ensuring that the sample category ratio is retained while dividing the entire training dataset into five independent subgroups. For each split, four-fifths of the dataset are used as the training set, while the remaining one-fifth serves as the test set. This process is repeated i times, $(i = 1, ..., 5)$, and the AUC metric is calculated on the ith test set, as described in [18]. After the cross-validation, we re-run our model on the test dataset to verify that our model does not overfit on our training data.

3   Experiment and Analysis

In this section, we present the results of our experimentation to evaluate the effectiveness of the proposed methodologies and models. The experiments were conducted on an Amazon Web Services (AWS) SageMaker instance with 8 vCPUs and 16 GB RAM, using Python 3.9.11 and its packages such as Pandas, Numpy, and Sklearn. The aim of this section is to provide a detailed analysis of the results obtained and to compare the performance of the proposed methodologies with other existing methods.

3.1   Feature Engineering

In this study, we applied feature engineering techniques to extract new features from the raw data. By leveraging our domain expertise, we were able to identify and extract characteristics, properties, and attributes from the data that were not immediately apparent. One of the major features used for categorization in the dataset was IP, so we combined it with one or two other attributes to create a dataset with more diverse and informative features (Table 2).

Additionally, the "attributed_time" column was removed and the "click time" column was separated into separate day and hour columns. This allowed us to improve the properties of the dataset and potentially improve the performance of our model.

Table 2. Engineered features description

Features	Format	Description
ipCountPerHour	int16	Count of similar IPs with the same hour
countIpApp	int16	Count of the unique combination of IP and App
countIpAppOs	int16	Count of the unique combination of IP and App and OS

3.2 Hyper Parameter Tuning

In order to optimize the performance of our XGBoost model, we implemented a technique called Hyperparameter Tuning. We used GridSearchCV, which is a method of searching for the optimal set of hyperparameters that results in the best performance of the model. The process of GridSearchCV involves specifying a set of hyperparameters and their possible values, and then training and evaluating the model for each combination of hyperparameters. In our case, we used a list of hyperparameters such as 'min_child_weight', 'gamma', 'subsample', 'colsample_bytree', 'max_depth', 'num_boost_round' and 'learning_rate' with specific range of values for each. This allowed us to systematically explore different combinations of hyperparameters and select the set that resulted in the best performance of the model, thus improving the accuracy and efficiency of the XGBoost algorithm. And the result of the grid search landed on these parameters:

- gamma : 1.0
- max_depth: 5,
- min_child_weight: 1,
- num_boost_round : 500
- learning_rate: 0.2

These parameters were used to train the final model and were found to provide the best results on the test dataset.

It is worth noting that grid search can be a time-consuming process, and this can impact the overall performance of the system. Specifically, the time required to execute a grid search depends on the size of the search space, which can increase rapidly with the number of hyperparameters and the range of values. As a result, a very large search space could lead to grid search taking an impractical amount of time to complete.

Despite the potential drawbacks and limitations of grid search, it remains a very useful method for hyperparameter tuning, especially when the practitioner has the necessary computational resources and time to execute it.

Moreover, the selection of hyperparameters based on previous experience and empirical results, as well as the practitioner's expertise in choosing the hyperparameter space to search, can help to minimize the computational cost and time required for grid search. In this way, grid search can still be an effective and practical method for hyperparameter tuning in a wide range of machine learning applications, including the prediction of click fraud using XGBoost.

3.3   Experiment Results

When it comes to machine learning, there is no single algorithm that is guaranteed to work in every situation. Instead, it is crucial to explore different algorithms and evaluate their performance using various metrics. In this section, we compare the XGBoost algorithm with other popular machine learning algorithms, such as logistic regression, decision tree, and random forest. Additionally, we also compare the proposed boosting algorithm with other established algorithms that have been used in similar studies in the literature, to see how it performs in comparison. This allows us to gain a better understanding of the strengths and weaknesses of the XGBoost algorithm and determine its suitability for a given task. By comparing XGBoost with other algorithms, we can also identify which algorithm performs best under different conditions and with different types of data.

To evaluate the performance of the different algorithms, we use two metrics: the AUC Score and $LogLoss$. The closer the AUC score is to 1, the better the algorithm will be. The results of the comparison are shown in Table 3, where we find that XGBoost reaches an AUC score of 0.96. The performance of the Random Forest algorithm is the closest to that of XGBoost among the algorithms compared.

Table 3. AUC and $LogLoss$ comparison to classical machine learning algorithms

	XGBoost	Logistic regression	Decision tree	Random forest
AUC	**0.96**	0.81	0.86	0.94
$LogLoss$	**0.15**	0.53	4.00	0.21

From Table 3, it is clear that our model compared to the rest of the learners performs better. While just from a first look to Table 4, it is clear that the proposed work does not perform significantly better then the other models in fact the result is basically the same as the ETCF model in terms of AUC.

Table 4. AUC Comparison To Previous Work

	SVM [17]	ETCF [17]	Proposed Model
AUC	0.93	0.96	**0.96**

From a first look in Table 4 it seems that our approach perform just as well to the ETCF model, we will discuss the meaning such result in the next secession.

4   Discussion

Based on the results presented in the previous section, it is clear that the XGBoost algorithm outperforms the other algorithms in terms of both AUC and $LogLoss$. With an AUC of 0.96 and a $LogLoss$ of 0.15, the XGBoost algorithm demonstrates the highest level of accuracy and lowest level of error.

In comparison, the logistic regression algorithm has an AUC of 0.81 and a $LogLoss$ of 0.53, indicating that it is less accurate and more prone to error than XGBoost. The decision tree algorithm has an AUC of 0.86 and a $LogLoss$ of 4.00, which is also lower than the XGBoost algorithm.

The Random Forest algorithm is the closest competitor to XGBoost, with an AUC of 0.94 and a $LogLoss$ of 0.21. While it is still not as accurate as XGBoost, it is still a good choice for certain types of problems.

Overall, these results suggest that the XGBoost algorithm is a suitable choice for classification problems with imbalanced data, particularly when the goal is to accurately identify fraudulent clicks. The results also highlights the importance of carefully preprocessing the data and avoiding data leakage in order to achieve the best possible results. It is worth noting that we performed hyperparameter tuning on the XGBoost algorithm using grid search, also helped to optimize the performance of the model even further.

We also compared our work to available literature, and from a first look it seems to perform similar to ETCF [17]. It is hypothesized that the difference in results between this work and previous work is primarily attributed to the preprocessing step. Specifically, the care taken in this work to ensure that the test set accurately emulates a real-world environment, as opposed to previous work where data leakage may have occurred due to the preprocessing and generation of new variables using the entire dataset prior to the train/test split. Additionally, it is hypothesized that the use of randomly selected rows for the test data in previous work, rather than the last rows of the original data, may have also contributed to the discrepancy in results.

It is true that some of the results may appear to be similar, and it may be tempting to question the value of this research. However, it is important to note that even a small improvement in AUC can lead to significant real-world benefits. Furthermore, our approach has been shown to be more stable, as evidenced by the better $logloss$. This suggests that our model is better able to handle the complexity of the data and make more accurate predictions. Additionally, our approach places a strong emphasis on reproducing a realistic setting in order to avoid data leakage and accurately mimic the distribution of the original data. This is an important consideration when evaluating the performance of a model in a real-world scenario.

5   Conclusion

In conclusion, this paper presented a click fraud prediction classification approach based on the XGBoost algorithm. The key contributions of this work include the use of feature engineering and preprocessing to capitalize on the usefulness of available data, the use of GridSearch to optimize the hyperparameters of the used algorithms, and the comparison of XGBoost with other classical machine learning models such as Random Forest, Logistic Regression, and Decision Tree. The results suggest that XGBoost outperforms all the other learners, with Random Forest being the closest in terms of performance.

It is important to note that although the difference in performance between XGBoost and other algorithms may seem small, a slight improvement in AUC can lead to a significant impact in real-world applications. Additionally, our approach was found to be more stable, as demonstrated by the better $LogLoss$ results.

In future research, we plan to apply our approach to other click fraud datasets, and explore the possibility of combining it with other algorithms to create an ensemble technique that could even outperform the current work. Another direction we could take is to explore CTR prediction data as it is closely related to click fraud in terms of structure. Overall, this work highlights the importance of feature engineering and preprocessing in improving the performance of machine learning models for click fraud prediction.

Software Implementation

The code for our implementation is available at: https://github.com/NadirSahllal/Forecasting-Click-Fraud-via-Machine-Learning-Algorithms

References

1. Digital advertising soared 35% to $189 billion in 2021 according to the IAB Internet Advertising Revenue Report. Retrieved 15 June 2022 (2022). https://www.iab.com/news/digital-advertising-soared-35-to-189-billion-in-2021-according-to-the-iab-internet-advertising-revenue-report/
2. Fourberg, N., et al.; Online Advertising: The Impact of Targeted Advertising on Advertisers, Market Access and Consumer Choice (2021). https://www.europarl.europa.eu/thinktank/en/document.html?reference=IPOL_STU%282021%29662913
3. Thejas, G.S., Boroojeni, K.G., Chandna, K., Bhatia, I., Iyengar, S.S., Sunitha, N.R.: Deep Learning-based model to fight against Ad click fraud. In; Proceedings of the 2019 ACM Southeast Conference. ACM SE 2019. ACM (2019). https://doi.org/10.1145/3299815.3314453
4. GS, T., Soni, J., Chandna, K., Iyengar, S.S., Sunitha, N.R., Prabakar, N.: Learning-based model to fight against fake like clicks on instagram posts. In: 2019 SoutheastCon. IEEE (2019). https://doi.org/10.1109/southeastcon42311.2019.9020533
5. Thejas, G.S., et al.: A multi-time-scale time series analysis for click fraud forecasting using binary labeled imbalanced dataset. In: 2019 4th International Conference on Computational Systems and Information Technology for Sustainable Solution (CSITSS). IEEE (2019). https://doi.org/10.1109/csitss47250.2019.9031036

6. Crussell, J., Stevens, R., Chen, H.: MAdFraud. In: Proceedings of the 12th Annual International Conference on Mobile Systems, Applications, and Services. MobiSys 2014. ACM (2014). https://doi.org/10.1145/2594368.2594391

7. Kwon, J., Kim, J., Lee, J., Lee, H., Perrig, A.: PsyBoG: power spectral density analysis for detecting botnet groups. In: 2014 9th International Conference on Malicious and Unwanted Software: The Americas (MALWARE). IEEE (2014). https://doi.org/10.1109/malware.2014.6999414

8. Kantardzic, M., Walgampaya, C., Yampolskiy, R., Joung Woo, R.: Click fraud prevention via multimodal evidence fusion by Dempster-Shafer theory. In: 2010 IEEE Conference on Multisensor Fusion and Integration for Intelligent Systems (MFI 2010). IEEE (2010). https://doi.org/10.1109/mfi.2010.5604480

9. Ge, L., Kantardzic, M., King, D.: CCFDP: collaborative click fraud detection and prevention system. In: 18th International Conference on Computer Application in Industry and Engineering - CAINE 2005, Honolulu (2005)

10. Iqbal, M.S., Zulkernine, M., Jaafar, F., Gu, Y.: FCFraud: fighting click-fraud from the user side. In: 2016 IEEE 17th International Symposium on High Assurance Systems Engineering (HASE). IEEE (2016). https://doi.org/10.1109/hase.2016.17

11. Batista, G.E., Prati, R.C., Monard, M.C.: A study of the behavior of several methods for balancing machine learning training data. ACM SIGKDD Explor. Newsl. 6(1), 20–29 (2004). https://doi.org/10.1145/1007730.1007735

12. Talkingdata Adtracking Fraud Detection Challenge. https://www.kaggle.com/competitions/talkingdata-adtracking-fraud-detection/data. Accessed 24 June 2022

13. Bergstra, J., Bengio, Y.: Random search for hyper-parameter optimization. J. Mach. Learn. Res. 13, 281–305 (2012)

14. Friedman, J. H.: Greedy function approximation: a gradient boosting machine. Ann. Stat. 29(5), 1189–1232 (2001). https://www.jstor.org/stable/2699986

15. Chen, T., Guestrin, C.: XGBoost. In: Proceedings of the 22nd ACM SIGKDD International Conference on Knowledge Discovery and Data Mining. KDD 2016. ACM (2016). https://doi.org/10.1145/2939672.2939785

16. Urbanowicz, R.J., Moore, J.H.: The application of Michigan-style learning classifiersystems to address genetic heterogeneity and epistasisin association studies. In: Proceedings of the 12th Annual Conference on Genetic and Evolutionary Computation. GECCO 2010. ACM (2010). https://doi.org/10.1145/1830483.1830518

17. Qiu, X., Zuo, Y., Liu, G.: ETCF: an ensemble model for CTR prediction. In: 2018 15th International Conference on Service Systems and Service Management (ICSSSM), pp. 1–5 (2018). https://doi.org/10.1109/ICSSSM.2018.8465044

18. Stone, M.: Cross-validatory choice and assessment of statistical predictions. J. Roy. Stat. Soc. Ser. B (Methodol.) 36(2), 111–147 (1974). https://www.jstor.org/stable/2984809

An Enhanced Anonymous ECC-Based Authentication for Lightweight Application in TMIS

Hind Idrissi[1,2(✉)] and Mohammed Ennahbaoui[2,3]

[1] National School of Applied Sciences of Khouribga (ENSAK),
Sultan Moulay Slimane University, Khouribga, Morocco
hind.idr@gmail.com
[2] LabMIA-SI, Faculty of Sciences, Mohammed V University in Rabat,
Rabat, Morocco
[3] High-Tech School of Rabat, Rabat, Morocco

Abstract. Technology has always had a significant role in medicine. Modern advancements in technology has revolutionized the health industry and totally changed the way we currently undertake healthcare. Telecare medicine information system (TMIS) is among the best new technological innovations shaping the medical field and taking its digitization to another logical step. It has made distance redundant and enabled patients to consult with specialists practically anywhere on the globe, which can be a lifesaver in emergency situations where immediate care is required. However, within TMISs, personal and sensitive information about patients and health professionals are exchanged over public networks and may be subject to several security attacks. Therefore, a wide variety of schemes have been proposed in literature to deal with user authentication and key agreement issues, yet, the majority of these works fail to achieve the essential security features. In this paper, we first provide a review of Ostad-Sharif et al. scheme and demonstrate its vulnerability to key compromise password and key compromise impersonation attacks. Consequently, to cover these security weaknesses, a robust mutual and anonymous three-factor authentication scheme with key agreement protocol is proposed for lightweight application in TMISs. Proof of security is given through an informal security analysis and a formal security verification using AVISPA. Our performance evaluation reveals that the proposed scheme is cost efficient in terms of computation, communication, storage and network impact overheads, as compared to other related recent schemes.

Keywords: TMIS · Security · Three-Factor Authentication · Key Agreement · ECC · Anonymity

1 Introduction

Nowadays, the world is witnessing a rapid emergence of phenomena like: growth of aging population, pollution, epidemics and pandemics, which causes an increase in the rate of illnesses and chronic diseases requiring a rapid intervention along with long-term care and frequent follow-up with hospitals, clinics and laboratories. This absolutely induces excessive effort, money and stress on patients, that find it difficult to take appointments in time, perform repeated trips to the healthcare center for treatment, and further, wait in queues for long time. At the other side, healthcare professionals are facing serious troubles: a growing request for better, cheaper and broader medical services, a need for costly infrastructure, a rising labor costs and staff shortages. Accordingly, we need a smart ecosystem that can guarantee remote and regular monitoring along with health management, so that patients may receive distant and home-based medical care, while affording facilities, data organization and less strained climate for health professionals.

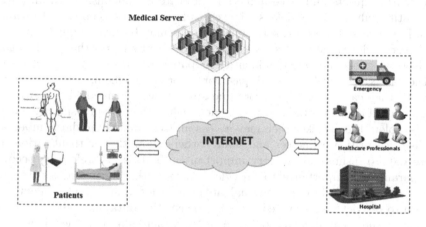

Fig. 1. Global Architecture of TMIS

Healthcare sector has recently drawn a wide interest from researchers and professionals owing to its complex nature and fast progress. With the advent of various advanced technologies such as Internet of Things (IoT) and 5G wireless communication, users are now able to exchange huge amounts of data freely and rapidly. The current outstanding digital revolution has promoted the information technology in several fields, of which healthcare is a part and necessitates certainly to keep up in the pace. Actually, health industry is changing to a hole new level with the widespread of new smart devices, on-body sensors, ingestibles and many other innovative medical equipment; all that working within broad connectivity and extensive centralization in order to improve care delivery and provide remote monitoring and treatment. Telecare medicine information systems (TMISs) are among the phenomenal recent achievements that allow patients and healthcare providers to share and access medical data and services anywhere and anytime via the Internet. They bring more convenience as they reduce patient's stress and expenses due to travel, hospitalization and readmission. Moreover, TMIS store patient's electronic medical records (EMR) in their servers, which enables doctors and medical professionals to retrieve patient's information, thus, make precise diagnosis, make appropriate decisions and prescribe accurate treatment.

Generally, a common architecture of TMISs includes four main entities: Patients, Health Providers, Medical Server and Internet, as illustrated in Fig. 1. However, since all communications and data exchanges happen through Internet which has an open nature, TMISs are subject to several security attacks and breaches. For example, an intruder may intercept the messages exchanged between the patient and his doctor, then modify them -which can put the patient's life in a real danger- or capture the sensitive information of the patient, such as his personal profile, device information, vital signs, medical history, payment information, etc; then uses them to ask for ransoms. At the server-side, multiple patients and medical professionals access the medical server at the same time. This can lead to denial of service situations, as an intruder may burden the server with requests and force it to communicate continuously with an authorized entity, which causes delays, or even outages, in responding to legitimate users. Even worse than that, sometimes attacks may be carried out from inside the server by legitimate users (patients or health providers) that exploit their privileges to guess the patient's identity or password. Moreover, a great deal of internet users keep utilizing weak passwords for easy remembrance, but unfortunately, they can undergo password guessing attack which could be performed in polynomial time. Another security issue is when the patient's smart device or card is stolen, the attacker then may access all the confidential data embedded.

These security weaknesses and many others show that authentication and secure data transmission are very important in TMISs. Therefore, it becomes of a paramount importance to provide TMISs with robust and secure solutions that ensure lightweight mutual authentication and key agreement with the aim to restrict unauthorized accesses to sensitive data maintained by medical servers and communicated between different actors and entities. It is worth to notice that most of authentication schemes in the literature regarding security of TMISs are two-factor authentications using password and identity. However, these schemes still suffer from various security limitations and weaknesses such as offline and online guessing password attack, privileged insider attack, stolen smart device/card attack, key compromise password attack, etc. In order to deal with these weaknesses and strengthen the ecosystem security, it is now recommended to develop authentication schemes with a third robust factor besides identity and password.

1.1   Threat Model

In this paper, we are following the two well-known threat models: Dolev-Yao (DY) threat model [3] and Canetti & Krawczyk (CK) adversary model [4], in which all communicating entities transmit the messages over an unsecured channel. An adversary attempts to take control over communication and data, and may be viewed as a hacker, an insider attacker, an untrusted third party or a malware robot. In order to highlight the adversary's capacity over the authentication scheme, some assumptions may be considered:

- An adversary may be aware of the authentication procedure and can take total control over the public channel;
- An adversary can eavesdrop communication, modify, delete, corrupt or replay any transmitted message via a public channel;
- An adversary may be a legitimate patient or vice versa;
- An adversary can steal the smart device/card of a legitimate patient, then, retrieve sensitive and personal data stored inside it;
- An adversary may compromise with a scanner device or directly with the patient's smart device in order to get precise information. For example, he/she can install a malicious software on the smart phone belonging to the patient, and transfer sensitive information to her/his node;
- However, an adversary is not able to intercept messages transmitted over a secure channel.

1.2 Motivation and Contribution

There are several works in the literature addressing security issues in TMISs. Unfortunately, a large amount of these schemes are found not suitable for healthcare application as they do not meet maximum security requirements and show high computational complexity with less scalability. Following, the main contributions in this work:

- A review and crypatanalysis of Ostad-Sharif et al.'s scheme [1] is provided to prove its vulnerability to two among the most harmful-attacks in the field: key compromise impersonation and key compromise password guessing.
- A robust mutual and anonymous authentication scheme with key agreement protocol has been proposed for lightweight application in smart healthcare to provide security against well-known attacks. The scheme provides three-factor authentication and makes use of elliptic curve cryptography (ECC), zero-knowledge protocol and Biometrics which are very hard to guess or forge and cannot be stolen, lost or copied.
- An informal security analysis regarding the various security features of the proposed scheme is provided.
- A formal security verification using the popular AVISPA simulator tool have been conducted to prove the correctness of our scheme and its resilience to various known attacks.
- At last, a comparison of the proposed scheme with recent existing schemes in literature is also carried out in terms of security features as well as communication, computation, storage and network throughput overheads.

1.3 Paper Organization

The rest of the paper is organized as follows. Section 2 investigates the recent existing related works in this field. Section 3 provides a review and security analysis of Ostad-Sharif et al.'s scheme [1]. In Sect. 4, the proposed scheme is rigorously described. Section 5 presents an informal security analysis of the proposed scheme against various attacks, while a formal security verification using AVISPA is discussed in Sect. 6. Our scheme is compared with other related schemes in terms of security features as well as communication, computation, storage and network throughput costs. The results of performance comparison are provided in Sect. 7. Finally, in Sect. 8, concluding remarks are given along with perspectives.

2   Related Works

In this section, we present a state-of-art of the recent security schemes dealing with authentication aspect in healthcare systems.

In 2018, Dhillon et al. [5] proposed an authentication protocol based on ECC for remote patient monitoring in Cloud-IoT environments. Their protocol dealing with prime security requirements (authentication, confidentiality and anonymity) makes use of three identity factors (biometrics, password and smart card), elliptic curve cryptography (ECC) and cloud-IoT network. Their approach was proved to be vulnerable to many attacks like DOS, stolen verifier and CS compromised attacks.

Ali et al. [6] first reviewed the user authentication scheme of Li et al. [7], then reported its ineffectiveness to withstand a wide range of offensive threats such as: user impersonation, privileged insider attack, password guessing attacks and smartcard theft. To provide resistance against these attacks and improve security in E-healthcare systems, Ali et al. [6] proposed a biometric-based remote user authentication scheme, and used BAN logic and random oracle model to validate their approach, which is proved to be vulnerable to MITM attack.

Srinivas et al. [8] presented a cloud-centric authentication method for wearable healthcare devices and medical data. Their scheme provided session-key security and demonstrated protection against active attacks such as replay, MIM attack and impersonation attack, but, did not resist smart device stolen attack.

Challa et al. [9] first reviewed Liu et al. [10] authentication scheme, and showed that it failed to provide proper mutual authentication and to resist attacks, such as stolen smart card, password guessing, privileged insider and user impersonation attacks. To overcome these security limitations, Challa et al. [9] designed a provably secure ECC-based three factor authentication (smartcard, user password and user biometrics) and key agreement protocol for WSN. Unfortunately, the security analysis proved that this scheme cannot ensure perfect forward secrecy (PFS) for secure communication.

Li et al. [11] introduced an original mutual authentication protocol endowed with anonymity to be employed in three-tier healthcare frameworks adopting wearables. Using BAN logic tool, the security analysis of the scheme shows it resists various types of attack, including impersonation, replay and MITM attack, but not protected against smart device stolen attack.

Amin et al. [12] proposed an architecture for patient monitoring health-care system in wireless medical sensors networks (WMSN) and then designed an anonymity-preserving mutual authentication protocol for mobile users. Ali et al. [13] first analyzed Amin et al. [12] scheme and pointed out that few security

features were available, such as off-line password guessing attack, user impersonation attack, known session-key temporary information attack, the revelation of
secret parameters, and identity guessing attack. To overcome the above vulnerabilities, Ali et al. [13] have proposed an enhanced three-factor based remote user
authentication protocol in wireless medical sensors networks (WMSNs) for heal-
htcare monitoring environments. The authors performed formal and informal
security analysis to validate their scheme's security, yet after all, their scheme
could not support Perfect Forward Secrecy (PFS).

In 2019, Chandrakar [14] designed a secure two-factor based remote authentication protocol for monitoring healthcare using wireless medical sensors networks (WMSNs). The authors used BAN logic to prove that the protocol provides session key agreement and mutual authentication securely, while resistance
to passive and attacks is validated through AVISPA tool. However, a detailed
description of the provided HLPSL file shows the vulnerability of the protocol
to MIM attack.

Liu et al. [15] proposed a privacy-preserving ECC-based mutual authentication scheme to ensure secure remote user authentication for mobile Edge-Cloud
architecture in Telecare Medical Information System (TMIS). This scheme supports patients (edge-servers) anonymity and forward-backward untraceability,
but, lacks user pre-verification and shows from excessive overhead.

Renuka et al. [16] first reviewed the authentication protocol proposed by He
et al.'s [17] for consumer USB mass storage devices and demonstrated that it
is prone to many attacks, basically forward/backward secrecy attacks, replay
attack and session specific information leakage attacks. With the aim to get over
the above vulnerabilities, Renuka et al. [16] presented a biometrics ECC-based
authentication protocol for application in healthcare systems taking benefit from
USB features. However, their scheme excessively exploits resources, raises latency
and does not support untraceability and pre-verification.

Sharma and Kalra [18] proposed a lightweight and secure hash function-based
authentication approach to be integrated with smart environments based remote
patient monitoring service model. Their approach was proved to satisfy all security requirements, and confirmed using AVISPA tool to resist most of active
and passive attacks. However, it does not achieve anonymity and untraceability, whereas it is also prone to threats like node compromise attack and insider
attack.

Gupta et al. [19] presented a lightweight anonymous user authentication and
key establishment scheme for wearable sensing devices in the TMIS. In order to
share a common session key among wearable devices and terminals, their proposed protocol simply employs primitive operations like hash and bitwise XOR.
Thus, it does not require a secure channel and shows high scalability. The formal
security verification using AVISPA attested the resilience of the protocol against
a wide range of well-known attacks, but, demonstrated in parallel that it is unsafe
facing various active attacks such as privileged-insider attack, desynchronization
attack and compromise sensors attacks.

Sharif et al. [1] first reviewed Amin et al. [20], Giri et al. [21] and Arshad et al. [22] authentication schemes, and demonstrated that they are all vulnerable to key compromise impersonation attack, in addition to the replay attack, the offline password guessing attack and non-support of perfect forward secrecy (PFS). To cover these security issues and build secure communication channels in TMIS, Sharif et al. [1] proposed a new efficient and trustworthy solution based on two-factor user authentication along with a session key agreement protocol. Their scheme is primarily based on elliptic curve cryptography and proved to be secure against several attacks, notably replay attack, session-specific temporary information attack and stolen smart card and mobile device attack. Unfortunately, a cryptanalysis being conducted on their scheme demonstrated that it cannot resist Man-in-The-Middle attack, key compromise password guessing attack and key compromise impersonation attack. This will be thoroughly discussed in the next section.

In 2020, Kumari et al. [23] proposed an ECC-based secure and efficient authentication framework for cloud-assisted smart medical system (SMS). They showed that their framework is secure against most of security attacks, such as MITM attack, impersonation attack, data non-repudiation, doctor anonymity, replay attack, known-key security property, message authentication, patient anonymity, data confidentiality, stolen-verifier attack, parallel session attack and session key security. However, it did not resist privileged insider attack and cloud server compromise attack.

Alzahrani et al. [24] first analyzed the work of Sharma and Kalra [18] and discovered that it is vulnerable to stolen smart card, session key compromise, and user impersonation attacks. In view of those drawbacks, Alzahrani et al. [24] have designed an efficient authentication protocol for remote patient health monitoring. The security features of the proposed protocol have been validated using BAN logic-based formal security analysis. Nonetheless, it fails to resist DoS and cloud server compromise attacks.

Dharminder et al. [25] presented a construction of an RSA based authentication scheme for authorized access to healthcare services and achieves desirable key attributes of authentication protocols. However, it is found that their scheme is not suitable for smart healthcare, because RSA based cryptosystem is not lightweight.

Sureshkumar et al. [26] designed a suitable architecture for smart healthcare systems involving a robust mutual authentication protocol with key establishment feature using chaotic map.

Many other schemes and protocols have been proposed recently and still in phase of evaluation by the community. In view of the above literature review and the investigations being conducted on existing schemes, we believe that healthcare systems and TMIS are still vulnerable to different security attacks. This motivates us to design and propose a new lightweight mutual authentication scheme for application in healthcare systems, and which can provide most of security features required.

3 Review and Cryptanalysis of Ostad-Sharif et al.'s Scheme

In this section, we first present an overview of Ostad-Sharif et al.'s scheme [1]. Then, we show through a cryptanalysis process proposed by Kumari et al. [2] that this scheme is vulnerable to two serious attacks: key compromise impersonation and key compromise password guessing.

3.1 Review of Ostad-Sharif et al.'s Scheme

The notations being used in Ostad-Sharif et al.'s protocol are listed in Table 1. Their protocol is composed of patient registration phase, login and authentication phase, illustrated respectively in Figs. 2 and 3, and then password change phase. To benefit from remote medical services, every patient should first register with the server, such that necessary login information are exchanged over a reliable channel. Once the registration process is completed, a common session key can be shared between the server and the patient through an authentication mechanism. Then, the agreed key may be utilized to secure their upcoming exchanges.

Table 1. Notations used in Ostad-Sharif et al.'s Scheme [1]

Notation	Description
ID_s	Server's Identity
ID_m	Mobile Device's Identity
ID_p	Patient's Identity
PW_p	Patient's Password
s	Private key of the server
r_s, x_s	Server's randoms
r_p, u_p, x_p	Patient's randoms
E	Elliptic curve
P	Base point of elliptic curve
$E_k(.)/D_k(.)$	Symmetric-key encryption/decryption using k
SK	Shared session key
T_p	Current timestamp
$h_0(.), h_1(.), h_2(.)$	Hash functions
$\|$	Concatenation
$\oplus$	XOR operation

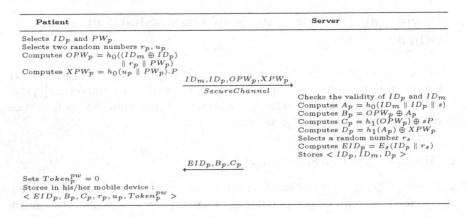

Patient	Server
Selects ID_p and PW_p	
Selects two random numbers r_p, u_p	
Computes $OPW_p = h_0((ID_m \oplus ID_p)$	
$\parallel r_p \parallel PW_p)$	
Computes $XPW_p = h_0(u_p \parallel PW_p).P$	

Patient → Server (over $SecureChannel$): ID_m, ID_p, OPW_p, XPW_p

Server computes:
- Checks the validity of ID_p and ID_m
- Computes $A_p = h_0(ID_m \parallel ID_p \parallel s)$
- Computes $B_p = OPW_p \oplus A_p$
- Computes $C_p = h_1(OPW_p) \oplus sP$
- Computes $D_p = h_1(A_p) \oplus XPW_p$
- Selects a random number r_s
- Computes $EID_p = E_s(ID_p \parallel r_s)$
- Stores $< ID_p, ID_m, D_p >$

Server → Patient: EID_p, B_p, C_p

Patient:
- Sets $Token_p^{pw} = 0$
- Stores in his/her mobile device : $< EID_p, B_p, C_p, r_p, u_p, Token_p^{pw} >$

Fig. 2. Registration Phase of Ostad-Sharif et al.'s Scheme [1]

3.2   Cryptanalysis of Ostad-Sharif et al.'s Scheme

Kumari et al. [2] have demonstrated that Ostad-Sharif at al.'s Scheme suffers from the key compromise password guessing attack and the key compromise impersonation attack. We present in the following how these attacks may happen according to [2].

Key Compromise Password Guessing Attack. Assume an adversary (A) holds the compromised secret key of the server s and procures the patient's device p. (A) can acquire the parameters $\{EID_p, B_p, C_p, r_p, u_p, Token_p^{pw}\}$ stored inside the mobile device. Then, (A) can guess the password of the patient in one of the following ways.

- (A) computes $(ID_p \parallel r_s) = D_s(EID_p)$ to obtain ID_p, tries to guess ID_m^* as the identity of the patient's mobile device. Then, (A) computes $A_p^* = h_0(ID_m^* \parallel ID_p \parallel s)$, $OPW_p^* = B_p \oplus A_p^*$, $h_1(OPW_p^*) = h_1(OPW_p) = C_p \oplus sP$, whence P is a public parameter. At this point, (A) compares $h_1(OPW_p^*)$ and $h_1(OPW_p)$, if they are equal, then the adversary (A) have successfully guessed the value of ID_m^*, else, he tries with other guess. It is worth to mention that with a correct ID_m, (A) also possesses the correct OPW_p and A_p. The next steps for (A) is to guess PW_p^* for possible patient's password, and compute $OPW_p^{**} = h_0((ID_m \oplus ID_p) \parallel r_p \parallel PW_p^*)$, such that r_p can be retrieved from the mobile device. If OPW_p^{**} and OPW_p are equal, then (A) have correctly guessed PW_p^*, else, he tries with another guess.
- Otherwise, (A) can obtain the exact value of ID_m from the server's database (S) where are stored $< ID_p, ID_m, Empty, D_p >$. With ID_p available, (A) computes $(ID_p \parallel r_s) = D_s(EID_p)$ and can easily select the entry $\{ID_p, ID_m, D_p\}$ relative to the patient from the stolen registration table of the server database. Afterwards, (A) guesses PW_p^* for possible patient's password, computes $A_p = h_0(ID_m^* \parallel ID_p \parallel s)$, $OPW_p = B_p \oplus A_p$. Then,

Patient/Mobile Device	Server

Fig. 3. Login and Authentication Phase of Ostad-Sharif et al.'s Scheme [1]

(A) computes $OPW_p^* = h_0((ID_m \oplus ID_p) \parallel r_p \parallel PW_p^*)$, whence r_p is available from the mobile device. If OPW_p^* and OPW_p are equal, then (A) have correctly guessed PW_p^*, else, he tries with another guess. Moreover, (A) can also compute $XPW_p = h_1(A_p) \oplus D_p$, $XPW_p^* = h_0(u_p \parallel PW_p^*)P$ whence u_p is available in the mobile device. At this point, (A) compares XPW_p^* and XPW_p, if they are equal, then (A) have correctly guessed PW_p^*, else, he tries with another guess.

Key Compromise Impersonation Attack. Assume an adversary (A) holds the compromised secret key of the server s. He can intercept the login message $\{Token_p^{pw}, EID_p, X_p, V_p, V_p^{pw}, T_p\}$ of the patient from public channel and find the value of $Token_p^{pw}$. (A) computes $(ID_p \parallel r_s) = D_s(EID_p)$ and obtains $\{ID_p, ID_m, D_p\}$ from the stolen registration table of the server database. Afterwards, (A) computes $A_p = h_0(ID_m \parallel ID_p \parallel s)$, produces a random number

x_{ep} and calculates $X_{ep} = h_0(ID_m \parallel ID_p \parallel x_{ep})P$ where P is a public parameter. If $Token_p^{pw} == 0$, (A) computes $V_{ep} = h_0(A_p \parallel X_{ep} \parallel sP \parallel T_{ep} \parallel Token_p^{pw})$ with T_{ep} is the current timestamp. Else if $Token_p^{pw} \geq 1$, (A) computes $XPW_p = h_1(A_p) \oplus D_p$ and $V_{ep}^{pw} = h_0(A_p \parallel X_{ep} \parallel sP \parallel T_{ep} \parallel XPW_p \parallel Token_p^{pw})$. To behave as the legitimate patient P, (A) sends $\{Token_p^{pw}, EID_p, X_{ep}, V_{ep}, V_{ep}^{pw}, T_{ep}\}$ as a login message to the server S. Obviously, the server will consider the received login message as T_{ep} is the current timestamp; EID_p involves the valid identities of the patient (ID_p), the mobile device (ID_m) and the fresh random r_s; further V_{ep} and V_{ep}^{pw} are computed with exact server key s according to the value of $Token_p^{pw}$, valid value of A_p and X_p have also being sent. Consequently, the server must trust that the received message is from the legal patient, and the adversary comes to impersonate as a legitimate patient.

4   Proposed Scheme

As demonstrated in the previous section, Ostad-Sharif et al.'s scheme [1] fails to achieve total security requirements. As result, we present an enhanced anonymous authentication and key agreement protocol providing robust security features to resist the aforementioned attacks. Our solution comprises basically three phases: patient registration, login and authentication, and makes use of elliptic curve cryptography along with a zero-knowledge protocol based on challenge-response commitment, in order to achieve key agreement and authentication without disclosing personal information during data exchanges. Table 2 lists the important notations to be used in the proposed scheme.

Table 2. Notations used in the Proposed Scheme

Notation	Description
ID_s	Server's Identity
ID_m	Mobile Device's Identity
ID_p	Patient's Identity
BID_p	Patient's Biometric Identity
PW_p	Patient's Password
x_s	Private key of server
x_p	Private key of patient
j, q_s	Server's Randoms
r_p, u_p, w_p, i, n_p	Patient's Randoms
E	Elliptic curve
P	Base point of elliptic curve
$Enc_k(.)/Dec_k(.)$	Symmetric-key encryption/decryption using k
$h_0(.), h_1(.), h_2(.)$	Hash functions
SK	Shared session key
T_i	Current timestamp
$\oplus$	XOR operation
$\parallel$	Concatenation

4.1   Registration Phase

Before benefiting from services of the medical server, every patient along with his mobile device must undergo a registration process. It is worth to notice that all exchanges in this phase take place over a secure channel. Figure 4 describes in detail the different steps of the registration phase.

Patient	Server
Selects ID_p, ID_m, BID_p and PW_p	
Generates four randoms r_p, u_p, w_p, i	
Computes $MI_p = h_0((ID_p \oplus ID_m) \parallel r_p)$	
Computes $MB_p = h_0(BID_p \parallel r_p)$	
Computes $OPW_p = h_0(MI_p \parallel MB_p \parallel$	
$PW_p \parallel u_p^i)$	
Computes $XPW_p = h_0(PW_p \parallel r_p \parallel u_p).P$	
Computes $PK_p = x_p.P$	

Secure Channel

$$\xrightarrow{\quad OPW_p, XPW_p, \quad \atop PK_p, w_p, u_p^i \quad}$$

	Computes $A_{s/p} = h_0(ID_s \parallel w_p \parallel x_s)$
	Computes $B_p = OPW_p \oplus A_{s/p}$
	Computes $PK_s = x_s.P$
	Computes $C_p = h_1(OPW_p \parallel A_{s/p} \parallel$
	$PK_s \parallel w_p) \oplus XPW_p$
	Selects a random number j
	Selects sec = secret commitment key
	Computes $Z_1 = Enc_{sec}((u_p^i)^j)$

$$\xleftarrow{\quad B_p, C_p, PK_s, Z_1 \quad}$$

| Stores $< r_p, u_p, w_p, i, B_p, C_p, Z_1 >$ | |
| in his/her mobile device | |

Fig. 4. Registration Phase of the Proposed Scheme

Step 1. Patient $\rightarrow$ Server : $\{OPW_p, XPW_p, PK_p, w_p, u_p^i\}$

The patient initiates the communication through selecting a digital identity ID_p, a biometric identity BID_p, an identity for the mobile device ID_m and a password PW_p. Then, he/she generates four random numbers r_p, u_p, w_p, i and computes $MI_p = h_0((ID_p \oplus ID_m) \parallel r_p)$ and $MB_p = h_0(BID_p \parallel r_p)$. In addition, the patient computes $OPW_p = h_0(MI_p \parallel MB_p \parallel PW_p \parallel u_p^i)$, $XPW_p = h_0(PW_p \parallel r_p \parallel u_p).P$ and its the public key $PK_p = x_p.P$, where P is the base point of the elliptic curve. Subsequently, he/she sends parameters $\{OPW_p, XPW_p, PK_p, w_p, u_p^i\}$ via a secure medium to the intended server.

Step 2. Server $\rightarrow$ Patient : $\{B_p, C_p, PK_s, Z_1\}$

Once receiving the patient parameters for registration, the server computes $A_{s/p} = h_0(ID_s \parallel w_p \parallel x_s)$ using its own identity ID_s, then, computes $B_p = OPW_p \oplus A_{s/p}$, its public key $PK_s = x_s.P$ and $C_p = h_1(OPW_p \parallel A_{s/p} \parallel$

$PK_s \parallel w_p) \oplus XPW_p$. Afterwards, the server generates a random number j and selects a secret commitment key sec to be used in the challenge-response protocol. In order to create the first challenge Z_1, The server computes $(u_p^i)^j$ and encrypts it using sec, i.e. $Z_1 = Enc_{sec}((u_p^i)^j)$. Finally, it sends to the patient the message $\{B_p, C_p, PK_s, Z_1\}$ via a reliable channel.

Step 3. Patient → Mobile Device : $\{r_p, u_p, w_p, i, B_p, C_p, PK_s, Z_1\}$

The patient stores the parameters $\{r_p, u_p, w_p, i, B_p, C_p, Z_1\}$ in his/her mobile device and then terminates the registration phase.

4.2 Login and Authentication Phase

Once the registration process is successfully completed, the patient is able from now on to use his/her mobile device to communicate at any time with the medical server. Figure 5 shows all steps of this phase.

Step 1. Patient → Server : $\{V_p, V_p^{pw}, w_p, T_p\}$

To start, the patient enters his/her identity ID_p, biometric identity BID_p and password PW_p. To verify that the current mobile device belongs to the legitimate patient and has not been robbed by an adversary, we proceed as follows. First, stored randoms r_p, u_p, i are retrieved from the memory of the mobile device in order to compute $MI_p^* = h_0((ID_p^* \oplus ID_m^*) \parallel r_p)$, $MB_p^* = h_0(BID_p^* \parallel r_p)$ and $OPW_p^* = h_0(MI_p^* \parallel MB_p^* \parallel PW_p^* \parallel u_p^i)$. Furthermore, the parameters B_p, C_p, w_p, PK_s are also retrieved from the memory to calculate $A_{s/p}^* = B_p \oplus OPW_p^*$, $XPW_p^* = h_0(PW_p^* \parallel r_p \parallel u_p).P$ and $C_p^* = h_1(OPW_p^* \parallel A_{s/p}^* \parallel PK_s \parallel w_p) \oplus XPW_p^*$, where P is the elliptic curve base point. At that moment, the parameter C_p^* being computed is compared to C_p stored in the mobile device. If both equal, then we can trust that the mobile device is possessed by its legal owner (i.e. patient). Subsequently, the patient generates a random number n_p and calculates the point $N_p = n_p.P$ on the elliptic curve. Using the public key of the server PK_s, the patient computes another point on the elliptic cure as an ephemeral key $key = n_p.PK_s = n_p.x_s.P = x_s.N_p$. He besides calculates $D_p = h_0(w_p \parallel i \parallel n_p).P$, encrypts (D_p, XPW_p^*, u_p) with the ephemeral key produced previously (key), then computes a verifier $V_p = Enc_{A_{s/p}^*}(Enc_{key}(D_p, XPW_p^*, u_p) \parallel N_p)$ an encrypted value using $A_{s/p}^*$. Next, the patient captures the current timestamp T_p and computes a second verifier basing the patient password $V_p^{pw} = h_0(A_{s/p}^* \parallel XPW_p^* \parallel D_p)$. At the end, he/she sends $\{V_p, V_p^{pw}, w_p, T_p\}$ through an unsecured channel to the targeted server.

Step 2. Server → Patient : $\{AuV_s, Z_2, Z_3, Q_s\}$

Patient/Mobile Device	Server
Enters his/her ID_p^*, BID_p^* and PW_p^*	

Retrieves r_p, u_p, i from the memory
Computes :
$$MI_p^* = h_0((ID_p^* \oplus ID_m^*) \parallel r_p)$$
$$MB_p^* = h_0(BID_p^* \parallel r_p)$$
$$OPW_p^* = h_0(MI_p^* \parallel MB_p^* \parallel PW_p^* \parallel u_p^i)$$
Retrieves B_p, C_p, w_p, PK_s from memory
Computes :
$$A_{s/p}^* = B_p \oplus OPW_p^*$$
$$XPW_p^* = h_0(PW_p^* \parallel r_p \parallel u_p).P$$
$$C_p^* = h_1(OPW_p^* \parallel A_{s/p}^* \parallel PK_s \parallel w_p)$$
$$\oplus XPW_p^*$$
Verifies $C_p^* =? C_p$
Generates a random number n_p
Computes :
$$N_p = n_p.P$$
$$key = n_p.PK_s = n_p.x_s.P = x_s.N_p$$
$$D_p = h_0(w_p \parallel i \parallel n_p).P$$
$$V_p = Enc_{A_{s/p}^*}(Enc_{key}(D_p, XPW_p^*, u_p)$$
$$\parallel N_p)$$
Captures current timestamp T_p
Computes $V_p^{pw} = h_0(A_{s/p}^* \parallel XPW_p^* \parallel D_p)$

$$\xrightarrow{\quad V_p, V_p^{pw}, \quad}$$
$$w_p, T_p$$

Checks the freshness of T_p
Computes $A_{s/p}^{**} = h_0(ID_s \parallel w_p \parallel x_s)$
$$Dec_{A_{s/p}^{**}}(V_p) = Enc_{key}(D_p, XPW_p^*, u_p)$$
$$\parallel N_p^*$$
Retrieves N_p^*
Computes $key^* = x_s.N_p^*$
$$Dec_{key^*}(Enc_{key}(D_p, XPW_p^*, u_p))$$
$$= (D_p^*, XPW_p^*, u_p)$$
Computes :
$$V_p^{pw^*} = h_0(A_{s/p}^{**} \parallel XPW_p^* \parallel D_p^*)$$
Verifies $V_p^{pw} =? V_p^{pw^*}$
Generates a random number q_s
Computes :
$$Q_s = q_s.N_p^* = n_p.q_s.P$$
$$Z_2 = Enc_{key^*}(u_p^j)$$
$$Z_3 = Enc_{(u_p^i)^j}(sec)$$
$$SK = h_2(D_p^* \parallel A_{s/p}^{**} \parallel N_p^* \parallel Q_s \parallel$$
$$(u_p^i)^j \parallel T_p)$$
$$AuV_s = h_2(V_p^{pw^*} \parallel D_p^* \parallel SK)$$

$$\xleftarrow{\quad AuV_s, Z_2, Z_3, Q_s \quad}$$

$Dec_{key}(Z_2) = u_p^j$
Computes $(u_p^j)^i$
$$Dec_{(u_p^j)^i}(Z_3) = sec$$
$$Dec_{sec}(Z_1) = (u_p^i)^j$$
Verifies $(u_p^i)^j =? (u_p^j)^i$
Computes :
$$SK = h_2(D_p \parallel A_{s/p}^* \parallel N_p \parallel Q_s \parallel (u_p^j)^i \parallel T_p)$$
$$AuV_p = h_2(V_p^{pw} \parallel D_p \parallel SK)$$
Verifies $AuV_p =? Auth_s$

Fig. 5. Login and Authentication Phase of the proposed scheme

At the reception of the message from the patient, the server first checks the freshness of the timestamp T_p, which at the same time guarantee the freshness of the overall message. Using its own identity ID_s, its private key x_s and the random w_p received in the previous step, the server computes its own version $A_{s/p}^{**} = h_0(ID_s \parallel w_p \parallel x_s)$ and uses it to decrypt the received V_p, i.e. $Dec_{A_{s/p}^{**}}(V_p) = Enc_{key}(D_p, XPW_p^*, u_p) \parallel N_p^*$. Now, in possession of N_p^*, the server is able to get the value of the ephemeral key, such as $key^* = x_s.N_p^*$, which can be then used to decrypt $Enc_{key}(D_p, XPW_p^*, u_p)$ and get the estimated values D_p^* and u_p^*. Subsequently, the sever computes $V_p^{pw^*} = h_0(A_{s/p}^{**} \parallel XPW_p^* \parallel D_p^*)$ and compares the obtained value with V_p^{pw} received from the patient. If not identical, the server rejects the session and terminates the communication. Otherwise, if both equal, then the server can trust the authenticity of the patient and the received message. Thereafter, the server generates a random number q_s and uses it to calculate $Q_s = q_s.N_p^* = n_p.q_s.P$. Next, to create the second challenge Z_2, the server computes (u_p^j), and encrypts it using key^*, i.e. $Z_2 = Enc_{key^*}(u_p^j)$. A third challenge is also computed as the encrypted value of the secret commitment key sec using $(u_p^i)^j$ calculated in the registration phase, i.e. $Z_3 = Enc_{(u_p^i)^j}(sec)$. At this stage, a session key is computed as $SK = h_2(D_p^* \parallel A_{s/p}^{**} \parallel N_p^* \parallel Q_s \parallel (u_p^i)^j \parallel T_p)$ along with an authentication verifier $AuV_s = h_2(V_p^{pw^*} \parallel D_p^* \parallel SK)$. Finally, the server sends the message $\{AuV_s, Z_2, Z_3, Q_s\}$ to the patient.

Step 3. Mutual Authentication and Key Agreement completed

Upon receiving the message from the server, the patient first decrypts Z_2 using key and gets (u_p^j). Then, he/she computes $(u_p^j)^i$ and uses it to decrypt Z_3 and obtain the secret commitment key sec. With the possession of sec, the patient is now able to decrypt the first challenge sent in the registration phase Z_1, and obtain $(u_p^i)^j$. At this moment, the patient verifies $(u_p^i)^j =? (u_p^j)^i$, if they match then the server is legitimate and can be trusted. Thereafter, the patient proceeds to the computation of the session key as $SK = h_2(D_p \parallel A_{s/p}^* \parallel N_p \parallel Q_s \parallel (u_p^j)^i \parallel T_p)$ and the authentication verifier $AuV_p = h_2(V_p^{pw} \parallel D_p \parallel SK)$, using its own parameters and the received Q_s. Then, he/she compares the received AuV_s with its own AuV_p previously calculated. If equal, then the server is authenticated and both parties are now agreed on a common session key.

5   Informal Security Analysis

5.1   Perfect Forward Secrecy

If an attacker succeeds in compromising the current session's secret keys, yet cannot find the previous session keys, it is called Perfect forward secrecy property (PFS). Our session key SK is calculated as $SK = h_2(D_p \parallel A_{s/p}^* \parallel N_p \parallel Q_s \parallel (u_p^j)^i \parallel T_p)$, where $D_p = h_0(w_p \parallel i \parallel n_p).P$ and $Q_s = q_s.N_p^* = n_p.q_s.P$. Thus, even if an adversary finds the server's private key x_s and the patient's password PW_p, he still needs to know the session-specific random numbers q_s and n_p to obtain the session key. However, this is not possible due to the elliptic curve discrete logarithm problem (ECDLP). Accordingly, our scheme can properly provide the perfect forward secrecy.

5.2   Known Key Security

This property is provided when a compromised session key could not affect the other session keys. In our scheme, the server and the patient separately generate two ephemeral secrets q_s and n_p during each session. These latter participate fairly in building a session key commonly shared by both entities. Hence, an adversary cannot guess any other session key given a corrupted one, which means the known-key security is properly provided.

5.3   Session Key Verification

In step 2 of the login and authentication phase from our scheme, the server produces the session key as $SK = h_2(D_p \parallel A^*_{s/p} \parallel N_p \parallel Q_s \parallel (u^j_p)^i \parallel T_p)$ and an authentication verifier as $AuV_s = h_2(V^{pw^*}_p \parallel D^*_p \parallel SK)$. Therefore, in step 3, the patient verifies the sessions key SK through examining whether its computed verifier AuV_p matches the received AuV_s. Consequently, the session key verification property is provided by the proposed scheme.

5.4   Anonymity and Unlinkability

Assume an adversary attempts to gather the patient's identity, he would fail to do it for many reasons. First, even the adversary steals or finds the patient's mobile device, he wouldn't obtain the patient's identities ID_p and BID_p since they were not directly stored in his mobile device. Second, none of the messages transmitted between the patient and the server includes ID_p and BID_p in clear, in addition, the adversary cannot acquire them from $V^{pw}_p = h_0(A^*_{s/p} \parallel XPW^*_p \parallel D_p)$ and $OPW_p = h_0(MI_p \parallel MB_p \parallel PW_p \parallel u^i_p)$. Moreover, the verifier V^{pw}_p is updated in each session, thus, the adversary cannot relate or link two messages to a specific patient. Accordingly, our scheme can provide strong anonymity and unlinkability.

5.5   Stolen Smart Device Attack

Our scheme can properly ensure security against this attack. Assume the mobile device of the patient is stolen, the adversary has no chance to impersonate as a legitimate authorized patient to gain access to the stored data in the medical server, because he/she does not know the patient's digital identity and biometric identities (ID_p, BID_p) which are not directly stored in the device. Moreover, the biometric identity is very hard to guess or forge and cannot be stolen, lost or copied.

5.6 Offline Password Guessing Attack

Our scheme resists well the offline password guessing attack for many reasons. Assume an adversary comes to obtain the mobile device of the patient and retrieves $<r_p, u_p, w_p, i, B_p, C_p, Z_1>$ from its memory, where $B_p = OPW_p \oplus A_{s/p}$ and $C_p = h_1(OPW_p \parallel A_{s/p} \parallel PK_s \parallel w_p) \oplus XPW_p$. The adversary cannot derive the identity of the patient as it is not included in any of the parameters retrieved. Moreover, he cannot guess the patient's password PW_p from the stored information because the mobile device don't preserve it. Indeed, the attacker needs first to know the value of OPW_p through the equation $B_p = OPW_p \oplus A_{s/p}$, hence he must find $A_{s/p}$, which is not feasible without the identity of the server ID_s and its private key x_s. Then, he should guess the patient's password PW_p from the equation $OPW_p = h_0(MI_p \parallel MB_p \parallel PW_p \parallel u_p^i)$, which is also not possible without knowing the value of MI_p and MB_p. Therefore, the present solution can properly resist this attack.

5.7 Replay Attack

In this attack, an adversary attempts to capture the exchanged messages with the aim to resubmit them later. It is indeed one of the challenging issues in cyber-security, and for distributed systems in particular. Our proposed scheme can prevent this attack due to the use of timestamps and session-specific ephemeral randoms. For example, an adversary can intercept a previously transmitted message between the patient and the server: $\{V_p, V_p^{pw}, w_p, T_p\}$ or $\{AuV_s, Z_2, Z_3, Q_s\}$ and try to replay it. For the server, a replay attack can be easily screened through examining the freshness of the timestamp associated with the message such as $\mid T_e - T_p \mid \le \Delta T$, such that T_e is the exact time the message has being received by the server and ΔT is the tolerated transmission delay. Similarly, the patient is also able to detect this attack through checking the verifier's equation $AuV_s =? AuV_p = h_2(V_p^{pw} \parallel D_p \parallel SK)$, where T_p is included in the calculated session key SK.

5.8 Man-in-the-Middle (MITM) Attack

In our solution, the server authenticates the patient in 2 steps: first verifies $V_p^{pw} =? V_p^{pw^*}$ where $V_p^{pw^*} = h_0(A_{s/p}^{**} \parallel XPW_p^* \parallel D_p^*)$ then, checks $(u_p^j)^i =? (u_p^i)^j$. Without the identity of the server ID_s, its private key x_s and the ephemeral randoms (n_p, u_p, i), an adversary can neither produce $A_{s/p}^{**}$, N_p and key, nor verify the challenge Z_3. At the other side, the patient authenticates the server through verifying $AuV_p =? Auth_s$ where $AuV_p = h_2(V_p^{pw} \parallel D_p \parallel SK)$, then examines $(u_p^i)^j =? (u_p^j)^i$. Without the ephemeral randoms (q_s, j), an adversary can neither find Q_s and SK, nor verify the challenge Z_1.

5.9 Key Replicating Attack

Being a version of the Man-in-the-Middle attack, key replicating attack would intercept and alter the exchanged messages between the patient and the server, with the aim to convince both parties to agree on an erroneous session key. In our scheme, we adopt key verification and confirmation procedure using verifiers that can only be properly and correctly computed the authentic communicating patient and server. Hence, our scheme is secure against this attack.

5.10   Privileged Insider Attack

The proposed scheme can properly provide security against this attack, because each patient in the registration phase sends $\{MI_p, OPW_p, XPW_p, PK_p, w_p, u_p^i\}$ to server via a reliable channel, where $OPW_p = h_0(MI_p \parallel MB_p \parallel PW_p \parallel u_p^i)$ and $XPW_p = h_0(PW_p \parallel r_p \parallel u_p).P$. Thus, an insider cannot acquire or guess the patient's password PW_p and the session key SK since he/she ignores the ephemeral randoms r_p and u_p, while PW_p is always merged with other parameters before being sent in a one-way hashed format.

5.11   Patient and Server Impersonation Attacks

In this attack, an adversary intercepts the exchanged messages with the aim to alter them and attempt to impersonate him/herself as a legitimate patient or server. Assume an adversary tries to impersonate as a legal patient to the server and captures the login message $\{V_p, V_p^{pw}, w_p, T_p\}$. To verify that the message is received from the right patient, the server computes $V_p^{pw*} = h_0(A_{s/p}^{**} \parallel XPW_p^* \parallel D_p^*)$ and then compares it with V_p^{pw} received from the patient. Thus, the adversary needs to calculate his own V_p^{pw} and hence his own $A_{s/p}$. However, the parameter $A_{s/p} = h_0(ID_s \parallel w_p \parallel x_s)$ depends on the server's identity ID_s and its private key x_s which are not within the reach of the adversary. Therefore, our scheme prohibits an attacker to impersonate as a patient. Similarly, an adversary may capture the message $\{AuV_s, Z_2, Z_3, Q_s\}$ and try to impersonate as a legal server to the patient. To do so, he/she needs to compute a valid verifier AuV_s, however, this is not feasible since the parameter D_p and the session key SK are unknown for him/her. Moreover, he/she would fail to guess the value of the challenges included in Z_2 and Z_3 as he/she ignores the ephemeral randoms (i, j), the secret commitment key sec, the server's private key x_s and the session key SK. Hence, our scheme can properly resist server impersonation attack.

5.12   Denial of Service (DoS) Attack

In DoS attacks, an adversary attempts to keep the server busy or inaccessible in terms of resources, services and response time through flooding it with requests and fake messages. For the proposed scheme, an adversary has no chance to lead and succeed this attack because we make use of hash-based verifiers with timestamps, which allows both patient and server shortly validating the integrity of received messages. Therefore, our scheme can withstand DoS attack.

5.13   Cloud Server Compromise Attack

Medical servers are usually implanted as cloud service providers, which are easily targeted by adversaries due to their open and accessible nature. This attack may cause serious damages and breaches when authorized users allow direct access to their sensitive data via a certain medium without referring to the cloud server. In our proposed scheme, the patient and the medical server mutually authenticate before exchanging sensitive data in an encrypted format using the unique session key.

5.14   Key Compromise Password Guessing Attack

Assume an adversary comes to compromise the secret key of the server x_s and obtains the mobile device of the patient, then, he/she can get the parameters $\{r_p, u_p, w_p, i, B_p, C_p, Z_1\}$ stored in the device. In this situation, can the adversary guess the password of the patient?. The answer is no. To get the patient's password PW_p, the adversary must extract OPW_p from the equation $B_p = OPW_p \oplus A_{s/p}$, and thus he/she first needs to guess the correct value of $A_{s/p} = h_0(ID_s \parallel w_p \parallel x_s)$, which is not feasible without knowing the server's identity ID_s. Suppose the adversary finds ID_s, he/she still needs to know the patient's identity ID_p and his biometric identity BID_p along with the identity of the mobile device ID_m, then try to guess the password from $OPW_p = h_0(MI_p \parallel MB_p \parallel PW_p \parallel u_p^i)$. However, the identities of the patient and mobile device are not directly stored or transmitted between communicating entities, they are kept private and inaccessible to the adversary. Subsequently, our proposed scheme can properly provide security against key compromise password guessing attack.

5.15   Key Compromise Impersonation Attack

Preventing this attack is among the serious concerns in authentication and key agreement schemes. Assume an adversary gets access to the private key of the server x_s, and can intercept the login message $\{V_p, V_p^{pw}, w_p, T_p\}$ sent by the patient over a public channel. To impersonate as a patient, he must create his/her own version of the login message. For that purpose, he/she needs to know the server identity ID_s to compute $A_{s/p} = h_0(ID_s \parallel w_p \parallel x_s)$, however, the server doesn't store any parameters in its registration table and the adversary has no chance to retrieve it. Otherwise, the adversary may try to get $A_{s/p}$ from the equation $A_{s/p} = B_p \oplus OPW_p$, where $OPW_p = h_0(MI_p \parallel MB_p \parallel PW_p \parallel u_p^i)$, but he/she still ignores the patient/device identities (ID_p, BID_p, ID_m), which are not directly stored in the device neither transmitted in clear throughout the communication. Moreover, without knowing the values of the ephemeral randoms (r_p, u_p, i), the adversary cannot compute its own D_p, V_p and V_p^{pw}. Finally, To verify that a message truly comes from the legitimate patient, the server first computes $V_p^{pw^*} = h_0(A_{s/p}^{**} \parallel XPW_p^* \parallel D_p^*)$ and then compares it with V_p^{pw} received from the patient. However, without the server identity ID_s, the adversary cannot calculate $A_{s/p}^{**}$. Hence, the attacker is absolutely not able to impersonate as the server or the patient, though their long-term secrets are divulged. As a result, our scheme can resist this attack.

6   Formal Security Verification Using AVISPA

Among the reliable and widely used tools to prove the security of authentication protocols and schemes over network, AVISPA [27] comes at the top of the list. The Automated Validation of Internet Security Protocols and Applications (AVISPA) is a push button formal technique for the security evaluation and validation of wide-ranging Internet security sensitive protocols and applications. AVISPA goes through a simulation and verification process using the HLPSL language, a HLPSL2IF translator and four checkers/ back-ends, with the aim to inspect several security properties, namely authentication, secrecy of keys, and resistance against passive and active attacks (replay attack, impersonation and MITM, etc). This tool comes with an incorporated graphical user interface, called security protocol animator (SPAN).

To simulate our proposed scheme using the AVISPA tool, we have first designed the HLPSL specifications for the patient and server roles as illustrated in Figs. 6 and 7. Thereafter, in Fig. 8, we have defined the HLPSL specification for the session as to describe the communication flow between the patient and the server. Moreover, the HLPSL specifications for the environment role are expressed in Fig. 9, where global information like sessions, intruder knowledge and global constants are indicated. Finally, Fig. 10 shows the intended security properties and goals.

In the patient role, state 0 refers to the registration phase where the patient transmits the message $\{OPWp'.XPWp'.PKp'.Wp'.Upi'\}$ to the medical server via a secure channel using symmetric key K and $SND()$ operation. The type declaration channel(dy) means that the channels follow the Dolev and Yao threat model. Thus, the goal $secrecy\_of$ $g1$ in the secret statement $secret(\{Wp', Upi'\}, g1, \{P, S\})$ means that the random number Wp' and the first challenge content Upi' are kept secret to the patient and the server. On the other hand, the goal $secrecy\_of$ $g2$ in the secret statement $secret(\{IDp, IDm, BIDp, PWp, Rp', Up', I', Xp'\}, g2, \{P\})$ means that the identities of the patient (IDp and $BIDp$), the mobile device identity IDm, the patient password PWp and the random numbers (Rp', Up', I', Xp') are only known by the patient. Thereafter, the login and authentication phases are represented in state 2 and state 4, where the goal $secrecy\_of$ $g3$ in the secret statement $secret(\{Np'\}, g3, \{P\})$ indicates that the nonce Np' is only known by the patient, while the goal $secrecy\_of$ $g4$ in the secret statement $secret(\{SK'\}, g4, \{P, S\})$ specifies that only the medical server and the patient know the value of the secret key SK'.

The server role includes two states. The state 1 refers to the registration phase with the goal $secrecy\_of$ $g5$ in the secret statement $secret(\{Xs', J', Sec'\}, g5, \{S\})$ to assert that the private key of the server Xs', the random J' and the secret commitment key Sec' are only known by the server. Besides, the state 3

```
role patient(P, S : agent,
             K : symmetric_key,
             Mul, Hash : hash_func,
             PP: text,
             SND, RCV : channel (dy))
played_by P
def=
  local State : nat,
  IDp, IDm, BIDp, Xp, PWp, Rp, Up, Wp : text,
  I, Np, Tp, Qs : text,
  OPWp, XPWp, Upi, MIp, MBp, PKp : message,
  Bp, Cp, Upij, Z1, Asp, NNp, PKs : message,
  Vp, VNNp, Vppw, Dp, Vpinit, QQs : message,
  Z2, Z3, AuVs, Upj, SK : message,
  Key : symmetric_key,

  init State := 0
  transition
      1. State = 0 /\ RCV(start) =|> State':= 2
         /\ Rp' := new()
         /\ Up' := new()
         /\ Wp' := new()
         /\ I' := new()
         /\ Xp' := new()
         /\ MIp' := Hash(xor(IDm,IDp).Rp')
         /\ MBp' := Hash(BIDp.Rp')
         /\ Upi' := exp(Up',I')
         /\ OPWp' := Hash(MIp'.MBp'.PWp. Upi')
         /\ XPWp' := Mul(Hash(PWp.Rp'.Up'),PP)
         /\ PKp' := Mul(Xp',PP)
         /\ SND({Na'.OPWp'.XPWp'.PKp'.Wp'.Upi'}_K)
         /\ secret ({Wp', Upi'}, g1, {P,S})
         /\ secret ({IDp, IDm, BIDp, PWp, Rp, Up', I',
                     Xp'}, g2, P)

      2. State = 2 /\ RCV({PKs'.Bp'.Cp'.Z1'}_K) =|> State':= 4
         /\ Np' := new()
         /\ Tp' := new()
         /\ Asp' := xor(Bp', OPWp)
         /\ NNp' := Mul(Np',PP)
         /\ Key' := Mul(Np',PKs')
         /\ Dp' := Mul(Hash(Wp.I.Np'),PP)
         /\ Vpinit' := {Dp'.XPWp.Up}_Key'
         /\ Vp' := {Vpinit'}_Asp'
         /\ VNNp' := {NNp'}_Asp'
         /\ Vppw' := Hash(Asp'.XPWp. Dp')
         /\ SND(Vppw'.Vp'.VNNp'. Wp. Tp')
         /\ witness(P,S,server_patient_np,Np')
         /\ secret({Np'},g3, P)

      3. State = 4 /\ RCV(AuVs'.Z2'.Z3'.QQs') =|> State':= 6
         /\ Upij' := exp(Upj, I)
         /\ SK' := Hash(Dp. Asp. Np. QQs'. Upij'.Tp)
         /\ AuVs' := Hash(Vppw. Dp. SK')
         /\ secret({SK'}, g4, {P,S})
         /\ request(P, S, patient_server_qs, Qs)

d role
```

Fig. 6. The HLPSL specification for the patient role

related to the login and authentication phase stands with the goal *secrecy_ of g6*
in the secret statement *secret*($\{Qs'\}$, $g6$, $\{S\}$) means that the random number
Qs' generated by the medical server is kept secret to it.

```
role server(P, S : agent,
            K : symmetric_key,
            Mul, Hash : hash_func,
            PP : text,
            SND, RCV : channel (dy))
played_by S
def=
  local State : nat,
        IDs, Wp, Xs, J, Tp, Np, Qs, Up, Sec : text,
        OPWp, XPWp, Upi, MIp, MBp, PKp, PKs : message,
        Asp, Bp, Cp, Upij, Z1, Vp, VNNp, Vppw : message,
        NNp, QQs, Dp, Upj, Z2, Z3, AuVs, SK : message,
        Key: symmetric_key,

  init State := 1
  transition
    1. State = 1 /\ RCV({Na'.OPWp'.XPWp'.PKp'.Wp'.Upi'}_K) =|>
          State':= 3
          /\ Xs' := new()
          /\ PKs' := Mul(Xs',PP)
          /\ Asp' := Hash(IDs.Wp'.Xs')
          /\ Bp' := xor(OPWp', Asp')
          /\ Cp' := xor(Hash(OPWp'.Asp'.PKs'.Wp'), XPWp')
          /\ J' := new()
          /\ Sec' := new()
          /\ Upij' := exp(Upi', J')
          /\ Z1' := {Upij'}_Sec'
          /\ SND({PKs'.Bp'.Cp'.Z1'}_K)
          /\ secret ({Xs' ,J', Sec'}, g5, S)

    2. State = 3 /\ RCV(Vppw'.Vp'.VNNp'. Wp. Tp') =|>
          State':= 5
          /\ Key' := Mul(Xs,NNp)
          /\ Vppw' := Hash(Asp,XPWp,Dp)
          /\ Qs' := new()
          /\ QQs' := Mul(Qs',NNp)
          /\ Upj' := exp(Up,J)
          /\ Z2' := {Upj'}_Key'
          /\ Z3' := {Sec}_Upij
          /\ SK' := Hash(Dp. Asp. NNp. QQs'. Upij. Tp')
          /\ AuVs' := Hash(Vppw'. Dp. SK')
          /\ SND (AuVs'.Z2'.Z3'.QQs')
          /\ secret ({Qs'}, g6, S)
          /\ witness(S, P, patient_server_qs, Qs')
          /\ request(S, P, server_patient_np, Np)

end role
```

Fig. 7. The HLPSL specification for the server role

Moreover, among the secrecy goals, we have *"authentication_ on patient_ server_ np"* and *"authentication_ on server_ patient_ qs"*. The first indicates that *np* is a nonce selected by the patient and then sent to the server to uniquely authenticate this patient. Similarly, the second goal means that *qs* is a nonce produced by the server and then sent to the patient to allow him uniquely authenticate the server.

Laking use of SPAN for simulation purposes, Figs. 11 and 12 illustrates the obtained outcomes under OFMC and the CL-AtSe, respectively. It is clearly demonstrated, according to provided summary, that our scheme is SAFE and can resist various attacks based on Dolev-Yao model. Moreover, it effectively

```
role session(P, S : agent,
         K : symmetric_key,
         Mul, Hash : hash_func,
         PP : text)
def=
 local S1, S2, R1, R2 : channel(dy)
 composition
    patient(P, S, K, Mul, Hash, PP, S1, R1)
    /\
    server(P, S, K, Mul, Hash, PP, S2, R2)
end role
```

Fig. 8. The HLPSL specification for the session role

```
role environment ()
def=
    const
      server_patient_np, patient_server_qs,
      g1, g2, g3, g4, g5, g6 : protocol_id,
      p, s : agent,
      k, kpi, ksi: symmetric_key,
      mul, hash : hash_func,
      pp : text

    intruder_knowledge = {p, s, mul, hash,
                                    kpi, ksi}
    composition
      session(p, s, k, mul, hash, pp) % normal
      %/\ session(p,i,ksi,mul,hash,pp)
      % intruder i impersonates s
      %/\ session(i,s,kpi,mul,hash,pp)
      % intruder i impersonates p
end role
```

Fig. 9. The HLPSL specification for the environment role

```
goal
    secrecy_of g1
    secrecy_of g2
    secrecy_of g3
    secrecy_of g4
    secrecy_of g5
    secrecy_of g6
    authentication_on patient_server_np
    authentication_on server_patient_qs
end goal
environment()
```

Fig. 10. The HLPSL specification of the security goals

satisfies the specified goals, namely the mutual authentication and privacy of the sensitive data.

7 Performance Evaluation

In this section, we evaluate the performance of our proposed scheme, compared to Dhillon et al.'s [5], Ali et al.'s [6], Srinivas et al.'s [8], Challa et al.'s [9], Li et al.'s [11], Amin et al.'s [12], Chandrakar's [14], Liu et al.'s [15], Renuka et al.'s [16], Sharma and Kalra's [18], Gupta et al.'s [19], Sharif et al.'s [1], Kumari et al.'s [23], Alzahrani et al.'s [24], Dharminder et al.'s [25] and Sureshkumar et al.'s [26] protocols. Our performance tests mainly focus on commonly evaluated metrics such as computation and communication overheads, storage cost and network throughput.

```
SUMMARY
  SAFE

DETAILS
  BOUNDED_NUMBER_OF_SESSIONS
  TYPED_MODEL

PROTOCOL
  /home/span/span/testsuite/results/AVISPA.if

GOAL
  As Specified

BACKEND
  CL-AtSe

STATISTICS

  Analysed   :  6 states
  Reachable  :  4 states
  Translation :  0.13 seconds
  Computation :  0.00 seconds
```

```
% OFMC
% Version of 2006/02/13
SUMMARY
  SAFE
DETAILS
  BOUNDED_NUMBER_OF_SESSIONS
PROTOCOL
  /home/span/span/testsuite/results/AVISPA.if
GOAL
  As_Specified
BACKEND
  OFMC
COMMENTS
STATISTICS
  parseTime: 0.00s
  searchTime: 0.21s
  visitedNodes: 4 nodes
  depth: 2 plies
```

Fig. 11. CL-AtSe back-end simulation result

Fig. 12. OFMC back-end simulation result

7.1 Comparison of Security Features

Table 3 depicts the security features of our proposed scheme compared to the aforementioned protocols in several functionality aspects. It is noticed that beyond half of the authentication schemes cannot resist offline password guessing attack, replay attack, privileged insider attack, denial of service attack, cloud server compromise attack and key compromise password guessing attack. Moreover, Ali et al.'s [6] and Gupta et al.'s [19] are proved to be the weakest protocols in terms of security as they fail to withstand a wide range of attacks and to provide substantial security properties. Ultimately, our proposed scheme satisfies all the security requirements as it was discussed in Sect. 5.

7.2 Computation and Communication Cost

For convenience with the aforementioned related schemes and to achieve a comparable level of security to 2048-bits RSA, we make use of the super-singular elliptic curve $E/F_p : y^2 = x^3 + x$ with a Tate pairing $e : G_1 \times G_1 \longrightarrow G_2$. The ECC point is 320 bits, the random number is 64 bits and the identity is 160, while the timestamp is 32 bits and the output of the hash functions is 256 bits. Moreover, we make use of AES [28] algorithm for symmetric encryption/decryption with a secret key of 256 bits length. Tables 4 and 5 provide the notations and the execution time of the operations performed during the authentication process at the patient side and the medical service side, separately.

Table 3. Comparison of security features for the different authentication and key agreement schemes

Scheme	[5]	[6]	[8]	[9]	[12]	[14]	[16]	[18]	[19]	[1]	[23]	[24]	[25]	Proposed
F_1	√	×	√	×	√	×	√	√	√	×	√	√	√	√
F_2	√	×	√	√	√	×	√	√	√	×	×	√	√	√
F_3	√	×	√	√	√	×	√	×	×	×	√	√	√	√
F_4	√	×	√	×	×	√	√	√	√	√	√	×	√	√
F_5	×	√	√	√	√	√	√	×	√	√	√	√	√	√
F_6	√	√	√	√	√		×	√	×	√	√	√	√	√
F_7	√	√	×	√	√	×	×	√	×	√	√	√	√	√
F_8	×	√	×	√	√	×	√	×	√	√		×	√	√
F_9	NA	NA	√	√	×	√	NA	NA	×	√	√	×	√	√
F_{10}	×	√	√	×	×	√	√	×	×	√	√	√	×	√
F_{11}	√	×	√	×	√	×	√	√	×	√	√	√	√	√
F_{12}	√	×	√	√	√	√	√	√	√	√	√	√	√	√
F_{13}	√	√	×	√	√	√	×	√	√	√	×	√	×	√
F_{14}	√	√	×	×	√	√	√	√	×	√	√	√	√	√
F_{15}	√	√	×	×	√	√	√	√	√	√	√	√	√	√
F_{16}	×	×	√	×	×	√	√	√	√	√	×	×	√	√
F_{17}	×	√	√	√	√	×	NA	NA	NA	×	×	×	√	√
F_{18}	NA	NA	√	√	×	√	NA	NA	√	×	√	√	×	√
F_{19}	NA	√	√	√	NA	√	√	NA	NA	×	√	√	√	√

F_1: Provide mutual authentication, F_2: Provide data confidentiality, F_3: Provide data integrity, F_4: Provide perfect forward secrecy, F_5: Provide known key security, F_6: Provide session key verification, F_7: Provide patient's strong anonymity and unlinkability, F_8: Resist stolen smart device/card attack, F_9: Resist offline password guessing attack, F_{10}: Resist replay attack, F_{11}: Resist MITM attack, F_{12}: Resist key replication attack, F_{13}: Resist privileged insider attack, F_{14}: Resist patient impersonation attack, F_{15}: Resist server impersonation attack, F_{16}: Resist denial of server attack, F_{17}: Resist cloud server compromise attack, F_{18}: Resist key compromise password guessing attack, F_{19}: Resist key compromise impersonation attack, NA: Not applicable, √: can provide/resist, ×: can not provide/resist

Table 4. Notations used in the authentication

Notation	Description
T_{pm}	ECC Point Multiplication
T_{pa}	ECC Point Addition
T_{bp}	Bilinear Pairing
T_{me}	Modular Exponentiation
T_h	Hash Function
T_{sig}	Signature using ECDSA
T_{sv}	Verification of ECDSA
T_{asym}	Asymmetric Encry/Decry
T_{sym}	Symmetric Encry/Decry
T_{cm}	Chaotic Map

Table 5. Computational cost of the different operations used in authentication

Operation	CU (s)	CSP/VS (s)
T_{pm}	0.0123	0.00758
T_{pa}	0.000756	0.000262
T_{bp}	0.0621	0.023
T_{me}	0.0119	0.0082
T_h	0.0005	0.0003
T_{sig}	0.00338	0.00108
T_{sv}	0.0284	0.0227
T_{asym}	0.3057	0.0619
T_{sym}	0.0059	0.0022
T_{cm}	0.0638	0.02102

Table 6. Comparison of computation and communication costs

Scheme	Operations and Execution Time (s)			#msg	Total Bits
	Patient/Mobile Device	Server	Total		
Srinivas et al. [8]	$23T_h + 1T_{me} + 1T_{asym}$	$24T_h + 1T_{asym}$	$\simeq0.11648$	3	2720
Challa et al. [9]	$8T_h + 2T_{pm} + 1T_{fe}$	$10T_h + 1T_{pm}$	$\simeq0.0749$	3	1728
Li et al. [11]	$2T_h + 4T_{pm} + 2T_{pa} + 5T_{sym}$	$2T_h + 4T_{pm} + 2T_{pa} + 4T_{sym}$	$\simeq0.1440$	4	4736
Amin et al. [12]	$12T_h$	$22T_h$	$\simeq0.0136$	4	2720
Chandrakar [14]	$11T_h$	$18T_h$	$\simeq0.0145$	6	5440
Renuka et al. [16]	$11T_h + 1T_{pm}$	$4T_h + 4T_{pm}$	$\simeq0.0903$	2	2456
Sharma & Kalra [18]	$20T_h + 10T_{xor}$	$12T_h + 6T_{xor}$	$\simeq0.207$	4	4416
Gupta et al. [19]	$11T_h + 8T_{xor}$	$5T_h + 3T_{xor}$	$\simeq0.0737$	5	3808
Sharif et al. [1]	$11T_h + 2T_{pm} + 2T_{pa}$	$8T_h + 2T_{pm} + 2T_{pa} + 2T_{sym}$	$\simeq0.2801$	2	1632
Kumari et al. [23]	$14T_h + 13T_{sym} + 1T_{sig} + 2T_{sv}$	$28T_h + 24T_{sym} + 2T_{sig} + 1T_{sv}$	$\simeq2.3401$	15	2976
Alzahrani et al. [24]	$11T_h + 1T_{sym}$	$12T_h + 1T_{sym}$	$\simeq0.243$	4	3552
Dharminder et al. [25]	$7T_h + 1T_{me}$	$2T_h + 1T_{me}$	$\simeq0.1322$	2	2216
Sureshkumar et al. [26]	$12T_h + 2T_{cm}$	$3T_h + 3T_{cm}$	$\simeq0.1116$	2	3392
Proposed	$9T_h + 3T_{pm} + 5T_{sym} + 2T_{me}$	$4T_h + 4T_{sym} + 1T_{me}$	$\simeq0.1129$	2	1684

Since login and authentication are the frequently executed phases, we analyze the computation and communication performance of our scheme with other existing schemes only for login and authentication. Table 6 presents the results of the analysis being performed.

In the login and authentication phases of the proposed scheme, the patient requires nine hash operations, three ECC point multiplications, five symmetric encryption/decryption and two modular exponentiation operations to be executed by his/her device. Therefore, the patient/mobile device demonstrates a computation overhead $9T_h + 3T_{pm} + 5T_{sym} + 2T_{me}$, which is equivalent to 0.0947 s. In addition, the server performs four hash operations, four symmetric encryption/decryption and one modular exponentiation. Therefore, the computational cost at the medical server side is $4T_h + 4T_{sym} + 1T_{me}$, which is 0.0182 s. As a result, the total execution time of the proposed scheme is 0.1129 s. As observed in Table 6, our proposed scheme shows in general less (or approximate) computational overhead than the majority of existing schemes, except for Challa et al.' [9], Amin et al.' [12], Chandrakar' [14], Renuka et al.' [16] and Gupta et al.' [19] schemes. Besides these schemes do not meet many of the necessary and substantial security features (see Table 3), they furthermore require more than 2 messages to perform the login and authentication, and thus, greater communication cost. Moreover, they are mostly designed basing only hash and xor functions, which require significantly less computation cost.

Concerning the communication cost, the login and authentication phase is performed only using two exchanged messages. First, the patient sends via his/her mobile device the message $\{V_p, V_p^{pw}, w_p, T_p\}$, which involves one hash value, one encrypted value, one random number and one timestamp, hence the total cost is $(256 + 256 + 64 + 32 =)$ 608 bits. Second, the medical server returns a response message $\{AuV_s, Z_2, Z_3, Q_s\}$, which includes one hash value, two encrypted values and one ECC point multiplication, thus the total cost is $(256 + 256 + 256 + 320 =)$ 1076 bits. Therefore, the total overhead of communication of our scheme is 1684 bits. This cost is less than all schemes being utilized for comparison, except for Ostad-Sharif et al.'s Scheme [1] whose communication cost is little more than ours of about 52 bits (see Table 6). However, Ostad-Sharif et al.'s Scheme [1] requires more computational cost ($\simeq 0.2801$ s) and suffers from various security vulnerabilities as discussed in Sect. 3 and displayed in Table 3. More precisely, their scheme fails to provide mutual authentication, data confidentiality and integrity, while it cannot resist cloud server compromise attack, key compromise password guessing attack and key compromise impersonation attack.

Eventually, in view of the present outcomes, our scheme is proved to be more appropriate in terms of reliability and efficiency compared to other schemes. Our scheme not only achieved all security features, but also demonstrated a high level of performance in terms of computation and communication. More importantly, the proposed scheme can properly resist most common attacks, namely, the key compromise password guessing and key compromise impersonation attacks, with only three ECC multiplication in overall.

7.3   Storage Cost

The efficiency of security protocols in general, and authentication scheme in particular, also depends on the storage cost needed to complete all operations and exchanges. This becomes of a paramount importance when restricted memory entities are involved, such as mobile devices, wearable sensors, gateways, etc. The key idea of our proposed scheme is to store as few parameters as possible and avoid storing the very sensitive data such as identities and passwords, with the aim to withstand security attacks targeting information in memories.

Table 7. Comparison of storage cost

Scheme	Storage Cost (in Bits)
Srinivas et al. [8]	$2112 + (256+160)n$
Challa et al. [9]	$1184 + (256+160)n$
Li et al. [11]	$4304 + (448+320)n$
Amin et al. [12]	$1344 + (256)n$
Chandrakar [14]	$768 + (256)n$
Renuka et al. [16]	1384
Sharma & Kalra [18]	$832 + (512)n$
Gupta et al. [19]	3776
Sharif et al. [1]	1472
Kumari et. [23]	3392
Alzahrani et al. [24]	1856
Dharminder et al. [25]	1344
Sureshkumar et al. [26]	1024
Proposed	1024

In our authentication scheme, no parameters are stored by the medical server. At the registration phase, the patient stores the four random numbers $<r_p, u_p, w_p, i>$, the two hash values $B_p = OPW_p \oplus A_{s/p}$ and $C_p = h_1(OPW_p \parallel A_{s/p} \parallel PK_s \parallel w_p) \oplus XPW_p$, and finally the challenge as a cipher $Z_1 = Enc_{sec}((u_p^i)^j)$. Knowing that a random is 64 bits, a hash value and a cipher are both 256 bits, then the total storage cost is 1024 bits, which is very admissible. Table 7 provides a comparison of storage cost between our scheme and other related schemes. Accordingly, our proposed scheme demonstrates the lowest cost and proves to be storage friendly. Sureshkumar et al.' [26] scheme also shows the same storage cost, but its communication overhead is relatively high and it depends only on hash functions to secure exchanges.

7.4   Impact of Network Throughput

Another important metric to examine is the network performance in terms of the throughput impact. Basically, the network throughput (NT) is measured as the amount of bits transferred per time unit. It can be formulated as: $NT = \frac{N \times S_p}{t_d}$, where N is the total number of packets received, S_p is the size of one packet, and t_d is the delivery time of packets.

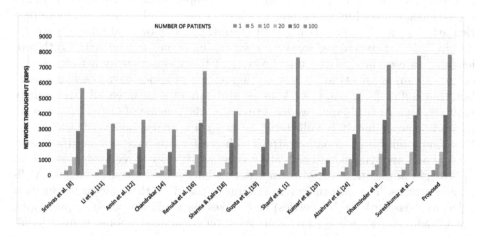

Fig. 13. Network Throughput of our proposed scheme compared to other related schemes

We make use of Iperf3 [29] to test the maximum throughput in IPv4 or IPv6 networks. It is a free and open source command line tool for measuring network throughput and bandwidth in real time, and it can report insightful information such as: max/min throughput and bandwidth, packet loss, latency, jitter, etc. In this evaluation, it was also interesting to watch the network performance when the number of patients requesting services from the medical server is continuously and simultaneously increasing. Figure 13 presents the network throughput outcomes (in Kbps) related to our solution compared to the other schemes. In the overall, our scheme shows better outputs in the long-term. We notice at the beginning that it was competing with Sureshkumar et al.' [26] and Sharif et al.' [1] schemes. It is actually a very little difference to the point of being negligible, especially that with increasing number of patients, our contribution exceeds both schemes. For more details, when one patient is communicating with the medical server, our scheme experiences a network throughput of 84.7 Kbps versus 87.3 Kbps and 86.5 Kbps for Sureshkumar et al.' [26] and Sharif et al.' [1], respectively. When the number of patients escalated to five, our scheme makes a network throughput of 420 Kbps versus 424.8 Kbps and 416 Kbps for Sureshkumar et al.' [26] and Sharif et al.' [1], respectively. However, for more than five patients, our scheme outperforms all related schemes. Subsequently, it is fair to say that our proposed scheme demonstrates its network scalability, in particular its ability to maintain its functionalities and performance in the event of high demand.

8   Conclusion

At the present time, TMISs play very important role to improve and manage healthcare sector. Through remote monitoring applications and smart care delivery services, human life has become much more easier and convenient, more particularly for elderly and patients with chronic diseases or disabilities. However, within TMISs, personal and sensitive information about patients and health professionals are exchanged and may be subject to various security attacks. In literature, many authentication and key agreement schemes have been proposed, but they suffer from many weaknesses and cannot guarantee all the security requirements. In this paper, we have reviewed the scheme of Ostad-Sharif et al. [1] and showed that it is vulnerable to key compromise password attack and key compromise impersonation attack. Thereafter, we have proposed a robust mutual and anonymous authentication scheme with key agreement protocol for lightweight application in TMISs in order to fully provide security against well-known attacks. The authentication scheme is based on three-factor verification (identity, password and biometrics) and makes use of elliptic curve cryptography (ECC) and zero-knowledge protocol based on challenge-response commitment. The informal security analysis demonstrates that our scheme provides all security properties and can properly resist numerous security attacks. Moreover, a formal security verification has been conducted using the widely accepted AVISPA tool. The simulation results confirm that our proposed scheme is safe and can withstand various attacks, specially MITM, impersonation and replay attacks. Regarding the performance evaluation, our scheme is proved to be secure and cost efficient in terms of computation, communication and storage capacities. As a result, in view of security and efficiency features, it is fair to assert that the present contribution is more suitable, reliable and secure for TMIS.

References

1. Ostad-Sharif, A., Abbasinezhad-Mood, D., Nikooghadam, M.: A robust and efficient ECC-based mutual authentication and session key generation scheme for healthcare applications. J. Med. Syst. **43**(1), 1–22 (2018). https://doi.org/10.1007/s10916-018-1120-5
2. Kumari, S., Chaudhary, P., Chen, C.M., Khan, M.K.: Questioning key compromise attack on Ostad-Sharif et al.'s authentication and session key generation scheme for healthcare applications. IEEE Access **7**, 39717–39720 (2019). https://ieeexplore.ieee.org/document/8669766
3. Dolev, D., Yao, A.: On the security of public key protocols. IEEE Trans. Inf. Theor. **29**(2), 198–208 (1983). https://ieeexplore.ieee.org/document/1056650
4. Canetti, R., Krawczyk, H.: Analysis of key-exchange protocols and their use for building secure channels. In: Pfitzmann, B. (ed.) EUROCRYPT 2001. LNCS, vol. 2045, pp. 453–474. Springer, Heidelberg (2001). https://doi.org/10.1007/3-540-44987-6_28
5. Dhillon, P.K., Kalra, S.: Multi-factor user authentication scheme for IoT-based healthcare services. J. Reliable Intell. Environ. **4**(3), 141–160 (2018). https://doi.org/10.1007/s40860-018-0062-5
6. Ali, R., Pal, A.K.: Cryptanalysis and biometric-based enhancement of a remote user authentication scheme for E-healthcare system. Arab. J. Sci. Eng. **43**(12), 7837–7852 (2018). https://doi.org/10.1007/s13369-018-3220-4
7. Li, X., Niu, J., Karuppiah, M., Kumari, S., Wu, F.: Secure and efficient two-factor user authentication scheme with user anonymity for network based E-health care applications. J. Med. Syst. **40**(12), 1–12 (2016). https://doi.org/10.1007/s10916-016-0629-8
8. Srinivas, J., Das, A.K., Kumar, N., Rodrigues, J.J.: Cloud centric authentication for wearable healthcare monitoring system. IEEE Trans. Dependable Secure Comput. **17**(5), 942–956 (2018). https://ieeexplore.ieee.org/document/8341758
9. Challa, S., et al.: An efficient ECC-based provably secure three-factor user authentication and key agreement protocol for wireless healthcare sensor networks. Comput. Electr. Eng. **69**, 534–554 (2018). https://doi.org/10.1016/j.compeleceng.2017.08.003
10. Liu, C.H., Chung, Y.F.: Secure user authentication scheme for wireless healthcare sensor networks. Comput. Electr. Eng. **59**, 250–261 (2017). https://dx.doi.org/10.1016/j.compeleceng.2016.01.002
11. Li, X., Ibrahim, M.H., Kumari, S., Kumar, R.: Secure and efficient anonymous authentication scheme for three-tier mobile healthcare systems with wearable sensors. Telecommun. Syst. **67**(2), 323–348 (2017). https://doi.org/10.1007/s11235-017-0340-1
12. Amin, R., Islam, S.H., Biswas, G.P., Khan, M.K., Kumar, N.: A robust and anonymous patient monitoring system using wireless medical sensor networks. Future Gener. Comput. Syst. **80**, 483–495 (2018). https://dx.doi.org/10.1016/j.future.2016.05.032
13. Ali, R., Pal, A.K., Kumari, S., Sangaiah, A.K., Li, X., Wu, F.: An enhanced three factor based authentication protocol using wireless medical sensor networks for healthcare monitoring. J. Ambient Intell. Humanized Comput. 1–22 (2018). https://doi.org/10.1007/s12652-018-1015-9
14. Chandrakar, P.: A secure remote user authentication protocol for healthcare monitoring using wireless medical sensor networks. Int. J. Ambient Comput. Intell. (IJACI) **10**(1), 96–116 (2019). https://doi.org/10.4018/IJACI.2019010106

15. Liu, X., Ma, W., Cao, H.: NPMA: a novel privacy-preserving mutual authentication in TMIS for mobile edge-cloud architecture. J. Med. Syst. **43**(10), 1–16 (2019). https://doi.org/10.1007/s10916-019-1444-9

16. Renuka, K., Kumari, S., Li, X.: Design of a secure three-factor authentication scheme for smart healthcare. J. Med. Syst. **43**(5), 133 (2019). https://doi.org/10.1007/s10916-019-1251-3

17. He, D., Kumar, N., Lee, J.H., Sherratt, R.S.: Enhanced three-factor security protocol for consumer USB mass storage devices. IEEE Trans. Consum. Electron. **60**(1), 30–37 (2014). https://doi.org/10.1109/TCE.2014.6780922

18. Sharma, G., Kalra, S.: A lightweight user authentication scheme for cloud-IoT based healthcare services. Iran. J. Sci. Technol. Trans. Electr. Eng. **43**(1), 619–636 (2019). https://doi.org/10.1007/s40998-018-0146-5

19. Gupta, A., Tripathi, M., Shaikh, T.J., Sharma, A.: A lightweight anonymous user authentication and key establishment scheme for wearable devices. Comput. Netw. **149**, 29–42 (2019). https://doi.org/10.1016/j.comnet.2018.11.021

20. Amin, R., Biswas, G.P.: An improved RSA based user authentication and session key agreement protocol usable in TMIS. J. Med. Syst. **39**(8), 1–14 (2015). https://doi.org/10.1007/s10916-015-0262-y

21. Giri, D., Maitra, T., Amin, R., Srivastava, P.D.: An efficient and robust RSA-based remote user authentication for telecare medical information systems. J. Med. Syst. **39**(1), 1–9 (2014). https://doi.org/10.1007/s10916-014-0145-7

22. Arshad, H., Rasoolzadegan, A.: Design of a secure authentication and key agreement scheme preserving user privacy usable in telecare medicine information systems. J. Med. Syst. **40**(11), 1–19 (2016). https://doi.org/10.1007/s10916-016-0585-3

23. Kumari, A., Kumar, V., Abbasi, M.Y., Kumari, S., Chaudhary, P., Chen, C.M.: CSEF: cloud-based secure and efficient framework for smart medical system using ECC. IEEE Access **8**, 107838–107852 (2020). https://doi.org/10.1109/ACCESS.2020.3001152

24. Alzahrani, B.A., Irshad, A., Alsubhi, K., Albeshri, A.: A secure and efficient remote patient-monitoring authentication protocol for cloud-IoT. Int. J. Commun. Syst. **33**(11), e4423 (2020). https://doi.org/10.1002/dac.4423

25. Dharminder, D., Mishra, D., Li, X.: Construction of RSA-based authentication scheme in authorized access to healthcare services. J. Med. Syst. **44**(1), 1–9 (2019). https://doi.org/10.1007/s10916-019-1471-6

26. Sureshkumar, V., Amin, R., Obaidat, M.S., Karthikeyan, I.: An enhanced mutual authentication and key establishment protocol for TMIS using chaotic map. J. Inf. Secur. Appl. **53**, 102539 (2020). https://doi.org/10.1016/j.jisa.2020.102539

27. Armando, A., et al.: The AVISPA tool for the automated validation of internet security protocols and applications. In: Etessami, K., Rajamani, S.K. (eds.) CAV 2005. LNCS, vol. 3576, pp. 281–285. Springer, Heidelberg (2005). https://doi.org/10.1007/11513988_27

28. Announcing the Advanced Encryption Standard (AES). Federal Information Processing Standards Publication 197, NIST, (2001)

29. Dugan, J., Elliott, S., Mah, B.A., Poskanzer, J., Prabhu, K.: iPerf3, tool for active measurements of the maximum achievable bandwidth on IP networks (2012). https://github.com/esnet/iperf

Discrete Mathematics

Symmetric 4-Adic Complexity of Quaternary Generalized Cyclotomic Sequences of Order Four with Period $2p^n$

Vladimir Edemskiy[✉] and Sofia Koltsova

Yaroslav-the-Wise Novgorod State University, Veliky Novgorod 173003, Russia
vladimir.edemsky@novsu.ru

Abstract. 4-adic complexity is an important characteristic of the unpredictability of a sequence. It is defined as the smallest order of feedback with carry shift register that can generate the whole sequence. In this paper, we estimate the symmetric 4-adic complexity of two classes of quaternary sequences with period $2p^n$. These sequences are constructed on generalized cyclotomic classes of order four and have a high linear complexity over the finite ring and over the field of order four. We show that the 4-adic complexity is good enough to resist the attack of the rational approximation algorithm.

Keywords: Quaternary sequences · Generalized cyclotomy · 4-adic complexity

1 Introduction

Pseudorandom sequences have a wide range of applications in the spread spectrum communication, radar navigation, code division multiple access, stream cipher, and so on. Such sequences can be efficiently generated by different shift registers. In 1990's Klapper and Goresky proposed a new register to design sequences which they call feedback with carry shift register (FCSR) and introduced a new characteristic of a sequence, its m-adic complexity [11], see also [4]. Sequences generated by FCSRs share many important properties enjoyed by linear feedback shift register sequences. Due to the rational approximation algorithm, m-adic complexity has become an important security criterion [10].

Binary and quaternary sequences are among the best known and most used. Quite a lot is known about the 2-adic complexity of binary sequences, see [13,15] and references here. However, it seems that the study of the 4-adic complexity of 4-ary sequences has not been fully developed. The 4-adic complexity of quaternary sequences with period $2p$ was studied in [3,12], series of interleaved quaternary sequences in [7,8]. A few papers are devoted to study of the 4-adic complexity of quaternary sequences with period equal to product of two primes [2,14], see also references here.

V. Edemskiy and S. Koltsova—were supported by Russian Science Foundation according to the research project No. 23-22-00516.

In this paper, we investigate the 4-adic complexity of quaternary generalized cyclotomic sequences of order four with period $2p^n$, which were constructed in [9]. According to [9], these sequences have high linear complexity over the residue class ring modulo four and over the finite field of order four.

In conclusion of introduction, we recall one studying method of the 4-adic complexity [4]. Let $s^\infty = (s_0, s_1, \ldots, s_N)^\infty$ be a quaternary sequence with period N, where N is a positive integer. Its generating polynomial is $S(x) = \sum_{i=0}^{N-1} s_i x^i \in \mathbb{Z}[x]$, where $\mathbb{Z}[x]$ is the polynomial ring with integer coefficients. Then the 4-adic complexity of s^∞ can be defined by

$$\Phi_4(s^\infty) = \left\lceil \log_4 \left(\frac{4^N - 1}{\gcd(S(4), 4^N - 1)} \right) \right\rceil, \tag{1}$$

where $\lceil x \rceil$ is the integer that more than x or equals x, and $\gcd(a,b)$ denotes the greatest common divisor of two integers a and b.

In [5], Hu et al. propose to consider the symmetric 2-adic complexity $\bar{\Phi}_2(s^\infty) = \min(\Phi_2(s^\infty), \Phi_2(\tilde{s}^\infty))$ for binary sequences, where $\tilde{s}^\infty = (s_{N-1}, s_{N-2}, \ldots, s_0)$ is the reciprocal sequence of s^∞. They claimed that the symmetric 2-adic complexity is better than the 2-adic complexity when measuring the security of binary sequences. Thus, it is also interesting to consider $\overline{\Phi}_4(s^\infty)$.

The remainder of this paper is organized as follows. In Sect. 2, we introduce some basic concepts. In Sect. 3, the properties of generalized polynomials of sequences and subsidiary Lemmas are given. In Sect. 4, we study some properties of generalized Gauss periods. Section 5 gives the main results and in Sect. 6 we estimate the symmetric 4-adic complexity of sequences.

2   Preliminaries

Throughout this paper, we will denote by $\mathbb{Z}_N$ the residue class ring modulo N for a positive integer N, and by $\mathbb{Z}_N^*$ the multiplicative group of $\mathbb{Z}_N$.

Let p be an odd prime such that $p \equiv 1 \pmod 4$ and n be a positive integer. Assume that g is an odd primitive root modulo p^2. Then g is also a primitive root modulo p^n and modulo $2p^n$ [6]. Below we recall the notation of Ding-Helleseth generalized cyclotomic classes of order four and the definition of generalized cyclotomic sequences proposed in [9].

For $j = 1, 2, \cdots, n$ and $i = 0, 1, 2, 3$, we put

$$D_i^{(p^j)} = \{g^{i+4t} \pmod{p^j} \mid 0 \le t < p^{j-1}(p-1)/4\};$$
$$D_i^{(2p^j)} = \{g^{i+4t} \pmod{2p^j} \mid 0 \le t < p^{j-1}(p-1)/4\}.$$

The cosets $D_i^{(p^j)}$, $i = 0, 1, 2, 3$ are called Ding-Helleseth generalized cyclotomic classes of order 4 with respect to p^j. By the definition, we have that $|D_i^{(p^j)}| = |D_i^{(2p^j)}| = p^{j-1}(p-1)/4$ for $i = 0, 1, 2, 3$.

It is obvious that $\left\{D_0^{(2p^j)}, D_1^{(2p^j)}, D_2^{(2p^j)}, D_3^{(2p^j)}\right\}$ forms a partition of $\mathbb{Z}_{2p^j}^*$ and

$$\mathbb{Z}_{2p^n} = \bigcup_{j=1}^{n} \bigcup_{t=0}^{3} p^{n-j}\left(D_t^{(2p^j)} \cup 2D_t^{(p^j)}\right) \cup \{0, p^n\}.$$

Let

$$C_t^{(2p^n)} = \bigcup_{j=1}^{n} p^{n-j} D_t^{(2p^j)} \text{ and } C_t^{(p^n)} = \bigcup_{j=1}^{n} 2p^{n-j} D_t^{(p^j)}, \ t = 0,1,2,3.$$

Throughout this paper, the subscripts in $D_i^{(p^j)}$, $D_i^{(2p^j)}$, $C_t^{(p^j)}$ and $C_t^{(2p^j)}$ are computed modulo 4. Denote by e integer such that $2 \bmod p \in D_e^{(p)}$.

We consider here two families of quaternary sequences be defined as in [9]. Let generalized quaternary cyclotomic sequence $v^\infty = (v_0, v_1, v_2, \dots)$ with period $2p^n$ defined by

$$v_i = \begin{cases} 0, & \text{if } i \ (\text{mod } 2p^n) \in C_2^{(2p^n)} \cup C_{-e}^{(p^n)} \cup \{0\}, \\ 1, & \text{if } i \ (\text{mod } 2p^n) \in C_0^{(2p^n)} \cup C_{2-e}^{(p^n)}, \\ 2, & \text{if } i \ (\text{mod } 2p^n) \in C_3^{(2p^n)} \cup C_{1-e}^{(p^n)} \cup \{p^n\}, \\ 3, & \text{if } i \ (\text{mod } 2p^n) \in C_1^{(2p^n)} \cup C_{3-e}^{(p^n)}. \end{cases} \tag{2}$$

and sequence $u^\infty = (u_0, u_1, u_2, \dots)$ with period $2p^n$ defined by

$$u_i = \begin{cases} 0, & \text{if } i \ (\text{mod } 2p^n) \in C_1^{(2p^n)} \cup C_{-e}^{(p^n)} \cup \{0\}, \\ 1, & \text{if } i \ (\text{mod } 2p^n) \in C_2^{(2p^n)} \cup C_{1-e}^{(p^n)}, \\ 2, & \text{if } i \ (\text{mod } 2p^n) \in C_3^{(2p^n)} \cup C_{2-e}^{(p^n)} \cup \{p^n\}, \\ 3, & \text{if } i \ (\text{mod } 2p^n) \in C_0^{(2p^n)} \cup C_{3-e}^{(p^n)} \end{cases} \tag{3}$$

The linear complexity of these sequences was also studied in [9]. In this paper, we will consider the symmetric 4-adic complexity of v^∞ and u^∞.

By (1) we need to study of $\gcd(S(4), 4^{2p^n} - 1)$. For this purpose, we consider the generalized Gauss periods. Using their properties, we estimate the symmetric 4-adic complexity of the above mentioned sequences.

3   Properties of the Generating Polynomial of Sequences

In this section, we give some subsidiary lemmas on the basis of the properties of the generating polynomial of sequences.

The properties of generalized cyclotomic classes are well-known, see for example [9]. Here we only list some necessary properties for further use in the following lemma.

Lemma 1. *Let l and k be two integers with $1 \le l < k \le n$. For $i = 0,1,2,3$, we have*

(i) $D_i^{(p^k)} \ (\text{mod } p^l) = D_i^{(p^l)}$ and $D_i^{(2p^k)} \ (\text{mod } 2p^l) = D_i^{(2p^l)}$;

(ii) *if $b \in 2D_i^{(p^l)}$, then $(b+2tp^l) \ (\text{mod } 2p^k) \in 2D_i^{(p^k)}$; and if $b \in D_i^{(2p^l)}$, then $(b+2tp^l)$ (mod $2p^k$) $\in D_i^{(2p^k)}$ for any integer t;*

(iii) $2D_i^{(p^k)} = \{b, b+2p^l, \dots, b+2(p^{k-l}-1)p^l \mid b \in 2D_i^{(p^l)}\}$ and $D_i^{(2p^k)} = \{b, b+2p^l, \dots, b+2(p^{k-l}-1)p^l \mid b \in D_i^{(2p^l)}\}$.

3.1 Subsidiary Lemmas

To obtain an estimate of the 4-adic complexity of quaternary periodic sequences, it is sufficient to determine $\gcd(S(4), 4^{2p^n} - 1)$. If d is a prime divisor of $4^{2p^n} - 1$ then d divides $4^{p^n} - 1$ or $4^{p^n} + 1$. Since

$$4^{p^n} \pm 1 = \frac{4^{p^n} \pm 1}{4^{p^{n-1}} \pm 1} \cdot \frac{4^{p^{n-1}} \pm 1}{4^{p^{n-2}} \pm 1} \cdot \ldots \cdot (4^p \pm 1),$$

there exists an integer m such that $d \neq 3, 5$ divides $(4^{p^{m+1}} \pm 1)/(4^{p^m} \pm 1)$ with $0 \leq m \leq n - 1$. To this end, we derive $S(4) \left(\bmod \frac{4^{p^{m+1}} \pm 1}{4^{p^m} \pm 1}\right)$ in this subsection.

Lemma 2. *Let* $m = 0, 1, \ldots, n - 1$ *and* $k = 1, 2, \ldots, n$. *For* $i = 0, 1, 2, 3$, *we have*

$$\sum_{f \in p^{n-k} D_i^{(2p^k)}} 4^f \quad \left(\bmod \frac{4^{2p^{m+1}} - 1}{4^{2p^m} - 1}\right) = \begin{cases} 4^{p^{n-k}} p^{k-1}(p-1)/4, & \text{if } k < n - m, \\ p^{n-m-1} \sum\limits_{f \in D_i^{(2p)}} 4^{fp^m}, & \text{if } k = n - m, \\ 0, & \text{if } k > n - m \end{cases}$$

and

$$\sum_{f \in 2p^{n-k} D_i^{(p^k)}} 4^f \quad \left(\bmod \frac{4^{2p^{m+1}} - 1}{4^{2p^m} - 1}\right) = \begin{cases} p^{k-1}(p-1)/4, & \text{if } k < n - m, \\ p^{n-m-1} \sum\limits_{f \in 2D_i^{(p)}} 4^{fp^m}, & \text{if } k = n - m, \\ 0, & \text{if } k > n - m. \end{cases}$$

Proof. We consider three cases for the proof of the first statement.

(i) Let $k < n - m$. In this case, $n - k > m$ and $4^f \equiv 4^{p^{n-k}} \pmod{4^{2p^{m+1}} - 1}$ for $f \in p^{n-k} D_i^{(2p^k)}$. We see that

$$\sum_{f \in p^{n-k} D_i^{(2p^k)}} 4^f \quad \left(\bmod \frac{4^{2p^{m+1}} - 1}{4^{2p^m} - 1}\right) = 4^{p^{n-k}} p^{k-1}(p-1)/4.$$

(ii) Suppose $k = n - m$, i.e., $n - k = m$. Using Lemma 1 (iii), for $l = 1$, we obtain

$$p^m D_i^{(2p^k)} = p^m \{b, b + 2p, \ldots, b + 2(p^{k-1} - 1)p \mid b \in D_i^{(2p)}\}.$$

Hence, we have

$$\sum_{f \in p^m D_i^{(2p^k)}} 4^f \quad \left(\bmod \frac{4^{2p^{m+1}} - 1}{4^{2p^m} - 1}\right) = \sum_{f \in D_i^{(2p)}} \sum_{t=0}^{p^{k-1}-1} 4^{p^m(f+2pt)} = p^{k-1} \sum_{f \in D_i^{(2p)}} 4^{fp^m}.$$

(iii) Let $k > n - m$. Then $m - n + k > 0$. By Lemma 1 (iii), for $l = m - n + k$, we get

$$D_i^{(2p^k)} = \{b, b + 2p^{m-n+k}, \ldots, b + 2(p^{n-m} - 1)p^{m-n+k} \mid b \in D_i^{(2p^{m-n+k})}\}.$$

Hence

$$\sum_{f\in p^{n-k}D_i^{(2p^k)}} 4^f = \sum_{b\in D_i^{(2p^{m-n+k})}} \left(4^{bp^{n-k}} + 4^{bp^{n-k}+2p^m} + \cdots + 4^{bp^{n-k}+2(p^{n-m}-1)p^m}\right).$$

Since

$$4^{bp^{n-k}} + 4^{bp^{n-k}+2p^m} + \cdots + 4^{bp^{n-k}+2(p^{n-m}-1)p^m} \equiv 0 \pmod{\frac{4^{2p^n}-1}{4^{2p^m}-1}},$$

it follows that $\sum\limits_{f\in p^{n-k}D_i^{(2p^k)}} 4^f \pmod{\frac{4^{2p^{m+1}}-1}{4^{2p^m}-1}} = 0$ in this case.

We can prove the second statement in the same way as the first one.   □

Define the subsidiary polynomials

$$S_t^{(2p^n)}(x) = \sum_{i\in C_t^{(2p^n)}} x^i \text{ and } S_t^{(p^n)}(x) = \sum_{i\in C_t^{(p^n)}} x^i, \ t = 0,1,2,3, \ m = 0,1,\ldots,n-1.$$

Let $S_v(x) = \sum_{i=0}^{2p^n-1} v_i x^i$ be the generating polynomial of v^∞ and $S_u(x) = \sum_{i=0}^{2p^n-1} u_i x^i$ be the generating polynomial of u^∞. By definitions of sequences and the subsidiary polynomials we see that

$$S_v(x) = S_0^{(2p^n)}(x) + 2S_3^{(2p^n)}(x) + 3S_1^{(2p^n)}(x) + S_{2-e}^{(p^n)}(x) + 2S_{1-e}^{(p^n)}(x) + 3S_{3-e}^{(p^n)}(x) + x^{p^n} \quad (4)$$

and

$$S_u(x) = S_2^{(2p^n)}(x) + 2S_3^{(2p^n)}(x) + 3S_0^{(2p^n)}(x) + S_{1-e}^{(p^n)}(x) + 2S_{2-e}^{(p^n)}(x) + 3S_{3-e}^{(p^n)}(x) + x^{p^n}. \quad (5)$$

The following lemma is very important for later on.

Lemma 3. *Let notation as before. Then*

(i) $S_t^{(2p^n)}(4) \pmod{\frac{4^{p^{m+1}}-1}{4^{p^m}-1}} = p^{n-m-1} \sum\limits_{f\in D_t^{(2p)}} 4^{fp^m} + (p^{n-m-1}-1)/4;$

(ii) $S_t^{(2p^n)}(4) \pmod{\frac{4^{p^{m+1}}+1}{4^{p^m}+1}} = p^{n-m-1} \sum\limits_{f\in D_t^{(2p)}} 4^{fp^m} - (p^{n-m-1}-1)/4;$

(iii) $S_t^{(p^n)}(4) \pmod{\frac{4^{2p^{m+1}}-1}{4^{2p^m}-1}} = p^{n-m-1} \sum\limits_{f\in 2D_t^{(p)}} 4^{fp^m} + (p^{n-m-1}-1)/4.$

Proof. By definitions we have

$$S_t^{(2p^n)}(4) = \sum_{k=1}^{n} \sum_{i\in p^{n-k}D_t^{(2p^k)}} 4^i = \sum_{k=1}^{n-m-1} \sum_{i\in p^{n-k}D_t^{(2p^k)}} 4^i$$

$$+ \sum_{i\in p^m D_t^{(2p^{n-m})}} 4^i + \sum_{k=n-m+1}^{n} \sum_{i\in p^{n-k}D_t^{(2p^k)}} 4^i.$$

According to Lemma 2, we get

$$S_t^{(2p^n)}(4)(\bmod \ \frac{4^{2p^{m+1}}-1}{4^{2p^m}-1}) = \frac{p-1}{4}\sum_{k=1}^{n-m-1}4^{p^{n-k}}p^{k-1}+p^{n-m-1}\sum_{f\in D_t^{(2p)}}4^{fp^m}.$$

Since $4^{p^{n-k}} \equiv 1 \ (\bmod \ 4^{p^{m+1}}-1)$ for $k \leq n-m-1$ and $4^{p^{n-k}} \equiv -1 \ (\bmod \ 4^{p^{m+1}}+1)$ for $k \leq n-m-1$, this completes the proof of the first and the second statements.

(iii) Here we get

$$S_t^{(p^n)}(4) = \sum_{k=1}^{n}\sum_{i\in 2p^{n-k}D_t^{(p^k)}}4^i = \sum_{k=1}^{n-m-1}\sum_{i\in 2p^{n-k}D_t^{(p^k)}}4^i$$

$$+ \sum_{i\in 2p^m D_t^{(p^{n-m})}}4^i + \sum_{k=n-m+1}^{n}\sum_{i\in 2p^{n-k}D_t^{(p^k)}}4^i.$$

Using Lemma 2, we get

$$S_t^{(p^n)}(4)(\bmod \ \frac{4^{2p^{m+1}}-1}{4^{2p^m}-1}) = \frac{p-1}{4}\sum_{k=1}^{n-m-1}p^{k-1}+p^{n-m-1}\sum_{f\in 2D_t^{(p)}}4^{fp^m}.$$

$\square$

Thus, to study the 4-adic complexity of sequences defined by (2) and (3), we need to investigate $\sum_{f\in D_t^{(2p)}}4^{fp^m}$ and $\sum_{f\in 2D_t^{(p)}}4^{fp^m}$. To this goal, we consider generalized Gauss periods and their properties in the next Section.

4   Generalized Gauss Periods

In this section, we generalize the notion of "Gauss periods" presented in [15] and study their properties.

Let $a = 16^{p^m}$. The generalized "Gauss periods" of order four is defined as follows:

$$\zeta_i(a) = \sum_{j\in D_i^{(p)}}a^j, \ i = 0,1,2,3.$$

It is clear that $\zeta_i(a^b) \equiv \zeta_i(a) \ (\bmod \ a^p - 1)$ for $b \in D_0^{(p)}$ and

$$\zeta_0(a) + \zeta_1(a) + \zeta_2(a) + \zeta_3(a) = \frac{a^p - 1}{a - 1} - 1. \tag{6}$$

Let $\omega_f(a) = \zeta_f(a) + \zeta_{f+2}(a)$, $f = 0, 1$. By definition, we get

$$\omega_0(a) + \omega_1(a) \equiv -1 \ (\bmod \ (a^p - 1)/(a-1)).$$

Lemma 4. *Let notation be as before. Then*

(i) $\displaystyle\sum_{j\in D_i^{(2p)}} 4^{jp^m} \equiv 4^{p^{m+1}}\zeta_{i-e}(16^{p^m})$ (mod $4^{2p^{m+1}}-1$) *for* $i=0,1,2,3$;

(ii) $\displaystyle\sum_{j\in 2D_i^{(p)}} 4^{jp^m} \equiv \zeta_i(16^{p^m})$ (mod $4^{2p^{m+1}}-1$) *for* $i=0,1,2,3$

Proof. By definition, we have

$$4^{p^{m+1}}\zeta_{i-e}(16^{p^m}) = \sum_{j\in D_{i-e}^{(p)}} 4^{2jp^m+p^{m+1}}.$$

Let $t\in\{2jp^m+p^{m+1}(\mathrm{mod}\ 2p^{m+1})\mid j\in D_{i-e}^{(p)}\}$. By condition $2\in D_e^{(p)}$, hence $t/p^m(\mathrm{mod}\ p)\in D_i^{(p)}$ and t is odd. Then $t/p^m(\mathrm{mod}\ 2p)\in D_i^{(2p)}$. Since $|D_i^{(2p)}|=|D_{i-e}^{(p)}|$, this completes the proof of the first statement.

Since the second statement can be proved by the same method as the first one, its proof is omitted here. $\qquad\square$

According to Lemmas 3, 4 and (4),(5), we get

$$S_v(4)\left(\mathrm{mod}\ \frac{4^{p^{m+1}}-1}{4^{p^m}-1}\right) =$$

$$(\zeta_{-e}(a)+2\zeta_{3-e}(a)+3\zeta_{1-e}(a)+\zeta_{2-e}(a)+2\zeta_{1-e}(a)+3\zeta_{3-e}(a))\,p^{n-m-1}+3p^{n-m-1}-1,$$

where $a=16^{p^m}$. By (6) we see that

$$S_v(4)(\mathrm{mod}\ \frac{4^{p^{m+1}}-1}{4^{p^m}-1}) = 2p^{n-m-1}+4\,(\zeta_{1-e}(a)+\zeta_{3-e}(a))\,p^{n-m-1}-1. \qquad (7)$$

We can obtain in the same way that

$$S_v(4)(\mathrm{mod}\ \frac{4^{p^{m+1}}+1}{4^{p^m}+1}) = p^{n-m-1}+2\,(\zeta_{2-e}(a)+\zeta_{3-e}(a))\,p^{n-m-1}-2, \qquad (8)$$

and

$$S_u(4)(\mathrm{mod}\ \frac{4^{p^{m+1}}-1}{4^{p^m}-1}) = 2(\zeta_{3-e}(a)-\zeta_{1-e}(a))p^{n-m-1}-1, \qquad (9)$$

$$S_u(4)(\mathrm{mod}\ \frac{4^{p^{m+1}}+1}{4^{p^m}+1}) = -4\zeta_{-e}(a)p^{n-m-1}-p^{n-m-1}-2. \qquad (10)$$

4.1 Properties of Generalized Gauss Periods

We need cyclotomic numbers to study the properties of generalized Gauss periods. Denote by $(k,f)_4$ the cyclotomic numbers of order four, $k,f\in\mathbb{N}$. Then $|(D_k+1)\cap D_f|=(k,f)_4$. We can prove the following Lemma using the usual cyclotomic method (see for example [1, 15]).

Lemma 5. *Let* $k, l = 0, 1, 2, 3$. *Then*

$$\zeta_l(a) \cdot \zeta_{l+k}(a) \equiv \sum_{f=0}^{3} (k, f)_4 \zeta_{f+l}(a) + \delta \quad (\bmod \ (a^p - 1)/(a-1)),$$

where $\delta = \begin{cases} (p-1)/4, & \text{if } p \equiv 1 (\bmod 8), \ k = 0 \text{ or } p \equiv 5 (\bmod 8), \ k = 2, \\ 0, & \text{otherwise.} \end{cases}$

We recall the formulae for calculating the cyclotomic numbers of order four. For $p \equiv 1 \ (\bmod 4)$ there always exist integers x and y such that $p = x^2 + 4y^2$, where $x \equiv 1$ (mod 4) and y is two-valued. We have Table 1 and Table 2 for cyclotomic numbers 16 of order four [1].

Table 1. $(p-1)/4$ is odd

$(i,j)_4$	0	1	2	3
0	A	B	C	D
1	E	E	D	B
2	A	E	A	E
3	E	D	B	E

Here $A = (p-7+2x)/16$, $B = (p+1+2x-8y)/16$, $C = (p+1-6x)/16$, $D = (p+1+2x+8y)/16$, $E = (p-3-2x)/16$.

Table 2. $(p-1)/4$ is even

$(i,j)_4$	0	1	2	3
0	F	G	K	I
1	G	I	J	J
2	K	J	K	J
3	I	J	J	G

Here $F = (p-11-6x)/16$, $G = (p-3+2x+8y)/16$, $K = (p-3+2x)/16$, $I = (p-3+2x-8y)/16$, $J = (p+1-2x)/16$.

Using Lemma 5 and formulae for cyclotomic numbers we can obtain the properties of ζ_f and ω_f presented in the following lemma. In this lemma and further, subscripts f in ζ_f and ω_f are all taken modulo 4 and 2, respectively. The modulo operation will be omitted when no confusion can arise. This statement was proved in [3] for $a = 16$. The proof for $a = 16^{p^m}$ is the same.

Lemma 6. *Let notations be as above and* $p = x^2 + 4y^2$, $x \equiv 1$ (mod 4), $e = ind_g 2$ (mod 4), $a = 16^{p^m}$, *and* $H(a) = \omega_0(a) - \omega_1(a)$. *Then* *(i)* $H^2(a) \equiv p \pmod{(a^p - 1)/(a - 1)}$.

(ii) For $p \equiv 5 \pmod 8$ we have

$$4\zeta_0(a)\zeta_2(a) \equiv (3p+1)/4 + (x-1)H(a)/2 \pmod{(a^p - 1)/(a-1)},$$
$$4\zeta_1(a)\zeta_3(a) \equiv (3p+1)/4 - (x-1)H(a)/2 \pmod{(a^p - 1)/(a-1)},$$
$$4(\zeta_0(a) - \zeta_2(a))^2 \equiv -2p - 2xH(a) \pmod{((a^p - 1)/(a-1))},$$
$$4(\zeta_1(a) - \zeta_3(a))^2 \equiv -2p + 2xH(a) \pmod{(a^p - 1)/(a-1)}.$$

(iii) For $p \equiv 1 \pmod 8$ we have

$$4\zeta_0(a)\zeta_2(a) \equiv -(p-1)/4 + (x-1)H(a)/2 \pmod{(a^p - 1)/(a-1)},$$
$$4\zeta_1(a)\zeta_3(a) \equiv -(p-1)/4 - (x-1)H(a)/2 \pmod{(a^p - 1)/(a-1)},$$
$$4(\zeta_0(a) - \zeta_2(a))^2 \equiv 2p - 2xH(a) \pmod{(a^p - 1)/(a-1)},$$
$$4(\zeta_1(a) - \zeta_3(a))^2 \equiv 2p + 2xH(a) \pmod{(a^p - 1)/(a-1)}.$$

Corollary 1. *(i) For $p \equiv 5 \pmod 8$ we have*

$$4(\zeta_0(a) + \zeta_1(a))(\zeta_2(a) + \zeta_3(a)) \equiv p + 1 - 2yH(a) \pmod{(a^p - 1)/(a-1)},$$
$$4(\zeta_1(a) + \zeta_2(a))(\zeta_0(a) + \zeta_3(a)) \equiv p + 1 - 2yH(a) \pmod{(a^p - 1)/(a-1)},$$

(ii) For $p \equiv 1 \pmod 8$ we have

$$4(\zeta_0(a) + \zeta_1(a))(\zeta_2(a) + \zeta_3(a)) \equiv -p + 1 + 2yH(a) \pmod{(a^p - 1)/(a-1)},$$
$$4(\zeta_1(a) + \zeta_2(a))(\zeta_0(a) + \zeta_3(a)) \equiv -p + 1 + 2yH(a) \pmod{(a^p - 1)/(a-1)}$$

Also we note that $\omega_0(a) \equiv (-1 + H(a))/2$ and $\omega_1(a) \equiv (-1 - H(a))/2 \pmod{(a^p - 1)/(a-1)}$.

5   4-Adic Complexity

Below is our first main result of this paper.

Theorem 1. *Let v^∞ be a generalized cyclotomic sequence defined by (2). Then $\Phi_4(v^\infty) > 2p^n - p^{n_0} - p^{n_1}$ when $n > 1$, where $n_0 = \lceil (2n-2)/3 \rceil$ and $n_1 = \lceil (4n-3)/3 \rceil$ and $\Phi_4(v^\infty) > 2p - 2\log_4(p+4)$ for $n = 1$.*

Proof. As before $S_v(x)$ is a generating polynomial of v^∞. To prove Theorem 1, it suffices to estimate $\gcd(S_v(4), 4^{2p^n} - 1)$.

First of all, we note that

$$S_v(4) \equiv (2 + 4 + 6)(p^n - 1)/2 + 2 \equiv 2 \pmod 3 \text{ and } S_v(4) \equiv -2 \pmod 5.$$

Hence 3 and 5 do not divide $\gcd(S_v(4), 4^{2p^n} - 1)$.

Let $d > 5$ be a prime divisor of $\gcd(S(4), 4^{2p^n} - 1)$. As we noted before, there exists an integer m such that d divides $(4^{p^{m+1}} \pm 1)/(4^{p^m} \pm 1)$ with $0 \leq m \leq n-1$. We consider two cases.

(i) Let d divide $(4^{p^{m+1}}-1)/(4^{p^m}-1)$ and $S_v(4)$. By (7) we get

$$4(\zeta_{1-e}(a)+\zeta_{3-e}(a))\,p^{n-m-1}+2p^{n-m-1}-1\equiv 0 \pmod{d},$$

where $a=16^{p^m}$ again. We observe that $\zeta_{1-e}(a)+\zeta_{3-e}(a)$ equals ω_0 or ω_1. Thus $\zeta_{1-e}(a)+\zeta_{3-e}(a)=(-1\pm H(a))/2$. Then

$$2(-1\pm H(a))p^{n-m-1}+2p^{n-m-1}-1\equiv 0 \pmod{d}$$

or

$$\pm H(a)p^{n-m-1}\equiv 1 \pmod{d}.$$

According to Lemma 4 (i) we get $p^{2n-2m-1}\equiv 1 \pmod{d}$. Using Fermat Little Theorem we obtain p^{m+1} divides $d-1$, hence $2n-2m-1>m+1$ or $3m<2n-2$, i.e., $m<(2n-2)/3$. This is impossible when $n=1$.

Let $n_0=\lceil (2n-2)/3\rceil$, i.e., $n_0=(2n-2)/3$ when $n\equiv 1 \pmod 3$ and $n_0=\lfloor (2n-2)/3\rfloor+1$ otherwise. Then, $S_v(4)$ is not divisible by $p^{m+1}-1$ for $m>n_0$. So, we have shown that $\gcd(S_v(4),4^{p^n}-1)\le 4^{p^{n_0}}-1$.

(ii) Let d divide $(4^{p^{m+1}}+1)/(4^{p^m}+1)$ and $S_v(4)$. In this case, by (8) we have

$$2(\zeta_{2-e}(a)+\zeta_{3-e}(a))p^{n-m-1}\equiv -p^{n-m-1}+2 \pmod{d}.$$

Hence,

$$4(\zeta_{2-e}(a)+\zeta_{3-e}(a))p^{n-m-1}(\zeta_{-e}(a)+\zeta_{1-e}(a))\equiv 2(-p^{n-m-1}+2)(\zeta_{-e}(a)+\zeta_{1-e}(a)) \pmod{d}.$$

By Corollary 1, we get

$$2(\zeta_{-e}(a)+\zeta_{1-e}(a))(-p^{n-m-1}+2)\equiv (1\pm p-2yH(a))p^{n-m-1} \pmod{d}.$$

Then

$$2(\zeta_{2-e}(a)+\zeta_{3-e}(a))p^{n-m-1}(-p^{n-m-1}+2)+2(\zeta_{-e}(a)+\zeta_{1-e}(a))(-p^{n-m-1}+2)p^{n-m-1}\equiv$$
$$\equiv (-p^{n-m-1}+2)^2+(1\pm p-2yH(a))p^{2n-2m-2} \pmod{d}.$$

or

$$-2p^{n-m-1}(-p^{n-m-1}+2)\equiv (-p^{n-m-1}+2)^2+p^{2n-2m-2}\pm p^{2n-2m-1}-2yH(a)p^{2n-2m-2} \pmod{d}.$$

Thus,

$$2yH(a)p^{2n-2m-2}\equiv -2p^{2n-2m-2}+4p^{n-m-1}+p^{2n-2m-2}-4p^{n-m-1}+4+p^{2n-2m-2}\pm p^{2n-2m-1} \pmod{d}$$

or

$$2yH(a)p^{2n-2m-2}\equiv \mp p^{2n-2m-1}+4 \pmod{d}.$$

Hence, by Lemma 4 (i) we observe that

$$4y^2p^{4n-4m-3}\equiv p^{4n-4m-2}\pm 8p^{2n-2m-1}+16 \pmod{d}.$$

Since $p = x^2 + 4y^2$, it follows that

$$x^2 p^{4n-4m-3} \pm 8p^{2n-2m-1} + 16 \equiv 0 \pmod{d}.$$

We have $x^2 p \pm 8p + 16 \equiv 0 \pmod{d}$ for $n = 1$. In this case, we get $\gcd(S_v(4), 4^p + 1) < p^2 + 8p + 16$. Again, since p^{m+1} divides $d - 1$, we get $4n - 4m - 2 > m + 1$ or $5m < 4n - 3$ when $n > 1$. Thus, we have shown that $\gcd(S_v(4), 4^{p^{n_1}} + 1) \leq 4^{p^{n_1}} - 1$, where $n_1 = \lceil (4n - 3)/5 \rceil$ and $n > 1$. The proof of Theorem 1 is completed. $\square$

Theorem 1 shows that the 4-adic complexity of these sequences is good enough to resist the attack of the rational approximation algorithm.

Our second main result of this paper is the following statement.

Theorem 2. *Let u^∞ be a generalized cyclotomic sequence defined by (3) when $n > 1$. Then $\Phi_4(u^\infty) > 2p^n - 2p^{n_1}$ when $n > 1$, where $n_1 = \lceil (4n - 3)/5 \rceil$ and $\Phi_4(u^\infty) > 2p - 2\log_4 p - 2$ for $n = 1$.*

Proof. To prove Theorem 2, it suffices to estimate $\gcd(S_u(4), 4^{2p^n} - 1)$, where $S_u(x)$ is the generating polynomial of u^∞.

In this case, 3 and 5 do not also divide $\gcd(S_u(4), 4^{2p^n} - 1)$.

We again consider two cases.

(i) Let d divide $(4^{p^{m+1}} - 1)/(4^{p^m} - 1)$ and $S_u(4)$. By (9) we have

$$2(\zeta_{3-e}(a) - \zeta_{1-e}(a))p^{n-m-1} \equiv 1 \pmod{d},$$

where $a = 16^{p^m}$. Then

$$4(\zeta_{3-e}(a) - \zeta_{1-e}(a))^2 p^{2n-2m-2} \equiv 1 \pmod{d}$$

or

$$(\pm p \pm xH(a))p^{2n-2m-2} \equiv 1 \pmod{d}$$

according to Lemma 4 (ii), (iii). We get $\pm xH(a)p^{2n-2m-2} \equiv \mp p^{2n-2m-1} + 1 \pmod{d}$
or

$$x^2 p^{4n-4m-3} \equiv p^{4n-4m-2} \pm 4p^{2n-2m-1} + 1 \pmod{d}.$$

Then

$$4y^2 p^{4n-4m-3} \pm 4p^{2n-2m-1} + 1 \equiv 0 \pmod{d}.$$

If $n = 1$ then $4y^2 p \pm 4p + 1 \neq 0$ and $d \leq (p^2 + 3p + 1)$.

As before we have p^{m+1} divides $d - 1$ and $4n - 4m - 2 > m + 1$ or $5m < 4n - 3$ when $n > 1$. Let $n_1 = \lceil (4n - 3)/5 \rceil$ as in Theorem 1. Thus, we have shown that $\gcd(S_u(4), 4^{p^n} - 1) \leq 4^{p^{n_1}} - 1$ for $n > 1$.

(ii) Let d divide $(4^{p^{m+1}} + 1)/(4^{p^m} + 1)$ and $S_u(4)$. In this case, according to (10) we obtain

$$4\zeta_{-e}(a)p^{n-m-1} \equiv -p^{n-m-1} - 2 \pmod{d}.$$

Hence,

$$4\zeta_{-e}(a)\zeta_{2-e}(a)p^{n-m-1} \equiv (-p^{n-m-1} - 2)\zeta_{2-e}(a) \pmod{d}.$$

Let $p \equiv 5 \pmod 8$. In this case, by Lemma 4 (ii), (iii) we have

$$(\zeta_{2-e}(a))(-p^{n-m-1}-2) \equiv ((3p+1)/4 \pm (x-1)H(a)/2)p^{n-m-1} \pmod d.$$

Then

$$4\zeta_{-e}(a))p^{n-m-1}(-p^{n-m-1}-2) + 4\zeta_{2-e}(a))(-p^{n-m-1}-2)p^{n-m-1} \equiv$$
$$\equiv (p^{n-m-1}+2)^2 + (3p+1\pm 2(x-1)H(a))p^{2n-2m-2} \pmod d$$

or

$$4p^{n-m-1}(p^{n-m-1}+2) \equiv p^{2n-2m-2}+4p^{n-m-1}+4+(3p+1)p^{2n-2m-2}\mp 2(x-1)H(a)p^{2n-2m-2} \pmod d.$$

Thus,

$$\pm 2(x-1)H(a)p^{2n-2m-2} \equiv (3p-2)p^{2n-2m-2} - 4p^{n-m-1}+4 \pmod d.$$

Hence,

$$4(x-1)^2 p^{4n-4m-3} \equiv ((3p-2)p^{2n-2m-2} - 4p^{n-m-1}+4)^2 \pmod d.$$

Since $(3p-1)^2 - 4(x-1)^2 p \equiv 0 \pmod d$ when $n = 1$, it follows that $d \le (3p-2)^2$ in this case.

Again, since p^{m+1} divides $d-1$, we get $4n-4m-2 > m+1$ or $5m < 4n-3$ when $n > 1$. Thus, in this case we have shown that $\gcd(S_u(4), 4^{p^n}+1) \le p^{n_1}+1$.

By (i) and (ii) we have $\gcd(S_u(4), 4^p+1) \le (p^2+3p+1)(3p-2)^2 < 16p^2$.

If $p \equiv 1 \pmod 8$ we get

$$4\zeta_{-e}(a))p^{n-m-1}(-p^{n-m-1}-2) + 4\eta_{2-e}(a))(-p^{n-m-1}-2)p^{n-m-1} \equiv$$
$$\equiv (p^{n-m-1}+2)^2 + (p-1\pm 2(x-1)H(a))p^{2n-2m-2} \pmod d$$

Thus, we can obtain the statement of this theorem in this case in the same way as earlier. The proof of Theorem 2 is completed.   □

Theorem 2 shows that the 4-adic complexity of these sequences is good enough to resist the attack of the rational approximation algorithm.

6   Symmetric 4-Adic Complexity

According to [5], the symmetric 2-adic complexity is better than the 2-adic complexity in measuring the security of a binary periodic sequence. In this regard, we also study the symmetric 4-adic complexity of v^∞ and u^∞.

Theorem 3. *Let v^∞ and u^∞ be the generalized cyclotomic sequences defined by (2) and (3) respectively. Then the estimates of the 4-adic complexity of v^∞ and u^∞ hold for* $\overline{\Phi}_4(v^\infty)$ *and* $\overline{\Phi}_4(u^\infty)$.

Proof. Let $\tilde{v}^\infty = (v_{2p^n-1}, v_{2p^n-2}, \ldots, v_0)^\infty$ and $\tilde{u}^\infty = (u_{2p^n-1}, u_{2p^n-2}, \ldots, u_0)^\infty$ be the reciprocal sequences of v^∞ and u^∞ respectively. Let $\tilde{S}_v(x)$ be the generating polynomial of $\tilde{v}^\infty$. Then $\tilde{S}_v(x) = \sum_{t=1}^{2p^n-1} u_{2p^n-t} x^{t-1}$ and

$$4\tilde{S}_v(4) = \sum_{t=1}^{2p^n} v_{2p^n-t} 4^t = \sum_{t=0}^{2p^n-1} v_{-t} 4^t + v_0 4^{2p^n} - v_0.$$

Hence,

$$4\tilde{S}(4) \equiv \sum_{t=0}^{2p^n-1} v_{-t} 4^t \pmod{4^{2p^n}-1}. \tag{11}$$

It is well known that $-1 \equiv g^{(p-1)/2} \pmod{p}$. We get $-1 \in D_0^{(2p^m)}$, $m = 1, 2, \ldots, n$ when $p \equiv 1 \pmod 8$. Hence, if $t \in C_i^{(2p^k)}$ or $t \in 2C_i^{(p^k)}$ then $-t \in C_i^{(2p^k)}$ or $-t \in 2C_i^{(p^k)}$ respectively. Thus, $v_{-t} = v_t$ and by (11) we have $4\tilde{S}_v(4) \equiv S_v(4) \pmod{4^{2p^n}-1}$. So, the statement of this theorem for $p \equiv 1 \pmod 8$ and the sequence v^∞ follows from Theorem 1. We can prove this for u^∞ in the same way.

Let $p \equiv 5 \pmod 8$. Then $-1 \in D_2^{(2p^m)}$, $m = 1, 2, \ldots, n$. In this case, if $t \in C_i^{(2p^k)}\left(2C_i^{(p^k)}\right)$ then $-t \in C_{i+2}^{(2p^k)}\left(2C_{i+2}^{(p^k)}\right)$. Thus, we get

$$v_{-i} = \begin{cases} 0, & \text{if } i \ (\text{mod } 2p^n) \in C_0^{(2p^n)} \cup C_{2-e}^{(p^n)} \cup \{0\}, \\ 1, & \text{if } i \ (\text{mod } 2p^n) \in C_2^{(2p^n)} \cup C_{-e}^{(p^n)}, \\ 2, & \text{if } i \ (\text{mod } 2p^n) \in C_1^{(2p^n)} \cup C_{3-e}^{(p^n)} \cup \{p^n\}, \\ 3, & \text{if } i \ (\text{mod } 2p^n) \in C_3^{(2p^n)} \cup C_{1-e}^{(p^n)}. \end{cases}$$

and

$$u_{-i} = \begin{cases} 0, & \text{if } i \ (\text{mod } 2p^n) \in C_3^{(2p^n)} \cup C_{2-e}^{(p^n)} \cup \{0\}, \\ 1, & \text{if } i \ (\text{mod } 2p^n) \in C_0^{(2p^n)} \cup C_{3-e}^{(p^n)}, \\ 2, & \text{if } i \ (\text{mod } 2p^n) \in C_1^{(2p^n)} \cup C_{-e}^{(p^n)} \cup \{p^n\}, \\ 3, & \text{if } i \ (\text{mod } 2p^n) \in C_2^{(2p^n)} \cup C_{1-e}^{(p^n)} \end{cases}$$

Then, according to Lemmas 3,4 and (6) we get

$$\sum_{t=0}^{2p^n-1} v_{-t} 4^t \pmod{\frac{4^{p^{m+1}}-1}{4^{p^m}-1}} =$$

$$(\zeta_{2-e}(a) + 2\zeta_{1-e}(a) + 3\zeta_{3-e}(a) + \zeta_{-e}(a) + 2\zeta_{3-e}(a) + 3\zeta_{1-e}(a))p^{n-m-1} + 3p^{n-m-1} - 1,$$

or

$$\sum_{t=0}^{2p^n-1} v_{-t} 4^t \pmod{\frac{4^{p^{m+1}}-1}{4^{p^m}-1}} = 4(\zeta_{1-e}(a) + \zeta_{3-e}(a))p^{n-m-1} + 2p^{n-m-1} - 1.$$

Similarly, we have

$$\sum_{t=0}^{2p^n-1} v_{-t} 4^t \pmod{\frac{4^{p^{m+1}}-1}{4^{p^m}-1}} = 2(\zeta_{-e}(a) + \zeta_{1-e}(a))p^{n-m-1} + p^{n-m-1} - 2.$$

Comparing this with (7) and (8), we see that the estimates of the 4-adic complexity obtained in Theorem 1 hold for $\Phi_4(\tilde{v}^\infty)$. Hence, they also hold for $\overline{\Phi}_4(v^\infty)$.

For u^∞ we get

$$\sum_{t=0}^{2p^n-1} u_{-t}4^t \pmod{\frac{4p^{m+1}-1}{4p^m-1}} =$$

$$(\zeta_{-e}(a)+2\zeta_{1-e}(a)+3\zeta_{2-e}(a)+\zeta_{3-e}(a)+2\zeta_{-e}(a)+3\zeta_{1-e}(a))p^{n-m-1}+3p^{n-m-1}-1,$$

or

$$\sum_{t=0}^{2p^n-1} u_{-t}4^t \pmod{\frac{4p^{m+1}-1}{4p^m-1}} = 2(\zeta_{1-e}(a)-\zeta_{3-e}(a))p^{n-m-1}-1.$$

Similarly, we have

$$\sum_{t=0}^{2p^n-1} u_{-t}4^t \pmod{\frac{4p^{m+1}-1}{4p^m-1}} = 4\zeta_{2-e}(a)p^{n-m-1}-p^{n-m-1}-2.$$

Again, we see that the estimates of the 4-adic complexity obtained in Theorem 2 hold for $\Phi_4(\tilde{u}^\infty)$. Hence, they also hold for $\overline{\Phi}_4(u^\infty)$.

□

Theorem 3 shows that the symmetric 4-adic complexity of these sequences is high.

7 Conclusion

We estimated the symmetric 4-adic complexity of two classes of quaternary generalized cyclotomic sequences of order four with period $2p^n$ and show that it is good enough to resist the attack of the rational approximation algorithm.

Acknowledgements. The authors are very grateful to the anonymous reviewers and the Editor for their valuable comments that improved the presentation and the quality of this paper. V. Edemskiy and S. Koltsova were supported by Russian Science Foundation according to the research project No. 23-22-00516.

References

1. Cusick, T.W., Ding, C., Renvall, A.: Stream Ciphers and Number Theory. North-Holland Publishing Co., Amsterdam (1998)
2. Edemskiy, V., Chen, Z.: 4-adic complexity of the two-prime quaternary generator. J. Appl. Math. Comput. **68**, 3565–3585 (2022)
3. Edemskiy, V., Koltsova, S.: Estimate of 4-adic complexity of unified quaternary sequences of length $2p$. Adv. Math. Commun. **16**(4), 733–740 (2022)
4. Goresky, M., Klapper, A.: Algebraic Shift Register Sequences. Cambridge University Press, Cambridge (2012)
5. Hu, H., Feng, D.: On the 2-adic complexity and the k-error 2-adic complexity of periodic binary sequences. IEEE Trans. Inf. Theory **54**(2), 874–883 (2008)

6. Ireland, K., Rosen, M.: A Classical Introduction to Modern Number Theory. Graduate Texts in Mathematics. Springer, Cham (1990)
7. Jing, X., Xu, Z., Yang, M., Feng K.: The 4-Adic Complexity of Interleaved Quaternary Sequences of Even Length with Optimal Autocorrelation (2022). arXiv:2209.10279v1
8. Jing, X., Yang, M., Feng K.: 4-adic complexity of interleaved quaternary sequences (2022). preprint, arXiv:2105.13826v1
9. Ke, P., Zhong, Y., Zhang, S.: Linear complexity of a new class of quaternary generalized cyclotomic sequence with period $2p^m$. Complexity (2020). https://doi.org/10.1155/2020/6538970
10. Klapper, A., Goresky, M.: Cryptanalysis based on 2-Adic rational approximation. In: Coppersmith, D. (ed.) CRYPTO 1995. LNCS, vol. 963, pp. 262–273. Springer, Heidelberg (1995). https://doi.org/10.1007/3-540-44750-4_21
11. Klapper, A., Goresky, M.: Feedback shift registers, 2-adic span, and combiners with memory. J. Cryptol. **10**, 111–147 (1997)
12. Qiang, S., Li, Y., Yang, M., Feng, K.: The 4-adic complexity of a class of quaternary cyclotomic sequences with period $2p$. CoRRabs/2011.11875 (2020)
13. Xiao, Z., Zeng, X.: 2-Adic complexity of two constructions of binary sequences with period 4N and optimal autocorrelation magnitude. Crypt. Commun. **13**(5), 865–885 (2021)
14. Zhang, C., Jing, X., Xu, Z.: The linear complexity and 4-adic complexity of quaternary sequences with period pq. J. Appl. Math. Comput. (2022). http://doi.org/10.1007/s12190-022-01822-y
15. Zhang, L., Zhang, J., Yang, M., Feng, K.: On the 2-Adic complexity of the Ding-Helleseth-Martinsen binary sequences. IEEE Trans. Inf. Theory **66**(7), 4613–4620 (2020)

Weightwise Perfectly Balanced Functions and Nonlinearity

Agnese Gini(✉) 🆔 and Pierrick Méaux 🆔

University of Luxembourg, Esch-sur-Alzette, Luxembourg
{agnese.gini,pierrick.meaux}@uni.lu

Abstract. In this article we realize a general study on the nonlinearity of weightwise perfectly balanced (WPB) functions. First, we derive upper and lower bounds on the nonlinearity from this class of functions for all n. Then, we give a general construction that allows us to provably provide WPB functions with nonlinearity as low as $2^{n/2-1}$ and WPB functions with high nonlinearity, at least $2^{n-1} - 2^{n/2}$. We provide concrete examples in 8 and 16 variables with high nonlinearity given by this construction. In 8 variables we experimentally obtain functions reaching a nonlinearity of 116 which corresponds to the upper bound of Dobbertin's conjecture, and it improves upon the maximal nonlinearity of WPB functions recently obtained with genetic algorithms. Finally, we study the distribution of nonlinearity over the set of WPB functions. We examine the exact distribution for $n = 4$ and provide an algorithm to estimate the distributions for $n = 8$ and 16, together with the results of our experimental studies for $n = 8$ and 16.

1 Introduction

Boolean functions have multiple applications in secure communications, therefore numerous criteria to determine suitable functions for the specific applications have been proposed during the last decades. In 2017, Carlet, Méaux, and Rotella began to study the cryptographic criteria of Boolean functions with restricted input set [CMR17], motivated by the cryptanalyzis of the FLIP stream cipher [MJSC16], introduced for hybrid homomorphic encryption. FLIP's peculiarity is that its filter function is evaluated on sets of Boolean vectors having constant Hamming weight. Thus, having functions with good properties also when restricted is crucial for examining its security. For instance, as generally working with balanced functions avoids biased output distributions, it is preferable for applications like FLIP to work with functions balanced when restricted over the slices $\mathsf{E}_{k,n} = \{x \in \mathbb{F}_2^n \mid \mathsf{w_H}(x) = k\}$ of the hypercube $\mathbb{F}_2^n$. To study this case, Carlet *et al.* [CMR17] introduced the notion of Weightwise Perfectly Balanced (WPB) functions, *i.e.* $f: \mathbb{F}_2^n \to \mathbb{F}_2$, such that $|\{x \in \mathsf{E}_{k,n} \mid f(x) = 0\}| = |\{x \in \mathsf{E}_{k,n} \mid f(x) = 1\}|$ for each $1 \leq k \leq n - 1$, and $f(0) = 0$ and $f(1) = 1$. The authors observed that these functions exist only when n is a power of two $n = 2^m$, and provided explicit constructions. Since then, many methods for constructing WPB functions have been proposed; *e.g.* [LM19, TL19, LS20, MS21, ZS21, MSL21, GS22, ZS22, MPJ+22, GM22a, GM22b, MKCL22, MSLZ22].

© The Author(s), under exclusive license to Springer Nature Switzerland AG 2023
S. El Hajji et al. (Eds.): C2SI 2023, LNCS 13874, pp. 338–359, 2023.
https://doi.org/10.1007/978-3-031-33017-9_21

In particular, Mandujano, Ku Cauich, and Lara recently investigated the problem of finding WPB functions with high nonlinearity via genetic algorithms [MKCL22]. While Boolean functions having the highest possible nonlinearity (*i.e.* bent functions) are known for $n = 2^m$, the problem of determining the maximal nonlinearity for a balanced 2^m-variable function is still open, and *a fortiori* for a WPB function. Indeed, being balanced, WPB functions cannot be bent (see *e.g.* [SZZ93, Car21]). In general, evolutionary algorithms give quite good results for small value of n [MCD97, PCG+16, MPJ+22], and in fact the authors of [MKCL22] were able to find a 8-variable function with nonlinearity 112, which was the maximal obtained so far for a WPB function. However, for larger values of n their results are limited due to the massive computational power required for this kind of approach.

Hence, the goal of this paper is to further investigate the nonlinearity of WPB functions, from a more algebraic point of view. Namely, we first discuss the known upper bound and determine novel lower bounds on the nonlinearity of a WPB function. For this purpose we introduce the notion of Non Perfect Balancedness (NPB), which measures the distance of Boolean function from the family of WPB functions. This notion is the analogous of the nonlinearity with respect to WPB functions instead of affine functions. Then, we address the problem of building WPB functions with prescribed nonlinearity. Specifically, our construction modifies the support of the input function on each slice to make it perfectly balanced, so that the output is a WPB function lying at minimal Hamming distance from the input function. By using this construction, we are able to exhibit both WPB functions with very low and very high nonlinearity for any n. Thereafter, we instantiate this strategy for 8 and 16 variables, obtaining two large families of WPB functions with almost optimal nonlinearity. For instance, we prove that for $n = 8$ our construction gives more than 2^{43} different functions with nonlinearity at least 112. We also provide explicit examples with nonlinearity $112, 114$ and 116, which is therefore the new highest value known (and reaching the highest nonlinearity observed for a 8-variable balanced functions). Finally, we study the nonlinearity distribution of WPB functions. As in [MCD97] the results obtained via genetic algorithms are compared with uniform distribution, in this paper we analyze the nonlinearity's behavior of WPB functions sampled uniformly at random. We followed the model established by [GM22a] for the weightwise nonlinearities of WPB functions. As a result of our experiments, we observed that extreme values are rare, concluding that we cannot expect in practice to find large families of functions, like those we exhibit from our construction, by sampling uniformly at random.

2 Preliminaries

For readability, we use the notation $+$ instead of $\oplus$ to denote the addition in $\mathbb{F}_2$ and $\sum$ instead of $\bigoplus$. In addition to classic notations we use $[a, b]$ to denote the subset of all integers between a and b: $\{a, a + 1, \ldots, b\}$. For a vector $v \in \mathbb{F}_2^n$ we denote by $\mathsf{w_H}(v)$ its Hamming weight $\mathsf{w_H}(v) = |\{i \in [1, n] \,|\, v_i = 1\}|$. For two vectors v and w of $\mathbb{F}_2^n$ we denote by $\mathsf{d_H}(v, w)$ the Hamming distance between v and w, $\mathsf{d_H}(v, w) = \mathsf{w_H}(v + w)$.

2.1   Boolean Functions and Weightwise Considerations

In this part we recall the main concepts on Boolean functions used in cryptography and their weightwise properties we will use in this article. We refer to *e.g.* [Car21] for Boolean functions and cryptographic parameters and to [CMR17] for the weightwise properties, also named as properties on the slices. For $k \in [0, n]$ we call slice of the Boolean hypercube (of dimension n) the set $\mathsf{E}_{k,n} = \{x \in \mathbb{F}_2^n \mid \mathsf{w}_\mathsf{H}(x) = k\}$. Thereafter, the Boolean hypercube is partitioned into $n + 1$ slices where the elements have the same Hamming weight.

Definition 1 (Boolean Function). *A Boolean function f in n variables is a function from $\mathbb{F}_2^n$ to $\mathbb{F}_2$. The set of all Boolean functions in n variables is denoted by $\mathcal{B}_n$.*

Definition 2 (Algebraic Normal Form (ANF) and degree). *We call Algebraic Normal Form of a Boolean function f its n-variable polynomial representation over $\mathbb{F}_2$ (i.e. belonging to $\mathbb{F}_2[x_1, \ldots, x_n]/(x_1^2 + x_1, \ldots, x_n^2 + x_n))$:*

$$f(x_1, \ldots, x_n) = \sum_{I \subseteq [1,n]} a_I \left(\prod_{i \in I} x_i \right)$$

where $a_I \in \mathbb{F}_2$. The (algebraic) degree of f, denoted by $\deg(f)$ is:

$$\deg(f) = \max_{I \subseteq [1,n]} \{|I| \mid a_I = 1\} \text{ if } f \text{ is not null}, 0 \text{ otherwise.}$$

To denote when a property or a definition is restricted to a slice we use the subscript k. For example, for a n-variable Boolean function f we denote its support by $\mathsf{supp}(f) = \{x \in \mathbb{F}_2^n \mid f(x) = 1\}$ and we refer to $\mathsf{supp}_k(f)$ for its support restricted to a slice, *i.e.* $\mathsf{supp}(f) \cap \mathsf{E}_{k,n}$.

Definition 3 (Balancedness). *A Boolean function $f \in \mathcal{B}_n$ is called balanced if $|\mathsf{supp}(f)| = 2^{n-1} = |\mathsf{supp}(f + 1)|$.*
    For $k \in [0, n]$ the function is said balanced on the slice k if $||\mathsf{supp}_k(f)| - |\mathsf{supp}_k(f+1)|| \leq 1$. In particular when $|\mathsf{E}_{k,n}|$ is even $|\mathsf{supp}_k(f)| = |\mathsf{supp}_k(f+1)| = |\mathsf{E}_{k,n}|/2$.

Definition 4 (Nonlinearity and weightwise nonlinearity). *The nonlinearity $\mathsf{NL}(f)$ of a Boolean function $f \in \mathcal{B}_n$, where n is a positive integer, is the minimum Hamming distance between f and all the affine functions in $\mathcal{B}_n$:*

$$\mathsf{NL}(f) = \min_{g, \deg(g) \leq 1} \{\mathsf{d}_\mathsf{H}(f, g)\},$$

where $g(x) = a \cdot x + \varepsilon$, $a \in \mathbb{F}_2^n, \varepsilon \in \mathbb{F}_2$ (where $\cdot$ is an inner product in $\mathbb{F}_2^n$, any choice of inner product will give the same value of $\mathsf{NL}(f)$).
    For $k \in [0, n]$ we denote by NL_k the nonlinearity on the slice k, the minimum Hamming distance between f restricted to $\mathsf{E}_{k,n}$ and the restrictions to $\mathsf{E}_{k,n}$ of affine functions over $\mathbb{F}_2^n$. Accordingly:

$$\mathsf{NL}_k(f) = \min_{g, \deg(g) \leq 1} |\mathsf{supp}_k(f + g)|.$$

We refer to the global weightwise nonlinearity of f as $\mathsf{GWNL}(f) = \sum_{k=0}^{n} \mathsf{NL}_k(f)$
[GM22a, Definition 4].

The functions reaching the maximal value of nonlinearity are called *bent*, and are deeply studied in the context of symmetric cryptography (see *e.g.* [Rot76, Tok15, Mes16]).

Definition 5 (Bent function). *Let $n \in \mathbb{N}^*$ be even. A Boolean function $f \in \mathcal{B}_n$ is bent if and only if* $\mathsf{NL}(f) = 2^{n-1} - 2^{n/2-1}$.

We also recall the concept of Walsh transform, and restricted Walsh transform [MMM+18], which are of particular interest to study the (restricted) nonlinearity or balancedness.

Definition 6 (Walsh transform and restricted Walsh transform). *Let $f \in \mathcal{B}_n$ be a Boolean function, its Walsh transform W_f at $a \in \mathbb{F}_2^n$ is defined as:*

$$W_f(a) := \sum_{x \in \mathbb{F}_2^n} (-1)^{f(x)+a \cdot x}.$$

Let $f \in \mathcal{B}_n$, $S \subset \mathbb{F}_2^n$, its Walsh transform restricted to S at $a \in \mathbb{F}_2^n$ is defined as:

$$W_{f,S}(a) := \sum_{x \in S} (-1)^{f(x)+a \cdot x}.$$

For $S = \mathsf{E}_{k,n}$ we denote $W_{f,\mathsf{E}_{k,n}}(a)$ by $\mathcal{W}_{f,k}(a)$, and for $a = 0_n$ we denote $\mathcal{W}_{f,k}(a)$ as $\mathcal{W}_{f,k}(0)$.

Property 1 (Nonlinearity and Walsh transform, *e.g.* [Car21]). *Let $n \in \mathbb{N}^*$, for every n-variable Boolean function f:*

$$\mathsf{NL}(f) = 2^{n-1} - \frac{\max_{a \in \mathbb{F}_2^n} |W_f(a)|}{2}.$$

Property 2 (Nonlinearity on the slice and restricted Walsh transform, adapted from [CMR17], Proposition 6). *Let $n \in \mathbb{N}^*, k \in [0, n]$, for every n-variable Boolean function f over $\mathsf{E}_{k,n}$:*

$$\mathsf{NL}_k(f) = \frac{|\mathsf{E}_{k,n}|}{2} - \frac{\max_{a \in \mathbb{F}_2^n} |\mathcal{W}_{f,k}(a)|}{2}.$$

Property 3 (Balancedness on the slice and restricted Walsh transform [GM22b]). *Let $n \in \mathbb{N}^*, k \in [0, n]$, $f \in \mathcal{B}_n$ is balanced over $\mathsf{E}_{k,n}$ if and only if:*

$$\mathcal{W}_{f,k}(0) = \begin{cases} 0 & \text{if } |\mathsf{E}_{k,n}| \text{ is even,} \\ \pm 1 & \text{if } |\mathsf{E}_{k,n}| \text{ is odd.} \end{cases}$$

2.2 Symmetric Functions

The n-variable *Boolean symmetric functions* are those that are constant on each slice $\mathsf{E}_{k,n}$ for $k \in [0, n]$. This class has been assiduously studied in the context of cryptography, see *e.g.* [Car04, CV05, BP05, SM07, QFLW09, Méa21, CM21]. In this paper we mainly consider two families of symmetric functions, which are both bases of the symmetric functions:

Definition 7 (Elementary symmetric functions). *Let $i \in [0, n]$, the elementary symmetric function of degree i in n variables, denoted by $\sigma_{i,n}$, is the function which ANF contains all monomials of degree i and no monomial of other degrees.*

Definition 8 (Slice indicator functions). *Let $k \in [0, n]$, the indicator function of the slice of weight k is defined as:*

$$\forall x \in \mathbb{F}_2^n, \quad \varphi_{k,n}(x) = 1 \text{ if and only if } \mathsf{w}_\mathsf{H}(x) = k.$$

Property 4 (Nonlinearity of $\sigma_{2,n}$). *Let $n \in \mathbb{N}^*$ even, the elementary symmetric function $\sigma_{2,n} = \sum_{1 \leq i < j \leq n} x_i x_j$ is bent, i.e. $\mathsf{NL}(\sigma_{2,n}) = 2^{n-1} - 2^{n/2-1}$.*

Property 5 (Weightwise restricted Walsh transform and addition of symmetric function ([GM22b], Proposition 4)). *Let $n \in \mathbb{N}^*$, $k \in [0, n]$ and $f \in \mathcal{B}_n$, the following holds on $f + \varphi_{k,n}$*

$$\forall a \in \mathbb{F}_2^n, \forall i \in [0, n] \backslash \{k\}, \mathcal{W}_{f+\varphi_{k,n},i}(a) = \mathcal{W}_{f,i}(a), \text{ and } \mathcal{W}_{f+\varphi_{k,n},k}(a) = -\mathcal{W}_{f,i}(a).$$

2.3 Weightwise Perfectly Balanced Functions

Definition 9 (Weightwise Perfectly Balanced Function (WPB)). *Let $m \in \mathbb{N}^*$ and f be a Boolean function in $n = 2^m$ variables. It will be called weightwise perfectly balanced (WPB) if, for every $k \in [1, n-1]$, f is balanced on the slice k, that is $\forall k \in [1, n-1], |\mathsf{supp}_k(f)| = \binom{n}{k}/2$, and:*

$$f(0, \ldots, 0) = 0, \quad \text{and } f(1, \ldots, 1) = 1.$$

The set of WPB functions in 2^m variables is denoted by $\mathcal{WPB}_m$.

Property 6 (WPB functions, alternative definition). *Let $m \in \mathbb{N}^*$, $n = 2^m$, f is a WPB function if:*

- $f(0_n) = 0$,
- $\forall k \in [1, n-1], \mathcal{W}_{f,k}(\mathbf{0}) = 0$,
- $f(1_n) = 1$.

2.4 Krawtchouk Polynomials and Properties

For some proofs we will use Krawtchouk polynomials and some of their properties, we give the necessary preliminaries here and refer to *e.g.* [MS78] for more details.

Definition 10 (Krawtchouk Polynomials). *The Krawtchouk polynomial of degree k, with $0 \leq k \leq n$ is given by:* $\mathsf{K}_k(\ell, n) = \sum_{j=0}^{k} (-1)^j \binom{\ell}{j} \binom{n-\ell}{k-j}$.

Property 7 (Krawtchouk polynomials relations). *Let $n \in \mathbb{N}^*$ and $k \in [0,n]$, the following relations hold:*

1. $\mathsf{K}_k(\ell, n) = \sum_{x \in \mathsf{E}_{k,n}} (-1)^{a \cdot x}$, *where $a \in \mathbb{F}_2^n$ and $\ell = \mathsf{w}_\mathsf{H}(a)$,*
2. $\mathsf{K}_{n-k}(\ell, n) = (-1)^\ell \mathsf{K}_k(\ell, n)$,
3. $\mathsf{K}_k(n - \ell, n) = (-1)^k \mathsf{K}_k(\ell, n)$,

Property 8 (Proposition 5 [DMS06]). *For n even, $k \in [0,n]$,*

$$\mathsf{K}_k(n/2, n) = \begin{cases} 0 & \text{if } k \text{ is odd,} \\ (-1)^{k/2} \binom{n/2}{k/2} & \text{if } k \text{ is even.} \end{cases}$$

3 Bounds on the Nonlinearity of a WPB Function

For n-variable Boolean functions the upper bound on the nonlinearity is a classic result, it is $2^{n-1} - 2^{n/2-1}$ and it can be reached only for n even, by bent functions. Since WPB functions are balanced, they cannot be bent (see *e.g.* [SZZ93, Car21]), therefore no WPB function can reach this bound, and we will consider as upper bound the one holding for all balanced functions. Therefore, from [SZZ93] Corollary 7, we have that a WPB function f has nonlinearity at most:

$$U_m = 2^{n-1} - 2^{n/2-1} - 2, \tag{1}$$

since $n = 2^m$ is even and f balanced. In this section we will focus on the lower bound on the nonlinearity of WPB functions, and provide different lower bounds.

First, we derive a lower bound based on the results on the weightwise nonlinearities of WPB functions.

Proposition 1. *Let $m \in \mathbb{N}^*$, $n = 2^m$ and $f \in \mathcal{WPB}_m$, then:*

$$\mu_n \leq \mathsf{GWNL}(f) \leq \mathsf{NL}(f),$$

where μ_n is the global minimum weightwise nonlinearity $\mu_n = \sum_{k=1}^{n-1} \min_{g \in \mathcal{WPB}_m} \mathsf{NL}_k(g)$.

Proof. The first inequality comes from the definition of GWNL (see Definition 4), and the second one comes from the fact that the nonlinearity considers the best affine approximation over $\mathbb{F}_2^n$ whereas the global weightwise nonlinearity considers the best affine approximation on each slice.   □

Thereafter, lower bounds on μ_n allow us to derive lower bounds on $\mathsf{NL}(f)$ when f is WPB. Using the results from [GM22a, Proposition 7], it gives:

$$\mathsf{NL}(f) \geq \begin{cases} 2 & \text{if } m = 3, \\ 4 & \text{if } m > 3, m \text{ even}, \\ 6 & \text{if } m > 3, m \text{ odd}. \end{cases}$$

To improve upon this bound we consider the distance between affine functions and WPB functions. To do so we introduce the notion of *Non Perfect Balancedness (NPB)*, similar to the nonlinearity.

Definition 11 (Non Perfect Balancedness). *Let $m \in \mathbb{N}^*$, $n = 2^m$, and f an n-variable Boolean function, the non perfect balancedness of f, denoted by $\mathsf{NPB}(f)$ is defined as:*

$$\mathsf{NPB}(f) = \min_{g \in \mathcal{WPB}_m} \mathsf{d_H}(f, g).$$

The NPB measures the distance to WPB functions, as the nonlinearity measures the distance to affine functions. In the following we give an expression of the NPB from the restricted Walsh transform.

Proposition 2 (NPB and restricted Walsh transform). *Let $m \in \mathbb{N}^*$, $n = 2^m$, and $f \in \mathcal{B}_n$, the following holds on its non perfect balancedness:*

$$\mathsf{NPB}(f) = \frac{2 - \mathcal{W}_{f,0}(0) + \mathcal{W}_{f,n}(0)}{2} + \sum_{k=1}^{n-1} \frac{|\mathcal{W}_{f,k}(0)|}{2}.$$

Proof. First, we rewrite the expression of NPB by partitioning $\mathbb{F}_2^n$ into the $n+1$ slices. For h a Boolean function we denote by $\mathsf{supp}_k(h)$ the support of h on $\mathsf{E}_{k,n}$ and by h_k the restriction of h on $\mathsf{E}_{k,n}$. Moreover, denoting by ν_k the binomial coefficient $\binom{n}{k}$ we have

$$\mathsf{NPB}(f) = \min_{g \in \mathcal{WPB}_m} \mathsf{d_H}(f, g) = \min_{g \in \mathcal{WPB}_m} \sum_{k=0}^{n} \mathsf{d_H}(f_k, g_k) \tag{2}$$

$$= |\mathsf{supp}_0(f)| + 1 - |\mathsf{supp}_n(f)| + \sum_{k=1}^{n-1} \min_{v \in \mathsf{E}_{\frac{\nu_k}{2}, \nu_k}} \mathsf{d_H}(f_k, v) \tag{3}$$

$$= |\mathsf{supp}_0(f)| + 1 - |\mathsf{supp}_n(f)| + \sum_{k=1}^{n-1} |\frac{\nu_k}{2} - |\mathsf{supp}_k(f)|| \tag{4}$$

$$= \frac{1 - \mathcal{W}_{f,0}(0)}{2} + \frac{1 + \mathcal{W}_{f,n}(0)}{2} + \sum_{k=1}^{n-1} \frac{|\mathcal{W}_{f,k}(0)|}{2}, \tag{5}$$

where Eq. 3 is obtained by using the definition of WPB functions (Definition 9), *i.e.* their value is 0 in 0_n and 1 in 1_n, and from the fact that each element of Hamming weight $\nu_k/2$ is the support of a WPB function on the slice $k \in [1, n-1]$. Finally, Eq. 5 comes from the expression of $\mathcal{W}_{f,k}(0)$:

$$\mathcal{W}_{f,k}(0) = \sum_{x \in \mathsf{E}_{k,n}} (-1)^{f(x)} = \nu_k - 2|\mathrm{supp}_k(f)|.$$

$\square$

Now, we show that we can express the non perfect balancedness of affine functions in terms of sum of Krawtchouk polynomials.

Lemma 1 (NPB of affine functions). *Let $m \in \mathbb{N}^*$, $n = 2^m$, and $f \in \mathcal{B}_n$ be an affine function. Let us denote $f = ax + \varepsilon$ with $a \in \mathsf{E}_{\ell,n}$ and $\varepsilon \in \{0,1\}$, its non perfect balancedness is:*

$$\mathsf{NPB}(f) = \varepsilon + (\ell + 1 + \varepsilon \mod 2) + \sum_{k=1}^{n/2-1} |\mathsf{K}_k(\ell, n)| + \frac{|\mathsf{K}_{\frac{n}{2}}(\ell, n)|}{2}.$$

Proof. First, we give the relation between $\mathcal{W}_{f,k}(0)$ and $\mathsf{K}_k(\ell, n)$ when $f = ax + \varepsilon$, using the first item of Property 7. For $k \in [0, n]$:

$$\mathcal{W}_{f,k}(0) = \sum_{x \in \mathsf{E}_{k,n}} (-1)^{a \cdot x + \varepsilon} = (-1)^{\varepsilon} \sum_{x \in \mathsf{E}_{k,n}} (-1)^{a \cdot x} = (-1)^{\varepsilon} \mathsf{K}_k(\ell, n).$$

Then, using Proposition 2 we get:

$$\mathsf{NPB}(f) = \frac{\sum_{k=1}^{n-1} |(-1)^{\varepsilon} \mathsf{K}_k(\ell, n)|}{2} + \frac{2 - (-1)^{\varepsilon} \mathsf{K}_0(\ell, n) + (-1)^{\varepsilon} \mathsf{K}_n(\ell, n)}{2} \tag{6}$$

$$= \sum_{k=1}^{n/2-1} |\mathsf{K}_k(\ell, n)| + \frac{|\mathsf{K}_{\frac{n}{2}}(\ell, n)|}{2} + \frac{2 + ((-1)^{\varepsilon+1} + (-1)^{\varepsilon+\ell}) \mathsf{K}_0(\ell, n)}{2} \tag{7}$$

$$= \sum_{k=1}^{n/2-1} |\mathsf{K}_k(\ell, n)| + \frac{|\mathsf{K}_{\frac{n}{2}}(\ell, n)|}{2} + 1 + \frac{(-1)^{\varepsilon+1} + (-1)^{\varepsilon+\ell}}{2}. \tag{8}$$

Equation 7 is obtained using Property 7 Item 2, and Eq. 8 comes from $\mathsf{K}_0(\ell, n) = 1$ using Definition 10. Finally, we rewrite $1 + \frac{(-1)^{\varepsilon+1} + (-1)^{\varepsilon+\ell}}{2}$ as $\varepsilon + (\ell + 1 + \varepsilon \mod 2)$, which can be verified considering the four cases:

- ℓ odd and $\varepsilon = 0$ giving 0,
- ℓ odd and $\varepsilon = 1$ giving 2,
- ℓ even and $\varepsilon = 0$ giving 1,
- ℓ even and $\varepsilon = 1$ giving 1.

$\square$

We highlight the NPB of particular affine functions, the linear functions having 0, 1 and $n/2$ monomials in their ANF.

Proposition 3. *Let* $m \in \mathbb{N}^*$ *and* $n = 2^m$, *we consider the three following n-variable Boolean functions* $f(x) = 0$, $g(x) = x_1$ *and* $h(x) = \sum_{i=1}^{n/2} x_i$. *Their non perfect balancedness is the following:*

- $\mathsf{NPB}(f) = 2^{n-1}$,
- $\mathsf{NPB}(g) = \binom{n-1}{n/2-1} - 1$,
- $\mathsf{NPB}(h) = 2^{n/2-1}$.

Proof. We begin with the expression of $\mathsf{NPB}(f)$ using Lemma 1. For $k \in [0, n]$ the Krawtchouk polynomial $\mathsf{K}_k(0, n)$ takes the value $\binom{n}{k}$, accordingly:

$$\mathsf{NPB}(f) = 1 + \sum_{k=1}^{n/2-1} \left| \binom{n}{k} \right| + \frac{\binom{n}{n/2}}{2} = \frac{1}{2} \sum_{k=0}^{n} \binom{n}{k} = 2^{n-1}.$$

Then, we give the expression of $\mathsf{NPB}(g)$ (using Lemma 1), using that for $k \in [0, n]$ $\mathsf{K}_k(1, n) = \binom{n-1}{k} - \binom{n-1}{k-1}$. Since for $k \in [1, n/2 - 1]$ we have $\binom{n-1}{k} \geq \binom{n-1}{k-1}$, $\mathsf{K}_k(1, n)$ is positive. Therefore,

$$\mathsf{NPB}(g) = \sum_{k=1}^{n/2-1} \binom{n-1}{k} - \binom{n-1}{k-1} + \frac{\left| \binom{n-1}{n/2} - \binom{n-1}{n/2-1} \right|}{2}$$

$$= \binom{n-1}{n/2-1} - \binom{n-1}{0} + 0 = \binom{n-1}{n/2-1} - 1.$$

Finally, we give the expression of $\mathsf{NPB}(h)$ using Lemma 1, Property 7 Item 2, and Property 8 for the value of Krawtchouk polynomials:

$$\mathsf{NPB}(h) = 1 + \sum_{k=1}^{n/2-1} |\mathsf{K}_k(n/2, n)| + \frac{|\mathsf{K}_{\frac{n}{2}}(n/2, n)|}{2} = \frac{1}{2} \sum_{k=0}^{n} |\mathsf{K}_k(n/2, n)|$$

$$= \frac{1}{2} \sum_{t=0}^{n/2} |(-1)^{2t/2} \binom{n/2}{2t/2}| = \frac{1}{2} \sum_{t=0}^{n/2} \binom{n/2}{t} = 2^{n/2-1}.$$

$\square$

Finally, we provide a lower bound on the nonlinearity of WPB functions using the NPB of affine functions.

Theorem 1 (Lower bound on the nonlinearity of WPB functions). *Let* $m \in \mathbb{N}$, $m \geq 2$, $n = 2^m$, *and* B_m *be the integer defined as:*

$$B_m = \min_{\substack{\ell \in [0, n/2] \\ \varepsilon \in \{0,1\}}} [\varepsilon + (\ell + 1 + \varepsilon \mod 2)] + \sum_{k=1}^{n/2-1} |\mathsf{K}_k(\ell, n)| + \frac{|\mathsf{K}_{\frac{n}{2}}(\ell, n)|}{2},$$

then, $\forall f \in \mathcal{WPB}_m$, $\mathsf{NL}(f) \geq B_m$.

Proof. Using Property 7 Item 3 and Lemma 1 we obtain that B_m is the NPB minimal over the n-variable affine functions. Then, using the definitions of nonlinearity and non perfect balancedness, for f WPB we obtain:

$$\mathsf{NL}(f) = \min_{g \text{ affine}} \mathsf{d}_\mathsf{H}(f, g) \geq \min_{\substack{g \text{ affine} \\ f \in \mathcal{WPB}_m}} \mathsf{d}_\mathsf{H}(f, g) = \min_{g \text{ affine}} \mathsf{NPB}(g) = B_m.$$

$\square$

Remark 1. We computed explicitly B_m for small value of m; see Table 1. From Proposition 3 we get that B_m is at most $2^{n/2-1}$, *i.e.* the non perfect balancedness given by a linear function with $\frac{n}{2}$ monomials in its ANF, *e.g.* $h(x) = \sum_{i=1}^{n/2} x_i$. Table 1 shows that actually for m up to 6, *i.e.* 64 variables, $B_m = \mathsf{NPB}(h)$.

Table 1. Concrete values of B_m and U_m for small values of m.

m	2	3	4	5	6
B_m	2	8	128	2^{15}	2^{31}
U_m	4	118	32638	$2^{31} - 2^{15} - 2$	$2^{63} - 2^{31} - 2$

4   Constructions of WPB Functions with Prescribed Nonlinearity

In this section we present a construction allowing to obtain a WPB function from any 2^m-variable Boolean function f. The principle of the construction is to modify the support of the input function on each slice to make it perfectly balanced, enabling us to obtain as output a WPB function g which lies at distance $\mathsf{NPB}(f)$ from the input function. We show thereafter how we can use this construction to build functions with low, or high nonlinearity.

Construction 1

Input: Let $m \in \mathbb{N}$, $m \geq 2$, $n = 2^m$ and f a n-variable function.
Output: $g \in \mathcal{WPB}_m$.
1: Initiate the support of g to $\mathsf{supp}(f)$.
2: If $0_n \in \mathsf{supp}(f)$ remove 0_n from $\mathsf{supp}(g)$.
3: If $1_n \notin \mathsf{supp}(f)$ add 1_n to $\mathsf{supp}(g)$.
4: **for** $k \leftarrow 1$ to $n-1$ **do**
5:    Compute $C_{k,n} = \mathcal{W}_{f,k}(0)/2$,
6:    **if** $C_{k,n} < 0$ **then**
7:       remove $|C_{k,n}|$ elements from $\mathsf{supp}_k(g)$,
8:    **else**
9:       **if** $C_{k,n} > 0$ **then**
10:          add $C_{k,n}$ new elements to $\mathsf{supp}_k(g)$,
11:       **end if**
12:    **end if**
13: **end for**
14: **return** g

Theorem 2 (Weightwise perfect balancedness and distance of Construction 1). *Let $m \in \mathbb{N}$, $m \geq 2$ and $n = 2^m$. Any function given by Construction 1 with input f is weightwise perfectly balanced, and $\mathsf{d_H}(f, g) = \mathsf{NPB}(f)$.*

Proof. First, we show that g is WPB, using the characterization from Property 6:

- $g(0_n) = 0$ since 0_n does not belong to $\mathsf{supp}(g)$.
- $g(1_n) = 1$ since 1_n belongs to $\mathsf{supp}(g)$.
- For $k \in [1, n-1]$, by construction if $C_{k,n}$ is inferior to zero then $\mathsf{supp}_k(g)$ has $|C_{k,n}|$ elements less than $\mathsf{supp}_k(f)$. We study what it implies on the restricted Walsh transform of g:

$$
\begin{aligned}
\mathcal{W}_{g,k}(\mathbf{0}) &= \sum_{x \in \mathsf{E}_{k,n}} (-1)^{g(x)} = |x \in \{\mathsf{E}_{k,n} \setminus \mathsf{supp}_k(g)\}| - |x \in \mathsf{supp}_k(g)| \\
&= |x \in \{\mathsf{E}_{k,n} \setminus \mathsf{supp}_k(f)\}| + |C_{k,n}| - (|x \in \mathsf{supp}_k(f)| - |C_{k,n}|) \\
&= \mathcal{W}_{f,k}(\mathbf{0}) + 2|C_{k,n}| = 0.
\end{aligned}
$$

In the other case, if $C_{k,n} = 0$, f is already balanced on the slice k then g is equal to f on this slice and $\mathcal{W}_{g,k}(\mathbf{0}) = \mathcal{W}_{f,k}(\mathbf{0}) = 0$. If $C_{k,n} > 0$ by construction $\mathsf{supp}_k(g)$ has $C_{k,n}$ elements more than $\mathsf{supp}_k(f)$, and similarly to the case $C_{k,n} < 0$ we obtain:

$$
\begin{aligned}
\mathcal{W}_{g,k}(\mathbf{0}) &= |x \in \{\mathsf{E}_{k,n} \setminus \mathsf{supp}_k(f)\}| - |C_{k,n}| - (|x \in \mathsf{supp}_k(f)| + |C_{k,n}|) \\
&= \mathcal{W}_{f,k}(\mathbf{0}) - 2|C_{k,n}| = 0.
\end{aligned}
$$

It allows us to conclude that $g \in \mathcal{WPB}_m$.

Then, we show that $\mathsf{d_H}(f, g) = \mathsf{NPB}(f)$. To do so we study the distance between f and g on each slice, denoting $\mathsf{d_{H,k}}(f, g) = |\{x \in \mathsf{E}_{k,n} \text{ such that } f(x) \neq g(x)\}|$.

- For $k = 0$, $\mathsf{supp}_0(g)$ is forced to be $\emptyset$, therefore $\mathsf{d_{H,0}}(f, g) = 0$ if $\mathsf{supp}_0(f) = \emptyset$ and $\mathsf{d_{H,0}}(f, g) = 1$ otherwise, which is equivalent to $\mathsf{d_{H,0}}(f, g) = (1 - \mathcal{W}_{f,0}(\mathbf{0}))/2$.
- For $k = n$, $\mathsf{supp}_n(g)$ is forced to be $\{1_n\}$, therefore $\mathsf{d_{H,0}}(f, g) = 1$ if $\mathsf{supp}_n(f) = \emptyset$ and $\mathsf{d_{H,n}}(f, g) = 0$ otherwise, which is equivalent to $\mathsf{d_{H,n}}(f, g) = (1 + \mathcal{W}_{f,n}(\mathbf{0}))/2$.
- For $k \in [1, n-1]$, $|C_{k,n}|$ elements are removed or added to $\mathsf{supp}_k(g)$ hence $\mathsf{d_{H,k}}(f, g) = |C_{k,n}| = |\mathcal{W}_{f,k}(\mathbf{0})|/2$.

Summing over all $k \in [0, n]$ and using Proposition 2 we can conclude:

$$
\mathsf{d_H}(f, g) = \frac{2 - \mathcal{W}_{f,0}(\mathbf{0}) + \mathcal{W}_{f,n}(\mathbf{0})}{2} + \sum_{k=1}^{n-1} \frac{|\mathcal{W}_{f,k}(\mathbf{0})|}{2} = \mathsf{NPB}(f).
$$

$\square$

As a first application we show how to obtain WPB functions with very low nonlinearity.

Proposition 4 (WPB function with low nonlinearity). *Let $m \in \mathbb{N}$, $m \geq 2$ and $n = 2^m$, there exists WPB functions g such that $\mathsf{NL}(g) = 2^{n/2-1}$.*

Proof. We prove the existence by exhibiting such functions. We define f as $\sum_{i=1}^{n/2} x_i$, such function is linear, and using Proposition 3 we have $\mathsf{NPB}(f) = 2^{n/2-1}$. Accordingly, using Construction 1 seeded with f, we obtain a function g WPB such that $\mathsf{d_H}(f, g) = 2^{n/2-1}$. Since the distance between two n-variable affine functions is at least 2^{n-1} (minimal distance of order-1 Reed-Muller code), f is the affine function the closest to g if $2^{n/2-1} \leq 2^{n-2}$, that is if $n \geq 2$. Thereafter, $\mathsf{NL}(g) = \mathsf{d_H}(f, g) = 2^{n/2-1}$. $\square$

Proposition 5 (WPB function with high nonlinearity). *Let $m \in \mathbb{N}$, $m \geq 2$ and $n = 2^m$. Consider $f_n = \sigma_{2,n} + \ell_{n/2}$ where $\ell_{n/2} = \sum_{i=1}^{n/2} x_i$. Construction 1 applied with f_n as input returns a WPB function g such that $\mathsf{NL}(g) \geq 2^{n-1} - 2^{n/2}$.*

Proof. Since $\sigma_{2,n}$ is a symmetric function giving 0 in 0_n and 1_n, it can be decomposed as a sum of $\varphi_{k,n}$ with $k \in [1, n-1]$, therefore using Property 5 we have:

- $\mathcal{W}_{f_n,0}(\mathbf{0}) = \mathcal{W}_{\ell_{n/2},0}(\mathbf{0})$,
- for $k \in [1, n-1]$, $\mathcal{W}_{f_n,0}(\mathbf{0}) = \pm\mathcal{W}_{\ell_{n/2},0}(\mathbf{0})$,
- $\mathcal{W}_{f_n,n}(\mathbf{0}) = \mathcal{W}_{\ell_{n/2},n}(\mathbf{0})$.

Therefore, using Proposition 2, we obtain $\mathsf{NPB}(f_n) = \mathsf{NPB}(\ell_{n/2})$, that is $\mathsf{NPB}(f_n) = 2^{n/2-1}$ from Proposition 3. Accordingly, using Construction 1 seeded with f_n, we obtain a function g WPB such that $\mathsf{d_H}(f_n, g) = 2^{n/2-1}$.

Since the function $\sigma_{2,n}$ is bent (Property 4) and $\ell_{n/2}$ is affine f_n is also bent (the nonlinearity is an extended affine equivalent criterion), that is $\mathsf{NL}(f_n) = 2^{n-1} - 2^{n/2-1}$. Finally, since the nonlinearity is a distance, the triangular equality gives $\mathsf{NL}(f_n) \leq \mathsf{NL}(g) + \mathsf{d_H}(f_n, g)$ hence $\mathsf{NL}(g) \geq \mathsf{NL}(f_n) - \mathsf{d_H}(f_n, g)$ that is $\mathsf{NL}(g) \geq 2^{n-1} - 2^{n/2}$. $\square$

Remark 2. The proven bound from Proposition 5 is high considering that the nonlinearity of WPB functions is upper bounded by $U_m = 2^{n-1} - 2^{n/2-1} - 2$.

Corollary 1. *Let $m \in \mathbb{N}$, $m \geq 2$ and $n = 2^m$. Let $f_n = \sigma_{2,n} + \ell_{n/2}$ and $C_{k,n} = \mathcal{W}_{f_n,k}(\mathbf{0})/2$. There exist at least*

$$\mathfrak{F}_n = \prod_{k=1}^{n-1} \left(\frac{\frac{1}{2}\binom{n}{k} + |C_{k,n}|}{|C_{k,n}|} \right) \tag{9}$$

WPB functions g such that $\mathsf{NL}(g) \geq 2^{n-1} - 2^{n/2}$.

Proof. Proposition 5 applies Construction 1 with the function $f_n = \sigma_{2,n} + \ell_{n/2}$, where $\ell_{n/2} = \sum_{i=1}^{n/2} x_i$, as input in order to obtain WPB functions with high nonlinearity. We count the number of different functions g that are reachable from f_n, considering the number of different possible support slice by slice. Since for f_n we have that $f_n(0_n) = \ell_{n/2}(0_n) = 0$ and $f_n(1_n) = \ell_{n/2}(1_n) = 0$, Construction 1 always adds 1_n to the support of g (the output WPB function). Then for $k \in [1, n-1]$, recall that $|\mathsf{supp}_k(f_n)| = |\mathsf{E}_{k,n}|/2 - C_{k,n}$ and by construction $|\mathsf{supp}_k(g)| = |\mathsf{E}_{k,n}|/2$. If $C_{k,n} < 0$, we have to subtract a set $\mathsf{S}_{k,n}$ of $|C_{k,n}|$ elements of from $\mathsf{supp}_k(f_n)$. Thus, there are $\binom{|\mathsf{E}_{k,n}|/2 - C_{k,n}}{|C_{k,n}|}$ different possible choices for $\mathsf{S}_{k,n}$. If $C_{k,n} > 0$, we have to add $C_{k,n}$ elements to $\mathsf{supp}_k(f_n)$. This corresponds to select a subset $\mathsf{S}_{k,n}$ of $\{\mathsf{E}_{k,n} \setminus \mathsf{supp}_k(f_n)\}$. Hence, we have $\binom{|\mathsf{E}_{k,n}|/2 + C_{k,n}}{C_{k,n}}$ possible of choices for $\mathsf{S}_{k,n}$. Therefore, by Construction 1 seeded with f_n we can produce

$$\prod_{k=1}^{n-1} \binom{\frac{1}{2}\binom{n}{k} + |C_{k,n}|}{|C_{k,n}|}$$

different WPB functions with nonlinearity greater than or equal to $2^{n-1} - 2^{n/2}$.

□

Applying this construction seeded with f_n we obtain a family of WPB functions with very high nonlinearity for each m. In particular, in the following subsection we discuss the explicit application of the construction as in Proposition 5, and we discuss the results in 8 and 16 variables. Recall that 112 is the maximal nonlinearity obtained experimentally in [MKCL22] through evolutionary algorithm for $n = 8$. Here, we obtain that any function g produced by Construction 1 seeded with $\sigma_{2,8} + \ell_4$ is such that $\mathsf{NL}(g) \geq 112$.

4.1   Concrete Examples in 8 and 16 Variables

Proposition 5 proves that Construction 1 seeded with the function $f_n = \sigma_{2,n} + \ell_{n/2}$, where $\ell_{n/2} = \sum_{i=1}^{n/2} x_i$, gives WPB functions with high nonlinearity. Implementing this in practice, we were able to construct multiple WPB functions in 8 and 16 with high nonlinearity.

We computed $C_{k,n} = \mathcal{W}_{f_n,k}(\mathbf{0})/2$. For $n = 8$ we have $C_{2,8} = C_{6,8} = 4$, $C_{4,8} = 6$ and for k odd $C_{k,8} = 0$. For $n = 16$ we have $C_{2,16} = C_{14,16} = 8$, $C_{4,16} = C_{12,16} = 28$, $C_{6,16} = C_{10,16} = 56$, $C_{8,16} = 70$ and for k odd $C_{k,16} = 0$. Therefore, from Corollary 1 we know that we can construct more than 2^{41} 8-variable WPB functions with nonlinearity at least 112, and more than 2^{1814} 16-variable WPB functions with nonlinearity at least 32512, as summarized in Table 2.

Table 2. Applying Construction 1 seeded with f_n as in Proposition 5 we obtain $\mathfrak{F}_n$ distinct WPB functions. For small values of n we report the size of $\mathfrak{F}_n$, the lower bound on the nonlinearity of these functions from Proposition 5, and the value of the general upper bound from Eq. 1.

n	4	8	16
$\mathfrak{F}_n$	6	$> 2^{43}$	$> 2^{1814}$
NL	4	≥ 112	≥ 32512
U_m	4	118	32638

Explicitly running Construction 1 seeded with f_n we reached nonlinearity up to 116 and 32598 for 8 and 16, respectively. Recall that the theoretical upper bound (1) is $U_3 = 118$ and $U_4 = 32638$, respectively.

Table 3 displays examples of 8-variable WPB functions of this family with nonlinearity value 112, 114 and 116. Each function is described by providing the points (represented as integers) to join to the support of f_8 for $k < 8$. Similarly, Table 4 contains examples of 16-variables WPB functions of this family with various nonlinearity values, described accordingly.

Table 3. To obtain an 8-variable WPB function g with nonlinearity NL given in the first column, we can set $\mathsf{supp}_k(g) = \mathsf{supp}_k(f_8) \cup \mathsf{S}_{k,8}$ and $g(255) = 1$.

NL	$S_{2,8}$	$S_{4,8}$	$S_{6,8}$
112	68, 136	90, 105, 204	125, 235
114	40, 129	147, 150, 153	187, 215
116	66, 136	85, 102, 170	123, 215

Table 4. To obtain a 16-variable WPB function g with nonlinearity NL as in the first column, we can set $\mathsf{supp}_k(g) = \mathsf{supp}_k(f_{16}) \cup \mathsf{S}_{k,16}$ and $g(65535) = 1$.

NL	$S_{2,16}$	$S_{4,16}$	$S_{6,16}$	$S_{8,16}$	$S_{10,16}$	$S_{12,16}$	$S_{14,16}$
32594	2052, 32770, 16416, 514	9256, 34884, 8840, 31040, 10960, 39424, 36898, 34960, 116, 89, 15, 163, 51, 53504, 9346	5702, 8998, 17801, 8350, 31040, 10960, 2103, 25032, 49481, 1861, 49812, 44545, 12952, 10533, 16505, 2853, 12849, 5646, 44552, 17177, 39712, 32981, 6438, 9160, 24882, 5729, 26721	26909, 23687, 21383, 57902, 36398, 6331, 14950, 14022, 44145, 30840, 41884, 7770, 54452, 38580, 29081, 50763, 30952, 45414, 13734, 6053, 8935, 11827, 29739, 26195, 20663, 30834, 27726, 46246, 21476, 46103, 5215, 6042, 19341	30073, 60660, 62196, 44725, 30413, 30456, 51051, 30039, 59066, 55786, 25335, 54963, 64916, 55782, 55917, 58857, 47829, 59859, 36813, 52907, 31356, 58326, 46057, 3582, 17343, 20333, 62095,	48093, 40863, 55163, 31710, 60271, 64719, 62460, 59381, 65496, 61039, 30671, 48871, 62439, 57069	64383, 32703, 32735, 57341
32596	16388, 272, 16416, 640	16650, 18564, 3077, 17428, 8738, 4481, 9345, 8722, 34945, 4385, 49155, 24588, 165, 16908	49430, 34148, 6482, 12579, 28745, 42784, 5058, 1257, 35341, 35210, 2886, 34438, 25762, 12040, 31008, 37395, 25192, 53300, 14418, 10627, 50340, 20836, 11337, 21168, 41316, 34256, 57425, 2236	29230, 43690, 3960, 13959, 4845, 44818, 44257, 14649, 44182, 7467, 27237, 11162, 45621, 22241, 43417, 27194, 58391, 33501, 25521, 40113, 7051, 55445, 41908, 53713, 21413, 7593, 6068, 14824, 45722, 16823, 879,11956, 38183, 22862,46913	40662, 60075, 47845, 15671, 24181, 28191, 55926, 32593, 8053, 26588, 41663, 42996, 34271, 19679, 8027, 31911, 20410, 33790, 55645, 58842, 14171, 59068, 14139, 52697, 27499, 52188, 55755, 44410	48765, 62439, 57022, 42495, 11775, 30590, 60991, 55271, 65512, 64250, 44975, 28605, 56307, 50943	32763, 57342, 49147, 57215
32598	8256, 2080, 4112, 2049	36912, 5264, 34840, 10264, 49169, 38400, 1632, 3075, 2570, 16800, 16908, 1569, 24612, 12417	29504, 17825, 37413, 18965, 41410, 16613, 5028, 35122, 21656, 61968, 42122, 8000, 24873, 9546, 21541, 10763, 35881, 57372, 45256, 42033, 37524, 19529, 7237, 16446, 17888, 20881, 26817, 49539	14964, 54452, 51612, 22981, 20723, 989, 46868, 50830, 11884, 1518, 5363, 36553, 43729, 39321, 50459, 55401, 37771, 52359, 5965, 8511, 18551, 58538, 14987, 53799, 44090, 10156, 29283, 27057, 58443, 61497, 35782, 44047, 22940, 7540, 19865	43961, 15221, 62179, 43927, 57240, 59741, 61867, 14190, 62511, 44665, 3067, 8107, 61937, 51161, 42937, 31835, 44725, 30435, 14324, 30381, 31964, 56506 54652, 59951, , 61206, 43993, 14310, 58959	32494, 24443, 32381, 62451, 44990, 62845, 36351, 32508, 61147, 56309, 32351, 48503	57215, 32751, 63483, 64510

5   Distribution of the Nonlinearity of WPB Functions

In this section we define the notion of distribution of the nonlinearity of WPB functions. Similarly to [GM22a], where the notion of distribution of the WPB functions has been first introduced, we define it as the discrete distribution describing the probability of getting a certain value of nonlinearity by sampling a WPB function uniformly at random:

Definition 12 (Nonlinearity distribution). *Let $m \in \mathbb{N}^*$, $n = 2^m$. The nonlinearity distribution $\mathfrak{N}_n$ is a discrete probability distribution describing the probability of getting a certain value of* NL *by taking a random WPB function, namely for any $x \in \mathbb{N}$*

$$p_{\mathfrak{N}_n}(x) = \frac{|\{f \in \mathcal{WPB}_m : \mathsf{NL}(f) = x\}|}{|\mathcal{WPB}_m|}.$$

The support of this distribution is the set of all values that can be realized as nonlinearity of a WPB function. Indeed, $y \in \mathsf{supp}(p_{\mathfrak{N}_n}) = \{a \in \mathbb{N} : p_{\mathfrak{N}_n}(a) \neq 0\}$ if and only if there exists $f \in \mathcal{WPB}_m$ such that $\mathsf{NL}(f) = y$. As for the weight-wise nonlinearities, this implies that the minimum and maximum nonlinearity of WPB functions are exactly the minimum and maximum of $\mathsf{supp}(p_{\mathfrak{N}_n})$.

The number of 4-variable WPB functions is $|\mathcal{WPB}_2| = 720$. Therefore, applying similar techniques as those in [GM22a], we can retrieve $\mathfrak{N}_4$ in less then 4 s on a simple laptop. The distribution is displayed in Fig. 1, note that B_2 and U_2 are both reached. However, for larger values of m an exhaustive computation is currently unfeasible, since *e.g.* $|\mathcal{WPB}_3| > 2^{243}$ and $|\mathcal{WPB}_4| > 2^{65452}$. Therefore, when $m > 2$ we can only compute an approximation of $\mathfrak{N}_{2^m}$.

x	2	4
$p_{\mathfrak{N}_n}(x)\%$	16.667	83.333
#	120	600

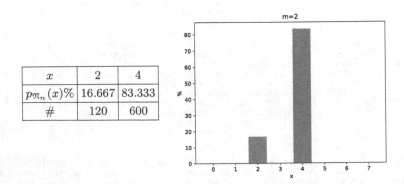

Fig. 1. Distribution $\mathfrak{N}_4$.

5.1   Experimental Approximation of $\mathfrak{N}_n$ for $n = 8$ and 16

To approximate the distribution $\mathfrak{N}_n$ we generate uniformly at random a sample S from $\mathcal{WPB}_m$ and we compute the distribution of the nonlinearity respectively to this sample. In fact, this strategy follows the same principle described in [GM22a] for approximating the distribution of the weightwise nonlinearities. Therefore, we can also apply the same computational techniques based on iterators and parallel computing.

More precisely, let $\mathbf{gen}_\pi(n)$ be a function that returns a random element of $\mathcal{WPB}_m$. Our strategy consists in sampling independently s functions and then computing their nonlinearity, in order to obtain a distribution $\mathfrak{N}'_n$ that is an approximation of $\mathfrak{N}_n$ given by a sample S of size s. Then, we set

$$p_{\mathfrak{N}'_n}(x) = \frac{|\{f \in S \colon \mathsf{NL}(f) = x\}|}{s}.$$

Algorithm 2 illustrates this strategy, denoting in pseudo-code by par-for the fact that the loop is performed in parallel.

Algorithm 2. Approximate nonlinearity distribution of WPB functions

---

Input: s sample size.
Output: $\mathfrak{N}'_n$.
1: $p = \mathbf{0} \in \mathbb{N}^u$, where u is an upper bound for the max NL.
2: **par-for** $i \in \{1, \ldots, s\}$ **do**
3:     $f \leftarrow \mathbf{gen}_\pi(n)$
4:     $x \leftarrow \mathsf{NL}(f)$
5:     $p_x = p_x + 1$
6: **end for**
7: $\mathfrak{N}'_n = (p_x/s \colon x \in [0, u-1])$
8: **return** $\mathfrak{N}'_n$

Results and Remarks. For $n = 8$, we obtained the approximated distribution $\mathfrak{N}'_8$ displayed by Fig. 2 and fully summarized by Table 5. $\mathfrak{N}'_8$ with $s > 2^{23}$ samples has maximal and minimal values 112 and 78, respectively. This implies that we can expect functions with nonlinearity outside of this range to be rare. Namely, our experiments show that sampling a random WPB function we can expect its nonlinearity to be almost always close to 104, and almost never larger than 112. However, notice that our approximation provides only a general intuition about the distribution $\mathfrak{N}_8$. Indeed, in Sect. 4 we prove the existence of 8-variable WPB functions with nonlinearity 8 and others with nonlinearity at least 112. In Sect. 4.1 we show that actually there exist WPB functions with nonlinearity 112, 114 and 116. More precisely, we provide a family 8-variables WPB functions (of size greater than 2^{43}) having nonlinearity at least 112. For $n = 16$ we obtained an approximated distribution $\mathfrak{N}'_{16}$ by $s > 2^{24}$ samples. $\mathfrak{N}'_{16}$ is summarized by Fig. 3 (and Table 8 and 9 in Appendix A). We can expect a WPB function in 16 variables sampled uniformly at random to have nonlinearity close to 32212 and neither smaller than 31886 nor larger than 32300. Again, this is only a general intuition since we prove in Sect. 4.1 that we can construct more than 2^{1814} functions having nonlinearity at least 32512.

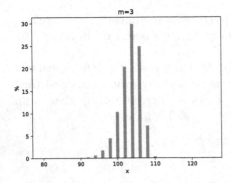

Fig. 2. Approximation of $\mathfrak{N}_8$ (via Table 5).

Fig. 3. Approximation of $\mathfrak{N}_{16}$ (via Table 8 and 9).

Table 5. Approximation of $\mathfrak{N}_8$ via Algorithm 2 with $s = 8585592 > 2^{23}$. See Fig. 2.

x	78	80	82	84	86	88	90	92	94
$p_{\mathfrak{N}_n}(x)\%$	0.000	0.000	0.000	0.001	0.005	0.018	0.063	0.202	0.606
#	2	8	27	115	411	1549	5402	17376	52011

x	96	98	100	102	104	106	108	110	112
$p_{\mathfrak{N}_n}(x)\%$	1.709	4.425	10.308	20.370	29.869	24.897	7.225	0.302	0.000
#	146762	379891	885042	1748852	2564407	2137525	620286	25889	37

6   Conclusion

In this article we studied the nonlinearity in the class of WPB functions. First, we discussed two lower bounds on the nonlinearity of a WPB function, introducing also the notion Non Perfect Balancedness (NPB). Then, we presented a new construction of WPB functions with prescribed nonlinearity, and by using this construction we are able to exhibit WPB functions with both low and high non linearity for any n. Finally, we studied the distribution of the nonlinearity of uniform WPB functions.

Up to 16 variables, we analyzed explicitly our construction of WPB functions with almost optimal nonlinearity, and the distribution of the nonlinearity of random functions. We concluded that functions like those we produced have a slim chance to be found by sampling uniformly at random. In Table 6 and Table 7 we summarize the state of the art (including our contributions) about the nonlinearity of WPB functions in 8 and 16 variables, respectively. The symbol * denotes the quantities observed from the approximation of the distributions in our experiments.

Table 6. Nonlinearity of 8-variable WPB constructions.

Construction	Nonlinearity
Minimum	8
Construction 1 seeded with ℓ_4	8
[TL19]	[66, 82]
[CMR17] f_8	88
[GM22b] $g_{6,8}$	96
Average*	103.49
Mode*	104
[MKCL22]	[110, 112]
Construction 1seeded with $\sigma_{2,8} + \ell_4$	[112, 116]
Upper Bound	118

Table 7. Nonlinearity of 16-variable WPB constructions.

Construction	Nonlinearity
Minimum	128
Construction 1 seeded with ℓ_8	128
[CMR17] f_{16}	29488
[GM22b] $g_{14,16}$	29824
[GM22b] h_{16}	30704
Average*	32199.25
Mode*	32212
Construction 1 seeded with $\sigma_{2,16} + \ell_8$	[32512, 32598]
Upper Bound	32638

Open Questions:

- *WPB functions with higher nonlinearity.* We have seen in Sect. 5 that there are 4-variable WPB functions reaching U_2. However, in Sect. 5.1 we did not found WPB functions with nonlinearity reaching U_3, but some attaining 116, which corresponds to the upper bound conjectured by Dobbertin [Dob95] and recently studied in [MMM22]. In 16 variables we did not observe WPB functions reaching this upper bound. A natural question is to determine the maximal nonlinearity of a WPB function, if it is provably lower than U_m or even lower than Dobbertin's bound for m greater than 3.
- *Nonlinearity and addition of symmetric functions.* In the proof of Proposition 5 we have seen that adding a symmetric function (null in 0_n and 1_n) does not modify the NPB of a function. Nevertheless, using Construction 1 with $\ell_{n/2}$ and $\ell_{n/2} + \sigma_{2,n}$ we witnessed that adding $\sigma_{2,n}$ can lead to WPB functions with very high nonlinearity from WPB functions with low nonlinearity. Hence, it would be interesting to determine how evolves the nonlinearity of WPB functions simply by adding symmetric functions.
- *NPB and other cryptographic criteria.* The non perfect balancedness turned out to be crucial for the construction of WPB functions introduced in Sect. 4. Since its definition is analog to the one of nonlinearity, it engages to study the implications of minimal and maximal NPB on other criteria such as degree, algebraic immunity, and nonlinearity.

Implementation. The concrete results in this paper, in 4, 8 and 16 variables, were computed explicitly via `sagemath` [The17]. We used `BooleanFunction` class from the module `sage.crypto.boolean_function` to encode the functions, and we applied the built-in method nonlinearity based on the Walsh transform. The code of our algorithms, and detailed results of our experiments are available at https://github.com/agnesegini/WAPB_pub. Experiments were partially hosted by https://hpc.uni.lu/ [VBCG14].

Acknowledgments. The two authors were supported by the ERC Advanced Grant no. 787390.

A   Approximation of $\mathfrak{N}_{16}$

Table 8. Approximation of $\mathfrak{N}_{16}$ via Algorithm 2 with $s = 18110464 > 2^{24}$ (Part 1). See Fig. 3.

x	31878	31880	31884	31886	31888	31890	31892	31894	31896	31898	31900	31902
$p_{\mathfrak{N}_n}(x)\%$	0.000	0.000	0.000	0.000	0.000	0.000	0.000	0.000	0.000	0.000	0.000	0.000
#	1	1	1	2	1	1	2	2	1	1	2	1
x	31904	31906	31908	31910	31912	31916	31918	31920	31922	31924	31926	31928
$p_{\mathfrak{N}_n}(x)\%$	0.000	0.000	0.000	0.000	0.000	0.000	0.000	0.000	0.000	0.000	0.000	0.000
#	1	1	4	3	1	5	4	11	3	4	8	2
x	31930	31932	31934	31936	31938	31940	31942	31944	31946	31948	31950	31952
$p_{\mathfrak{N}_n}(x)\%$	0.000	0.000	0.000	0.000	0.000	0.000	0.000	0.000	0.000	0.000	0.000	0.000
#	11	10	7	7	9	11	13	21	13	19	28	19
x	31954	31956	31958	31960	31962	31964	31966	31968	31970	31972	31974	31976
$p_{\mathfrak{N}_n}(x)\%$	0.000	0.000	0.000	0.000	0.000	0.000	0.000	0.000	0.000	0.000	0.000	0.000
#	25	23	26	35	27	38	50	48	43	60	65	74
x	31978	31980	31982	31984	31986	31988	31990	31992	31994	31996	31998	32000
$p_{\mathfrak{N}_n}(x)\%$	0.000	0.001	0.001	0.001	0.001	0.001	0.001	0.001	0.001	0.001	0.001	0.001
#	80	93	95	95	94	147	134	159	169	191	195	240
x	32002	32004	32006	32008	32010	32012	32014	32016	32018	32020	32022	32024
$p_{\mathfrak{N}_n}(x)\%$	0.001	0.001	0.002	0.002	0.002	0.002	0.002	0.003	0.003	0.003	0.003	0.004
#	254	267	292	325	372	394	441	492	504	541	631	716
x	32026	32028	32030	32032	32034	32036	32038	32040	32042	32044	32046	32048
$p_{\mathfrak{N}_n}(x)\%$	0.004	0.005	0.005	0.005	0.006	0.006	0.007	0.008	0.008	0.009	0.010	0.011
#	777	821	867	981	1080	1129	1272	1410	1500	1626	1804	1943
x	32050	32052	32054	32056	32058	32060	32062	32064	32066	32068	32070	32072
$p_{\mathfrak{N}_n}(x)\%$	0.012	0.013	0.014	0.016	0.018	0.018	0.020	0.022	0.024	0.026	0.029	0.031
#	2088	2357	2587	2814	3238	3342	3615	3958	4413	4735	5196	5576
x	32074	32076	32078	32080	32082	32084	32086	32088	32090	32092	32094	32096
$p_{\mathfrak{N}_n}(x)\%$	0.034	0.036	0.040	0.043	0.047	0.052	0.055	0.060	0.066	0.071	0.077	0.083
#	6087	6570	7185	7760	8446	9462	9971	10862	11963	12786	13960	15004

Table 9. Approximation of $\mathfrak{N}_{16}$ via Algorithm 2 with $s = 18110464 > 2^{24}$ (Part 2). See Fig. 3.

x	32098	32100	32102	32104	32106	32108	32110	32112	32114	32116	32118	32120
$p_{\mathfrak{N}_n}(x)\%$	0.092	0.098	0.107	0.114	0.124	0.136	0.147	0.160	0.173	0.185	0.198	0.216
#	16643	17679	19410	20710	22377	24605	26541	28948	31245	33485	35878	39032
x	32122	32124	32126	32128	32130	32132	32134	32136	32138	32140	32142	32144
$p_{\mathfrak{N}_n}(x)\%$	0.234	0.253	0.274	0.294	0.318	0.339	0.368	0.395	0.428	0.453	0.490	0.527
#	42349	45765	49650	53182	57629	61402	66557	71506	77511	82064	88690	95420
x	32146	32148	32150	32152	32154	32156	32158	32160	32162	32164	32166	32168
$p_{\mathfrak{N}_n}(x)\%$	0.562	0.602	0.646	0.695	0.739	0.791	0.846	0.902	0.963	1.025	1.089	1.156
#	101851	109070	116977	125949	133882	143285	153179	163369	174408	185596	197313	209364
x	32170	32172	32174	32176	32178	32180	32182	32184	32186	32188	32190	32192
$p_{\mathfrak{N}_n}(x)\%$	1.229	1.297	1.375	1.450	1.523	1.606	1.695	1.773	1.858	1.938	2.018	2.100
#	222611	234952	248929	262600	275734	290871	306909	321097	336415	351029	365403	380364
x	32194	32196	32198	32200	32202	32204	32206	32208	32210	32212	32214	32216
$p_{\mathfrak{N}_n}(x)\%$	2.171	2.251	2.322	2.380	2.442	2.501	2.540	2.576	2.604	2.614	2.608	2.598
#	393218	407735	420543	431073	442322	452937	460029	466583	471623	473496	472316	470558
x	32218	32220	32222	32224	32226	32228	32230	32232	32234	32236	32238	32240
$p_{\mathfrak{N}_n}(x)\%$	2.570	2.539	2.476	2.403	2.326	2.228	2.123	1.999	1.871	1.742	1.592	1.450
#	465477	459756	448388	435231	421306	403534	384544	362026	338889	315447	288252	262553
x	32242	32244	32246	32248	32250	32252	32254	32256	32258	32260	32262	32264
$p_{\mathfrak{N}_n}(x)\%$	1.303	1.155	1.018	0.878	0.751	0.632	0.525	0.430	0.345	0.269	0.207	0.158
#	235999	209170	184350	159016	135944	114468	95066	77860	62407	48738	37488	28564
x	32266	32268	32270	32272	32274	32276	32278	32280	32282	32284	32286	32288
$p_{\mathfrak{N}_n}(x)\%$	0.117	0.083	0.059	0.040	0.027	0.018	0.011	0.007	0.004	0.002	0.001	0.001
#	21264	15050	10746	7251	4951	3222	2054	1248	702	353	222	98
x	32290	32292	32294	32296	32298	32300						
$p_{\mathfrak{N}_n}(x)\%$	0.000	0.000	0.000	0.000	0.000	0.000						
#	61	28	12	6	3	1						

References

[BP05] Braeken, A., Preneel, B.: On the algebraic immunity of symmetric Boolean functions. In: Maitra, S., Veni Madhavan, C.E., Venkatesan, R. (eds.) INDOCRYPT 2005. LNCS, vol. 3797, pp. 35–48. Springer, Heidelberg (2005). https://doi.org/10.1007/11596219_4

[Car04] Carlet, C.: On the degree, nonlinearity, algebraic thickness, and nonnormality of Boolean functions, with developments on symmetric functions. IEEE Trans. Inf. Theory **50**(9), 2178–2185 (2004)

[Car21] Carlet, C.: Boolean Functions for Cryptography and Coding Theory. Cambridge University Press, Cambridge (2021)

[CM21] Carlet, C., Méaux, P.: A complete study of two classes of Boolean functions: direct sums of monomials and threshold functions. IEEE Trans. Inf. Theory **68**(5), 3404–3425 (2021)

[CMR17] Carlet, C., Méaux, P., Rotella, Y.: Boolean functions with restricted input and their robustness; application to the FLIP cipher. IACR Trans. Symmetric Cryptol. **3**, 2017 (2017)

[CV05] Canteaut, A., Videau, M.: Symmetric Boolean functions. IEEE Trans. Inf. Theory **51**(8), 2791–2811 (2005)

[DMS06] Dalai, D.K., Maitra, S., Sarkar, S.: Basic theory in construction of Boolean functions with maximum possible annihilator immunity. Des. Codes Crypt. **40**, 41–58 (2006). https://doi.org/10.1007/s10623-005-6300-x

[Dob95]   Dobbertin, H.: Construction of bent functions and balanced Boolean functions with high nonlinearity. In: Preneel, B. (ed.) FSE 1994. LNCS, vol. 1008, pp. 61–74. Springer, Heidelberg (1995). https://doi.org/10.1007/3-540-60590-8_5

[GM22a]   Gini, A., Méaux, P.: On the weightwise nonlinearity of weightwise perfectly balanced functions. Discret. Appl. Math. **322**, 320–341 (2022)

[GM22b]   Gini, A., Méaux, P.: Weightwise almost perfectly balanced functions: secondary constructions for all n and better weightwise nonlinearities. In: Isobe, T., Sarkar, S. (eds.) Progress in Cryptology (INDOCRYPT 2022). LNCS, vol. 13774, pp. 492–514. Springer, Cham (2022). https://doi.org/10.1007/978-3-031-22912-1_22

[GS22]   Guo, X., Sihong, S.: Construction of weightwise almost perfectly balanced Boolean functions on an arbitrary number of variables. Discret. Appl. Math. **307**, 102–114 (2022)

[LM19]   Liu, J., Mesnager, S.: Weightwise perfectly balanced functions with high weightwise nonlinearity profile. Des. Codes Cryptogr. **87**(8), 1797–1813 (2019)

[LS20]   Li, J., Sihong, S.: Construction of weightwise perfectly balanced Boolean functions with high weightwise nonlinearity. Discret. Appl. Math. **279**, 218–227 (2020)

[MCD97]   Millan, W., Clark, A., Dawson, E.: An effective genetic algorithm for finding highly nonlinear Boolean functions. In: Han, Y., Okamoto, T., Qing, S. (eds.) ICICS 1997. LNCS, vol. 1334, pp. 148–158. Springer, Heidelberg (1997). https://doi.org/10.1007/BFb0028471

[Méa21]   Méaux, P.: On the fast algebraic immunity of threshold functions. Cryptogr. Commun. **13**(5), 741–762 (2021)

[Mes16]   Mesnager, S.: Bent Functions. Springer, Cham (2016). https://doi.org/10.1007/978-3-319-32595-8

[MJSC16] Méaux, P., Journault, A., Standaert, F.-X., Carlet, C.: Towards stream ciphers for efficient FHE with low-noise ciphertexts. In: Fischlin, M., Coron, J.-S. (eds.) EUROCRYPT 2016. LNCS, vol. 9665, pp. 311–343. Springer, Heidelberg (2016). https://doi.org/10.1007/978-3-662-49890-3_13

[MKCL22] Mandujano, S., Ku Cauich, J.C., Lara, A.: Studying special operators for the application of evolutionary algorithms in the seek of optimal Boolean functions for cryptography. In: Pichardo Lagunas, O., Martínez-Miranda, J., Martínez Seis, B. (eds.) Advances in Computational Intelligence (MICAI 2022). LNCS, vol. 13612, pp. 383–396. Springer, Cham (2022). https://doi.org/10.1007/978-3-031-19493-1_30

[MMM+18] Maitra, S., Mandal, B., Martinsen, T., Roy, D., Stănică, P.: Tools in analyzing linear approximation for Boolean functions related to FLIP. In: Chakraborty, D., Iwata, T. (eds.) INDOCRYPT 2018. LNCS, vol. 11356, pp. 282–303. Springer, Cham (2018). https://doi.org/10.1007/978-3-030-05378-9_16

[MMM22]   Maitra, S., Mandal, B., Roy, M.: Modifying Bent functions to obtain the balanced ones with high nonlinearity. In: Isobe, T., Sarkar, S. (eds.) Progress in Cryptology (INDOCRYPT 2022). LNCS, vol. 13774, pp. 449–470. Springer, Cham (2022). https://doi.org/10.1007/978-3-031-22912-1_20

[MPJ+22] Mariot, L., Picek, S., Jakobovic, D., Djurasevic, M., Leporati, A.: Evolutionary construction of perfectly balanced Boolean functions. In: 2022 IEEE Congress on Evolutionary Computation (CEC), pp. 1–8. IEEE (2022)

[MS78] MacWilliams, F.J., Sloane, N.J.A.: The Theory of Error-Correcting Codes, 2nd edn. North-Holland Publishing Company (1978)

[MS21] Mesnager, S., Su, S.: On constructions of weightwise perfectly balanced Boolean functions. Cryptogr. Commun. **13**, 951–979 (2021). https://doi.org/10.1007/s12095-021-00481-3

[MSL21] Mesnager, S., Su, S., Li, J.: On concrete constructions of weightwise perfectly balanced functions with optimal algebraic immunity and high weightwise nonlinearity. Boolean Funct. Appl. (2021)

[MSLZ22] Mesnager, S., Sihong, S., Li, J., Zhu, L.: Concrete constructions of weightwise perfectly balanced (2-rotation symmetric) functions with optimal algebraic immunity and high weightwise nonlinearity. Cryptogr. Commun. **14**(6), 1371–1389 (2022)

[PCG+16] Picek, S., Carlet, C., Guilley, S., Miller, J.F., Jakobovic, D.: Evolutionary algorithms for Boolean functions in diverse domains of cryptography. Evol. Comput. **24**(4), 667–694 (2016)

[QFLW09] Qu, L., Feng, K., Liu, F., Wang, L.: Constructing symmetric Boolean functions with maximum algebraic immunity. IEEE Trans. Inf. Theory **55**(5), 2406–2412 (2009)

[Rot76] Rothaus, O.S.: On "bent" functions. J. Comb. Theory Ser. A. **20**(3), 300–305 (1976)

[SM07] Palash Sarkar and Subhamoy Maitra. Balancedness and correlation immunity of symmetric boolean functions. Discrete Mathematics, pages 2351–2358, 2007

[SZZ93] Seberry, J., Zhang, X.-M., Zheng, Y.: Nonlinearly balanced Boolean functions and their propagation characteristics. In: Stinson, D.R. (ed.) CRYPTO 1993. LNCS, vol. 773, pp. 49–60. Springer, Heidelberg (1994). https://doi.org/10.1007/3-540-48329-2_5

[The17] The Sage Developers: SageMath, the Sage mathematics software system (Version 8.1) (2017). https://www.sagemath.org/

[TL19] Tang, D., Liu, J.: A family of weightwise (almost) perfectly balanced Boolean functions with optimal algebraic immunity. Cryptogr. Commun. **11**(6), 1185–1197 (2019)

[Tok15] Tokareva, N.: Bent Functions: Results and Applications to Cryptography. Academic Press, Cambridge (2015)

[VBCG14] Varrette, S., Bouvry, P., Cartiaux, H., Georgatos, F.: Management of an academic HPC cluster: the UL experience. In: 2014 International Conference on High Performance Computing and Simulation (HPCS), pp. 959–967. IEEE (2014) Sébastien Varrette, Pascal Bouvry, Hyacinthe Cartiaux, and Fotis Georgatos. Management of an academic HPC cluster: The UL experience. In 2014 International Conference on High Performance Computing & Simulation (HPCS), pages 959–967, 2014

[ZS21] Zhang, R., Su, S.: A new construction of weightwise perfectly balanced Boolean functions. Adv. Math. Commun. (2021)

[ZS22] Zhu, L., Sihong, S.: A systematic method of constructing weightwise almost perfectly balanced Boolean functions on an arbitrary number of variables. Discret. Appl. Math. **314**, 181–190 (2022)

Chudnovsky-Type Algorithms over the Projective Line Using Generalized Evaluation Maps

Stéphane Ballet and Bastien Pacifico[✉]

Institut de Mathématiques de Marseille,
169 Avenue de Luminy, 13009 Marseille, France
{stephane.ballet,bastien.pacifico}@univ-amu.fr

Abstract. Recently, it was shown that the Chudnovsky-type algorithms over the projective line enable a generic recursive construction of multiplication algorithms in finite fields $\mathbb{F}_{q^n}$. This construction is based on the method introduced by D. V. and G. V. Chudnovsky (1987), that generalizes polynomial interpolation to the use of algebraic curves, and specialized to the case of the projective line. More precisely, using evaluation at places of increasing degrees of the rational function field over $\mathbb{F}_q$, it has been proven that one can construct in polynomial time algorithms with a quasi-linear bilinear complexity with respect to the extension degree n. In this paper, we discuss how the use of evaluation with multiplicity, using generalized evaluation maps, can improve this construction.

1 Introduction

The seek for efficient algorithms for multiplication in finite fields is very active lately, especially due to its potential applications for cryptography and error correcting codes. Let q be a prime power, and n be a positive integer. In this paper, we consider the problem of the multiplication in a finite extension $\mathbb{F}_{q^n}$ of an arbitrary finite field $\mathbb{F}_q$. Such an algorithm involves different kind of operations in $\mathbb{F}_q$: additions, scalar multiplications (by a constant), and bilinear multiplications, that depend on the two elements being multiplied. Different models can be used to measure the performance of these algorithms. Among them, the model of the bilinear complexity [8, Chapter 14] focuses only on the number of bilinear multiplications in the base field used by the algorithm.

Definition 1.1. *Let $\mathcal{U}$ be an algorithm for the multiplication in $\mathbb{F}_{q^n}$ over $\mathbb{F}_q$. Its number of bilinear multiplications is called its bilinear complexity, written $\mu(\mathcal{U})$. The bilinear complexity of the multiplication in $\mathbb{F}_{q^n}$ over $\mathbb{F}_q$, denoted by $\mu_q(n)$, is the quantity:*

$$\mu_q(n) = \min_{\mathcal{U}} \mu(\mathcal{U}),$$

where $\mathcal{U}$ is running over all multiplication algorithms in $\mathbb{F}_{q^n}$ over $\mathbb{F}_q$.

S. El Hajji et al. (Eds.): C2SI 2023, LNCS 13874, pp. 360–375, 2023.
https://doi.org/10.1007/978-3-031-33017-9_22

While the degree of the extension is lower than $\frac{1}{2}q + 1$, polynomial interpolation gives algorithm reaching the optimal bilinear complexity $\mu_q(n) = 2n - 1$ [10,14]. The case of $n = \frac{1}{2}q + 1$ can be solved using the evaluation of the leading coefficient of the polynomial, usually called evaluation at infinity. However, the polynomial interpolation cannot be used for larger extension, due to the lack of elements of $\mathbb{F}_q$ to be evaluated.

The method of Chudnovsky and Chudnovsky [9] is an answer to this problematic, allowing the evaluation at rational points of algebraic curves, or equivalently rational places of algebraic function fields. By the Hasse-Weil bound, the number of rational places is bounded relatively to the genus of the function field. The original strategy then consists in the construction Chudnovsky-Chudnovsky Multiplication Algorithm (CCMA) using function fields of genus increasing relatively to the degree of the extension. This allowed to prove that the bilinear complexity of the multiplication in finite field extensions is linear with respect to the extension degree ([1], see [7]). The main problem of these algorithms is that there are not generically constructible, and thus there are very few results on their total complexity nor their implementation.

The method has since been extended, for instance to the evaluation at places of arbitrary degrees, or to the evaluation with multiplicity. Lately, Ballet, Bonnecaze and Pacifico introduced a recursive construction of Chudnovsky-type algorithms over the projective line. Using the rational function field only, and taking places by increasing degrees, they proved the existence of Chudnovsky-type algorithms with a quasi-linear bilinear complexity, that are constructible generically, deterministically and in polynomial time [6]. This paper is dedicated to show that the use of evaluation with multiplicity can improve the algorithms given by this construction.

2   Chudnovsky-Type Multiplication Algorithms

2.1   Background and Notations

Let $F/\mathbb{F}_q$ be a function field of genus $g = g(F)$ over $\mathbb{F}_q$. For $\mathcal{O}$ a valuation ring, the place P is defined to be $P = \mathcal{O} \setminus \mathcal{O}^\times$. We denote by F_P the residue class field at the place P, that is isomorphic to $\mathbb{F}_{q^d}$, d being the degree of the place. A rational place is a place of degree 1. A divisor $\mathcal{D}$ is a formal sum $\mathcal{D} = \sum_i n_i P_i$, where P_i are places and n_i are relative integers. The support $supp\ \mathcal{D}$ of $\mathcal{D}$ is the set of the places P_j for which $n_j \neq 0$, and $\mathcal{D}$ is effective if all the n_i are positive. The degree of $\mathcal{D}$ is defined by $\deg \mathcal{D} = \sum_i n_i$. The Riemann-Roch space associated to the divisor $\mathcal{D}$ is denoted by $\mathcal{L}(\mathcal{D})$. A divisor $\mathcal{D}$ is said to be non-special if $\dim \mathcal{L}(\mathcal{D}) = \deg(\mathcal{D}) + 1 - g$. Details about algebraic function fields can be found in [13].

2.2   The Algorithm

First, let us recall a definition generalized evaluation maps.

Definition 2.1. *For any divisor* $\mathcal{D}$*,* P *a place of degree* d *and the multiplicity* $u \geq 1$ *an integer, we define the generalized evaluation map*

$$\varphi_{\mathcal{D},P,u} : \left| \begin{array}{l} \mathcal{L}(\mathcal{D}) \longrightarrow (\mathbb{F}_{q^d})^u \\ f \longmapsto (f(P), f'(P), \dots, f^{(u-1)}(P)) \end{array} \right. \tag{1}$$

where the $f^{(k)}(P)$ *are the coefficients of the local expansion*

$$f = f(P) + f'(P)t_P + f''(P)t_P^2 + \dots + f^{(k)}(P)t_P^k + \dots \tag{2}$$

of f *at* P *with respect to the local parameter* t_P*, i.e. in* $\mathbb{F}_{q^d}[[t_P]]$*.*

Note that the evaluations with multiplicity are also called derivative evaluations. Furthermore, our algorithms require to compute multiplications in these rings, and it is relevent to consider the bilinear complexity in this context.

Definition 2.2. *The bilinear complexity of the multiplication in the power series ring of the truncated local expansions of order* u *at a place* P *of degree* d*, i.e. in* $\mathbb{F}_{q^d}[[t_P]]/(t_P^u)$*, is denoted by* $\mu_q(d, u)$*.*

Using these definitions, we can introduce a specialization of the latest version of the algorithm [7], provided that we first give the definition of the generalized Hadamard product:

Definition 2.3. *Let* q *be a prime power. The generalized Hadamard product in* $\mathbb{F}_{q^{d_1}} \times \cdots \times \mathbb{F}_{q^{d_N}}$*, denoted by* $\odot$*, is given for all* $(a_1, \dots, a_N), (b_1, \dots, b_N) \in \mathbb{F}_{q^{d_1}} \times \cdots \times \mathbb{F}_{q^{d_N}}$ *by*

$$(a_1, \dots, a_N) \odot (b_1, \dots, b_N) = (a_1 b_1, \dots, a_N b_N).$$

Theorem 2.1. *Let* q *be a prime power and* n *be a positive integer. Let* $F/\mathbb{F}_q$ *be an algebraic function field of genus* g*,* Q *be a degree* n *place,* $\mathcal{D}$ *be a divisor of* $F/\mathbb{F}_q$*,* $\mathcal{P} = \{P_1, \dots, P_N\}$ *be a set of places of arbitrary degrees (lower than* n*) of* $F/\mathbb{F}_q$*, and* $\underline{u} = (u_1, \dots, u_N)$ *be positive integers. We suppose that* $\operatorname{supp} \mathcal{D} \cap \{Q, P_1, ..., P_N\} = \emptyset$ *and that*

(i) the evaluation map

$$Ev_Q : \mathcal{L}(\mathcal{D}) \rightarrow F_Q$$
$$f \longmapsto f(Q)$$

   is surjective,

(ii) the evaluation map

$$Ev_{\mathcal{P}} : \mathcal{L}(2\mathcal{D}) \rightarrow (\mathbb{F}_{q^{\deg P_1}})^{u_1} \times \cdots \times (\mathbb{F}_{q^{\deg P_N}})^{u_N}$$
$$f \longmapsto (\varphi_{2\mathcal{D},P_1,u_1}(f), \dots, \varphi_{2\mathcal{D},P_N,u_N}(f))$$

   is injective.

Then,

(1) we have a multiplication algorithm $\mathcal{U}_{q,n}^{F,\mathcal{P},\underline{u}}(\mathcal{D},Q)$ such that for any two elements x, y in $\mathbb{F}_{q^n}$:

$$xy = E_Q \circ Ev_{\mathcal{P}}|_{ImEv_{\mathcal{P}}}^{-1}\left(E_{\mathcal{P}} \circ Ev_Q^{-1}(x)\underline{\odot}E_{\mathcal{P}} \circ Ev_Q^{-1}(y)\right), \qquad (3)$$

where E_Q denotes the canonical projection from the valuation ring $\mathcal{O}_Q$ of the place Q in its residue class field F_Q, $E_{\mathcal{P}}$ the extension of $Ev_{\mathcal{P}}$ on the valuation ring $\mathcal{O}_Q$ of the place Q, $Ev_{\mathcal{P}}|_{ImEv_{\mathcal{P}}}^{-1}$ the restriction of the inverse map of $Ev_{\mathcal{P}}$ on its image, $\odot$ the generalized Hadamard product and $\circ$ the standard composition map;

(2) the algorithm $\mathcal{U}_{q,n}^{F,\mathcal{P},\underline{u}}(\mathcal{D},Q)$ defined by (3) has bilinear complexity

$$\mu(\mathcal{U}_{q,n}^{F,\mathcal{P},\underline{u}}(\mathcal{D},Q)) = \sum_{i=1}^{N}\mu_q(\deg P_i, u_i).$$

2.3   Chudnovsky-Type Algorithms over the Projective Line

The following definition gives the specialization to the rational function field introduced in [6], that does not use evaluation with multiplicities.

Definition 2.4. *Let q be a prime power and n be a positive integer. A recursive Chudnovsky-type algorithm $\mathcal{U}_{q,n}^{\mathcal{P}_n}(Q)$ over the projective line is an algorithm $\mathcal{U}_{q,n}^{F,\mathcal{P},\underline{u}}(\mathcal{D},Q)$ satisfying the assumptions of Theorem 2.1 such that:*

- *$F/\mathbb{F}_q$ is the rational function field $\mathbb{F}_q(x)$,*
- *Q is a place of degree n of $\mathbb{F}_q(x)$,*
- *$\mathcal{D} = (n-1)P_\infty$, where P_∞ is the place at infinity of $\mathbb{F}_q(x)$,*
- *$\mathcal{P}_n$ is a set of places of degrees lower than n such that*

$$\sum_{P \in \mathcal{P}_n} \deg P = 2n - 1,$$

- *$\underline{u} = (1,\ldots,1)$*
- *the multiplication in $F_P \simeq \mathbb{F}_{q^d}$, where $d = \deg P$, is computed by $\mathcal{U}_{q,d}^{P_d}(P)$, where $P \in \mathcal{P}_n$.*

The bilinear complexity of these algorithms is given by

$$\mu_b(\mathcal{U}_{q,n}^{\mathcal{P}_n}(Q)) = \sum_{P \in \mathcal{P}_n} \mu_b(\mathcal{U}_{q,d}^{P_d}(P)).$$

Note that the evaluation at P_∞ is defined specifically in this context, since P_∞ is in the support of $\mathcal{D}$.

Definition 2.5. *Let k be a positive integer and P_∞ be the place at infinity of $\mathbb{F}_q(x)$. Let $\mathcal{D} = kP_\infty$, and let $f = \sum_{i=0}^{k-1} f_i x^i \in \mathcal{L}(\mathcal{D})$. The evaluation of f at P_∞ is given by*

$$f_{\mathcal{D}}(P_\infty) = f_{k-1},$$

the leading coefficient of f.

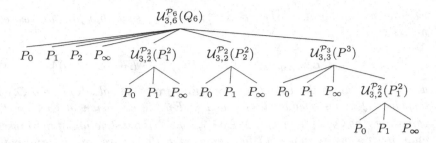

Fig. 1. Diagram of $\mathcal{U}_{3,6}^{P_6}(Q_6)$

Example 2.1. An example of such an algorithm is given by Fig. 1. This algorithm was introduced as an example of recursive Chudnovsky-type algorithm over the projective line in [6]. It evaluates on the 4 rational places of $\mathbb{F}_3(x)$, two of its degree 2 places, and one place of degree 3.

3 Chudnovsky-Type Algorithms over the Projective Line Using Generalized Evaluation Maps

When specializing canonically (as in Sect. 2.3) the general Chudnovsky type algorithm on the projective line (cf. [6]) we have to take into account in a more specific way than usually the evaluation in the place at infinity, because the Riemann-Roch spaces involved are spaces of polynomials. This leads us to modify the definition of the application $Ev_\mathcal{P}$ involved in the algorithm of Theorem 2.1 by considering the application $\tilde{Ev}_\mathcal{P}$. This modification is crucial if we want to maintain genericity (i.e. without using a Riemann-Roch space involving rational fractions) and if we want to deal with the case of extensions of degree $n = \frac{1}{2}q + 1$ without evaluating at places other than rational ones. This trick allows in particular to find Karatsuba's algorithm in the case of $\mathbb{F}_{2^2}$ (see [6, Sect. 3.3]). Also, when introducing the derived evaluations, we maintain this generality condition. One can furthermore define the generalized evaluation map at P_∞ as follows.

Definition 3.1. *Let k be a positive integer and P_∞ be the place at infinity of $\mathbb{F}_q(x)$. Let $\mathcal{D} = kP_\infty$. The generalized evaluation map at P_∞ with multiplicity u is defined by*

$$\varphi_{\mathcal{D},P_\infty,u} : \left| \begin{array}{ccc} \mathcal{L}(\mathcal{D}) & \longrightarrow & (\mathbb{F}_q)^u \\ f = \sum_{i=0}^{k-1} f_i x^i & \longmapsto & (f_{k-1}, f_{k-2}, \ldots, f_{k-u}) \end{array} \right.$$

Including this definition, a Chudnovsky-type algorithm over the projective line using generalized evaluation map is given by the following.

Proposition 3.1 (Polynomial interpolation CCMA on the projective line). *Let*

– $\mathbb{F}_q(x)$ *be the rational function field over $\mathbb{F}_q$,*

- n be a positive integer,
- Q be a degree n place of $\mathbb{F}_q(x)$,
- $\mathcal{P} = \{P_\infty, P_0, P_1, \ldots, P_N\}$ be a set of places of $\mathbb{F}_q(x)$, such that P_∞ is the place at infinity, P_0 is the place associated to the polynomial x, and $P_1, \ldots, P_N$ are places of arbitrary degrees,
- $\underline{u} = (u_\infty, u_0, u_1, \ldots, u_N)$, where $u_\infty, u_0, u_1, \ldots, u_N$ are positive integers.

We set $\mathcal{D} = (n-1)P_\infty$. If

$$\sum_{i \in \{\infty, 0, 1, \ldots, N\}} u_i \deg P_i = 2n - 1, \tag{4}$$

then

(i) the evaluation map

$$Ev_Q : \mathcal{L}(\mathcal{D}) \to F_Q$$
$$f \mapsto f(Q)$$

is bijective,

(ii) the evaluation map

$$\tilde{Ev}_\mathcal{P} : \mathcal{L}(2\mathcal{D}) \to \mathbb{F}_q^{u_\infty} \times \mathbb{F}_q^{u_0} \times \cdots \times (\mathbb{F}_{q^{\deg P_N}})^{u_N}$$
$$f \mapsto (\varphi_{2\mathcal{D}, P_\infty, u_\infty}(f), \varphi_{2\mathcal{D}, P_0, u_0}(f), \ldots, \varphi_{2\mathcal{D}, P_N, u_N}(f))$$

is an isomorphism of vector spaces.

Moreover,

(1) for any two elements x, y in $\mathbb{F}_{q^n}$, we have a multiplication algorithm $\mathcal{U}_{q,n}^{\mathcal{P}, \underline{u}}(Q)$ of type polynomial interpolation such that:

$$xy = E_Q \circ \tilde{Ev}_\mathcal{P}^{-1} \left(\tilde{E}_\mathcal{P} \circ Ev_Q^{-1}(x) \odot \tilde{E}_\mathcal{P} \circ Ev_Q^{-1}(y) \right), \tag{5}$$

where E_Q denotes the canonical projection from the valuation ring $\mathcal{O}_Q$ of the place Q in its residue class field F_Q, $\tilde{Ev}_\mathcal{P}^{-1}$ the inverse map of $\tilde{Ev}_\mathcal{P}$, $\odot$ the generalized Hadamard product in $\mathbb{F}_q \times \mathbb{F}_q^{u_0} \times (\mathbb{F}_{q^{\deg P_1}})^{u_1} \times \cdots \times (\mathbb{F}_{q^{\deg P_N}})^{u_N}$, $\circ$ the standard composition map, and

$$\tilde{E}_\mathcal{P} : \mathcal{L}(\mathcal{D}) \to \mathbb{F}_q^{u_\infty} \times \mathbb{F}_q^{u_0} \times \cdots \times (\mathbb{F}_{q^{\deg P_N}})^{u_N}$$
$$f \mapsto (\varphi_{\mathcal{D}, P_\infty, u_\infty}(f), \varphi_{\mathcal{D}, P_0, u_0}(f), \ldots, \varphi_{\mathcal{D}, P_N, u_N}(f))$$

(2) the algorithm $\mathcal{U}_{q,n}^{\mathcal{P}, \underline{u}}(Q)$ defined by (5) has bilinear complexity

$$\mu(\mathcal{U}_{q,n}^{\mathcal{P}, \underline{u}}) = \sum_{i \in \{\infty, 0, 1, \ldots, N\}} \mu_q(\deg P_i, u_i).$$

Proof. Since $\mathcal{D} = (n-1)P_\infty$, $\mathcal{L}(\mathcal{D})$ is isomorphic to $\mathbb{F}_{q^n}$, and we associate elements of $\mathcal{L}(\mathcal{D})$ to elements of $\mathbb{F}_{q^n}$. For $f, g \in \mathcal{L}(\mathcal{D})$, if we compute the Generalized Hadamard product of $\tilde{E}_P(f)$ and $\tilde{E}_P(g)$, we get

$$\tilde{E}_P(f) \odot \tilde{E}_P(g) = \begin{pmatrix} \varphi_{\mathcal{D},P_\infty,u_\infty}(f) \\ \varphi_{\mathcal{D},P_0,u_0}(f) \\ \varphi_{\mathcal{D},P_1,u_1}(f) \\ \vdots \\ \varphi_{\mathcal{D},P_N,u_N}(f) \end{pmatrix} \odot \begin{pmatrix} \varphi_{\mathcal{D},P_\infty,u_\infty}(g) \\ \varphi_{\mathcal{D},P_0,u_0}(g) \\ \varphi_{\mathcal{D},P_1,u_1}(g) \\ \vdots \\ \varphi_{\mathcal{D},P_N,u_N}(g) \end{pmatrix}$$

$$= \begin{pmatrix} \varphi_{\mathcal{D},P_\infty,u_\infty}(f)\varphi_{\mathcal{D},P_\infty,u_\infty}(g) \\ \varphi_{\mathcal{D},P_0,u_0}(f)\varphi_{\mathcal{D},P_0,u_0}(g) \\ \varphi_{\mathcal{D},P_1,u_1}(f)\,\varphi_{\mathcal{D},P_1,u_1}(g) \\ \vdots \\ \varphi_{\mathcal{D},P_N,u_N}(f)\,\varphi_{\mathcal{D},P_N,u_N}(g) \end{pmatrix}$$

$$= \begin{pmatrix} \varphi_{2\mathcal{D},P_\infty,u_\infty}(fg) \\ \varphi_{2\mathcal{D},P_0,u_0}(fg) \\ \varphi_{2\mathcal{D},P_1,u_1}(fg) \\ \vdots \\ \varphi_{2\mathcal{D},P_N,u_N}(fg) \end{pmatrix} = \tilde{Ev}_P(fg).$$

We have to prove that $\tilde{Ev}_P$ is bijective. Let $f = f_0 + f_1 x + \cdots + f_{2n-2}x^{2n-2}$ be a function in $\mathcal{L}(2\mathcal{D})$ such that $f \in \ker \tilde{Ev}_P$. In particular, $\varphi_{2\mathcal{D},P_\infty,u_\infty}(f) = 0$ implies that $f_{2n-2} = \ldots = f_{2n-1-u_\infty} = 0$. Then, $f = \sum_{i=0}^{2n-2-u_\infty} a_i x^i \in \mathcal{L}((2n-2-u_\infty)P_\infty)$ and

$$(\varphi_{2\mathcal{D},P_0,u_0}(f), \varphi_{2\mathcal{D},P_1,u_1}(f), \ldots, \varphi_{2\mathcal{D},P_N,u_N}(f)) = (0, 0, \ldots, 0).$$

Hence, $f \in \ker \tilde{Ev}_P \subseteq \mathcal{L}((2n-2-u_\infty)P_\infty - \sum_{i=0}^N u_i P_i)$. But, the divisor $(2n-2-u_\infty)P_\infty - \sum_{i=0}^N u_i P_i$ is of degree -1 so $f = 0$ and $\ker \tilde{Ev}_P = \{0\}$. Thus $\tilde{Ev}_P$ is injective, and bijective since between two vector spaces of same dimension. For all $f, g \in \mathcal{L}(\mathcal{D})$, we obtain

$$fg = \tilde{Ev}_P^{-1}(\tilde{E}_P(f) \odot \tilde{E}_P(g)),$$

and finally, with $f = Ev_Q^{-1}(x)$ and $g = Ev_Q^{-1}(y)$ for any $x, y \in \mathbb{F}_{q^n}$,

$$xy = E_Q \circ \tilde{Ev}_P^{-1}\left(\tilde{E}_P \circ Ev_Q^{-1}(x) \odot \tilde{E}_P \circ Ev_Q^{-1}(y)\right),$$

where E_Q denotes the canonical projection from the valuation ring $\mathcal{O}_Q$ of the place Q in its residue class field F_Q. Hence, we obtain an algorithm of polynomial interpolation, since functions in the Riemann-Roch spaces are polynomials. Its bilinear multiplications are first given by the $\varphi_{\mathcal{D},P_i,u_i}(f)\varphi_{\mathcal{D},P_i,u_i}(g)$, that require $\mu_q(\deg P_i, u_i)$ bilinear multiplications over $\mathbb{F}_q$ for each $i = \infty, 0, 1, \ldots, N$. Thus the bilinear complexity of the algorithm $\mathcal{U}_{q,n}^{P,u}(Q)$ is the same for all possible Q, and is given by $\mu(\mathcal{U}_{q,n}^{P,u}) = \sum_{i \in \{\infty,0,1,\ldots,N\}} \mu_q(\deg P_i, u_i)$.

This proposition suppose that the multiplications in the power serie rings of local expansions are computed using algorithms that are optimal in terms of bilinear complexity. In a more pratical point of view, one can consider that the multiplication in $\mathbb{F}_{q^d}[[t_P]]/(t_P)^u$ are computed by an algorithm $\mathcal{U}_{q,d,u}(P)$. In this case, the bilinear complexity of an algorithm defined in Proposition 3.1 is given by

$$\mu(\mathcal{U}_{q,n}^{\mathcal{P},\underline{u}}) = \sum_{i \in \{\infty,0,1,\ldots,N\}} \mu\left(\mathcal{U}_{q,\deg P_i, u_i}(P_i)\right).$$

A possibility to improve the bilinear complexity of the Chudnovsky-type algorithms over the projective line of [6] is hence to use derivative evaluations. For example, we can use derivative evaluations instead of one of the places of the highest degree in an algorithm $\mathcal{U}_{q,n}^{\mathcal{P}}$ constructed taking places by increasing degrees. An illustration of this process is given in the following example.

Example 3.1. We define $\mathcal{U}_{3,6}^{\mathcal{P}',\underline{u}}$ with $\mathcal{P}' = \{P_\infty, P_0, P_1, P_2, P_1^2, P_2^2, P_3^2\}$, and $\underline{u} = (2,1,\ldots,1)$. This construction is illustrated in Fig. 2, where $2P_0$ means that we evaluate at P_0 with multiplicity 2 and P_0' is the second coefficient of the local expansion at P_0. Its bilinear complexity reaches the best-known bilinear complexity bound [7, Table 2].

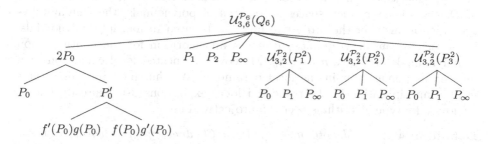

Fig. 2. Diagram of $\mathcal{U}_{3,6}^{\mathcal{P}',\underline{u}}(Q)$.

Table 1 shows some improvements of [6, Table 2], thanks to some derivative evaluations at rational places with multiplicity 2 only, as in Example 3.1. A result is underlined when it equalizes the best-known bilinear complexity.

This is a first improvement of the bilinear complexity of recursive Chudnovsky-type algorithms over the projective line. In what follows, we refine the strategy introduced in [6]. This requires to introduce a construction of Chudnovsky-type algorithms over the projective line to multiply the truncated local expansions.

Table 1. Some improvements of [6] thanks to derivative evaluations.

n	2	3	4	5	6	7	8	9	10	11	12	13	14	15	16	17	18
$\mu(\mathcal{U}_{2,n}^{P',u})$	–	–	10	14	–	22	28	32	38	42	48	52	58	64	68	76	80
$\mu(\mathcal{U}_{3,n}^{P',u})$	–	–	–	–	15	–	23	27	–	35	39	–	47	51	–	59	63

4 Multiplication of Truncated Local Expansions Using Chudnovsky-Type Algorithms over the Projective Line

Let d and u be positive integers. The best results on the bilinear complexity $\mu_q(d, u)$ of the multiplication in the power series ring of truncated local expansions of order u at a place of degree d are given by Rambaud in [11] (see [7, Table 3]). However, our goal is to introduce a generic construction, and we approach this problem by using only Chudnovsky-type algorithms over the projective line.

In this section, we focus on the construction of Chudnovsky-type algorithms for the multiplication of the truncated local expansions of order u at place P of degree d, i.e. in $\mathbb{F}_{q^d}[[t_P]]/(t_P^u)$, where t_P is a local parameter at the place P. In fact, by generically using the rational function field with only P_∞ in the support of $\mathcal{D}$, the Riemann-Roch spaces are spaces of polynomials, the Chudnovsky-type algorithms over the projective line can be used to multiply polynomials. In particular, an algorithm $\mathcal{U}_{q,n}$ provides an algorithm for the multiplication of polynomials of degree n over $\mathbb{F}_q$. Moreover, truncated local expansions can be seen as polynomials in the local parameter. We thus introduce algorithms for the multiplication of the truncated local expansions using already known Chudnovsky-type algorithms over the projective line.

Definition 4.1. *We denote by $\mathcal{U}_{q,d,u}(P)$ a Chudnovsky-type algorithm for the multiplication of the power series ring of truncated local expansions of order u at place P of degree d.*

In what follows, ouf construction process does not depend on the choice of P, thus we denote such an algorithm by $\mathcal{U}_{q,d,u}$, of bilinear complexity $\mu(\mathcal{U}_{q,d,u})$. These algorithms give an upper bound for the bilinear complexity in these algebras, i.e.

$$\mu_q(d, u) \leq \mu(\mathcal{U}_{q,d,u}).$$

One can obtain a first result by using directly the known results for he multiplication in finite extensions of finite fields.

Proposition 4.1. *Let q be a prime power, let $d \geq 1$ and $u > 1$ be positive integers. There exists a Chudnovsky-type algorithm over the projective line $\mathcal{U}_{q,d,u}$ such that*

$$\mu(\mathcal{U}_{q,d,u}) = \mu(\mathcal{U}_{q,d})\mu(\mathcal{U}_{q^d,u})$$

where $\mathcal{U}_{q,d}$ is a Chudnovsky type algorithm for the multiplication in $\mathbb{F}_{q^d}$ over $\mathbb{F}_q$ and $\mathcal{U}_{q^d,u}$ is a Chudnovsky type algorithm for the multiplication in $\mathbb{F}_{(q^d)^u}$ over $\mathbb{F}_{q^d}$.

Proof. Let $f, g \in \mathbb{F}_{q^d}[[t]]/(t^u)$. Then, one can write $f = \sum_{i=0}^{u-1} f_i t^i$ and $g = \sum_{j=0}^{u-1} g_j t^j$, where the f_i and g_i belong to $\mathbb{F}_{q^d}$. Then, the product $\overline{fg}$ in the truncated local expansion is given by

$$\overline{fg} = \sum_{k=0}^{u-1} \left(\sum_{i+j=k} f_i g_j \right) t^k.$$

The algorithm $\mathcal{U}_{q^d,u}$ allows one to compute the product fg of f and g seen as polynomials in $\mathbb{F}_q[t]_{\leq u-1}$, and thus allows to obtain the truncated product $\overline{fg}$. This algorithm involves $\mu(\mathcal{U}_{q^d,u})$ bilinear multiplications in $\mathbb{F}_{q^d}$. Then, each of these multiplication in $\mathbb{F}_{q^d}$ can be computed over $\mathbb{F}_q$ using an algorithm $\mathcal{U}_{q,d}$ of bilinear complexity $\mu(\mathcal{U}_{q,d})$. Finally, this defines the algorithm $\mathcal{U}_{q,d,u}$ of bilinear complexity $\mu(\mathcal{U}_{q,d,u}) = \mu(\mathcal{U}_{q,d})\mu(\mathcal{U}_{q^d,u})$.

The rest of this section is dedicate to obtain a better result using a trick for the multiplication of the truncated expansions at rational places. More precisely, we obtain an improvement of the latest construction by multiplying the local expansions at a place P of degree d at order $u - 1$ instead of u, and compute two more bilinear multiplications.

Proposition 4.2. *Let q be a prime power and $u > 1$ be a positive integer. There exists a Chudnovsky-type algorithm over the projective line $\mathcal{U}_{q,1,u}$ such that*

$$\mu(\mathcal{U}_{q,1,u}) = \mu(\mathcal{U}_{q,u-1}) + 2,$$

where $\mathcal{U}_{q,u-1}$ is a Chudnovsky type algorithm for the multiplication in $\mathbb{F}_{q^{u-1}}$ over $\mathbb{F}_q$.

Proof. We use the multiplication of polynomials of degree $u-2$ instead of $u-1$. Let $\tilde{f}, \tilde{g} \in \mathbb{F}_q[[t]]/(t^{u-1})$ be truncated series at order $u - 1$. Then, one can write $\tilde{f} = \sum_{i=0}^{u-2} f_i t^i$ and $\tilde{g} = \sum_{j=0}^{u-2} g_j t^j$, where the f_i and g_i belong to $\mathbb{F}_q$. Then, the product $\tilde{f}\tilde{g}$ is given by

$$\tilde{f}\tilde{g} = \sum_{k=0}^{2u-4} \left(\sum_{i+j=k} f_i g_j \right) t^k,$$

where $i, j \leq u - 2$. This product can be computed using $\mathcal{U}_{q,u-1}$ with $\mu(\mathcal{U}_{q,u-1})$ bilinear multiplications in $\mathbb{F}_q$. Let us denote by $\overline{\tilde{f}\tilde{g}}$ the truncation of $\tilde{f}\tilde{g}$ at order u. Then, the truncated product of fg is given by $\overline{fg} = \overline{\tilde{f}\tilde{g}} + (f_0 g_{u-1} + f_{u-1} g_0) t^{u-1}$. Thus, there exists an algorithm $\mathcal{U}_{q,d,u}$ such that

$$\mu(\mathcal{U}_{q,1,u}) = \mathcal{U}_{q,u-1} + 2.$$

This latest proposition together with Proposition 4.1 gives directly the following corollary.

Corollary 4.1. *Let q be a prime power, $d \geq 1$ and $u > 1$ be positive integers. There exists a Chudnovsky-type algorithm over the projective line $\mathcal{U}_{q,d,u}$ such that*

$$\mu(\mathcal{U}_{q,d,u}) = \mu\left(\mathcal{U}_{q,d}\right)\left(\mu(\mathcal{U}_{q^d,u-1}) + 2\right)$$

where $\mathcal{U}_{q,d}$ is a Chudnovsky type algorithm for the multiplication in $\mathbb{F}_{q^d}$ over $\mathbb{F}_q$ and $\mathcal{U}_{q^d,u-1}$ is a Chudnovsky type algorithm for the multiplication in $\mathbb{F}_{(q^d)^{u-1}}$ over $\mathbb{F}_{q^d}$.

5   A Better Construction Strategy

The strategy introduced in [6] to construct multiplication algorithms at finite distance, i.e. for a given extension degree n, consists in constructing the set of places $\mathcal{P}$ by taking all places by increasing degree until the sum is exactly equal to $2n - 1$. More precisely, if the sum gets bigger than this value, it is sufficient to remove a place of the appropriate degree. It is noticed that this strategy is not optimal, because the ratio $\frac{\mu(\mathcal{U}_{q,n})}{n}$ is not strictly increasing. Moreover this strategy does not include evaluation with multiplicity.

5.1   Generic Strategy

In this section, we introduce a new generic strategy of construction of Chudnovsky-type algorithms over the projective line including the use of derivative evaluations. This also provides an answer to the flaw of the not strictly increasing ratio of the construction taking places by increasing degrees. In order to introduce this strategy, we define the relative bilinear complexity of an algorithm.

Definition 5.1. *Let $\mathcal{U}_{q,d,u}$ be an algorithm for the multiplication in the power series ring of truncated local expansions of order u at place P of degree d. Its relative bilinear complexity is given by*

$$\frac{\mu(\mathcal{U}_{q,d,u})}{du}.$$

This ratio is useful in our strategy since it measures the bilinear complexity of an algorithm in relation to its use (see Table 3). For $u = 1$, the problem of the non-strictly increasing ratio stated earlier can be addressed if we take places by increasing relative bilinear complexity instead of by increasing degrees. This definition moreover generalizes the ratio given in the beginning of this section to the use of evaluation with multiplicity. Our strategy is thus to construct the set of places $\mathcal{P}$ and multiplicities $\underline{u}$ by increasing relative bilinear complexity.

Recall that from [6, Sect. 4.2], one can iteratively compute the number of places of each degree of the rational function field over $\mathbb{F}_q$. Then, for any prime power q we can iteratively compute a table of the $\mu(\mathcal{U}_{q,d,u})$ using increasing relative bilinear complexity. More precisely, we know that for any q, the algorithm $\mathcal{U}_{q,1,1}$ is just a bilinear multiplication in $\mathbb{F}_q$, and thus $\mu(\mathcal{U}_{q,1,1}) = 1$. Then, we process as follows.

Given the table of the $\mu(\mathcal{U}_{q,d,u})$, for $1 \leq d, u \leq n - 1$, we compute $\mu(\mathcal{U}_{q,n,1})$ by constructing the parameters $\mathcal{P}$ and $\underline{u}$ by taking places and multiplicities by increasing relative bilinear complexity and fill the table. The process is the following.

1. Add places in $\mathcal{P}$ and increase the corresponding the multiplicity until we have $\sum_i u_i \deg P_i \geq 2n - 1$ following the increasing relative bilinear complexity.
2. If the sum gets strictly greater than $2n - 1$, remove some places or reduce the multiplicity following decreasing relative bilinear complexity.
3. Fill the table of the $\mathcal{U}_{q,d,u}$, for $1 \leq d, u \leq n$ using Proposition 4.2 and Corollary 4.1.

Example 5.1. Let $q = 2$. We consider the table of the $\mu(\mathcal{U}_{q,d,u})$, for $1 \leq, d, u \leq 3$. From the results of [6] we know the values of $\mu(\mathcal{U}_{q,d,1})$ for $d = 1, 2, 3$. The values obtained for $u = 2, 3$ are given by Corollary 4.1. Hence, we have the following Table 2.

Table 2. Bilinear complexity of $\mathcal{U}_{2,d,u}$ for $1 \leq d, u \leq 3$.

$\mu(\mathcal{U}_{2,d,u})$	$u = 1$	$u = 2$	$u = 3$
$d = 1$	1	3	5
$d = 2$	3	9	15
$d = 3$	6	18	30

Now, consider the corresponding table of the relative bilinear complexities.

Table 3. Relative bilinear complexity of $\mathcal{U}_{2,d,u}$ for $1 \leq d, u \leq 3$.

$\frac{\mu(\mathcal{U}_{2,d,u})}{du}$	$u = 1$	$u = 2$	$u = 3$
$d = 1$	1	1.5	1.67
$d = 2$	1.5	2.25	2.50
$d = 3$	2	3	3.33

– In order to multiply in the extension of degree 4 of $\mathbb{F}_2$, recall that $\mathbb{F}_2(x)$ contains 3 rational places and one place of degree 2. The algorithm constructed using places of increasing degrees as in [6] uses two rational places, the place of degree 2 and one place of degree 3. Its bilinear complexity is then equal to $2\mu(\mathcal{U}_{q,1,1}) + \mu(\mathcal{U}_{q,2,1}) + \mu(\mathcal{U}_{q,3,1}) = 2 + 3 + 6 = 11$. According our new strategy, we start by including in $\mathcal{P}$ the three rational places and the place of degree 2. Using the table of the relative bilinear complexity, we see that it is more

profitable to use derivative evaluations at rational places instead of including
a place of degree 3. We finally obtain an algorithm $\mathcal{U}_{2,4,1}$ using one rational
place with multiplicity $u = 1$, two rational places with multiplicity $u = 2$
and the place of degree 2 with multiplicity $u = 1$. Its bilinear complexity is
$\mu(\mathcal{U}_{2,4,1}) = 2\mu(\mathcal{U}_{q,1,2}) + \mu(\mathcal{U}_{q,1,1}) + \mu(\mathcal{U}_{q,2,1}) = 2 \times 3 + 1 + 3 = 10$.

- By Proposition 4.2, we have $\mu(\mathcal{U}_{2,1,4}) = \mu(\mathcal{U}_{2,3,1}) + 2 = 8$.
- For $2 \leq d, u \leq 4$, we have that $u - 1 \leq \frac{1}{2}q^d + 1$. Thus the algorithm $\mathcal{U}_{q^d,u-1}$ is
  of optimal bilinear complexity $\mu(\mathcal{U}_{q^d,u-1}) = 2(u - 1) - 1$. Thus, by Corollary
  4.1, we obtain the remaining values of Table 4.

Table 4. Bilinear complexity of $\mathcal{U}_{2,d,u}$ for $1 \leq d, u \leq 4$.

$\mu(\mathcal{U}_{2,d,u})$	$u = 1$	$u = 2$	$u = 3$	$u = 4$
$d = 1$	1	3	5	8
$d = 2$	3	9	15	21
$d = 3$	6	18	30	42
$d = 4$	10	30	50	70

5.2 Experimental Results

Finally, our goal is to push forward the calculations to compare on a larger scale
the results obtained with this new strategy to the one of the places of increasing
degrees given in [6]. In order to obtain a fully automatized simulation and to
avoid heavy or not directly related computations, we consider the following to
construct a multiplication algorithm in $\mathbb{F}_{q^n}$.

- We construct the table of the $\mu(\mathcal{U}_{q,d,u})$ for d, u in logarithmic size compared
  to the extension degree n.
- We fill the table only when no extra calculation is required. For instance, we
  give bilinear complexity of $\mathcal{U}_{q,d,u}$ for $d, u > 1$ only if $u - 1 \leq \frac{1}{2}q^d + 1$, and
  thus $\mathcal{U}_{q^d,u-1}$ has optimal bilinear complexity, so we do not have to determine
  how to construct this algorithm nor to compute its bilinear complexity.

Using the table of the $\mu(\mathcal{U}_{2,d,u})$ for $d, u \leq 10$, we computed the bilinear
complexity obtained for the multiplication in finite extensions $\mathbb{F}_{2^n}$, for $n \leq 500$.

In Fig. 3, the curves represent the bilinear complexity obtained by the following constructions:

- (1) is the Karatsuba algorithm ($\mathcal{O}(n^{\log_2 3})$ bilinear multiplications),
- (2) is the best asymptotical theoretical bound [3]. Th is bound is linear relatively to the extension degree while the recursive construction presented in
  this paper is supposed to be quasi-linear, as in [6]. Thus, for n sufficiently
  large, the curves of the constructions (3) and (4) will cross this line.
- (3) is the recursive Chudnovsky-type algorithms over the projective line, taking places by increasing degrees and without multiplicity,

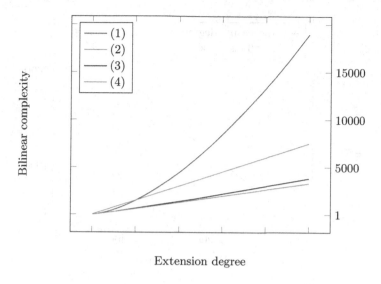

Fig. 3. Comparison of the bilinear complexity

– (4) is the the new result of recursive Chudnovsky-type algorithms over the projective line using evaluation with multiplicity, constructed using increasing relative bilinear complexity.

Note that there is no other generic construction of algorithms based on the method of Chudnovsky that can be included in this figure. Table 4 compares more precisely the two recursive constructions of Chudnovsky-type algorithms over the projective line.

Remark 5.1. We arbitraty chose to treat the example of extensions of $\mathbb{F}_2$. The low number of places of $\mathbb{F}_2(x)$ makes it the worst case from the point of view of Chudnovsky-type algorithms. However, even in this case we see the gain obtained with the use of derivative evaluations.

Remark 5.2. It would be interesting to consider our recursive construction over the projective line with the derivative evaluations from an asymptotic point of view with respect to the degree n of the extensions $\mathbb{F}_{q^n}$. Indeed, this would allow on the one hand to compare it to the recursive construction over the projective line without the derivative evaluations studied in the article [6] (in particular with the uniform bounds of the bilinear complexity but also bounds of the construction complexity); on the other hand it would allow to compare also according to other criteria as for example the use of places of degree k versus the use of rational places with derivative evaluations of order $\leq k$ or the comparison between the derivative evaluation of order 1 (resp. of order 3) and the quadratic (resp. quartic) embedding by analogy with the case of the classical construction strategy based on the increasing genus.

Let us recall what is at stake in these comparisons in the case of the classical strategy of increasing genus. Originally, because of the Drinfeld-Vladut bound, in

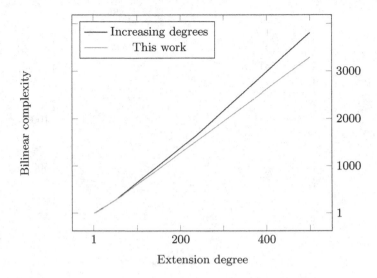

Fig. 4. Comparison of the bilinear complexity of generic recursive constructions of Chudnovsky-type algorithms over the projective line

the case of small basis fields $\mathbb{F}_2$ respectively $\mathbb{F}_q$ with $3 \leq q < 9$, we initially select the method of the quartic respectively quadratic embedding. More precisely, as a consequence of [1, Theorem 1.1] (Condition $N_1(F/\mathbb{F}_q) > 2n + 2g - 2$), the asymptotic use of CCMA requires to have an infinite family $\mathcal{F} = (F_k/\mathbb{F}_q)$ of algebraic function fields $F_k/\mathbb{F}_q$ defined over $\mathbb{F}_q$ of genus g_k having $N_1(F_k) > 2g_k$. But, $A(\mathcal{F}) = \limsup_{k \to \infty} \frac{N_1(F_k)}{g_k} \leq A(q)$ where $A(q)$ denotes the Ihara constant defined by $A(q) = \limsup_{g \to \infty} N_q(g)/g$ with $N_q(g) = max\{N_1(F) \mid$ F is a function field over $\mathbb{F}_q\}$. By the Drinfeld-Vladut bound, we have $A(q) \leq q^{\frac{1}{2}} - 1$. Hence, as we need a family $\mathcal{F}$ satisfying $A(\mathcal{F}) \geq 2$, we cannot directly use CCMA for families defined over the small fields $\mathbb{F}_q$ with $q < 9$. However, we can avoid this difficulty by embedding these small fields $\mathbb{F}_q$ in an suitable extension $\mathbb{F}_{q^m}$ namely, $m = 4$ (resp. $m = 2$) if $q = 2$ (resp. $3 \leq q < 9$) and by using CCMA with an asymptotical family defined over $\mathbb{F}_{q^m}$. In this situation, we clearly have $\mu_q(n) \leq \mu_q(mn) \leq \mu_q(m).\mu_{q^m}(n)$ by Lemma 1.2 in [9]. Note that, in these cases, instead of the embeddings, it is possible to use places of degree four and respectively two which is not a method equivalent to the above embedding method and generally gives better bilinear complexities (cf. [2,5] and [3] with respect to [1, Corollary 4.3]). It is also possible in this framework to combine the use of places of degree >1 and the derived evaluations, which allows to obtain better bounds [3,4].

In the fixed genus strategy, as in our recursive construction on the projective line, we find a similar situation, namely the use of places of degree > 1 with the possibility of using also the derivative evaluations. In the context of a future work, the first questions we can ask ourselves are the following:

1) What are the asymptotic bounds (if it is possible to determine them) for the recursive construction over the projective line with derivative valuations compared to those obtained in [6]?
2) When is it better to use derivative valuations of order $\leq k$ at a rational place rather than an evaluation at a place of degree k?

References

1. Ballet, S.: Curves with many points and multiplication complexity in any extension of $\mathbb{F}_q$. Finite Fields Appl. **5**, 364–377 (1999)
2. Ballet, S., Le Brigand, D., Rolland, R.: On an application of the definition field descent of a tower of function fields. In: Proceedings of the Conference Arithmetic, Geometry and Coding Theory (AGCT 2005), vol. 21, pp. 187–203. Société Mathématique de France, sér. Séminaires et Congrès (2009)
3. Ballet, S., Pieltant, J.: On the tensor rank of multiplication in any extension of $\mathbb{F}_2$. J. Complex. **27**, 230–245 (2011)
4. Ballet, S., Pieltant, J.: Tower of algebraic function fields with maximal Hasse-Witt invariant and tensor rank of multiplication in any extension of $\mathbb{F}_2$ and $\mathbb{F}_3$. J. Pure Appl. Algebra **222**(5), 1069–1086 (2018)
5. Ballet, S., Rolland, R.: Multiplication algorithm in a finite field and tensor rank of the multiplication. J. Algebra **272**(1), 173–185 (2004)
6. Ballet, S., Bonnecaze, A., Pacifico, B.: Multiplication in finite fields with Chudnovsky-type algorithms on the projective line. arXiv (2020)
7. Ballet, S., Chaumine, J., Pieltant, J., Rambaud, M., Randriambololona, H., Rolland, R.: On the tensor rank of multiplication in finite extensions of finite fields and related issues in algebraic geometry. Uspekhi Math. Nauk **76**(1(457)), 31–94 (2021)
8. Bürgisser, P., Clausen, M., Shokrollahi, A.: Algebraic Complexity Theory. Springer, Heidelberg (1997). https://doi.org/10.1007/978-3-662-03338-8
9. Chudnovsky, D., Chudnovsky, G.: Algebraic complexities and algebraic curves over finite fields. J. Complex. **4**, 285–316 (1988)
10. De Groote, H.: Characterization of division algebras of minimal rank and the structure of their algorithm varieties. SIAM J. Comput. **12**(1), 101–117 (1983)
11. Rambaud, M.: Courbes de Shimura et algorithmes bilinéaires de multiplication dans les corps finis. Ph.D. thesis, Telecom ParisTech (2017). Written in English
12. Seroussi, G., Lempel, A.: On symmetric algorithms for bilinear forms over finite fields. J. Algorithms **5**(3), 327–344 (1984)
13. Stichtenoth, H.: Algebraic Function Fields and Codes. No. 254 in Graduate Texts in Mathematics, 2nd edn. Springer, Heidelberg (2008). https://doi.org/10.1007/978-3-540-76878-4
14. Winograd, S.: On multiplication in algebraic extension fields. Theoret. Comput. Sci. **8**, 359–377 (1979)

Coding Theory

Security Enhancement Method Using Shortened Error Correcting Codes

Tomohiro Sekiguchi[✉] and Hidema Tanaka

National Defense Academy of Japan, 1-10-20 Hashirimizu,
Yokosuka, Kanagawa 239-8686, Japan
tosekiguc@gmail.com, hidema@nda.ac.jp

Abstract. This paper proposes two methods that combine high error correcting capability with security enhancement to enable cryptographic communication even under high noise. The first method is a combination of symmetric key cryptography and Shortened LDPC, which enables two-way communication. It can be regarded as one type of mode of operation. The second method combines the McEliece method and Shortened QC-MDPC to realize one-way communication. It has the advantage of fast processing speeds compared to general asymmetric key cryptography and the ability to centrally manage key updates for many IoT modules. We performed computer simulations and analysed practical parameterization and security enhancement. Both methods are found to provide sufficient security and are expected to have a wide range of applications.

Keywords: Shortened error correcting code · LDPC · QC-MDPC · High noise communication environment · Cryptographic communication · Security enhancement

1 Introduction

The expansion of high-speed, high-capacity wireless networks has led to an explosion of wireless IoT modules. With this situation, communication errors due to electromagnetic noise and communication interference have become a problem. Especially for large data communications, even small errors cause retransmission requests, leading to an increase in communication traffic. On the other hand, security issues cannot be ignored, as wireless communication is easy to eavesdrop on. We are therefore in a situation where both error correcting capability and security are needed. In the development of Post Quantum Cryptography (PQC), code-based [1,2,13] and lattice-based methods [4,6] are known to make active use of errors. However, in many cases they are discussed in security analyses and have not been evaluated in their error correcting capability. On the other hand, in the case of symmetric key cryptography, encryption process and error correcting code process are independent, and there is no discussion of making them compatible. However, key lengths tend to be longer due to quantum computer countermeasures.

Error correcting codes applying shortened techniques have been shown to be highly effective in communications under high noise. For example, in previous study, the effectiveness of the Shortened Low Density Parity Check (LDPC) has been evaluated in detail by computer experiments [15]. In general, eavesdropping itself is often not feasible under high noise, so such a communication channel can itself be regarded as a secure communication. Usually, in security evaluation, the attacker assumes the same error rate of communication as the receiver, but if a cryptographic process with high error correcting capability can be realized, it can provide a very high level of security in practical usage.

This paper proposes two methods that combine such error correcting capability with security enhancement. The first is two-way communication, which aims at establishing a general one-to-one cryptographic communication. The second is one-way communication, which focuses on easy key updating with public keys and is a many-to-one communication for centralized management of IoT modules. The features of each are summarized as follows.

Two-way:

- It can be regarded as a kind of mode of operation, since it applies existing symmetric key cryptography.
- High noise is deliberately applied for security enhancement.
- Highly effective for security enhancement.

One-way:

- Applies code-based asymmetric key cryptography, but has the properties of symmetric key cryptography because it uses a pre-shared key.
- Faster processing than general asymmetric key cryptography and suitable for continuous communication.
- The effect of security enhancement in security analysis is limited, but it is expected to be very effective in practical terms (the attacker's assumption in security analysis is too strong).

2   Preliminaries

2.1   Linear Code

Let (n,k) be code word length n [bit] and information word length k [bit] of linear code C. $\mathbf{G} = [\ \mathbf{I}_k|\ \mathbf{P}\ ]$ denotes a generator matrix whose size is $n \times k$ over $\mathbb{F}_2$, where $\mathbf{I_k} \in \mathbb{F}_2^{k \times k}$ denotes the identity matrix and $\mathbf{P} \in \mathbb{F}_2^{k \times (n-k)}$ denotes submatrix. Let $Enc(\cdot)$ and $Dec(\cdot, \cdot)$ be encoding and decoding function as follows.

$$\mathbf{c} = Enc(\ \mathbf{i}\ ) = \mathbf{G}\mathbf{i}^T,$$
$$\mathbf{i} = Dec(\ \mathbf{c},\ \mathbf{p}\ ) \ \text{ and } \ \mathbf{p} = \mathbf{H}\mathbf{c}^T, \tag{1}$$

where $\mathbf{i} \in \mathbb{F}_2^k$, $\mathbf{c} \in \mathbb{F}_2^n$ and $\mathbf{p} \in \mathbb{F}_2^{n-k}$ denote information word, code word and parity check word respectively. Matrix $\mathbf{H} = [\mathbf{P}|\ \mathbf{I}_{n-k}]$ which holds $\mathbf{G}\mathbf{H}^T = 0$, denotes parity check matrix of $(n - k) \times n$ over $\mathbb{F}_2$. Given error vector $\mathbf{e} \in \mathbb{F}_2^n$, we have received code word $\mathbf{y} = (\mathbf{c} + \mathbf{e}) \in \mathbb{F}_2^n$. Using matrix $\mathbf{H}$, we can calculate parity check word as follows.

$$\mathbf{p} = \mathbf{H}\mathbf{y}^T = \mathbf{H}(\mathbf{c}^T + \mathbf{e}^T) = \mathbf{H}\mathbf{e}^T \tag{2}$$

In the followings, $\text{Hw}(\cdot)$ denotes hamming weight and especially $\text{Hw}(\mathbf{H})$ denotes one of row in $\mathbf{H}$. The error correcting capability depends on encoding and decoding algorithm, however, almost decoding function is polynomial time algorithm.

2.2 LDPC and MDPC Codes

Low Density Parity Check (LDPC) code is one of linear codes, and error correcting capability achieves the Shannon limit [8]. Its parity check matrix is sparse and $\text{Hw}(\mathbf{H}) = \mathcal{O}(\log n)$. There are many constructions ways for such parity check matrix, shown by a Gallager, Mackay [10], Reed Solomon based [7], and so on. If $\text{Hw}(\mathbf{H}) = \mathcal{O}(\sqrt{n})$, it can be redefined as Moderate Density Parity Check (MDPC).

Definition 1 (Quasi Cyclic(QC)-code). *(n_q, k_q) quasi cyclic code is a (n, k) linear code. Generator matrix is block circulant matrix, which l_q denotes order and matrix size. Then, code word length becomes $n = l_q n_q$, and information word length becomes $k = l_q k_q$.*

Parity check matrix can be also rewritten as

$$\mathbf{H}_q = \{\, \mathbf{H}_0 \mid \mathbf{H}_1 \mid, ..., \mid \mathbf{H}_{n_q-1} \}, \tag{3}$$

where $\mathbf{H}_i, (0 \leq i \leq n_q - 1)$ denotes $l_q \times l_q$ sub-matrix. A generator matrix $\mathbf{G}_q$ can be derived from $\mathbf{H}_q$. Note that l_q-shifted code words are included in the elements of the set of code words. By using such matrices, we can construct a (n_q, k_q) QC-code. Generator matrix can be defined as follows.

$$\mathbf{G}_q = \left(\quad \mathbf{I}_{n-k} \quad \left| \begin{array}{c} (\mathbf{H}_{n_q-1}^{-1}\mathbf{H}_0)^T \\ (\mathbf{H}_{n_q-1}^{-1}\mathbf{H}_1)^T \\ \vdots \\ (\mathbf{H}_{n_q-1}^{-1}\mathbf{H}_{n_q-2})^T \end{array} \right. \right) \tag{4}$$

Definition 2 (QC-MDPC code). *(n_q, k_q, l_q) QC-MDPC code satisfies a (n_q, k_q) QC-code with code length $n = n_q l_q$, parity check length $k = k_q l_q$ and order l_q which is a prime number. We have $\text{Hw}(\mathbf{H}) = \mathcal{O}(\sqrt{n})$ and $\text{Hw}(\mathbf{e}) = \mathcal{O}(\sqrt{n})$.*

2.3 Shortened LDPC Codes

To improve coding efficiency and error correcting capability, many techniques are known; Length, Expansion, Puncturing, Ejection, Filtering, Shortened, and

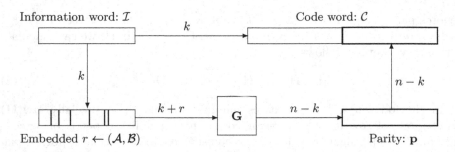

Fig. 1. Shortened LDPC

so on. Among these techniques, we focus on Shortened technique because its high performance in error correcting capability. Figure 1 shows outline of Shortened LDPC coding.

> Code word $\mathcal{C} = (c_0, c_1, \ldots, c_{n-1})$
> Information word $\mathcal{I} = (i_0, i_1, \ldots, i_{k-1})$ (5)
> Index set $\mathcal{A} = \{a_0, a_1, \ldots, a_{r-1}\}$, $r < k$ and $a_j \in \mathbb{F}_r$ $(0 \leq r \leq r-1)$

Note that the values of a_j are different each other. As shown in Fig. 1, $\mathcal{C}$ is concatenation of $\mathcal{I}$ and **p**. To generate **p**, encoding process embeds bits corresponding to $\mathcal{A}$ to $\mathcal{I}$ and then apply **G**. $\mathcal{A}$ denotes the bit position for interruption to embed, and in general, such embedded bits are fixed to zero. $\mathcal{A}$ is necessary for decoding phase, it is pre-shared between sender and receiver and is not sent in the communication phase. To improve more error correcting capability, we can set the value of $\mathcal{A}$ according to the distribution of noise in the communication environment [15].

Definition 3 (Shortened code). *Given (n, k) linear code $\mathcal{C}$, $\mathcal{A} = \{a_0, \ldots, a_{r-1}\}$ s.t. $a_j \in \mathbb{F}_r$ ($r < k, 0 \leq j \leq r-1$) and shortened code $\mathcal{C}_\mathcal{A}$ using indices from set $\mathcal{A}$, which embeds bit positions $a_0, \ldots, a_{r-1}$, and its values. The shortened code has code word length n and information word length k and parity length $n - k$.*

3   Proposal Method

3.1   Basic Idea

In the case of wireless secure communication, the sender encrypts the plain texts and then encodes them using error correcting code. The resultant code word is transmitted to radio wave using D/A converter. At this time, it is affected by noise according to the communication environment. We assume Additive White Gaussian Noise (AWGN) model. The receiver uses A/D conversion on the received code word, and error correcting decode them.

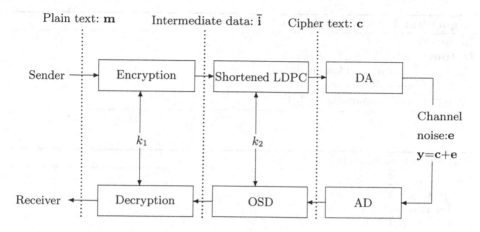

Fig. 2. Outline of proposed method

As mentioned above, encryption and error correcting code are generally performed independently. If the values of $\mathcal{A}$ and the bits to be embedded are kept secret for the aforementioned Shortened LDPC, it can be regarded as a mode of operation method for block cipher that performs encryption and error correcting code simultaneously. Furthermore, LDPC allows communication under high noise, so that the cipher text itself, which contains many errors, can be made more secure. This is the basic idea of our proposed method.

Let k_1 be the secret key of the symmetric key cipher (eg. AES-128 [5]). Let $\mathcal{B} = (b_0, b_1, \ldots, b_{r-1})$ be r [bit] random binary value. We define secret keys k_1 and k_2 as follows.

$$k_1 \in \mathbb{F}_2^{|k_1|}$$
$$k_2 = (\mathcal{A} , \mathcal{B}) \in \mathbb{N}^r \times \mathbb{F}_2^r \tag{6}$$

Figure 2 shows outline of our proposed method. "OSD" in the diagram denotes Order Statistic Decoding, which is considered optimal for Shortened LDPC [15]. The advantages of the proposed method are as follows.

- Shortened LDPC has a very high error correcting capability, it enables communication under high noise.
- Intermediate data $\bar{\mathbf{i}}$ is an encrypted output, so it is uniformly random and unpredictable to attackers.
- The cost of attack simply increases because error correcting code has also secret information.

3.2 Proposed Method

Secret Key k_2 Generation. The values of $\mathcal{A}$ and $\mathcal{B}$ in k_2 should be randomly generated. The size of $\mathcal{A}$ is selected by the Shortened LDPC code generation manner. The following **Algorithm 1** is the generator of secret keys $k_2 = (\mathcal{A}, \mathcal{B})$.

Algorithm 1. Secret key k_2 generation

Input: k, r
Output: $k_2 = (\mathcal{A}, \mathcal{B}) \in \mathbb{N}^r \times \mathbb{F}_2^r$
1: $a_j \leftarrow$ uniformly random $[0, |k| - 1]$
2: $b_j \leftarrow$ uniformly random $[0, 1]$
3: repeat 1~2, r times then $(\mathcal{A}, \mathcal{B}) \leftarrow (a_j, b_j)$.

Algorithm 2. Encryption algorithm

Input: $\mathbf{m} \in \mathbb{F}_2^b, k_1, k_2$
Output: $\mathbf{y} \in \mathbb{F}_2^n$
1: $\bar{\mathbf{i}} = \mathrm{E}(\mathbf{m}, k_1)$
2: $\mathbf{c} = (\bar{\mathbf{i}} \mid \mathbf{G}(\bar{\mathbf{i}}, k_2))$
3: $\mathbf{y} = \mathbf{c} + \mathbf{e}$
4: repeat 1~7, N times.

Encryption and Decryption Algorithm. Our encryption and decryption algorithms are shown in **Algorithm 2** and **Algorithm 3**. Where $\mathrm{E}(\cdot, \cdot)$ and $\mathrm{D}(\cdot, \cdot)$ denote the encryption and decryption functions of the symmetric key cipher, respectively. In addition, $\mathbf{G}(\cdot, \cdot)$ and $\mathrm{OSD}(\cdot, \cdot)$ denote encoding function of Shortened LDPC and OSD decoding function using k_2. The value of $|k_1|$ is determined by the specification of the symmetric key cipher, however, 128 to 256 [bit] is standard. In case the applied symmetric key cipher is a block cipher, the relationship between the block size b and k should be noted. When $b \leq k$, the proposed method needs to be executed $N = \lceil \frac{k}{b} \rceil$ times to process one plain text block. In the case of $b \geq k$, it is $N = \lceil \frac{b}{k} \rceil$ times. Thus, N cipher text blocks are generated for one $\bar{\mathbf{i}}$. Note that in the case of stream ciphers, one cipher text block is generated for each $\bar{\mathbf{i}}$, because this case can be processed as $b = k$.

In the following, for simplicity, we consider the condition of $\mathbf{m} \in \mathbb{F}_2^b$. Also, Shortened LDPC can correct errors below $\mathrm{Hw}(\mathbf{e})$, however in the following, it is assumed for simplicity that $\mathrm{Hw}(\mathbf{e})$ errors always occur. In practice, $\mathrm{Hw}(\mathbf{e})$ depends on the communication environment, but it is possible to achieve situations where errors are deliberately introduced and $\mathrm{Hw}(\mathbf{e})$ errors occur.

Algorithm 3. Decryption algorithm

Input: $\mathbf{y} \in \mathbb{F}_2^n, k_1, k_2$
Output: $\mathbf{m} \in \mathbb{F}_2^b$
  1: $\bar{\mathbf{i}} = \mathrm{OSD}(\mathbf{y}, k_2)$
  2: $\mathbf{m} = \mathrm{D}(\bar{\mathbf{i}}, k_1)$.
  3: repeat 1~2, N times.

---

4 Security Evaluation

4.1 Security Model

We consider security evaluation in the chosen plain text attack manner. Therefore attacker can freely manipulate plain text $\mathbf{m}$ but attacker can not distinguish whether cipher text $\mathbf{c}$ and received code word $\mathbf{y}$ are correct or not (see Fig. 2). We assume that attacker knows the specification of our proposed method; k, n and $\mathrm{Hw}(\mathbf{e})$. In addition, we also assume that $\mathbf{G}$ is sparse matrix and unpredictable for attacker.

We consider the following three models. In these models, since the value of $\bar{\mathbf{i}}$ denotes the output from a symmetric key cipher using k_1, the probability of successful estimation of this value is $1/2^{|k_1|}$. In addition, the attacker can get $\mathbf{y}$, however, can not determine $\mathbf{c}$ because of error bits. Let $\mathcal{O}_{\mathcal{L}}$ be the computational complexity of OSD.

Model 1 $\mathbf{G}$ is open and (k_1, k_2) are secret.
Model 2 $(\mathbf{G}, k_1)$ are secret and k_2 is open.
Model 3 $(\mathbf{G}, k_1, k_2)$ are secret.

4.2 Detailed Evaluation

Model 1. This model assumes that the specification of error correcting codes is open. When $\mathbf{G}$ is open, attacker can estimate $\mathbf{H}$ from $\mathbf{G}$. Under the condition of Model 1, if attacker can determine k_2, attacker can perform error correction and obtain $\mathbf{c}$. If no errors exist, the value of k_2 can be determined by deriving a simultaneous linear equation with unknown k_2 under the condition of known $\mathbf{H}$ and $\mathbf{y}$. Since k_2 has $\binom{k+1}{r} 2^r$ different values, it is necessary to collect $\binom{k+1}{r}$ 2^r kinds of different $(\mathbf{m}, \mathbf{y})$. However, there are $\binom{k}{\mathrm{Hw}(\mathbf{e})}$ different combinations in which errors can occur. As a result, the necessary number of independent linear equations becomes $u = \binom{k}{\mathrm{Hw}(\mathbf{e})} \binom{k+1}{r} 2^r$. By using Gaussian elimination, the computational complexity becomes $\mathcal{O}(u^3) \mathcal{O}_{\mathcal{L}}$. After determining k_2, attacker can obtain u kinds of true $(\mathbf{m}, \bar{\mathbf{i}})$. Since it is assumed that the secret key cipher satisfies computational security, there are no other attack methods other than brute force search. As a result, the necessary computational cost for k_1 becomes

$\mathcal{O}(2^{|k_1|})$. Note that the attack for k_1 does not require anything other than $(\mathbf{m}, \mathbf{y})$ used in the attack for k_2 and computational complexity for k_1 and k_2 are independent. As a result, the total computational complexity is $\mathcal{O}(u^3)\mathcal{O}_{\mathcal{L}} + \mathcal{O}(2^{|k_1|})$ and necessary number of chosen plain texts is u. The probability of successful attack is 1.0.

Model 2. This model assumes that the value of k_2 is secret and fixed, however its value is revealed. Although unlike Model 1, the specification of error correcting codes is also secret. In this case, since $\mathbf{G}$ is still secret, attacker needs to estimate $\mathbf{H}$ to obtain $\mathbf{c}$. The matrix $\mathbf{H}$ has linearly independent binary vector with hamming weight of $\mathrm{Hw}(\mathbf{H}) = \mathcal{O}(\sqrt{n})$ and length of $(n-k)$. Therefore, $\mathbf{H}$ is constructed by selecting $(n-k)$ vectors among linearly independent $v = \binom{n-k}{\mathrm{Hw}(\mathbf{H})}$ vectors. As a result, there are total $_v P_{n-k}$ kinds of candidates of $\mathbf{H}$ and attacker can obtain $\mathbf{c}$ for each candidate. As the same way of Model 1, by using brute force search for k_1, attacker can obtain $_v P_{n-k}$ kinds of $(\mathbf{m}, \bar{\mathbf{i}}, k_1)$. Therefore, the total computational complexity becomes $_v P_{n-k} \mathcal{O}_{\mathcal{L}} \mathcal{O}(2^{|k_1|})$. Only one $(\mathbf{m}, \mathbf{y})$ is sufficient for this attack, however, the probability of successful attack is $1/_v P_{n-k}$, because $(\mathbf{m}, \mathbf{y})$ is correctly established for all candidates of $(k_1, \mathbf{H})$, so it is not possible to distinguish which $(k_1, \mathbf{H})$ is correct.

Model 3. This case can be easily derived by combining the result of Model 2 and the result of k_2 analysis shown in Model 1. From these results, we can conclude that the computational complexity of $u_v P_{n-k} \mathcal{O}_{\mathcal{L}} \mathcal{O}(2^{|k_1|})$ and necessary number of chosen plain texts is u. As a result of this attack, attacker obtains total $u_v P_{n-k}$ kinds of $(k_1, k_2, \mathbf{H})$. Therefore the probability of successful attack is $1/u_v P_{n-k}$.

4.3   Results of Security Evaluation

We show the results of security evaluation in Table 1. Note that $u = \binom{k}{\mathrm{Hw}(\mathbf{e})}$ $\binom{k+1}{r} 2^r$ and $v = \binom{n-k}{\mathrm{Hw}(\mathbf{H})}$. However, since the error correcting process is a linear operation, $\mathcal{O}_{\mathcal{L}}$ is sufficiently small to be negligible. Here we assume that $\mathcal{O}_{\mathcal{L}} = 1$. From the results of Model 1, the following conditions must be satisfied in order to obtain the effect of security enhancement even if $\mathbf{G}$ is open.

$$\mathcal{O}(u^3) > \mathcal{O}(2^{|k_1|}) \tag{7}$$

From the above, we can derive following condition.

$$u = \binom{k}{\mathrm{Hw}(\mathbf{e})}\binom{k+1}{r} 2^r > 2^{\frac{|k_1|}{3}} \tag{8}$$

However, this requires impractical code lengths. Therefore, we can conclude that $\mathbf{G}$ must be kept secret.

Table 1. Results of security evaluation

	Data	Computational complexity	Successful probability
Model 1	u	$\mathcal{O}(u^3)\mathcal{O}_\mathcal{L} + \mathcal{O}(2^{|k_1|})$	1.0
Model 2	1	$_vP_{n-k}\,\mathcal{O}(2^{|k_1|})\mathcal{O}_\mathcal{L}$	$1/_vP_{n-k}$
Model 3	u	$u_vP_{n-k}\mathcal{O}(2^{|k_1|})\mathcal{O}_\mathcal{L}$	$1/u_vP_{n-k}$

When v is sufficiently large for $(n - k)$, the following approximation holds.

$$_vP_{n-k} \simeq v^v \tag{9}$$

Using above, the amount of computational complexity required for attacks can be estimated as follows.

$$\text{Model 2: } v^v\mathcal{O}(2^{|k_1|}) \tag{10}$$

$$\text{Model 3: } uv^v\mathcal{O}(2^{|k_1|}) \tag{11}$$

As already mentioned, the probability of identifying the correct (k_1, k_2) is very small even after solving the huge computational complexity problem. As a result, we can conclude that our proposed method can achieve sufficient computational security and has the effect of security enhancement.

5   Application to Two-Way Cryptographic Communication Under High Noise Environment

In this section, we examine the communication efficiency and the effect of security enhancement of our proposed method, assuming a high noise communication environment. In the case that error correction is failed, the data must be retransmitted. As a result, data transmission efficiency becomes low. On the other hand, the security enhancement cannot be realized, if Hw($\mathbf{e}$) is small. Therefore, we need to determine the effective number of error bits that sufficiently increases security without reducing transmission efficiency.

To confirm these, the relationship between DFR (Decoding Failure Rate) and Hw($\mathbf{H}$) is verified by computer experiments. DFR is an indicator to assess communication efficiency, as described above. Since Hw($\mathbf{H}$) affects the number of error-correctable bits Hw($\mathbf{e}$), it is an indicator that evaluates communication efficiency in the same as DFR and has a significant impact on security enhancement as shown in Sect. 4.3. In this experiment, we assume AES-128 and consider the cipher text in a truncated (shortened) process. Therefore, (240,112)-Shortened LDPC is assumed and the Sum-Product Decoding (OSD) is set to 100 for the number of iterations in the error correcting process. The results of the computer experiments are averaged over 10 times. Figure 3 shows the results.

Since a relationship of small DFR and large Hw($\mathbf{H}$) is clearly desirable, it can be concluded that Hw($\mathbf{H}$) = 11 is the most appropriate setting. As a result, we

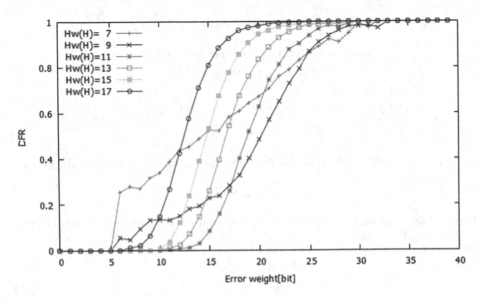

Fig. 3. Density of generator matrix (LDPC)

can set $(\mathrm{Hw}(\mathbf{H}), r) = (11, 16)$ for the communication conditions of $\mathrm{Hw}(\mathbf{e}) = 15$ and $\mathrm{DFR} = 0.09$. Since $|\mathcal{A}| = \binom{112 + 1}{16}$ and $|\mathcal{B}| = 16$ [bit], the size of k_2 can be calculated as $2^{63.27+16}$. Therefore we can determine k_2 is 80 [bit]. Since k_1 is 128 [bit], the total size of key (k_1, k_2) becomes 208 [bit].

The computational complexity required for Model 2 can be calculated using $v \simeq 2^{63.52}$ as follows.

$$v^v \mathcal{O}(2^{|k_1|}) \simeq (2^{63.52})^{2^{63.52}} 2^{128} = 2^{2^{63.52}} 2^{128} \tag{12}$$

In the same way, the computational complexity required for Model 3 can be calculated as follow.

$$uv^v \mathcal{O}(2^{|k_1|}) \simeq 2^{79.27} 2^{2^{63.52}} 2^{128} \tag{13}$$

Therefore, the computational complexity requirements for these attack methods are much greater than for brute search for (k_1, k_2). From the above, we can confirm the effectiveness of security enhancement of our proposed method.

Conversely, we can conclude that brute force search would be most effective for our proposed method. The condition of $\bar{\mathbf{i}} \in \mathbb{F}_2^{112}$ for $\mathbf{m} \in \mathbb{F}_2^{128}$, resulting in 16 [bit] redundancy. This fact can be seen as 16 [bit] entropy in the brute force search for k_1 (in other word, 16 [bit] of the key will be undefined). There are $\binom{240}{15} \simeq 2^{77.71}$ kinds of $\mathbf{c} \in \mathbb{F}_2^{240}$ to be back-calculated from $\mathbf{y} \in \mathbb{F}_2^{240}$, depending on the condition of $\mathrm{Hw}(\mathbf{e}) = 15$. The most effective brute force search for k_2 requires $\mathbf{c}$ to be uniquely determined (0 [bit] of entropy in $\mathbf{c}$). However, this case has 77.71 [bit] of entropy in $\mathbf{c}$. Note that the maximum value of entropy is 112 [bit], since $\mathbf{y}, \mathbf{c} \in \mathbb{F}_2^{240}$ but $\bar{\mathbf{i}} \in \mathbb{F}_2^{112}$. Therefore, there exists a total entropy of $16+77.71=93.71$ [bit], so the probability of successful attack by the brute force search of 2^{128+80} is $2^{-93.71}$. As a result, we can conclude that with the addition of 80 bits of k_2, we can achieve security enhancement of 93.71 [bit].

Thus, the security enhancement for the brute force search is obtained by entropy (uncertainty), where the key cannot be determined. Entropy is determined by $(r, \mathrm{Hw}(\mathbf{e}))$, which is determined by the communication environment.

We also add the condition that $\mathbf{G}$ is secret from the results presented in Sect. 4.2.1. Including this in the secret key would result in an explosion in the size of the key. To solve this, the columns of $\mathbf{G}$ need to be randomly permuted. We can solve this by using the initial value for this random permutation as the secret key and sequentially swapping the columns of $\mathbf{G}$. This allows $\mathbf{G}$ to be kept practically secret and also provides a higher degree of security. However, it is necessary to develop a cryptographically secure method to randomise the sequence of $\mathbb{N}^r$, which is our future work.

6 Application for Asymmetric Key Cryptography

6.1 Motivation and Background

From the view point of general cryptographic communication, our proposed method shown in previous sections realizes general two-way communication. However, the actual communication method does not necessarily have to be two-way. For example, continuous one-way communication under high noise environment is also general, such as surveillance camera movie using drones or remote sensing from satellites.

In this section, we propose an one-way encrypted communication method applying McEliece method using Shortened (n_q, k_q, l_q) QC-MDPC code. The methods presented in the previous section make it easy to apply them to QC-MDPC, however, only one-way communication can be achieved from the mechanism of asymmetric key cryptography. On the other hand, RSA, for example, is generally not used for streaming distribution because the computational cost required for the encryption and decryption process is very high. However, McEliece method is almost same as an error-correcting coding process, and has a great advantage as asymmetric key cryptography for such applications.

6.2 Proposed Method

To avoid confusion, we again define pre-shared secret key $k_3 = (\mathcal{A}, \mathcal{B})$ (see Eq. (6)). Note that this differs from the general asymmetric key cryptography assumption in this respect. On the other hand, the generation of public and private keys is the same as the existing method [11]. These procedures are the derivation of keys and after that, it is similar to the two-way case to realize security enhancement by error bits.

Reciver | Sender

$$k_3 \longleftrightarrow k_3$$

$$(\mathbf{H}_q, \mathbf{G}_q) \longrightarrow \mathbf{G}_q$$

m:randomized plain text

$$\mathbf{y} \xleftarrow[\;\mathbf{y} = \mathbf{c} + \mathbf{e}\;]{\text{Channel Noise}} \quad \mathbf{c} = Enc(\mathbf{m}, \mathbf{G}_q, k_3)$$

$$\mathbf{m} = Dec(\mathbf{y}, \mathbf{H}_q, k_3)$$

Fig. 4. Proposed method

Algorithm 4. Key generation of proposed method

1: Generation of private key

$h_i \in \mathcal{R}_{\frac{\mathrm{Hw}(\mathbf{H_q})}{n_q}} \leftarrow$ uniformly random $([0,\,1]),\ 0 \le i \le n_q - 1.$

$\mathcal{R}_{\frac{\mathrm{Hw}(\mathbf{H_q})}{n_q}}$: Ring over $\mathbb{F}_2/(X^{l_q} - 1).$

2: Generation of public key

Construct $\mathbf{H_i}$ from h_i,

$$\mathbf{H}_q = \{\ \mathbf{H}_0 \mid \mathbf{H}_1 \mid, ..., \mid \mathbf{H}_i \mid, ..., \mid \mathbf{H}_{n_q-1}\ \}.$$

Construct $\mathbf{G_q}$ from $\mathbf{H_q}$,

$$\mathbf{G}_q = \left(\ \mathbf{I}_{n-k} \ \left|\ \begin{array}{c} (\mathbf{H}_{n_q-1}^{-1}\mathbf{H}_0)^T \\ (\mathbf{H}_{n_q-1}^{-1}\mathbf{H}_1)^T \\ \vdots \\ (\mathbf{H}_{n_q-1}^{-1}\mathbf{H}_{n_q-2})^T \end{array}\ \right.\right).$$

3: Generation of pre-shared key

$k_3 = $ **Algorithm 1** $(k_q l_q,\ r).$

Figure 4 and **Algorithm** 4 show the outline of proposed method. In the diagram, $Enc(\cdot, \cdot, \cdot)$ and $Dec(\cdot, \cdot, \cdot)$ denote the encode and decode functions of proposed Shortened QC-MDPC with keys, respectively. In addition, **m** in the diagram denotes randomized plain text. As already mentioned in Sect. 3, it is necessary to prevent plain text from appearing in the cipher text if it is processed as is. This is achieved using a symmetric key cipher, but the secret key may be determined again independently of k_3. The reasons for this are the same as in Sect. 3, but for limited space, the details are omitted in this paper. Almost notation is the same as in Sect. 3, but we add following supplemental information. The coefficients of the polynomial h_i is binary and their hamming weights are $\sum_{i=0}^{n_q-1} \mathrm{Hw}(h_i) = \mathrm{Hw}(\mathbf{H}_q)$ with $\mathrm{Hw}(h_i) \approx \frac{\mathrm{Hw}(\mathbf{H}_q)}{n_q}$. Note that $\mathrm{Hw}(\cdot)$ in this section, denotes the hamming weight of polynomial $\mathcal{R}$, which is similar to vector Hamming weights and the coefficients of the polynomial over the ring are treated as a vector. We assume that the distribution of "1"s in $\mathbf{H}_q$ is unpredictable random. Let $\mathcal{R}_w$ be the ring over $\mathbb{F}_2/(X^{l_q} - 1)$ and whose hamming weight is less than or equal to w. Let e_i be the error over h_i, we have $\sum_{i=0}^{n_q-1} \mathrm{Hw}(e_i) = \mathrm{Hw}(\mathbf{e})$ with $\mathrm{Hw}(e_i) \approx \frac{\mathrm{Hw}(\mathbf{e})}{n_q}$.

6.3   Security Evaluation (2)

The mechanism of McEliece method allows attacker to use $\mathbf{G}_q$ to obtain $\mathbf{c}$ for any $\mathbf{m}$. To determine $\mathbf{H}_q$ under these conditions, Syndrome Decoding Problem (SDP) [3] or Code word Finding Problem (CFP) [14] must be solved. The security of McEliece method is based on hardness of these problems and Information Set Decoding (ISD) algorithm [12] is known as the optimal solution. The computational complexity in the case of (n_q, k_q, l_q)QC-MDPC is shown as follows [11].

$$\text{SDP: } W_{SDP} = \frac{2^{\mathrm{Hw}(\mathbf{e})\log_2 \frac{n}{n-k}}}{\sqrt{l_q}} \tag{14}$$

$$\text{CFP: } W_{CFP} = \frac{2^{\mathrm{Hw}(\mathbf{H}_q)\log_2 \frac{n}{n-k}}}{l_q} \tag{15}$$

Note that above is simpler than [11], but modified in advantageous for attacker.
   There are two possible models of attack against our proposed method.

Model 4 Generate $\mathbf{c}$ for any $\mathbf{m}$ and use them to determine $\mathbf{H}_q$.
Model 5 Find $\mathbf{e}$ for the observed $\mathbf{y}$ and determine $\mathbf{H}_q$.

   For Model 4, only the application of CFP should be considered. However, to apply $\mathbf{H}_q$, k_3 needs to be estimated and r embedded in $\mathbf{c}$. Therefore, computational complexity of $|k_3|$ times is required.

$$|k_3|W_{CFP} = |k_3|\frac{2^{\mathrm{Hw}(\mathbf{H}_q)\log_2 \frac{n}{n-k}}}{l_q} \tag{16}$$

Since asymmetric key cryptography allows the attacker to eliminate the effects of communication errors, the high noise communication environment itself does not contribute to security enhancement for Model 4.
   For Model 5, the application of SDP should be considered. This attack must calculate syndrome from $\mathbf{y}$ to determine $\mathbf{e}$, and obtain $\mathbf{c}$. The calculation of syndrome requires estimating k_3 and embedding r in $\mathbf{y}$. As in the case of Model 4, computational complexity of $|k_3|$ times is required for SDP. After obtaining $\mathbf{c}$

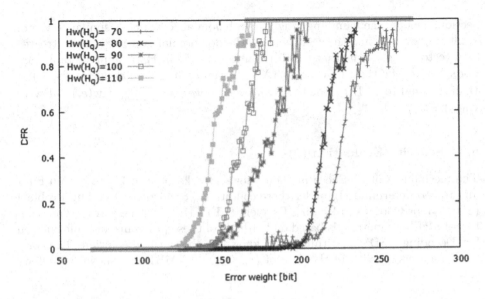

Fig. 5. Density of generator matrix (QC-MDPC)

from $(\mathbf{y}, \mathbf{e})$, it is the same as in Model 4. Therefore, the necessary computational complexity is as follows.

$$|k_3|(W_{SDP} + W_{CFP}) = |k_3|(\frac{2^{\text{Hw}(\mathbf{e})\log_2 \frac{n}{n-k}}}{\sqrt{l_q}} + \frac{2^{\text{Hw}(\mathbf{H}_q)\log_2 \frac{n}{n-k}}}{l_q}) \qquad (17)$$

For noise in the communication channel to contribute to security enhancement, the following condition must satisfied.

$$\text{Hw}(\mathbf{e}) \geq \text{Hw}(\mathbf{H}_q) + \log_2(\sqrt{l_q} - \frac{n}{n-k}) \qquad (18)$$

Whether this condition is satisfied or not depends on the decoding algorithm applied. This is confirmed by computer simulations in the next section.

6.4 Application to One-Way Cryptographic Communication Under High Noise Environment

As in Sect. 5, the relationship between $\text{Hw}(\mathbf{H}_q)$ and DFR is reviewed. Previous work has shown that the McEliece method using $(2,1,4801)$ QC-MDPC can achieve security of 2^{80} [11]. Considering the above facts, we consider McEliece method with Shortened $(2,1,4801)$ QC-MDPC. Furthermore, as in Sect. 5, we set $r = 16$. Therefore, $(n,k) = (9618, 4801)$ and there are $\binom{4801+1}{16} 2^{16} = 2^{167.4}$ combinations of k_3, we have $|k_3| = 168$ [bit]. The decoding algorithm is also the same as in Sect. 5, OSD with 20 iterations.

Figure 5 shows the results of computer simulations. This result shows that $\text{Hw}(\mathbf{H}_q) = 80$ has the highest error correcting capability and in this case

Hw($\mathbf{e}$) = 180 can achieve DFR$\simeq$ 0. For Model 4, the computational complexity of attack becomes $|k_3|W_{CFP} = 2^{235.2}$. For Model 5, this result clearly satisfies the conditions of Eq. (18), which shows that high noise contributes sufficiently to improve security enhancement. For Model 5, the computational complexity of attack becomes $2^{340.8}$.

7 Conclusions

Two types of security enhancement methods using shortened error correcting codes are proposed in this paper. Both methods enable communication under high noise and have a wide range of possible applications. Their practicality can be confirmed by computer simulations to determine the specific configuration parameters. We plan to implement hardware modules and verify its practicality.

QC-MDPCs are Hw($\mathbf{H}$) = $\mathcal{O}(\sqrt{n})$ and Hw($\mathbf{e}$) = $\mathcal{O}(\sqrt{n})$, as Definition 2 indicates. However, the results of the computer simulation in Sect. 6.4 are different ,we chose Hw($\mathbf{H}$) = 80 and Hw($\mathbf{e}$) = 180. Shortened QC-MDPC in the proposed method has $r = 16$, so hamming weight of the embedded bits is expected to be around 8. It can therefore be expected to have an effect of around $80 + 8$ with regard to Hw($\mathbf{H_q}$). As for Hw($\mathbf{e}$), it is expected to have an effect on OSD and its iterations setting. These issues affect the effectiveness of the security enhancement of the proposed method. A detailed analysis of these issues is our future work.

On the other hand, $\mathbf{G}$ and $\mathbf{G}_q$ are responsible for the following drawbacks in operating the proposed method.

Two-way: $\mathbf{G}$ needs to be kept secret.
One-way: The fact that $\mathbf{G}_q$ is public makes it easy to attack.

Since both LDPC and QC-MDPC are linear codes, they can function as error-correcting codes without efficiency loss if columns in $\mathbf{G}$ and $\mathbf{G}_q$ are shuffled. For example, consider a pseudo random shuffle with k_2 or k_3 as initial values. This pseudo random shuffle can solve the above drawback by sequentially changing $(\mathbf{G}, \mathbf{H})$ or $(\mathbf{G}_q, \mathbf{H}_q)$. On the other hand, research results on random shuffle are immature and only algorithm P [9] and Fisher-Yates shuffle are known. The development of cryptographically secure random shuffles is also our future work.

References

1. Albrecht, M.R., et al.: Classic mceliece: conservative codebased cryptography. Submission to the NIST post quantum standardization process (2020). https://classic.mceliece.org/nist/mceliece-20201010.pdf
2. Aragon, N., et al.: Bike: bit flipping key encapsulation. Submission to the NIST post quantum standardization process (2020). https://bikesuite.org/
3. Berlekamp, E.R., McEliece, R.J., van Tilborg, H.C.A.: On the inherent intractability of certain coding problems (corresp.). IEEE Trans. Inf. Theory **24**(3), 384–386 (1978). https://doi.org/10.1109/TIT.1978.1055873

4. Bos, J.W., et al.: CRYSTALS - kyber: a cca-secure module-lattice-based KEM. IACR Cryptol. ePrint Arch., p. 634 (2017). http://eprint.iacr.org/2017/634
5. Daemen, J., Rijmen, V.: The Design of Rijndael: AES - The Advanced Encryption Standard. Information Security and Cryptography, Springer, Berlin, Heidelberg (2002). https://doi.org/10.1007/978-3-662-04722-4
6. D'Anvers, J., Karmakar, A., Roy, S.S., Vercauteren, F.: Saber: module-LWR based key exchange, CPA-secure encryption and CCA-secure KEM. IACR Cryptol. ePrint Arch., p. 230 (2018). http://eprint.iacr.org/2018/230
7. Djurdjevic, I., Xu, J., Abdel-Ghaffar, K., Lin, S.: A class of low-density parity-check codes constructed based on reed-solomon codes with two information symbols. In: Fossorier, M., Høholdt, T., Poli, A. (eds.) AAECC 2003. LNCS, vol. 2643, pp. 98–107. Springer, Heidelberg (2003). https://doi.org/10.1007/3-540-44828-4_12
8. Gallager, R.G.: Low-density parity-check codes. IRE Trans. Inf. Theory 8(1), 21–28 (1962). https://doi.org/10.1109/TIT.1962.1057683
9. Knuth, D.E.: The Art of Computer Programming, Volume III: Sorting and Searching. Addison-Wesley, Boston (1973)
10. MacKay, D.J.C.: Good error-correcting codes based on very sparse matrices. IEEE Trans. Inf. Theory 45(2), 399–431 (1999). https://doi.org/10.1109/18.748992
11. Misoczki, R., Tillich, J.P., Sendrier, N., Barreto, P.S.L.M.: Mdpc-mceliece: new mceliece variants from moderate density parity-check codes. IACR Cryptology ePrint Archive 2012, 409 (2012). http://dblp.uni-trier.de/db/journals/iacr/iacr2012.html#MisoczkiTSB12
12. Prange, E.: The use of information sets in decoding cyclic codes. IRE Trans. Inf. Theory 8, 5–9 (1962)
13. Singh, H.: Code based cryptography: Classic mceliece. CoRR abs/1907.12754 (2019). http://arxiv.org/abs/1907.12754
14. Vardy, A.: Algorithmic complexity in coding theory and the minimum distance problem. In: Leighton, F.T., Shor, P.W. (eds.) Proceedings of the Twenty-Ninth Annual ACM Symposium on the Theory of Computing, El Paso, Texas, USA, 4–6 May 1997, pp. 92–109. ACM (1997). https://doi.org/10.1145/258533.258559
15. Watanabe, K., Kaguchi, R., Shinoda, T.: Shortened LDPC codes accelerate OSD decoding performance. EURASIP J. Wirel. Commun. Netw. 2021(1), 22 (2021). https://doi.org/10.1186/s13638-021-01901-x

An Updated Database of $\mathbb{Z}_4$ Codes and an Open Problem About Quasi-cyclic Codes

Nuh Aydin$^{(\boxtimes)}$ (ID), Yiyang Lu, and Vishad Onta

Kenyon College, Gambier, OH 43022, USA
{aydinn,lu1,onta1}@kenyon.edu

Abstract. Research on codes over finite rings has intensified after the discovery that some of the best binary nonlinear codes can be obtained as images of $\mathbb{Z}_4$-linear codes. Codes over various finite rings have been a subject of much research in coding theory after this discovery. Many of these rings are extensions of $\mathbb{Z}_4$ and numerous new linear codes over $\mathbb{Z}_4$ have been found in the last decade. Due to the special place of $\mathbb{Z}_4$, an online database of $\mathbb{Z}_4$ codes was created in 2007. The original database on $\mathbb{Z}_4$ codes recently became unavailable. The purpose of this paper is to introduce a new and updated database of $\mathbb{Z}_4$ codes. We have made major updates to the original database by adding 8699 new linear codes over $\mathbb{Z}_4$. These codes have been found through exhaustive computer searches on cyclic codes and by an implementation of the ASR search algorithm that has been remarkably fruitful to obtain new linear codes from the class of quasi-cyclic (QC) and quasi-twisted (QT) codes over finite fields. We made modifications to the ASR algorithm to make it work over $\mathbb{Z}_4$. The initial database contained few codes that were not free. We have now added a large number of non-free codes. In fact, of the 8699 codes we have added, 7631 of them are non-free. Our database will be further updated by incorporating data from [16]. We also state an open problem of great theoretical interest that arose from computational observations.

Keywords: Quaternary codes · Cyclic codes · Quasi-cyclic codes · Gray map · Binary nonlinear codes · Search algorithms for linear codes

1 Introduction and Motivation

Codes over finite rings have received much attention from coding theory researchers in the last few decades. This all started with the discovery in 1992 [13] and subsequent comprehensive development in 1994 [17] that some of the best binary nonlinear codes can be obtained as images of $\mathbb{Z}_4$-linear codes. Later, new binary non-linear codes were obtained from images of $\mathbb{Z}_4$ codes, such as the $(92, 2^{24}, 28)$ code in [4] that was obtained from a QC code over $\mathbb{Z}_4$ which was based on the lift of the binary Golay code to $\mathbb{Z}_4$. The quaternary Golay code

---

This research was supported by Kenyon College Summer Science Scholars research program. N. Aydin is the corresponding author.

S. El Hajji et al. (Eds.): C2SI 2023, LNCS 13874, pp. 395–406, 2023.
https://doi.org/10.1007/978-3-031-33017-9_24

was used in [11] to construct the Leech lattice, which is considered the simplest known construction of the Leech lattice to date.

Various kinds of finite rings have been considered as the code alphabet in recent decades. However, the ring $\mathbb{Z}_4$ and its extensions have a special places among finite rings in coding theory.

There are several online databases for various types of codes and alphabets. For example, M. Grassl maintains a database at [14] that holds records of best known linear codes (BKLC) over small finite fields of order up to 9. A similar database is available in the Magma software [22]. Grassl also maintains a database of best known additive quantum codes over the binary field. Chen maintains a table of best known QC and QT codes at [12]. A table of nonlinear binary codes is available at [18]. There are several other databases of interest for coding theorists that are listed at [14].

Due to the special place of $\mathbb{Z}_4$ in coding theory, a database of $\mathbb{Z}_4$ codes was created in 2007 and a paper that introduced it was published in 2009 [2]. The database was populated with codes obtained from various search algorithms but it was not complete, especially in terms of non-free codes. Researchers have found many new codes over the years that have been added to the database. However, it is still incomplete and there is room for additional entries. Moreover, the original database (whose URL was http://z4codes.info/) recently became unavailable. We have created a new database of $\mathbb{Z}_4$ codes and updated it with many more codes. The URL for the new database is http://quantumcodes.info/Z4/. (We also created a new database of quantum codes recently, available at http://quantumcodes.info/) After completing this manuscript, we became aware of another database of $\mathbb{Z}_4$-codes available at [16] which covers a smaller range of parameters (length up to 99 instead of 128), and dimension ($k = 2k_1 + k_2$) restricted to ≤ 16. On the other hand, the database [16] is more complete (for its parameter sets) than ours and contains codes with better parameters. We will incorporate the data from [16] into our database, hence present a more complete and up-to-date database for researchers.

This work describes how we obtained the new codes for the database. We have used exhaustive searches for both free and non-free cyclic codes over $\mathbb{Z}_4$, and adapted the highly effective ASR search algorithm for $\mathbb{Z}_4$. An implementation of these search algorithms resulted in the discovery of many new linear codes over $\mathbb{Z}_4$, as well as rediscovering several binary BKLCs through the original Gray map. Two nonlinear binary codes with new parameters have been found as well.

2 Basic Definitions

A code C of length n over $\mathbb{Z}_4$ is a subset of $\mathbb{Z}_4^n$. If C is an additive subgroup of $\mathbb{Z}_4^n$, then C is a also submodule of $\mathbb{Z}_4^n$ and it is a linear code over $\mathbb{Z}_4$. A codeword is an element of C, and a generator matrix is a matrix whose rows generate C. Any linear code C over $\mathbb{Z}_4$ is equivalent to a code over that ring with a generator matrix G of the form

$$\begin{bmatrix} I_{k_1} & A & B \\ 0 & 2I_{k_2} & 2C \end{bmatrix}$$

where A and C are $\mathbb{Z}_2$-matrices and B is a $\mathbb{Z}_4$-matrix. We then say that C is of type $4^{k_1}2^{k_2}$, which is also the size of C. We express the parameters of C as $[n, k_1, k_2, d_L]$ or just $[n, k_1, k_2, d]$, where n is the length of C and d_L or d is the minimum Lee distance of C. Besides the Lee distance, Euclidean and Hamming distances are also considered for codes over $\mathbb{Z}_4$, however, in this paper we primarily consider the Lee distance because it is the most relevant metric when we consider binary images of $\mathbb{Z}_4$-codes and compare them with existing binary codes. The Euclidean distance is important for the notion of Type II codes [10]. A $\mathbb{Z}_4$-linear code is not necessarily a free module, a module with a basis. It is so if and only if $k_2 = 0$. If k_2 is zero, we call C a free code. Otherwise, it is non-free.

The Gray map $\phi : \mathbb{Z}_4^n \to \mathbb{Z}_2^{2n}$ is the coordinate-wise extension of the bijection $\mathbb{Z}_4 \to \mathbb{Z}_2^2$ defined by

$$0 \to 00,$$
$$1 \to 01,$$
$$2 \to 11,$$
$$3 \to 10.$$

The image $\phi(C)$ of a linear code C over $\mathbb{Z}_4$ of length n by the Gray map is a binary code of length $2n$. We know that ϕ is not only a weight-preserving map from

$$(\mathbb{Z}_4^n, \text{Lee weight } (w_L)) \text{ to } (\mathbb{Z}_2^{2n}, \text{Hamming weight } (w_H))$$

but also a distance-preserving map from

$$(\mathbb{Z}_4^n, \text{Lee distance } (d_L)) \text{ to } (\mathbb{Z}_2^{2n}, \text{Hamming distance } (d_H)).$$

We also know that for any linear code C over $\mathbb{Z}_4$, its Gray map image $\phi(C)$ is distance invariant, so its minimum Hamming distance d_H is equal to the minimum Hamming weight w_H. Thus, we know that the minimum Hamming distance of $\phi(C)$ is equal to the minimum Lee weight d_L of C. Additionally, we know that

$$w_L = w_H = d_H = d_L.$$

Thus, $\phi(C)$ is a binary code, not necessarily linear because the Gray map is not linear. We refer the reader to [21] for more details on codes over $\mathbb{Z}_4$.

Remark 1. Let C be a linear code over $\mathbb{Z}_4$ with parameters $[n, k_1, k_2, d]$ (where d is the Lee distance) and let $B = \phi(C)$ be its Gray image. We use the notation $[2n, 2k_1 + k_2, d]$ to denote the parameters of B, although it is more standard to use the notation $(2n, 2^{2k_1+k_2}, d)$ for a nonlinear code. We find this notation more convenient and we note that the Gray image of a $\mathbb{Z}_4$-linear code is distance-invariant, a property that is not possessed by arbitrary nonlinear codes.

3   Cyclic Search over $\mathbb{Z}_4$

With the usual identification of vectors $v = (v_0, v_1, \ldots, v_{n-1})$ with the corresponding polynomials $v(x) = v_0 + v_1 x + \cdots + v_{n-1} x^{n-1}$, cyclic codes of length n over $\mathbb{Z}_4$ are ideals of the quotient ring $\mathbb{Z}_4[x]/\langle x^n - 1 \rangle$. The factorization of $x^n - 1$ and the algebraic structure of $\mathbb{Z}_4[x]/\langle x^n - 1 \rangle$ are similar to the field case when n is odd. We started the search process on cyclic codes for odd lengths.

The $\mathbb{Z}_4$ database contains data on codes for length up to 128. We first exhaustively search all cyclic codes over $\mathbb{Z}_4$ of odd lengths. Hence, we examine all cyclic codes of odd length up to 127. To do so, we calculate all divisors of $x^n - 1$ from $n = 1$ to $n = 127$, generate all cyclic codes, and compute their minimum Lee distances. For large lengths and dimensions, the minimum distance calculations take too long. Therefore, we used the following restrictions.

1. When $n \leq 61$, we calculate Lee weight without time limit.
2. When $n \geq 63$ and $\min(2k_1 + k_2, 2n - 2k_1 - k_2) \leq 60$, we calculate Lee weight with a prescribed fixed time limit.
3. When $n \geq 63$ and $\min(2k_1 + k_2, 2n - 2k_1 - k_2) > 60$, we skip the code without calculating its Lee weight.

For an odd integer n, have the unique factorization of $x^n - 1$ over $\mathbb{Z}_4$ and many other similarities to the field case. Hence computations are easier in this case. Specifically, we have the following theorem.

Theorem 1.   [4] *Let n be an odd positive integer. Then $x^n - 1$ can be factored into a product of finitely many pairwise coprime basic irreducible polynomials over $\mathbb{Z}_4$, say, $x^n - 1 = g_1(x) g_2(x) \cdots g_r(x)$. Also, this factorization is unique up to ordering of the factors. In fact, we have the following: if $f_2(x) \mid (x^n - 1)$ in $\mathbb{Z}_2[x]$ then there is a unique monic polynomial $f(x) \in \mathbb{Z}_4[x]$ such that $f(x) \mid (x^n - 1)$ in $\mathbb{Z}_4[x]$ and $f(x) = f_2(x)$, where $f_2(x)$ denotes the reduction of $f(x)$ mod 2.*

The polynomial $f(x)$ in the above theorem is called the Hensel lift of $f_2(x)$. Other fundamental facts about cyclic codes over $\mathbb{Z}_4$ are given in the following theorems.

Theorem 2.   [4,20,21] *Let n be an odd integer and let I be an ideal in $\mathbb{Z}_4[x]/\langle x^n - 1 \rangle$. Then there are unique monic polynomials $f(x), g(x), h(x)$ over $\mathbb{Z}_4[x]$ such that $I = \langle f(x)h(x), 2f(x)g(x) \rangle = \langle f(x)h(x) + 2f(x) \rangle$ where $f(x)g(x)h(x) = x^n - 1$ and $|I| = 4^{\deg(g(x))} 2^{\deg(h(x))}$*

Theorem 3.   [4] *Let I be a cyclic code over $\mathbb{Z}_4$ of odd length n. Then I is a free module of rank k if and only if the generator polynomial $p(x)$ of the corresponding ideal divides $x^n - 1$ and $\deg(p(x)) = n - k$.*

From the theorems above, we get the following important consequences.

Corollary 1.   *Let C be a cyclic code over $\mathbb{Z}_4$ of odd length n. Then*

1. C is a principal ideal.

2. *The number cyclic codes of length n is 3^r and the number of free cyclic codes of length n is 2^r, where r is the number of basic irreducible divisors of $x^n - 1$ as in Theorem 1.*

3. *There is a one-to-one correspondence between divisors of $x^n - 1$ and free cyclic codes of length n over $\mathbb{Z}_4$.*

In searching for cyclic codes over $\mathbb{Z}_4$, we first generated all free cyclic codes of odd length by finding all divisors of $x^n - 1$ from its factorization into basic irreducibles. This is the same process as constructing cyclic codes over a finite field. We then constructed all cyclic codes that are not free using Theorem 2. This part is different from the field case. We have found a total of 6332 new linear codes over $\mathbb{Z}_4$ as cyclic codes by this search.

4   ASR Search Method for New QC Codes

The second search method we implemented was adapting the ASR search algorithm to $\mathbb{Z}_4$. First introduced in [6] (named after the authors later) and refined and generalized in more recent works ([1,5,7–9,19]), the ASR search algorithm produced a large number of new, record breaking codes over small finite fields from the class of quasi-cyclic (QC) and quasi-twisted codes (QT). Our implementation of the ASR search algorithm for $\mathbb{Z}_4$ yielded 2369 new linear $\mathbb{Z}_4$ codes. Before describing our method, we review some basics.

A QC code is a generalization of a cyclic code, where a cyclic shift of a codeword by ℓ positions gives another codeword. Such a code is called an ℓ-QC code, or a QC code of index ℓ. Algebraically, a QC code of length $n = m \cdot \ell$ and index ℓ is an R-submodule of R^ℓ where $R = \mathbb{Z}_4[x]/\langle x^m - 1\rangle$. A generator matrix of a QC code can be put into the form

$$\begin{bmatrix} G_{1,1} & G_{1,2} & \dots & G_{1,\ell} \\ G_{2,1} & G_{2,2} & \dots & G_{2,\ell} \\ \vdots & \vdots & \ddots & \vdots \\ G_{r,1} & G_{r,2} & \dots & G_{r,\ell} \end{bmatrix}$$

where each $G_{i,j} = Circ(g_{i,j})$ is a circulant matrix defined by some polynomial $g_{i,j}(x)$. Such a code is called an r-generator QC code. Most of the work on QC codes in the literature is focused on the 1-generator case. A generator matrix of a 1-generator QC code can be put into the form

$$[G_1 G_2 \dots G_\ell]$$

The class of QC codes is known to contain many codes with good parameters. There have been various types of search algorithms on the class of QC codes. The ASR search method is one that has been shown to be particularly effective for 1-generator QC codes. It is based on the following theorem, and it is essentially an implementation of this theorem. More information about the ASR search can be found in several publications including [5,6,19].

Theorem 4. [6] *Let C be a 1-generator ℓ-QC code over $\mathbb{F}_q$ of length $n = m\ell$ with a generator of the form:*

$$(f_1(x)g(x), f_2(x)g(x), ..., f_\ell(x)g(x)),$$

where $x^m - 1 = g(x)h(x)$ and $\gcd(h(x), f_i(x)) = 1$ for all $i = 1, ..., \ell$. Then C is an $[n, k, d']$ code where $dim(C) = m - \deg(g(x))$, and $d' > \ell \cdot d$ where d is the minimum distance of the cyclic code C of length m generated by $g(x)$.

4.1   Adapting the ASR Algorithm for Free QC Codes over $\mathbb{Z}_4$

When we adopt the ASR search algorithm for $\mathbb{Z}_4$, we consider two cases: The case where the starting cyclic code that forms the the building blocks of the components of the QC code is free (case 1) and non-free (case 2). The former case is similar to the field case. To determine whether two polynomials are relatively prime over $\mathbb{Z}_4$, we use the following lemma.

Lemma 1. [21] *Let $f_1(x)$ and $f_2(x) \in \mathbb{Z}_4[x]$ and denote their image in $\mathbb{Z}_2[x]$ under - by $\bar{f}_1(x)$ and $\bar{f}_2(x)$, respectively. Then $f_1(x)$ and $f_2(x)$ are coprime in $\mathbb{Z}_4[x]$ if and only if $\bar{f}_1(x)$ and $\bar{f}_2(x)$ are coprime in $\mathbb{Z}_2[x]$.*

We begin the search process by finding all divisors of $x^m - 1$ over the binary field. For each divisor $g(x)$, we compute its Hensel lift $g_4(x)$ to $\mathbb{Z}_4$. Hence, $g_4(x)$ is a divisor of $x^m - 1$ over $\mathbb{Z}_4$ and it generates a free cyclic code. We then form a generator of a QC code as in Theorem 4 using $g_4(x)$ as the "seed", the common term in each block. The QC codes obtained this way are also free (Theorem 3.1 in [4]).

4.2   Adapting ASR for Non-free QC Codes and an Open Problem

Adapting ASR with free cyclic codes over $\mathbb{Z}_4$ as seed only produces QC codes that are also free. It is desirable to obtain some non-free codes as well since the database was lacking non-free codes. For this we fed the same algorithm in the previous subsection with the generators (seeds) of non-free cyclic codes we obtained in the initial part of the process. We indeed obtained many new $\mathbb{Z}_4$ codes that are not free. While most of these codes turned out to be non-free, it is still possible to obtain free QC codes using a non-free seed when there is no restriction on the polynomials f_i. We do not yet know if there is a condition on f_i's that would guarantee that all 1-generator QC codes given in Theorem 4 with a non-free seed $g(x)$ have the same k_1 and k_2 as the non-free cyclic code generated by $g(x)$. We formally state this problem as follows:

Problem 1. Let $C_g = \langle g(x) \rangle$ be a cyclic code of odd length m over $\mathbb{Z}_4$ of type $4^{k_1} 2^{k_2}$ with $k_2 > 0$. Consider 1-generator QC codes C over $\mathbb{Z}_4$ of the form

$$(f_1(x)g(x), f_2(x)g(x), ..., f_\ell(x)g(x)),$$

where $f_i(x) \in \mathbb{Z}_4[x]$.

(a) Determine a sufficient (or a necessary and sufficient) condition on the polynomials $f_i(x)$ (and possibly on $g(x)$) so that C has the same type as C_g.

(b) Determine a sufficient (or a necessary and sufficient) condition on the polynomials $f_i(x)$ (and possibly on $g(x)$) so that C is free. What is its size in this case?

5   New Linear Codes over $\mathbb{Z}_4$

We classify the codes with good parameters that we have found into a few types: decent, good, very good, and great codes. The classification is shown in Table 1. Decent codes are those whose Gray images are nonlinear and they have minimum Lee weight d_L equal to the minimum weight of the best known binary linear code. This means that if the code parameters we found are $[n, k_1, k_2, d_L]$ and parameters of the best know binary linear code are $[2n, 2k_1 + k_2, d]_2$ and $d = d_L$, then this code is a decent code.

A code is a good code if it satisfies either of the two sets of conditions. First, if the code we found has a nonlinear Gray map image and its parameters $[n, k_1, k_2, d_L]$ beat the parameters of the best known binary linear code $[2n, 2k_1 + k_2, d]_2$ but its weight does not exceed the best known upper bound (d_u) on the minimum weight of a binary linear code of length $2n$ and dimension $2k_1 + k_2$, then this code is a good code. Second, a code can also be a good code if it has a linear Gray map image and its parameters are the same as the parameters of the best known linear code over $\mathbb{Z}_2$.

Table 1. Classification of $\mathbb{Z}_4$-linear codes based on Gray image

linearity of image	$d_L = d$	$d_L > d$ but $d_L \leq d_u$	$d_L > d_u$
linear	good	great	not possible
nonlinear	decent	good	very good

To be a very good code, a code needs to have nonlinear Gray map image and its minimum Lee weight d_L must beat the best known upper bound on the minimum weight, d_u, of a binary linear code over $\mathbb{Z}_2$ with the comparable length and dimension. Such codes are also called BTL (better-than-linear) in the literature ([15]). And to be a great code, a code needs to have not only a linear Gray image but also parameters that beat the parameters of the best known binary linear code. Now we give details of how many new codes we obtained from each category.

1. Free cyclic codes of odd length: A total of 613 new linear $\mathbb{Z}_4$ codes of this type have been found of which 135 are decent codes, 70 good codes, and 4 very good codes. Table 2 below shows a small sample of codes from this category. All of the new codes from this category have been added to the database. We

represent a polynomial as a string of its coefficients in ascending order of its terms. For example, the string 323001 on the first row of Table 2 represents the polynomial $g(x) = x^5 + 3x^2 + 2x + 3$.

Table 2. Examples of new free cyclic codes from exhaustive search

$[n, k_1, k_2, d]$	Gray map image	classification	g
$[31, 26, 0, 4]$	nonlinear	decent code	323001
$[47, 24, 0, 16]$	nonlinear	good code	331123310332331020110201
$[117, 90, 0, 6]$	nonlinear	—	302033000010011022210012321

2. Non-free cyclic codes of odd length: A total of 5717 new linear $\mathbb{Z}_4$ codes of this type have been found of which 134 are decent codes and 271 are good codes. Table 3 below shows a few examples of codes from this category. All of the new codes from this category have been added to the database.

Table 3. Examples of new non-free cyclic codes from exhaustive search

$[n, k_1, k_2, d]$	Gray map image	classification	g
$[21, 17, 4, 2]$	linear	good code	32311
$[45, 24, 1, 8]$	nonlinear	—	120111221202011303211
$[105, 19, 1, 44]$	nonlinear	—	3202320312303021332301133333002 3212013210103113330103020003000 10003013100010100230111010101
$[125, 120, 5, 2]$	linear	good code	100001

3. QC codes where m is odd, and the seed codes are free cyclic codes: A total of 452 new $\mathbb{Z}_4$-linear codes of this type have been found of which 76 are decent codes, 3 are good codes, and 1 is a very good code. Table 4 below shows a few examples of codes from this category. All of the new codes from this category have been added to the database.

4. QC codes where the seed polynomials generate non-free cyclic codes: A total of 1917 new $\mathbb{Z}_4$ linear codes of this type have been found of which 119 are decent codes, 127 are good codes, and 1 is a very good code. Table 5 below shows a few examples of codes from this category. All of the new codes from this category have been added to the database. There are 3 new free QC codes found in this search. The third code in Table 5 is one of these three codes.

5. New binary nonlinear codes: We found 2 new binary nonlinear codes based on the comparison with the database [18]. These two codes however have the same parameters as the corresponding BKLCs. We also rediscovered the free cyclic codes with parameters [47,24,0,16] and [47,23,0,18]. These two codes

Table 4. Examples of new free QC codes found via the ASR algorithm

$[n, k_1, k_2, d]$	ℓ	Gray map image	classification	g	f
$[22, 10, 0, 12]$	2	nonlinear	decent code	31	$f_1 = 2101311121$ $f_2 = 1123112011$
$[30, 9, 0, 18]$	2	nonlinear	—	1021311	$f_1 = 01030023$ $f_2 = 31003013$
$[35, 4, 0, 32]$	7	nonlinear	decent code	31	$f_1 = 0303$ $f_2 = 3221$ $f_3 = 102$ $f_4 = 311$ $f_5 = 2311$ $f_6 = 3213$ $f_7 = 33$
$[54, 21, 0, 22]$	2	nonlinear	—	1001001	$f_1 = 2321012031$ 3033223332 2 $f_2 = 2320013322$ 3130002020 2
$[75, 10, 0, 54]$	5	nonlinear	—	321231	$f_1 = 1230312011$ $f_2 = 2332233233$ $f_3 = 0022320232$ $f_4 = 1302320302$ $f_5 = 2113222122$

were found in [3] but they are not included in the database [18] which, apparently, has not been updated for a long time and it does not seem to incorporate the data from [14]. The database [18] was constructed to give information on $A(n, d)$, the size of the largest binary code of length n and minimum distance d. As such, both linear and nonlinear codes must be considered in determining $A(n, d)$. Hence, the data from [14] must be taken into account in determining $A(n, d)$. Of the two binary nonlinear codes we have found, Table 6 exhibits the one from the exhaustive search of non-free cyclic codes. The other code is from a search of free QC codes by the ASR algorithm and is shown in Table 7.

Table 5. Examples of new QC codes found via the ASR algorithm

$[n, k_1, k_2, d]$	ℓ	Gray map image	classification	g	f
$[6, 1, 2, 4]$	2	linear	—	311	$f_1 = 3$ $f_2 = 3$
$[28, 0, 3, 32]$	4	linear	good code	31101	$f_1 = 2$ $f_2 = 222$ $f_3 = 202$ $f_4 = 022$
$[45, 5, 0, 40]$	3	nonlinear	decent code	3032233011 1	$f_1 = 30121$ $f_2 = 21021$ $f_3 = 30103$
$[63, 4, 9, 40]$	3	nonlinear	—	1323002332 10003121	$f_1 = 3021$ $f_2 = 3303$ $f_3 = 1211$
$[66, 1, 12, 44]$	2	linear	—	3001023221 2032230010 2100100100 1	$f_1 = 111$ $f_2 = 331$
$[112, 4, 3, 92]$	16	nonlinear	—	1121	$f_1 = 3111$ $f_2 = 3332$ $f_3 = 1001$ $f_4 = 0311$ $f_5 = 1033$ $f_6 = 3011$ $f_7 = 0213$ $f_8 = 0121$ $f_9 = 3131$ $f_{10} = 0313$ $f_{11} = 3213$ $f_{12} = 1132$ $f_{13} = 3211$ $f_{14} = 1032$ $f_{15} = 1101$ $f_{16} = 0113$

Table 6. The new binary nonlinear code from non-free cyclic codes

$[n, k_1, k_2, d]$	Gray map image	classification	g
$[51, 10, 8, 28]$	nonlinear	decent code	10000012131032001222 23001111010223122032 31

Table 7. The new binary nonlinear code from a free QC code

$[n, k_1, k_2, d]$	l	Gray map image	classification	g	f
$[51, 16, 0, 26]$	3	nonlinear	decent code	31	$f_1 = 3223033120003033$ $f_2 = 2122003313031103$ $f_3 = 0232111300112321$

6   Conclusion and Further Research

Codes over $\mathbb{Z}_4$ have a special place in coding theory. A database of $\mathbb{Z}_4$ codes was constructed in 2007 but it became unavailable recently. We have created a new database of $\mathbb{Z}_4$ codes and updated the original one substantially by adding 8699 new codes. Of these, a total 433 are decent codes, 426 are good codes, 5 are very good codes, and 2 are new nonlinear binary codes. These codes have been found by implementing search algorithms for cyclic and QC codes. Based on observations on computational results, we formulated an open problem of great theoretical interest and invite researchers to resolve it. Still more codes can be found and added to the database by conducting similar searches by considering cyclic codes of even length and related searches for QC codes. Moreover, data from a similar database will be incorporated into this database. This will result in a most up-to-date database of $\mathbb{Z}_4$ codes for researchers. We also note that the database [18] of nonlinear binary codes is in need of an update.

Acknowledgements. We thank the anonymous reviewers for their many useful comments and suggestions, in particular bringing the similar database [16] to our attention.

References

1. Akre, D., Aydin, N., Harrington, M.J.: New binary and ternary quasi-cyclic codes with good properties. Comp. Appl. Math. **42**, 102 (2023). https://doi.org/10.1007/s40314-022-01946-8
2. Aydin, N., Asamov, T.: A database of Z4 codes. J. Comb. Inf. Syst. Sci. **34**(1–4), 1–12 (2009)
3. Aydin, N., Gulliver, T.A.: Some good cyclic and quasi-twisted $\mathbb{Z}_4$-linear codes. ARS Comb. **99**, 503–518 (2011)
4. Aydin, N., Ray-Chaudhuri, D.K.: Quasi-cyclic codes over $\mathbb{Z}_4$ and some new binary codes. IEEE Trans. Inf. Theory **48**(7), 2065–2069 (2002)

5. Aydin, N., Lambrinos, J., VandenBerg, O.: On equivalence of cyclic codes, generalization of a quasi-twisted search algorithm, and new linear codes. Des. Codes Crypt. **87**(10), 2199–2212 (2019). https://doi.org/10.1007/s10623-019-00613-0

6. Aydin, N., Siap, I., Ray-Chaudhuri, D.K.: The structure of 1-generator quasi-twisted codes and new linear codes. Des. Codes Crypt. **24**(3), 313–326 (2001)

7. Aydin, N., Siap, I.: New quasi-cyclic codes over $\mathbb{F}_5$. Appl. Math. Lett. **15**(7), 833–836 (2002)

8. Aydin, N., Connolly, N., Grassl, M.: Some results on the structure of constacyclic codes and new linear codes over GF(7) from quasi-twisted codes. Adv. Math. Commun. **11**(1), 245–258 (2017)

9. Aydin, N., Guidotti, T.H., Liu, P., Shaikh, A.S., VandenBerg, R.O.: Some generalizations of the ASR search algorithm for quasi-twisted codes. Involve, J. Math. **13**(1), 137–148 (2020)

10. Bonnecaze, A., Solé, P., Bachoc, C., Mourrain, B.: Type II codes over $\mathbb{Z}_4$. IEEE Trans. Inf. Theory **43**(3), 969–976 (1997)

11. Bonnecaze, A., Solé, P., Calderbank, A.R.: Quaternary quadratic residue codes and unimodular lattices. IEEE Trans. Inf. Theory **41**(2), 366–377 (1995)

12. Chen, E.: Quasi-Cyclic Codes: Bounds on the parameters of of QC codes. http://www.tec.hkr.se/chen/research/codes/qc.htm. Accessed 18 Dec 2022

13. Forney Jr, G.D., Sloane, N.J., Trott, M.D.: The Nordstrom-Robinson code is the binary image of the octacode. In: Coding and Quantization: DIMACS/IEEE Workshop, pp. 19–26 (1992). Amer. Math. Soc.

14. Grassl, M.: Code Tables: Bounds on the parameters of of codes. http://www.codetables.de/. Accessed 18 Dec 2022

15. Kiermaier, M., Wassermann, A., Zwanzger, J.: New upper bounds on binary linear codes and a $\mathbb{Z}_4$-code with a better-than-linear gray image. IEEE Trans. Inf. Theory **62**(12), 6768–6771 (2016)

16. Kiermaier, M., Zwanzger, J.: Best known linear codes over $\mathbb{Z}_4$. https://www.mathe2.uni-bayreuth.de/20er/codedb/Z4/index.html

17. Hammons, A.R., Kumar, P.V., Calderbank, A.R., Sloane, N.J., Solé, P.: The $\mathbb{Z}_4$-linearity of kerdock, preparata, goethals, and related codes. IEEE Trans. Inf. Theory **40**(2), 301–319 (1994)

18. Litsyn, S., Rains, E.M., Sloane, N.J.A.: Table of Nonlinear Binary Codes. http://www.eng.tau.ac.il/litsyn/tableand/index.html. Accessed 18 Dec 2022

19. Pandey, S.R., Aydin, N., Harrington, M.J., Akre, D.: A generalization of the ASR search algorithm to 2-generator quasi-twisted codes. In: 2022 IEEE International Symposium on Information Theory (ISIT 2022), pp. 2136–2141 (2022). https://doi.org/10.1109/ISIT50566.2022.9834522

20. Pless, V.S., Qian, Z.: Cyclic codes and quadratic residue codes over $\mathbb{Z}_4$. IEEE Trans. Inf. Theory **42**(5), 1594–1600 (1996)

21. Wan, Z.-X.: Quaternary Codes. World Scientific, Singapore (1997)

22. Magma computer algebra system. http://magma.maths.usyd.edu.au/

Author Index

S. El Hajji et al. (Eds.): C2SI 2023, LNCS 13874, pp. 407–408, 2023.
https://doi.org/10.1007/978-3-031-33017-9

Printed in the United States
by Baker & Taylor Publisher Services